INTRODUCTORY
SECOND EDITION

Technology in Action

GO!

Alan Evans   Kendall Martin   Mary Anne Poatsy

PEARSON
Prentice
Hall

Upper Saddle River, New Jersey

Technology in Action
Introductory Edition/Alan Evans, Kendall Martin, Mary Anne Poatsy

Vice President/Publisher: Natalie E. Anderson
Executive Editor, Media: Jodi McPherson
Executive Editor, Print: Stephanie Wall
Project Manager, Editorial and Media: Jodi Bolognese
Editorial Assistants: Alana Meyers, Sandra Bernales, Bambi Marchigano, Brian Hoehl
Developmental Editor: Shannon LeMay-Finn
Senior Marketing Manager: Emily Williams Knight
Marketing Assistant: Lisa Taylor
Senior Project Manager, Production: April Montana
Production Assistant: Sandra Bernales
Manufacturing Buyer: April Montana
Senior Media Project Manager: Cathleen Profitko
Design Manager: Maria Lange
Art Director: Blair Brown
Cover Design: Blair Brown
Composition: Quorum Creative Services.
Full-Service Project Management: Bookmasters, Inc.
Cover Printer: Phoenix Color
Printer/Binder: Courier Kendallville

Credits and acknowledgments borrowed from other sources and reproduced, with permission, in this textbook appear on appropriate page within text (or on pages 423–430).

Microsoft® and Windows® are registered trademarks of the Microsoft Corporation in the U.S.A. and other countries. Screen shots and icons reprinted with permission from the Microsoft Corporation. This book is not sponsored or endorsed by or affiliated with the Microsoft Corporation.

Pearson Education LTD.   Pearson Education Australia PTY, Limited
Pearson Education Singapore, Pte. Ltd   Pearson Education North Asia Ltd
Pearson Education, Canada, Ltd   Pearson Educación de Mexico, S.A. de C.V.
Pearson Education–Japan   Pearson Education Malaysia, Pte. Ltd

10 9 8 7 6 5 4 3 2
ISBN 0-13-148905-4

Dedication

For my wife Patricia, whose patience, understanding,
and support continue to make this work possible. And
for my parents who always believed that I had a book
lurking in me somewhere!

—Alan Evans

For all the teachers, mentors, and gurus who have
popped in and out of my life.

—Kendall Martin

For my husband Ted, who unselfishly continues
to take on more than his fair share to support me
throughout this process; and for my children,
Laura, Carolyn, and Teddy, whose encouragement
and love have been inspiring.

—Mary Anne Poatsy

ABOUT THE AUTHORS

Alan D. Evans, MS, CPA
aevans@mc3.edu

Alan is currently the director of computer science for Montgomery County Community College. Alan's parents instilled in him a love of education at an early age. After a successful career in business, Alan finally realized his true calling was education. He has been a teacher and an administrator at the collegiate level for the past five years.

Alan makes presentations at technical conferences and meets regularly with computer science faculty and administrators from other colleges to discuss curriculum development. Currently, he is researching computer literacy standards for first-year college students.

Kendall E. Martin, PhD
kmartin@mc3.edu

Kendall has been teaching since 1988 at a number of institutions, including Villanova University, DeSales University, Arcadia University, Ursinus College, County College of Morris, and Montgomery County Community College, at both the undergraduate and master's degree level.

Kendall's education includes a B.S. in Electrical Engineering from the University of Rochester and an M.S. and Ph.D. in Engineering from the University of Pennsylvania. She has industrial experience in research and development environments (AT&T Bell Laboratories) as well as experience from several start-up technology firms.

At Ursinus College, Kendall developed a successful faculty training program for distance education instructors, and she makes conference presentations during the year.

Mary Anne Poatsy, MBA, CFP
mpoatsy@mc3.edu

Mary Anne is an adjunct faculty member at Montgomery County Community College, teaching various computer application and concepts courses in face-to-face and online environments.

Mary Anne holds a B.A. in Psychology and Elementary Education from Mount Holyoke College and an MBA in Finance from Northwestern University's Kellogg Graduate School of Management. Mary Anne has more than nine years of educational experience, ranging from elementary and secondary education to Montgomery County Community College, Muhlenberg College, and Bucks County Community College, as well as training in the professional environment. Prior to teaching, Mary Anne was a vice president at Shearson Lehman Hutton in the Muncipal Bond Investment Banking department.

ACKNOWLEDGMENTS

First, we would like to thank our students. We constantly learn from them while teaching, and they are a continual source of inspiration and new ideas.

We could not have written this book without the loving support of our families. Our spouses and children made sacrifices (mostly in time not spent with us) to permit us to make this dream into a reality.

Our heartfelt thanks go to Shannon LeMay-Finn, our developmental editor. Shannon took three authors and helped them become a cohesive team. She continues to go above and beyond the requirements of her job in a quest to make this book special.

Although working with the entire team at Prentice Hall was a truly enjoyable experience, a few individuals deserve special mention. Jodi McPherson, our executive editor, was inspirational from the very start. She helped us grow the ideas that we had into an actual book. Jodi's support and encouragement, along with that of our executive acquisitions editor, Stephanie Wall, made this book live! Jodi Bolognese, our editorial project manager, can juggle more balls in the air at one time than anyone on the planet! She really kept the book moving along toward completion. As senior media project manager, Cathi Profitko worked tirelessly to ensure that the media accompanying the text was professionally produced and delivered in a timely fashion. Despite the inevitable problems that always crop up when producing multimedia, she handled all challenges with a smile. She is absolutely one of the hardest working individuals we have ever known. Emily Knight, who is in charge of marketing our text, has been a great supporter of this project since the beginning. Her enthusiasm is contagious as she displays a remarkable work ethic. And we can't forget Natalie Anderson, vice president of information technology business publishing, who is our publisher. Natalie has a wonderful sense of humor, which helps smooth over the inevitable bumps in the road encountered on a project of this magnitude. Our heartfelt appreciation also goes to April Montana, senior project manager of production, who contines to work tirelessly to ensure our book is always published on time and looks fabulous. The timelines are always short, our art is complex, and there are many people with whom she has to coordinate tasks. She makes it look easy. Her dedication and hard work help make this book a reality.

There were many people we did not meet in person at Prentice Hall, and elsewhere, who made significant contributions by designing the book, illustrating, composing the pages, producing multimedia, and securing permissions. We thank them all, particularly supplement authors Bob Koziel, Diane Coyle, and Jerri Williams.

Also deserving of thanks are the many experienced textbook authors who provided invaluable advice and encouragement to three neophytes at the start of this project.

Many of our colleagues at Montgomery County Community College made suggestions and provided advice during this project. We appreciate all the help everyone provided, but we would particularly like to thank John Mack, Jerri Williams, Diane Coyle, and Dianne Meskauskas, who worked directly on the supplements to the book.

And finally, we would like to thank the following reviewers and the many others who contributed their time, ideas, and talents to this project. We appreciate the time and energy that you put into your comments because they helped us turn out a better product.

Reviewers

Wilma Andrews .... Virginia Commonwealth University
LeeAnn Bates
Susan Birtwell .... Kwantlen University College
Jeff Burton .... Daytona Beach Community College
Gerianne Chapman .... Johnson & Wales University
Gail Cope...................................... Sinclair Community College
Doug Cross.................................... Clackamas Community College
Susan N. Dozier .... Tidewater Community College
Annette Duvall............................. Albuquerque Technical Vocational Institute
Laurie Eakins............................... Eastern Carolina University
Susan Hanson............................... Albuquerque Technical Vocational Institute
Marie Hartlein.............................. Montgomery County Community College
Catherine Hines .... Albuquerque Technical Vocational Institute
Mary Carole Hollingsworth ...... Georgia Perimeter College
Norm Hollingsworth................... Georgia Perimeter College
Glen Johansson .... Spokane Community College
David Kight .... Brewton-Parker College
Yvonne Leonard .... Coastal Carolina University
Toni Marucco .... Lincoln Land Community College
Lisa Nademlynsky....................... Johnson & Wales University
Judy Ogden .... Johnson County Community College
Connie O'Neill .... Sinclair Community College
Brenda Parker............................... Middle Tennessee State University
Patricia Rahmlow........................ Montgomery County Community College
Mirella Shannon .... Columbia College
John Taylor.................................... Hillsborough Community College—Brandon Campus
Dennie Templeton .... Radford University
Catherine Werst............................ Cuesta College
Barbara Yancy .... Community College of Baltimore County—Essex Campus
Mary Zajac.................................... Montgomery County Community College

We would also like to thank the following reviewers of the first edition:

Wilma Andrews	Virginia Commonwealth University
Linda Belton	Springfield Technical Community College
Julie Boyles	
Gerald U. Brown Jr.	Tarrant County College
Judy Cestaro	California State University—San Bernardino
Debra Chapman	The University of South Alabama
Françoise Corey	CSU, Long Beach
Thad Crews	Western Kentucky University
John Cusaac	Fullerton College
Susan N. Dozier	Tidewater Community College
Annette Duvall	Albuquerque Technical Vocational Institute
Catherine L. Ferguson	University of Oklahoma
Beverly Fite	Amarillo College
Richard A. Flores	Citrus College
Sherry Green	Purdue—Calumet
Debra Gross	The Ohio State University
Judy Irvine	Seneca College
Kathy Johnson	DeVry Chicago
Stephanie Jones	South Plains College
Robert R. Kendi	Lehigh University
Jackie Lamoureux	Albuquerque Technical Vocational Institute
Judith Limkilde	Seneca College—King Campus
Richard Linge	Arizona Western College
Joelene Mack	Golden West College
Dana McCann	Central Michigan University
Lee McClain	West Washington University
Daniela Marghitu	Auburn University
Laura Melella	Fullerton College
Josephine G. Mendoza	California State University—San Bernardino
Rebecca A. Mundy	University of Southern California
Linda Mushet	Golden West College
Omar Nooraldeen	Cape Fear Community College
Woody Pekoske	North Carolina State University
Paul Quan	Albuquerque Technical Vocational Institute
Kriss Stauber	El Camino College
Neal Stenlund	Northern Virginia Community College
Song Su	East Los Angeles College
Goran Trajkovski	Towson University
Linda Turpen	Albuquerque Technical Vocational Institute
Bill VanderClock	Bentley Business University
Mary Anne Zlotow	College of DuPage

Why We Wrote This Book

Our 16 years of teaching computer concepts have coincided with sweeping innovations in computing technology that have affected every facet of society. From ATMs to the Web, computers are more than ever a fixture of our daily lives—and the lives of our students. But although today's students have a greater comfort level with their digital environment than previous generations, their textbooks haven't caught up. Even the best books spend too much time introducing hardware students already know, and not enough time explaining all the fun and productive things that same hardware can do.

We wrote *Technology in Action* to address this problem by focusing on today's student. Instead of a history lesson on the microchip, we focus on what tasks students can accomplish with their PC and skills they can apply immediately in the workplace and at home. The result is a book that sparks student interest by focusing on the material they want to learn (such as how to set up a home network), while teaching the material they need to learn (such as how networks work). The sequence of topics is carefully set up to mirror the typical student learning experience.

As they read through this text, your students will progress through stages of increasing difficulty:

1. Examining why it's important to be computer fluent and how computers impact our society

2. Examining the basic components of the computer

3. Connecting to the Internet

4. Exploring software

5. Learning the operating system and personalizing the computer

6. Evaluating and upgrading the PC

7. Exploring home networking and keeping the computer safe from hackers

8. Going mobile with cell phones, PDAs, tablet PCs, and laptops

The focus of the early chapters is on practical uses for the computer, with real-world examples to help the learner place computing in a familiar context. For students ready to go beyond the basics, special BEHIND THE SCENES chapters venture deeper into the realm of computing through in-depth explanations of how elements of the system unit (CPU, motherboard, RAM) work. They are specifically designed to keep more experienced students engaged and challenge them with interesting research assignments.

We have also developed a comprehensive multimedia program to reinforce the material taught in the text and support both classroom lectures and distance learning. New HELPDESK training content, created specifically for *Technology in Action*, enables students to take on the role of a helpdesk operator and work through common questions asked by computer users. Exciting SOUND BYTE multimedia—fully integrated with the text—accelerates student mastery of complex topics.

In addition, we have included DIG DEEPER sections throughout the book to encourage further study by taking an in-depth look at a topic of student interest, such as how a firewall works or how speech-recognition software works, that they can explore at their own pace.

Now that the computer has become a ubiquitous tool in our lives, a new approach to computer concepts is warranted. This book is designed to reach the students of the 21st century.

What's Inside

■ **Questions Students Ask**
These section headings reflect the natural progression of a typical PC learning experience by integrating questions students ask consistently every semester.

■ **Sound Bytes**
These dynamic multimedia tutorials help explain complex concepts.

■ **Dig Deeper**
These sections cover technical topics in depth to challenge more advanced students.

■ **Bits and Bytes**
In these sections, students learn how to maintain their computers, how to develop good habits for safe computing, as well as other interesting facts about computers.

■ **Trends in IT**
These sections explore new and emerging technologies, computers in society, careers in computing, and ethical considerations involved in computing.

What's New in This Edition

The world of technology is always changing, and we've updated this second edition to reflect these changes. In addition, we've improved the book by listening to your feedback. In this second edition you'll find the following:

New Helpdesk Simulation Our new interactive student training places the student in the role of a helpdesk staffer fielding questions from callers. Feedback and gentle guidance is provided by a virtual supervisor to keep student learning on track.

New and Improved Art We listened to your suggestions and made certain diagrams even clearer to illustrate hard-to-explain concepts for students. We've also inserted new pieces of art throughout to illustrate our expanded coverage and to provide the most up-to-date images possible.

Expanded Career Coverage in Chapter 1 You asked for more examples of how technology is used in today's careers. We responded by increasing coverage of computer usage in the arts, medical fields, shipping and fulfillment, law enforcement, and education.

Expanded Internet Coverage in Chapter 3 Based on your feedback, our discussion of the Internet now includes the future of the Internet, the history of the Internet, as well as blogs.

New and Updated Sound Bytes We've improved and updated our popular Sound Bytes to keep your students engaged and current. The new high-tech design, improved navigation, and updated content mean enhanced presentation both in the lab and online.

New and Updated TechTV Clips We've improved and updated the TechTV clips found on the book's companion Web site.

An Even More Reader-Friendly Design By streamlining the design that was so popular in the first edition, we've made this edition even easier for students to navigate.

About the Multimedia—
Designed by the Authors

Technology in Action features a unique and innovative student resource—interactive multimedia labs written specifically to the text—that demystify even the most complex topics. These Sound Bytes are indicated by an icon; at least two appear in each chapter.

The Sound Byte labs all include a multimedia lesson with a video or animation clip to illustrate a concept. After viewing the lesson students can take a multiple-choice quiz to assess their retention of the material and then immediately apply their knowledge with fun and interesting activities specifically tailored to each Sound Byte.

For example, your student reads about random access memory in Chapter 6—seeing the Sound Byte icon, she views the accompanying multimedia lab entitled "Installing RAM." She takes the quiz, reinforcing the objective information, and then does the activity, which sends her to the Crucial Technology Web site to find information on matching the correct RAM type to her system and gathering the latest prices.

For students very new to computers there are lessons in the features of PDA devices, laptop tours, and more; for those ready to go beyond the basics, lessons include creating a database in Access and writing a simple Web page in Word.

For your convenience, the Sound Bytes are included on the Instructor's Resource DVD and are also available to students on a CD or on the Companion Web site.

THE SOUND BYTES AVAILABLE ARE:

- Best Utilities for Your Computer (p. 108)
- CD and DVD Reading & Writing Interactive (p. 235)
- Connecting to the Internet (p. 91)
- *New!* Connecting with Bluetooth (p. 320)
- Creating a Web-Based E-Mail Account (p. 102)
- *New!* Creating Web Queries with Excel (p. 126)
- Customizing Windows XP (p. 196)
- Enhancing Photos with Image-Editing Software (p. 140)
- File Compression (p. 205)
- File Management (p. 199)
- Finding Information on the Web (p. 101)
- Hard Disk Anatomy Interactive (pp. 207, 233)
- Healthy Computing (p. 57)
- Installing a CDRW Drive (p. 236)

- Installing a Computer Network (p. 266)
- Installing a Personal Firewall (p. 285)
- Installing RAM (p. 229)
- Letting Your Computer Clean Up after Itself (p. 208)
- PDA on the Road and at Home (p. 332)
- Port Tour (p. 54)
- Protecting Your Computer (p. 290)
- Questions to Ask Before You Buy a Computer (p. 23)
- Securing Your Wireless Networks (p. 274)
- Tablet and Laptop Tour (p. 341)
- Using Speech-Recognition Software (p. 133)
- Using Windows XP to Evaluate CPU Performance (p. 225)
- Virtual Computer Tour (pp. 21, 55)
- Welcome to the Web (p. 94)

Instructor Resources

The new and improved Prentice Hall Instructor's Resource Center DVD includes the tools you expect from a Prentice Hall computer concepts text such as the following:

- Helpdesk Simulation
- The Instructor's Manual in Word and PDF formats
- Solutions to questions and exercises from the book and Web site
- Multiple, customizable PowerPoint slide presentations for each chapter
- Computer concepts animations
- TechTV videos
- Image library of IT and computer-related images
- Sound Bytes
- Test bank with TestGen and QuizMaster Software

This DVD is an interactive library of assets and links. This DVD writes custom "index" pages that can be used as the foundation of a class presentation or online lecture. By navigating through this DVD, you can collect the materials that are most relevant to your interests, edit them to create powerful class lectures, copy them to your own computer's hard drive, and/or upload them to an online course management system.

OneKey

OneKey lets you in to the best teaching and learning resources all in one place. OneKey for *Technology in Action* is all your students need for out-of-class work conveniently organized by chapter to reinforce and apply what they've learned in class and from the text. OneKey is all you need to plan and administer your course through Blackboard, WebCT, or Course Compass. All your instructor resources are in one place to maximize your effectiveness and minimize your time and effort. OneKey for convenience, simplicity, and success.

TechTV

Formed by the May 2004 merger of G4 and TechTV, G4TechTV is the one and only 24-hour television network that is plugged into every dimension of games, gear, gadgets, and gigabytes. Headquartered in Los Angeles, the network features all original programming dedicated to the passions and lifestyle of the gamer generation. To learn more, log on to **www.g4techtv.com** or contact your local cable or satellite provider to get G4TechTV in your area.

TestGen Software

TestGen is a test generator program that enables you to view and easily edit test bank questions, transfer them to tests, and print in a variety of formats suitable to your teaching situation. The program also offers many options for organizing and displaying test banks and tests. Powerful search and sort functions enable you to locate questions easily and arrange them in the order you prefer.

QuizMaster, also included in this package, enables students to take tests created with TestGen on a local area network. The QuizMaster Utility built into TestGen enables instructors to view student records and print a variety of reports. Building tests is easy with TestGen, and exams can be easily uploaded into WebCT, Blackboard, and Course Compass.

Tools for Online Learning

Train & Assess IT

Training and Assessment Software
www.prenhall.com/taitdemo

Technology in Action features brand-new computer-based Train & Assess IT content to help reinforce material covered in the text. Developed by the authors specifically for *Technology in Action*, this interactive Helpdesk training enables students to assume the role of helpdesk operator to talk a caller through concepts questions related directly to the text. Additionally, a supervisor is available at all times to provide guidance, feedback, and more information to help the student understand the concepts underlying each question and response.

The Helpdesk calls are fully integrated with the book's content and multimedia package, including ready access to the Sound Bytes, as well as 3-D art from the book and original animations to help illustrate concepts. In addition, students have direct access to the Bits & Bytes features as shown in the book and links to Web sites for more information. Students will also be able to navigate throughout the call to find more information on specific topics. At the end of each call, students are presented with a handy summary of all the information they've learned, helping to further reinforce key chapter material.

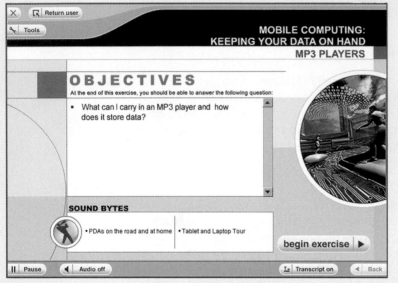

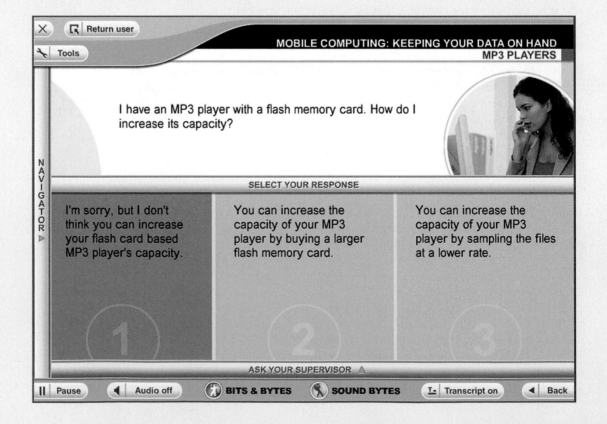

Companion Web Site

www.prenhall.com/techinaction

This text is accompanied by a companion Web site at **www.prenhall.com/techinaction**. Features of this new site include an interactive study guide, downloadable supplements, additional Web Research Projects, TechTV videos, Web resource links such as Careers in IT and crossword puzzles, plus bonus chapters on the latest trends and hottest topics in information technology. All links to Web Research Projects will be constantly updated to ensure accuracy.

Unique to the *Technology in Action* Web site is a series of innovative multimedia labs written specifically to the text that demystify even the most complex topics. These Sound Bytes are indicated by an icon with at least two appearing per chapter and are also available on the CD that accompanies the text. (For a list of available Sound Bytes, please see page x.)

CourseCompass

www.coursecompass.com

CourseCompass is a dynamic, interactive online course-management tool powered exclusively for Pearson Education by Blackboard. This exciting product enables you to teach market-leading Pearson Education content in an easy-to-use, customizable format.

Blackboard

www.prenhall.com/blackboard

Prentice Hall's abundant online content combined with Blackboard's popular tools and interface results in robust Web-based courses that are easy to implement, manage, and use—taking your courses to new heights in student interaction and learning.

WebCT

www.prenhall.com/webct

Course management tools within WebCT include page tracking, progress tracking, class and student management, a grade book, communication tools, a calendar, reporting tools, and more. Gold Level Customer Support, available exclusively to adopters of Prentice Hall courses, is provided free of charge upon adoption and provides you with priority assistance, training discounts, and dedicated technical support.

Using This Book

This book is arranged in the order you would most likely follow when exploring a computer. You'll start in the second chapter by looking at your computer as you would if you were assembling it for the first time, exploring each piece and its function within your system. Next, because so many people use the Internet to communicate, conduct research, and shop, Chapter 3 explores the Internet and its many features. Even if you're an experienced Internet user, this chapter will help you use the Internet more effectively and more safely.

In Chapter 4, you'll look more closely at the application software that you'll most likely encounter in your daily life, both at work and at home. Then, in Chapter 5, you'll explore your computer's operating system. In doing so, you'll learn about the different system software programs you can use to keep your computer in top shape, as well as ways you can keep your files and folders organized.

Once you understand the pieces of your system and the three elements that make it a useful tool (the Internet, application software, and the operating system), Chapter 6 will help you evaluate your computer system to see if it is meeting your needs. By exploring and evaluating your system's parts, you'll learn whether you need to upgrade your computer and how to go about doing so.

It's likely that you have more than one computer in your home, workplace, or school. To share common resources between computers, you need to know about networking. Thus, in Chapter 7, you'll learn about home computer networks, as well as how to protect yourself from hackers and viruses. Then, in Chapter 8, you'll explore mobile computing devices such as cell phones, personal digital assistants (PDAs), laptops, and tablet PCs.

Finally, in Chapter 9, you'll find out just how your computer's hardware really works. You'll learn more about your central processing unit (CPU) and the types of random access memory (RAM) available on the market today, and how these components affect the performance of your computer.

Along the way, *Technology in Focus* features will teach you more about digital technology, protecting your computer and the data on it, as well as the history of the personal computer.

No matter how much you use the computer, you probably still have a lot of questions about how to use it *best*. Throughout this book, you'll find references to multimedia components called **Sound Bytes** that *show* you the answers to some frequently asked questions, such as how to set up a firewall and how to use antivirus software effectively.

SOUND BYTE

QUESTIONS TO ASK BEFORE YOU BUY A COMPUTER

This Sound Byte will help you consider some important questions you need to ask when you buy a computer, such as whether you should get a laptop or a desktop, or whether you should purchase a new computer or a used or refurbished one.

In each chapter, you'll also find **Bits and Bytes**, boxes that contain interesting facts and helpful tips on how to maintain and better use your computer.

Also scattered throughout the book are **Trends in IT** features that examine computer-related ethical issues, careers in technology, applications of computers in society, as well as emerging technologies.

Finally, throughout the book you'll find **Dig Deeper** features. These features take an in-depth look at various computer concepts, such as how a hard disk drive or a computer firewall works.

The wonderful thing about computers is that there is something new to learn about them every day. Developing an understanding of how computers can make your life easier is critical to your future success. So, let's get started on our exploration of computers.

Please visit the Web site at **www.prenhall.com/techinaction** where you will find bonus chapters on the latest trends in information technology, an interactive study guide, online end-of-chapter materials, Careers in IT features, TechTV videos, technology updates, crossword puzzles, and more.

BITS AND BYTES

Keeping Your Keyboard Clean

To keep your computer running at its best, it's important that you occasionally clean your keyboard. To do so, follow these steps:

1. Turn off your computer.
2. Disconnect the keyboard from your system.
3. Turn the keyboard upside down and *gently* shake out any loose debris. You may want to spray hard-to-reach places with compressed air (found in any computer store) or use a vacuum device made especially for computers. Don't use your home vacuum, because the suction is too strong and may damage your keyboard.
4. Wipe the keys with a cloth or cotton swab lightly dampened with a diluted solution of dishwashing liquid and water or iso-propyl alcohol and water. Don't spray or pour cleaning solution directly onto the keyboard. Make sure you hold the keyboard upside down or at an angle to prevent drips from running into the circuitry.

TRENDS IN IT

Emerging Technologies: Tomorrow's Displays

Most of us grew up with CRT monitors on our computers. Large and heavy but providing excellent resolution and clarity, these monitors were the main display for computers until the early 2000s. Soon, though, you may only find these clunky dinosaurs in the Smithsonian.

Today, LCD screens are where it's at. First introduced in 2000, these monitors have taken the desktop market by storm, and with prices steadily dropping, they now out-sell CRTs. Lighter and less bulky than CRT monitors, they can be easily moved and take up less real estate on a desk. Still, current LCD technology does have limitations. LCD screens are relatively fragile (although less so than CRT monitors) and viewing angles are limited. In addition, LCDs can't display full-motion video as well as CRT monitors, making them unpopular with hard-core gamers.

Despite their limitations, LCDs will continue to be the predominant display device for computers, cell phones, and PDAs in the next few years. But according to sources like *PC Magazine*, new technologies are being developed that take LCD displays to the next level.

Flexible Screens
The most promising displays currently under development are *organic light-emitting displays* (OLEDs). These displays, currently used in [...] organic compounds that p[...] an electric current. OLEDs [...] other flat-screen technolog[...] portable battery-operated [...] research is being geared to[...] (*FOLEDs*). Unlike LCDs an[...] faces such as glass, FOLED[...] on lightweight, inexpensiv[...] transparent plastics or met[...] 2.28, the computer screen [...] into an easily transported [...]

FOLEDs would allow ac[...] new dimension. Screens co[...] are hung now (such as on b[...] transmission of data to the [...] advertisers to display easil[...] images. Combining transp[...]

FIGURE 2.28

There's no need to lug around a heavy computer monitor. With FOLED technology, you'll be able to unroll a computer screen wherever you need it from a container the size of a pen. The prototype shown is currently being developed by Universal Display Corporation and may be available within two to three years.

DIG DEEPER

How Ink-Jet and Laser Printers Work

Ever wonder how a printer knows what to print, and how it puts ink in just the right places? Most ink-jet printers use *drop-on-demand* technology in which the ink is "demanded" and then "dropped" onto the paper. Two separate processes use drop-on-demand technology: thermal bubble, used by Hewlett-Packard and Canon, and piezoelectric, used by Epson. The difference between the two processes is how the ink is heated within the print cartridge reservoir (the chamber inside the printer that holds the ink).

In the thermal bubble process, the ink is heated in such a way that it expands (like a bubble) and leaves the cartridge reservoir through a small opening, or nozzle. Figure 2.16 shows the general process for thermal bubble. In the piezoelectric process, each ink nozzle contains a crystal at the back of the ink reservoir that receives an electrical charge, causing the ink to vibrate and drop out of the nozzle.

Laser printers use a completely different process. Inside a laser printer is a big metal cylinder (or drum) that is charged with static electricity. When you ask the printer to print something, it sends signals to the laser in the laser printer, telling it to "uncharge" selected spots on the charged cylinder, corresponding to the document you wish to print. Toner, a fine powder that is used in place of liquid ink, is attracted to only those areas on the drum that are not charged. (These uncharged areas are the characters and images you want to print.) The toner is then transferred to the paper as it feeds through the printer. Finally, the toner is melted onto the paper. All unused toner is swept away before the next job starts the process all over again.

FIGURE 2.16

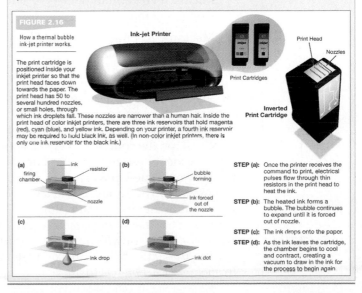

How a thermal bubble ink-jet printer works.

The print cartridge is positioned inside your inkjet printer so that the print head faces down towards the paper. The print head has 50 to several hundred nozzles, or small holes, through which ink droplets fall. These nozzles are narrower than a human hair. Inside the print head of color inkjet printers, there are three ink reservoirs that hold magenta (red), cyan (blue), and yellow ink. Depending on your printer, a fourth ink reservoir may be required to hold black ink, as well. (In non-color inkjet printers, there is only one ink reservoir for the black ink.)

Ink-jet Printer

Print Head

Nozzles

Print Cartridges

Inverted Print Cartridge

(a) firing chamber / ink / resistor / nozzle

(b) bubble forming / ink forced out of the nozzle

(c) ink drop

(d) ink dot

STEP (a): Once the printer receives the command to print, electrical pulses flow through thin resistors in the print head to heat the ink.

STEP (b): The heated ink forms a bubble. The bubble continues to expand until it is forced out of nozzle.

STEP (c): The ink drops onto the paper.

STEP (d): As the ink leaves the cartridge, the chamber begins to cool and contract, creating a vacuum to draw in the ink for the process to begin again

TECHNOLOGY IN ACTION

Browser Tune-Up

To take full advantage of the numerous multimedia resources that accompany *Technology in Action*, be sure you have the right technology at your fingertips. This includes a good Web browser and appropriate plug-ins.

Browsers

Netscape   Microsoft
Internet Explorer

The Web and the tools used to publish on it are changing every day. If you are using an older version of a browser that cannot handle advanced features of Hypertext Markup Language (HTML), some portions of this course may not work for you.

We recommend that you use the latest version of Netscape or Microsoft Internet Explorer.

Plug-ins, Players, and Viewers

In order to use certain Technology in Action multimedia elements, such as Sound Bytes, your Web browser needs to be equipped with special helper applications, called plug-ins, players, or viewers, that enable it to play the multimedia properly. These are common plug-ins, players, and viewers that are used on the Web and that you will need to view all of the multimedia content available for this course:

- Adobe Reader is free software that enables you to view and print Adobe Portable Document Format (PDF) files.

- Apple QuickTime player is for viewing video in Apple's QuickTime format. It works with over 30 audio, video, and image formats.

- Microsoft PowerPoint Viewer 97 is for viewing and printing PowerPoint presentations. Download this if you do not already have PowerPoint installed on your computer.

- Macromedia Shockwave and Flash are for viewing interactive content in various Macromedia formats.

If you encounter an element (such as video or an animation) that requires one of these helpers and you do not have the proper version installed on your system, you may get an error message from your browser.

To make sure you are using the most recent versions of these tools, visit the BROWSER TUNE-UP on the companion Web site (**www.prenhall.com/techinaction**), your *Technology in Action* Student Resource CD, or your online course (Blackboard, WebCT, or CourseCompass). The Browser Tune-Up will run an analysis of your system and show you what tools you need to download. The Tune-Up will also provide you with links you can follow to download and install these players and plug-ins.

Please note that if working in a lab, you may need to check with your professor or lab instructor before downloading any additional materials.

Once these downloads are complete, you'll be ready to access all the unique multimedia *Technology in Action* has to offer!

CONTENTS AT A GLANCE

CONTENTS

CHAPTER 4

Application Software: Programs That Let You Work and Play ... 122

TECHNOLOGY IN FOCUS

Digital Entertainment ... 164

CHAPTER 5

Using System Software: The Operating System, Utility Programs, and File Management ... 178

CHAPTER 6

CHAPTER 7

TECHNOLOGY IN FOCUS

Protecting Your Computer and Backing Up Your Data ... 302

CHAPTER 8

Mobile Computing: Keeping Your Data on Hand ... 314

CHAPTER 9

Behind the Scenes: Inside the System Unit … 354

Technology in Action

CHAPTER 1

OBJECTIVES

After reading this chapter, you should be able to answer the following questions:

- What does it mean to be "computer fluent"? (p. 3)

- How does being computer fluent make you a savvy computer user and consumer? (pp. 4–5)

- How can becoming computer fluent help you in a career? (pp. 5–15)

- How can becoming computer fluent help you understand and take advantage of future technologies? (pp. 16–18)

- What kinds of challenges do computers bring to a digital society and how does becoming computer fluent help you deal with these challenges? (pp. 18–19)

- What exactly is a computer and what are its four main functions? (p. 19)

- What is the difference between data and information? (pp. 19–20)

- What are bits and bytes and how are they measured? (pp. 20–21)

- What hardware does a computer use to perform its functions? (pp. 21–22)

- What are the two main types of software you find in a computer? (p. 22)

- What different kinds of computers are there? (pp. 22–23)

SOUND BYTES

- Virtual Computer Tour (p. 21)
- Questions to Ask Before You Buy a Computer (p. 23)

2

Why Computers Matter to You:

Becoming Computer Fluent

TECHNOLOGY IN ACTION:
BECOMING COMPUTER FLUENT

It's safe to say that computers are nearly everywhere in our society. You find them in schools, cars, airports, shopping centers, toys, medical devices, homes, and in many people's pockets. If you're like most Americans, you interact with computers almost every day, sometimes without even knowing it. Whenever you buy something with a credit card, you interact with a computer. Simply turning on your car engine requires that you use a computer. And, of course, most of us can't imagine our lives without e-mail. If you don't yet have a home computer and don't feel comfortable using one, you still can't have escaped the impact of technology: countless ads for computers, cell phones, digital cameras, and an assortment of Web sites surround us each day. We're constantly reminded of the ways in which computers, the Internet, and technology are integral parts of our lives.

So, just by being a member of our society you know quite a bit about computers. But why is it important to learn more about computers, becoming what is called **computer fluent**? Being computer fluent means being familiar enough with computers that you understand their capabilities and limitations and know how to use them. But being computer fluent means more than just knowing about the parts of your computer. The following are some other benefits:

- Becoming computer fluent will help you use your computer more wisely and be a more knowledgeable consumer.

- Becoming computer fluent will help you in your career.

- Becoming computer fluent will help you better understand and take advantage of future technologies.

In addition, understanding computers and their ethical, legal, and societal implications will make you a more active and aware participant in society.

Anyone can become computer fluent—no matter what your degree of technical expertise. Being computer fluent doesn't mean you need to know enough to program a computer or build one yourself. Just like with a car, if you drive one, you should know enough about it to take care of it and to use it effectively, but that doesn't mean you have to know how to build one. You should try to achieve the same familiarity with computers. In this chapter, we'll look at the ways in which computers can affect your life, now and in the future. We'll also look at just what a computer does as well as which parts help it perform its tasks.

Becoming a Savvy Computer User and Consumer

One of the benefits of becoming computer fluent is being a savvy computer user and consumer. What does this mean? The following are just a few examples of what it may mean to you:

- **Avoiding hackers and viruses.** Do you know what hackers and viruses are? Both can pose threats to computer security. Being aware of how hackers and viruses operate and knowing the damage they can do to your computer can help you avoid falling prey to them.

- **Protecting your privacy.** You've probably heard of identity theft—you see and hear news stories all the time of people whose "identities" are stolen and whose credit ratings are ruined by "identity thieves." But do you know how to protect yourself from identity theft when you're online?

- **Understanding the *real* risks.** Part of being computer fluent means being able to separate the *real* privacy and security risks from things you don't have to worry about. For example, do you know what a cookie is? Do you know whether it poses a privacy risk for you when you're on the Internet? What about a firewall? Do you know what one is? Do you really need one to protect your computer?

- **Using the Internet wisely.** Anyone who has ever searched the Web can attest that finding information and finding good information are two very different things. People who are computer fluent make the Internet a powerful tool and know how to find the information they want effectively. How familiar with the Web are you and how effective are your searches?

- **Avoiding Internet headaches.** If you have an e-mail account, chances are you have received the electronic form of junk mail called spam. What do you do when your e-mail inbox is crowded with spam? How can you keep from being overwhelmed by it? Computer fluency means avoiding spam and other Internet headaches.

- **Being able to maintain, upgrade, and troubleshoot your computer.** Learning how to care for and maintain your

FIGURE 1.1

Although you may not need to repair or construct a computer, computer fluency includes learning how to perform basic upgrades and maintenance.

computer (Figure 1.1) and knowing how to diagnose and fix problems can save you a lot of time and hassle. Do you know how to upgrade your computer if you want more memory, for example? Do you know which software and computer settings can help you keep your computer in top shape?

- **Making good purchasing decisions.** Everywhere you go you see ads like the one in Figure 1.2 for computers and other devices: laptops, printers, monitors, cell phones, digital cameras, and personal digital assistants (PDAs). Do you know what all the words in the ads mean? What is RAM? What is a CPU? What are MB, GB, GHz, and cache? How fast do you need your computer to be and how much memory should you have? Understanding computer "buzz words" and keeping up-to-date with technology will help you better determine which computers and devices match your needs.

- **Knowing how to integrate the latest technology with your equipment.** Finally, becoming computer fluent means knowing how to be a better computer user in the future (see Figure 1.3). It means knowing which technologies are

FIGURE 1.2

Do you know what all the words in a computer ad mean?

Type: Personal computer/Mini tower
Dimensions (WxDxH)/Weight: 6.6 in x 16.8 in x 17.6 in/26 lbs.
Processor: 1 x Intel Pentium 4 3.4 GHz
Cache Memory: 512 KB L2 cache
RAM: 512 MB (installed)/2 GB(max)- DDR SDRAM-dual-channel-400 MHz
Storage Floppy Drive: 1.44 MB -3.5" HD
Storage Hard Drive: 1 x 120 GB - standard - DMA/ATA-100 (Ultra)
Optical Storage: 1 x CD-RW -48x (read), - internal
Optical Writer: 1 x DVD-RW -12x (read), 4x (write) - internal
Video Output: Graphics card - ATI Radeon 9800 256MB DDR
Audio Output: Sound Blaster Audigy 2 ZS Sound Card - PCI - stereo
Ports: 6 USB 2.0 (2 front, 4 back) - 2 IEEE 1394 (1 front, 1 back)
OS Provided: Microsoft Windows XP Professional

data is available), the U.S. Department of Labor indicated that 53.5 percent of U.S. workers use a computer on the job, and this percentage will only increase. Meanwhile, the U.S. Department of Agriculture has found that employees who use a computer on the job earn 10 to 11 percent more than those who don't.

In fact, even getting a job often means having a rudimentary knowledge of computers. Drafting a résumé and cover letter requires a basic understanding of word processing software, and you need to be at least a little familiar with the Internet to use job search Web sites (such as Monster.com).

Becoming truly computer fluent—understanding the capabilities and limitations of computers and what you can do with them—will help you perform your job more effectively. If you're pursuing an engineering or business degree, you already know how important it is for you to learn as much as you can about computers. But if you're pursuing another career, you may not think you need computer skills. In this section, we discuss interesting ways in which computers are used in all sorts of careers.

on the horizon (some of which we'll discuss in this chapter) and how to integrate these technologies into your home setup when possible. Can you connect your laptop to a wireless network? What is "Bluetooth" and does your computer "have" it? Can a device with a USB 2.0 connector be plugged into an old USB 1.0 port? (For that matter, what is a USB port?) How much memory should your cell phone have? Knowing the answers to these and other questions will help you make better decisions as you consider whether investing in new technologies is right for you.

Being Prepared for Your Career

Regardless of which profession you pursue, if computers are not already in everyday use in that career, they most likely will be soon. As of 2001 (the most recent year for which

FIGURE 1.3

Becoming computer fluent means knowing how to be a better consumer and computer user in the future. Will you know whether your computer and devices work well with each other and with future technologies?

COMPUTERS IN BUSINESS: WORKING IN A DATA MINE?

Businesses accumulate a lot of data. Sometimes businesses have so much data that they find it difficult to separate the anomalies from the trends. How do businesses manage to make meaning of all this data? They use a process known as *data mining*. For instance, large retailers often study the data gathered from register terminals to determine which products are selling on a given day and in a specific location. This helps managers gauge how much merchandise they need to order to replace stock that is sold. Managers also use mined data to determine that for a certain product to sell well, they must lower its price—especially if they cut the price at one store and saw sales increase, for example. Data mining thus allows retailers to respond to consumer buying patterns.

In the music business, managers can subscribe to a music watch service from companies such as Big Champagne. Big Champagne monitors music-sharing sites such as Kazaa and keeps track of which music people are downloading and the geographic areas in which they live. This provides marketing personnel in the music companies with information that they can use to drive sales. If the latest 50 Cent single is being downloaded like crazy in Detroit yet local record stores are failing to order significant quantities of the CDs, record executives can use this information to convince record stores that demand will increase for the CD and to up their orders. Using data-mining techniques such as this is music to management ears!

COMPUTERS IN RETAIL: LET ME LOOK THAT UP FOR YOU

Many students have part-time jobs in retail stores. These jobs are often far from glamorous, but they do provide employees with experience using a host of computers, from the mundane to the complex. Most retail employees use simple computers when they process a transaction. These point-of-sale terminals (formerly known as cash registers) are in turn often connected to complex inventory and sales computer systems that provide immediate data to retail store managers and customers (see Figure 1.4). Sales clerks can perform searches for customers to determine which stores might have an item in stock that the customer couldn't find. And by analyzing their constantly updated records, managers can evaluate how their business is doing.

Before computers, if managers wanted to know how well a certain style of shoes was selling, for example, they would have to take inventory physically (count the remaining shoes). However, when a point-of-sale terminal records sales as they are made, it's easy for managers to query a sales database and determine how products are performing. As noted earlier, understanding which data can be captured by computers and how it can be analyzed—or mined—to spot trends is key to running a successful retail business.

FIGURE 1.4

Point-of-sale terminals not only update sales and inventory databases, but retail clerks can use them to search databases based on customer inquiries.

COMPUTERS IN SHIPPING: UPS DATA ON THE GO

Did you know that United Parcel Service (UPS) handles over 13 million packages *per day*? That's a lot of packages. But just how does the "brown" company ensure all its customers' packages get from point A to point B without ending up forever in point C? The company uses a sophisticated database and a very efficient package-tracking system that follows the packages as they move around the world.

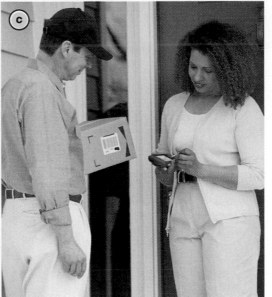

FIGURE 1.5

(a) Package tracking starts at the point of sending by the generation of a smart label for the package.
(b) Scanning is accomplished by wearable scanners.
(c) Delivery personnel carry delivery acquisition devices that feature wireless networking capability, internal modems, infrared scanners, Global Positioning System (GPS) capabilities, and an electronic pad to capture customer signatures.

For UPS, package tracking starts when the sender drops off a package and the company creates a "smart label" for the package (see Figure 1.5a). In addition to the standard postal bar code and a bar code showing UPS customer numbers, this smart label contains something called a MaxiCode. The MaxiCode is a specially designed scannable sticker that resembles an inkblot and contains all the important information about the package (class of service, destination, etc.). When the package is handled in processing centers, UPS workers scan the MaxiCode using wearable scanners (see Figure 1.5b). Worn on the employee's hands, these scanners use Bluetooth technology to transmit the scanned data through radio waves to a terminal the workers wear. This terminal then sends the data across a wireless network, where it is recorded in the UPS database.

To track package delivery, UPS carriers use delivery acquisition devices (see Figure 1.5c) that feature wireless networking capability, infrared scanners (to scan the smart labels and transmit the information back to the UPS database), and an electronic pad to capture customer signatures. By capturing all of this data and making it available on its Internet database, UPS enables its customers to track their packages through the delivery process. UPS is also able to make informed decisions about staffing and deploying equipment (trucks, airplanes, etc.) based on the volume and type of packages in the system at any given time. Today, even something as seemingly simple as package delivery makes use of sophisticated computer devices.

COMPUTERS IN THE ARTS: SHALL WE DANCE?

Some art students think that because they're studying art, there is no sense in their studying computers. However, unless you plan on being a starving artist (!), you'll probably want to sell your work. To do so, you'll need to advertise to the public and/or contact art galleries to convince them to purchase or display your work. Wouldn't it be helpful if you knew how to create a simple Web site like the one shown in Figure 1.6?

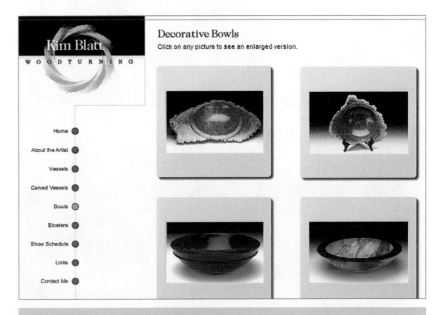

FIGURE 1.6

Kim Blatt, a Pennsylvania woodturning artist, uses his web site (**www.kimblatt woodturning.com**) to familiarize prospective customers with his work.

(a) A dancer is wired up with sensors to capture his movements for digitization on a computer. (b) While live dancers are performing center stage, virtual dancers are projected on either side to provide a new sensory experience for the audience.

But using computers in the arts goes way beyond using the Internet. For example, the Atlanta Ballet, in conjunction with the Georgia Institute of Technology, is using computers to create virtual dancers and new performances for audiences. As shown in Figure 1.7, live dancers are wired with sensors that are connected to a computer that captures the dancers' movements. Based on the data it collects, the computer generates a virtual dancer on a screen. The computer operator can easily manipulate this virtual dancer as well as change the dancer's costume with a click of a mouse. This allows the ballet company to create new experiences for the audience by pairing virtual dancers with live dancers.

Computers even figure directly into the development of artworks themselves. For example, artist Camille Utterback used a computer and video clips of pedestrians in Tokyo to create her visual art piece entitled *Liquid Time* (see Figure 1.8). When no one is near the visual art piece, the screen displays a static, blank image. However, as onlookers in the gallery move closer to the work, a camera mounted on the ceiling of the art gallery captures the movements and dimensions of the onlookers in the gallery. A computer with specialized software then uses this captured data and causes the video playing in the *Liquid Time* piece to ripple. Because the rippling effect is based on the movement and size of the gallery patrons, the work looks different to each person looking at it. As viewers move away from the work, the video returns to a static display. More and more today, artists are combining their skills with new technologies to create novel and inventive works.

Computers even figure directly into the development of artworks. Camille Utterback used video clips of pedestrians in Tokyo in her work entitled *Liquid Time*.

COMPUTERS IN THE MEDICAL FIELD: BRING THE VIRTUAL PATIENT IN, DOCTOR

If you watch *ER* or have been to a doctor's office lately, you know that computers are a staple at medical facilities. Among other things, doctors and nurses use them to update patient records and to keep in touch with their patients by e-mail. But computer use in the medical field extends beyond simple computers. Imagine the following conversation at a medical facility:

Doctor:	He's going into cardiac arrest. Adrenaline heart needle, stat!
Head Nurse:	Blood pressure is 70 over 40 and falling, Doctor!
Doctor:	Darn it, where's that needle!
OR Nurse:	Adrenaline, Doctor.
Head Nurse:	60 over 30, Doctor.
Doctor:	Another 50 cc's of adrenaline.
Head Nurse:	I've lost the pulse!
Doctor:	We need to defibrillate . . . charging paddles . . . prepare to shock him . . . CLEAR!
Head Nurse:	No response, Doctor. We've lost him.
Doctor:	Darn! Well, let's boot him up and try again.

Training for physicians and nurses can be difficult at best. Often, the best way for medical students to learn is to experience a real emergency situation. The problem is that students are then confined to watching as the emergency unfolds while trained personnel actually care for the patient. Students rarely get to train in real-life situations, and when they do, a certain level of risk is involved.

Medical students are now getting access to better training opportunities thanks to a computer technology called a **patient simulator** (shown in Figure 1.9). Patient simulators are life-sized mannequins that can speak, breathe, and blink (their eyes respond to external stimuli). They have a pulse and a heartbeat and respond just like humans to procedures such as the administration of intravenous drugs.

Medical students can train on patient simulators and experience firsthand how a human would react to their treatments without any risk to a live patient. The best thing about these patients is that if they die, students can restart the computer simulation

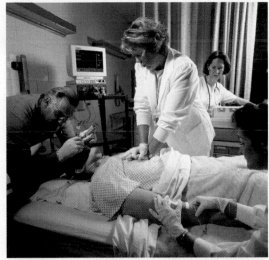

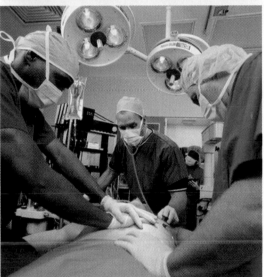

FIGURE 1.9

Patient simulators (made by Medical Education Technologies, Inc.) allow health care students to practice medical procedures without risk of injury or death to the patient.

and try again. Teaching hospitals, universities, and medical schools are currently deploying patient simulators. In addition, the U.S. military is using patient stimulators to train doctors, nurses, and medics to respond to terrorist attacks that employ chemical and biological agents.

Surgeons are even using computer-guided robots, such as the da Vinci Surgical System from Intuitive Surgical, to perform complicated surgery. Surgeons are often limited by their manual dexterity and can have trouble making small, precise incisions. So how can robots help? Robotic surgery devices can exercise much finer control when making delicate incisions than can a human being guiding a scalpel or a laser. To use the robots, doctors look into a computer-guided surgery control device where they manipulate controls that move the robotic devices hovering over the patient (see Figure 1.10, p. 10). One robot control arm contains a slender imaging

techtv
For more information on how surgeons use three-dimensional gaming technology, see "Hot Topic: New Operation for 3-D Graphics," a TechTV clip found at www.prenhall.com/techinaction.

Surgeons use computer-guided robots, such as the da Vinci Surgical System from Intuitive Surgical, to perform surgery. Here, a doctor looks into the control device where he manipulates controls that move the robotic devices hovering over the patient.

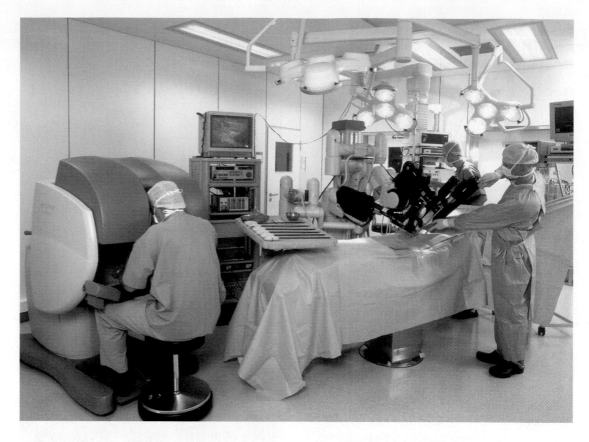

rod that allows the doctor to see inside the patient when the rod is inserted into the patient. For instance, doctors can now perform a coronary bypass by making two small incisions in the patient and inserting the imaging rod in one incision and another robotic device with a cutting tool (scalpel) attachment into the other. The ability to make small incisions in the patient instead of the large ones required by conventional surgery means less trauma and blood loss for the patient. Although it hasn't been done yet, theoretically, doctors do not even have to be in the same room as the patient. They could be thousands of miles away controlling the movements of the robotic devices from a control station. Obviously, doctors and nurses need to be familiar with computers to use this revolutionary equipment.

Doctors are also using specialized software to turn their handheld computers (PDAs) into powerful reference tools, enabling them to look up the symptoms of illnesses and the drugs used to treat them. When writing prescriptions, doctors can use their PDAs to verify dosages and check the safety of prescribing certain drugs in combination. And using wireless technology, doctors can download a patient's medical history to their PDAs in a matter of seconds—no need

to pull medical records from filing cabinets buried in the dark recesses of the hospital basement. Doctors can make notations to a patient's records and place orders for medication and tests electronically through the PDA, and technicians and nurses no longer have to struggle to decipher a doctor's handwriting.

COMPUTERS IN LAW ENFORCEMENT: PUT DOWN THAT MOUSE—YOU'RE UNDER ARREST!

When you think of a private investigator, what do you think of? Images of undercover agents sitting in a car at night with binoculars trained on a window hoping to catch a glimpse of an unfaithful spouse? Or countless hours spent trailing suspects on foot? Today, wearing out shoe leather to solve crimes is far from the only method available to investigators. Just like on *CSI*, computers are being used in police cars and crime labs to solve an increasing number of crimes. As an investigator today, you can save a great deal of time if you're a bit computer savvy.

One technique modern detectives are using to solve crimes is to employ computers to search the vast number of databases on the

Internet. Proprietary law enforcement databases such as the FBI's National Crime Information Center database enable police detectives to track down a wealth of information about individuals and businesses to help them solve crimes. Detectives are also using their knowledge of wireless networking to intercept and read suspects' e-mail or chat sessions while they are online, all from the comfort of a car parked outside the suspect's home (where legally permissible, that is).

As detective work goes more high tech, so, too, does crime. To fight such high-tech crime, a law enforcement specialty called **computer forensics** (Figure 1.11) is growing. Already being used to send criminals behind bars, computer forensics is the application of computer systems and techniques to gather potential legal evidence. The ability to recover and read deleted or damaged files from a criminal's computer could provide evidence for a trial. The tried and true techniques of personally interviewing and observing suspects are still crucial to investigative work, but using computers can make the entire process more efficient.

Do you think there will ever be a day when crime can actually be predicted? Every day, businesses across the world use complicated forecasting models to make predictions about their sales, inventory levels, prices, and so on. Thanks to recent technological advancements, law enforcement officials might soon have access to specialized computer software that can forecast criminal activity, allowing police officers hopefully to take preventative measures to stop crime before it occurs.

Don't believe it? Criminologist Jacqueline Cohen and computer scientist Andreas Olligschlaeger received funding from the U.S. Justice Department to study police reports from Rochester, New York, and Pittsburgh, Pennsylvania. After entering the data about criminal offenses, precinct staffing, and patrol routes, the two researchers used trend-spotting programs developed for business data mining to analyze the data. The result: the program was able to predict criminal activity before it happened an astounding 80 percent of the time. The key to the analysis was identifying and studying leading indicators that trigger crime sprees. Whereas consumer researchers may look at consumer spending patterns and levels of disposable income, criminologists study soft crime statistics such as disorderly conduct, trespassing, and mischief. Increases in these types of crimes indicate that serious

FIGURE 1.11

Computer forensics is the application of computer systems and techniques to gather potential legal evidence.

crimes may soon be on the rise. When a trend is identified, patrols in the area can be stepped up to try to head off crimes before they occur. Building, analyzing, and fine-tuning the models will keep law enforcement officials busy for years.

Even something as simple as parking enforcement uses computers today. Smart meters, such as the one made by the Australian company Reino, shown in Figure 1.12, are being installed in major cities around the globe. Each computerized meter can manage up to 10 parking spaces. When you park in a space, you go to the meter and pay with cash, credit card, or your cell phone. The meter can even send a text message to your cell phone when your time is almost up so you can pay for more time. The meter reports revenue and any malfunctions to the parking authority's central computer on a regular basis. Parking officials can access the meter remotely and change parking rates in response to usage patterns, scheduling of special events, or the time of day. Parking enforcement officers have special PDAs that communicate wirelessly with the meters to determine when parked cars are in violation. The meters send information (such as the time, date, and location of the violation)

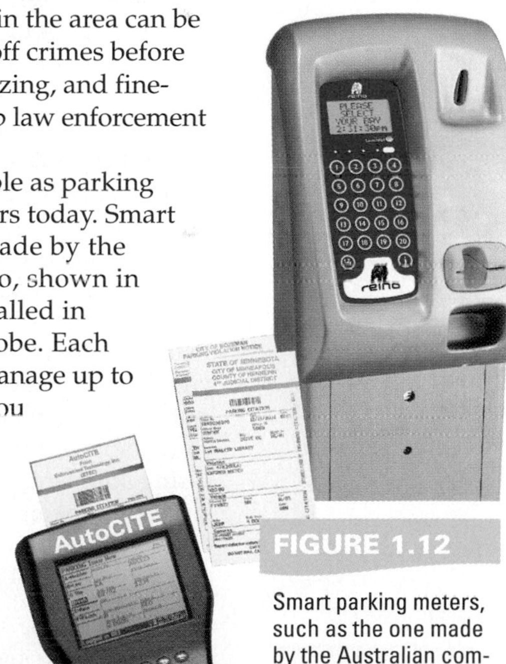

FIGURE 1.12

Smart parking meters, such as the one made by the Australian company Reino, are being installed in major cities around the globe. When you park in a space, you go to the meter and pay with cash, credit card, or cell phone. The meter can even send a text message to your cell phone when your time is almost up so you can pay for more time without returning to the meter.

to the PDAs, which makes generating tickets quicker and more accurate. Beating the meter maid just became a lot harder!

Technology is even being used to thwart graffiti artists. A company called Traptec has pioneered a graffiti detection system called Taggertrap. When the Taggertrap system detects the telltale sound of the graffiti artist plying his trade (the sound of a spray can being used), the system alerts the police by cell phone and uses miniature cameras to record the crime in progress. The video footage is sent immediately by e-mail so the police have evidence of the crime before dispatching officers to the scene. Tests in San Diego already caught six offenders in the act.

COMPUTERS IN THE LEGAL FIELDS: WELCOME TO THE VIRTUAL COURTROOM

In courtrooms today, video records of crimes in progress (often captured by cameras at convenience stores or gas stations) are sometimes displayed to the jury to help them understand how the crime unfolded. But what happens if no surveillance camera recorded the crime? Paper diagrams, models, and still photos of the crime scene used to be the only choice for attorneys to illustrate their case. Now there is a much more exciting and lively alternative: computer forensics animations.

Computer forensics animations are extremely detailed (and often lifelike) re-creations that have been generated with computers based on forensic evidence, depositions of witnesses, and the opinions of experts. Using sophisticated animation programs, similar to the ones Pixar Studios uses to

create movies such as *Toy Story* and *Monsters, Inc.*, forensic animators can depict one side's version of how events occurred, allowing the jury to watch it unfold. Hearing witnesses describe an auto accident can't compare to watching it (see Figure 1.13), and testimony of a person being shot is much more compelling when accompanied by a video re-creation of the event.

Before an animation can be shown to a jury, it must pass careful examinations by the opposing attorney and the judge to ensure it meets the standards set for admissibility to the courtroom. Certain judges contend that forensic animations prejudice the jury and so prohibit the animations from being admitted into evidence. But as more courts accept these animations as evidence, forensic animation will be as commonplace in the courtroom as a judge's black robe. Chances are if you are entering the legal profession, you will encounter this type of evidence frequently.

COMPUTERS IN EDUCATION: AND ON THE LEFT, YOU SEE THE *MONA LISA*

When teaching today, you need to be at least as computer savvy as your students. Computers are part of most schools, even preschools. And in many colleges, students are required to purchase their own computers. So, teachers must have a working knowledge of computers to integrate computer technology effectively into the classroom.

The Internet has obvious advantages in the classroom as a research tool for students, and effective use of the Internet allows teachers to expose students to places they otherwise

FIGURE 1.13

This still excerpt from an animation depicts the collision of a tractor trailer and a passenger van.

could not. Many museums and institutions have virtual tours on their Web sites that allow students to examine objects in the museum collections. Often, these virtual tours include three-dimensional photos that can be viewed from all angles. So, even if you teach in Topeka, Kansas, you can take your students on a virtual tour of the National Air and Space Museum in Washington, D.C., for example (see Figure 1.14). No field trip expenses or permission slips needed.

But what about when you actually want to take your students to visit museums firsthand? Today, technology is often used to enhance visitors' experiences at museums. London's Tate Modern Museum, for example, offers free PDA tours that provide visitors with additional information about the art they are viewing (see Figure 1.15). By simply using a PDA, you can listen to music that the artist listened to while she was creating the work or look at other works that are not contained in the museum that reflect similar techniques or themes to the one you are viewing. For more modern artists, you can watch interviews with the artist explaining her motivation for the work. You can even use the PDA to contact other members of your group and direct them to specific works you want them to see. Knowing how to use a PDA effectively just may help make a museum tour even more memorable.

Meanwhile, many teachers today are extending the reach of their courses beyond the classroom by using course management software. Course management software (such as Blackboard or WebCT) are computer programs that enable instructors and students to post messages (such as schedules) and

Can't fit in a trip to Washington, D.C., this semester? As a teacher, you can still conduct a virtual museum tour for your students using the Internet. This picture of the Wright Flyer from the National Air and Space Museum would be a natural conversation starter for a discussion about powered flight.

other files (such as syllabi) to a course Web site they can access anytime. Although originally designed for online classes, course management software over the past few years has become a popular tool for traditional face-to-face classes as well.

Computers in the classroom will become more prevalent as prices continue to fall and parents demand their children be provided with the necessary computer skills they need to be successful in the workplace. Therefore, as an educator, being computer

FIGURE 1.15

Digital audio tours have been standard in visitor attractions worldwide for some time, providing interpretation in multiple languages and descriptions of displays for visually-impaired people. Now multimedia tours using PDAs and wireless technologies are also being introduced at museums and galleries like the Tate Modern in London, opening up even more ways to enhance the visitor experience and reach a wider range of audiences. The multimedia tour provides contextual information for exhibits, showing images of related objects in other museums, videos of artists at work, and interviews with experts. Through a wireless network, the PDA also allows visitors to respond to opinion polls and even send instant messages to other visitors in the museum, while interactive maps and location-based services help everyone find what they're looking for. For deaf and hard-of-hearing people, handheld computers offer the first chance to tour the galleries in complete independence, watching videoed sign language interpretation with subtitles. Researchers and museum staff can also use wireless computers in the galleries to access databases of information on the art and artists and other administrative applications.

fluent will help you plan constructive computerized lessons for your students and use technology to interact with them.

COMPUTERS AND THE SCIENCES: PROGRAMMING THE PERFECT STORM

As we all know, weather forecasting is not an exact science. Who hasn't had a trip to the beach ruined by unexpected rain? But thanks to a partnership between the National Severe Storms Lab and the National Center for Supercomputing Applications (NCSA), tornado forecasting may be getting more accurate. Using data collected during a tornado in South Dakota in June 2003, scientists have been able to create digitally the most advanced color-coded storm model known to date (see Figure 1.16). The model is so detailed it takes *nine days* for a supercomputer (the most powerful computer on earth) to generate the simulation, even though the computer is executing four billion operations *a second*. By studying the data produced by this simulation, forecasters hope to improve their predictions as to where tornadoes will form and touch down.

Other technological applications in the sciences are being used on some of the oldest sites on earth. The ancient site of Pompeii has been under the intense scrutiny of tourists and archaeologists for decades. Sadly, all the foot traffic and exposure to the elements is eroding portions of the ruins. Today scientists are using three-dimensional scanners and imaging software to capture a detailed record of the current condition of the ruins (see Figure 1.17). The virtual re-creation of the ruins is so lifelike that archaeologists can study the ruins on-screen instead of at the actual site. Using the scans as well as satellite imagery, aerial photography, and other data, scientists will eventually be able to re-create missing portions of the ruins in a virtual model. And scientists won't stop at Pompeii. This method will soon be used to make records of other decaying sites. Archaeologists of tomorrow, get set for a different sort of fieldwork!

COMPUTER GAMING CAREERS: NOW BIGGER THAN HOLLYWOOD!

It's amazing but true: in 2003, revenues from computer gaming in the United States surpassed revenues from Hollywood. In fact, computer gaming is now a $9 billion industry and is projected to continue to grow rapidly over the next decade. If you're a gamer, you know games must be creative to grab their audience. Large-scale games are impossible to create on your own—you must be part of a team. These creative teams have to meet face-to-face on a daily basis to swap ideas. The good news is that because computer games are best developed for a local market by people native to that market, game development will most likely stay in the United States instead of being outsourced to other countries

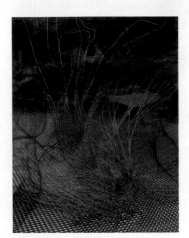

FIGURE 1.16

A color-coded representation of a tornado forming. The red balls in the center forming the tornado funnel will change to yellow as the storm's intensity decreases.

FIGURE 1.17

Digital re-creation of the ruins of Pompeii allows archaeologists to study the ruins without even being there, as well as extrapolate missing portions of the structures.

(as many programming jobs have been). Obviously, you'll need an in-depth knowledge of computers to pursue a career in game programming or as a gaming artist. Mastering software animation tools such as Lightwave 3D, shown in Figure 1.18, will enable you to create the characters and scenery you need to populate game worlds.

COMPUTERS AT HOME: JUST PROGRAM IT AND FORGET IT

Running a household and raising children are time-intensive activities rivaling the commitment needed in any other profession. You may be familiar with many computerized entertainment products for the home (such as Sony PlayStation and Nintendo GameCube), but these won't help you get your home maintenance work done any sooner. However, knowing how to use computers—being computer fluent—will help you be aware of the vast array of labor- and time-saving technological products being marketed to consumers.

Sick of cleaning your home or mowing the lawn? Robots are not just found in science labs and industrial settings anymore. Robotic "maintenance workers" are now emerging for the home market. Why should you have to waste time mowing the lawn or vacuuming the floors when robots can do these tasks for you? Is security a concern in your home? Why not have a robot customized to patrol your home as a security guard. Figure 1.19 shows a few of the robots you could be using to help make the lives of dual-career parents a little less stressful.

Meanwhile, so-called smart devices—devices such as temperature controls, lights, and security devices that contain computer chips—are becoming widely available for the home. Smart devices can control functions in the home without human intervention. And although attempts have been made to launch Internet-connected appliances (such as refrigerators that order food over the Internet when you're running low), these have not yet met with widespread success. Will your oven one day prepare your food without your supervision? Only time will tell. You can keep tabs on the latest products available to make your home easier to manage at sites such as **www.smarthome.com**.

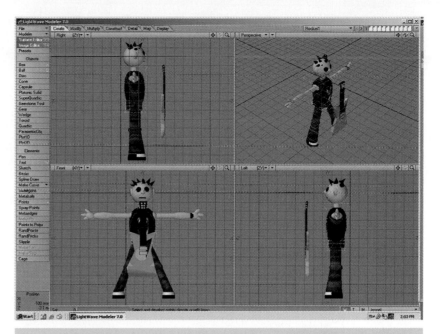

FIGURE 1.18

Lightwave 3D animation software can be used to create interesting animated figures such as the rock band member shown here.

FIGURE 1.19

(a) White Box Robotics's 912 robot acts as a home security device when equipped with webcams, facial-recognition software, and wireless communications (for contacting authorities if it detects unauthorized persons). You can also access the robot's webcam by using the Internet to keep tabs on your house. (b) The RoboMower from Friendly Robotics mows your lawn for you. (c) The iRobot Roomba vacuum relieves you of the dreariness of vacuuming your floors.

Getting Ready for the Technology of Tomorrow

If you're computer fluent, you'll be a smarter computer user and you'll be prepared for virtually any career. But what are the other benefits of computer fluency? By understanding computers and how they work today, you'll be better able to take advantage of and understand the technologies of tomorrow. Let's take a look at some emerging technologies and how they may affect your life.

NANOSCIENCE: THE NEXT "BIG" THING

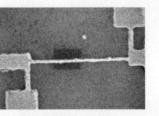

FIGURE 1.20

Comprising several types of atomic particles layered together, this nanowire could eventually be used to conduct electrical signals within a nanoscale computer—a computer smaller than a pencil eraser but more powerful than today's desktop computers.

Have you ever heard of *nanoscience*? Developments in computing based on the principles of nanoscience are being touted as the next big wave in computing. Ironically, this realm of science focuses on very small objects. In fact, **nanoscience** involves the study of molecules and structures (called *nanostructures*) whose size ranges from 1 to 100 nanometers.

How big is this? The prefix *nano* stands for one-billionth. Therefore, a nanometer is one-billionth of a meter. To put this in perspective, a human hair is approximately 50,000 nanometers wide. Put side by side, 10 hydrogen atoms (the simplest atom) would measure approximately 1 nanometer. Anything smaller than a nanometer is just a stray atom or particle floating around in space. Therefore, nanostructures represent the smallest human-made structures that can be built.

Nanotechnology is the science revolving around the use of nanostructures to build devices on an extremely small scale. You may wonder what nanoscience and nanotechnology have to do with you and your life. Right now, not much, but someday scientists hope to use nanostructures to build computing devices too small to be seen by the naked eye. Nanowires, such as the one shown in Figure 1.20, could be used to create extremely small pathways in computer chips. Developments such as this could lead to computers the size of a pencil eraser that are far more powerful than today's desktop computers. Meanwhile, nanomachines (mechanical devices built on the nanoscale) could be designed to float through the human bloodstream and clear arterial blockages that lead to heart attacks and strokes.

If you watch *Star Trek*, you know that "nanoprobes" (tiny machines that can be injected into the bloodstream) have already been envisioned on the TV series' twenty-fourth-century world. But nanotechnology is a relatively new field (less than 15 years old). Although we can create a carbon nanotube (Figure 1.21), we are still a long way from developing nanoscale machines. However, universities and government laboratories are investing billions of dollars in nanotechnology research every year. If you have an interest in science and engineering, this is the time to pursue an education in nanoscience, because you could be on the forefront of the next big technological breakthrough.

BIOMEDICAL CHIP IMPLANTS: COMBINING HUMANS WITH MACHINES?

Mention implanting technology into the human body and some people conjure up images of the Borg, human-based life forms on *Star Trek* that have replaced parts of their bodies with cybernetic implants. The Borg are aliens that capture humans and install technology in their bodies to ensure obedience and enslavement to Borg society (the collective). Unlike the Borg, however, the goal of modern-day biomedical chip research is not to "assimilate" humans into a Borg-like collective. Rather, the goals are to provide technological solutions to physical problems (see Figure 1.22, p. 17) and to provide a means for positively identifying individuals.

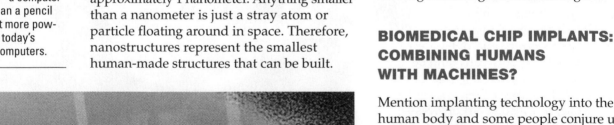

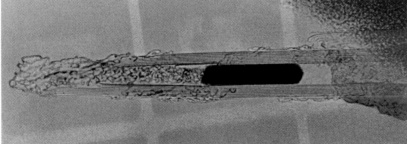

FIGURE 1.21

A carbon nanotube developed in a laboratory. Nanotubes have approximately 60 times the tensile strength of steel. Although they can't be manufactured on a large scale yet, scientists envision using nanotubes to construct extremely durable goods and structures.

One potential application of biomedical chip implants is to provide sight to the blind. Macular degeneration and retinitis pigmentosa are two diseases that account for the majority of blindness in developing nations. Both diseases result in damage to the photoreceptors contained in the retina of the eye. (Photoreceptors convert light energy into electrical energy that is transmitted to the brain, allowing us to see.) Researchers are experimenting with chips that contain microscopic solar cells and are implanted in the damaged retina of patients. The idea is to have the chip take over for the damaged photoreceptors and transmit electrical images to the brain. Although these chips have been tested in patients, they have not yet restored anyone's sight. But uses of biomedical chips such as these are illustrative of the type of medical devices you may "see" in the future.

One form of biomedical chip already entering the market is a technology that can be used to verify a person's identity. Called the VeriChip, this "personal ID chip" is being marketed by a company called Applied Digital Solutions. VeriChips, about the size of a grain of rice (see Figure 1.23), are implanted underneath the skin. When exposed to radio waves from a scanning device, the chip emits a signal that transmits its unique serial number to the scanner. The scanner then connects to a database that contains the name, address, and serious medical conditions of the person in whom the chip has been implanted.

The company envisions the VeriChip speeding up airport security and being used together with other devices (such as electronic ID cards) to provide tamperproof security measures. If someone stole your credit card, that person couldn't use it if a salesclerk verifies your identity by scanning a chip before authorizing a transaction. Chips could eventually be developed so that they contain a vast wealth of information about the person in whom they are implanted. However, it remains to be seen whether the general public will accept having personal data implanted into their bodies.

ARTIFICIAL INTELLIGENCE: WILL COMPUTERS BECOME HUMAN?

Science fiction shows and movies such as *Star Wars* have always been populated with robots that emulate humans, seemingly

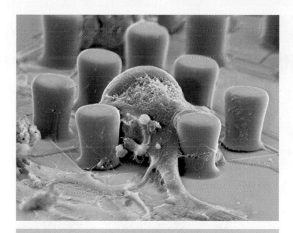

FIGURE 1.22

Researchers are currently experimenting with implantable chips such as the one shown. Here, we see a nerve cell on a silicon chip. The cell was cultured on the chip until it formed a network with nearby cells. The chip contains a transistor that stimulates the cell above it, which in turn passes the signal to neighboring neurons.

FIGURE 1.23

The VeriChip is small device implanted directly under the skin. A special scanner is then able to read the information stored on it.

effortlessly. So, when will we have C-3PO or R2-D2 helping us in our home or office?

The answer is not anytime soon, although advances are being made. **Artificial intelligence (AI)** is the science that attempts to produce machines that display the same type of intelligence that humans do. Current computers can perform both calculations and the tasks that are programmed into them much faster than humans. As mentioned earlier, there are already robots on the market that can be programmed to do tasks such as lawn mowing. In addition, industrial robots, such as the one shown in

FIGURE 1.24

Industrial robots such as this one can be programmed to lift heavy objects and to perform repetitive tasks such as painting and welding. However, robots such as these cannot think yet. They are just performing preprogrammed tasks.

Figure 1.24, are used to perform tasks such as welding, painting, and heavy lifting in factories. However, the performance of these tasks is based on preprogrammed algorithms, not independent thought.

Currently, no computers can emulate the human thought process. The human brain is superior to computers in a very important way: it is capable of processing almost a limitless number of tasks at the same time. Just to write a letter on your computer, your brain coordinates thousands of nerve impulses that control your hands, eyes, and thought processes. Although computers can multitask, not even the most powerful computers can handle the multitasking load of a human brain.

The reason computers can't emulate human thought yet is because no one fully understands how the human brain works. Scientific studies have confirmed that electrical activity between neurons somehow coalesces into thoughts, but scientists aren't quite sure how that happens. Until the human brain is fully understood, progress in the area of artificial intelligence is likely to proceed quite slowly, but you'll no doubt experience artificial intelligence breakthroughs in your lifetime.

Understanding the Challenges Facing a Digital Society

Part of becoming computer fluent is also being able to understand and form knowledgeable opinions on the challenges facing a digital society. Although computers offer us a world of opportunities, they also pose ethical, legal, and moral challenges and questions. For example, how do you feel about the following:

In 2003, a man named Jay Walker (who founded the Web site Priceline.com) suggested a program called "US HomeGuard" to the federal government. The objective of the program is to install high-tech webcams (cameras connected to the Internet) in places that need to be protected from terrorist activities, such as airports, nuclear power plants, and reservoirs (see Figure 1.25). A central agency would be responsible for the webcam monitoring and would employ up to one million stay-at-home citizens as "spotters" to monitor the webcams for suspicious activity.

The webcams would take photos every 45 seconds or so and computers would

FIGURE 1.25

Should the government be allowed to install cameras like the one shown, or do you think such technology should be outlawed?

compare the photos to the previous ones, noting any changes. If there was a change, such as a person throwing an object over a reservoir fence, the photo would be transmitted to at least three spotters. If the spotters saw something odd, the system would capture more photos from the camera in question (and surrounding cameras) and send the images to another 10 spotters. If the second group confirmed the alert, security forces at the facility being attacked would swing into action.

Opponents of this technology say that it harkens back to George Orwell's book *1984*, in which citizens of a futuristic society are constantly under surveillance by a government entity known as Big Brother. Advocates of the plan say that only restricted areas would be under surveillance, and that the security benefits outweigh the privacy risks. The government is considering funding a pilot program to the tune of $40 million to see if the system is feasible. What do you think of this technology? Should the government be allowed to install such webcams?

This is just one example of the kind of question active participants in today's digital society need to be able to think about, discuss, and, at times, take action on. Being computer fluent enables you to form *educated* opinions on these issues and to take stands based on accurate information rather than media hype and misinformation. Here are a few other questions you, as a member of our digital society, may be expected to think about and discuss:

- What privacy risks do biomedical chips such as the VeriChip pose? Do the privacy risks of such chips outweigh the potential benefits?

- Should companies be allowed to collect personal data from Web site visitors without their permission?

- Should spam be illegal? If so, what penalties should be levied on people who send spam?

- Is it ethical to download music off the Web without paying for it? What about copying a friend's software onto your computer?

- What are the risks involved with humans attempting to create computers that can learn and become more human?

- Should we rely solely on computers to provide security for sensitive areas such as nuclear power plants?

As a computer user, you must consider these and other questions to define the boundaries of the digital society in which you live.

Becoming Computer Fluent

By now you can see why becoming computer fluent is so important. But where do you start? As mentioned in the introduction, you glean some knowledge about computers just from being a member of our society. However, although you certainly know what a computer *is*, do you really understand how it works, what all its parts are, and what these parts do? In this section, we'll discuss what a computer does that makes it such a useful machine.

COMPUTERS ARE DATA PROCESSING DEVICES

Strictly defined, a **computer** is a data processing device that performs four major functions:

1. It gathers data (or allows users to input data).

2. It processes that data into information.

3. It outputs data or information.

4. It stores data and information.

To understand these four functions, you need to understand the distinction between the terms *data* and *information*. People often use these terms interchangeably. Although in a simple conversation they may mean the same thing, when discussing computers, the distinction between *data* and *information* is an important one.

In computer terms, **data** is a representation of a fact or idea. Data can be a number, a word, a picture, or even a recording of sound. For example, the number 6165553297 and the names David and Johnson are pieces of data. But how useful are these chunks of data to you? **Information** is data that has been organized or presented in a meaningful fashion. When your computer provides you with a contact listing that indicates David Johnson can be reached by telephone at (616) 555-3297, the data mentioned earlier suddenly becomes useful—that is, it is information.

Computers are very good at processing data into information. When you first arrived

FIGURE 1.26

Computers are very
good at processing
data into information.

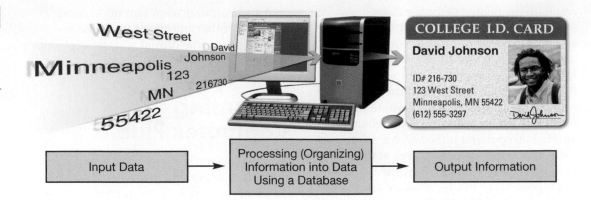

on campus, you probably were directed to a place where you could get an ID card. You most likely provided a clerk with personal data (such as your name and address) that was entered into a computer. The clerk then took your picture with a digital camera (collecting more data). This information was then processed appropriately so that it could be printed on your ID card (see Figure 1.26). This organized output of data on your ID card is useful information. Finally, the information was probably stored as digital data on the computer for later use.

BITS AND BYTES: THE LANGUAGE OF COMPUTERS

How do computers process data into information? Unlike humans, computers work exclusively with numbers (not words). In order to process data into information, computers need to work in a language they understand. This language, called **binary language**, consists of just two numbers: 0 and 1. Everything a computer does (such as process data or print a report) is broken down into a series of 0s and 1s. Each 0 and 1 is a **binary digit**, or **bit** for short. Eight binary digits (or bits) combine to create 1 **byte**. In computers, each letter of the alphabet, each number, and each special character (such as the @ sign) consists of a *unique* combination of 8 bits, or a string of eight 0s and 1s. So, for example, in binary (computer) language, the letter K is represented as 01001011. This equals 8 bits, or 1 byte. (We'll discuss binary language in more detail in Chapter 9.)

You've probably heard the terms kilobyte (KB) and megabyte (MB) before. But how do these fit into the bit and byte discussion here? Not only are bits and bytes used as the

FIGURE 1.27   How Much Is a Byte?

NAME	ABBREVIATION	NUMBER OF BYTES	RELATIVE SIZE
BYTE	B	1 byte	Can hold one character of data.
KILOBYTE	KB	1,024 bytes	Can hold 1,024 characters or about half of a typewritten page double-spaced.
MEGABYTE	MB	1,048,576 bytes	A floppy disk holds approximately 1.4 MB of data, or approximately 768 pages of typed text.
GIGABYTE	GB	1,073,741,824 bytes	Approximately 786,432 pages of text. Since 500 sheets of paper is approximately 2 inches, this represents a stack of paper 262 feet high.
TERABYTE	TB	1,099,511,627,776 bytes	This represents a stack of typewritten pages almost 51 miles high.
PETABYTE	PB	1,125,899,906,842,624 bytes	The stack of pages is now 52,000 miles high, or about one-fourth the distance from the Earth to the moon.

language that tells the computer what to do, they are also what the computer uses to represent the data and information it inputs and outputs. Word processing files, digital pictures, and even software programs are all represented inside a computer as a series of bits and bytes. These files and applications can be quite large, containing many millions of bytes. To make it easier to measure the size of these files, we need larger units of measure than a byte. Kilobytes, megabytes, and gigabytes are therefore simply amounts of bytes. As shown in Figure 1.27, a **kilobyte (KB)** is approximately 1,000 bytes, a **megabyte (MB)** is about a million bytes, and a **gigabyte (GB)** is about a billion bytes. As our information processing needs have grown, so too have our storage needs. Today, some computers can store up to a petabyte of data—that's more than one quadrillion bytes!

COMPUTER HARDWARE

You've no doubt heard the term *hardware* used in reference to computers. An anonymous person once said that **hardware** is any part of a computer that you can kick when it doesn't work properly. A more formal definition of hardware is any part of the computer you can physically touch. All hardware on the computer helps the computer to perform its various tasks (see Figure 1.28).

Most computer systems have hardware devices that you use to enter, or input, data (text, images, and sounds) into your computer. These devices, such as a keyboard and a mouse, are called **input devices**. In addition to the keyboard and the mouse, input devices include scanners (which input text and photos), microphones (which input sounds), and digital cameras (which input photos and video).

You also use input devices to provide the steps and tasks the computer needs to process data into usable information. These steps and tasks are called **instructions**. Instructions may be in the form of a user response to a question posed while working in a software application or in the form of a command in which you instruct the computer what to do (such as clicking an icon with your mouse).

As noted earlier, once data is entered into a computer, the computer processes that data. Those components that process data

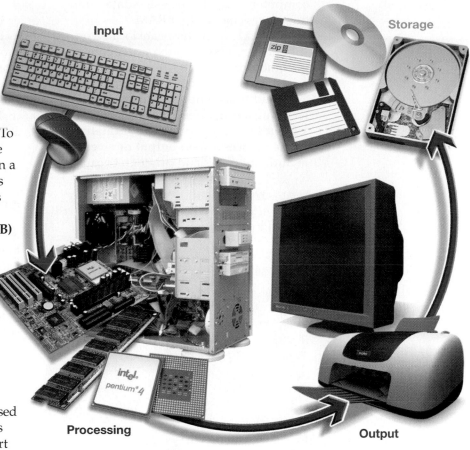

Input

Storage

Processing

Output

FIGURE 1.28

Each part of the computer serves a special function.

---

are located inside the **system unit**. The system unit is the metal or plastic case that holds all the physical parts of the computer together. The part of the system unit that is responsible for the processing (or the "brains" of the computer) is called the **central processing unit**, or **CPU**.

Another component inside the system unit that helps process data into information is **memory**. Memory chips hold (or store) the instructions or data that the CPU processes. The most common type of memory that a

SOUND BYTE

VIRTUAL COMPUTER TOUR

In this Sound Byte, you'll take a video tour of the inside of a system unit. From opening the cover to locating the power supply, CPU, and memory, you'll become more familiar with what's inside your computer.

computer uses for processing data is random access memory, or RAM.

The CPU and memory are located on a special circuit board in the system unit called the **motherboard**. Once this data has been processed, it is classified as information.

In addition to input devices and the system unit, a computer includes devices that let you see your processed information. These devices, called **output devices**, include monitors and printers. Because they output sound, speakers are also considered output devices.

Finally, when your data has been input, processed, and output, you may want to store the data or information so that you can access and use it again. Specialized **storage devices** such as hard disk drives, floppy disk drives, and CD drives allow you to store your data and information.

We'll discuss all the hardware you find on a computer in much more detail in Chapter 2.

COMPUTER SOFTWARE

A computer needs more than just hardware to work: it also needs some form of software. Think of a book without words or a CD without music. Without words or music, these two common items are just shells that hold nothing. Similarly, a computer without software is a shell full of hardware components that can't do anything. **Software** is the set of computer programs that enables the hardware to perform different tasks. There are two broad categories of software: application software and system software.

When you think of software, you are most likely thinking of application software. **Application software** is the set of programs you use on a computer to help you carry out tasks. If you've ever typed a document, created a spreadsheet, or edited a digital photo, for example, you've used a form of application software (see Figure 1.29).

System software is the set of programs that enables your computer's hardware devices and application software to work together. The most common type of system software is the **operating system (OS)**, the program that controls the way in which your computer system functions. It manages the hardware of the computer system, including the CPU, memory, and storage devices, as well as input and output devices such as the mouse, keyboard, and printer. The operating system also provides a means by which users can interact with the computer. We'll cover software in greater depth in Chapter 4 and Chapter 5.

FIGURE 1.29

Software is the set of computer programs that enable the hardware to perform different tasks.

COMPUTER PLATFORMS: PCS AND MACS

The kind of operating system software you have depends on your computer's **platform.** The two most common platform types are the PC (short for personal computer, named after the original IBM personal computer) and the Apple Macintosh (or Mac). Macs and PCs use different CPUs, and therefore, each system processes information very differently. Correspondingly, their operating systems are also different. Macintosh computers use the Macintosh operating system (or Mac OS), whereas PCs generally run on the Microsoft Windows operating system. But that's where their differences end. You can still use both PCs and Macs to perform the same types of tasks (word processing and so on). The PC is not necessarily better than the Mac (or vice versa), but PCs have by far the larger market share (see Figure 1.30). Although the vast majority of consumers use PCs, Macs are the platform of choice for professions such as graphic design and animation.

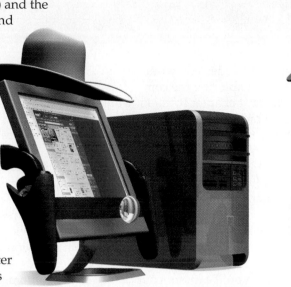

FIGURE 1.30

Ever since the early 1980s, PCs and Macs have been gunning for each other's market share. Although PCs have a much larger market share, Macs are still the platform of choice for many professions, such as graphic design.

SPECIALTY COMPUTERS

PCs and Macs (whether desktop or laptop units) are obviously not the only computers you may encounter. There are smaller, more mobile computers that you can carry around, such as PDAs. In addition, there are computers you may never come in direct contact with but that are important to our society nonetheless:

- **Servers** are computers that provide resources to other computers connected in a network. When you connect to the Internet, for example, your computer is communicating with a server at your Internet service provider (ISP). This server provides your computer with services that allow it to access the Internet. One server can provide services to many computers.

- **Mainframes** are large, expensive computers that support hundreds or thousands of users simultaneously. Mainframes excel at executing many different computer programs at the same time. Although many large companies still use mainframes, smaller and cheaper PC-based servers have replaced mainframes in many companies.

- **Supercomputers** are specially designed computers that can perform complex calculations extremely rapidly. They are used in situations in which complex

models requiring intensive mathematical calculations are needed (such as weather forecasting or atomic energy research). Supercomputers are the fastest and most expensive computers. The main difference between a supercomputer and a mainframe is that supercomputers are designed to execute a few programs as quickly as possible, while mainframes are designed to handle many programs running at the same time (but at a slower pace).

No matter what the size, computers are an integral part of our lives, and they are constantly changing. Whether you're a novice or an experienced computer user or fall somewhere in between, you need to learn as much as you can about computers so that you can use them wisely.

SOUND BYTE

QUESTIONS TO ASK BEFORE YOU BUY A COMPUTER

This Sound Byte will help you consider some important questions you need to ask when you buy a computer, such as whether you should get a laptop or a desktop, or whether you should purchase a new computer or a used or refurbished one.

Using This Book

This book is arranged in the order you would most likely proceed when exploring the computer. You'll start in the next chapter by looking at your computer as you would if you were assembling it for the first time, exploring each piece and its function within your system. Next, Chapter 3 explores the Internet and its many features. Even if you're an experienced Internet user, this chapter will help you use the Internet more effectively and more safely.

In Chapter 4, you'll look more closely at the application software that you'll most likely encounter in your daily life, both at work and at home. Then, in Chapter 5, you'll explore your computer's operating system. In doing so, you'll learn about the different system software programs you can use to keep your computer in top shape, as well as ways in which you can keep your files and folders organized.

Once you understand the pieces of your system and the three elements that make it a useful tool (the Internet, application software, and the operating system), Chapter 6 will help you evaluate your computer system to see if it's meeting your needs. By exploring and evaluating your system's parts, you'll learn whether you need to upgrade your computer and how to go about doing so.

It's likely that you have more than one computer in your home, workplace, or school. To share common resources among computers, you need to know about networking. Thus, in Chapter 7, you'll learn about home computer networks as well as how to protect yourself from hackers and viruses. Then, in Chapter 8, you'll explore mobile computing devices such as cell phones, PDAs, portable computers, and tablet PCs.

Finally, in Chapter 9, you'll find out just how your computer's hardware really works. You'll learn more about your CPU and the types of RAM available on the market today and how these components affect your computer's performance.

Along the way, Technology in Focus features will teach you more about the history of the personal computer, digital technology, and how to protect your computer and the data on it. You'll also find more material on the book's companion Web site, at **www.prenhall.com/techinaction**.

No matter how much you use the computer, you probably still have a lot of questions about how to use it *best*. Throughout this book, you'll find references to multimedia components called Sound Bytes (like the one shown in Figure 1.31) that *show* you the answers to some frequently asked questions, such as how to set up a firewall and how to use antivirus software effectively. You'll find these Sound Bytes on the book's CD as well as on the companion Web site **www.prenhall.com/techinaction**.

In each chapter, you'll also find Bits and Bytes (like the one shown in Figure 1.32), boxes that contain interesting facts and helpful tips on how to best maintain and use your computer.

Also scattered throughout the book are Trends in IT features (like the one shown in Figure 1.33) that examine computer-related ethical issues, careers in technology, applications of computers in society, as well as emerging technologies.

Finally, throughout the book you'll find Dig Deeper features (like the one shown in Figure 1.34). These features take an in-depth look at various computer concepts, such as how a hard disk drive or a computer firewall works.

The wonderful thing about computers is that there is something new to learn about them every day. Developing an understanding of how computers can make your life easier is critical to your future. So, let's get started on our exploration of computers. In the next chapter, you'll learn all about the parts of your computer and how these parts make computers such useful tools.

SOUND BYTE

QUESTIONS TO ASK BEFORE YOU BUY A COMPUTER

This Sound Byte will help you consider some important questions you need to ask when you buy a computer, such as whether you should get a laptop or a desktop, or whether you should purchase a new computer or a used or refurbished one.

FIGURE 1.31

BITS AND BYTES

Keeping Your Keyboard Clean

To keep your computer running at its best, it's important that you occasionally clean your keyboard. To do so, follow these steps:

1. Turn off your computer.
2. Disconnect the keyboard from your system.
3. Turn the keyboard upside down and *gently* shake out any loose debris. You may want to spray hard-to-reach places with compressed air (found in any computer store) or use a vacuum device made especially for computers. Don't use your home vacuum, because the suction is too strong and may damage your keyboard.
4. Wipe the keys with a cloth or cotton swab lightly dampened with a diluted solution of dishwashing liquid and water or isopropyl alcohol and water. Don't spray or pour cleaning solution directly onto the keyboard. Make sure you hold the keyboard upside down or at an angle to prevent drips from running into the circuitry.

FIGURE 1.32

TRENDS IN IT

Emerging Technologies: Tomorrow's Displays

Most of us grew up with CRT monitors on our computers. Large and heavy but providing excellent resolution and clarity, these monitors were the main display for computers until the early 2000s. Soon, though, you may only find these clunky dinosaurs in the Smithsonian.

Today, LCD screens are where it's at. First introduced in 2000, these monitors have taken the desktop market by storm, and with prices steadily dropping, they now out-sell CRTs. Lighter and less bulky than CRT monitors, they can be easily moved and take up less real estate on a desk. Still, current LCD technology does have limitations. LCD screens are relatively fragile (although less so than CRT monitors) and viewing angles are limited. In addition, LCDs can't display full-motion video as well as CRT monitors, making them unpopular with hard-core gamers.

Despite their limitations, LCDs will continue to be the predominant display device for computers, cell phones, and PDAs in the next few years. But according to sources like *PC Magazine*, new technologies are being developed that take LCD displays to the next level.

Flexible Screens

The most promising displays currently under development are *organic light-emitting displays* (OLEDs). These displays, currently used in some Kodak cameras, use organic compounds that produce light when exposed to an electric current. OLEDs tend to use less power than other flat-screen technologies, making them ideal for portable battery-operated devices. However, most research is being geared toward *flexible OLEDs* (FOLEDs). Unlike LCDs and CRTs, which use rigid surfaces such as glass, FOLED screens would be designed on lightweight, inexpensive, flexible material such as transparent plastics or metal foils. As shown in Figure 2.28, the computer screen of the future might roll up into an easily transported cylinder the size of a pen!

FOLEDs would allow advertising to progress to a new dimension. Screens could be hung where posters are hung now (such as on billboards). And wireless transmission of data to these screens would allow advertisers to display easily updatable full-motion images. Combining transparency and flexibility would

...eavy computer monitor. With FOLED technology, ... screen wherever you need it from a container ...own is currently being developed by Universal ...vailable within two to three years.

FIGURE 1.33

DIG DEEPER

How Ink-Jet and Laser Printers Work

Ever wonder how a printer knows what to print, and how it puts ink in just the right places? Most ink-jet printers use *drop-on-demand* technology in which the ink is "demanded" and then "dropped" onto the paper. Two separate processes use drop-on-demand technology: thermal bubble, used by Hewlett-Packard and Canon, and piezoelectric, used by Epson. The difference between the two processes is how the ink is heated within the print cartridge reservoir (the chamber inside the printer that holds the ink).

In the thermal bubble process, the ink is heated in such a way that it expands (like a bubble) and leaves the cartridge reservoir through a small opening, or nozzle. Figure 2.16 shows the general process for thermal bubble. In the piezoelectric process, each ink nozzle contains a crystal at the back of the ink reservoir that receives an electrical charge, causing the ink to vibrate and drop out of the nozzle.

Laser printers use a completely different process. Inside a laser printer is a big metal cylinder (or drum) that is charged with static electricity. When you ask the printer to print something, it sends signals to the laser in the laser printer, telling it to "uncharge" selected spots on the charged cylinder, corresponding to the document you wish to print. Toner, a fine powder that is used in place of liquid ink, is attracted to only those areas on the drum that are not charged. (These uncharged areas are the characters and images you want to print.) The toner is then transferred to the paper as it feeds through the printer. Finally, the toner is melted onto the paper. All unused toner is swept away before the next job starts the process all over again.

FIGURE 2.16

How a thermal bubble ink-jet printer works.

Ink-jet Printer

The print cartridge is positioned inside your inkjet printer so that the print head faces down towards the paper. The print head has 50 to several hundred nozzles, or small holes, through which ink droplets fall. These nozzles are narrower than a human hair. Inside the print head of color inkjet printers, there are three ink reservoirs that hold magenta (red), cyan (blue), and yellow ink. Depending on your printer, a fourth ink reservoir may be required to hold black ink, as well. (In non-color inkjet printers, there is only one ink reservoir for the black ink.)

Print Cartridges

Print Head

Nozzles

Inverted Print Cartridge

(a) firing chamber — ink — resistor — nozzle

(b) bubble forming — ink forced out of the nozzle

(c) ink drop

(d) ink dot

STEP (a): Once the printer receives the command to print, electrical pulses flow through thin resistors in the print head to heat the ink.

STEP (b): The heated ink forms a bubble. The bubble continues to expand until it is forced out of nozzle.

STEP (c): The ink drops onto the paper.

STEP (d): As the ink leaves the cartridge, the chamber begins to cool and contract, creating a vacuum to draw in the ink for the process to begin again.

FIGURE 1.34

Summary

1. What does it mean to be "computer fluent"?

Computer fluency goes way beyond knowing how to use a mouse and send e-mail. If you are computer fluent, you understand the capabilities and limitations of computers and know how to use them wisely. Being computer fluent also enables you to make informed purchasing decisions, use computers in your career, understand and take advantage of future technologies, and understand the many ethical, legal, and societal implications of technology today.

2. How does being computer fluent make you a savvy computer user and consumer?

By understanding how a computer is constructed and how its various parts function, you'll be able to get the most out of your computer. Among other things, you'll be able to avoid hackers, viruses, and Internet headaches; protect your privacy; separate the real risks from those you don't have to worry about; be able to maintain, upgrade, and troubleshoot your computer; and make good purchasing decisions.

3. How can becoming computer fluent help you in a career?

As computers become more a part of our daily lives, it is difficult to imagine any career that does not use computers in some fashion. Understanding how to use computers effectively will help you be a more productive and valuable employee, no matter which profession you choose.

4. How can becoming computer fluent help you understand and take advantage of future technologies?

The world is changing every day, and many changes are a result of new computer technologies. Understanding how today's computers function should help you utilize technology effectively now. And by understanding computers and how they work today, you can contribute to the technologies of tomorrow by providing manufacturers with suggestions on what you need to do that you can't do with current technology.

5. What kinds of challenges do computers bring to a digital society and how does becoming computer fluent help you deal with these challenges?

Although computers offer us a world of opportunities, they also pose ethical, legal, and moral challenges and questions. Being computer fluent enables you to form *educated* opinions on these issues and to take stands based on accurate information rather than media hype and misinformation.

6. What exactly is a computer and what are its four main functions?

Computers are data processing devices. They help organize, sort, and categorize data to turn it into information. The computer's four major functions are (1) it gathers data (or allows users to input data), (2) it processes that data (performs calculations or some other manipulation of the data), (3) it outputs data or information (displays information in a form suitable for the user), and (4) it stores data and information for later use.

7. What is the difference between data and information?

Data is a representation of a fact or idea. The number 3 and the words *televisions* or *Sony* are pieces of data. Information is data that has been organized or presented in a meaningful fashion. An inventory list that indicates that "3 Sony televisions" are in stock is processed information. It allows a retail clerk to answer a customer query about the availability of merchandise. Information is more powerful than raw data.

8. What are a bit and a byte and how are they measured?

To process data into information, computers need to work in a language they understand. This language, called binary language, consists of two numbers: 0 and 1. Each 0 and 1 is a binary digit, or bit. Eight bits create one byte. In computers, each letter of the alphabet, each number, and each special character consists of a unique combination of eight bits (1 byte), or a string of eight 0s and 1s. For describing large amounts of storage capacity, the terms kilobyte (approximately 1,000 bytes) megabyte (approximately 1 million bytes), and gigabyte (approximately 1 billion bytes) are used.

9. What hardware does a computer use to perform its functions?

Hardware is any part of the computer you can touch. Most computers have input devices that you use to input data into your computer. Those components that process that data are located inside the system unit. They include the CPU (central processing unit), memory, and motherboard. Output devices (such as monitors and printers) are used to display information (after processing) in a format suitable for users. Finally, storage devices (such as hard disk drives) are used to preserve data and information for future use.

10. What are the two main types of software you find in a computer?

The two broad categories of software are application software and system software. Application software is the set of programs you use on a computer to help you carry out tasks (such as writing a letter). System software is the set of programs that enables your computer's hardware devices and application software to work together. The most common type of system software is the operating system.

11. What different kinds of computers are there?

Aside from PCs and Macs, you'll find mobile computing devices (such as laptops and PDAs), as well as servers, mainframes, and supercomputers. Servers are computers that provide resources to other computers connected in a network. Mainframes are large, expensive computers specifically designed to provide services to hundreds (or thousands) of users at the same time. Supercomputers are designed to perform a small number of calculations as rapidly as possible.

Key Terms

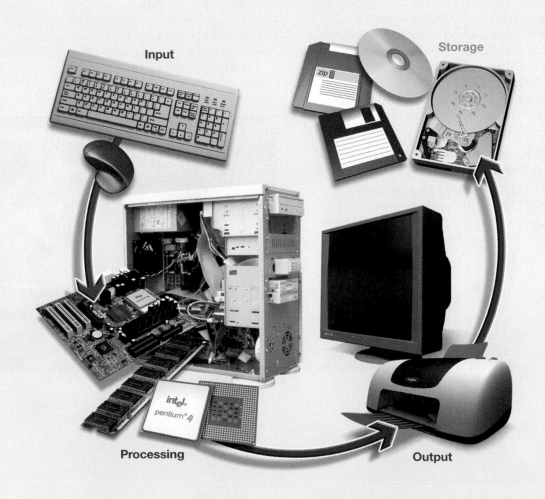

Input

Storage

Processing

Output

Buzz Words

Word Bank

- input
- CPU
- data
- platform
- biomedical chips
- application software
- mainframe

- output
- nanotechnology
- byte
- supercomputer
- information
- server
- storage

- processing
- computer forensics
- system software
- bit
- megabyte
- gigabyte

Instructions: Fill in the blanks using the words from the Word Bank above.

Because of the integration of computers into business and society, many fields of study are available now that were unheard of a few years ago. (1) _____, the study of very small computing devices built at the molecular level, will provide major advances in the miniaturization of computing. (2) _____ is already taking criminologists beyond what they could accomplish with conventional investigation techniques. And as (3) _____ become widespread, individuals will benefit from having computing devices implanted right in their bodies.

At the lowest level, computers manipulate data in units called (4) _____s. Because these units are too small to define data on their own (say, standing for the letter Q), they are grouped together to form (5) _____s. (6) _____ represents raw facts or ideas. (7) _____ represents facts or ideas that have been organized or processed in some fashion to make them more meaningful. When storing data, large quantities of space are needed. The capacity of most hard drives today is measured in (8) _____s, which represents over 1 billion bytes of information.

For data to be acted upon by a computer, various components of the computer must interact with the data. Mice and keyboards are examples of (9) _____ devices that are used to enter data into the computer. The CPU is an example of a (10) _____ device that helps turn data into information. (11) _____ devices, such as monitors and printers, allow computers to provide information in a usable format. To save information and data for later use, (12) _____ devices such as hard disk drives and CD drives are used.

Organizing Key Terms

Instructions: This chapter introduces many new terms and concepts. In the following illustration, fill in each of the blanks with key terms or concepts from the chapter in order to show how categories of ideas fit together.

CAREERS AND POSITIONS USING COMPUTERS	REASONS TO BUILD COMPUTER FLUENCY	FUTURE OF COMPUTING

RETAIL

1. _____
2. _____

ART

3. _____
4. _____

MEDICINE

5. _____
6. _____

7. _____

● *Detectives*

● *Lawyers*

8. _____

EDUCATION

9. _____
10. _____

11. _____

● *Protect privacy*

12. _____
13. _____

● *Artificial intelligence*

14. _____
15. _____

Making the Transition to . . . Next Semester

1. Computer Literacy

In your college career, you'll be spending time understanding the requirements of the degree program you choose. At many schools, computer literacy requirements exist, either as incoming requirements (skills students must have before they are admitted) or outgoing requirements (skills students must prove they have before graduating). Does your program require specific computer skills? Should these be required? How can students efficiently prove that they have these skills?

2. Future Hardware/Software Needs

Think about the schedule of courses you will be taking next semester. How many courses will require you to produce papers in electronic format? How many will require you to use course management software, such as Blackboard or WebCT? Will any require you to use some specialty software product such as a nutrition monitoring program or a statistics training application? Do any courses require specialized hardware for your computer?

3. Future System Needs

Consider the number of years you are planning to continue your studies. Will you be purchasing a computer system? Will you need to upgrade your existing system? If you do buy a new system today, might you need to buy/upgrade another system before the end of your collegiate career?

4. Using New Technologies

Do you think you are taking advantage of the latest technologies for learning? Can you record lectures on a cell phone? Can you read posted lecture notes from a PDA? Can you copy files you need to take home from the school network to an iPod MP3 player?

Making the Transition to . . . the Workplace

1. Computer-Free Workplaces?

In this chapter we listed a number of careers that demand computer skills. How are computers used in the profession you are in or plan to enter? Can you think of any careers in which people do not use computers? Can you imagine computers being used in these careers in the future? How?

2. Medical Computing Applications

In their training and their work, doctors and nurses rely on computers. What about patients? Does having access to a computer and computer skills help a patient create better health care options? Does having access to a computer help in filing an insurance claim? Does it help in finding the best doctor or hospital for a specific procedure?

3. Preparing for a Job

An office is looking for help and needs an employee able to manipulate data on Excel spreadsheets, to coordinate the computer file management for the office, and to conduct backups of critical data. How could you prove to the interviewer that you have the skills to handle the job? How could you prove you have the ability to learn the job?

4. Career Outlook

Which career fields are growing the fastest? (Suggestion: Try asking Jeeves at **www.ask.com**.) What computer skills and knowledge do the top 10 of these career paths demand?

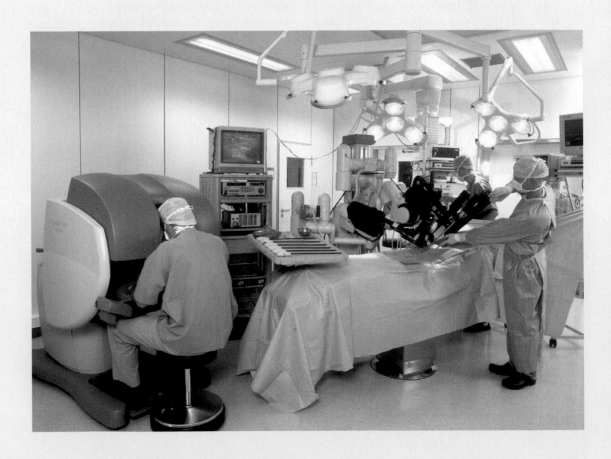

Critical Thinking Questions

Instructions: Albert Einstein used "Gedanken experiments," or critical thinking questions, to develop his theory of relativity. Some ideas are best understood by experimenting with them in our own minds. The following critical thinking questions are designed to demand your full attention but require only a comfortable chair—no technology.

1. Rating Your Computer Fluency

This chapter lists a number of ways in which knowing about computers (or becoming computer fluent) will help you. How much do you know about computers? What else would you like to know? How do you think learning more about computers will help you in the future?

2. Data Mining

This chapter briefly discusses data mining, a technique companies use to study sales data and gather information from it. Have you heard of data mining before? How might a company like Wal-Mart or Target use data mining to better run their business? Can you think of any privacy risks data mining might pose?

3. Nanotechnology

As you learned in the chapter, nanotechnology is the science revolving around the use of nanostructures to build devices on an extremely small scale. What applications of tiny computers can you think of? How might nanotechnology impact your life?

4. Biomedical Chips

This chapter discusses various uses of biomedical chips. Many biomedical chip implants that will be developed in the future will most likely be aimed at correcting vision loss, hearing loss, or other physical impediments. But chips could also be developed to improve physical or mental capabilities of healthy individuals. For example, chips could be implanted in athletes to make their muscles work better together, thereby allowing them to run faster. Or, your memory could be enhanced by providing additional storage capacity for your brain.

a. Should biomedical implant devices that increase athletic performance be permitted in the Olympics? What about devices that repair a problem (such as blindness in one eye) but then increase the level of visual acuity in the affected eye so that it is better than normal vision?

b. Would you be willing to have a chip implanted in your brain to improve your memory? Would you be willing to have a VeriChip implanted under your skin?

5. Artificial Intelligence

Artificial intelligence is the science that attempts to produce machines that display the same type of intelligence that humans do. Do you think humans will ever create a machine that can think? In your opinion, what are the ethical and moral implications associated with artificial intelligence?

6. IT Careers

Information technology (IT) careers are suited to a wide range of people at different points in their lives.

a. Would an IT career have advantages for a single parent? How?

b. Would an IT career be able to help someone pursue a later career in a nontechnical field?

c. How might an IT career assist someone in completing a college degree?

Team Time   Promoting Future Technologies

Problem:

People are often overwhelmed by the relentless march of technology. Accessibility of information is changing the way we work, play, and interact with our friends, family, and coworkers. In this Team Time, we consider the future and reflect on how the advent of new technologies will affect our daily lives 10 years in the future.

Task:

Your group has just returned from a trip in a time machine 10 years into the future. Amazing changes have taken place in just a short time. To a large extent, consumer acceptance of technology makes or breaks a new technology. Your mission is to create a creative marketing strategy to promote the technological changes you observed in the future and accelerate their acceptance.

Process:

Divide the class into three or more teams.

1. With the other members of your team, use the Internet to research up-and-coming technologies (**www.howstuffworks.com** is a good starting point). Prepare a list of innovations that you believe will occur in the next 10 years. Determine how they will be integrated into society and the effect they will have on our culture.
2. Present your group's findings to the class for debate and discussion. Note specifically how the rest of the class reacts to your reports on the innovations. Are they excited? Skeptical? Incredulous? Did they laugh off your ideas or become wildly enthusiastic?
3. Write a marketing strategy paper detailing how you would promote the technological changes that you envision for the future. Also note some barriers for acceptance the technology may have to overcome, as well as any legal or ethical challenges or questions you see the new technology posing.

Conclusion:

The future path of technology is determined by dreamers. If not for innovators such as Edison, Bell, and Einstein, we would not be as advanced a society as we are today. Innovators come from all walks of life and our creative energies must be exercised to keep them in tune. Don't be afraid to suggest technological advancements that seem outrageous today. In 1966, when the original *Star Trek* series was on television, handheld communicators seemed astounding and beyond our reach. Yet the dreamers who created those communication devices for a science fiction series spawned a multi-billion-dollar cell phone industry in the twenty-first century. The next technological wave may be started in your imagination!

Materials on the Web

In addition to the review materials presented here, you'll find extra materials on the book's companion Web site (**www.prenhall.com/techinaction**) that will help reinforce your understanding of the chapter content. These materials include the following:

Sound Byte Lab Guides

For each Sound Byte mentioned in the chapter, there is a corresponding lab guide located on the book's companion Web site. These guides review the material presented in the Sound Byte and direct you to various Web resources that examine the material. The Sound Byte Lab Guides for this chapter include these:

- Virtual Computer Tour
- Questions to Ask When You Buy a Computer

True/False and Multiple-Choice Quizzes

The book's Web site includes a true/false and a multiple-choice quiz for this chapter. You can take these quizzes, automatically check the results, and e-mail the results to your instructor.

Web Research Projects

The book's Web site also includes a number of Web research projects for this chapter. These projects ask you to search the Web for information on computer-related careers, milestones in computer history, important people and companies, emerging technologies, and the applications and implications of different technologies.

Technology in Action also features unique interactive Help Desk training, in which you'll assume the role of Help Desk operator taking calls about concepts learned in each chapter. The Help Desk calls for this chapter include:

- Understanding Bits and Bytes

CHAPTER 2

OBJECTIVES

After reading this chapter, you should be able to answer the following questions:

- What devices do you use to get data into the computer? (pp. 38–43)

- What devices do you use to get information out of the computer? (pp. 43–49)

- What's on the front of your system unit? (pp. 50–53)

- What's on the back of your system unit? (pp. 53–54)

- What's inside your system unit? (pp. 54–56)

- How do you set up your computer to avoid strain and injury? (pp. 56–59)

 **SOUND BYTES**

- Port Tour (p. 54)
- Virtual Computer Tour (p. 55)
- Healthy Computing (p. 57)

Looking at Computers:

Understanding the Parts

Jillian has just bought a new computer and is setting it up. Because she lives in a dorm, she spent more than she had planned to buy a flat-panel monitor, which she places on her small desk. It takes up far less room than her old monitor, which was big and bulky. Next she pulls out her system unit, which she knows is the component she'll connect all the other pieces of her system to. Although she wanted to buy the most powerful computer on the market, she bought one that was slightly less expensive. Still, it came with a Zip drive, CD-RW/DVD combo player, a 100-GB hard drive, and what the computer salesperson said was enough memory and power to do almost anything. She sets it on the floor next to her desk and attaches the monitor to it.

Next she pulls out her keyboard. She looked into buying a wireless keyboard, but since her budget was tight, she bought a standard keyboard instead. The box tells her it is a "USB" keyboard, so she finds what looks to be the right port on the back of her system unit and plugs it in. Her mouse also needs a USB port. Finding another USB port, she attaches the mouse there. She's glad that her system has plenty of USB ports.

She sets up her speakers next. Although the salesperson told her she'd probably want to upgrade them, she decided to wait until she can afford it. She arranges them on her desk, then finds two round ports on her system unit that match their plugs. She sees the ports are labeled "speaker out" and "mic in," so she inserts the speakers into the "speaker out" port.

Last is her printer. She debated over which type of printer to buy, but decided to buy an ink-jet because she prints a lot of color copies and photos. She finds the right port on her system unit and connects it. She then plugs the monitor, speakers, printer, and system unit into the surge protector, which the salesperson told her would protect her devices from power surges. All that's left is to make sure her setup is comfortable, and she's ready to go.

What kind of computer setup do you have? Do you know all the options available and what the different components of your system do? In this chapter, we'll take a look at your computer's basic parts. You'll learn about input devices (such as the mouse and keyboard), output devices (such as monitors and printers), storage devices (such as the hard drive), as well as components inside the computer that help it to function. Finally, you'll learn how to set up your computer so that it's comfortable to work on.

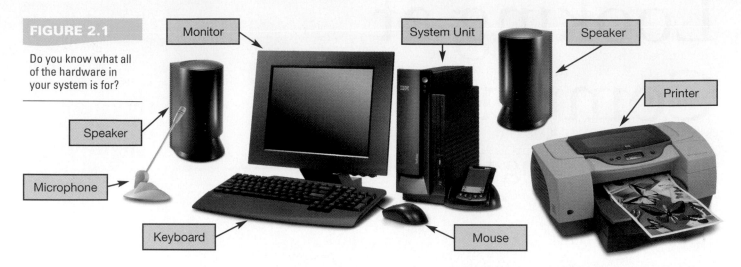

FIGURE 2.1

Do you know what all of the hardware in your system is for?

Monitor · System Unit · Speaker · Printer · Speaker · Microphone · Keyboard · Mouse

Your Computer's Hardware

For the amount of amazing things computers can do, they are really quite simple machines. You learned in Chapter 1 that a basic computer system is made up of software and hardware. In this chapter, we look more closely at your computer's **hardware**, the parts you can actually touch (see Figure 2.1). Hardware components consist of the **system unit**, the box that contains the central electronic components of the computer, and **peripheral devices**, those devices such as monitors and printers that are connected to the computer. Together the system unit and peripheral devices perform four main functions: they enable the computer to input data, process that data, and output and store the data and information. We begin our exploration of hardware by taking a look at your computer's input devices.

Input Devices

An **input device** enables you to enter data (text, images, and sounds) and instructions (user responses and commands) into the computer. The most common input devices are the **keyboard** and the **mouse**. You use keyboards to enter typed data and commands, whereas you use the mouse to enter user responses and commands. There are other input devices as well: microphones input sounds, while scanners and digital cameras input text and images.

KEYBOARDS

Aren't all keyboards the same? Most desktop computers come with a standard keyboard, which uses the **QWERTY keyboard** layout, as shown in Figure 2.2a. This layout gets its name from the first six letters in the top-left row of alphabetic keys on the keyboard. Over the years, there has been some debate over what is the best layout for keyboards. The QWERTY layout was originally designed for typewriters, not computers, and was meant to slow typists to prevent typewriter keys from jamming. The QWERTY layout is therefore considered inefficient because it slows typing speeds. Now that technology can keep up with faster typing, other keyboards are being considered.

The **Dvorak keyboard** is the leading alternative keyboard, although it is not

FIGURE 2.2

(a) The first six keys in the top-left row of alphabetic keys give the QWERTY keyboard its name. QWERTY is the standard keyboard that comes with most computers. (b) With a Dvorak keyboard, you can type most of the more commonly used words in the English language with the letters found on "home keys," the keys in the middle row of the keyboard.

nearly as common as the QWERTY. The Dvorak keyboard puts the most commonly used letters in the English language on "home keys," the keys in the middle row of the keyboard, as shown in Figure 2.2b. The Dvorak keyboard's design reduces the distance your fingers travel for most keystrokes, increasing typing speed.

How can I use my keyboard most efficiently? All keyboards have the standard set of alpha and numeric keys that you regularly use when typing. As shown in Figure 2.3, there are also other keys on a keyboard that have special functions. Knowing how to use these special keys will help you improve your efficiency with the keyboard:

• The **numeric keypad** allows you to enter numbers quickly.

• **Function keys** act as shortcut keys you press to perform special tasks. They are sometimes referred to as the "F" keys because they start with the letter *F* followed by a number. Each software application has its own set of tasks assigned to the function keys, although some are more universal. For example, the F1 key is usually the Help key in software applications. However, the F4 key performs a different shortcut in Microsoft Word than it does in Microsoft Excel.

• The **Control key** is used in combination with other keys to perform shortcuts and special tasks. For example, holding down the Control key while pressing the letter *B* adds bold formatting to selected text. Similarly, you use the **Alt**

BITS AND BYTES

Keeping Your Keyboard Clean

To keep your computer running at its best, it's important that you occasionally clean your keyboard. To do so, follow these steps:

1. Turn off your computer.
2. Disconnect the keyboard from your system.
3. Turn the keyboard upside down and *gently* shake out any loose debris. You may want to spray hard-to-reach places with compressed air (found in any computer store) or use a vacuum device made especially for computers. Don't use your home vacuum, because the suction is too strong and may damage your keyboard.
4. Wipe the keys with a cloth or cotton swab lightly dampened with a diluted solution of dishwashing liquid and water or isopropyl alcohol and water. Don't spray or pour cleaning solution directly onto the keyboard. Make sure you hold the keyboard upside down or at an angle to prevent drips from running into the circuitry.

key with other keys for additional shortcuts and special tasks. (On Macintosh computers, the Control key is the Apple or Command key while the Alt key is the Option key.)

• The **Windows key** is specific to the Windows operating system. Used alone, it brings up the Start menu; however, it's used most often in combination with other keys as shortcuts. For example, pressing the Windows key plus the letter *E* starts Windows Explorer.

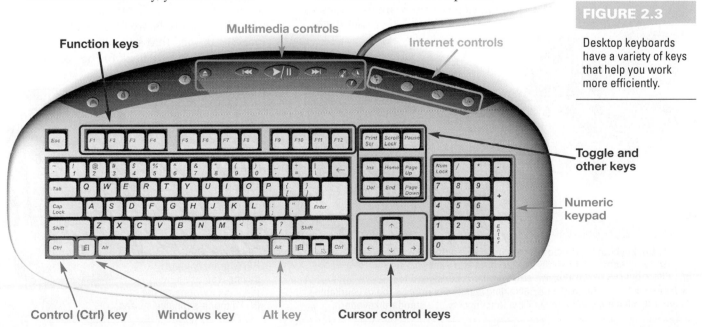

Desktop keyboards have a variety of keys that help you work more efficiently.

Function keys

Multimedia controls

Internet controls

Toggle and other keys

Numeric keypad

Control (Ctrl) key   Windows key   Alt key   Cursor control keys

Some keyboards (such as the one shown in Figure 2.3) also include multimedia and Internet keys or buttons that enable you to open a Web browser, view e-mail, access Help features, or control your CD/DVD player. Unlike the other keys on a standard keyboard, these buttons are not always in the same position on every keyboard, but the symbols on top of the buttons generally help you determine their function.

Another set of controls on standard keyboards are the **cursor control keys** that move your **cursor**, the flashing | symbol on the monitor that indicates where the next character will be inserted. The arrow keys move the cursor one space at a time in a word document, either up, down, left, or right.

Above the arrow keys, you'll usually find keys that move the cursor up or down one full page or to the beginning (Home) or end (End) of a line. The Delete (Del) key allows you to delete characters, whereas the Insert key allows you to insert or overwrite characters within a document. The Insert key is a **toggle key** because its function changes each time you press it: when toggled on, the Insert key inserts new text within a line of existing text. When toggled off, the Insert key *replaces* (or overwrites) existing characters with new characters as you type. Other toggle keys include the Num Lock key and the Caps Lock key, which toggle between an on/off state.

Are keyboards different on laptops?
Laptop keyboards, like that shown in Figure 2.4a, need to be more compact than standard keyboards and therefore have fewer keys. Still, a lot of the laptop keys have alternate functions so that you get the same capabilities

from the limited keys as you do from the special keys on standard keyboards. You can also hook up traditional keyboards to most laptops, or you can use a specially designed keyboard, shown in Figure 2.4b, that fits on top of the laptop.

What about keyboards for PDAs?
Generally, you enter data and commands into a personal digital assistant (PDA) by using a **stylus**, a pen-shaped device that you use by tapping or writing on the PDA's touch-sensitive screen, as shown in Figure 2.5. However, some PDAs have built-in keyboards that allow you to type in text just as you would with a normal keyboard. If your PDA doesn't include a built-in keyboard, you can buy keyboards that attach to the PDA. We'll discuss PDA keyboards in more detail in Chapter 8.

Are there wireless keyboards? As its name indicates, a wireless keyboard doesn't use cables to connect to your computer. Rather, it's powered by batteries and sends data to the computer using a form of wireless technology. Infrared wireless keyboards communicate with the computer using infrared light waves (similar to how a remote control communicates with a TV). The computer receives the infrared light signals through a special infrared port. The disadvantage to infrared keyboards is that you need to point the keyboard directly at the infrared port on the computer for it to work.

What are the best wireless keyboards? The best wireless keyboards send data to the computer using radio frequency (RF). These keyboards contain a radio transmitter that sends out radio wave signals. These signals are received by a small receiver device that sits on your desk and is plugged into the back of the computer where the keyboard would normally plug in. Unlike infrared technology, RF technology doesn't require that you point the keyboard at the receiver for

FIGURE 2.4

(a) Laptop keyboards are more compact than traditional desktop keyboards, and usually don't include extra keys such as the numeric keypad. (b) This full-size keyboard is designed to work with a laptop. With its special folding legs, it sits right on top of your laptop keyboard, allowing you to have all the functionality of a standard keyboard.

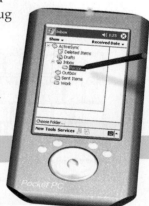

FIGURE 2.5

The stylus is the PDA's primary input device. You use it by tapping or writing on the PDA's touch-sensitive screen.

BITS AND BYTES

Keystroke Shortcuts

You may know that you can combine certain keystrokes to take shortcuts within the Windows operating system. The following are a few of the most helpful shortcuts to make your time at the computer more efficient.

TEXT FORMATTING	FILE MANAGEMENT	CUT/COPY/PASTE	WINDOWS CONTROLS
CTRL+B Applies (or removes) **bold** formatting to selected text	**CTRL+O** Opens the Open dialog box	**CTRL+X** Cuts (removes) selected text from document	**Alt+F4** Closes the current window
	CTRL+N Opens a new document		**Ctrl+Esc** Opens the Start menu
CTRL+I Applies (or removes) *italic* formatting to selected text	**CTRL+S** Saves a document	**CTRL+C** Copies selected text	**Windows Key+F1** Opens Windows Help
	CTRL+P Opens the Print dialog box	**CTRL+V** Pastes selected text (previously cut or copied)	
CTRL+U Applies (or removes) <u>underlining</u> to selected text			**Windows Key+F** Opens the Search (Find Files) dialog box

it to work. RF keyboards used on home computers can be placed as far as 6 to 30 feet from the computer, depending on their quality. RF keyboards used in business conference rooms or auditoriums can be placed as far as 100 feet away from the computer, but they are far more expensive than most home users can afford.

MICE AND OTHER POINTING DEVICES

What kinds of mice are there?
The mouse you're probably most familiar with, like the one shown in Figure 2.6a, has a rollerball on the bottom, which moves when you drag the mouse across a mousepad. The movement of the rollerball controls the movement of your **pointer**, the I-beam or arrow that appears on the screen. Mice also have two or three buttons that enable you to execute commands and open shortcut menus. (Mice for Macintoshes sometimes have only one button.) Some newer mice have additional programmable buttons and wheels that let you scroll through documents or Web pages.

Do I always need a mousepad? You need a mousepad with a traditional rollerball mouse because the mousepad creates the friction needed to move the mouse's rollerball. But you don't need to use a mousepad with every mouse. A **trackball**

mouse, shown in Figure 2.6b, is basically a traditional mouse that has been turned on its back. The rollerball sits on top or on the side of the mouse and you move the ball with your fingers, allowing the mouse to remain stationary. A trackball mouse doesn't demand much wrist motion, so it's considered healthier on the wrists than a traditional mouse.

Another mouse that doesn't use a mousepad is the **optical mouse**, shown in Figure 2.6c. Instead of a rollerball, the optical

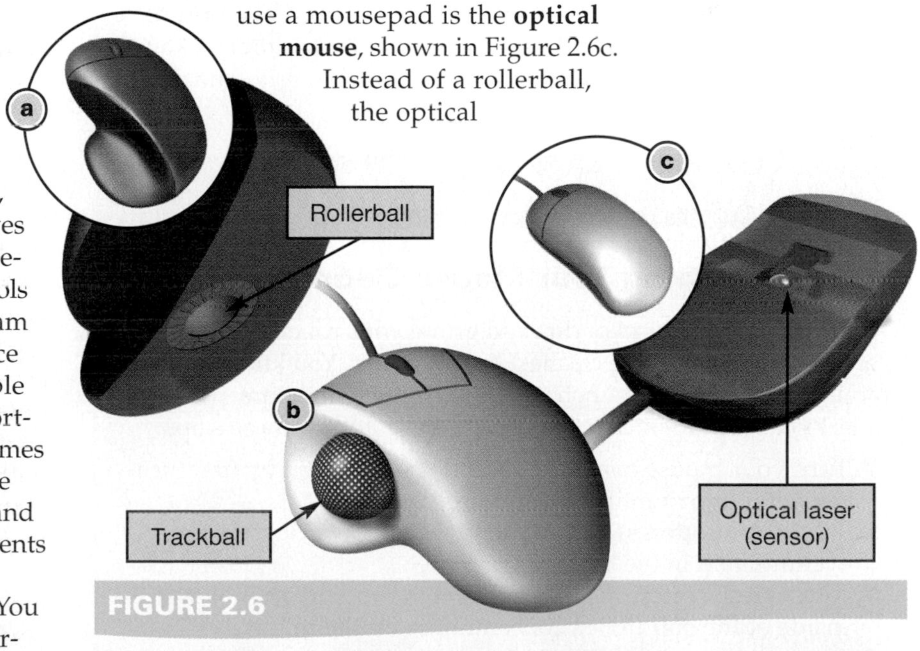

Rollerball

Trackball

Optical laser (sensor)

FIGURE 2.6

(a) A traditional mouse has a rollerball on the bottom, which moves when you drag the mouse across a mousepad. (b) A trackball mouse turns the traditional mouse on its back, allowing you to control the rollerball with your fingers. (c) An optical mouse has an optical laser (or sensor) on the bottom that detects its movement.

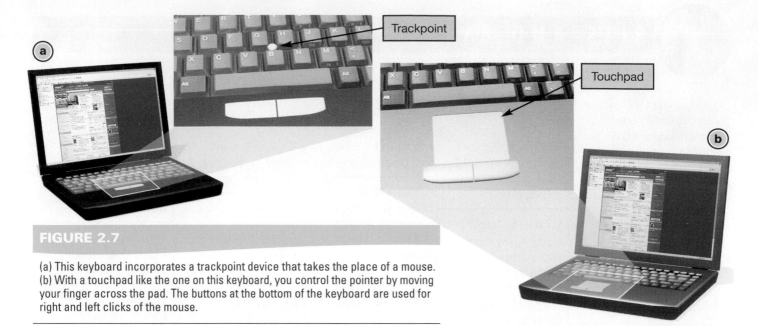

FIGURE 2.7

(a) This keyboard incorporates a trackpoint device that takes the place of a mouse. (b) With a touchpad like the one on this keyboard, you control the pointer by moving your finger across the pad. The buttons at the bottom of the keyboard are used for right and left clicks of the mouse.

mouse uses an internal sensor or laser to detect the mouse's movement. The sensor sends signals to the computer, telling it where to move the pointer on the screen. Optical mice are often a bit more expensive than traditional mice, but because they have no moving parts on the bottom, they have small advantages over traditional mice: there is less chance of parts breaking down and no way for dirt to interfere with the mechanisms.

Are there wireless mice? Just as there are wireless keyboards, there are wireless mice, both standard and optical. Wireless mice are similar to wireless keyboards in that they use batteries and send

data to the computer by radio or light waves. If you also have an RF wireless keyboard, your RF wireless mouse and keyboard can share the same RF receiver.

What about mice for laptops? Due to the limited space on laptops, the mouse is built into the keyboard area. Some laptops incorporate a trackball-like mechanism as a mouse. Others incorporate a **trackpoint**, a small, joystick-like nub that allows you to move the cursor with the tip of your finger. Other laptops have a **touchpad**, a small, touch-sensitive screen at the base of the keyboard. To use the touchpad, you simply move your finger across the pad. Some touchpads are also sensitive to taps, interpreting them as mouse-button clicks. Figure 2.7 shows some of the mouse options you'll find in laptops. Of course, if you prefer, you can always hook up a traditional mouse to your laptop as well.

Are game controls considered mice? Game controls (such as joysticks and steering wheels) are not mice per se, but they are considered input devices because they send data to the computer. Force-feedback joysticks and steering wheels deliver data in both directions: they translate your movements to the computer and translate its responses as forces on your hands, creating a richer simulated experience. If you like to move around a lot while you play games, you can purchase wireless game controllers at most computer stores.

Can I use a mouse with a PDA? As we mentioned earlier, the input device you use with PDAs is a *stylus*. You don't use a

BITS AND BYTES

Keeping Your Mouse Clean

It's amazing what kind of dirt and grime your rollerball mouse can pick up, even in the cleanest environment. You know your mouse needs cleaning when it becomes sluggish, nonresponsive, or jerky in its motion. To clean your mouse, follow these steps:

1. Turn your mouse over and remove the rollerball by first turning and removing the surrounding disk.
2. Take a dry cotton swab and remove any loose dust that has accumulated in the ball area.
3. Run a fresh cotton swab dampened in rubbing alcohol over the inside of the ball cavity, concentrating on the rollers.
4. Clean the mouse ball with rubbing alcohol to remove any oil and grime.
5. Let the components dry before putting them back together.

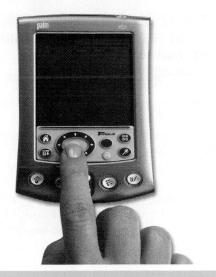

FIGURE 2.8

This PDA "mouse" is a stick-on device that offers mouselike controls and eliminates the need for a stylus.

traditional mouse. However, some PDAs with built-in keyboards do include touchpads and trackpoint controls similar to those found in laptops. Although you can't hook up a traditional desktop mouse to a PDA, there are micelike devices made especially for PDAs that eliminate the need for a stylus, as shown in Figure 2.8.

INPUTTING SOUND

What's the best microphone to have? A **microphone** allows you to capture sound waves (such as your voice) and transfer them to digital format on your computer. Microphones come with most computers, but if you didn't get a microphone with your computer, you may want to buy a desktop microphone if you plan to record your own audio files (see Figure 2.9). A headset microphone is the best type of microphone for videoconferencing and speech-recognition uses. **Videoconferencing** technology allows a person sitting at a computer equipped with a personal video camera and a microphone to transmit video and audio across the Internet (or other communications medium). All computers participating in a videoconference need to have a microphone and speakers installed so that participants can speak to and hear one another.

In **speech-recognition systems**, you operate your computer through a microphone, telling it to perform specific commands (such as to open a file) or to translate your spoken words into data input. Speech recognition

has yet to truly catch on, but its popularity is growing. In fact, it's included in the software applications found in Office 2003. We discuss speech-recognition software in more detail in Chapter 4.

Are expensive microphones worth the money? Microphone quality varies widely. For personal use, an inexpensive microphone is probably sufficient. However, if you plan to create professional products and sell them to others, you'll most likely need a professional recording studio microphone that could cost upward of $250. Speech-recognition software requires a high degree of voice clarity, so it's best to have a headset-style microphone for this application.

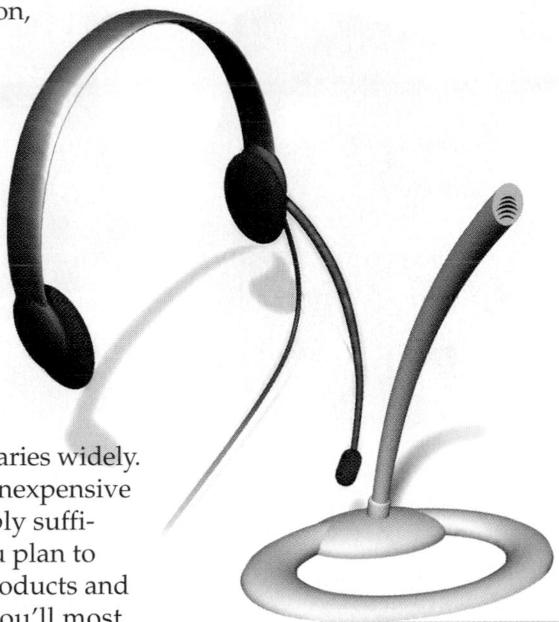

FIGURE 2.9

Headset and desktop microphones offer convenient, hands-free voice input.

Output Devices

As you learned in Chapter 1, **output devices** enable you to send processed data out of your computer. This can take the form of text, pictures (graphics), sounds (audio), and video. One common output device is a **monitor** (sometimes referred to as a **display screen**), which displays text, graphics, and video as *soft copies* (copies you can see only on-screen). Another common output device is the **printer**, which creates tangible or hard copies (copies you can touch) of text and graphics. Speakers are obviously the output devices for sound.

MONITORS

What are the different types of monitors? There are two basic types of monitors: CRTs and LCDs. If your monitor looks like a traditional television set, it has a picture tube device called a **cathode-ray tube (CRT)** like the one shown in Figure 2.10a. If your monitor is flat, such as those found in laptops, it's using **liquid crystal display (LCD)** technology (see Figure 2.10b, p. 44), similar to that used in digital watches. LCD monitors (also called *flat-panel monitors*) are

FIGURE 2.10

(a) CRT monitors are big and bulky and look like television sets. (b) LCDs (flat-panel monitors) save precious desktop space and weigh considerably less than CRT monitors.

lighter and more energy efficient than CRT monitors, making them perfect for portable computers such as laptops.

CRT Monitors
How does a CRT monitor work? A CRT
screen is a grid made up of millions of **pixels**, or tiny dots. Simply put, illuminated pixels are what create the images you see on your monitor. The pixels are illuminated by an electron beam that passes back and forth across the back of the screen very quickly—60 to 75 times a second—so that the pixels appear to glow continuously. Figure 2.11 shows in more detail how a CRT monitor works.

What factors affect the quality of a CRT monitor? A couple of factors affect the quality of a CRT monitor. One is the monitor's refresh rate. **Refresh rate** (sometimes referred to as *vertical refresh rate*) is the number of times per second the electron beam scans the monitor and recharges the illumination of each pixel. Common monitors have refresh rates that range between 75 and 85 hertz (Hz). While some monitors have higher refresh rates, they do not offer any user benefits. Hertz is a unit of frequency indicating cycles per second, in this case meaning the electron beam scans the monitor 75 to 85 times each second. The faster the refresh rate, the less the screen will flicker, the clearer the image will be, and the less eyestrain you'll experience.

The clearness or sharpness of the image—its **resolution**—is controlled by the number of pixels displayed on the screen. The higher the resolution, the sharper and clearer the image. Monitor resolution is listed as a number of pixels. A high-end monitor may have a maximum resolution of 1,600 x 1,200, meaning it contains 1,600 vertical columns with 1,200 pixels in each column. Note that most monitors allow you to adjust their resolution within a certain range. (We discuss setting your monitor's resolution in more detail in Chapter 6.) Dot pitch is another factor

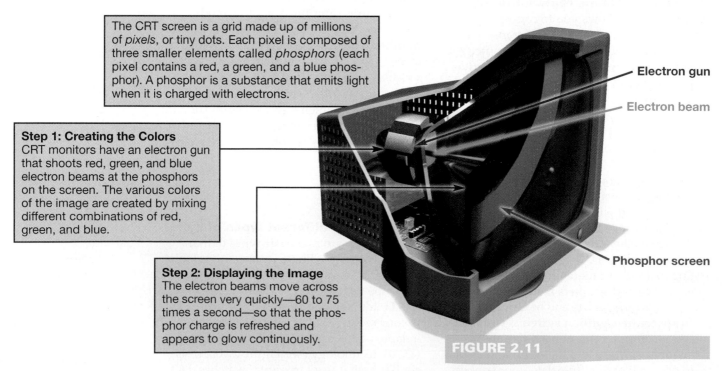

The CRT screen is a grid made up of millions of *pixels*, or tiny dots. Each pixel is composed of three smaller elements called *phosphors* (each pixel contains a red, a green, and a blue phosphor). A phosphor is a substance that emits light when it is charged with electrons.

Step 1: Creating the Colors
CRT monitors have an electron gun that shoots red, green, and blue electron beams at the phosphors on the screen. The various colors of the image are created by mixing different combinations of red, green, and blue.

Step 2: Displaying the Image
The electron beams move across the screen very quickly—60 to 75 times a second—so that the phosphor charge is refreshed and appears to glow continuously.

Electron gun

Electron beam

Phosphor screen

FIGURE 2.11

How a CRT monitor works.

FIGURE 2.12 CRT Monitors vs. LCD Monitors

CRT MONITOR ADVANTAGES	LCD MONITOR ADVANTAGES
Images viewable from all angles (LCD monitors often have limited viewing angle)	Take up less space and weigh less than CRT monitors
Resolution can be adjusted more completely	Cause less eyestrain than CRT monitors
Better color accuracy and clarity	Are more environmentally friendly than CRT monitors
Less expensive than LCD monitors	Larger viewable area compared with similar sized CRT (17-inch viewable area on 17-inch monitor compared with 15-inch viewable area on a 17-inch CRT monitor)
Better for gaming and watching DVDs due to quicker pixel response time and higher color accuracy	

that affects monitor quality. **Dot pitch** is the diagonal distance, measured in millimeters, between pixels of the same color on the screen. A smaller dot pitch means that there is less blank space between pixels, and thus a sharper, clearer image. A good CRT monitor has a dot pitch of 0.28 mm or less.

So, if you're buying a new CRT monitor, choose the one with the highest refresh rate, the highest maximum resolution, and the smallest dot pitch.

LCD Monitors
How does an LCD monitor work? Like a CRT screen, an LCD screen is composed of a grid of pixels. However, instead of including a cathode-ray tube, LCD monitors are made of two sheets of material filled with a liquid crystal solution. A fluorescent panel at the back of the LCD monitor generates light waves. When electric current passes through the liquid crystal solution, the crystals move around, either blocking the fluorescent light or letting the light shine through. This blocking or passing of light by the crystals causes images to be formed on the screen.

Are all LCD monitors the same? You'll generally find two types of LCD monitors on the market: **passive-matrix displays** and **active-matrix displays**. Less expensive LCD monitors use passive-matrix displays, whereas more expensive monitors use active-matrix displays. With passive-matrix technology, electrical current passes through the liquid crystal solution and charges groups of pixels, either in a row or a column. This causes the screen to brighten with each pass of electrical current and subsequently fade. With active-matrix displays, each pixel is charged individually, as needed. The result

is that an active-matrix display produces a clearer, brighter image.

LCD vs. CRT
Are LCD monitors better than CRT monitors? LCD monitors have a number of advantages over CRT monitors, as shown in Figure 2.12. Certainly, size is an advantage, because LCD monitors take up far less space on a desktop than a CRT monitor. Additionally, LCD monitors weigh less, making them the obvious choice for mobile devices. LCD technology also causes less eyestrain than the refreshed pixel technology of a CRT.

BITS AND BYTES

Cleaning Your Monitor

Have you ever noticed how quickly your monitor attracts dust? It's important to keep your monitor clean because dust buildup can act like insulation, keeping heat in and causing the electronic components to wear out much faster. To clean your monitor, follow these steps:

1. Shut off the monitor.
2. For a CRT monitor, wipe the monitor's surface using a sheet of fabric softener or a soft cloth dampened with window cleaner or water. Never spray anything directly onto the monitor. (Check your monitor's user manual to see if there are cleaning products you should avoid using.) For an LCD (flat panel) monitor, use a 50/50 solution of isopropyl alcohol and water on a soft cloth and wipe the screen surface gently.
3. In addition to the screen, wipe away the dust from around the case.

Finally, don't place anything on top of the monitor because the items may block air from cooling it, and avoid placing magnets (including your speaker system's subwoofer) anywhere near the monitor because they can interfere with the mechanisms inside the monitor.

For information on printer-assisted crime see "Counterfeit Computing," a TechTV clip found at www.prenhall.com/ techinaction.

Also, because of their different technologies, you can see more of an LCD screen than you can with the same size CRT monitor. For example, there are 17 inches of viewable area on a 17-inch LCD monitor but only 15 inches of viewable area on a 17-inch CRT monitor. LCDs are also more environmentally friendly, emitting less than half the electromagnetic radiation and using less power than their CRT counterparts.

One of the few disadvantages of LCD monitors is their limited viewing angle. Even with the most expensive models, you may have a hard time seeing the screen image clearly from an angle. Additionally, the resolution on a LCD screen is fixed and cannot be modified to the same degree as that of a CRT. CRT monitors also have better color accuracy than LCD monitors. Finally, LCD monitors are often more expensive than CRTs.

PRINTERS

What are the different types of printers? There are two primary categories of printers: *impact* and *nonimpact*. **Impact printers** have tiny hammer-like keys that strike the paper through an inked ribbon, thus making a mark on the paper. The most common impact printer is the dot-matrix printer.

In contrast, **nonimpact printers** don't have mechanisms that strike the paper. Instead, they spray ink or use laser beams to make marks on the paper. The most common nonimpact printers are ink-jet printers and laser printers. Such nonimpact printers have replaced dot-matrix printers almost entirely. They tend to be less expensive, quieter, faster, and offer better print quality than dot-matrix printers.

FIGURE 2.13

Ink-jet printers are popular for home users, especially for color printing.

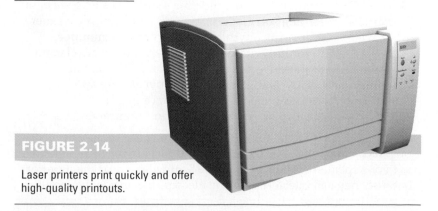

FIGURE 2.14

Laser printers print quickly and offer high-quality printouts.

What were dot-matrix printers used for? You may remember the printers that used paper with perforated edges and track-feed holes down the side. Those were **dot-matrix printers**, the first computer printers. They were revolutionary at the time because they allowed users to print a copy of the information displayed on their computer screens—something that hadn't been possible before. In addition to being slow and noisy, the output of the first dot matrix-printers wasn't nearly as good as that produced by typewriters.

Do people still use dot-matrix printers? Although ink-jet and laser printers have replaced dot-matrix printers for everyday use, dot-matrix printers are still used for printing multipart forms such as invoices or contracts. This is because the pressure of the hammer-like keys can penetrate the multiple layers of paper.

What are the advantages of ink-jet printers? Compared with dot-matrix printers, **ink-jet printers** are quieter, faster, and offer higher-quality printouts (see Figure 2.13). In addition, even high-quality ink-jet printers are affordable. Ink-jet printers work by spraying tiny drops of ink onto paper. The first ink-jet printers suffered from clogged ink jets, but over time, that problem was resolved. Their initial advantage, which continues today, is that ink-jets print color images. In fact, when using the right paper, higher-end ink-jet printers print images that look like professional-quality photos. Because of their high quality and low price, ink-jet printers are the most popular printer for color printing.

Why would I want a laser printer? **Laser printers** are often preferred for their quick and quiet production and high-quality printouts (see Figure 2.14). Because they print quickly, laser printers are often used in schools and offices where multiple computers share one printer. Although more expensive to buy than ink-jet printers, over the long run, laser printers are more economical than ink-jets (they cost less per printed black-and-white page) when you include the price of ink and special paper in the overall cost.

What kind of printer could I use for my laptop? Although any printer that is suitable for your desktop is appropriate to use with your laptop, you may want to consider a portable printer for added mobility and flexibility. Portable printers are compact

BITS AND BYTES

Does It Matter What Paper I Print On?

The quality of your printer is only part of what controls the quality of a printed image. The paper you use is equally important. If you're printing text-only documents for personal use, using low-cost paper is fine. However, if you're printing documents for more formal use, such as résumés, you may want to choose a higher-quality paper. To do so, consider the paper's weight, whiteness, and brightness.

The *weight* of paper is measured in pounds, with 24 pounds being standard. A heavier paper may be best for projects such as brochures, but be sure to check that your printer can handle the added thickness. It is a matter of personal preference as to the degree of paper *whiteness*. Generally, the whiter the paper, the brighter

colors appear. However, in some more formal printings such as résumés, you may want to use a creamier color. The *brightness* of paper usually varies from 85 to 94. The higher the number, the brighter the paper and the easier it is to read. Opacity, or thickness of the paper, is especially important if you're printing on both sides of the paper.

If you're printing photos, paper quality can have a big impact on the results. Photo paper is more expensive than regular paper and comes in a variety of textures ranging from matte to high gloss. For a photo-lab look, high-gloss paper is the best choice. Semigloss (often referred to as satin) is good for portraits, while a matte surface is often used for black-and-white printing.

---

enough to fit in a briefcase, are lightweight, and run on battery power.

Are there wireless printers?
Infrared-compatible, or wireless printers, allow you to print from your handheld device, laptop computer, or even your digital camera. These printers work using Bluetooth, a wireless short-range radio technology we'll discuss in more detail in Chapter 8.

Are there any other types of specialty printers?
A **multifunction printer**, or an all-in-one printer, is a device that combines the functions of a printer, scanner, copier, and fax into one machine. Popular for their space-saving convenience, all-in-one printers can be either ink-jet or laser-based.

Plotters are large printers used to produce oversize pictures that require precise continuous lines to be drawn, such as maps or architectural plans. Plotters use a computer-controlled pen that provides a greater level of precision than the series of dots that laser or ink-jet printers are capable of making.

Thermal printers, such as the one shown in Figure 2.15, are another kind of specialty printer. These printers work by either melting wax-based ink onto ordinary paper (in a process called *thermal wax transfer printing*) or by burning dots onto specially coated paper (in a process called *direct thermal printing*). They are used in stores to print receipts and in airports for electronic ticketing, among other places. Thermal printers are also emerging as a popular tech-

nology for mobile and portable printing, for example, in conjunction with PDAs. Many models feature wireless infrared technology for complete portability.

Choosing a Printer
How do I select the best printer? There are several factors to consider when choosing a printer:

- **Speed**. A printer's speed determines how many pages it can print per minute (called pages per minute, or ppm). A reasonable printing speed for an ink-jet printer is 10 ppm for text and slightly less for graphics. Laser printers print more quickly than ink-jet printers (up to 30 or so ppm) but are more expensive.

- **Resolution**. A printer's resolution (or printed image clarity) is measured in dots per inch (dpi), or the number of dots of ink in a 1-inch line. The higher the dpi, the greater the level of detail and quality of the image. You'll sometimes see dpi represented as a horizontal number multiplied by a vertical number, such as 600 x 600, but you may also see the same resolution simply stated as 600 dpi. For general-purpose printing, 300 dpi is sufficient. If you're going to print photos, 1,200 dpi is better. The dpi for professional photo–quality printers is twice that.

FIGURE 2.15

Thermal printers are ideal for mobile computing because they are compact, lightweight, and require no ink cartridges. Here you see a PDA set into a thermal printer.

DIG DEEPER

How Ink-Jet and Laser Printers Work

Ever wonder how a printer knows what to print, and how it puts ink in just the right places? Most ink-jet printers use *drop-on-demand* technology in which the ink is "demanded" and then "dropped" onto the paper. Two separate processes use drop-on-demand technology: thermal bubble, used by Hewlett-Packard and Canon, and piezoelectric, used by Epson. The difference between the two processes is how the ink is heated within the print cartridge reservoir (the chamber inside the printer that holds the ink).

In the thermal bubble process, the ink is heated in such a way that it expands (like a bubble) and leaves the cartridge reservoir through a small opening, or nozzle. Figure 2.16 shows the general process for thermal bubble. In the piezoelectric process, each ink nozzle contains a crystal at the back of the ink reservoir that receives an electrical charge, causing the ink to vibrate and drop out of the nozzle.

Laser printers use a completely different process. Inside a laser printer is a big metal cylinder (or drum) that is charged with static electricity. When you ask the printer to print something, it sends signals to the laser in the laser printer, telling it to "uncharge" selected spots on the charged cylinder, corresponding to the document you wish to print. Toner, a fine powder that is used in place of liquid ink, is attracted to only those areas on the drum that are not charged. (These uncharged areas are the characters and images you want to print.) The toner is then transferred to the paper as it feeds through the printer. Finally, the toner is melted onto the paper. All unused toner is swept away before the next job starts the process all over again.

FIGURE 2.16

How a thermal bubble ink-jet printer works.

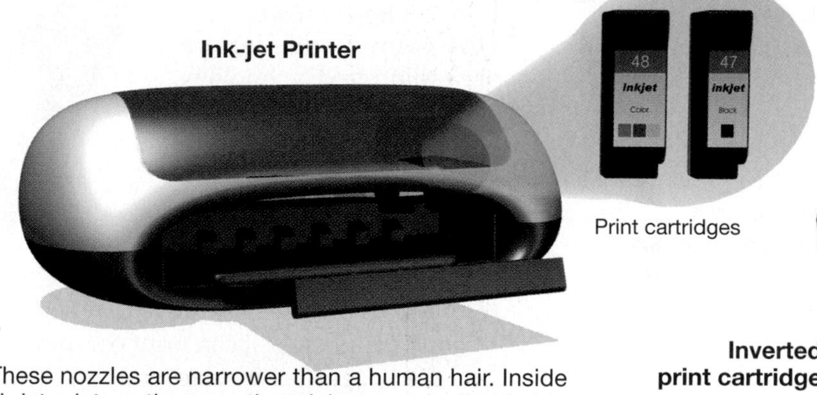

The print cartridge is positioned inside your inkjet printer so that the print head faces down toward the paper. The print head has 50 to several hundred nozzles, or small holes, through which ink droplets fall. These nozzles are narrower than a human hair. Inside the print head of color ink-jet printers, there are three ink reservoirs that hold magenta (red), cyan (blue), and yellow ink. Depending on your printer, a fourth ink reservoir may be required to hold black ink, as well. (In non-color ink-jet printers, there is only one ink reservoir for the black ink.)

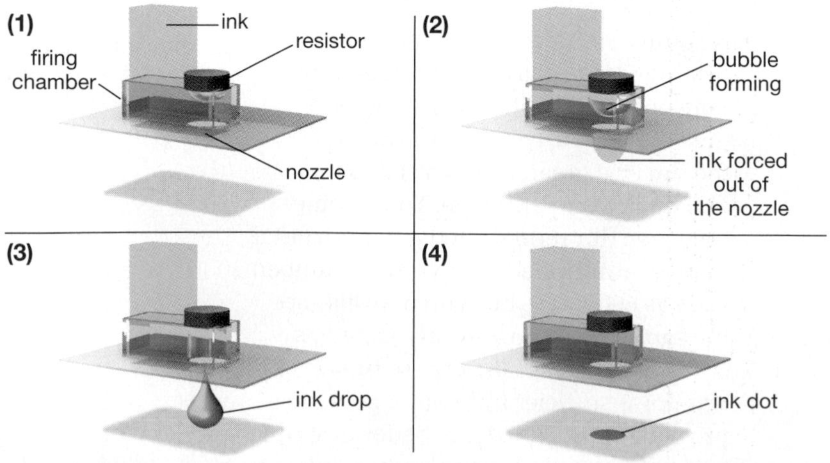

Ink-jet Printer

Print cartridges

Print head

Nozzles

Inverted print cartridge

(1)
ink
resistor
firing chamber
nozzle

(2)
bubble forming
ink forced out of the nozzle

(3)
ink drop

(4)
ink dot

STEP (1): Once the printer receives the command to print, electrical pulses flow through thin resistors in the print head to heat the ink.

STEP (2): The heated ink forms a bubble. The bubble continues to expand until it is forced out of the nozzle.

STEP (3): The ink drops onto the paper.

STEP (4): As the ink leaves the cartridge, the chamber begins to cool and contract, creating a vacuum to draw in the ink for the process to begin again.

BITS AND BYTES

Maintaining Your Printer

In general, printers require very little maintenance. Occasionally, it's a good idea to wipe the case of the printer with a damp cloth to free it from accumulated dust. However, do not wipe away any ink residue that has accumulated inside the printer. If you are experiencing streaking or blank areas on your printed paper, your print head nozzles may be clogged. To fix this, run the printer's cleaning cycle. (Check your printer's manual for instructions, because every

printer is different.) If this doesn't work, you may want to use a cleaning sheet to brush the print head clean. These sheets often come with printers or with reams of photo paper. If you still have a problem, try a cleaning cartridge. Cleaning cartridges contain a special fluid that scrubs the print head. Such cartridges can be found where most ink cartridges are sold (just make sure you buy one that is compatible with your printer).

- **Color output**. If you're using an ink-jet printer to print color images, buy a four-color (cyan, magenta, yellow, and black) or six-color printer (four-color plus light cyan and light magenta) for the highest-quality output. Some printers come with one ink cartridge for all colors, whereas others have two ink cartridges, one for black and one for color. The best setup is to have individual ink cartridges for each color so you can replace only the specific color cartridge that is empty. Color laser printers have separate toner cartridges for each color.

- **Memory**. Printers need memory in order to print. Ink-jet printers run slowly if they don't have enough memory. If you plan to print small text-only documents on an ink-jet printer, 1 to 2 megabytes (MB) of memory should be enough. You need about 4 MB of memory if you expect to print large text-only documents and 8 MB if you print graphic-intense files. Unlike ink-jet printers, laser printers won't print at all without sufficient memory. To ensure your laser printer meets your printing needs, buy one with 16 MB of memory. Some printers allow you to add more memory later.

- **Use and cost**. If you will be printing mostly black-and-white, text-based documents or will be sharing your printer with others, a laser printer is best because of its printing speed and overall economies for volume printing. If you're planning to print color photos and graphics, an ink-jet is the better, more economical choice.

OUTPUTTING SOUND

What is the output device for sound?
As noted earlier, most computers include inexpensive speakers as an output device for sound. These speakers are sufficient to play the standard audio clips you find on the Web and usually enable you to participate in teleconferencing. However, if you plan to watch a lot of DVDs or are particular about how your music sounds, you may want to upgrade to a more sophisticated speaker system, such as one that includes subwoofers (special speakers that produce only low bass sounds) and surround-sound (speaker systems set up in such a way that they surround you with sound). We discuss how to evaluate and upgrade your speaker system in more detail in Chapter 6.

The System Unit

We just looked at the components of your computer that you use to input and output data in some form. But where does the processing take place and where is the data stored? The *system unit* is the box that contains the central electronic components of the computer, including the computer's processor (its brains), its memory, and the many circuit boards that help the computer function. You'll also find the power source and all the storage devices (CD/DVD drive, Zip drive, and hard drive) in the system unit.

What styles of system units are there? The most common styles of system units on desktop computers are *desktop boxes*, which sit horizontally on top of your desk, and *tower configurations*, which typically sit vertically on the floor below your desk

(see Figure 2.17b). Some creatively designed desktop system units, such as the Apple iMac (see Figure 2.17a), house not just the computer's processor and memory, but its monitor as well. No matter the design, every computer—be it a desktop computer or a laptop—has a system unit.

Which is the best system unit style? The choice between a desktop box and a tower configuration is ultimately up to you because both styles contain the parts needed to run the computer. The tower configuration may have a few advantages over the desktop style because tower configurations don't take up desktop space. In addition, tower configurations have more spaces reserved on the inside of the system unit that you can use to install additional devices that didn't come with your system, such as an additional DVD or CD drive.

ON THE FRONT PANEL

What's on the front panel of my computer? No matter whether you choose a desktop or tower design, the front panel of your computer provides you with access to power controls as well as to the storage devices on your computer. Figure 2.18 shows the front panel of a typical system. Although your system might be slightly different, chances are it includes many of the same features.

Power Controls
What's the best way to turn my computer on and off? If your system has two buttons on the front panel, the larger button is the button you press to turn on (or power on) the system. (You also find power-on buttons on some keyboards.) Although you use this button to turn on your system, you don't want to use it to turn off (or power off) your system. Modern operating systems want control over the shutdown procedure, so you turn off the power by clicking on a shutdown icon on the desktop, not by pushing the main power button.

If you do shut off the power using the main power button without shutting down your operating system first, nothing on your system will be permanently damaged.

CD/RW drive

DVD/RW drive

Memory card reader

Floppy drive (optional)

Productivity ports: audio, FireWire, USB

Power button

FIGURE 2.18

The front panel of your computer provides you with access to power controls as well as to the storage devices on your computer.

However, some files and applications may not close properly, so the operating system may need to do some extra work the next time you start your computer.

Why do some computers have two buttons on the front panel? The second and generally smaller button on some front panels *restarts* the computer. Restarting the system while it's powered on is called a **warm boot**. You might need to perform a warm boot if the operating system or other software application stops responding. It takes less time to perform a warm boot than to power down completely and then restart all of your hardware. Doing a complete power down and restart is a **cold boot**. You do a cold boot each time you start the computer after it's been powered down completely. Note that if your computer does not have a restart button, you can perform a warm boot by pressing the Ctrl, Alt, and Delete keys at the same time.

Should I turn off my computer every time I'm done using it? Some people say you should leave your computer on at all times. They argue that turning your computer on and off throughout the day subjects its components to stress as the heating and cooling process forces the components to expand and contract repeatedly. Other people say you should shut down your computer when you're not using it. They claim that you'll end up wasting money on electricity to keep the computer running all the time. However, modern operating systems include power-management settings that allow the most power-hungry components of the system (the hard drive and monitor) to shut down after a short idle period.

So, if you use the computer sporadically throughout the day, it may be best to keep it on while you're apt to use it and power it down when you're done using it for the day. However, if you only use your computer for a little while each day, you'll be paying electricity charges during long periods of nonuse. If you're truly concerned about the stresses incurred from powering on and off your computer, you may want to buy a warranty with the computer, which will undoubtedly cost less than the extra power you'd use to keep your computer constantly running.

Can I "rest" my computer without turning it off completely? As mentioned earlier, your computer has power-management settings that help it conserve energy. These settings are called *standby*

Using the hibernation and standby settings is not only good for the environment, but it is also good for your pocketbook.

mode and *hibernation*. When your computer is in **standby mode**, its more power-hungry components, such as the monitor and hard drive, are put in idle. In essence, the computer is napping. To wake it up, you tap a key on the keyboard or move the mouse. When the computer is in **hibernation**, it saves an image of your desktop and powers down. When you wake the computer from hibernation (by pushing the power button), the computer reloads everything to your desktop so that it is exactly as it was before it went into hibernation. You can find the settings for standby and hibernation modes in the Performance and Maintenance option in the Control Panel menu (see Figure 2.19).

Drive Bays: Your Access to Storage Devices
What else is on the front panel? Besides the power button, the other features that can be seen from the front of your system unit are **drive bays**. These bays are special shelves reserved for storage devices, those devices that hold your data and applications when the power is shut off. There are two kinds of drive bays:

1. Internal drive bays cannot be seen or accessed from outside the system unit. Generally, internal drive bays are reserved for hard disk drives.

2. External drive bays can be seen and accessed from outside the system unit. External drive bays house floppy disk and CD drives, for example. Empty external drive bays are covered by a faceplate.

By looking at the front panel of your system unit, you can tell which devices have been installed, and often how many bays remain available for expansion.

What kinds of external drive bays do most PCs have? Some PCs still have a bay for a **floppy disk drive**, which reads and writes to easily transportable floppy disks, which hold a limited amount of data. Some computers also feature a **Zip disk drive**, which resembles a floppy disk drive but has a slightly wider opening. Zip disks work just like standard floppies but can carry much more data.

On the front panel, you'll also see one or two bays for other storage devices such as CD drives. **CD-ROM drives** read CDs, whereas **CD-RW drives** can both read from and write data to CDs. Some computers may also come with a separate **DVD-RW drive** that allows the computer to read and write DVDs. DVDs are the same size and shape as CDs but can hold more than 25 times as much data. DVD-RW drives are especially useful if you're creating digital movies. Today, many computers come with a "combo" CD-RW/DVD drive, a device that can read and write CDs and play DVDs.

Several manufacturers now also include slots on the front of the system unit in which you can insert portable **flash memory cards** such as Memory Sticks and CompactFlash cards. Many laptops also include slots for flash memory cards. Flash memory cards let you transfer digital data between your computer and devices such as digital cameras, PDAs, video cameras, and printers. Although incredibly small—some are just the size of a postage stamp—these memory cards have capacities that match that of a Zip disk.

Other flash devices, sometimes referred to as *Jumpdrives* or *flash drives*, plug into universal serial bus (USB) ports. These devices, again not much larger than your thumb, can hold up to 1 GB of data. The size, convenience, and portability of these devices may indeed make them the chosen replacement for Zip and floppy disks in the very near future. We discuss flash memory in more detail in Chapter 8.

Figure 2.20 shows the storage capacities of the various portable storage media (such as floppy disks and CD-ROMs) used in your computer's drive bays. As you learned in Chapter 1, storage capacity is measured in bytes. A kilobyte (KB) equals about 1,000 bytes, a megabyte (MB) equals about a million bytes, and a gigabyte (GB) equals about a billion bytes.

Ports
What are the ports on the front of my computer for? **Ports** are the places on the system unit where peripheral devices attach

---

FIGURE 2.20 Storage Media Capacities

STORAGE MEDIUM	CAPABILITIES	STORAGE CAPACITY
CD CD-RW	Read-only Read and write	700 MB
DVD DVD+RW	Read-only Read and write	9.4 GB
Flash Memory Cards	Read and write	16 MB to 1 GB
Floppy Disk	Read and write	1.44 MB
Zip Disk	Read and write	100 MB, 250 MB, or 750 MB

to the computer so data can be exchanged between them. Traditionally, ports have been located on the back of the system unit. However, because so many portable devices (such as digital cameras) need to be plugged into the computer, and because ports on the front of the system unit are easier to access than are ports on the back, many manufacturers are designing ports on the front of the system unit as well (see Figure 2.21). These front-panel ports allow you easily to connect your computer to a digital camera, MP3 player, or PDA, for example.

ON THE BACK

What's on the back of my system unit? Peripheral devices, such as monitors, printers, and keyboards, connect to the system unit through ports. Because peripheral devices exchange data with the computer in various ways, a number of different ports have been created to accommodate these devices (see Figure 2.22). Serial ports and parallel ports have long been used to connect input and output devices to the computer. **Serial ports** send data one bit (or piece of data) at a time and are often used to connect modems to the computer. Sending data one bit at a time is a slow way to communicate. Data sent over serial ports is transferred at a speed of 115 kilobits per second (Kbps), or 115,000 bits per second. A **parallel port** sends data between devices in groups of bits at speeds of 500 Kbps and is therefore much faster than a serial port. Parallel ports are often used to connect printers to computers.

Universal **serial bus (USB) ports** are fast replacing serial and parallel ports as the means to connect input and output devices to the computer. This is mainly because of their ability to transfer data quickly—at approximately 12 megabits per second, or Mbps (that's 12,000 Kbps). USB ports can connect a wide variety of peripherals to the computer, including keyboards, printers, Zip drives, and digital cameras.

Which ports help me connect with other computers? Another set of ports on your computer helps you communicate with other computers. Called **connectivity ports**, these ports give you access to networks and the Internet and enable your computer to function as a fax machine. To find connectivity ports, look for a port that resembles a standard phone jack. This jack is the **modem**

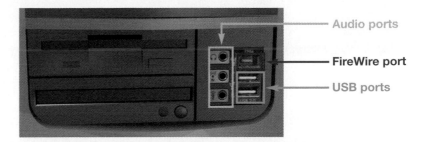

Front-panel ports allow you easily to connect to your devices.

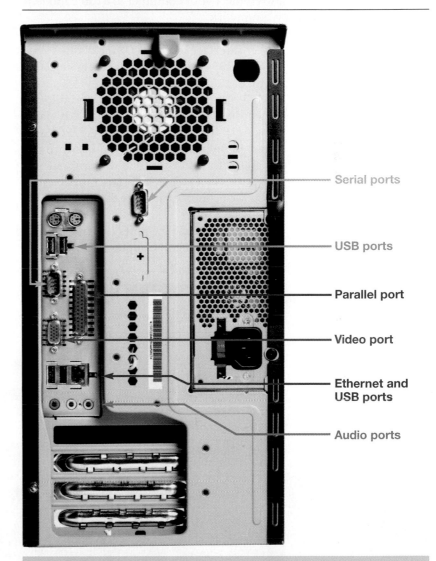

The back of your computer probably looks a lot like this one. There are several different ports because many devices exchange data with the computer in various ways.

port. It uses a traditional telephone signal to connect two computers. Most computers now come configured with a second connectivity port called an **Ethernet port**. This port is slightly larger than a standard phone jack

SOUND BYTE
PORT TOUR

In this Sound Byte, you'll take a tour of both a desktop system and a laptop system to compare the number and variety of available ports. You'll also learn about the different types of ports and compare their speed and expandability.

and transfers data up to 100 Mbps. You use it to connect your computer to a cable modem or a network.

What are the fastest ports available? Newer interfaces such as **USB 2.0**, **FireWire** (or **IEEE 1394**), and the latest **FireWire 800** are the fastest ports available. Devices such as MP3 players, digital cameras, and digital camcorders all benefit from the speedy data transfer of USB 2.0 and FireWire. USB 2.0 transfers data at 480 Mbps and is approximately 40 times faster than the original USB port. The FireWire interface moves data at 400 Mbps, while FireWire 800 doubles the rate to 800 Mbps.

We'll explore all the ports on your system unit in more detail in Chapter 6.

INSIDE THE SYSTEM UNIT

What's inside the system unit? Figure 2.23 shows the layout common to many system units. As you can see, a **power supply** is housed inside the system unit to regulate the wall voltage to the voltages required by computer chips. The **hard disk drive** (or just **hard drive**) is also inside the system unit. The hard disk drive holds all permanently stored programs and data. Inside the system unit, you'll also find many printed circuit boards, which are flat, thin boards made of material that won't conduct electricity. On top of this material, thin copper lines are traced, allowing designers to connect a set of computer chips.

The various circuit boards have specific functions that augment the computer's basic functions. Some provide connections to other devices, so they are usually referred to as **expansion cards** (or **adapter cards**). Typical expansion cards found in the system unit are the sound card and video card. A **sound card** provides a connection for the speakers and microphone, while a **video card** provides a connection for the monitor. There is also the **modem card**, which provides the computer with a connection to the Internet, and a **network interface card (NIC)**, which enables your computer to connect with other computers.

On the bottom or side of the system unit, you'll find the largest printed circuit board, called the **motherboard**. The motherboard is named such because all of the other boards (video cards, sound cards, and so

FIGURE 2.23

Inside the system unit.

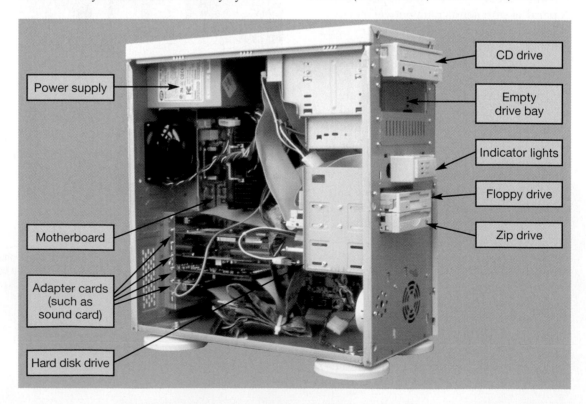

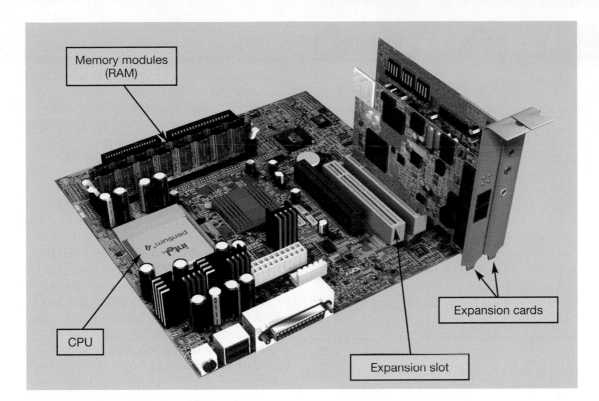

FIGURE 2.24

A motherboard contains the CPU, the memory (RAM) cards, and slots available for expansion cards.

Memory modules (RAM)

CPU

Expansion cards

Expansion slot

on) connect to it to receive power and to communicate—therefore, it's the "mother" of all boards.

What's on the motherboard? The motherboard contains the set of chips that powers the system, including the central processing unit (CPU). The motherboard also houses the chips that provide the short-term memory for the computer as well as a set of slots available for expansion cards (see Figure 2.24).

What is the CPU? The **central processing unit** (**CPU**, or **processor**) is the largest and most important chip in the computer. It is sometimes referred to as the "brains" of the computer because it controls all the functions performed by the computer's other components and processes all the commands issued to it by software instructions. Modern CPUs can perform three billion tasks a second without error, making them extremely powerful components.

What exactly is RAM? Because the CPU processes data so rapidly, there needs to be a way to store data and commands nearby so they can be fed to the CPU very quickly. **Random access memory (RAM)** is that storage space. If you look at a motherboard, you'll see RAM as a series of small cards (called *memory cards* or *memory modules*) plugged into slots on the motherboard. The CPU can request the contents of RAM,

which can be located, opened, and delivered to the CPU for processing in a few billionths of a second (or *nanoseconds*).

Sometimes RAM is referred to as *primary storage* for this reason, but it should not be confused with other types of *permanent* storage devices. Because all the contents of RAM are erased when you turn off the computer, RAM is the *temporary* or **volatile storage** location for the computer. To save data more permanently, you need to save it to the hard drive or to another permanent storage device such as a floppy disk, CD, or Zip disk.

Does the system unit contain any other kinds of memory besides RAM? In addition to RAM, the motherboard also contains a form of memory called **read-only memory (ROM)**. ROM holds all the instructions the computer needs to start up. Unlike data stored in RAM, the instructions stored in ROM are permanent, making ROM a

SOUND BYTE

VIRTUAL COMPUTER TOUR

This Sound Byte will take you on a video tour inside your system unit. From opening the cover to locating the power supply, CPU, and RAM, to examining the expansion slots available, this video guide will teach you to be more familiar with what's inside your computer.

BITS AND BYTES

Opening Up Your System Unit

Many people use a computer for years without ever needing to open their system unit. But there are two reasons you might want or need to do so: to replace a defective expansion card or device or to upgrade your computer. If your hard drive or CD-ROM drive fails, with a bit of guidance, you can open the system unit yourself and replace it. Adding additional memory or adding a DVD-RW drive are upgrade procedures that you can do safely at home. However, it's important that you follow the device's specific installation instructions. These instructions will detail any safety procedures you'll need to observe, such as unplugging the computer or grounding yourself to avoid static electricity, which can damage internal components. It's also important to check with the manufacturer of your system to see if opening up the case will void the system's warranty.

You generally don't see the hard disk drive because it's enclosed in a sealed protective case. The hard disk drive holds all the data and instructions that the computer needs, even after the power is turned off.

nonvolatile storage location. This means it does not get erased when the power is turned off.

What kind of data is saved on the hard disk drive? As noted earlier, the hard disk drive is the storage device you use to hold the data and instructions your computer needs permanently, even after the computer is turned off. This makes the hard disk a nonvolatile storage location.

Today's hard drives, with capacities of up to 500 GB, can hold hundreds of billions of pieces of data.

As noted earlier, the hard disk drive is generally installed inside the system unit with all the other drive bays (see Figure 2.25). However, unlike the other drive bays, you can't access the hard disk drive from the outside of the system unit, making it a form of *nonportable* permanent storage.

Setting It All Up: Ergonomics

It's important that you understand not only your computer's components and how they work together, but also how to set up these components safely. *Merriam-Webster's*

Dictionary defines **ergonomics** as "an applied science concerned with designing and arranging things people use so that the people and things interact most efficiently and safely." In terms of computing, ergonomics refers to how you set up your computer and other equipment to minimize your risk of injury or discomfort.

Why is ergonomics important? Workplace injuries related to musculoskeletal disorders occur frequently in the United States. Approximately 1.8 million workers experience such disorders annually, with 600,000 needing to take time off from work. The Occupational Safety and Health Administration, or OSHA (**www.osha.gov**), reports that these types of injuries cost businesses and taxpayers up to $20 billion annually in workers' compensation and up to $40 billion in other expenses such as medical care.

How can I avoid injuries when I'm working at my computer? The following are some guidelines that can help you avoid discomfort, eyestrain, or injuries while you're working at your computer:

- **Position your monitor correctly**. Studies suggest it's best to place your monitor at least 25 inches from your eyes. You may need to decrease the screen resolution to make text and images more readable at that distance. Also, experts recommend the monitor be positioned so that it is at eye level or at an angle 20 to 50 degrees below your line of sight.

- **Purchase an adjustable chair**. Adjust the height of your chair so that your feet touch the floor. (You may need to use a footrest to get the right position.) Back support needs to be adjustable so that you can position it to support your lumbar (lower back) region. You should also be able to move the seat or adjust the back so you can sit without exerting pressure on your knees. If your chair doesn't adjust, placing a pillow behind your back can provide the same support.

- **Assume a proper position while typing**. A repetitive strain injury (RSI) is a painful condition caused by repetitive or awkward movements of a part of the body. Improperly positioned keyboards are one of the leading causes of RSIs in computer users. Your wrists should be flat (unbent) with respect to the keyboard and your forearms parallel to the floor. You can either adjust the height of your chair or install a height-adjustable keyboard tray to ensure a proper position. Specially designed ergonomic keyboards like the one in Figure 2.26 can help you achieve the proper position of your wrists.

- **Take breaks from computer tasks**. Remaining in the same position for long periods of time increases stress on your body. Shift your position in your chair and stretch your hands and fingers periodically. Likewise, staring at the screen for long periods of time can lead to eyestrain, so rest your eyes by periodically taking them off the screen and focusing them on an object at least 20 feet away.

- **Ensure the lighting is adequate**. Assuring proper lighting in your work area is a good way to minimize eyestrain. To do so, eliminate any sources of direct glare (light shining directly into your eyes) or reflected glare (light shining off the computer screen) and ensure there is enough light to read comfortably.

Figure 2.27 illustrates how you should arrange your monitor, chair, body, and keyboard to avoid injury or discomfort while you're working on your computer.

FIGURE 2.26

Ergonomic keyboards that curve and contain built-in wrist rests help you maintain proper hand position to minimize strain on your wrists.

SOUND BYTE
HEALTHY COMPUTING

In this Sound Byte, you'll see how to set up your workspace in an ergonomically correct way. You'll learn the proper location of the monitor, keyboard, and mouse, as well as ergonomic features to look for in choosing the most appropriate chair.

FIGURE 2.27

Achieving comfort and a proper typing position is the way to avoid repetitive strain injuries and other aches and pains while working at a computer. To achieve this, obtain equipment that boasts as many adjustments as possible. Every person is a different shape and size, requiring each workspace to be individually tailored.

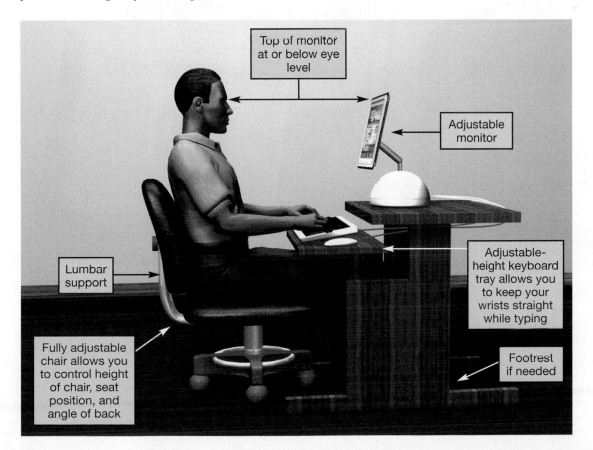

Top of monitor at or below eye level

Adjustable monitor

Lumbar support

Adjustable-height keyboard tray allows you to keep your wrists straight while typing

Fully adjustable chair allows you to control height of chair, seat position, and angle of back

Footrest if needed

TRENDS IN IT

Emerging Technologies: Tomorrow's Displays

Most of us grew up with CRT monitors on our computers. Large and heavy but providing excellent resolution and clarity, these monitors were the main display for computers until the early 2000s. Soon, though, you may only find these clunky dinosaurs in the Smithsonian.

Today, LCD screens are where it's at. First introduced in 2000, these monitors have taken the desktop market by storm, and with prices steadily dropping, they now out-sell CRTs. Lighter and less bulky than CRT monitors, they can be easily moved and take up less real estate on a desk. Still, current LCD technology does have limitations. LCD screens are relatively fragile (although less so than CRT monitors) and viewing angles are limited. In addition, LCDs can't display full-motion video as well as CRT monitors, making them unpopular with hard-core gamers.

Despite their limitations, LCDs will continue to be the predominant display device for computers, cell phones, and PDAs in the next few years. But according to sources like *PC Magazine*, new technologies are being developed that take LCD displays to the next level.

Flexible Screens

The most promising displays currently under development are *organic light-emitting displays* (*OLEDs*). These displays, currently used in some Kodak cameras, use organic compounds that produce light when exposed to an electric current. OLEDs tend to use less power than other flat-screen technologies, making them ideal for portable battery-operated devices. However, most research is being geared toward *flexible OLEDs* (*FOLEDs*). Unlike LCDs and CRTs, which use rigid surfaces such as glass, FOLED screens would be designed on lightweight, inexpensive, flexible material such as transparent plastics or metal foils. As shown in Figure 2.28, the computer screen of the future might roll up into an easily transported cylinder the size of a pen!

FOLEDs would allow advertising to progress to a new dimension. Screens could be hung where posters are hung now (such as on billboards). And wireless transmission of data to these screens would allow advertisers to display easily updatable full-motion images. Combining transparency and flexibility would

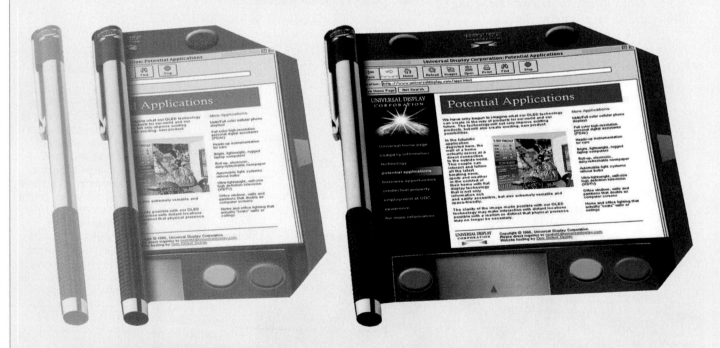

FIGURE 2.28

There's no need to lug around a heavy computer monitor. With FOLED technology, you'll be able to unroll a computer screen wherever you need it from a container the size of a pen. The prototype shown is currently being developed by Universal Display Corporation and may be available within two to three years.

FIGURE 2.29

A prototype developed by MicroOptical Corporation features a microdisplay embedded in a pair of glasses. To users, it appears as though the display is projected right in front of them. Within a few years, you'll be able to buy a microdisplay when you buy glasses at stores such as LensCrafters. Microdisplays such as this can significantly cut the weight of portable computers.

also allow these displays to be mounted on windshields or eyeglasses. Who needs paper maps when you can examine directions right on your windshield without taking your eyes off the road?

There are some obstacles to be overcome before these screens will be widely available. Currently, the compounds that create blue hues age much faster than the ones that produce reds and greens. This makes it difficult to maintain balanced colors over long time periods. And the compounds used to form the OLEDs can be contaminated by exposure to water vapor or oxygen. However, once these problems are overcome, flexible displays should be popping up everywhere.

Wearable Screens

Who needs a screen when you can just wear one? Microdisplays are screens that, measured diagonally, are 1 inch or less in size. These displays are currently in use or are in development and can be used in head-mounted displays, such as the glasses shown in Figure 2.29. Eventually, these displays could replace heavier screens on laptops, desktops, and even PDAs.

"Bistable" Screens

Your computer screen constantly changes its images when you are surfing the Internet or playing a game. However, PDA and cell phone screens don't necessarily change that often. Therefore, something called a "bistable" display may one day be used in these devices. A *bistable display* has the ability to retain its image even when the power is turned off. In addition, bistable displays are lighter than LCD displays and reduce overall power consumption, resulting in longer battery life. As the market for portable devices continues to explode, you can expect to see bistable technologies in mobile computer screens.

So, when will the current LCD technology be displaced once and for all? Because scientific research still must be conducted before these technologies are commercially viable, it is difficult to say. But certainly within the next 10 years these and other as yet undreamed-of technologies should replace current LCDs.

Summary

1. What devices do you use to get data into the computer?

An input device enables you to enter data (text, images, and sounds) and instructions (user responses and commands) into the computer. You use keyboards to enter typed data and commands, whereas you use the mouse to enter user responses and commands. Keyboards are distinguished by the layout of the keys as well as the special keys found on the keyboard. The most common keyboard is the QWERTY keyboard. However, over the years, there has been some debate over what is the best layout for keyboards. The Dvorak keyboard is a leader in alternative keyboards. The Dvorak keyboard puts the most commonly used letters in the English language on "Home Keys," the keys in the middle row of the keyboard.

Laptop keyboards are more compact and have fewer keys than standard keyboards. Still, a lot of the laptop keys have alternate functions so that you get the same capabilities from the limited number of keys as you do the special keys on standard keyboards. PDAs use a stylus instead of a keyboard.

Most computers come with a standard two-button mouse, but you can also find optical mice, trackball mice, and wireless mice. In a trackball mouse, the rollerball sits on top of the mouse and you move the ball with your fingers. An optical mouse uses an internal sensor or laser to control the mouse's movement. Wireless mice use batteries and send data to the computer via radio or light waves.

Laptops incorporate the mouse into the keyboard area. Laptop mice include trackball mice, trackpoints, and touchpads.

Microphones are the devices used to input sounds, while scanners and digital cameras input text and images.

2. What devices do you use to get data out of the computer?

Output devices enable you to send processed data out of your computer. This can take the form of text, pictures, sounds, and video. Monitors display soft copies of text, graphics, and video, while printers create hard copies of text and graphics.

There are two basic types of monitors: CRTs and LCDs. If your monitor looks like a TV set, it has a picture tube device called a CRT (cathode ray tube). If it is flat, it's using LCD (liquid crystal display) technology. LCD monitors take up less space and are lighter and more energy efficient than CRT monitors, making them perfect for portable computers. However, CRT monitors are less expensive, have higher resolutions, can be viewed at an angle, and offer better color quality.

There are two primary categories of printers: impact and non-impact. Impact printers have hammer-like keys that strike the paper through an inked ribbon. Non-impact printers spray ink or use laser beams to make marks on the paper. The most common non-impact printers are inkjet printers and laser printers. Specialty printers are also available. These include multifunction printers, plotters, and thermal printers. When choosing a printer, you should be aware of factors such as speed, resolution, color output, memory, and cost.

Speakers are the output devices for sound. Most computers include speakers. However, you may want to upgrade to a more sophisticated speaker system, such as one that includes sub-woofers and surround-sound.

3. What's on the front of your system unit?

The system unit is the box that contains the central electronic components of the computer. On the front of the system unit, you'll find the power source as well as access to the storage devices (CD/DVD drive, floppy disk drive, and Zip disk drive) in your computer. Most PCs still have a bay for a floppy disk drive. Some have a Zip disk drive. Most also include one or two bays for storage devices such as CD drives and DVD drives. Several manufacturers now also include a slot on the front of the system unit in which you can insert portable flash memory cards such as Memory Sticks and Compact Flash cards. Some computers also include ports on the front panel.

4. What's on the back of your system unit?

On the back of the system unit you'll find a wide variety of ports that allow you to hook up peripheral devices (such as your monitor and keyboard) to your system. The most common ports found on the back of the system unit are serial ports, parallel ports, and USB ports.

Serial ports send data one bit (or piece of data) at a time at speeds of 56 Kbps and are sometimes used to connect mice and keyboards to the computer.

Parallel ports send data between devices in *groups* of bits at speeds of 92 Kbps.

USB ports are fast replacing serial and parallel ports and transfer data at approximately 12 Mbps.

Ports that provide even faster data transfer include Ethernet, USB 2.0, and FireWire ports.

Connectivity ports give you access to networks and the Internet and enable your computer to function as a fax machine. Connectivity ports include modem ports and Ethernet ports.

5. What's inside your system unit?

The system unit contains the main electronic components of the computer, including the motherboard, the main circuit board of the system. On the motherboard is the computer's central processing unit (CPU), which coordinates the functions of all other devices on the computer.

RAM, the computer's volatile memory, is also located on the motherboard. RAM is where all the data and instructions are held while the computer is running. ROM, a permanent type of memory, is responsible for housing instructions to help start up the computer.

The hard drive (the permanent storage location) and other storage devices (CD/DVD drives, floppy drives) are also located inside the system unit, as are circuit boards (such as sound, video, modem, and network interface cards) that help the computer perform special functions.

6. How do you set up your computer to avoid strain and injury?

Ergonomics refers to how you arrange your computer and equipment to minimize your risk of injury or discomfort. This includes positioning your monitor correctly, buying an adjustable chair that ensures you have good posture while using the computer, assuming a proper position while typing, and making sure the lighting is adequate. Other good practices include taking frequent breaks as well as using other ergonomically designed equipment such as keyboards.

Key Terms

Buzz Words

Word Bank

- USB
- CRT
- mouse
- drive bay
- LCD
- keyboard
- trackpoint
- monitor
- speakers
- RAM
- QWERTY
- CD-RW
- ink-jet
- ergonomics
- ROM
- CPU
- floppy
- optical
- hard drive
- flash memory
- Dvorak
- laser printer
- system unit
- parallel
- microphone

Instructions: Fill in the blanks using the words from the Word Bank above.

Austin had been getting a sore back and stiff arms when he sat at his desk, so he redesigned the (1)_____ of his computer setup. He placed the (2)_____ so that it was 25 inches from his eyes and bought an adjustable chair. He also decided to improve his equipment in other ways. His (3)_____ was old, so he replaced it with an (4)_____ mouse that didn't need a mousepad. To plug in the mouse, he used a (5)_____ port on the back of his (6)_____. He considered buying an alternative keyboard to replace the (7)_____ keyboard he got with his computer, but he didn't know much about alternative keyboards like the (8)_____ keyboard, so he decided to wait.

Because he prints a lot of flyers for his band, Austin decided to buy a printer that can print text-based pages quickly. Although he decided to keep his (9)_____ printer to print out photos, he decided to purchase a new (10)_____ to print out his heavy document load much faster. While looking at new printers, Austin also noticed (11)_____ monitors that would take up far less space on his desk than the (12)_____ monitor he had. Unfortunately, he couldn't afford to invest in a new monitor, so he decided to keep his old one. However, he decided he could afford new (13)_____, since the ones that came with his computer weren't that good and didn't have subwoofers. He bought a professional (14)_____ a while back so he could record music at home. Finally, knowing his system could probably use a bit more memory, Austin checked out prices for additional (15)_____.

Organizing Key Terms

Instructions: *This chapter introduces many new terms and concepts. In the following illustration, fill in each of the blanks with key terms or concepts from the chapter to show how categories of ideas fit together.*

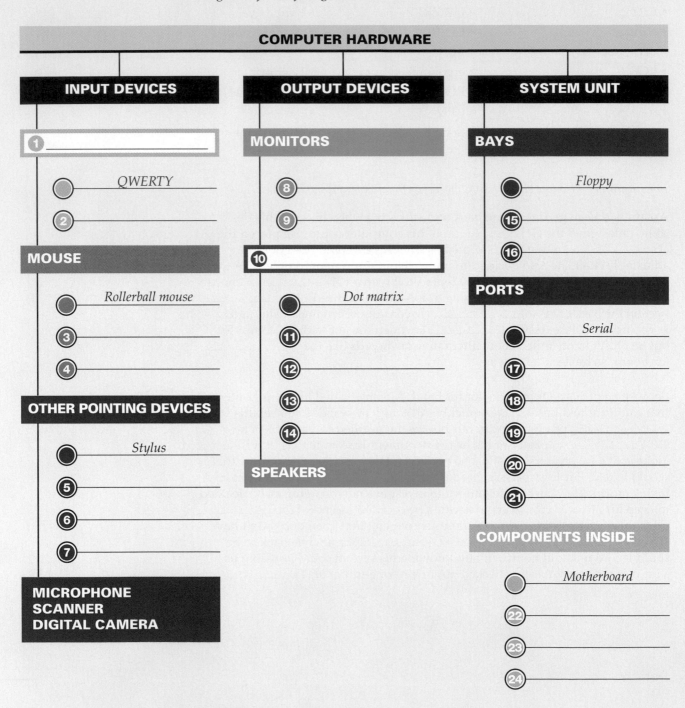

COMPUTER HARDWARE

INPUT DEVICES

1 _____

    QWERTY

2 _____

MOUSE

    Rollerball mouse

3 _____

4 _____

OTHER POINTING DEVICES

    Stylus

5 _____

6 _____

7 _____

**MICROPHONE
SCANNER
DIGITAL CAMERA**

OUTPUT DEVICES

MONITORS

8 _____

9 _____

10 _____

    Dot matrix

11 _____

12 _____

13 _____

14 _____

SPEAKERS

SYSTEM UNIT

BAYS

    Floppy

15 _____

16 _____

PORTS

    Serial

17 _____

18 _____

19 _____

20 _____

21 _____

COMPONENTS INSIDE

    Motherboard

22 _____

23 _____

24 _____

Making the Transition to . . . Next Semester

1. Choosing the Best Keyboard

Once you become more familiar with software products such as Microsoft Office, you may want to migrate to a customized keyboard design. Although keyboards have similar setups, some keyboards provide special keys and buttons to support different users. For example, some keyboards are designed specifically for multimedia use, Internet use, and office use. Which one is best for you?

a. Examine the various keyboard setups at the Microsoft Web site (**www.microsoft.com/hardware/keyboard**). Which keyboard would best suit your needs and why? What features would be most useful to you? How would you evaluate the additional costs vs. the benefits?

b. What advantages would a wireless keyboard give you? How much do wireless keyboards cost? What price would you be willing to pay to go wireless?

c. When would you need a keyboard for your PDA? What is the current price for a portable folding PDA keyboard?

2. Choosing the Best Mouse

On the Web, research the different kinds of mice available and list their special features, functions, and costs. Of these mice, which do you think would be most useful to you? Why?

3. Pricing Computer Upgrades

Investigate the following on the Internet:

a. How much would it cost to add a CD or DVD drive to your computer? Does your system have an extra drive bay to install an extra CD/DVD drive?

b. How much would it cost to buy new 17-inch CRT and LCD monitors? What kind of monitor would be best to view DVDs?

c. How much do various computer speaker systems cost? What speakers would be best to listen to CDs?

d. Do you know whether your current sound card and video card support the new devices? How could you find this out?

4. Exploring Scanners

One input device you did not explore in the text is a scanner. Conduct research on the Web to find out about scanners.

a. What are the different kinds of scanners on the market?

b. What qualities do good scanners have?

c. How much do scanners cost?

d. Create a table comparing all the specifications listed earlier for several different scanners. Highlight the scanner you would be most interested in purchasing.

5. Setting Up the Computer

You have successfully completed an introductory course in computer science and are now the "family expert." Your parents have purchased a computer system and have called you to help them set it up. The problem is, you are a plane ride away, so you need to design a step-by-step guide you can e-mail to them. In your guide, make sure you describe each component and use proper terminology (especially when referring to ports) to ensure your parents hook everything up correctly. Don't forget power cords.

Making the Transition to . . . the Workplace

1. PCs vs. Macs

There are two main types of computers in the workplace: PC-style computers (manufactured by a variety of companies) and Apple Macintosh and G Series computers (manufactured by Apple Computer).

a. What system are you used to using?

b. What questions would you need to ask if you walked into a new job and found a different system on your desk?

2. What System Will You Use?

When you arrive at a new position for a company, you'll most likely be provided with a computer. Based on the career you are in now or are planning to pursue, answer the following questions:

a. What kind of computer system would you most like to use (PC, Macintosh, tower configuration, desktop configuration, laptop, PDA, etc.)?

b. What kind of keyboard, mouse, monitor, and printer would you like to have?

c. Would you need any additional input or output devices to perform your job?

3. What Hardware Will You Use?

What types of computer hardware would make your work life more efficient? What adjustments would you need to make on your current system to accommodate those hardware devices? (For example, does your computer have the right kind of port or enough ports to support additional hardware devices?)

4. Choosing the Best Printer

You are looking for a new printer for your home business. You have always had an ink-jet printer, but now that costs for laser printers are dropping, you're considering buying a laser printer. However, you're still unsure since they're more expensive than ink-jet printers, although you've heard that there is an overall cost savings with laser printers when the cost of toner/ink and paper is taken into consideration.

a. Using the Internet, investigate the merits of different ink-jet and laser printers. Narrow in on one printer in each category and note the initial cost of each.

b. Research the cost of ink/toner for each printer. Calculate the cost of ink/toner supplies for each printer, assuming you will print 5,000 black-and-white pages per year. How much will it cost per page of printing, not including the initial cost of the printer itself?

c. Investigate the multipurpose printers that also have faxing, scanning, and copying capabilities. How much more expensive are they than a traditional ink-jet or laser printer? Are there any drawbacks to these multipurpose machines? Do they perform each function as well as their stand-alone counterparts?

d. Based on your research, which printer would be the most economical?

5. Office Ergonomics

Your boss has designated you "ergonomics coordinator" for the department. She has asked you to design a flyer to be posted around the office informing your coworkers of the proper computer setup as well as the potential risks if such precautions are avoided. Create an ergonomics flyer, making sure it fits on an 8.5" x 11" piece of paper.

Critical Thinking Questions

Instructions: Albert Einstein used "Gedanken experiments," or critical thinking questions, to develop his theory of relativity. Some ideas are best understood by experimenting with them in our own minds. The following critical thinking questions are designed to demand your full attention but require only a comfortable chair—no technology.

1. Keyboard of the Future

What do you think the keyboard of the future will look like? What capabilities will it have that keyboards currently don't have? Will it have ports? Cables? Special communications abilities?

2. Mouse of the Future

What do you think the mouse (or other pointing device) of the future will look like? What sorts of improvements on the traditional mouse can you imagine? Do you think there will ever be a day when we won't need mice and keyboards to use our computers?

3. Storage Devices of the Future

How do you think storage devices will change in the future? Will increased storage capacity and decreased size affect the ways in which we use computers?

4. Computers Decreasing Productivity?

Can you think of any situations in which computers actually decrease productivity? Why? Should we always expect computers to increase our productivity? What do you think the impact of using computers would be:

a. in a third-grade classroom?
b. in a manager's office for a large chain supermarket?
c. for a retired couple who purchase their first PC?

5. "Smart" Homes

The Smart Medical Home project of the University of Rochester's Center for Future Health is researching how to use technology to monitor many aspects of your health. The Smart Medical Home is the creation of a cross-disciplinary group of scientists and engineers from the college, the Medical Center, and the university's Center for Future Health. This particular "smart home" includes a sophisticated computer system that helps keep track of items such as eyeglasses or keys, and the kitchen is equipped with a new kind of packaging to signal the presence of dangerous bacteria in food. Spaces between ordinary walls are stuffed with gadgetry, including banks of powerful computers.

a. What abilities should a smart home have to safeguard and improve the quality of your life?
b. Could there be potential hazards of a smart home?

6. Toy or Computer?

When do you think a toy becomes a computer? The Microsoft Xbox has a hard disk drive, a CD-ROM, internal RAM, and a built-in Ethernet port. Is this a computer or a toy?

Team Time   PCs vs. Apples: Which Is Best?

Problem:

As you learned in Chapter 1, there are two major classes of computer systems in the marketplace today: PCs and Apple computers. Many people have chosen one camp with an almost religious fervor. In this exercise, each team will explore the trade-offs between a PC and an Apple computer and defend their allegiance to one system or the other.

Task:

Split your class into two teams:

Team A   is a group of PC diehards. They believe these computers perform as well as Apple systems and cost less, providing better value.

Team B   is a group of hard-working Apple-loving software developers. They believe there are no systems as user friendly and reliable as those made by Apple.

Look at the following list of settings for computer labs. Each team should decide why their particular system would be the best choice in each of these settings.

1. An elementary school considering incorporating more technology into the classroom
2. A small accounting firm expanding into new offices
3. A video production company considering producing digital video
4. A computer system for a home office for an aspiring author

Process:

STEP 1:   Form the two teams. Think about what your goals are and what information and resources you need to tackle this project.

STEP 2:   Research and then discuss the components of each system you are recommending. Are any components better suited for each particular need? Consider all the input, output, processing, and storage devices. Are any special devices or peripherals required?

STEP 3:   Write a summary position paper. For each of the four settings, support your system recommendation for

Team A   Some kind of PC computer system

Team B   An Apple system

Conclusion:

There are a number of competing designs for computer systems. Being aware of the options in the marketplace and knowing how to analyze the trade-offs in different designs allows you to become a better consumer as well as a better computer user.

Becoming Computer Fluent

Now that you have taken a computer course, all your friends and relatives are coming to you with their computer questions. Two people in particular are asking you for advice on which computer system to buy. One friend cannot afford much, but wants a good basic system. The other, your cousin, can pick out whichever computer he would like and his new employer will pay for it, so price is not a factor. However, your cousin needs a powerful machine to handle all the multimedia files he uses and creates.

Instructions: Use the Internet to research two different computer systems—the most expensive system you can find, and the cheapest (but still reliable) system you can find. Create a table describing these systems. Consider possible trade-offs in price vs. quality that your friend and cousin might want to consider.

Materials on the Web

In addition to the review materials presented here, you'll find extra materials on the book's companion Web site (**www.prenhall.com/techinaction**) that will help reinforce your understanding of the chapter content. These materials include the following:

Sound Byte Lab Guides

For each Sound Byte mentioned in the chapter, there is a corresponding lab guide located on the book's companion Web site. These guides review the material presented in the Sound Byte and direct you to various Web resources that examine the material. The Sound Byte lab guides for this chapter include:

- Port Tour
- Virtual Computer Tour
- Healthy Computing

True/False and Multiple-Choice Quizzes

The book's Web site includes a true/false and a multiple-choice quiz for this chapter. You can take these quizzes, automatically check the results, and e-mail the results to your instructor.

Web Research Projects

The book's Web site also includes a number of Web research projects for this chapter. These projects ask you to search the Web for information on computer-related careers, milestones in computer history, important people and companies, emerging technologies, and the applications and implications of different technologies.

Technology in Action also features unique interactive Help Desk training, in which you'll assume the role of Help Desk operator taking calls about concepts learned in each chapter. The Help Desk calls for this chapter include:

- Using Input Devices
- Using Output Devices

The History of THE PC

Do *you ever wonder how big the first personal computer was, or how much the first portable computer weighed?* Computers are such an integral part of our lives that we don't often stop to think about how far they've come or where they got their start. But in just 30 years, computers have evolved from expensive, huge machines that only corporations owned to small, powerful devices found in millions of homes. In this *Technology in Focus* feature, we look at the history of the computer. Along the way, we discuss some developments that helped make the computer powerful and portable, as well as the people who contributed to its development. But first, we start with the story of the personal computer and how it grew to be as integral to our lives as the automobile.

The First Personal Computer: The Altair

Our journey through the history of the personal computer starts in 1975. At that time, most people were unfamiliar with the mainframes and supercomputers that large corporations and the government owned. With price tags exceeding the cost of buildings, and with few if any practical home uses, these monster machines were not appealing or attainable to the vast majority of Americans. But that began to change when the January 1975 cover of *Popular Electronics* announced the debut of the **Altair 8800**, touted as the first personal computer (see Figure 1). For just $395 for a do-it-yourself kit or $498 for a fully assembled unit (about $1,000 in today's dollars), the price was reasonable enough so that computer fanatics could finally own their own computers.

The Altair was a very primitive computer, with just 256 bytes (not kilobytes, just bytes) of memory. It didn't come with a keyboard, nor did it include a monitor or printer. Switches on the front of the machine were used to enter data in unfriendly machine code (strings of 1s and 0s). Flashing lights on the front indicated the results of a program. User-friendly it was not—at least not by today's standards.

Despite its limitations, computer "hackers" (as computer enthusiasts were called then) flocked to the machine. Many who bought the Altair had been taught to program, but until that point had access only to big, clumsy computers. They were often hired by corporations to program "boring" financial, statistical, or engineering programs in a workplace environment. The Altair offered these enthusiasts the opportunity to create their own programs. Within three months, Micro Instrumentation and Telemetry Systems (MITS), the company behind the Altair, received more than 4,000 orders for the machine.

The release of the Altair marked the start of the personal computer (PC) boom. In fact,

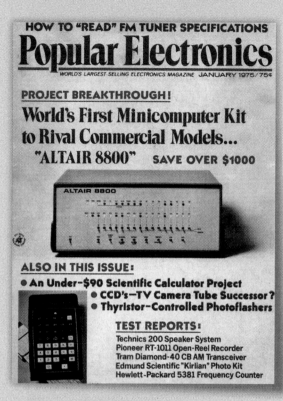

FIGURE 1
In 1975, the Altair was touted as the "world's first minicomputer" in the January issue of *Popular Electronics*.

two men who would play large roles in the development of the PC were among the first Altair owners. Recent high school grads Bill Gates and Paul Allen were so enamored by this "minicomputer," as these personal computers were called at the time, that they wrote a compiling program (a program that translates user commands into those that the computer can understand) for the Altair. The two friends later convinced its developer, Ed Roberts, to buy their program. This marked the start of a small company called Microsoft. But we'll get to that story later. First, let's see what their future archrivals were up to.

Why Was It Called the "Altair"?

For lack of a better name, the Altair's developers originally called the computer the PE-8, short for *Popular Electronics* 8-bit. However, Les Soloman, the *Popular Electronics* writer who introduced the Altair, wanted the machine to have a catchier name. The author's daughter, who was watching *Star Trek* at the time, suggested the name Altair (that's where the *Star Trek* crew was traveling that week). The first star of the PC industry was born.

FIGURE 2
Steve Jobs (a) and Steve Wozniak (b) were two computer hobbyists who worked together to form the Apple Computer Company.

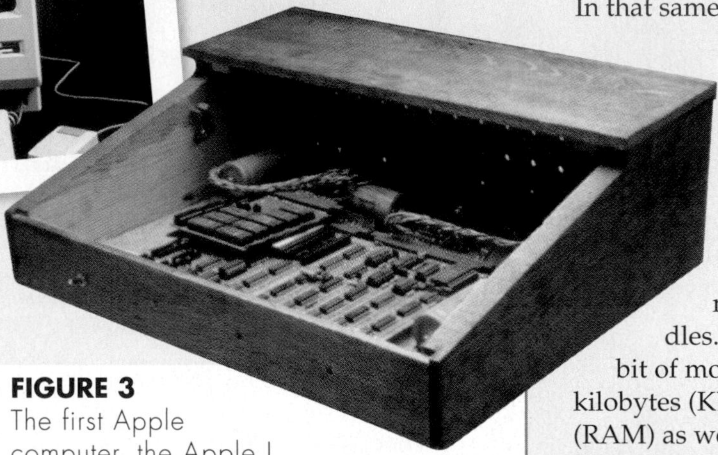

FIGURE 3
The first Apple computer, the Apple I, looked like a typewriter in a box. It was one of the first computers to incorporate a keyboard.

Original Apple II

FIGURE 4
The Apple II came with the addition of a monitor and an external floppy disk drive.

The Apple I and II

Around the time the Altair was released, **Steve Wozniak**, an employee at Hewlett-Packard, was becoming fascinated with the burgeoning personal computer industry and was dabbling with his own computer design. He would bring his computer prototypes to meetings of the Homebrew Computing Club, a group of young computer fans who met to discuss computer ideas in Palo Alto, California. **Steve Jobs**, who was working for computer game manufacturer Atari at the time, liked Wozniak's prototypes and made a few suggestions. Together, the two built a personal computer, later known as the **Apple I**, in Wozniak's garage (see Figures 2 and 3). In that same year, on April 1, 1976, Jobs and Wozniak officially formed the **Apple Computer Company**.

No sooner had the Apple I hit the market, Wozniak was working to improve it. A year later, in 1977, the **Apple II** was born (see Figure 4). The Apple II included a color monitor, sound, and game paddles. Priced around $1,300 (quite a bit of money in those days), it included 4 kilobytes (KB) of random access memory (RAM) as well as an optional floppy disk drive that enabled users to run additional programs. Most of these programs were games. However, for many users, there was a special appeal to the Apple II: the program that made the computer function when the power was first turned on was stored in read-only memory (ROM). Previously, such routine-task programs had to be rewritten every time the computer was turned on. This automation made it possible for the least technical computer enthusiast to write programs.

An instant success, the Apple II would be the most successful in the company's line, outshining even its successor, the **Apple III**, released in 1980. Eventually, the Apple II included a spreadsheet program, word processing, and desktop publishing software. These programs gave personal computers like the Apple functions beyond just gaming and special programming, leading to their increased popularity. We talk more about these advances later. For now, other players were entering the market.

Why Is It Called "Apple"?

Steve Jobs wanted Apple Computer to be the "perfect" computer company. Having recently worked at an apple orchard, Jobs thought of the apple as the "perfect" fruit—it was high in nutrients, came in a nice package, and was not easily damaged. Thus, he and Wozniak decided to name their new computer company Apple.

Enter the Competition

Around the time Apple was experiencing success with its computers, a number of competitors entered the market. The largest among them were Commodore, RadioShack, and IBM. As Figure 5 shows, just years after the introduction of the Altair, the market was filled with personal computers from a variety of manufacturers.

The Commodore PET and TRS-80

Among Apple's strongest competitors were the **Commodore PET 2001,** shown in Figure 6, and Tandy RadioShack's **TRS-80,** shown in Figure 7. Commodore introduced the PET in January 1977. It was featured on the cover of *Popular Science* in October 1977 as the "new $595 home computer." Tandy RadioShack's home computer also garnered immediate popularity. Just one month after its release in 1977, the TRS-80 sold approximately 10,000 units. Priced at $599.95, the easy-to-use machine included a color display and 4 KB of memory. Many other manufacturers followed suit over the next decade, launching new desktop products, but none were as successful as the TRS-80 and the Commodore.

FIGURE 5
Personal Computer Development

YEAR	APPLE	IBM	OTHERS
1975			MITS Altair
1976	Apple I		
1977	Apple II		Tandy RadioShack's TRS-80 Commodore PET
1980	Apple III		
1981		IBM PC	Osborne
1983	Lisa		
1984	Macintosh	286-AT	IBM PC clones

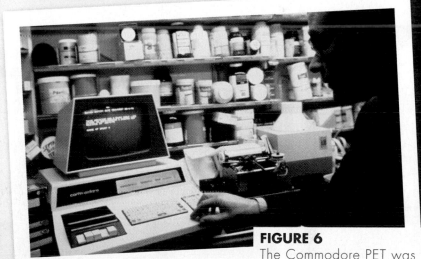

FIGURE 6
The Commodore PET was well received because of its all-in-one design.

FIGURE 7
The TRS-80 hid its circuitry under the keyboard. The computer was nicknamed "trash-80," which was more a play on its initials than a reflection of its capabilities.

The Osborne

The Osborne Company introduced the **Osborne** in April 1981 as the industry's first portable computer (see Figure 8). Although portable, the computer weighed 24.5 pounds, and its screen was just 5 inches wide. In addition to its hefty weight, it came with a hefty price tag of $1,795. Still, the Osborne included 64 KB of memory, two floppy disk drives, and software programs installed (such as word processing and spreadsheet software). The Osborne was an overnight success, with sales quickly reaching 10,000 units per month. However, despite the Osborne's popularity, the release of a successor machine, called the **Executive,** reduced sales of the Osborne significantly, and the Osborne Company eventually closed. Compaq bought the Osborne design and later produced its first portable in 1983.

IBM PCs

By 1980, IBM recognized it needed to get its feet into the personal computer market. Up until that point, the company had been a player in the computer industry, but primarily with mainframe computers, which it sold only to large corporations. It had not taken the smaller, personal computer seriously. In August 1981, however, IBM released its first personal computer, appropriately named the **IBM PC.** Because many companies were already familiar with IBM mainframes, they readily adopted the IBM PC. The term *PC* soon became the term used to describe personal computers.

The IBM PC came with up to 256 KB of memory and started at $1,565. IBM marketed its PC through retail outlets such as Sears and Computerland in order to reach the home market, and it quickly dominated the playing field. In January 1983, *Time* magazine, playing on its annual "man of the year" issue, named the computer "1982 machine of the year" (see Figure 9).

FIGURE 8
The Osborne was introduced as the first portable personal computer. It weighed a whopping 24.5 pounds and contained just 64 KB of memory.

FIGURE 9
The IBM PC was the first (and only) non-human object chosen as "man of the year" (actually, "machine of the year") by *Time* magazine in its January 1983 issue. This designation indicated the impact the PC was having on the general public.

Other Important Advancements

It was not just the *hardware* of the personal computer that was developing during the 1970s and 1980s. At the same time, advances in programming languages and operating systems and the influx of application software were leading to more useful and powerful machines.

The Importance of BASIC

The software industry began in the 1950s with the development of programming languages such as FORTRAN, ALGOL, and COBOL. These languages were used mainly by businesses to create financial, statistical, and engineering programs for corporate enterprises. But the 1964 introduction of **Beginners All-Purpose Symbolic Instruction Code (BASIC)** revolutionized the software industry. BASIC was a programming language that the beginning programming student could easily learn. It thus became enormously popular—and the key language of the PC. In fact, **Bill Gates** and **Paul Allen** (see Figure 10) used BASIC to write the program for the Altair. As we noted earlier, this program led to the creation of **Microsoft**, a company that produced software for the micro computer.

The Advent of Operating Systems

Because data on the earliest personal computers was stored on audiocassettes (not floppies), many programs were not saved or reused. Rather, programs were rewritten as needed. Then Steve Wozniak developed a floppy disk drive called the **Disk II**, which he introduced in July 1978. With the introduction of the floppy drive, programs could be saved with more efficiency, and operating systems (OSs) developed.

OSs were (and still are) written to coordinate with the specific processor chip that controlled the computer. Apples run on a Motorola chip, while PCs (IBMs and so on) run on an Intel chip. **Disk Operating System (DOS)**, developed by Wozniak and introduced in December 1977, was the OS that controlled the first Apple computers. The **Control Program for Microcomputers (CP/M)**, developed by Gary Kildall, was the

FIGURE 10
Bill Gates and Paul Allen are the founders of Microsoft.

first OS designed for the Intel 8080 chip (the processor for PCs). Intel hired Kildall to write a compiling program for the 8080 chip, but Kildall quickly saw the need for a program that could store computer operating instructions on a floppy disk rather than on a cassette. Intel wasn't interested in buying the CP/M program, but Kildall saw a future for the program and thus founded his own company, Digital Research.

In 1980, when IBM was considering entering the personal computer market, it approached Bill Gates at Microsoft to write an OS program for the IBM PC. Although Gates had written versions of BASIC for different computer systems, he had never written an OS. He therefore recommended IBM investigate the CP/M OS, but no one from Digital Research returned IBM's call. Microsoft reconsidered the opportunity and developed **MS-DOS** for IBM computers. (This was one phone call Digital Research certainly regrets not returning!)

MS-DOS was based on an OS called **Quick and Dirty Operating System (QDOS)** developed by Seattle Computer Products. Microsoft bought the nonexclusive rights to QDOS and distributed it to IBM. Eventually, virtually all personal computers running on the Intel chip used MS-DOS as their OS. Microsoft's reign as one of the dominant players in the PC landscape had begun. Meanwhile, many other software programs were being developed, taking personal computers to the next level of user acceptance.

The Software Application Explosion: VisiCalc and Beyond

Inclusion of floppy disk drives in personal computers not only facilitated the storage of operating systems, but also set off a software application explosion, because the floppy disk was a convenient way to distribute software. Around that same time, in 1978,

FIGURE 11
Dan Bricklin and Bob Frankston created VisiCalc, the first business application developed for the personal computer.

FIGURE 12
Software Application Development

YEAR	APPLICATION
1978	**VisiCalc:** First electronic spreadsheet application. **WordStar:** First word processing application.
1980	**WordPerfect:** Thought to be the best word processing software for the PC. WordPerfect was eventually sold to Novell, then later acquired by Corel.
1982	**Lotus 1-2-3:** Added integrated charting, plotting, and database capabilities to spreadsheet software.
1983	**Word for MS-DOS:** Introduced in *PC World* magazine with the first magazine-inserted demo disk.
1985	**Excel:** One of the first spreadsheets to use a graphical user interface. **PageMaker:** First desktop publishing software.

Harvard Business School student Dan Bricklin recognized the potential for a spreadsheet program that could be used on PCs. He and his friend Bob Frankston (see Figure 11) thus created the program **VisiCalc**. VisiCalc not only became an instant success, it was also one of the main reasons for the rapid increase in PC sales. Finally, ordinary home users could see how owning a personal computer could benefit their lives. More than 100,000 copies of VisiCalc were sold in its first year.

After VisiCalc, other electronic spreadsheet programs entered the market. **Lotus 1-2-3** came on the market in 1982, and **Microsoft Excel** entered the scene in 1985. These two products became so popular that they eventually put VisiCalc out of business.

Meanwhile, word processing software was gaining a foothold in the PC industry. Up to this point, there were separate, dedicated word processing machines, and the thought hadn't occurred to enable the personal computer to do word processing. Personal computers, it was believed, were for computation and data management. However, once **WordStar**, the first word processing application, came out in disk form in 1979 and was available on personal computers, word processing became another important use for the PC. In fact, word processing is now one of the most common PC applications. Competitors such as **Word for MS-DOS** (the precursor to Microsoft Word) and **WordPerfect** soon entered the market. Figure 12 lists some of the important dates in software application development.

The Graphical User Interface

Another important advancement in personal computers was the introduction of the **graphical user interface (GUI)**, which allowed users to interact with the computer more easily. Until that time, users had to use complicated command- or menu-driven interfaces to interact with the computer. Apple was the first company to take full commercial advantage of the GUI, but competitors were fast on its heels, and soon the GUI became synonymous with personal computers. But who developed the idea of the GUI? You'll probably be surprised to learn that a company known for its photocopiers was the real innovator.

Xerox

In 1972, a few years before Apple had launched its first PC, photocopier manufacturer **Xerox** was hard at work in its Palo Alto Research Center (PARC) designing a personal computer of its own. Named the **Alto** (shown in Figure 13), the computer included a word processor, based on the What You See Is What You Get (WYSIWYG) principle, that was a file management system with directories and folders. It also had a mouse and could connect to a network. None of the other personal computers of the time had any of these features. Still, for a variety of reasons, Xerox never sold the Alto commercially. Several years later, it developed the Star Office System, which was based on the Alto. Despite its convenient features, the Star never became popular, because no one was willing to pay the $17,000 asking price.

The Lisa and the Macintosh

Xerox's ideas were ahead of their time. But many of the ideas of the Alto and Star would soon catch on. In 1983, Apple introduced the **Lisa**, shown in Figure 14. Named after Apple founder Steve Job's daughter, the Lisa was the first successful PC brought to market to use a GUI. Legend has it that Jobs had seen the Alto during a visit to PARC in 1979 and was influenced by its GUI. He therefore incorporated a similar user interface into the Lisa, providing features such as windows, drop-down menus, icons, a hierarchical file system with folders and files, and a point-and-click device called a mouse. The only problem with the Lisa was its price. At $9,995 ($20,000 in today's dollars), few buyers were willing to take the plunge.

A year later, in 1984, Apple introduced the **Macintosh**, shown in Figure 15. The Macintosh was everything the Lisa was and then some, and at about a third of the cost. The Macintosh was also the first personal computer to introduce 3.5-inch floppy disks with a hard cover, which were smaller and sturdier than the previous 5.25-inch floppies.

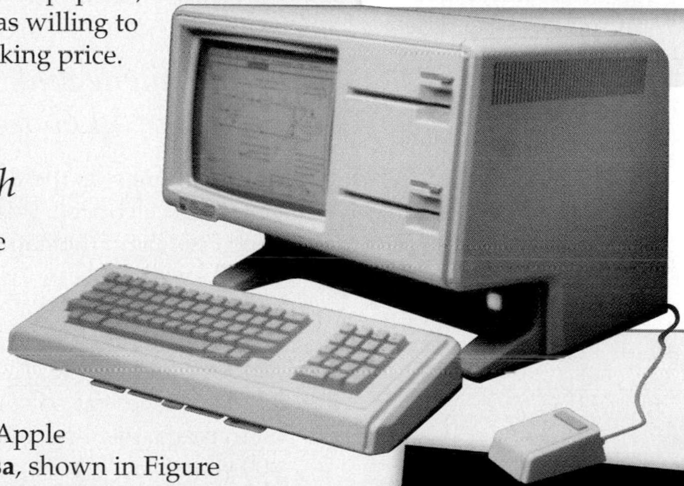

FIGURE 13
The Alto was the first computer to use a graphical user interface, and it provided the basis for the GUI that Apple used. However, because of marketing problems, the Alto never was sold.

FIGURE 14
The Lisa was the first computer to introduce a GUI to the market. Priced too high, it never gained the popularity it deserved.

Macintosh in 1984

FIGURE 15
The Macintosh became one of Apple's best-selling computers, incorporating a graphical user interface along with other innovations such as the 3.5-inch floppy disk drive.

The Internet Boom

The GUI made it easier for users to work on the computer. The Internet provided another reason for consumers to buy computers. Now they could conduct research and communicate with each other in a new and convenient way. In 1993, the Web browser **Mosaic** was introduced. This browser allowed users to view multimedia on the Web, causing Internet traffic to increase by nearly 350 percent. Meanwhile, companies discovered the Internet as a means to do business, and computer sales took off. IBM-compatible PCs became the personal computer system of choice when, in 1995, Microsoft (the predominant software provider to PCs) introduced **Internet Explorer**, a Web browser that integrated Web functionality into Microsoft Office applications, and **Windows 95**, the first Microsoft OS not based on MS-DOS.

Making the PC Possible: Early Computers

Since the first Altair was introduced in the 1970s, more than a billion personal computers have been distributed around the globe. Because of the declining prices of computers and the growth of the Internet, it's estimated that a billion more computers will be sold within the next decade. But what made all this possible? The computer is a compilation of parts, all of which are the result of individual inventions. From the earliest days of humankind, we have been looking for a more systematic way to count and calculate. Thus, the evolution of counting machines has led to the development of the computer we know today.

The Pascalene and the Jacquard Loom

The **Pascalene** was the first accurate mechanical calculator. This machine, created by the French mathematician **Blaise Pascal** in 1642, used revolutions of gears to count by tens, similar to odometers in cars. The Pascalene could be used to add, subtract, multiply, and divide. The basic design of the Pascalene was so sound that it lived on in mechanical calculators for more than 300 years.

Nearly 200 years later, **Joseph Jacquard** revolutionized the fabric industry by creating a machine that automated the weaving of complex patterns. Although not a counting or calculating machine, the **Jacquard Loom** (shown in Figure 16) was significant because it relied on stiff cards with punched holes to automate the process. Much later this process would be adopted as a means to record and read data by using punch cards in computers.

FIGURE 16
The Jacquard Loom used holes punched in stiff cards to make complex designs. This technique would later be used in the form of punch cards to control the input and output of data in computers.

Babbage's Engines

Decades later, in 1834, **Charles Babbage** designed the first automatic calculator, called the **Analytical Engine** (see Figure 17). The machine was actually based on another machine called, the **Difference Engine**, which was a huge steam-powered mechanical calculator Babbage designed to print astronomical tables. Babbage stopped working on the Difference Engine to build the Analytical Engine. Although it was never developed, Babbage's detailed drawings and descriptions of the machine include components similar to those found in today's computers, including the store (RAM), the mill (central processing unit), as well as input and output devices. This invention gave Charles Babbage the title of the "father of computing."

FIGURE 17
The Analytical Engine, designed by Charles Babbage, was never fully developed, but included components similar to those found in today's computers.

The Hollerith Tabulating Machine

In 1890, **Herman Hollerith**, while working for the U.S. Census Bureau, was the first to take Jacquard's punch card concept and apply it to computing. Hollerith developed a machine called the **Hollerith Tabulating Machine** that used punch cards to tabulate census data. Up until that time, census data had been tabulated in a long, laborious process. Hollerith's tabulating machine automatically read data that had been punched onto small punch cards, speeding up the tabulation process. Hollerith's machine became so successful that he left the Census Bureau in 1896 to start the Tabulating Machine Company. His company later changed its name to International Business Machines, or IBM.

The Z1 and Atanasoff-Berry Computer

German inventor **Konrad Zuse** is credited with a number of computing inventions. His first, in 1936, was a mechanical calculator called the **Z1**. The Z1 is thought to be the first computer to include features that are integral to today's systems, including a control unit and separate memory functions, noted as important breakthroughs for future computer design.

In late 1939, John Atanasoff, a professor at Iowa State University, and his student, Clifford Berry, built the first electrically powered digital computer, called the **Atanasoff-Berry Computer (ABC)**, shown in Figure 18. The computer was the first to use vacuum tubes to store data instead of the mechanical switches used in older computers. Although revolutionary at its time, the machine weighed 700 pounds, contained a mile of wire, and took about 15 seconds for each calculation. (In comparison, today's personal computers can calculate more than 300 billion operations in 15 seconds.) Most important, the ABC was the first to use the binary system. It was also the first to have memory that repowered itself upon booting. The design of the ABC would end up being central to that of future computers.

FIGURE 18
The Atanasoff-Berry Computer laid the design groundwork for many computers to come.

The Harvard Mark I

From the late 1930s to the early 1950s, **Howard Aiken** and **Grace Hopper** designed the Mark series of computers at Harvard University. The U.S. Navy used these computers for ballistic and gunnery calculations. Aiken, an electrical engineer and physicist, designed the computer, while Hopper did the programming. The **Harvard Mark I**, finished in 1944, could perform all four arithmetic operations (addition, subtraction, multiplication, and division).

However, many believe Hopper's greatest contribution to computing was the invention of the **compiler**, a program that translates English language instructions into computer language. The team was also responsible for a common computer-related expression. Hopper was the first to "debug" a computer when she removed a moth that had flown into the Harvard Mark I. The moth caused the computer to break down. After that, problems that caused the computer to not run were called "bugs."

The Turing Machine

Meanwhile, in 1936, the British mathematician **Alan Turing** created an abstract computer model that could perform logical operations. The **Turing Machine** was not a real machine but rather a hypothetical model that mathematically defined a mechanical procedure (or algorithm). Additionally, Turing's concept described a process by which the machine could read, write, or erase symbols written on squares of an infinite paper tape. This concept of an infinite tape that could be read, written to, and erased was the precursor to today's RAM.

The ENIAC

The **Electronic Numerical Integrator and Computer (ENIAC)**, shown in Figure 20, was another U.S. government–sponsored machine developed to calculate the settings used for weapons. Created by **John W. Mauchly** and **J. Presper Eckert** at the University of Pennsylvania, it was placed in operation in June 1944. Although the ENIAC is generally thought of as the first successful high-speed electronic digital computer, it

FIGURE 19
Grace Hopper coined the term *computer bug* referring to a moth that had flown into the Harvard Mark I, causing it to break down.

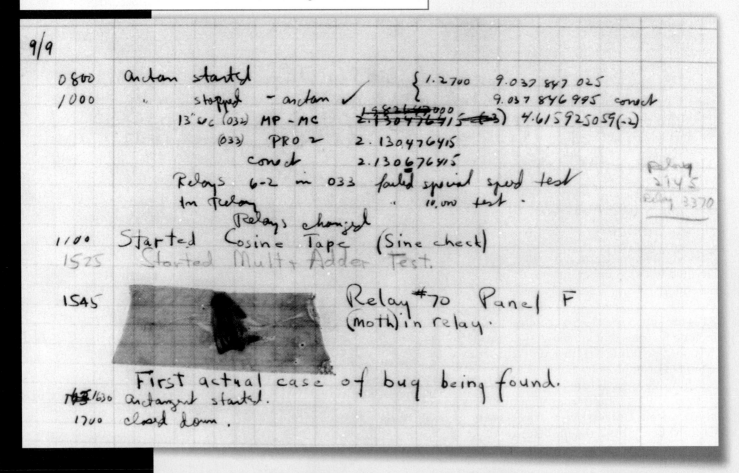

was big and clumsy. The ENIAC used nearly 18,000 vacuum tubes and filled approximately 1,800 square feet of floor space. Although inconvenient, the ENIAC served its purpose and remained in use until 1955.

The UNIVAC

The **Universal Automatic Computer**, or **UNIVAC**, was the first commercially successful electronic digital computer. Completed in June 1951 and owned by the company Remington Rand, the UNIVAC operated on magnetic tape (as opposed to its competitors, which ran on punch cards). The UNIVAC gained notoriety when, in a 1951 publicity stunt, it was used to predict the outcome of the Stevenson-Eisenhower presidential race. By analyzing only 5 percent of the popular vote, the UNIVAC correctly identified Dwight D. Eisenhower as the victor. After that, the UNIVAC soon became a household name. The UNIVAC and computers like it were considered **first-generation computers** and were the last to use vacuum tubes to store data.

Transistors and Beyond

Only a year after the ENIAC was completed, scientists at the Bell Telephone Laboratories in New Jersey invented the **transistor** as a means to store data. The transistor replaced the bulky vacuum tubes of earlier computers and was smaller and more powerful. It was used in almost everything, from radios to phones. Computers that used transistors were referred to as **second-generation computers**. Still, transistors were limited as to how small they could be made.

A few years later, in 1958, **Jack Kilby**, while working at Texas Instruments, invented the world's first **integrated circuit**, a small chip capable of containing thousands of transistors. This consolidation in design enabled computers to become smaller and lighter. The computers in this early integrated circuit generation were considered **third-generation computers**.

Other innovations in the computer industry further refined the computer's speed,

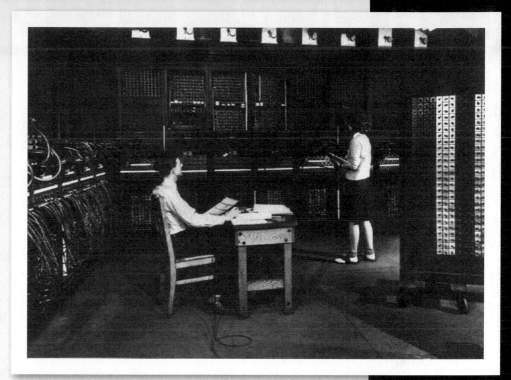

FIGURE 20
The ENIAC took up an entire room and required several people to manipulate it.

accuracy, and efficiency. However, none were as significant as the 1971 introduction by the Intel Corporation of the **microprocessor chip**, a small chip containing millions of transistors. The microprocessor functions as the central processing unit (CPU), or brains, of the computer. Computers that used a microprocessor chip were called **fourth-generation computers**. Over time, Intel and Motorola became the leading manufacturers of microprocessors. Today, the Intel Pentium 4 chip, shown in Figure 21, contains more than 42 million transistors.

As you can see, personal computers have come a long way since the Altair and have a number of inventions and people to thank for their amazing popularity. What will the future bring? If current trends continue, computers will be smaller, lighter, and more powerful. The advancement of wireless technology will also certainly play a big roll in the development of the personal computer.

FIGURE 21
The Pentium 4 chip contains more than 42 million transistors.

CHAPTER 3

OBJECTIVES

After reading this chapter, you should be able to answer the following questions:

- ■ What is the origin of the Internet? (p. 84)

- ■ How does data travel on the Internet? (pp. 84–85)

- ■ What are my options for connecting to the Internet? (pp. 86–90)

- ■ How do I choose an Internet service provider? (pp. 90–91)

- ■ What is a Web browser? (pp. 92–93)

- ■ What is a URL and what are its parts? (pp. 93–94)

- ■ How can I use hyperlinks and other tools to get around the Web? (pp. 93–96)

- ■ How do I search the Internet using search engines and subject directories? (pp. 96–99)

- ■ What are Boolean operators and how do they help me search the Web more effectively? (pp. 98–99)

- ■ How can I communicate through the Internet with e-mail, chat, IM, and newsgroups? (pp. 101–105)

- ■ What is e-commerce and what e-commerce safeguards protect me when I'm online? (pp. 106–108)

- ■ What are cookies and what risks do they pose? (p. 108)

- ■ What are the various kinds of multimedia files found on the Web? (pp. 109–110)

- ■ What kind of software do I need to enjoy multimedia on the Web? (p. 109)

- ■ What will the Internet of the future look like? (pp. 110–111)

SOUND BYTES

- • Connecting to the Internet (p. 91)
- • Welcome to the Web (p. 94)
- • Finding Information on the Web (p. 101)

- • Creating a Web-based E-mail Account (p. 102)
- • Best Utilities for Your Computer (p. 108)

Using the Internet:

Making the Most of the Web's Resources

It's 10:00 P.M. as Max sits down to begin his online coursework. Although it's been a long day, he likes taking the online course because it lets him finish his degree and still keep his full-time job. While downloading the assignment file from the course Web site, he switches to his Instant Messenger (IM) account to see if any of his friends are online. Seeing his friend Tom is logged on, he chats with him for a while. Like a lot of his friends, Max has become a fan of IM. He uses it almost as much as he does e-mail.

Still waiting for his file to finish downloading, he visits ESPN.com to check out the score of the Red Sox game. He then goes to his favorite search engine, Google, and starts researching the topic he plans to write about for his class. As he conducts his searches, he experiments with some Web search techniques he learned about in his online class. He's amazed at how much information he can find when he searches the Web, yet how hard it is to find truly *useful* information.

Finally, Max sees that the assignment file has finished down-loading. Tired of waiting what seems like forever for files to download over his modem, he vows to get a faster Internet con-nection, probably DSL or cable. He checks his e-mail one last time and finds the usual spam as well as a message from the student loan office reminding him his payment is due. He opens Microsoft Internet Explorer and clicks on the link for the bank from his Favorites list. With a few more clicks, he transfers enough money from his savings account to his checking account to cover his payment.

Does this level of Internet interaction sound at all like yours? If you're like many Americans, you use the Internet as much as you do your television, maybe even more. But do you really know how to get the most out of your Internet experience and which connection option is best for you? In this chapter, you'll learn what you should know about the Internet in order to use it to your best advantage. We'll look at the options you have for connecting to the Internet, as well as what you should know about the companies that provide you with Internet access. We'll then discuss how you can navigate and search the Web effectively so that your time spent on the Internet is useful. Finally, we'll investigate other Internet features you probably use, such as communication technologies (e-mail, IM, and the like), e-commerce, and multimedia experiences. But first, let's start by looking at the origin of the Internet and how data travels across this big network.

Internet Basics

You've no doubt been on the Internet countless times. According to the U.S. Census Bureau, over 57.6 percent of American homes are connected to the Internet, a number that grows each day. But what exactly is the Internet? The **Internet** is the largest network in the world, actually a network of networks, connecting millions of computers from more than 65 countries. Today, most people use the Internet to communicate with others, although online shopping and entertainment activities follow close behind. Yet these uses are a far cry from the original intention of the Internet.

THE ORIGIN OF THE INTERNET

Why was the Internet created? To understand why the Internet was created, you need to understand what was happening in the early 1960s in the United States. At this time, the Cold War with Russia was raging, and military leaders and civilians alike were concerned about a Russian nuclear or conventional attack on the United States. Meanwhile, the U.S. armed forces were becoming increasingly dependent on computers to coordinate and plan their activities. For the U.S. armed forces to operate efficiently, computer systems located in various parts of the country needed to have a reliable means of communication—one that could not be disrupted easily. Thus, the U.S. government funded much of the early research into the Internet to facilitate computer communications for the military.

At the same time, researchers also hoped the Internet would address the problems involved with getting different computers to communicate with each other. Although computers had been networked together since the early 1960s, there was no reliable way to connect computers from different manufacturers because these computers used different proprietary methods of communication. What was lacking was a common communications method that *all* computers could use, regardless of the differences in their individual designs. The Internet was therefore created to respond to these two concerns: to establish a safe form of military communications and to create a means by which all computers could communicate.

Who invented the Internet? The modern Internet evolved from an early "internetworking" project called the **Advanced Research Projects Agency Network (ARPANET)**. Funded by the U.S. government for the military in the late 1960s, ARPANET was the first attempt to allow computers to communicate over vast distances in a reliable manner. What started as a group of four computers networked together in the ARPANET has grown into millions of computers connected to the Internet today.

Although many people participated in the creation of the ARPANET, two men who worked on the project, Vinton Cerf and Robert Kahn, are generally acknowledged as the "fathers" of the Internet. They earned this honor because they were primarily responsible for developing the communications protocols (or standards) still in use on the Internet today.

THE WEB VS. THE INTERNET

So are the Web and the Internet the same thing? Because the **World Wide Web (WWW** or the **Web)** is the part of the Internet we use the most, we sometimes think of the "Net" and the "Web" as being interchangeable. However, the Web is only a part of the Internet. Other parts of the Internet include communications systems such as e-mail and instant messaging and information exchange technologies such as File Transfer Protocol (FTP) and newsgroups, all of which we discuss later in this chapter. What distinguishes the Web from the rest of the Internet is (1) its use of common communication protocols (such as TCP/IP) and special languages (such as the Hypertext Markup Language or HTML) that enable different computers to talk to each other and display information in compatible formats and (2) its use of special links (called hyperlinks) that enable users to jump from one place to another on the Web.

THE INTERNET'S CLIENTS AND SERVERS

How does the Internet work? Computers connected to the Internet communicate (or "talk") to each other in a similar fashion as we do when we ask a question and get an answer. Thus, a computer connected to the Internet acts in one of two ways: it is either a **client**, a computer that asks for data, or a **server**, a computer that receives the request and returns the data to the client. Because the Internet uses clients and servers, it is referred to as a **client/server network**.

How do computers talk to each other? Suppose you want to access the Web to check out snow conditions at your favorite ski area. As Figure 3.1 illustrates, when you type the Web site address of the ski area in your **Web browser** (software that allows you to access the Web) your computer acts as a *client computer* because you are asking for data from the ski area's Web site. Your browser's request for this data travels along several pathways, similar to interstate highways. The largest and fastest pathway is the main artery of the Internet, called the **Internet backbone**, to which all intermediary pathways connect. All data traffic flows along the backbone and then on to smaller pathways until it reaches its destination, which is the server computer for the ski area's Web site. The server computer returns the requested data to your computer by using the most expedient pathway system (which may be different from the pathway the request took). Your Web browser then interprets the data and displays it on your monitor.

How does the data get sent to the correct computer? Each time you connect to the Internet, your computer is assigned a unique identification number. This number, called an **Internet Protocol (IP) address**, is a set of four numbers separated by dots, such as 123.45.245.91. IP addresses are the means by which all computers connected to the Internet identify each other.

Similarly, each Web site is assigned an IP address that uniquely identifies it. However, because the long strings of numbers that make up IP addresses are difficult for humans to remember, Web sites are given text versions of their IP addresses. So, the ski area Web site mentioned earlier may have an IP address of 234.59.180.37 and a text name of **www.skislope.com**. When you type **www.skislope.com** into your browser window, your computer (with its own unique IP address) looks for the ski area's IP address (234.59.180.37). Data is exchanged between the ski area's server computer and your computer using these unique IP addresses.

FIGURE 3.1

How the Internet's client/server network works.

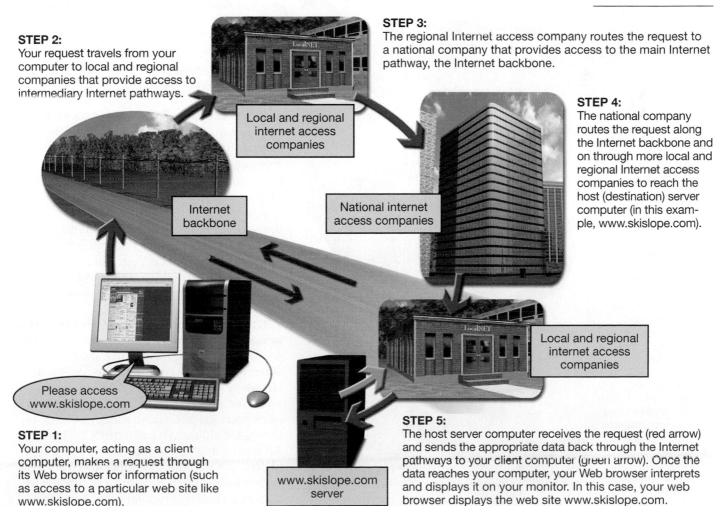

STEP 2:
Your request travels from your computer to local and regional companies that provide access to intermediary Internet pathways.

STEP 3:
The regional Internet access company routes the request to a national company that provides access to the main Internet pathway, the Internet backbone.

STEP 4:
The national company routes the request along the Internet backbone and on through more local and regional Internet access companies to reach the host (destination) server computer (in this example, www.skislope.com).

Local and regional internet access companies

Internet backbone

National internet access companies

Local and regional internet access companies

Please access www.skislope.com

www.skislope.com server

STEP 1:
Your computer, acting as a client computer, makes a request through its Web browser for information (such as access to a particular web site like www.skislope.com).

STEP 5:
The host server computer receives the request (red arrow) and sends the appropriate data back through the Internet pathways to your client computer (green arrow). Once the data reaches your computer, your Web browser interprets and displays it on your monitor. In this case, your web browser displays the web site www.skislope.com.

CONNECTING TO THE INTERNET

To take advantage of the resources the Internet offers, you need a means to connect your computer to it. Home users have several connection options available. The most common method is a **dial-up connection**. With dial-up connections, you connect to the Internet using a standard telephone line. Other connection options, collectively called **broadband connections**, offer faster means to connect to the Internet. Broadband connections include cable, satellite, and DSL.

DIAL-UP CONNECTIONS

How does a dial-up connection work?

A dial-up connection is the least costly method of connecting to the Internet, needing only a standard phone line and a modem (see Figure 3.2). A **modem** is a device that converts (modulates) the digital signals the computer understands to the analog signals that can travel over phone lines. In turn, the computer on the other end must also have a modem to translate (*dem*odulate) the received analog signal back to a digital signal for the receiving computer to understand.

Although external modems do exist, modern desktop computers generally come with internal modems built into the system unit. Laptops usually use either internal modems or small credit card–sized devices called **PC cards** (sometimes called **PCMCIA cards**) that are inserted into a special slot on the laptop. Current modems have a maximum data transfer rate of 56 kilobits per second (Kbps, usually referred to as 56K). **Data transfer rate**, or **throughput**, is the measurement of how fast data travels between computers. It is also informally referred to as *connection speed*. When you use a 56K modem, you actually connect to the Internet at a speed lower than 56 Kbps because of interference such as line noise.

What are the advantages of a dial-up Internet connection?

A dial-up connection is the least costly way to connect to the Internet. Although slower than broadband connections, dial-up connections, with today's 56K modems, are often fine for casual Internet users who do not need a very fast connection.

What are the disadvantages of dial-up?

In a word: speed. Even at 56 Kbps, moving through the Internet with a dial-up connection can be a slow and frustrating experience. Web pages can take a long time to load, especially if they contain multimedia files. Similarly, if you visit many Web sites at the same time or receive or send large files while you're on the Internet, you'll find that a dial-up connection is very slow. Another disadvantage to dial-up is that when you're on the Internet, you tie up your phone line if you don't have a separate line.

Can I avoid tying up my phone line when I use a dial-up connection?

One solution to this problem is to install an additional phone line for your Internet connection. However, this can be costly. Alternatively, if you have a call-waiting feature with your phone service, you can use a device such as Catch-A-Call, shown in Figure 3.3. These devices enable you to receive incoming phone calls without disconnecting from the Internet. When you receive a call, the device displays a flashing red light. To accept the

FIGURE 3.2

Dial-up connection modem options.
(a) A dial-up Internet connection often uses a standard phone cord that connects a phone jack and your computer's internal modem, which is a card located inside the system unit.
(b) External modems are peripheral devices that sit outside the system unit. Although you can still find external modems, most computers now come with internal modems.
(c) Laptops use small credit card–sized devices, called PC cards, to connect to the Internet.

Modem Jack

Modem Card

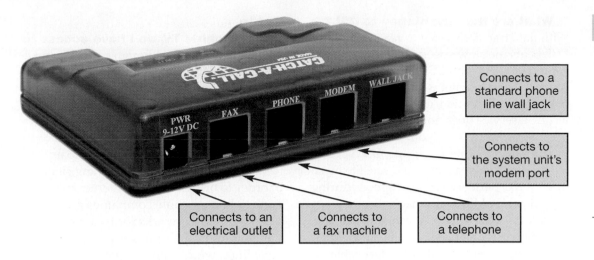

Connects to a standard phone line wall jack

Connects to the system unit's modem port

Connects to an electrical outlet

Connects to a fax machine

Connects to a telephone

FIGURE 3.3

Devices such as Catch-A-Call temporarily place your Internet connection on hold while you answer incoming calls or receive faxes. This makes sharing one phone line for Internet access and phone service less inconvenient.

call, you pick up your phone and the device automatically puts your Internet connection on hold. If neither of these options works for you, you may want to pursue other means of connecting to the Internet besides a dial up connection, such as broadband connections.

BROADBAND CONNECTIONS

What broadband options do I have?
The two leading broadband home Internet connection technologies are *DSL*, which uses a standard phone line to connect your computer to the Internet, and *cable*, which uses your television's cable service provider to connect to the Internet. Some users, especially those located in rural areas, connect to the Internet by *satellite*.

DSL
How does DSL work? Similar to a dial-up connection, **DSL** (short for **Digital Subscriber Line**) uses telephone lines to connect to the Internet. However, unlike dial-up, DSL allows phone and data transmission to share the same line, thus eliminating the need for an additional phone line. Phone lines are made of twisted copper wires known as **twisted-pair wiring**. Think of this twisted copper wiring as a three-lane highway with only one lane being used to carry voice data. DSL uses the remaining two lanes to send and receive data separately, at much higher frequencies. Thus, although it uses a standard phone line, a DSL connection is much faster than a dial-up connection.

Can anyone with a phone line have DSL? Just because you have a traditional phone line in your house doesn't mean that you have access to DSL service. Your local phone company must have special DSL technology to offer you the service. Although more phone companies are acquiring DSL technology, many areas in the United States, especially rural ones, still do not have DSL service available.

You also need a special **DSL modem**, like the one shown in Figure 3.4. Although it's called a modem, a DSL modem doesn't actually function like the dial-up modems described earlier. Rather than modulating/demodulating analog and digital data, DSL modems use modulation techniques to separate the types of signals into voice and data signals so they can travel in the right "lane" on the twisted-pair wiring. Voice data is sent at the lower speed, while digital data is sent at frequencies ranging from 128 Kbps to 1.5 megabits per second (Mbps).

Are there different types of DSL service? The more typical DSL transmissions download (or receive) data from the Internet faster than they can upload (or send) data. Such transmissions are referred to as **Asymmetrical Digital Subscriber Line (ADSL)**. Other DSL transmissions, called **Symmetrical Digital Subscriber Line (SDSL)**, upload and download data at the same speed. If you upload data to the Internet often (if you design and update your own Web site, for example), you may want to investigate the range of sending-speed capabilities of your DSL connection, or check to see if your DSL provider offers SDSL service.

FIGURE 3.4

You need a special DSL modem like this one to connect to the Internet using DSL.

What are the advantages to DSL?
With data transfer rates that reach 1.5 Mbps, DSL beats the slow speeds of dial-up by a great deal. And with DSL service, you can connect to the Internet without tying up your phone line. In addition, unlike cable and satellite, DSL service does not share the line with other network users in your area. Therefore, in times of peak Internet usage, DSL speed is not affected, whereas cable and satellite hookups often experience reduced speeds during busy times. Additionally, bad weather does not affect DSL service as it can with satellite, and DSL service is less susceptible to the radio frequency interference that hinders cable.

Are there drawbacks to DSL? As mentioned earlier, DSL service is not available in all areas. If you do have access to DSL service, the quality and effectiveness of your service depend on your proximity to a phone company central office (CO). A CO is the place where a receiving DSL modem is located. Data is sent through your DSL modem to the DSL modem at the CO. For the DSL service to work correctly, you need to be within approximately three miles of a CO because the signal quality and speed weaken drastically at distances beyond 18,000 feet. A simple call to your local phone company can determine your proximity to a CO and whether DSL service is available. You can also find out whether DSL is available in your area by checking **www.dsl.com** or **www.getconnected.com**.

Cable
If I have cable TV, do I have access to cable Internet? Although cable TV and a **cable Internet connection** both use coaxial cable, they are separate services. In fact, even though you may have cable TV in your home, cable Internet service may not be available in your area. Cable TV is a one-way service in which the cable company feeds your television programming signals. In order to bring two-way Internet connections to homes, cable companies must upgrade their networks for two-way data transmission capabilities and with fiber-optic lines, which transmit data at close to the speed of light along glass fibers or wires. Because data sent through fiber-optic lines is transmitted at the speed of light, transmission speeds are much faster than those along other conventional copper wire technologies.

What do I need to hook up to cable Internet? Cable Internet connection requires a **cable modem**, as shown in Figure 3.5. Generally, the modem is located somewhere near your computer. The cable modem is then connected to an expansion (or adapter) card called a **network interface card (NIC)**, located inside your system unit. The cable modem works similarly to a traditional dial-up modem in that it modulates/demodulates the cable signal into digital data and back again. Because the cable TV signal and Internet data can share the same line, you can watch cable TV and be on the Internet at the same time.

FIGURE 3.5

Cable Internet connection hardware. (a) In order to gain cable Internet access, you must install a cable modem in your home. (b) This modem connects to a network interface card located inside your computer's system unit.

Why would I choose a cable connection? The speed of a cable Internet connection is slightly better than the speed of a DSL connection. With cable Internet, you can receive data at speeds up to 4 Mbps and send data at approximately 300 Kbps. As technology improves, these transfer rates also will improve, and some cable companies are already offering data transfer rates of up to 6 Mbps. However, the availability of cable Internet compared to DSL may be the main reason you choose cable. Although cable service is not available in all areas, it is quickly rolling out and may be available where DSL is not. Check your local cable TV provider to determine whether cable Internet is available where you live and the transfer rates in your area.

Cost may also be a consideration in choosing cable. Installation fees tend to be lower, especially with the do-it-yourself kits found in most computer accessory stores. Monthly charges for cable are also slightly lower than for DSL, and packaged deals for cable TV subscribers may also be available.

Are there any disadvantages to cable Internet? Because you share your cable connection with your neighbors, you may experience periodic decreases in connection speeds during peak usage times with cable Internet connections. Although your connection speeds are still faster than a dial-up alternative, your ultimate speed depends on how many other users are trying to transmit data at the same time as you are.

Satellite
What is satellite all about? Satellite Internet is another way to connect to the Internet that most people choose when other high-speed options are not available. To take advantage of satellite Internet, you need a satellite dish, which is placed outside your home and connects to your computer with **coaxial cable**, the same type of cable used for cable TV. As shown in Figure 3.6, data from your computer is transmitted between your personal satellite dish and the satellite company's receiving satellite dish by a satellite that orbits the earth. A major provider for satellite Internet is DirecPC, the same company that offers DirecWay satellite television.

What are the advantages to satellite Internet connections? Because several major telecommunications companies maintain satellites in orbit above the equator, almost anyone in the United States can

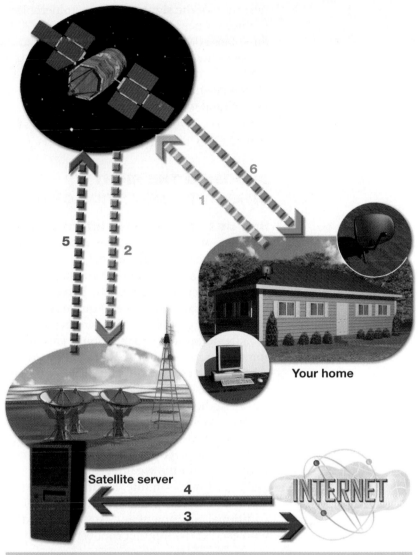

FIGURE 3.6

(1) Request for information from the Internet is sent by a satellite that is orbiting the equator directly to (2) the satellite server. The satellite server retrieves (3,4) the Internet information and (5) returns it directly back through the orbiting satellite (6) to your home computer.

receive satellite service. It is therefore a particularly popular choice for those who live in rural areas of the country where neither cable nor DSL service is available.

Are there any drawbacks to satellite? Because other broadband services may not be available, satellite broadband may be your only alternative to dial-up. However, restrictions to this service do apply. Because it takes longer for data to be transferred with satellite broadband than with cable or DSL, this type of connection is not best for some Internet uses such as online gaming. Additionally, because download transmissions are not "wired," but rather are sent as radio waves, the strength and reliability of the signal are more vulnerable to interference. Last, your satellite dish must face south for the best line of sight to the satellites circling the earth's equator. If high buildings, mountains, or other tall objects obstruct your southern exposure, your signal may be blocked. Unfavorable weather conditions can also block or interfere with the satellite transmission signal.

CHOOSING THE RIGHT INTERNET CONNECTION OPTION

How do I choose which Internet connection option is best for me? Dial-up is the most common means of Internet connection, but also the slowest. If you need a faster connection, you should choose one of the broadband alternatives. Your location plays the biggest role in choosing among broadband options. As mentioned earlier, some areas aren't able to offer DSL and/or cable Internet service. Additionally, you may need to consider which other services you want bundled into your payment, such as cable or satellite TV, and which service inconveniences you are willing to live with, such as the slower peak time rates associated with cable and the weather interference associated with satellite. Figure 3.7 shows the data transfer rates, monthly costs, and additional equipment and fees associated with each of the Internet connection options.

Finding an Internet Service Provider

Once you have chosen the method by which you'll connect to the Internet, whether it's dial-up or broadband, you need a way to access the Internet. **Internet service providers (ISPs)** are national, regional, or local companies that connect individuals, groups, and other companies to the Internet. EarthLink, for example, is a well-known national ISP.

As mentioned earlier, the Internet is a network of networks, and the central component of the Internet network is the *Internet backbone*. The Internet backbone is the main pathway of high-speed communications lines through which all Internet traffic flows. Large communications companies, such as AT&T, MCI, and Sprint, are backbone providers that control access to the main lines of the Internet backbone. These backbone providers supply Internet access to ISPs, which, in turn, supply access to other users.

Large businesses and educational facilities connect to the Internet through one of the *regional* ISPs that then connect to the backbone. Local cable and telephone companies fit into this category of regional ISPs. Home or small business users connect to the Internet through *local* ISPs or through **online service providers (OSPs)**, which are

FIGURE 3.7   Comparing Internet Connection Options

CONNECTION OPTION	DATA TRANSFER RATE (APPROXIMATE)	MONTHLY COSTS (APPROXIMATE)	ADDITIONAL EQUIPMENT	ADDITIONAL FEES (APPROXIMATE)
Dial-Up	56 Kbps (max)	Local phone rates	Internal or external modem	None
DSL (ADSL)	128 Kbps upload 8.45 Mbps download	$40–$320	DSL modem	Installation $100–$200
DSL (SDSL)	1.5 Mbps upload/download	$40–$370	DSL modem	Installation $100–$200
Cable	128–384 Kbps upload 1–3.5 Mbps download	$30–$70	Cable modem	Installation $75–$200
Satellite	56 Kbps upload 400 Kbps download	$40–$50	Dish	Installation $125–$250

Note: The data transfer rates listed in this table are approximations. As technologies improve, so too do data transfer rates. Costs and fees are also subject to change.

Internet access providers such as America Online (AOL) that have their own proprietary online content.

Where do I find an ISP? If you have a broadband connection, your broadband provider *is* your ISP. If you're accessing the Internet from a dial-up connection, you need to determine which ISPs are available in your area. Look in the phone book, check ads in the newspaper, or ask friends which ISP they use. You're no doubt familiar with many of them already. Additionally, you can go to sites such as The List (**www.thelist.com**) or All Free ISP (**www. all-free-isp.com**) for listings of national and regional ISPs.

How exactly are OSPs different from ISPs? OSPs and ISPs both provide you with access to the Internet so you can visit Web sites and send e-mail to your friends. However, OSPs (such as CompuServe, AOL, and Microsoft's MSN) go a step further than standard ISPs by offering unique content and special services and areas that only their subscribers can access. Initially, when getting around the Internet was more cumbersome, the streamlined content and directory-like searching mechanisms OSPs offered were worth the higher monthly fees. Now, with efficient sites such as Yahoo!, many people find it is more cost-effective and equally convenient to connect to the Internet with a local or national ISP.

CHOOSING AN ISP

What factors should I consider in choosing an ISP? If you're in the market for an ISP, you'll need to consider the following:

- How much does the ISP cost for monthly Internet access and what other services does it offer?
- How are services paid for and how are renewals handled? (For example, does the ISP automatically charge your credit card each month?)
- Does the ISP have a local access number so that you can avoid long-distance phone charges while you use the Internet?
- Will you need more than one e-mail account? If so, how many accounts does the ISP provide?

SOUND BYTE

CONNECTING TO THE INTERNET

In this Sound Byte, you'll learn the basics of connecting to the Internet from home, including the various types of Internet connections as well as useful information on selecting the right ISP.

- If you travel a lot, does the ISP have local access in the areas where you'll be traveling or an available 800 number to connect to?
- Does the ISP allow you to access your e-mail by using the Web?
- Are you planning on having a Web site? If so, does the ISP have available space for your Web site on its server?
- Is there a trial period? Trial periods enable you to check out availability during peak and off-peak hours before committing to the ISP long-term.
- How is the ISP's customer service? The best ISPs provide customer service that is accessible by phone and the Web.

It's important that you carefully select the right ISP for your needs. Although one ISP may be perfect for your friends, their needs may be different from yours. Remember, too, that changing your ISP can be both time-consuming (you may need to change connections) and inconvenient (if your e-mail address changes, you'll need to notify everyone).

BITS AND BYTES

Connecting Personal Digital Assistants (PDAs) and Cell Phones to the Internet

Connecting your PDA or cell phone requires that you have a *wireless Internet service provider*, such as Verizon or T-Mobile. The connection is by no means fast—wireless devices connect at a maximum speed of 14.4 Kbps. However, to make such Internet connections worthwhile, Web sites are beginning to create content specifically designed for wireless devices. This specially designed content is text-based, contains no graphics, and is designed so that it fits the display screens of cell phones and PDAs. You'll learn more about how mobile devices connect to the Internet in Chapter 8.

TRENDS IN IT

Emerging Technologies: How Will You Connect to the Internet Tomorrow?

In the 1990s, most home users connected to the Internet with a dial-up modem. In those early days, dial-up data transfer rates crawled along at a speed of 14.4 Kbps. Today you can connect to the Internet with a dial-up modem at speeds of 56 Kbps. Meanwhile, DSL technology and cable connections provide even faster connections, and satellite is available where other technologies are not. In fact, today, nearly 25 percent of all American homes have some form of broadband access to the Internet. Estimates are that the demand for broadband access will increase to nearly 50 percent in a few years.

Yet despite these advances, consumers are demanding even faster Internet connections, and new technologies are being developed to satisfy the need for speed. Fiber-optic technology, currently available only to corporate and urban America, is slowly making its way to the suburbs and rural areas. This technology not only enables the transmission of data at close to the speed of light, but also provides an uninterrupted data pathway that makes the delivery of communications more reliable. The backbone to this fiber-optic revolution is already being formed, as networks of fiber-optic cable are being laid throughout the country.

But there is more on the horizon than just increased fiber-optic reach. Numerous companies are exploring a technology that sends data, voice, and video signals over normal electric power lines. That's right, someday, you may be able to connect to the Internet through your normal wall outlet. Called "power-line connectivity," this technology is being tested in Europe and Australia, as well as a few cities in the United States, although there is still a lot of research required before it will be considered viable. With a power-line Internet connection, you could one day transfer exobits of data—that's 1 with 18 zeros after it—per second through ordinary power lines. Now that's *fast*.

Proponents of power-line Internet connectivity say that the technology has benefits beyond speed. Unlike cable or DSL, power-line Internet access requires no new wires, and connections would be available in any room with a power outlet. That means as long as you're connected to a power line, you would have high-speed Internet access. Thus, power-line technology resolves the "last mile" delivery dilemma currently encountered by fiber-optic technology because fiber-optic networks struggle to lay the last mile of cable into homes. Despite these advantages, within the United States, extra hurdles will need to be jumped to resolve regulatory issues involving the Federal Communications Commission (FCC), local public utility commissions, and power companies.

Hopes are that power-line Internet access will be a cheaper means of connecting to the Internet. And with access to the Internet through power lines, we may see more household appliances (such as refrigerators and ovens) being connected to the Internet, too. A totally networked home may be closer than you think.

Navigating the Web: Web Browsers

Once you're connected to the Internet and have an ISP to access its services, you're free to explore the many features the Internet has to offer, including the Web. However, in order to explore the Web, you need more than an ISP—you also need a *Web browser*. As defined earlier, a Web browser is software installed on your computer system that allows you to locate, view, and navigate the Web. The most common browser in use today is Microsoft's **Internet Explorer (IE)**, while other Internet users prefer **Netscape Navigator**. These browsers are graphical browsers, meaning they can display pictures (graphics) in addition to text, as well as other forms of multimedia, such as sound and video.

What features do browsers offer? As you can see in Figure 3.8, a browser's toolbars provide convenient navigation and Web page management tools. Whether you are like most surfers using Internet Explorer or are one of the few still using Netscape Navigator, the toolbar navigation features are virtually the same.

What popular alternative Web browsers are there? Although Netscape and IE are the most-used Web browsers, you do have other options:

• Opera (**www.opera.com**) is a browser that has a small but dedicated following. Opera's advantage over Netscape and IE is that it can preserve your surf sessions: When you launch Opera, it loads and opens all the Web sites you had open when you last used it.

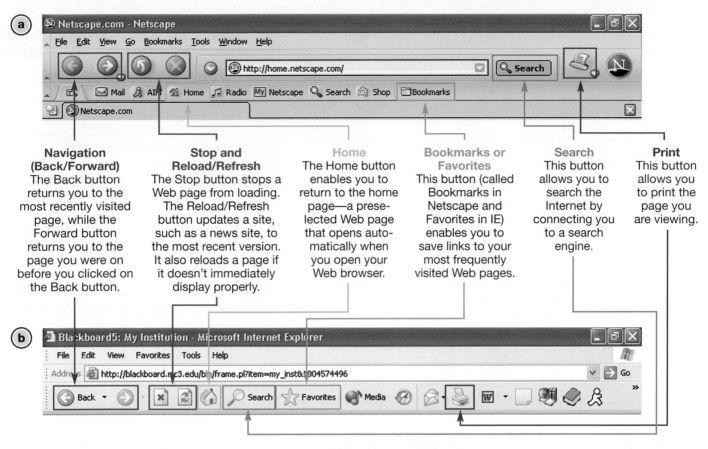

Navigation (Back/Forward)
The Back button returns you to the most recently visited page, while the Forward button returns you to the page you were on before you clicked on the Back button.

Stop and Reload/Refresh
The Stop button stops a Web page from loading. The Reload/Refresh button updates a site, such as a news site, to the most recent version. It also reloads a page if it doesn't immediately display properly.

Home
The Home button enables you to return to the home page—a preselected Web page that opens automatically when you open your Web browser.

Bookmarks or Favorites
This button (called Bookmarks in Netscape and Favorites in IE) enables you to save links to your most frequently visited Web pages.

Search
This button allows you to search the Internet by connecting you to a search engine.

Print
This button allows you to print the page you are viewing.

- Lynx (**http://lynx.isc.org**) is an alternative text-only browser that you navigate by highlighting emphasized words on the screen with the up and down arrow keys, and then pressing Enter.

- Mozilla (**www.mozilla.org**) is a free browser based on Netscape Navigator's code. It is rapidly gaining popularity because of its user-friendly style. Some popular features of Mozilla include a pop-up blocker that is incorporated directly into the browser and tabbed Web pages that enable you to open many Web pages in one browser window and to bookmark a group of several tabbed pages in one bookmark.

Getting Around the Web: URLs, Hyperlinks, and Other Tools

Unlike text in a Microsoft Word document, which is linear (meaning you read it from top to bottom, left to right, one page after another), the Web is anything but linear. As its name implies, the Web is a series of connected paths or links that connect you to different

Web sites, or locations on the Web. You gain initial access to a particular Web site by typing in its unique address, or **Uniform Resource Locator** (**URL**, pronounced "you-are-ell"). For example, the URL of the Web site for *Popular Science* magazine is **http://www.popsci.com**. By typing in this URL for *Popular Science* magazine, you connect to the **home page**, or main page, of the Web site. Once in the home page, you can move all around the site by clicking on specially formatted pieces of text called *hyperlinks*. Let's look at these and other navigation tools in more detail.

URLs

What do all the parts of the URL mean? As noted earlier, a URL is a Web site's address. And, like a regular street address, a URL is composed of several parts that help identify the Web document for which it stands, as shown in Figure 3.9. The

Domain name

http://www.**nytimes**.com/**pages/cartoons**

Protocol   Host Top-Level   Path or
                   Domain   Subdirectory
                   (TLD)

FIGURE 3.8

Although the names are different, both Netscape (a) and IE (b) offer similar navigational tools.

FIGURE 3.9

The parts of a URL.

SOUND BYTE
WELCOME TO THE WEB

In this Sound Byte, you'll visit the Web in a series of guided tours of useful Web sites. This tour serves as an introductory guide for Web newcomers as well as a great resource for more experienced users.

first part of the URL indicates the set of rules (or the **protocol**) used to retrieve the specified document. The protocol is generally followed by a colon, two forward slashes, *www* (indicating World Wide Web), and then the **domain name**.

What's the protocol? For the most part, URLs begin with *http*, which is short for the **Hypertext Transfer Protocol (HTTP)**. The protocol allows files to be transferred from a Web server so that you can see them on your computer using a browser. Another common protocol used to transfer files over the Internet is **File Transfer Protocol (FTP)**. FTP is used to upload and download files from one computer to another. FTP files use an FTP file server, whereas HTTP files use a Web server. In order to connect to most FTP servers, you need a user ID and a password. **ftp://ftp.uwp.edu** is a typical FTP address. (In this case, the site is used to transfer files to the University of Wisconsin at the Parkside campus.) To upload and download files from FTP sites, you can use a Web browser or file transfer software, such as WS-FTP, Fetch, or CuteFTP.

What's in a domain name? Domain names consist of two parts: the first part indicates who the site's **host** is. For example, in the URL **www.berkeley.edu**, berkeley.edu is the domain name and berkeley is the host. The three-letter suffix in the domain name (such as .com or .edu) is called the **top-level domain (TLD)**. This suffix indicates the kind of organization the host is. Figure 3.10 lists the top-level domains that are currently approved and in use.

In addition to the domains listed in Figure 3.10, there are also TLDs for each country in the world. These are two-letter designations such as .uk for the United Kingdom and .us for the United States. Within a country-specific domain, further subdivisions can be made for regions or states. For instance, the .us domain contains subdomains for each state, using the two-letter abbreviation of the state. For example, the URL for the state of Pennsylvania's Web site is **www.state.pa.us**.

What's the information after the domain name that I sometimes see? When the URL is only the domain name (such as **www.nytimes.com**), you are requesting a site's home page. However, at times, a forward slash and additional text follow the domain name, such as **www.nytimes.com/pages/cartoons**. The information after the slash indicates a particular file or **path** (or **subdirectory**) within the Web site. In this example, you would connect to the cartoon pages in the *New York Times* site.

HYPERLINKS AND BEYOND

What's the best way to get around in a Web site? As mentioned earlier, once you've reached a Web site, you can jump from one location, or Web page, to another within the Web site or to another Web site altogether by clicking on specially coded text called **hyperlinks**, shown in Figure 3.11. Generally, text that operates as a hyperlink appears in a different color (often blue)

FIGURE 3.10   Current Top-level Domains and Their Authorized Users

DOMAIN NAME	WHO CAN USE THE DOMAIN NAME
.aero	Members of the air transport industry
.biz	Businesses
.com	Originally for commercial sites, can be used by anyone now
.coop	Cooperative associations
.edu	Degree granting institutions
.gov	United States government
.info	Information service providers
.mil	United States military
.museum	Museums
.name	Individuals
.net	Originally for networking organizations, is no longer restricted
.org	Organizations (often nonprofits)
.pro	Credentialed professionals

and/or is underlined. Sometimes images also act as hyperlinks. When you pass your cursor over a hyperlinked image, the cursor changes to a hand with a finger pointing upward. To access the hyperlink, you simply click on the image.

To get back to your original location or a Web page you viewed previously, you can also use the browser's Back and Forward buttons (shown previously in Figure 3.8). If you want to back up more than one page, you can use the down arrow next to the Back button to access a list of most recently visited Web sites. By clicking on any one of these sites in the list, you can return to that page without having to navigate back through other Web sites and Web pages you've visited.

The **History list** on your browser's toolbar is also a handy feature. The History list shows all the Web sites and pages that you've visited over a certain period of time. These Web sites are organized according to date and can go back as far as three weeks.

As another way to retrace your steps, some sites also provide a **breadcrumb list**—a list of links you've visited that usually appears at the top of a page. Figure 3.11 shows an example of a breadcrumb list. Breadcrumbs get their name from the Hansel and Gretel fairy tale in which the children dropped breadcrumbs on the trail to find their way back out of the forest.

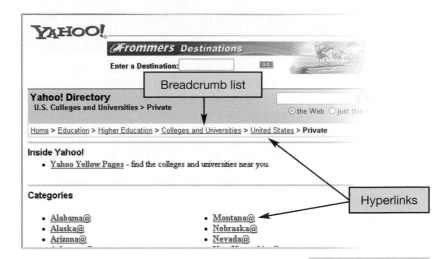

FAVORITES AND BOOKMARKS

What's the best way to mark a site so I can return to it later? If you want an easy way to return to a specific Web page, you can use your browser's **Favorites** or **Bookmark** feature (shown previously in Figure 3.8). (IE calls this feature Favorites; Netscape calls the same feature a Bookmark.) These features place a marker of the site's URL in an easily retrievable list in your browser's toolbar. To add a Web page to your list of Favorites in IE, from within the site you wish to mark, click on the Favorites menu and select Add to Favorites. As shown in Figure 3.12, you can modify

When you click on a hyperlink, you jump from one location in a Web site to another. When you click on the links in a breadcrumb list, you can navigate your way back through a Web site.

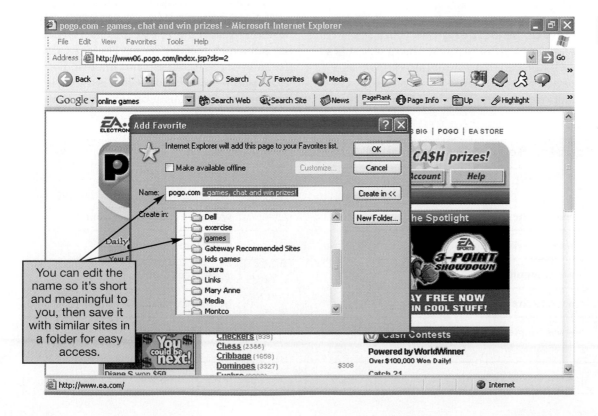

You can edit the name so it's short and meaningful to you, then save it with similar sites in a folder for easy access.

Using the IE Favorites feature makes returning to an often-used or hard-to-find Web page much easier.

the name of the Web page on your Favorites list to make it more meaningful. (The process for adding and modifying a Bookmark in Netscape is very similar.) If your list of Favorites or Bookmarks becomes long, you can create folders to organize the sites into categories.

Searching the Web: Search Engines and Subject Directories

The Internet, with its billions of Web pages, offers its visitors access to masses of information on virtually any topic. There are two main tools you can use to find information on the Web: a **search engine** is a set of programs that searches the Web for specific words (or **keywords**) you wish to query (or look for) and then returns a list of the Web sites on which those keywords are found. Popular search engines include Google and AlltheWeb. You can also search the Web using a **subject directory**, which is a structured outline of Web sites organized by topics and subtopics. Yahoo! is a popular subject directory. Figure 3.13 lists popular search engines and subject directories and their URLs.

SEARCH ENGINES

How do search engines work? Search engines have three parts. The first part is a program called a **spider** (also known as a **crawler** or **bot**). The spider constantly collects data on the Web, following links in

Web sites and reading Web pages. Spiders get their name because they crawl over the Web using multiple "legs" to visit many sites simultaneously. As the spider collects data, the second part of the search engine, an *indexer* program, organizes the data into a large database. When you use a search engine, you interact with the third part: the search engine software. This software searches the indexed data, pulling out relevant information according to your search. The resulting list appears in your Web browser as a list of **hits**, or sites that match your search.

Why don't I get the same results from all search engines? Each search engine uses a unique formula, or algorithm, to formulate the search and create the resulting index, as shown in Figure 3.14. In addition, search engines differ in how they rank the search results. Most search engines rank their results based on the *frequency* of the appearance of your queried keywords in Web sites as well as the *location* of those words in the sites. Thus, sites that include the keywords in their URL or site name most likely appear at the top of the hit list. After that, results vary because of differences in each engine's proprietary formula.

In addition, search engines differ as to which sites they search. For instance, Google and AlltheWeb search nearly the entire Web, whereas specialty search engines search only sites that have been specifically identified as being relevant to the particular subject. Specialty search engines exist for almost every industry or interest. For example, **www.dailystocks.com** is a search engine used primarily by investors that

FIGURE 3.13   Popular Search Engines and Subject Directories

SEARCH ENGINES		SUBJECT DIRECTORIES	
AlltheWeb	**www.alltheweb.com**	CompletePlanet	**www.completeplanet.com**
AltaVista	**www.altavista.com**	LookSmart	**www.looksmart.com**
Dogpile	**www.dogpile.com**	Lycos	**www.lycos.com**
Excite	**www.excite.com**	MSN	**http://search.msn.com**
Google	**www.google.com**	Open Directory Project	**www.dmoz.org**
Teoma	**www.teoma.com**	Yahoo!	**www.yahoo.com**

searches for corporate information to help them make educated decisions.

What are the advantages of using the different kinds of search engines? Using a search engine with a large index such as Google can be advantageous in conducting a search on hard-to-find information because it searches that many more indexed Web sites. However, if you're looking for only a few sites that have a high relevancy to your search, a search engine that has a smaller database, such as the Ask Jeeves search engine Teoma, may be more helpful. If you can't decide which search engine is best, you may want to try a **meta search engine**, such as Dogpile (**www.dogpile.com**). Meta search engines search other search engines rather than individual Web sites.

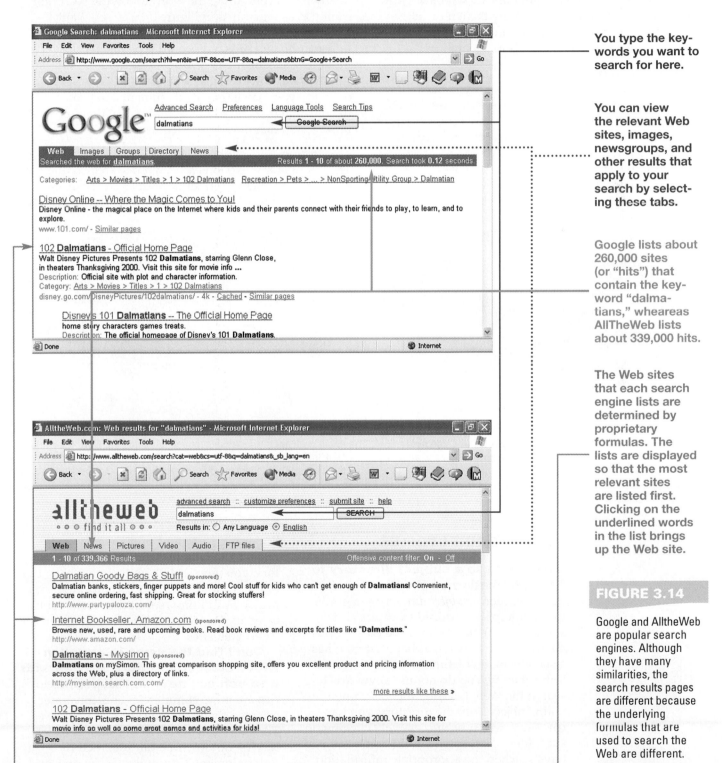

You type the keywords you want to search for here.

You can view the relevant Web sites, images, newsgroups, and other results that apply to your search by selecting these tabs.

Google lists about 260,000 sites (or "hits") that contain the keyword "dalmatians," wheareas AlltheWeb lists about 339,000 hits.

The Web sites that each search engine lists are determined by proprietary formulas. The lists are displayed so that the most relevant sites are listed first. Clicking on the underlined words in the list brings up the Web site.

FIGURE 3.14

Google and AlltheWeb are popular search engines. Although they have many similarities, the search results pages are different because the underlying formulas that are used to search the Web are different.

DIG DEEPER

Refining Your Web Searches: Boolean Operators

When you conduct Web searches, you often receive a list of hits that includes thousands—even millions—of Web pages that have no relevance to the topic you're trying to search. **Boolean operators** are words you can use to refine your searches, making them more effective. These words—AND, NOT, and OR—describe the relationships between keywords in a search.

Narrowing Searches

Using the Boolean AND operator helps you narrow (or limit) the results of your search. When you use the AND operator to join two keywords, the search engine returns only those documents that include both keywords (not just one). For example, if you type *Norway AND Sweden* into the search engine's search box, it will list only Web sites with pages that contain *both* the word *Norway and* the word *Sweden*, as illustrated in Figure 3.15.

You can also narrow your search by using the NOT operator. When you use the NOT operator to join two keywords, the search engine doesn't show the results of any pages containing the word following NOT. For example, as illustrated in Figure 3.16, if you want information on buying cars but you don't want any information on Fords, you could type *cars NOT Ford* into the search box.

Be aware, however, that when you use the NOT operator, you may eliminate documents that contain the unwanted keyword but that also contain important information that may have been useful to you.

Expanding Searches

The OR operator expands a keyword search so that the search results include either or both keywords. For example, if you type *laptop OR notebook* into the search

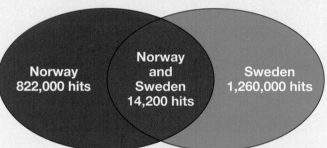

FIGURE 3.15

Using the AND operator will narrow your search because the search engine will return only those pages that include *both* the words *Norway* and *Sweden*, indicated by the shaded area in the diagram.

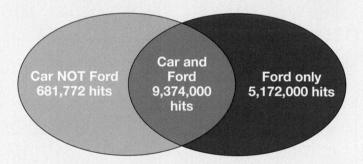

FIGURE 3.16

Using the NOT operator will narrow your search because the search engine will not return those pages that include the word following NOT. In this case, the search engine will list only those hits containing the word *car* but not the word *Ford*, as indicated in the shaded area.

SUBJECT DIRECTORIES

How can I use a subject directory to find information on the Web? As mentioned earlier, a *subject directory* is a guide to the Internet organized by topics and subtopics. Yahoo! is one of the most popular subject directories, although it now has a search engine feature, as well. With a subject directory, you do not use keywords to search the Web. Instead, after selecting the main subject from the directory, you narrow your search by successively clicking on subfolders that match your search until you have reached the appropriate information.

For example, to find previews on newly released movies in Yahoo's subject directory, you would click on the main category of Entertainment, select the subcategory Movies and Films, select the further subcategory Preview, and then open one of the listed Web sites.

Can I find the same information with a subject directory as I can with a search engine? Most subject directories are more commercial and consumer-oriented than academic- or research-based. The main categories in the subject directory of Yahoo!, for example, include Entertainment, Computers & Internet, and

box, it will list Web sites with pages that contain *either* the word *laptop* or the word *notebook* or both, as shown in Figure 3.17. Boolean OR searches are particularly helpful if there are a variety of synonymous keywords you could use in your search.

Other Helpful Search Strategies

Combining terms produces more specific results. To do so, though, you must use parentheses to add order to your search. For example, if you are looking for tutorials or lessons to better use the program Microsoft Excel, you can search for *(Tutorials OR Lessons) AND Excel*. Similarly, if you want to know how to better use the entire Microsoft Office suite with the exception of Access, you can search for *(Tutorials OR Lessons) AND (Office NOT Access)*.

To search for an exact phrase, you simply place quotation marks around your keywords. The search engine will look for only those Web sites that contain the words in that *exact order*. For example, if you want information on the movie *Lord of the Rings* and you type in these words without quotation marks, your search results will contain Web pages that include any of the words *Lord*, *of*, *the*, and *Rings*, although not necessarily in that order. Typing in *"Lord of the Rings"* in quotes guarantees all search results will include this exact phrase.

Some search engines also let you use the plus sign (+) and minus sign (–) instead of the words AND and NOT, respectively. Additionally, you can use the asterisk (*) to replace a series of letters and the percent sign (%) to replace a single letter in a word. These symbols, called **wildcards**, are helpful when you're searching for

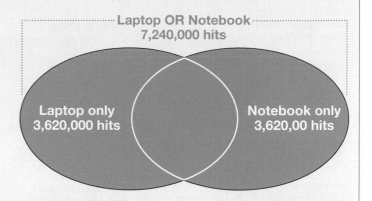

FIGURE 3.17

Using the OR operator will broaden your search because the search engine will return pages that include either of the keywords. In this case, the search engine will list all hits containing the words *laptop* and/or *notebook*, as indicated by the shaded area.

a keyword but are unsure of its spelling, or if a word can be spelled in different ways or may contain different endings. For example, if you're doing a genealogy project and are searching for the name *Goldsmith*, you might want to use *Goldsm&th* to take into consideration alternate spellings of the name (such as Goldsmyth). Similarly, if you're searching for sites related to psychiatry and psychology and you type *psych**, the search results will include all pages containing the words *psychology*, *psychiatry*, *psychedelic*, and so on.

Using Boolean search techniques can make your Internet research a lot more efficient. With the simple addition of a few words, you can narrow your search results to a more manageable and more meaningful list.

Recreation & Sports. Even within categories such as Reference, you find consumer-oriented subcategories such as Phone Numbers and Quotations.

Many subject directories, such as Yahoo! and MSN, are part of a larger Web site that focuses on offering its visitors a variety of information, such as the weather, news, sports, and shopping guides. This type of Web site is referred to as a **portal**.

When should I use a subject directory instead of a traditional search engine? Directory searches are great for finding information on general topics (such as sports and hobbies) rather than narrowing

in on a specific or unusual piece of information. For example, conducting a search on the keyword *hobbies* on a search engine does not provide you with a convenient list of hobbies, as does a subject directory. And although most directories tend to be commercially oriented, there are academic and professional directories whose sites subject experts select and annotate. These directories are created specifically to facilitate the research process. The Librarians' Index to the Internet (**www.lii.org**), in Figure 3.18 (p. 100), for example, is an academic directory whose index lists librarian-selected Web sites that have little if any commercially sponsored content.

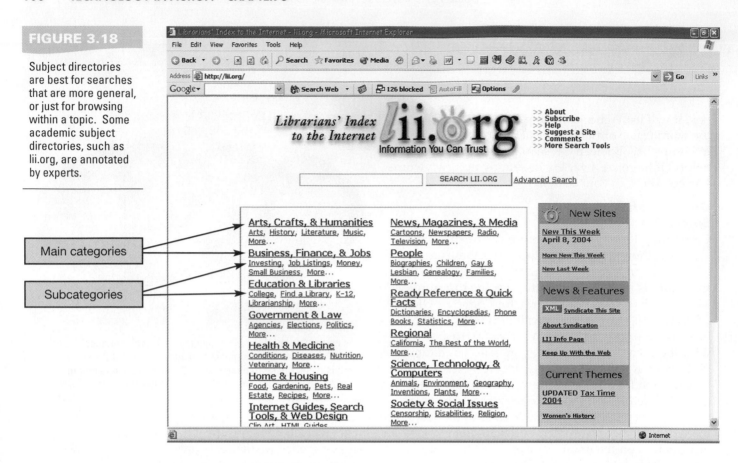

Subject directories are best for searches that are more general, or just for browsing within a topic. Some academic subject directories, such as lii.org, are annotated by experts.

EVALUATING WEB SITES

How can I make sure the Web site is appropriate to use for research?

When you're using the Internet for research, you shouldn't assume that everything you find is accurate and appropriate to use. Before you use an Internet resource, ask yourself the following questions:

1. **Who is the author of the article or the sponsor of the site?** If the author is well known or the site is published by a reputable news source (such as the *New York Times*), you can feel more confident using it as a source than if you are unable to locate information about the author or do not know who sponsors the site. (Note: Some sites include a page with information about the author or the site's sponsor.)

2. **For what audience is the site intended?** Ensure that the content, tone, and style of the site match your needs. You probably wouldn't want to use information from a site geared toward teens if you're writing for adults, nor use a site that has a casual style and tone for serious research.

3. **Is the site biased in any way?** The purpose of many Web sites is to sell you a product or service, or to persuade rather than inform. These sites, although useful in some situations, present a biased point of view. Look for sites that offer several sets of facts or consider opinions from several sources.

4. **Is the information in the site current for your needs?** Material can last a long time on the Web. Some research projects (such as historical accounts) depend on older records. However, if you're writing about cutting-edge technologies, you need to look for the most recent sources. Therefore, look for a date on information to make sure it is current.

5. **Are the links available and appropriate?** Check out the links provided on the site to determine whether they are still working and appropriate for your needs. Don't assume that the links provided are the only additional sources of information. Investigate other sites on your topic as well.

The answers to these questions will help you decide whether you should consider a Web site a good source of information.

Communicating Through the Internet: E-Mail and Other Technologies

For better or worse, **e-mail** (short for **electronic mail**) is fast becoming the primary means of communication in the twenty-first century. However, it is not the only form of Internet-based communication: *weblogs, chat rooms, instant messaging,* and *newsgroups* are also popular forms. Like any other means of communication, you need to know how to use these tools efficiently to get the best out of them.

E-MAIL

Why did e-mail catch on so quickly?

The quick adoption of e-mail was caused, in part, by the fact that it's fast and convenient and reduces the costs of postage and long-distance telephone charges. In addition, with e-mail, the sender and receiver don't have to be available at the same time in order to communicate. Because of these and other reasons, more than 90 percent of Americans who access the Internet claim that their main activity is sending and receiving e-mail. The question facing e-mail users today is not *how* to use e-mail, but how best to *manage* e-mail.

How can I organize my e-mail? If you connect to your e-mail through your ISP and use a software program such as Microsoft Outlook or Eudora to view your e-mail, you can use special features of these programs to manage your e-mail inbox. As you can see in Figure 3.19, you can choose to organize your e-mail by task, sender, or priority using color codes or distributing your messages to designated folders within your inbox. Additionally, you can automatically filter out unwanted e-mail and sort the remaining e-mail into topic-specific folders.

FIGURE 3.19

You can organize your e-mail by color coding it and assigning messages to specific folders. You can also use e-mail management software to delete unwanted e-mail automatically based on criteria you select.

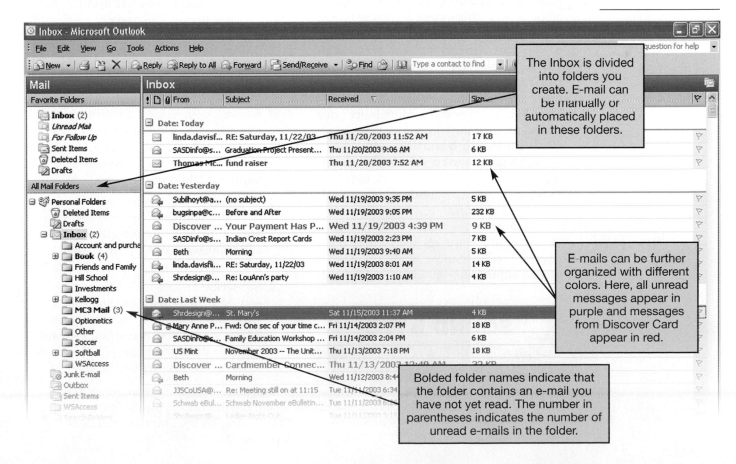

Do I need more than one e-mail account? Your primary e-mail account is most likely a **client-based e-mail** account. Client-based e-mail is dependent on an e-mail account provided by your ISP and a client software program, such as Outlook or Eudora. To access client-based e-mail accounts, you must connect with your ISP, such as EarthLink, and configure your computer with Outlook or Outlook Express or Eudora.

Web-based e-mail uses the Internet as the client; therefore, you can access a Web-based e-mail account from any computer that has access to the Web—no special client software is needed. Yahoo! and Hotmail offer free Web-based e-mail accounts. AOL is another popular Web-based e-mail provider, though not free. Many ISPs such as EarthLink now provide Web-based e-mail options as well.

Why should I have a Web-based e-mail account if I already have a client-based account? Web-based e-mail accounts are good to have for several reasons. As just mentioned, if you have a Web-based e-mail account, your e-mail is accessible from any computer as long as you have access to the Internet. This is helpful if you travel and aren't able to connect to your client-based e-mail accounts on your home computer. A secondary Web-based e-mail account also provides you with a more permanent e-mail address. Your other e-mail accounts and addresses may change when you switch ISPs or change employers, so having a permanent e-mail address is important. Finally, if you need to send personal e-mails from work, using a Web-based e-mail account keeps your private e-mail off the company's system.

With all these benefits, why wouldn't I just want a free Web-based e-mail account? One drawback to free Web-based e-mail accounts is that they have storage limits. For example, Yahoo! gives users 100 megabytes (MB) of free storage, while Hotmail gives users just 2 MB of free storage. If you want more storage, you have to pay an annual fee—ranging from around

$20 for 2 GB of storage. Also, with Web-based e-mail you don't have the organizing and management capabilities you get with Outlook or Eudora. Thus, if you want those types of features, it's best to stick with client-based e-mail.

Spam

Would having a Web-based e-mail account help reduce the spam I receive? Companies that send out **spam**, unwanted or junk e-mail, find your e-mail address from either a list they purchase or with software that looks for e-mail addresses on the Internet. If you've used your e-mail address when purchasing anything online or opening up an online account, or if you've participated in a newsgroup or a chat room, your e-mail address will eventually appear on one of the lists spammers get. You can use your Web-based e-mail address when you fill out forms on the Web and avoid having your primary account filled with spam. Additionally, both Hotmail and Yahoo! prescreen for spam. But if your Web-based e-mail account is saturated with spam, you can abandon that account with little inconvenience. It's much harder to abandon your primary e-mail address.

How else can I prevent spam? There are several ways you can prevent spam:

1. Install antispam software. At **www.download.com**, for instance, you'll find several free programs that block spam.

2. Before registering on a Web site, read its privacy policy to see how it uses your e-mail address. Don't give the site permission to pass on your e-mail address to third parties.

3. Don't reply to spam to remove yourself from the spam list. By replying, you are confirming your e-mail address is active. Instead of stopping spam, you may receive more.

4. Subscribe to an e-mail forwarding service such as **www.emailias.com** or **www.sneakemail.com**. These services screen your e-mail messages, forwarding only those messages you designate as being OK to accept.

For more information on preventing spam, see the Technology in Focus feature "Protecting Your Computer and Backing Up Your Data."

SOUND BYTE

CREATING A WEB-BASED E-MAIL ACCOUNT

In this Sound Byte, you'll see a step-by-step demonstration explaining how to create a free Yahoo! Web-based e-mail account. You'll also learn the options available with such accounts.

BITS AND BYTES

Why Is It Called "Spam"?

Why and how unwanted e-mail has been dubbed "spam" is not really known, but one theory is that the name came from the Monty Python song that praises the canned processed meat product SPAM. The song is an endless repetition of the term *spam*, much like the endless repetition of useless text that constitutes the unwanted e-mail. Also, electronic spam, like its canned ham namesake, is rarely asked for but often served. When served, it's rarely eaten and generally pushed out of the way, similar to electronic spam that is often received but rarely read.

Phishing and Internet Hoaxes
Besides spam, what other headaches are associated with e-mail? One of the more recent scams involving the Internet is phishing (pronounced "fishing"). Phishing lures Internet users into revealing personal information such as credit card or social security numbers, banking information, passwords, or other sensitive information that could lead to identity theft. The scammers send e-mails that look like they are from a legitimate business the recipient deals with, such as an online bank or Internet service such as AOL. The e-mail states that the recipient needs to update or confirm his or her account information, and sends the recipient to a Web site that looks like a legitimate Web site but is really a fraudulent copy the scammer has created. Once the e-mail recipient confirms his or her personal information, the scammers capture it and can begin using it for their own personal use.

How can I avoid being caught by phishing scams? The best way to avoid falling for such scams is to avoid replying directly to any e-mail asking you for personal information. Check with the company asking for the information and only give the information if you are certain it is needed, and only over the phone. Never give personal information over the Internet unless you know the site is a secure one. We discuss ways you can make sure a site is secure later in this chapter.

What is an Internet hoax? Internet **hoaxes** contain information that is untrue. Hoax e-mail messages may request that you send money to cover medical costs for an impoverished and sick child or ask you to pass on bogus information, such as how to avoid a virus. Chain e-mail letters are also considered a form of Internet hoax.

Why are hoaxes so bad? The sheer number of e-mails generated by hoaxes can cost millions in lost opportunity costs caused by time spent reading, discarding, or resending the message, and they can clog up the Internet system. If you receive an e-mail you think might be a hoax, don't pass it on. First determine whether it is a hoax by visiting the U.S. Department of Energy's Hoaxbusters site at **http://hoaxbusters.ciac.org**.

WEBLOGS (BLOGS)

What is a blog? Weblogs (or **blogs**) are personal logs, or journal entries, that are posted on the Web. The beauty of blogs is that they are simple to create, simple to manage, and simple to read. Although different types of blogs exist, there are some basic similarities: first, blogs are arranged as a listing of entries on a single page, with the most recent blog appearing on the top of the

BITS AND BYTES

Want to Stop Pop-Ups?

If you've spent any time on the Internet, you have no doubt had a session interrupted by pop-ups, those annoying advertisement windows that appear in your Web browser. Here are some ways to stop pop-ups:

1. **Remove adware or spyware programs.** Adware and spyware that lurk on your computer often cause pop-ups. Several effective programs such as SpyBot Search & Destroy are available as free downloads.
2. **Install ad-blocking software.** This is a quick and easy way to block pop-up ads. Panicware's Pop-up Stopper is just one of many free programs available.
3. **Switch Web browsers.** Although Internet Explorer is the most widely used Web browser, it is the only one that doesn't have pop-up ad blocking capabilities. Mozilla's Firefox and Apple's Safari both have built-in pop-up blocking capabilities. (A note for IE users: Microsoft has plans to release a service pack for Windows to add pop-up blocking capabilities to IE.)

list. Second, blogs are public. Everyone who has a Web browser and access to the Internet can read the blog. Finally, blogs are searchable, making them user friendly.

What do people write in blogs? Many people use blogs as a sort of personal scrapbook. They just write a stream-of-conscious flow of thoughts or a report of their daily activities whenever the urge strikes. Many blogs, however, focus on a particular topic. For example, **www.rottentomatoes.com** is a blog site that contains reviews and opinions about movies. **www.gizmodo.com** is a blog site that devotes itself to discussing techno-gadgets such as cell phones, PDAs, digital cameras, and tablets, to name a few (see Figure 3.20).

You'll also find blogs that contain hyperlinks to other pages with the blogger's opinion of the linked material incorporated into the blog.

How do I create a blog? It is easy to write and maintain a blog, and you'll find many Web sites that provide the necessary tools for you to create your own blog. Two sites that offer blog hosting for free are **www.blogger.com** and **www.livejournal.com**. For a relatively small annual fee, you can add other features to your blog, such as pictures or subpages. Another alternative is to host your blog yourself. Hosting your own weblog requires that you have an IP address (like 32.168.87.145) and a URL, such as **www.mydailydribble.org** in order for other people to access it online.

CHAT ROOMS

What's a chat room? A chat room is an area on the Web where many people come together to communicate online. The conversations are in real time and are visible to everyone in the chat room. Usually, chat rooms are created to address a specific topic or area of interest, and chances are you can find an active chat room on any subject of interest to you. Yahoo.com is a good source to locate chat rooms.

Do people know who I am in a chat room? When you enter a chat room, you sign in with a username and password. It's best to not disclose your true identity but rather to "hide" behind a username, thus protecting your privacy. On the other hand, the people you are chatting with are also hiding their identities. Some chatters use this veil of privacy to cover dishonest intentions. Undoubtedly, you have heard stories of individuals, especially young teenagers, being deceived (and sometimes harmed) by someone they've met in a chat room. A number of Web sites, such as **www.chatdanger.com**, try to protect vulnerable people such as children from malicious chat room users (see Figure 3.21).

Netiquette
Are there special ways to behave in a chat room? General rules of etiquette (often referred to as "**netiquette**") exist across chat rooms and other online forums, including obvious standards of behavior such as introducing yourself when you enter the room and specifically addressing the person you are talking to. Chat room users are also expected to refrain from swearing, name calling, and using explicit or prejudiced language and are

FIGURE 3.20

Blogs like the one shown here from **www.gizmodo.com** can be online reviews organized by category or personal journals recording the blogger's thoughts, viewpoints, and feelings.

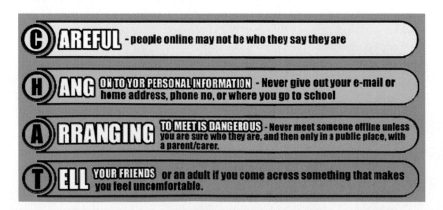

FIGURE 3.21

Chatdanger.com is produced by Childnet International, a nonprofit organization working to help make the Internet safe for children.

not allowed to harass other participants. In addition, chat room users cannot repeatedly post the same text with the intent to disrupt the chat. (This behavior is called *scrolling*.) Similarly, users shouldn't type in all capital letters, because this is interpreted as shouting.

INSTANT MESSAGING

How does instant messaging work?
Instant messaging (IM) services are programs that enable you to communicate in real time with friends who are also online. AOL's Instant Messenger (AIM or IM), shown in Figure 3.22, is one of the most popular instant messaging services. When you use IM, you set up a list of contacts, often called a *Buddy List*. To communicate with someone from your Buddy List, that person must be online at the same time as you are. When someone is trying to communicate with you when you're online, you are notified and can then accept or reject the communication. If you want to chat with more than one person, you can either hold simultaneous individual conversations, or if you all want to talk together, you can create custom IM chat rooms.

What's the difference between a chat room and IM? When you use IM services, you have private conversations with people you know. With chat rooms, anyone who enters the chat room can take part in the conversation.

BITS AND BYTES

Want to Call Your Buddies over IM?

Would you rather talk to your Buddy than have a typed conversation? You each need only AOL IM or MSN Messenger and a microphone. After you have decided on the Buddy you want to talk to, right-click on the Buddy's screen name, select Connect to Talk from the drop-down menu, and then select Connect. The Talk box will contact your Buddy, see if he or she wants to talk, then try to make a connection. When a connection has been made, you can begin to talk to each other. Talking over IM is like talking on a walkie-talkie. While you are talking, you need to hold down the Push to Talk button and release it to hear your Buddy.

NEWSGROUPS

What's a newsgroup? A **newsgroup** (sometimes referred to as a **discussion group**) is an online discussion forum in which people post messages and read and reply to messages from other members of the newsgroup. Newsgroups exist for more than 30,000 topics, from games and hobbies to science and computers to current issues and debates. The best directory of newsgroups is the Tile.Net Usenet Newsgroups Directory, available at **www.tile.net**. You can also find newsgroups through Google Groups, which is a directory of newsgroups that appears as a separate tab when you log onto Google's home page.

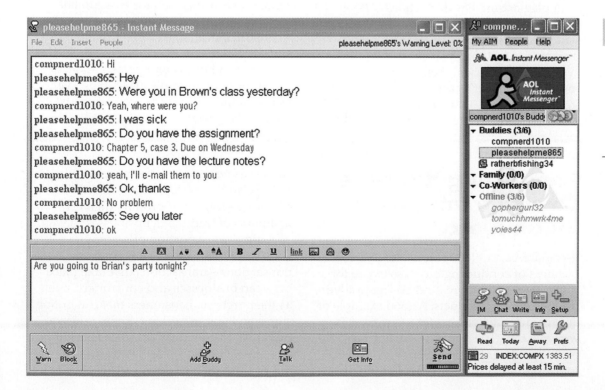

FIGURE 3.22

Instant messaging services such as AOL Instant Messenger enable you to have real-time online conversations with friends and family.

TRENDS IN IT

Ethics: What Can You Borrow from the Internet?

You've no doubt heard of *plagiarism*—taking another person's words as your own. And you've probably heard the term *copyright violation*, especially if you've been following the music industry's battle to keep "free" music off the Web. But what constitutes plagiarism and what constitutes copyright violation? And what can you borrow from the Web? Consider these scenarios:

- You find a political cartoon that would be terrific in a PowerPoint presentation you're creating for your civics class. You copy it into your presentation.
- Your hobby is cooking. You design a Web site that includes videos of you preparing recipes, as well as the recipes themselves. Some of these recipes you take from your favorite cookbooks, others you get from friends. You don't cite your sources, nor obtain permission from the originators of the recipes you post to your Web site.
- You're pressed for time and need to do research for a paper due tomorrow. You find information on an obscure Web site and copy it into your paper without documenting the source.
- You download a song from the Internet and incorporate it into a PowerPoint presentation for a school project. Because you figure everyone knows the song, you don't credit it in your sources.

Which of the preceding scenarios represent copyright violations? Which represent plagiarism? The distinctions between these scenarios are narrow in some cases, but it's important to understand the differences.

As noted earlier, plagiarism occurs when you use someone else's ideas or words and represent them as your own. In today's computer society, it's easy to copy information from the Internet and paste it into a Word document, change a few words, and call it your own.

To avoid plagiarism, use quotation marks around all words you borrow directly and credit your sources for any ideas you paraphrase or borrow. Avoiding plagiarism means properly crediting *all* information you obtain from the Internet, including words, ideas, graphics, data, and audio and video clips.

Copyright violation is more serious because it is punishable by law. The law assumes that all original work including text, graphics, software, multimedia, audio or video clips, and even ideas is copyrighted, regardless of whether the work displays the copyright symbol (©). Copyright violation occurs when you use another person's material for your own personal *economic* benefit, or when you take away from the economic benefit of the originator. Don't assume that by citing a source you're abiding by copyright laws. In most cases, you need to seek *and receive* written permission from the copyright holder. There are exceptions to this rule. For example, there is no copyright on government documents; therefore, you can download and reproduce material from NASA, for example, without violating copyright laws. The British Broadcasting Corporation (BBC) is also beginning to digitize and make available its archives of material to the public without copyright restrictions.

Teachers and students also receive special consideration regarding copyright violations. This special consideration falls under a provision called *academic fair use*. As long as the material is being used for educational purposes, limited copying and distribution is allowed. For example, an instructor can make copies of a newspaper article and distribute it to her class or a student can include a cartoon in a PowerPoint presentation without seeking permission from the artist. However, to avoid plagiarism in these situations, you still must credit your sources of information.

Conducting Business Over the Internet: E-Commerce

E-commerce, or **electronic commerce**, is the business of conducting business online for purposes ranging from fund-raising to advertising to selling products. A good example of an e-commerce business (or e-business) is **www.dell.com**. The company's online presence offers customers a convenient way to shop for computer systems and accessories. Its

success is because of creative marketing, an expanding product line, and reliable customer service and product delivery—all hallmarks of traditional businesses as well.

A significant portion of e-commerce consists of **business-to-consumer (B2C)** transactions—transactions that take place between businesses and consumers, such as the purchases consumers make at online stores and online banking. There is also a **business-to-business (B2B)** portion of e-commerce; this consists of businesses buying and selling goods and services to other businesses. Finally, the **consumer-to-consumer (C2C)** portion of e-commerce consists of consumers selling to each other through online auction sites such as eBay.

What are the advantages and disadvantages of online businesses? The main advantage to online businesses is that they can reach a wider market by taking advantage of the Internet's global reach. In addition, traditional stores that have an online presence (referred to as **click-and-brick businesses**) are able to provide a variety of services on their sites. Customers can visit their sites to check the availability of items or to get store locations and directions. The disadvantages of e-commerce include the costs of operating an e-business, such as those related to setting up the system and ensuring that the Web site is marketed appropriately.

What are the most popular e-commerce activities? According to **www.consumerreports.com**, consumers buy books, music and videos, movie and event tickets, and toys and games more often online than in retail stores. Auction sites such as eBay are becoming the online equivalent to the weekend yard sale and have dramatically increased in popularity.

But e-commerce encompasses more than just shopping opportunities. Today, anything you can do inside your bank you can do online, and over 25 percent of U.S. households do some form of online banking. Most people use online services to check their account balances, while checking stock and mutual fund performances is another popular activity. With services such as **www.lendingtree.com**, shopping for mortgages and personal loans has become an accepted online activity. Credit card companies also provide online services allowing you to view your credit card statement and conduct investment activities. And you can also pay your bills online (although some companies charge a fee for this service).

E-COMMERCE SAFEGUARDS

Just how safe are online transactions? When you buy something over the Web, you most likely use a credit card; therefore, the exchange of money is done directly between you and a bank. Because online shopping eliminates a sales clerk or other human intermediary from the transaction, it can actually be safer than traditional retail shopping. Still, because users are told to be wary of online

transactions and because the integrity of online transactions is the backbone of e-commerce, businesses must have some form of security certification to give their customers a level of comfort. Businesses hire security companies such as VeriSign to certify that their online transactions are secure. Thus, if the Web site displays the VeriSign seal, you can trust that the information you submit to the site is protected.

Another indication that a Web site is secure is the appearance of a small icon of a closed padlock (IE) or key (Netscape) on the status bar at the bottom of the screen, as shown in Figure 3.23. Additionally, the beginning of the URL of the site will change from http:// to https://, the s standing for "secure."

How else can I shop safely online? To ensure that your online shopping experience is a safe one, follow these guidelines:

• Shop at well-known, reputable sites. If you aren't familiar with a site, investigate it with the Better Business Bureau (**www.bbb.org**), or at **www.bizrate.com** or **www.webassured.com**.

• When you place an order, print a copy of the order and make sure you receive a confirmation number.

• Make sure the company has a phone number and street address in addition to a Web site.

For tips on how to make a good web log, see "Top Five Tips for Webloggers," a TechTV clip found at www.prenhall.com/techinaction.

FIGURE 3.23

The VeriSign seal, a closed padlock icon, and *https* in the URL are indications that the site is secure.

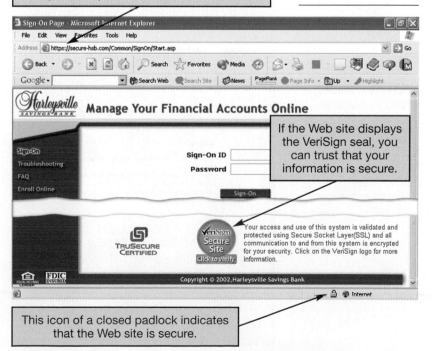

When the beginning of the URL changes from http:// to https://, the Web site is secure.

If the Web site displays the VeriSign seal, you can trust that your information is secure.

This icon of a closed padlock indicates that the Web site is secure.

- Always pay by credit card. The U.S. federal consumer credit card protection laws protect credit card purchases.
- Check the return policy. Print it out and save it in case the site disappears overnight.

COOKIES

What are cookies? Cookies are small text files that some Web sites automatically store on your computer's hard drive when you visit the site. When you log on to a Web site that uses cookies, a cookie file assigns a unique ID number to your computer. The unique ID is intended to make your return visit to a Web site more efficient and better geared to your particular interests. The next time you log on to that Web site, the site marks your visit and keeps track of it in its database.

What do Web sites do with cookie information? Cookies provide Web sites with information about your browsing habits, such as the advertisements you've opened, the products or sites you've looked at, and the time and duration of your visits. Cookies also remember personal information you enter into Web site forms, such as your credit card information, name, mailing address, and phone number. Companies use this information to determine the traffic flowing through their Web site and the effectiveness of their marketing strategy and Web site placement. By tracking which pages you view,

how long you stay on the site, and how many times you come back to the site, cookies enable companies to differentiate between users and their preferences.

Can companies get my personal information when I visit their sites? Cookies do not go through your hard drive in search of personal information such as passwords or financial data. Moreover, cookies cannot determine your name. The only personal information a cookie obtains is the information you supply when you fill out forms online.

Do privacy risks exist with cookies? Some sites sell the personal information their cookies collect to companies such as DoubleClick or Abacus. These companies are Web advertisers that are building huge databases of consumer preferences and habits, collecting personal and business information such as credit card numbers, phone numbers, credit reports, and the like. The ultimate concern is that advertisers will use this information indiscriminately, thus infiltrating your privacy.

Should I delete cookies from my hard drive then? Since cookies pose no *security* threat (because it is virtually impossible to hide a virus in a cookie), take up little room on your hard drive, and offer you small conveniences on return visits to Web sites, there is no great reason for you to delete them. Deleting your cookie files could also cost you the inconvenience of reentering data you have already entered once into Web site forms. However, if you're uncomfortable with the accessibility of your personal information, you can periodically delete cookies or configure your browser to block certain types of cookies, as shown in Figure 3.24. Software programs such as Cookie Pal also exist to help monitor cookies for you. For more information on cookies, see the Technology in Focus feature "Protecting Your Computer and Backing Up Your Data."

FIGURE 3.24

Tools are available, either through your browser or as a separate software application, to sort between cookies you want to keep and cookies that you don't want on your system.

SOUND BYTE

BEST UTILITIES FOR YOUR COMPUTER

In this Sound Byte, you'll explore various utilities that you can use to avoid Internet annoyances. You'll learn how to install and use specific utilities and find out where to download some of them for free.

Web Entertainment: Multimedia and Beyond

Internet radio, MP3 music files, streaming video, and interactive gaming are all part of a growing entertainment world available over the Internet. What makes the Web appealing to many people is its enriched multimedia content. **Multimedia** is anything that involves one or more forms of media in addition to text.

Many types of multimedia are used on the Web. Graphics—drawings, charts, and photos—are the most basic form of multimedia on the Web. Audio files are what give sound to the Web—the clips of music you hear when you visit certain Web sites, MP3 files that you download, or live broadcasts you can listen to through Internet radio. Video files on the Internet range from the simple (such as short video clips) to the complex (such as hour-long live concerts). In addition to movies, you can watch live or prerecorded television broadcasts, movie trailers, and sporting events.

What is streaming audio and video? If you've been on the Web a lot, you've probably encountered streaming audio and video. Some Web sites, especially those offering live broadcasts, use **streaming audio** to enhance the listening process. Streaming audio enables audio files to be fed to your browser continuously. In this way, you can avoid having to download an entire file completely before

you listen to it—you can listen to it in streaming fashion, as it downloads from the site to your computer. Likewise, **streaming video** continuously feeds a video file to your browser so you can watch large files as they download instead of first having to download the files completely.

Do I need anything besides a browser to view or hear multimedia on the Web? Without any additional software, most graphics on the Web will appear in your browser when you visit a site. However, to view and hear some multimedia files on the Web, you need a special software program called a **plug-in** (or **player**). Figure 3.25 lists the most popular plug-ins.

If you've purchased your computer over the past several years, you'll find plug-ins already installed with your browser. For those you don't have, the Web site requiring the plug-in usually displays a message on the screen that includes links to a site where you can download the plug-in free of charge. For example, to use streaming audio on a Web site, your browser might send you to **www.macromedia.com**, where you can download Shockwave Player.

Do I need to update players and plug-ins? Like most technological resources, improvements and upgrades are available for players and plug-ins. Most plug-ins and players will alert you to check for and download upgrades when they are available. It is best to

FIGURE 3.25   Popular Plug-ins/Players and Their Uses

PLUG-IN/PLAYER NAME	WHERE YOU CAN GET THE PLUG-IN/PLAYER	WHAT THE PLUG-IN/PLAYER DOES
Adobe Acrobat Reader	www.adobe.com	Lets you view and print Portable Document Format (PDF) files
Authorware Player	www.macromedia.com	Helps you view animations
Flash Player	www.macromedia.com	Lets you play animation and other graphics files on the Web
QuickTime Player	www.apple.com/quicktime	Lets you play animation, music, Musical Instrument Digital Interface (MIDI), audio, and video files on the Web
RealOne	www.real.com	Lets you play streaming audio, video, animations, and multimedia presentations on the Web
Shockwave Player	www.macromedia.com	Lets you play interactive games, multimedia, graphics, and streaming audio and video on the Web
Windows Media Player	www.microsoft.com	Lets you play MP3 and WAV files, listen to music files and live audio, and view movies and live video broadcasts on the Web

keep the players and plug-ins as current as possible so that you get the full effects of the multimedia running with these players.

Are there any risks with using plug-ins? When a browser requires a plug-in to display particular Web content, it usually automatically accesses the plug-in, generally without you giving consent to start the plug-in. This automatic access can present security risks. To minimize such risks, update your plug-ins and browser software frequently so that you will have the most up-to-date remedies against identified security flaws.

Is there any way to get multimedia Web content to load faster? When you're on the Internet, your browser keeps track of the Web sites you've visited so it can load them faster the next time you visit them. This cache (or hiding place) of the HTML text pages, images, and video files from recently visited Web sites can make your Internet surfing more efficient, but it can also congest your hard drive. To keep your system running efficiently, delete your Temporary Internet Cache periodically. For Internet Explorer 6, select Tools, Internet Options, then in the Temporary Internet Files area, select Delete Files. For Netscape Navigator 6, select Edit, Preferences, Advanced, Cache, and then select Clear Disk Cache.

The Future of the Internet

What does the future hold in store for the Internet? Certainly, the Internet of the future will have more bandwidth, offer increased services, and reach more of the world's population than it does today. Two major projects currently under way in the United States to develop advanced technologies for the Internet are the Large Scale Networking (LSN) program and Internet2. In addition, plans are under way to wire the solar system—the next logical expansion of the Internet once the planet Earth is fully connected. And all the while, new Internet experiences are being developed for us all to enjoy.

THE LARGE SCALE NETWORKING PROGRAM AND INTERNET2

What are the Large Scale Networking and Internet2 programs? Out of a project entitled the Next Generation Internet

(which ended in 2002), the U.S. government created the **Large Scale Networking (LSN)** program. LSN's aim is to fund the research and development of cutting-edge networking and wireless technologies and to increase the speed of networks.

The **Internet2** is an ongoing project sponsored by over 200 universities (supported by government and industry partners) to develop new Internet technologies and disseminate them as rapidly as possible to the rest of the Internet community. The Internet2 backbone supports extremely high-speed communications (up to 9.6 gigabits per second, or Gbps) and provides an excellent test bed for new data transmission technologies. It is hoped that the Internet2 will solve the major problem plaguing the current Internet: lack of bandwidth. Once the Internet2 is fully integrated with the current Internet, greater volumes of information should flow more smoothly.

AN INTERPLANETARY INTERNET?

Will the Internet actually expand into outer space in the future? Many scientists think that a manned mission to Mars could happen within the next 20 years. Before the end of the century, a colony on Mars is not out of the question. To accomplish these lofty goals, many more unmanned missions to Mars must be undertaken. Reliable communications between Mars and Earth must be established to ensure spacecraft en route to Mars and ground stations on Earth can communicate. We have already seen how scientists communicate with the devices that have landed on Mars, remotely correcting hardware and software issues. Because the Internet allows virtually instantaneous communications between any point on the Earth, researchers are hoping to take advantage of this technology and create an interplanetary Internet, a network that spans across planets.

How would an interplanetary Internet be constructed? Unfortunately, there are a few physical obstacles to overcome. Communications require line of sight to be maintained. The orbital dynamics of planets need to be taken into consideration to ensure that line of sight between Earth and Mars is not obstructed for any great length of time. However, this problem has already been addressed on Earth by the installation of the Deep Space Network. The Deep Space Network is comprised of three antenna installations located in California,

Spain, and Australia. These installations provide for almost continuous transmission of data to outer space regardless of the orbital position of the Earth. A series of seven satellites has been proposed to be orbited around Mars to provide similar coverage on that end (see Figure 3.26).

What are the benefits of installing an interplanetary Internet? Aside from enhanced communication between spacecraft and Earth home bases, webcams could be installed on other planets, which would allow people on Earth to take virtual tours of distant celestial bodies. The interplanetary Internet would provide the same functionality to astronauts in the International Space Station or to colonists on Mars that the Internet does to regular users here on Earth. You wouldn't want to be on a three-year mission to Mars and not be able to check your e-mail, would you?

THE EXPANDING FEATURES OF THE INTERNET

What new experiences will the Internet provide in the future? When using the Internet today, we use our senses of sight and hearing to view various multimedia. But what about our senses of smell and taste? In 2002, TriSenx (**www.trisenx.com**) launched the Sensory Enhanced Net Experience machine, or the "Senx device." This device reads embedded Web page commands and uses specialized software to generate fragrances and aromas. The desktop device plugs into a port on your computer and is priced at around $370. With smell technology conquered, can the sense of taste be far behind? Certainly not! Printer-like devices could generate printed flavor cards in the near future. Several companies are working on bringing these devices to market.

But why would I want to smell and taste the Internet? Imagine watching a *Star Wars* DVD on your computer and being able to smell the ozone when a laser cannon evaporates an Imperial TIE fighter. In addition, advertisers could increase sales by inducing consumers to buy products after they've had a whiff of them. For example, Internet banner ads could be embedded with the sweet aroma of cookies, which might make you want to dash off to the store to buy some. If the smell doesn't do it, you can just download and print an ice-cream flavor

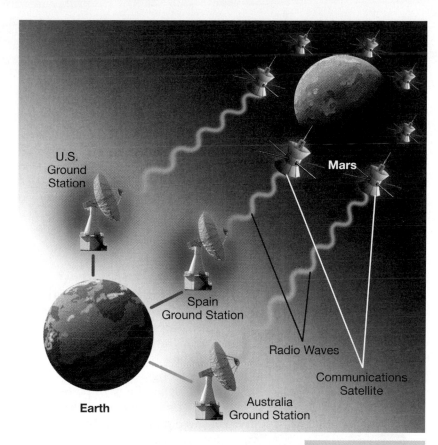

card from the Internet and be able to taste it before you buy any.

How else will the Internet become a more integral part of our lives? In the future, you can expect to use the Internet to assist you with many day-to-day tasks that you now do manually. For example, already popular in upscale housing developments, Internet-enabled appliances and household systems allow your home virtually to run itself. For example, refrigerators can monitor their contents and go online to order more diet soda when they detect that the supply is getting low. Meanwhile, Internet heating and cooling systems can monitor weather forecasts and order fuel deliveries when supplies run low or bad weather is expected. These appliances will become more widespread as the price of equipment drops.

The uses for the Internet are limited only by our imaginations and the current constraints of technology. But as you enter the workforce perhaps you will invent the next killer consumer application (the next eBay?) or contribute to the development of key technologies (nanotech circuits?) that will drive the speed of the Internet to new heights. Think about what you will want to use the Internet for tomorrow—then make it a reality.

FIGURE 3.26

Seven satellites orbiting Mars (proposed) and three ground stations on Earth (existing) could provide continuous communications for spacecraft traveling between the two planets. Only one ground station on Earth and one satellite orbiting Mars (in direct line of sight) are needed to complete a connection.

Summary

1. What is the origin of the Internet?

The Internet is the largest network in the world, connecting millions of computers. Government and military officials developed the Internet as a reliable means of communications in the event of war. Eventually, scientists and educators used the Internet to exchange research. Today, we use the Internet and the Web (which is a part of the Internet) to shop, research, communicate, and as a form of entertainment.

2. How does data travel on the Internet?

A computer connected to the Internet acts as either a client, a computer that asks for information, or a server, a computer that receives the request and returns the information to the client. Data travels between clients and servers along a system of communication lines, or pathways. The largest and fastest of these pathways is the Internet backbone. To ensure that data is sent to the correct computer along the pathways, IP addresses (unique ID numbers) are assigned to all computers connected to the Internet.

Your home

Satellite server

3. What are my options for connecting to the Internet?

Home users have many options for connecting to the Internet, the most common of which is a dial-up connection, in which you connect to the Internet using a standard phone line. Other connection options, called broadband connections, are faster. Broadband connections include cable, satellite, and DSL.

4. How do I choose an Internet service provider?

Internet service providers (ISPs) are national, regional, or local companies that connect individuals, groups, and other companies to the Internet. Factors to consider in choosing an ISP include cost, quality of service, and availability.

5. What is a Web browser?

In order to locate, navigate to, and view Web pages, you need special software called a Web browser installed on your system. The most common Web browsers are Netscape Navigator and Microsoft Internet Explorer.

6. What is a URL and what are its parts?

You gain access to a Web site by typing in its address, or Uniform Resource Locator (URL). A URL is composed of several parts, including the protocol, the host, the top-level domain, and, occasionally, paths (or subdirectories).

7. How can I use hyperlinks and other tools to get around the Web?

One unique aspect of the Web is that you can jump from place to place by clicking on specially formatted pieces of text called hyperlinks. You can also use tools such as Back and Forward buttons, History lists, breadcrumb lists, and Favorites or Bookmarks to navigate the Web.

8. How do I search the Internet using search engines and subject directories?

A search engine is a set of programs that searches the Web for specific keywords you wish to query and then returns a list of the Web sites on which those keywords are found. A subject directory is a structured outline of Web sites organized by topics and subtopics.

9. What are Boolean operators and how do they help me search the Web more effectively?

Sometimes, search engines return lists with thousands or millions of hits. Boolean operators are words (AND, NOT, and OR) you can use to refine your searches, making them more effective.

10. How can I communicate through the Internet with e-mail, chat, IM, and newsgroups?

Communication was one of the reasons the Internet was developed and is one of the primary uses of the Internet today. E-mail allows users to communicate electronically without the parties involved being available at the same time, while chat rooms are public areas on the Web where different people communicate. Instant messaging enables you to communicate in real time with friends who are also online, and newsgroups are online discussion forums in which people post messages and read and reply to messages from other newsgroup members.

11. What is e-commerce and what e-commerce safeguards protect me when I'm online?

E-commerce is the business of conducting business online. E-commerce includes transactions between businesses (B2B), between consumers (C2C), and between businesses and consumers (B2C). Because more business is conducted online, numerous safeguards have been put in place to ensure transactions are protected.

12. What are cookies and what risks do they pose?

Cookies are small text files that some Web sites store on your hard drive when you visit their site. Cookies provide Web sites with information about your browsing habits, such as the advertisements you've opened, the products or sites you've looked at, and the time and duration of your visits. Although cookies present no security threat because it's virtually impossible to hide a virus in a cookie, they can pose a threat to your privacy should the company pass on your personal information. It's important to read privacy statements on Web sites before supplying personal information.

13. What are the various kinds of multimedia files found on the Web?

The Web is appealing because of its enriched multimedia content. Multimedia is anything that involves text in addition to one or more forms of media, including graphics, audio, and video clips.

14. What kind of software do I need to enjoy multimedia on the Web?

Sometimes you need a special software program called a plug-in (or player) to view and hear multimedia files. Plug-ins are often installed in new computers or are offered free of charge at manufacturers' Web sites.

15. What does the Internet of the future look like?

The Internet of the future will have higher bandwidth and will be able to provide additional services as a result of projects such as the Large Scale Networking (LSN) program and Internet2. As more exploratory missions of the solar system are launched, development of an interplanetary Internet to facilitate communication between planets will progress. Design enhancements to the Internet will engage more of our senses, including smell and taste. The Internet will become more ingrained into our daily lives as Internet-enabled appliances and household systems will provide more remote-control features for your home.

Key Terms

Buzz Words

Word Bank

- Internet service provider
- dial-up
- AOL
- hyperlink
- plug-in
- wildcard
- newsgroup
- Bookmark

- DSL
- satellite
- browser
- breadcrumb list
- search engine
- spam
- keyword
- chat room

- portal
- cable modem
- PC card
- host
- subject directory
- Buddy List
- cookie(s)
- URLs

Instructions: Fill in the blanks using the words from the Word Bank above.

The day finally arrived when Juan no longer was a victim of slow Internet access through a traditional (1)_____ connection. He could finally hook up to the Internet through his new high-speed (2)_____. He had been investigating broadband access for a while and thought that connecting through his existing phone lines with (3)_____ would be convenient. Unfortunately, it was not available in his area. Where Juan lived, a clear southern exposure did not exist, so he did not even entertain the idea of a (4)_____ connection. Although Juan relished the speedy access, he was faced with changing from (5)_____, his online service provider, to a different (6)_____ through his cable company. Although he needed to change his e-mail address, he was glad he didn't have to give up instant messaging, because his (7)_____ of online contacts had grown to be quite extensive. Juan knew he could access instant messaging through the (8)_____ Netscape Navigator.

Juan clicked on his list of favorite Web sites and found the movie review site he had saved as a (9)_____ the day before. He prefers to use this feature rather than entering in the (10)_____ of the sites he often visits. Juan navigated through the site, clicking on (11)_____ that took him immediately to the pages he was most interested in. Finding the movie he wanted to see, Juan ordered tickets online. The credit card information he input during an earlier visit to the site automatically appeared. Juan is glad that Web sites use (12)_____ to capture personal information.

Then, using the (13)_____ at the top of the Web site, he traced his steps back to his starting point. Juan next typed in the address for Google, his preferred (14)_____, and typed in the (15)_____ to begin his search for a good restaurant in the area.

Organizing Key Terms

Instructions: *This chapter introduces many new terms and concepts. In the following illustration, fill in each of the blanks with key terms or concepts from the chapter in order to show how categories of ideas fit together.*

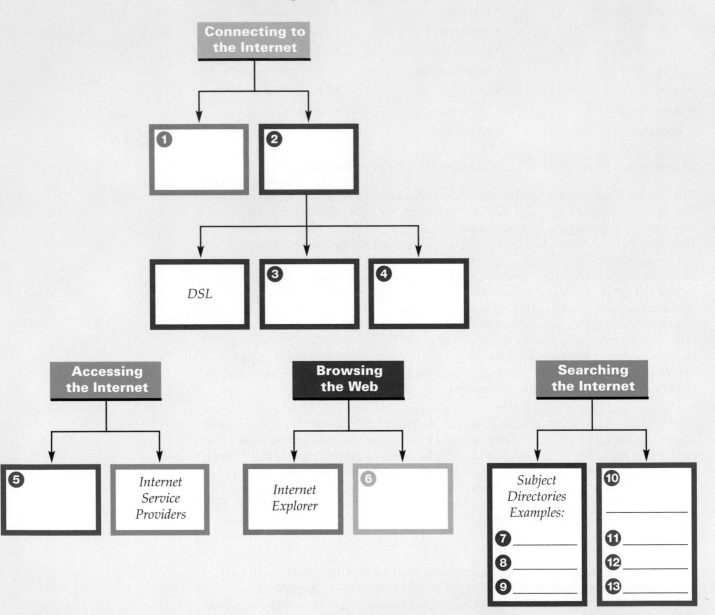

Becoming Computer Fluent

Instructions: *Using keywords from the chapter, write a letter to your local cable company imploring it to bring cable modem service to your neighborhood. In the letter, include your dissatisfaction with dial-up as well as your opinion on why cable is better than DSL (which is currently being offered in your neighborhood) and satellite. Also include the activities on the Internet you think people in the community could benefit from by using high-speed cable access.*

Making the Transition to . . . Next Semester

1. Online Support Facilities

Your school most likely has many online support facilities. Do you know what they are? Go to your school's Web site and search for online support.

a. Is there online tutoring?

b. Can you reserve a book from the library online?

c. Can you register for classes online?

d. Can you take classes online?

e. Can you buy books online?

2. Plagiarism Policies

Does your school have a plagiarism policy?

a. Search your school's Web site to find the school's plagiarism policy. What does it say?

b. How well do you paraphrase? Find some Web sites that help test or evaluate your paraphrasing skills.

3. Advanced Web Searches

Using search engines effectively is an important tool. Some search engines help you with Boolean-type searches using advanced search forms. Choose your favorite search engine and select the Advanced Search option. (If your favorite search engine does not have an advanced search feature, try Yahoo! or Google.)

a. Conduct a search for inexpensive vacation spots for spring break using Boolean search terms. Record your results along with your search queries.

b. Conduct the same search but use the advanced search form with your favorite search engine. Were the results the same? If there were any differences, what were they? Which was the best search method to use in this case and why?

4. Internet Connection Options

You are planning on moving to an apartment next semester and will be leaving behind the comforts of broadband access of the residence halls. Evaluate the Internet options available in your area.

a. Create a table that includes information on various dial-up ISPs, cable Internet, DSL, and satellite broadband service providers. The table should include the name of the provider, the cost of the service, the upload and download transfer rates, and the installation costs (service and parts). Also include whether a Web-based e-mail account will be available. Include the URL of each ISP or broadband service provider's Web site.

b. Based on the table you create, write a brief paragraph describing which service you would choose and why.

Making the Transition to . . . the Workplace

1. Online Résumé Resources

Using a search engine, locate several Web resources that offer assistance in writing a résumé. For example, the University of Minnesota (**www.umn.edu/ohr/ecep/resume**) has a resume tutor that guides you as you write your résumé.

a. What other Web sites can you find that help you write a résumé?
b. Do they all offer the same services and have the same features?
c. Which Web site features do you think work best?

2. Online Cover Letter Resources

Your résumé will need to be accompanied by a cover letter. Research Web sites that offer advice for and samples of cover letters.

a. Which Web sites do you feel offer the best advice on how to write a cover letter?
b. Which style cover letter works best for you?
c. What do the Web sites say you should include in your cover letter and why?

3. Evaluating Web Content

You have noticed that your coworkers are using the Internet to conduct research. However, they are not careful to check the validity of the Web sites they find before using the information.

a. Research the Internet for Web site evaluation guidelines. Print out your sources and findings.
b. Using the material from Step (a), create a scorecard or set of guidelines that will help others determine whether a Web site is reliable.

4. Internet Connection Speed

You would like to know how fast your Internet connection speed is. Your coworker in the Information Technology (IT) department recommended the following sites for you to check out.

www.testmyspeed.com
www.bandwidthplace.com
www.pcpitstop.com
www.computingcentral.msn.com/internet/speedtest.asp

a. List reasons why you would be interested in measuring your Internet connection speed.
b. List four factors that can affect your connection speed.
c. Discuss why "defragging" your hard drive may help improve your connection speed.

5. E-Mail Privacy

"An e-mail is no more private than a postcard."

a. Search the Internet for resources that can help you support or oppose the preceding statement. Print out sources for both sides of the argument.
b. Write a paragraph that summarizes your position.

Critical Thinking Questions

Instructions: Albert Einstein used "Gedanken experiments," or critical thinking questions, to develop his theory of relativity. Some ideas are best understood by experimenting with them in our own minds. The following critical thinking questions are designed to demand your full attention but require only a comfortable chair—no technology.

1. Internet and Society

The Internet was initially created in part to enable scientists and educators to share information quickly and efficiently. It is evident the advantages the Internet brings to our lives, but does Internet access also cause problems?

a. What advantages and disadvantages does the Internet bring to your life?

b. What positive and negative effects has the Internet had on our society as a whole?

c. Some people argue that conducting searches on the Internet provides answers but does not inspire thoughtful research. What do you think?

d. Should use of the Internet be banned, or at least limited, for research projects in schools? Why or why not?

2. File Swapping Ethics

The original file-swapping site Napster's unprecedented rise to fame came to a quick halt because of accusations of copyright infringements. However, downloading music from the Internet still occurs.

a. What's your opinion on having the ability to download music files of your choice? Do you think the musicians who oppose online music sharing make valid points?

b. Discuss the differences you see in sharing music files online and sharing CDs with your friends.

3. The Power of Google

Google is the largest and most popular search engine on the Internet today. Because of its size and popularity, some people claim that Google has enormous power to influence a Web user's search experience solely by its Web site ranking processes. What do you think about this potential power? How could it be used in negative or harmful ways?

a. Some Web sites pay search engines to list them near the top of the results pages. These sponsors therefore get priority placement. What do you think of this policy?

b. What effect (if any) do you think that Google has on Web site development? For example, do you think Web site developers intentionally include frequently searched words in their pages so that they will appear in more hits lists?

c. When you "google" someone, you type their name in the Google search box to see what comes up. What privacy concerns do you think such "googling" could present? Have you ever googled yourself or your friends?

4. Charging for E-Mail?

Should there be a charge placed on sending e-mail or on having IM conversations? What would be an appropriate charge? If a charge is placed on e-mail and IM conversations, what would happen to their use?

Team Time   Comparing Internet Search Methods

Problem:

With millions of sites on the Internet, finding useful information can be a daunting—at times, impossible—task. However, there are methods to make searching easier, some of which have been discussed in this chapter. In this Team Time, each team will search for specific items or pieces of information on the Internet and compare search methodologies.

Task:

Split your group into two or more teams depending on class size. Each group will search for the same items. No restrictions on search processes are to be made. The only requirement is to document the entire search process, as described here.

Search Items:

- What was America's first penny candy to be individually wrapped?
- On which fraternity in which college was the movie *Animal House* based?
- What are the previous names for the American League baseball team the Anaheim Angels?
- What is the cheapest price to purchase a copy of the latest version of Microsoft Office Professional?
- Where can you go to buy the least expensive pink fuzzy bathrobe?

Process:

STEP 1:   Teams are positioned at computers connected to the Internet.

STEP 2:   Each team is given the list of search items. Teams can use whichever search strategies they feel will best reach the desired goal with the most accuracy in the least amount of time.

STEP 3:   Teams compare notes as to which search methods they used to find each item.

Conclusion:

Were subject directories better than search engines for certain searches? Which methods were used to narrow down choices? How were final answers determined?

Materials on the Web

In addition to the review materials presented here, you'll find extra materials on the book's companion Web site (**www.prenhall.com/techinaction**) that will help reinforce your understanding of the chapter content. These materials include the following:

Sound Byte Lab Guides

For each Sound Byte mentioned in the chapter, there is a corresponding lab guide located on the book's companion Web site. These guides review the material presented in the Sound Byte and direct you to various Web resources that examine the material. The Sound Byte Lab Guides for this chapter include:

- Connecting to the Internet
- Welcome to the Web
- Finding Information on the Web
- Creating a Web-Based E-mail Account
- The Best Utilities for Your Computer

True/False and Multiple-Choice Quizzes

The book's Web site includes a true/false and a multiple-choice quiz for this chapter. You can take these quizzes, automatically check the results, and e-mail the results to your instructor.

Web Research Projects

The book's Web site also includes a number of Web research projects for this chapter. These projects ask you to search the Web for information on computer-related careers, milestones in computer history, important people and companies, emerging technologies, and the applications and implications of different technologies.

Technology in Action also features unique interactive Help Desk training, in which you'll assume the role of Help Desk operator taking calls about concepts learned in each chapter. The Help Desk calls for this chapter include:

- Connecting to the Internet
- Getting Around the Web
- Using Subject Directories and Search Engines
- Staying Secure on the Internet

CHAPTER 4

OBJECTIVES

After reading this chapter, you should be able to answer the following questions:

SOUND BYTES

Application Software:

Programs That Let You Work and Play

Finals are this week. Jenna sits down to tackle the last project for her technology information class. She's actually looking forward to working on the project, because it's a research assignment on "simulation" software. She's a fan of the *Sims* software games and is researching how different professions are using simulation software to train workers. Her instructor said the class can use any format for the project, so Jenna decides to do a PowerPoint presentation. With the Insert Slides from Outline feature, she transfers the outline she has already prepared in Word to PowerPoint slides. Using that as the basis for her presentation, she embellishes the slides with photographs and other illustrations, being careful to include references to her sources.

With the bulk of this presentation completed, she takes a break from her project and shifts her focus to balancing her checkbook and recording her income and expenses. Because she records all her banking transactions in the financial planning application Quicken, balancing her checkbook against the bank's records and monitoring her budget are a breeze. She then downloads the information into TurboTax, a tax-preparation software program, so that she can do her taxes herself more easily. She's saved a lot of money by doing her own taxes, and the programs were quite simple to learn.

Before going to dinner, she returns her attention to her presentation. After adding a background color and other effects to her slides, she finds an audio track she can run in the background as she presents her project. Although a lot is riding on this presentation, she's actually excited to show it off.

How often do you use software and what kinds of software are you familiar with? Do you know what software programs are on the market and what their most important features are? In this chapter, you'll learn about the kinds of software you can use to perform a variety of tasks, from simple word processing to digital image editing. We'll then discuss how you can buy software, what the different versions of software mean, and how you can legally get software for free off the Web. Finally, we'll look at how you can install and uninstall software safely on your system.

The Nuts and Bolts of Software

A computer without software is like a sandwich with no filling. Although the computer hardware is obviously critical, a computer system does nothing without software. What is software? Technically speaking, the term **software** refers to a set of instructions that tells the computer what to do. These instruction sets, also called **programs**, provide a means for us to interact with and use the computer, all without specialized computer programming skills. Your computer has two basic types of software: *system software* and *application software*:

- **System software** helps run the computer and coordinates instructions between application software and the computer's hardware devices. System software includes the operating system and utility programs (programs in the operating system that help manage system resources). We discuss system software in detail in Chapter 5.

- **Application software** is what you use to do tasks at home, school, and work. You can do a multitude of things with application software, such as writing letters, sending e-mail, balancing a budget, creating presentations, editing photos, taking an online course, and playing games, just to name a few.

Figure 4.1 shows the various types of application software available. In this chapter, we look at all of these types in detail.

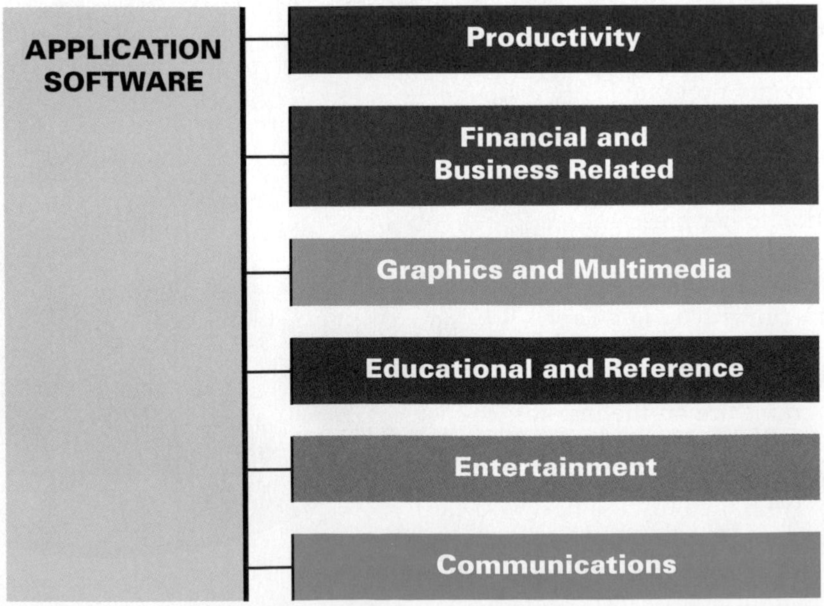

Productivity Software

It's safe to say you already regularly use some form of productivity software. **Productivity software** includes programs that enable you to perform various tasks generally required in home, school, and business. This category includes word processing, spreadsheet, presentation, personal information manager (PIM), and database programs.

WORD PROCESSING SOFTWARE

What is the best software to use to create general documents? Most students use **word processing software** to create and edit written documents such as papers, letters, and résumés. Microsoft Word and Corel's WordPerfect are popular word processing programs. Because of its general usefulness, word processing software is the most widely used software application. Word processing software has a key advantage over its ancestral counterpart, the typewriter: you can make revisions and corrections without having to retype an entire document. You can quickly and easily insert, delete, and move pieces of text. Similarly, you can remove and insert text from one document into another seamlessly.

How do I control the way my documents look? Another advantage of word processing software is that you can easily format, or change the appearance of your document. As a result, you can produce highly sophisticated documents without having to send them to a professional printer. With formatting options, you can change fonts, font styles, and sizes; add colors to text; adjust the margins; add borders to portions of text or whole pages; insert bulleted and numbered lists; and organize your text into columns. You can also insert pictures from your own files or from a precreated

APPLICATION SOFTWARE

- Productivity
- Financial and Business Related
- Graphics and Multimedia
- Educational and Reference
- Entertainment
- Communications

FIGURE 4.1

Application software categories

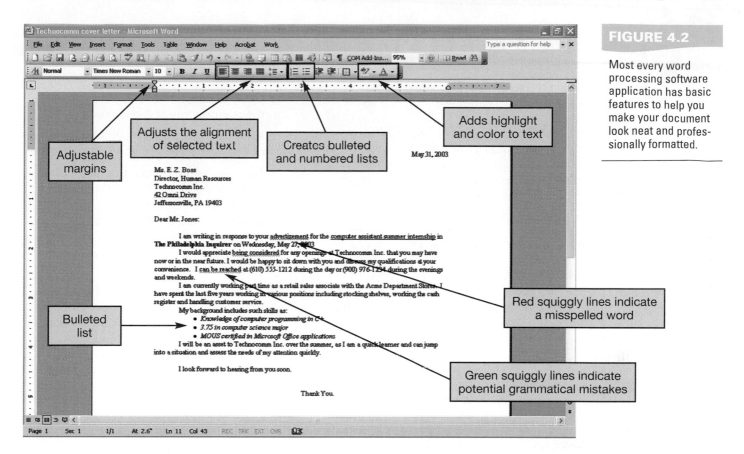

FIGURE 4.2

Most every word processing software application has basic features to help you make your document look neat and professionally formatted.

gallery of images called *clip art* that is included with the software. Using formatting tools, you can also spice up the look of your document by creating an interesting background or by adding a "theme" throughout your document with coordinated colors and styles. Figure 4.2 shows an example of some of the formatting options.

What special tools do word processing programs have? You're probably familiar with the basic tools of word processing software. Most applications come with some form of spelling/grammar checker, for example. Another popular tool is the search/replace tool, which allows you to search for text in your document and automatically replace it with other text.

However, the average user is unaware of many interesting word processing software tools. For example, did you know that you could translate words or phrases to another language or automatically correct your spelling as you type? You can also automatically summarize key points in a text document. In Microsoft Word, you access these tools from the Tools menu (see Figure 4.3).

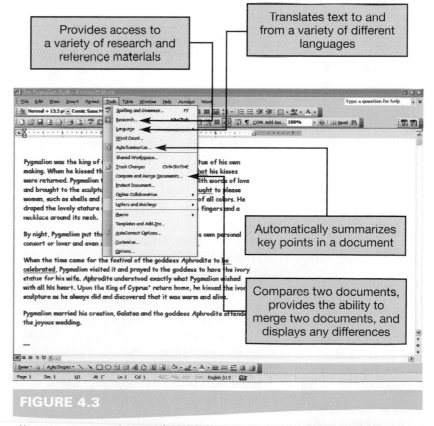

FIGURE 4.3

You can access word processing tools from the Tools menu in Microsoft Word.

BITS AND BYTES

What's the Difference Between Save and Save As?

Imagine you're working on a Word document. Before you leave for class, you (1) save the document to your hard drive for the first time. Later, you open the file to add some finishing touches. When you're done, you (2) save the file again. The next day, you (3) save the file to a Zip disk. In these three situations, when do you use the Save command and when do you use Save As?

When you save a file for the first time (situation 1), you use Save As to give the file a name and designate where it should be located. (When you save a file for the first time, the Save command also brings you to the Save As dialog box.) When you have already saved the file and are saving changes to it (situation 2), you use the Save command. However, if you want to change the name or location of a file that you saved previously (situation 3), you use the Save As command. The following table illustrates these three options.

WHEN TO USE	SAVE AS	SAVE
First time saving a file	X	X
Saving changes to file contents but not filename or location		X
Saving changes to filename and/or location	X	

SPREADSHEET SOFTWARE

Why would I need to use spreadsheet software? Spreadsheet software, such as Microsoft Excel or Lotus 1-2-3, enables you to do calculations and numerical analyses easily. You can use spreadsheet software to track your expenses and to create a simple budget. You can also use spreadsheet software to figure out how much you should be paying on your student loans, car loans, or credit card bills each month. You know you should pay more than the minimum payment to spend less on interest, but how much more should you pay and for which loan? Spreadsheet software can help you easily evaluate different scenarios such as planning the best payment strategy.

How do I use spreadsheet software? The basic element in a spreadsheet program is the *worksheet*, which is a grid consisting of columns and rows. As shown in Figure 4.4, the columns and rows form individual boxes called *cells*. Each cell can be identified

according to its column and row position. For example, a cell in column A row 1 is referred to as cell A1. There are several types of data you can enter into a cell:

- *Labels* are descriptive text that identifies the components of the worksheet.

- *Values* are numeric data either entered in directly or as a result of a calculation.

- *Formulas* are equations that you build yourself using addition, subtraction, multiplication, and division, as well as values and cell references. For example, in Figure 4.4, you would type the formula =B8-B24 to calculate your net income for September.

- *Functions* are formulas that are preprogrammed into the spreadsheet software. Functions help you with calculations ranging from the simple (such as adding groups of numbers) to the complex (such as determining monthly loan payments), without you needing to know how to write the exact formula. So, in Figure 4.4, to calculate your average earned income in September, you could use the built-in AVERAGE function, which would look like this: =AVERAGE(B4:B7).

The primary benefit of spreadsheet software is its ability to recalculate all functions and formulas in the spreadsheet automatically when assumptions are changed. For example, in Figure 4.4, you can insert an additional budget row, such as "Savings", and recalculate the results without having to redo the worksheet from scratch. The ability for spreadsheets to recalculate automatically after changes are made is the primary benefit to working with spreadsheet software.

Because automatic recalculation enables you to see immediately the effects that different options have on your spreadsheet, you can quickly test different assumptions in the same analysis. This is called a *"what-if" analysis*. Look again at Figure 4.4 and ask, "What if my tuition goes up another $100? What impact will that have on my savings?" By adding another $100 to your tuition shown in the budget, you will automatically know the impact a tuition increase will have on your total savings.

How do I change the way my spreadsheets look? To make important data more apparent or an entire spreadsheet

SOUND BYTE

CREATING WEB QUERIES WITH EXCEL

In this Sound Byte, you'll learn what a web query is, how it's used, and how you can use Excel to create your own.

Where rows and columns intersect is a cell. This is cell A1.

Cells A1 to A23 are labels.

These cells are values.

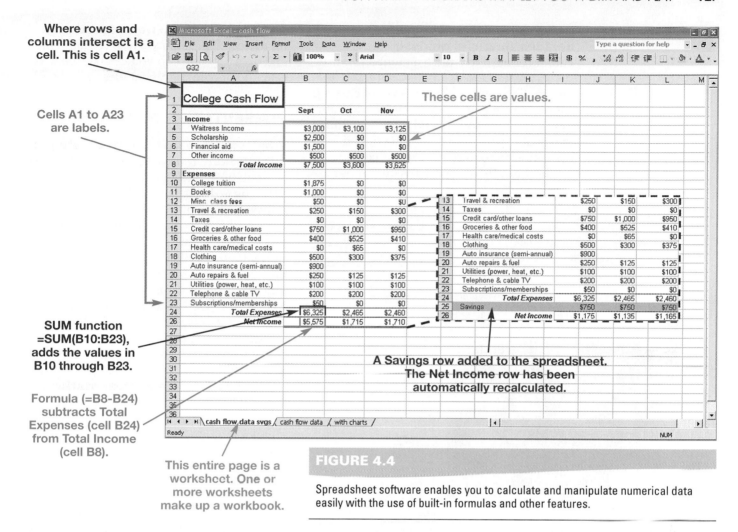

SUM function =SUM(B10:B23), adds the values in B10 through B23.

Formula (=B8-B24) subtracts Total Expenses (cell B24) from Total Income (cell B8).

A Savings row added to the spreadsheet. The Net Income row has been automatically recalculated.

This entire page is a worksheet. One or more worksheets make up a workbook.

FIGURE 4.4

Spreadsheet software enables you to calculate and manipulate numerical data easily with the use of built-in formulas and other features.

more readable, you may want to adjust the size of cells or add colors to text labels. Spreadsheet software offers similar formatting options to those found in word processing software, including the ability to change the font and style of text and numbers. In addition, you can add colored shading and borders, change the height and width of rows and columns, and apply symbols to currency ($) and percentage (%) values.

What kinds of graphs and charts can I create with spreadsheet software? Sometimes it's easier to see the meaning of numbers when they are shown in a graphical format, or a *chart*. As shown in Figure 4.5, most spreadsheet applications allow you to create a variety of charts, including basic column charts, pie charts, and line charts, with or without three-dimensional (3-D) effects. In addition to these basic charts, you can use stock charts (for investment analysis) and scatter charts (for statistical analysis), as well as create custom charts.

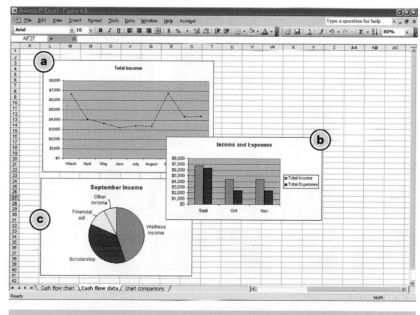

FIGURE 4.5

(a) Line charts show trends over time. (b) Column charts show comparisons. (c) Pie charts show how parts contribute to the whole.

Are spreadsheets used for anything besides financial analysis? Even if you never need to crunch a number, spreadsheets are good tools for keeping track of information such as addresses or for creating simple lists of your CD collection. Excel, for example, offers sorting and filtering features that enable you to sort through your address book quickly to find a particular contact or a subset of contacts, perhaps only those people to whom you want to send party invitations. Spreadsheets also contain time and date functions, so you can use them as calendar and appointment files.

PRESENTATION SOFTWARE

What software do I use to create presentations? You've probably sat through presentations during which the speaker's dialogue is displayed in slides projected on a screen. These presentations can be very basic outlines, containing only a few words and simple graphics, or elaborate multimedia presentations with animated text, graphic objects, and colorfully formatted backgrounds. You use **presentation software** such as Microsoft PowerPoint or Corel Presentations to create these types of dynamic slide shows. Because these applications are so simple to use, you can produce high-quality presentations without a lot of training.

How do I create a presentation? Using the basic features included in presentation software, creating a slide show is very simple. To arrange text and graphics on your slides easily, you can choose from a variety of *slide layouts*. These layouts give you the option of using a single or double column of bulleted text as well as various combinations of bulleted text and other content such as clip art, graphs, photos, and even video clips.

You can also lend a theme to your presentation by choosing from different *design templates*, preformatted slides that add coordinated background, fonts, and styles to your slides. You can use animation effects to control how and when text and other objects enter and exit each slide. Similarly, slide transitions control how slides move from one to the next during the presentation.

Are there different ways to view my slides while I'm working on my presentation? There are several different formats with which you can view your presentation. The most common is Normal (or Slide) view (see Figure 4.6a). In recent versions of PowerPoint, this view consists of three panes: the left pane shows either small versions of the slides or an outline of the presentation; the middle pane shows the slide you are currently working on; and the bottom pane shows speaker notes. Speaker notes are helpful notes to yourself while you give your presentation.

Another common view is Notes view (see Figure 4.6b). When you work on a

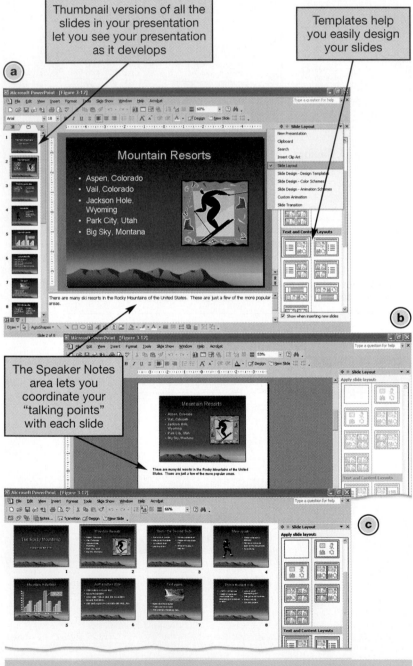

Thumbnail versions of all the slides in your presentation let you see your presentation as it develops

Templates help you easily design your slides

The Speaker Notes area lets you coordinate your "talking points" with each slide

FIGURE 4.6

Using PowerPoint, you can view your slides in three views: (a) Normal, (b) Notes, and (c) Slide Sorter.

presentation in Notes view, you see just the slide and your speaker notes. Finally, you can view the slides in your presentation in Slide Sorter view (see Figure 4.6c). In this view, you can see up to 12 thumbnail versions of your slides at one time. It is easiest to rearrange slides and add transitions and other effects when you're in Slide Sorter view.

DATABASE SOFTWARE

How can I use database software?
Database software, such as Corel Paradox and Microsoft Access, is basically a complex electronic filing system. As mentioned earlier, most spreadsheet applications can handle small databases such as a simple address book. Database software is best used for larger and more complicated groups of data that require more than one table, and where it's necessary to group, sort, and retrieve data, and to generate reports.

Traditional databases are organized into fields, records, and tables, as shown in Figure 4.7. A *field* is a data category such as "First Name," "Last Name," or "Street Address." A *record* is a collection of related fields, such as "Douglas Seaver, Printing Solutions, 7700 First Avenue, Topeka, KS, (888) 988-2678." A table groups related records together, such as "SalesDeptContactInfo."

How do businesses use database software?
Many online businesses use database applications because users can easily open, view, and update live data within a Web browser from anywhere. For example, many online companies have their inventory in a database that is automatically

BITS AND BYTES

What Is Personal Information Manager Software?

Most productivity software suites contain some form of **personal information manager (PIM) software**, such as Microsoft Outlook or Lotus Organizer. These programs strive to replace the various management tools found on a traditional desk, such as a calendar, address book, notepad, and to-do lists. Some PIMs contain e-mail management features so that you can not only receive and compose e-mail messages, but also organize them into various topical folders, prioritize them, and coordinate them with other activities in your calendar. If other people you know use the same PIM software, you can coordinate group schedules as well as check classmates' or coworkers' availability before scheduling meeting times. If you are working on a team project, you can create and electronically assign tasks to group members. With the Keep Me Updated feature, you can track each person's progress to ensure that the team finishes the project on time.

revised as each order is placed. Companies such as FedEx and UPS let customers search their online databases for tracking numbers, allowing customers to get instant information on the status of their packages. Other businesses use databases to keep track of clients, invoices, or personnel information.

PRODUCTIVITY SOFTWARE TOOLS

What tools can help me work more efficiently with productivity software?
Whether you are working on a word document, spreadsheet, database, or slide

---

This entire group of records represents the SalesDeptContactInfo table

Microsoft Access - [SalesDeptContactInfo : Table]

File   Edit   View   Insert   Format   Records   Tools   Window   Help

Type a question for help

	ContactID	First Name	Last Name	CompanyName	Street Address	City	State	Business Phone
▶	1	Susan	Scantosi	eWidgetPlus	363 Rogue Street	St. Louis	MO	(612) 444-1236
	2	Thomas	Mazeman	BooksRUs	2165 Piscotti Ave	Springfield	IL	(888) 234-6983
	3	Douglas	Seaver	Printing Solutions	7700 First Ave	Topeka	KS	(888) 988-2678
	4	Amir	Ramiv	TechStands	1436 Riverfront Place	St. Louis	MO	(877) 867-7656
	5	Franklin	Scott	WorksSuite	8789 Ploughman Drive	Tulsa	OK	(800) 864-2390
	6	Ronald	Komeika	Creekside Financia	1264 Pond Hill Road	Toledo	OH	(343) 333-3333
	7	Barbara	Mitchell	Market Tenders	9823 Bridge Street	LaPorte	IN	(888) 238-2123
*	(AutoNumber)							

The category First Name is a field

All the information for Douglas Seaver represents one record

FIGURE 4.7

Databases help us organize information. Similar information is organized by main topic into tables, then broken down into categories called fields. Each individual row of data is called a record.

presentation, there are several tools you can use to increase your efficiency. These tools walk you through tasks, help you begin a project, or allow you to automate tasks:

- **Wizards** are step-by-step guides that walk you through the necessary steps to complete a complicated task. At each step, the wizard asks you questions. Based on your responses, the wizard helps you complete that portion of the task. After the series of questions is done, your task will be complete. Many productivity software applications include wizards. For example, you can easily create charts in Excel using the Excel Chart Wizard.

- **Templates** are forms included in many productivity applications that provide the basic structure for a particular kind of document, spreadsheet, or presentation. Templates can include specific page layout designs, special formatting and styles relevant to that particular document, as well as automated tasks (macros).

- **Macros** are small programs that group a series of commands to run as a single command. Macros are best used to automate a routine task (to save time) or to automate a complex series of commands that must be run frequently. For example, a teacher may write a macro to sort the grades in her grade book automatically in descending order and to highlight those grades that are below a C average with red formatting. Every time she adds the results of an assignment or test, she can set up the macro to run through those series of steps automatically. Using a macro is much easier than

doing the series of steps repeatedly with each addition to the grade book.

INTEGRATED SOFTWARE APPLICATIONS VS. SOFTWARE SUITES

Are there different ways to buy productivity software? You can buy productivity software as individual stand-alone programs, as integrated software applications, or as a suite of software applications.

Integrated Software Applications

What's an integrated software application? An **integrated software application** is a single software program that incorporates the most commonly used tools of many productivity software programs into one *integrated* stand-alone program. In essence, integrated software applications are "software lite" because they don't include many of the more complex features of the stand-alone productivity software applications. Microsoft Works is an example of an integrated software application.

As discussed earlier, most productivity software applications include templates for frequently developed documents such as résumés, cover letters, and invoices. Integrated software programs offer hundreds of nonstandard templates, such as fitness workout tracking worksheets and CD inventory databases. Some of these templates enable you to accomplish tasks that would perhaps be too complicated to tackle without a template. For example, such software programs often include templates that help users calculate a mortgage payment schedule. Without needing to know the complicated calculations involved in creating such a schedule, you can prepare one by simply inputting data into the template.

Figure 4.8 shows the Task Launcher for Microsoft Works (the Task Launcher is the first window that opens when you launch Microsoft Works). As you can see, this integrated software application includes word processing, spreadsheet, and database features as well as templates, calendar, encyclopedia, and map features.

Why would I use an integrated software application instead of individual stand-alone programs? Integrated software applications are perfect if you don't need the more advanced features found in the individual productivity software

BITS AND BYTES

Productivity Software Tips and Tricks

Looking for tips on how to make better use of your productivity software? A number of Web sites send subscribers daily e-mails full of tips, tricks, and shortcuts to their favorite software programs. **NerdyBooks.com**, for example, sends subscribers a free tip each day to their e-mail account. NerdyBooks's free *Who Knew?* weekly newsletter is also full of software tips. *Dummies Daily* (**http://etips.dummies.com**), based on the For Dummies series of help books, offers subscribers tips on a variety of topics, including productivity software applications. Most of these services are free, although some require that you subscribe to an ancillary product.

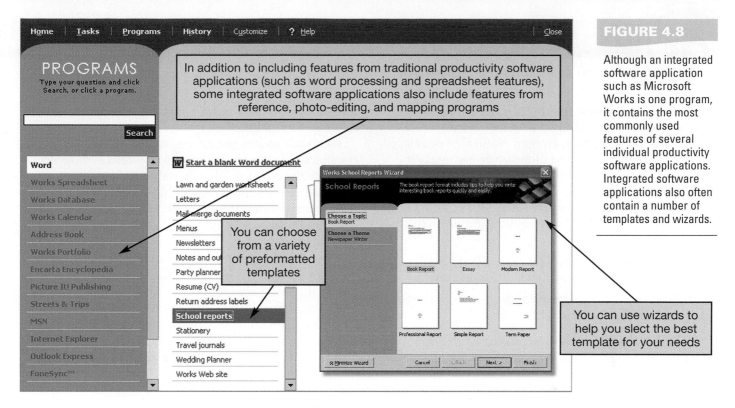

FIGURE 4.8

Although an integrated software application such as Microsoft Works is one program, it contains the most commonly used features of several individual productivity software applications. Integrated software applications also often contain a number of templates and wizards.

(within figure) In addition to including features from traditional productivity software applications (such as word processing and spreadsheet features), some integrated software applications also include features from reference, photo-editing, and mapping programs

(within figure) You can choose from a variety of preformatted templates

(within figure) You can use wizards to help you slect the best template for your needs

applications. Also, if you often use preformatted forms and templates, integrated software programs are the better choice because they contain far more template options than do individual software applications. Integrated software programs are also less expensive than their full-featured counterparts. However, if you find your needs go beyond the limited capabilities of an integrated program, you might want to consider buying those individual programs that meet your particular requirements, or you may want to consider buying a software suite.

Software Suites
What's a software suite? A **software suite** is a collection of software programs that have been bundled together as a package. You can buy software suites for many different categories of applications, including productivity, graphics, and virus protection. Microsoft Office is just one example of the many types of software suites on the market today (see Figure 4.9). You can also buy different versions of the same suite, the difference being the combination of software applications included in each version.

Which software applications do productivity software suites contain? Most productivity software suites contain the same basic software programs such as word processing, spreadsheet, presentation,

and PIM software. The Microsoft Office suite bundles together the word processing program Microsoft Word, the spreadsheet program Excel, the presentation program PowerPoint, and the PIM program Outlook. However, depending on the version and manufacturer, some suites also include other programs, such as database programs and speech-recognition software.

FIGURE 4.9

Software suites provide users with a cheaper method of obtaining all of the software they want to buy in one bundle.

DIG DEEPER

Speech-Recognition Software

Speech-recognition software (or **voice-recognition software**) translates your spoken words into typed text. ScanSoft's product, Dragon NaturallySpeaking, is one of the leading stand-alone voice-recognition software applications on the market. Microsoft has incorporated speech recognition software features into its word processing, spreadsheet, and presentation programs in Office 2003. Speech-recognition software works in two ways:

- It can perform dictation, meaning that it will "type" the words you speak into a document.

- It can execute the formatting and file management commands you give to it.

Figure 4.10 shows how you can use Microsoft Word's built-in speech-recognition software to instruct the software to carry out simple voice commands to select and format text.

Although speech recognition can be useful, getting a computer to understand your spoken words and correctly translate them into printed digital content is difficult. Improvements to the process continue to be made, and current accuracy rates for Dragon NaturallySpeaking v7 are in the 90 percent range. How does the software work? It's an extremely complicated process. As you speak, the speech-recognition software divides each second of your speech into 100 individual samples, or sounds. It then compares these individual sounds with a database (called a codebook) containing samples of every sound a human being can make. When a match is made, your voice sound is given a number that corresponds to the number of the similar sound in the database.

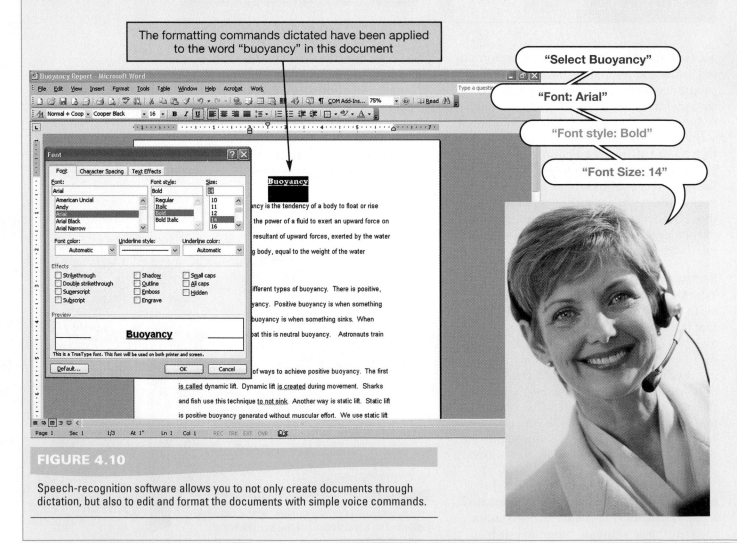

The formatting commands dictated have been applied to the word "buoyancy" in this document

"Select Buoyancy"

"Font: Arial"

"Font style: Bold"

"Font Size: 14"

FIGURE 4.10

Speech-recognition software allows you to not only create documents through dictation, but also to edit and format the documents with simple voice commands.

Once your voice sounds are assigned values, these values are matched with another database containing phonemes for the language being spoken. A *phoneme* is the smallest phonetic unit that distinguishes one word from another. For example, "b" and "m" are both phonemes that distinguish the words *bad* and *mad* from each other in the English language. A typical language such as English is comprised of thousands of different phonemes. And because of differences in pronunciation, some phonemes may actually have several different corresponding matching sounds.

Once all the sounds are assigned to phonemes, word and phrase construction can begin. The phonemes are matched against a word list that contains transcriptions of all known words in a particular language. Because pronunciation can vary (for example, *the* can be pronounced so that it rhymes with *duh* or *see*), the word list must contain alternate pronunciations for many words. Each phoneme is worked on separately; the phonemes are then chained together to form words that are contained in the word list. Because a variety of sounds can be put together to form many different words, the software analyzes all the possible values and picks the one value that it determines has the best probability of correctly matching your spoken word. The word is then displayed on the screen or is acted upon by the computer as a command.

Why are there problems with speech-recognition software? We don't always speak every word the same way, and accents and regional dialects result in great variations in pronunciations. Therefore, speech recognition is not perfect and requires significant training. Training entails getting the computer to recognize your particular way of speaking, a process that involves reading prepared text into the computer so the phoneme database can be adjusted to your specific speech patterns.

Another approach to speech inconsistencies is to restrict the word list to a few key words or phrases and then have the computer guess the probability that a certain phrase is being said. This is how cell phones that respond to voice commands work. The phone doesn't really figure out you said "call home" by breaking down the phonemes. It just determines how likely it is that you said "call home" as opposed to "call office." This cuts down on the processing power needed and reduces the chance of mistakes. However, it also restricts the words you can use to achieve the desired results.

Although not perfect, speech-recognition software programs can be of invaluable service for individuals who can't type very well or who have physical limitations that prevent them from using a keyboard or mouse. For those whose careers depend on a lot of typing, using speech-recognition software reduces the chances of their incurring debilitating repetitive strain injuries. Additionally, because most people can speak faster than they can write or type, speech-recognition software can help you work more efficiently. It can also help you to be productive during generally nonproductive times. For example, you can dictate into a digital recording device while doing other things such as driving, then later download the digital file to your computer and let the program type up your words for you.

Speech recognition should continue to be a hot topic for research over the next decade. Aside from the obvious benefits to persons with disabilities, many people are enamored with the idea of talking to their computers!

SOUND BYTE

USING SPEECH-RECOGNITION SOFTWARE

In this Sound Byte, you'll see a demonstration of the speech-recognition software included with Microsoft Office. You'll also learn how to access and train speech-recognition software so that you can create and edit documents without typing.

FIGURE 4.11 Software Suites

	WORD PROCESSING	SPREADSHEET	PRESENTATION	PIM	DATABASE	OTHER INCLUDED SOFTWARE
MICROSOFT OFFICE 2003	**WORD**	**EXCEL**	**POWERPOINT**	**OUTLOOK**	**ACCESS**	**PUBLISHER**
Professional	x	x	x	x	x	x
Standard	x	x	x	x		
Academic*	x	x	x	x		
Small Business	x	x	x	x		x

*Academic edition is priced lower than Standard edition and is for non-commercial use only.

WORDPERFECT OFFICE 12	**WORDPERFECT**	**QUATTRO PRO**	**PRESENTATIONS**	**ADDRESS BOOK**	**PARADOX**	**MICROSOFT VISUAL BASIC**
Standard	x	x	x	x		x
Professional	x	x	x	x	x	x
Academic	x	x	x	x	x	

LOTUS SMARTSUITE	**WORDPRO**	**LOTUS 1-2-3**	**FREELANCE**	**ORGANIZER**	**APPROACH**	
SmartSuite	x	x	x	x	x	

BITS AND BYTES

Sun's StarOffice: Looking for a More Affordable Productivity Suite?

If you're looking for a more affordable software suite than the big three, Sun Microsystems StarOffice 7 may be worth a try. StarOffice 7 is a productivity software suite based on the open-source productivity software OpenOffice. The original StarOffice suite was initially available as a free download, but as of May 2002, Sun began charging for its upgraded version. You can find StarOffice 7 in most retail stores that sell productivity software applications. Even as a retail product, its price is substantially lower than the mainstream suites. StarOffice contains similar applications to those found in other productivity suites and integrates well with them, so you can easily open files created in other applications. Similarly, users of other productivity suites can easily open files you create in StarOffice. Although you won't find all the features you're used to seeing in competing products, StarOffice does offer a wide variety of features, including a large image gallery and spelling, grammar, and thesaurus tools to meet most general needs.

What are the most popular productivity software suites? As illustrated in Figure 4.11, there are three primary developers of productivity software suites: Microsoft, Corel, and Lotus. Microsoft and Corel offer different bundled packages with different combinations of software applications, whereas Lotus offers only SmartSuite.

Why would I buy a software suite instead of individual programs? Most people buy software suites because suites are cheaper than buying each program individually. In addition, because the programs bundled together in a software suite come from the same developer, they work well together (that is, they provide for better integration) and share common features, toolbars, and menus. For example, say you own Corel's WordPerfect, a stand-alone word processing software application, and Microsoft's stand-alone spreadsheet program Excel. If you want to incorporate an Excel chart into a WordPerfect document, you may have trouble because the two programs come from different developers. However, with a software suite such as Microsoft Office, you can easily incorporate an Excel chart into a Word document simply by clicking an icon.

Financial and Business-Related Software

Financial and business-related software can be grouped into three main categories:

- Personal financial software that helps you perform businesslike tasks at home, such as preparing your taxes and managing your personal finances
- General business software used in different capacities across industries
- Specialized business software designed for particular industries

PERSONAL FINANCIAL SOFTWARE

What software can I use to do my taxes? Tax-preparation software such as Intuit's TurboTax and H&R Block's TaxCut enable you to prepare your state and federal taxes on your own rather than having to hire a professional. Each program offers a complete set of tax forms and instructions as well as expert advice on how to complete each form. Error-checking systems are built into the programs to help catch your mistakes. Furthermore, TurboTax offers you guidance on financial planning for the following year to help you effectively plan and manage your financial resources (see Figure 4.12).

What software can I use to help keep track of my finances? Financial planning software helps you manage your daily finances. Intuit's Quicken and Microsoft Money are popular examples. These programs include electronic checkbook registers and automatic bill payment tools, as shown in Figure 4.13, p. 136. With these features, you can print checks from your computer or pay your regular monthly payments such as your rent and student loans with automatically scheduled online payments or printed checks. The software automatically records all transactions, even online payments, in your checkbook register. You assign categories to each transaction, use these categories to analyze your spending patterns, and can

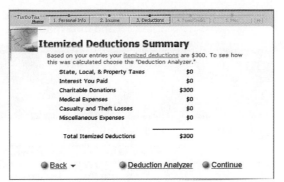

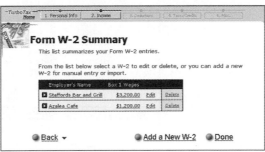

Tax-preparation software, such as Intuit's TurboTax, enables you to prepare your taxes on your own through a guided step-by-step process.

even compare your spending habits to a budget you set up.

Financial planning programs also coordinate with tax-preparation software. Quicken, for example, coordinates seamlessly with TurboTax so you never have to go through your checkbook and bills to find tax deductions and tax-related income or expenses. In addition, many banks and credit card companies offer online services that download into Quicken or Money. Quicken even offers a credit card. All your purchases are organized into categories and are downloaded easily to your Quicken file to further streamline your financial planning and record keeping. You can also purchase a Pocket PC version of Quicken to install on your personal digital assistant (PDA) so your financial records are always at your fingertips.

What programs are good for people with small businesses? If you have a small business or a hobby that produces income, you know the importance of keeping

FIGURE 4.13

When you write checks with personal financial planning software, your transactions are entered automatically in an electronic checkbook.

Other account services and information

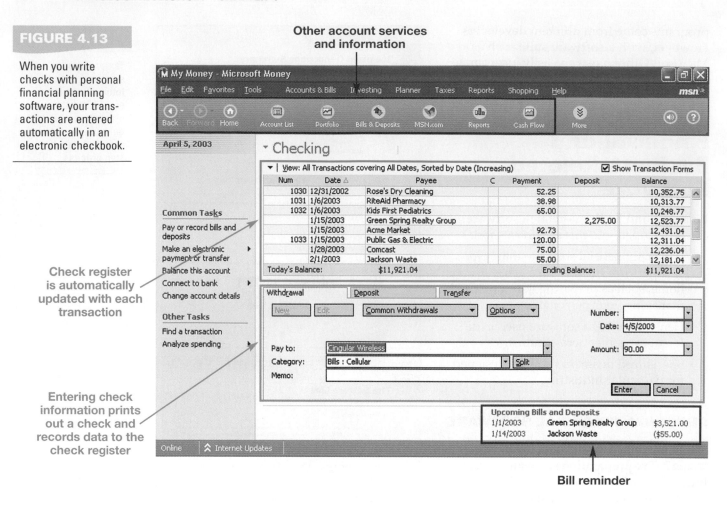

Check register is automatically updated with each transaction

Entering check information prints out a check and records data to the check register

Bill reminder

good records and tracking your expenses and income. **Accounting software** helps small business owners manage their finances more efficiently by providing tools for tracking accounts receivable and accounts payable. In addition, these applications also offer inventory management plus payroll

and billing tools. Examples of accounting software applications include Intuit's QuickBooks and Peachtree Accounting. Both programs include templates for invoices, statements, and financial reports so that small business owners can create common forms and reports.

GENERAL BUSINESS SOFTWARE

What financial and business-related software do bigger businesses use?

As indicated earlier, some business software is task-specific and used across a variety of industries. This type of software includes programs such as Palo Alto Software's Business Plan Pro and Marketing Plan Pro, which help businesses write strategic and development plans.

Another good example of general business software is **project management software**, such as Microsoft Project. Such software helps project managers easily create and modify project management scheduling charts like the one shown in Figure 4.14. Charts like these help project managers plan

BITS AND BYTES

Need a Way to Share Files? Try Acrobat

Say you've created a file in Microsoft Excel, but the person to whom you want to send it doesn't have Excel, or any spreadsheet software, installed on his computer. Or say your sister owns a Mac and you own a PC. You are constantly running into file-sharing problems. What do you do in these situations? Create a PDF file. Portable Document Format (PDF) is a file format you can create with Adobe Acrobat. This program transforms any file, regardless of its application or platform, into a document that can be shared, viewed, and printed by anyone who has Adobe Reader. The good news? Adobe Reader is a free download available at **www.adobe.com**.

and track specific project tasks as well as coordinate personnel resources.

What other kinds of software do businesses often use? Mapping programs such as Rand McNally's StreetFinder and Microsoft's Streets & Trips are perfect for businesses that require a lot of travel. These programs provide street maps and written directions to locations nationwide, and you can customize the maps so that they include landmarks and other handy traveling sites such as airports, hotels, and restaurants.

These programs are often available in versions for PDAs and for cars and work in conjunction with a Global Positioning System (GPS) device to help you navigate your way around. Mapping programs are essential for sales representatives or delivery-intensive businesses. Of course, mapping programs are also good for nonprofessionals planning trips and traveling to unfamiliar locations.

Businesses also use **customer relationship management (CRM) software** to store sales and client contact information in one central database. Sales professionals use CRM programs to get in touch and follow up with their clients. These programs also include tools that enable businesses to assign quotas and to create reports and charts to document and analyze actual and projected sales data. CRM programs coordinate well with PIM software such as Outlook and can be set up to work with PDAs. GoldMine Business Contact Manager from FrontRange Solutions is an example of a CRM program.

SPECIALIZED BUSINESS SOFTWARE

What kinds of specialized business software are there? Some software applications are tailored to the needs of a particular company or industry. For example, the construction industry uses software such as Intuit's Master Builder, which features estimating tools to help construction companies bid on prospective jobs. It also integrates project management functions and accounting systems that are unique to the construction industry.

Other examples of specialized business software include property management software for real estate professionals; ambulance

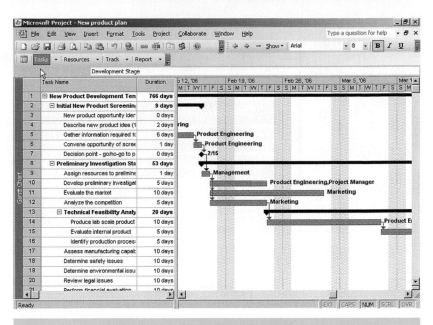

FIGURE 4.14

A Gantt chart in Microsoft Project provides project managers with a visual tool for assigning personnel and scheduling and managing tasks.

scheduling and dispatching software for emergency assistance organizations; and library automation software for cataloging, circulation, inventory, online catalog searching, and custom report printing at libraries.

In addition to these specific business software applications that companies can buy off the shelf, programs are often custom developed to address the specific needs of a particular company. This is often referred to as **proprietary software**, because it is owned and controlled by the company it is created by or for.

Graphics and Multimedia Software

Graphics software encompasses a wide range of programs home users and professionals alike use to design and create attractive documents, images, illustrations, and Web pages. In addition, graphics software allows engineers and other professionals to create three-dimensional models and drawings to help them visualize construction plans. Graphics software is a part of a larger group of software: multimedia software. **Multimedia software** includes video and audio editing software, animation software,

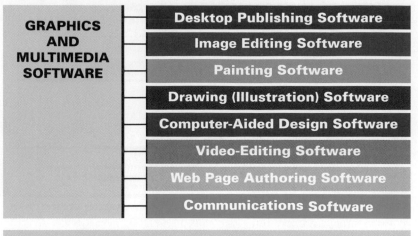

GRAPHICS AND MULTIMEDIA SOFTWARE

- Desktop Publishing Software
- Image Editing Software
- Painting Software
- Drawing (Illustration) Software
- Computer-Aided Design Software
- Video-Editing Software
- Web Page Authoring Software
- Communications Software

FIGURE 4.15

There are many varieties of graphics and multimedia software.

and other special software required to produce computer games. In this section, we look at a number of popular types of graphics and multimedia software, shown in Figure 4.15.

DESKTOP PUBLISHING SOFTWARE

What software can I use to lay out and design newsletters and other publications? Desktop publishing (DTP) **software** allows you to incorporate and arrange graphics and text in your documents in creative ways. Although many word processing applications allow you to use some of the features that are hallmarks of desktop publishing, specialized desktop publishing software such as QuarkXPress

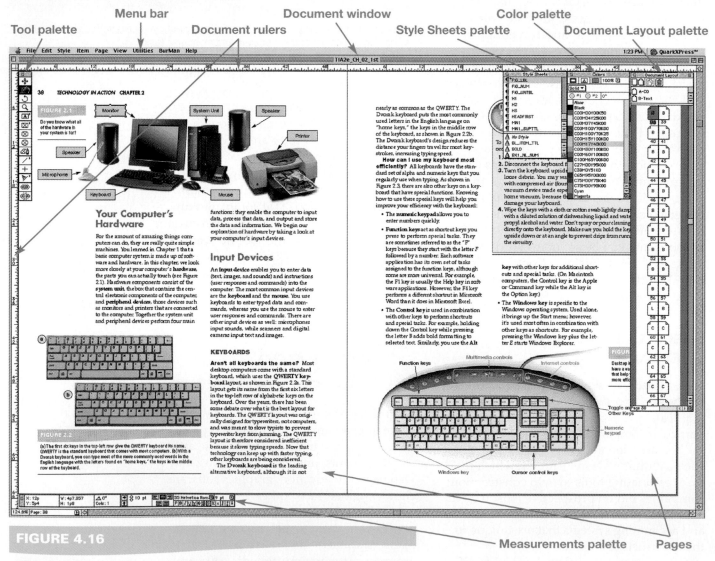

FIGURE 4.16

Major publishing houses use professional desktop publishing programs such as QuarkXPress to lay out the pages of textbooks such as this one.

and Adobe PageMaker allows professionals to design and lay out complex books and other publications (see Figure 4.16).

What tools do desktop publishing programs include? Desktop publishing programs offer a variety of tools with which you can format text and graphics. With text formatting tools, you can easily change the font, size, and style of your text as well as arrange text on the page in different columns, shapes, and patterns. You can import files into your documents from other sources, including elements from other software programs (such as an Excel chart or text from Word) or graphics files. You can readily manipulate graphics with tools that can crop, flip, or rotate images or modify the image's color, shape, and size. Desktop publishing programs also include features that allow you to publish to the Web.

IMAGE-EDITING SOFTWARE

What software do I use to edit my photos? Image-editing software (sometimes called photo-editing software) programs enable you to edit photographs and other images. Image-editing software includes tools for basic modifications to digital images such as removing red-eye, modifying color hues, and removing scratches or rips from scanned images of old photos.

Like image-editing software, **painting software** is used to modify photographs. However, painting software also includes an extensive set of painting tools such as brushes, pens, and artistic-type mediums (paints, pastels, oils) that allows you to create realistic-looking images as well. Many graphic designers use digital photos and images as a basis for their design and then modify these images with painting software to create their final product.

Adobe Photoshop and Jasc Paint Shop Pro 7 are full-featured image-editing and painting software applications, respectively. Some painting programs offer more sophisticated tools such as those for layering images (placing pictures on top of each other) and masking images (hiding parts of layers to create effects such as collages) (see Figure 4.17). Designers use these more sophisticated tools to create the enhanced digital images used commercially in logos, advertisements, and on book and CD covers.

Can a nonprofessional use image-editing software? As more and more people buy digital cameras, the need for software that allows users to manipulate these digital images is growing. There are many image-editing programs designed specifically for the casual user that are perfect for when you want to view or modify a digital image (picture or photo). If you want to use a program that offers you more than basic features but that is still easy to use, Adobe Photoshop Elements is a good basic program for the novice. With this program, you can improve the color balance of an image,

FIGURE 4.17

With some image-editing and painting software, you can take two individual pictures and combine them into one picture.

For more information on graphics software, see "Low-End vs. Professional Photo Software," a TechTV clip found at www.prenhall.com/techinaction.

touch up an image (by removing red-eye, for example), add creative effects to an image, or group images together to create montages.

Do I get image-editing or painting software when I buy a digital camera or computer? Image-editing programs such as ArcSoft, Microsoft Picture It!, and Roxio PhotoSuite are often included with digital cameras. With these applications, you can perform the most common image-editing tasks, such as taking out red-eye and cropping and resizing pictures. You can even add creative effects such as borders and frames. Some programs have templates in which you can insert your favorite pictures into preformatted calendar pages or greeting cards (see Figure 4.18). They may also have photo fantasy images that let you paste a face from your digital image onto the body of a professional athlete or other famous person.

Microsoft Paint is a basic painting program incorporated in the Microsoft Windows operating system. With Paint you can perform

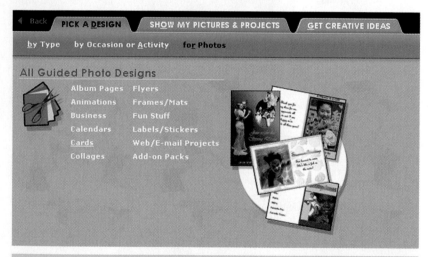

FIGURE 4.18

Some image-editing software applications provide templates with which you can create greeting cards and calendars.

SOUND BYTE

ENHANCING PHOTOS WITH IMAGE-EDITING SOFTWARE

In this Sound Byte, you'll learn tips and tricks on how to best use image-editing software. You'll learn how to remove the red-eye from photos and incorporate borders, frames, and other enhancements to produce professional effects.

basic tasks such as cropping and flipping images. Paint also allows you to create simple designs and images using standard object and drawing tools.

DRAWING SOFTWARE

What kind of software should I use for simple illustrations? Drawing software (or illustration software) programs let you create or edit two-dimensional line-based drawings. You use drawing software to create technical diagrams or original non-photographic drawings, animations, and illustrations using standard drawing and painting tools such as pens, pencils, and paintbrushes. You can also drag geometric objects from a toolbar onto the canvas area to create images and use paint bucket, eye-dropper, and spray can tools to add color and special effects to the drawings.

Are there different types of drawing software? Drawing software is used in both creative and technical drawings. Software applications such as Adobe Illustrator include tools that let you create professional-quality illustrations. The Illustrator image controls let you create complex designs and use special effects, and its warping tool allows you to bend, stretch, and twist portions of your image or text. Because of its many tools and features, Illustrator is one of the preferred drawing software programs of most graphic artists.

Microsoft Visio is a program used to create technical drawings, maps, basic block diagrams, networking and engineering flowcharts, and project schedules. Visio uses project-related templates with special objects that you drag onto a canvas. For example, using the Visio floor template and dragging furniture and other interior objects onto it, you can create an interior design like the one shown in Figure 4.19. In addition to these uses, Visio also provides mind-mapping templates that help you organize your thoughts and ideas.

Are there programs that combine drawing and painting capabilities? Many graphic artists create their initial designs with drawing software because of the ease with which modifications and manipulations can be made to the design. Afterward, the artists often convert these designs to a painting image for further color refinement and image changes. Although professionals may use individual programs for each of these processes, some programs, such as CorelDRAW Graphics Suite and Deneba Canvas, combine features from both drawing and painting software programs. CorelDRAW Graphics Suite is a set of individual applications including CorelDRAW, Photo Paint, and RAVE. Deneba is an integrated application that lets you create illustrations, edit photos, as well as lay out Web pages and create other Web designs.

COMPUTER-AIDED DESIGN SOFTWARE

What software is used to make 3-D models? Computer-aided design (CAD) programs are a form of 3-D modeling engineers use to create automated designs, technical drawings, and model visualizations. Specialized CAD software is used in industries such as architecture, automotive, aerospace, and medical engineering. This list keeps growing as more and more industries realize the benefits CAD can bring to their product development and manufacturing process.

With CAD software, architects can build virtual models of their plans and readily visualize all aspects of design prior to actual construction. Engineers use CAD software to design everything from factory components to bridges (see Figure 4.20). The 3-D nature of these programs allows engineers to rotate the model and make adjustments to their designs where necessary, thus eliminating costly building errors.

CAD software is also being used in conjunction with GPS systems for accurate placement of fiber-optic networks around the country. The medical engineering community uses

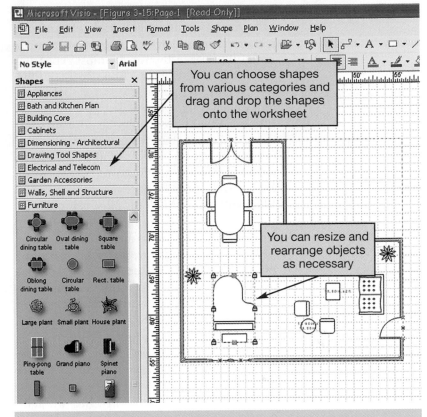

FIGURE 4.19

The drawing program Visio lets you create different types of diagrams easily with drag-and-drop options.

CAD to create anatomically accurate solid models of the human anatomy to develop medical implants quickly and accurately.

VIDEO-EDITING SOFTWARE

What kind of software can I use to edit my digital videos? With the boom of digital camcorders and increasing graphics capabilities on home computers, many people

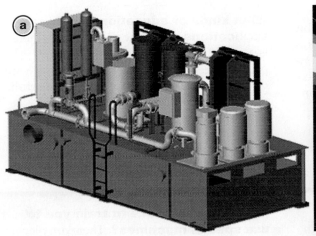

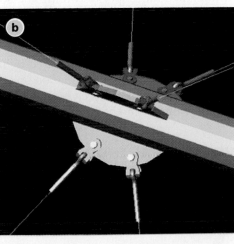

FIGURE 4.20

CAD software assists engineers in designing everything from (a) factory components to (b) bridge supports. This allows designs to be tested and refined before construction takes place.

are experimenting with **digital video–editing software**. There are quite a few video-editing software applications on the market at a wide range of prices. Although the most expensive products (such as Adobe Premiere) offer the widest range of special effects and tools, there are some moderately priced video-editing programs that have enough features to keep the casual user happy. Some software developers offer free trial versions for you to test run before buying them. Others, such as Microsoft Movie Maker, can be downloaded for free. Microsoft Movie Maker is fairly simple to use and is available from the Microsoft Web site for those running Windows XP.

Does video-editing software support all kinds of video files? Video files come in a number of formats. Many of the affordable video-editing software packages support only a few types of video files. For example, one application may support Windows Media Player video files, whereas another may support QuickTime or RealOne Player video files instead. Fortunately, software boxes list which types of video files the software supports. You should buy the least expensive application with the greatest number of supported file formats.

How do I incorporate or edit sound in digital videos? Adding music to or editing sounds in digital videos can change a standard video into a work of art. If you have Microsoft Windows on your computer, you already have Sound Recorder. With this program you can record simple sounds, adjust volume to fade in or fade out sounds, and even add echo and other special effects to your video. Sony's Sound Forge and other similar applications incorporate a variety of features that enable you to edit sounds and music by removing and rearranging sound clips in addition to adding special volume and sound effects. Professionals and real audio enthusiasts use higher-end products such as Adobe Premiere, but the high price of these programs tends to limit them from being used by non-professionals. For more information on video-editing software, see the Tech in Focus feature, "Digital Entertainment," on page 164.

WEB PAGE AUTHORING SOFTWARE

What software do I use to create a Web page? Web page authoring software allows even the novice user to design interesting and interactive Web pages, without knowing any Hypertext Markup Language (HTML) code. Web page authoring applications often include wizards, templates, and reference materials to help you easily complete most Web page authoring tasks. More experienced users can take advantage of the advanced features included in this software, including features that enable you to add headlines and weather information, stock tickers, and maps to make your Web content current, interactive, and interesting. Microsoft FrontPage and Macromedia Dreamweaver are two of the leading programs to which both professionals and casual Web page designers turn.

Are there other ways to create Web pages? If you need to produce only the occasional Web page and do not need a separate Web page authoring program, you'll find that many software applications include features that enable you to convert your document into a Web page easily. In some Microsoft Office applications, you can choose to save the file as a Web page and the application will automatically convert the file to a Web-compatible format.

Educational and Reference Software

Educational software refers to the variety of software applications on the market that offer some form of instruction or training. Software applications that act as sources for reference materials, such as the standard atlases, dictionaries, and thesauri, are referred to collectively as **reference software**.

EDUCATIONAL SOFTWARE

What kinds of educational software applications are there? Although there is a multitude of educational software products geared to the younger set, software developers have by no means ignored adult markets. In addition to all the products relating to the younger audience, there are software products that teach users new skills such as typing, languages, cooking, or playing the guitar. Test preparation software is popular for students taking the SAT, GMAT, LSAT, or MCAT exams.

Is there software to train you to use special machines? There are plenty of programs with tutorial-like training for many popular computer software applications. These programs use illustrated step-by-step instructions to guide the user through unfamiliar skills. Some training programs use simulation techniques where the learning is done in a realistic environment. Such simulation training programs include commercial and military flight training, surgical instrument training, and machine operation training.

A benefit of these simulated training programs is they safely allow users to experience potentially dangerous situations. Consequently, users of these training programs are more likely to take risks and learn from their mistakes—something they could not afford to do in real-life situations. Remember the doctors who used simulated patients in Chapter 1? Simulated training programs save costly errors. Should something go awry, the cost of the error is only restarting the simulation program as opposed to the high costs of a real-life error.

Do I need special software to take courses online? Taking classes over the Internet is fast becoming a popular method of learning because it offers greater schedule flexibility for busy students. Although some courses are run from an individually developed Web site, many online courses are run through **course management software** programs such as Blackboard and WebCT (see Figure 4.21). These programs provide traditional classroom tools such as calendars and grade books over the Internet. There are also special areas for students to exchange ideas and information in chat rooms, discussion forums, and e-mail messages. Of course, there are areas where assignments, lectures, and other pertinent information to the class can be posted.

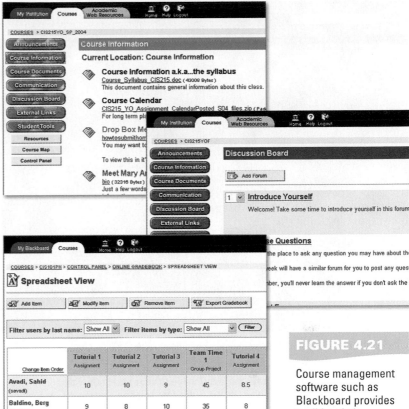

REFERENCE SOFTWARE

How can I use software to research information? Encyclopedias are no longer those massive sets of books in the library. Now you can find full sets of encyclopedias on small CD-ROMs. In addition to containing all the information found in traditional paper encyclopedias, electronic encyclopedias include multimedia content such as interactive maps, video, and audio clips. When researching famous sports figures, for example, you not only can read about Jackie

FIGURE 4.21

Course management software such as Blackboard provides traditional classroom features such as important classroom document (syllabus, calendar), classroom discussions, and a grade book in an online environment.

BITS AND BYTES

What Is "Edutainment"?

Many educational programs for children disguise the learning process by combining it with interactive puzzles, games, and other fun activities. Because it combines education and entertainment, this software is referred to as *edutainment*. Often these programs include a theme or story that is carried throughout the program, and learners are rewarded with prizes when they've correctly answered questions. Edutainment software is most popular with preschool and early elementary-aged students, but adult edutainment programs exist to assist older learners in mastering certain skills such as typing or English as a second language.

Jackie Robinson Leads the Way

Jackie Robinson broke major league baseball's color barrier in 1947.

FIGURE 4.22

Encyclopedias on CD, such as Encarta, bring life to your research with videos and audio clips. While you read about Jackie Robinson, you can also watch of video of him in an actual game and hear the words of the game announcer.

Robinson, but also can view a video of Robinson in play (see Figure 4.22).

What other types of reference software are there? As with all other categories of software, reference software is a growing field. In addition to the traditional atlases, dictionaries, and thesauri available on CD, many other types of reference software are available. Medical and legal reference software is available for basic information you would have previously had to pay a professional to obtain. For example, medical references such as *Franklin Physicians' Desk Reference* enable you to access information on Food and

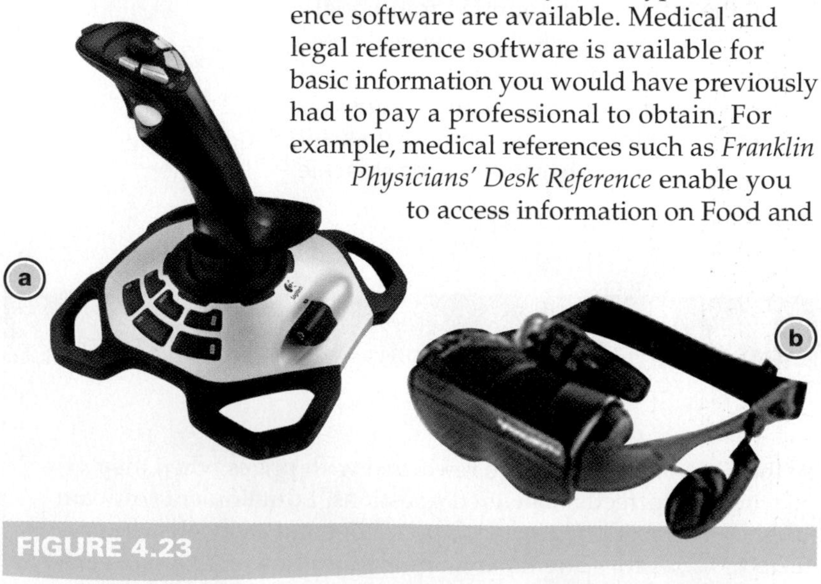

FIGURE 4.23

(a) You need a joystick to play some computer games. (b) Virtual reality games require special equipment such as goggles to deliver the three-dimensional effects.

Drug Administration (FDA)–approved drugs, whereas legal software packages such as Family Lawyer provide standard legal forms.

Entertainment Software

Entertainment software is, as its name implies, designed to provide users with entertainment. Computer games make up the vast majority of entertainment software. These digital games began with Pong, Pacman, and Donkey Kong and have evolved to include many different categories, including action, adventure, driving, puzzle, role-playing, card-playing, sports, strategy, and simulation. Entertainment software also includes other types of computer applications, such as **virtual reality programs**, which turn an artificial environment into a realistic experience.

Do I need special equipment to run entertainment software? As with any computer software, you need to make sure your system has enough resources such as random access memory (RAM) and hard disk capacity to run the program. Because entertainment programs generally incorporate many sophisticated multimedia features, you need to ensure your system has the appropriate sound cards, video cards, speakers, monitor, and CD or DVD drives as well.

Some software may require a joystick to play the game. Virtual reality programs also require specialized equipment such as goggles or gloves, so you can't run these programs on just any machine (see Figure 4.23).

COMPUTER GAMES

How do I tell what computer games are appropriate for a certain user? The Entertainment Software Rating Board (ESRB) established a rating system in 1994 that suggests an age-appropriate rating for computer and video entertainment (see **www.esrb.org**). Since that time, more than 8,000 game titles have been given an ESRB rating. Figure 4.24 shows these ratings and symbols.

You can find the rating symbols on the front lower-right or left corner of the software package. In addition to the rating label, a content descriptor located on the back of the box describes particular game elements that may be of interest or concern. The ESRB also provides rating information for online games. Many Web sites display the ESRB rating; the descriptors appear as ScreenTips when you place your cursor on the rating symbol.

Can I make my own video games? Creating video games is catching on as a new career opportunity for video game enthusiasts. Professionally created video games involve some careful programming and use fairly sophisticated software applications that are not recommended for the casual home enthusiast. However, if you should want to try your hand at creating your own video games, multimedia software applications such as Macromedia Flash RPG Maker will certainly provide you with enough tools to create games for your personal entertainment.

MP3 PROGRAMS

What can I do with MP3 files? MP3 is the audio compression format that lets you store and play music on computers and distribute it swiftly and easily over the Internet. Hundreds of software applications are available to allow you to copy (or rip), play, edit, and organize MP3 files, as well as to record and distribute your own music online. Most MP3 programs fall into one of the following categories:

- **MP3 recording software**: MP3 recording software allows you to record directly from streaming audio and other software or microphone sources to MP3 format.

- **Ripping software**: Ripping software allows you to convert CDs to MP3 format.

- **MP3 burners**: Burning software allows you to record MP3 files onto a CD.

- **Encoding and decoding/format conversion**: Encoders are programs that convert files to MP3 format at varying levels of quality. Decoding/format conversion programs allow you to convert MP3 files to another audio format such as WAV, Windows Media Audio (WMA), or AIFF.

Can I modify or edit my MP3 files? Audio-editing software includes tools that make editing your MP3 files as easy as editing your text files. Such software enables you to do some basic editing such as cutting dead-air space from the beginning or end of the song

ENTERTAINMENT SOFTWARE RATING BOARD
Rating Symbols

FIGURE 4.24

ESRB ratings can be found on most game software and on the homepages of many online games and Web sites to indicate the age-appropriate content.

or cutting a portion out in the middle. You can also add special sound effects or smooth abrupt starts and finishes on your MP3 files.

How can I manage all the MP3 files on my hard drive? Software such as MP3 File Editor allows you to organize your MP3 and other audio files so that you can sort, filter, and search your collection by artist, album, or category. Using these programs, you can manage individual tracks, generate play lists, and even export the files to a database or spreadsheet application for further manipulation.

Communications Software

The advent of the computer and other technologies has broadened our ability to communicate with each other beyond the standard phone call and written letter. Today, we have other means of communications available that combine computer hardware and software. For example, e-mail and instant messaging, which are discussed in Chapter 3, are fast replacing more traditional means of communications. **Groupware**, software that helps people who are in different locations work together using e-mail and online scheduling tools, is fast becoming a popular means for communication. For example, software that supports the distribution of files over networks, such as File Transfer Protocol (FTP) and Usenet, are members of the groupware software family.

TRENDS IN IT

Emerging Technologies: Is It Real or Is It Virtual?

The applications of virtual reality, beyond familiar video games, are almost endless. Three-dimensional environments created by computers are getting better and better at helping people experience new things, or experience familiar things in new ways.

Overcoming fear is another growing application. Dentists, for instance, are trying virtual reality headsets for their patients to help them reduce anxiety about getting their teeth cared for. And fear of flying can be treated with virtual reality therapy. Gradual exposure to takeoff and landing in a virtual environment allows would-be travelers to face their phobias and prepare to take the next step into a real flight. Fear of heights, spiders, thunderstorms, and even public speaking (which is many people's greatest fear) have been treated with virtual reality therapy.

Other medical applications include the opportunity for people with disabilities to practice maneuvering wheelchairs or to become familiar with public transportation before venturing into a new city or town. Surgeons can practice difficult procedures on a virtual patient without risk. And therapy for burn patients that incorporates virtual reality seems to ease pain more when used with medication than does medication alone (see Figure 4.25). While being treated, patients wear virtual reality goggles and immerse themselves in a world apart from their pain. Psychologists say that patients are so absorbed in the virtual reality experience that they are not as aware of their pain.

You won't lose any weight or get in shape in a virtual gym. But you can get instant coaching feedback and see a visual replay of your performance. And you can do it without getting hurt, which is a big advantage for coaches in risky sports such

as football and skiing. Swiss Olympic skier Simon Ammann used a virtual reality program to compare his jumps wearing two different pairs of skis to determine which was best. He and his coach believe the change in skis that resulted from the experiment was a factor in his gold-medal performance at the 2002 Winter Olympics.

Of course, if you'd rather travel, you can always use the virtual reality program created at UCLA to explore the world of ancient Rome in A.D. 400, through simulations of 22 temples, courts, and monuments. The ancient cityscape is loaded into a supercomputer with a special spherical screen that fills the viewer's field of vision. You can not only see the monuments, but you can also move around them and even levitate for a closer look. See you there!

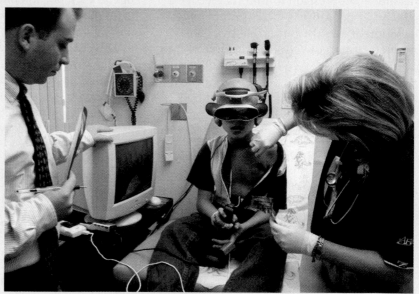

FIGURE 4.25

Burn patients who incorporate virtual reality into their therapy sometimes experience less pain.

What other kinds of group communications software exist? To enhance long-distance group communications, businesses often utilize videoconferencing technologies. **Videoconferencing** involves the transmission of audio (voice) and video (picture) data over computer networks. Videoconferencing systems can be quite complex or as simple as a computer setup enhanced with a camera on top of a monitor, microphone, and speakers (see Figure 4.26). Improvements in videoconferencing technology have made this form of communication much more efficient and effective than it was when it was first introduced.

Do I need special software to have phone conversations over the Internet? Telephony technology, often

Businesses that have offices in diverse geographical locations use videoconferencing software to hold meetings.

referred to as Voice over Internet Protocol (VoIP), is the transmission of telephone calls over the Internet. VoIP can take place between two computers, between a computer and a phone with an adapter, or between two phones with adapters. If you are not using phones to make your phone calls, your computer system needs a microphone and speakers. In any case, the data from the phone call is sent over the Internet, so you'll need an Internet connection as well as a software client, a small software application that is provided by the VoIP provider to run on its server.

How do I make a phone call with VoIP? Depending on the service, there are two ways to make a phone call with VoIP. One is to use a traditional telephone and an adapter that connects to your cable/Digital Subscriber Line (DSL) broadband connection. The other is to use a microphone headset that is plugged into your computer. You dial the phone number using the number pad on your keyboard, and the call is then routed through the Internet connection. Either way, once dialed, the call goes through your local telephone company to a VoIP provider, over the Internet to the called party's local telephone company, and finally to the party you wish to speak to.

Getting Help with Software

If you need help while you work with software, there are several different resources you can access to find answers to your questions. For general help or information about the product, many Web sites offer **frequently asked questions (FAQs)** for answers to the most common questions.

Some programs also offer online help and support. Sometimes, online help is comparable to a user's manual. However, many times, online help also allows you to chat (using the Internet) with a member of an online support team. Some applications are context-sensitive and offer help based on what task you're doing or ScreenTips to explain where your cursor is resting.

In Microsoft Office applications, on the far right of the menu bar, you'll find the Ask a Question box in which you can type your question. The Office Assistant, generally an animated paper clip (also known as Clippy; see Figure 4.27, p. 148), automatically provides tips on tasks while you're working or answers your specific questions.

Finally, there is the Help menu on the menu bar where you can choose to search an index or content outline or activate

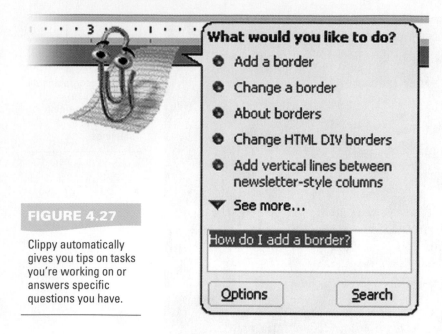

Clippy automatically gives you tips on tasks you're working on or answers specific questions you have.

the What's This? Help feature to find out the nature of almost any feature of a Microsoft application.

Where do I go for tutorials and training on an application? If you need help learning how to use a product, sometimes the product's developer offers online tutorials or program tours that show you how to use the software features. Often, you can find good tutorials simply by searching the Internet. **PCShowandTell.com**, for example, includes more than 40,000 multimedia help files and is accessible for a small annual fee. **Webnests.com**, an online company dedicated to online hosting products, offers free tutorials for many software applications.

BITS AND BYTES

The Microsoft Knowledge Base

If your problem is more technical, such as a problem in the software or an error message, you can check the Microsoft Knowledge Base, a collection of more than 250,000 articles written by Microsoft support professionals reflecting their resolution of customer issues and problems. The Knowledge Base, located at **support.microsoft.com**, is a terrific online resource for resolving problems with Microsoft products. The problem is that the Knowledge Base has grown so big that it can be difficult to search effectively. Therefore, to get the most from the Knowledge Base, use a high-quality search engine such as Google to search it for you. To do so, go to Google (**www.google.com**) and select the Advanced Search option. Type in your search terms but specify *support.microsoft.com* as the domain to be searched.

Buying Software

These days, you no longer need to go to a computer supply store to buy software. You can find software in almost any retail environment. Additionally, you can purchase software in nontraditional ways such as online, through catalogs, or at auctions.

STANDARD SOFTWARE

What application software comes with my computer? Virtually every new computer comes with some form of application software, though the applications depend on the hardware manufacturer and computer model. You can usually count on your computer having some form of productivity software preinstalled. Lower-end computer models generally offer an integrated application such as Microsoft Works, whereas higher-end models offer a productivity suite such as Microsoft Office.

Multimedia-enriched computers may also offer graphics software or a productivity suite that includes Web page authoring software. Most computers will have some form of PIM software, such as Outlook or Outlook Express for e-mail management as well as some form of financial planning software.

If you know you'll need a particular type of software not offered as standard on your new computer, you may want to see if the computer manufacturer has an offer to add that particular software. Sometimes, initially buying software through the hardware manufacturer is less expensive than buying software on the retail market.

DISCOUNTED SOFTWARE

Is it possible to buy software at a discount? Software manufactures understand that students and educators often need to use software for a short period of time because of a specific class or project. Additionally, software developers want to encourage you to learn with their product, hoping you'll become a long-term user of their software. Therefore, if you're a student or an educator, you can purchase software that is no different from regularly priced software at prices that are sometimes substantially less than general consumer prices. (Figure 4.11 shows what applications are included in the academic versions of productivity software suites.)

Sometimes, campus computer stores or college bookstores also offer discounted prices to students and faculty who possess a valid ID. Online software suppliers such as **JourneyEd.com**, **Edtech-cps.com**, and **AcademicSuperstore.com** also offer the same software applications available in the store to students at reduced prices. You can also find software through mail-order companies. Check out **Catalogs.Google.com** for an extensive listing of companies that offer software by mail order.

Can I buy used software? Often, you can buy software through online auction sites such as eBay. If you do so, you need to ensure you are buying licensed (legal) copies. Computer shows that display state-of-the-art computer equipment are generally good sources for software. However, here, too, you must exert a bit of caution to ensure you are buying licensed copies and not pirated versions.

Can I buy software directly from the Internet? You can also buy software on the Internet that is custom developed to your specific needs. Companies such as First Internet Software House (**www.fishouse.com**) act as intermediaries between you, the software user, and a software developer. With custom-developed software, the developer tweaks open-source software code to meet your particular needs.

Microsoft, through its .NET program, offers software over the Internet for *all* devices—not just computers—that have a connection to the Internet. Therefore, you can download software specifically for your PDA or wireless phone by using .NET. Additionally, if you have a Microsoft .NET account (available free of charge at the Microsoft Web site), you can connect to any other .NET-connected device.

FREEWARE AND SHAREWARE

Can I get software for free legally?
Freeware is any copyrighted software that you can use for free. Plenty of freeware exists on the Web, ranging from games and screen savers to business, educational, graphics, home and hobby, and system

utility software programs. To find freeware, simply type *freeware* in your search engine. One good source of freeware offering a large variety of programs is **FreewareHome.com**.

Although they do not charge a fee, some developers release free software and request that you mail them a postcard or send them an e-mail message to thank them for their time in developing the software and to give them your opinion of it. Such programs are called *postcardware* and *e-mailware*, respectively.

Can I try out new software before it is really released? In addition to freeware, some software developers offer **beta versions** of their software free of charge. Beta versions are still under development. By distributing free beta versions, developers hope to have users report errors or bugs they find in the program. This helps the developers correct any errors before they launch the software on the market at retail prices.

Is it still freeware if I'm asked to pay for the program after using it for a while? Software that allows users to test software (run it for a limited time free of charge) is referred to as **shareware**. Shareware is not freeware. If you use the software after the initial trial period is over, you will be breaking the software license agreement.

Software developers put out shareware programs to get their products into users' hands without the added expense and hassle of marketing and advertising. Therefore, quite a few great programs are available as shareware that can compete handily with programs on retail shelves. For example, **TechSmith.com** offers screen capture and desktop recording software applications such as SnagIt and Camtasia as shareware. You can try these products for free for a 30-day period. For a listing of other shareware programs, visit **Download.com** or **Shareware.com**.

Can shareware programmers make me pay for the shareware once I have it? The whole concept of shareware assumes users will behave ethically and abide by the license agreement. However, to protect themselves, many developers have incorporated code into the program to stop it from working completely, or to alter the output slightly, after the 30-day trial period expires. On WinZip programs a reminder that the product is not free appears on the screen, like the one shown in Figure 4.28. With CorelDRAW, for example, once the trial period is over, you cannot open the program.

Are there risks associated with installing beta versions, freeware, and shareware? Not all files available as shareware and freeware will work on your computer. You can easily crash your system and may even need to reinstall your operating system as a result of loading a freeware or shareware program that was not written for your computer's operating system.

Of course, by their very nature, beta products are most likely not bug free, so you always run the risk of something going awry with your system. Unless you're willing to deal with potential problems, it may be best to wait until the last beta version is released. By that time, most of the serious bugs have been worked out. As a matter of precaution, you should be comfortable with the reliability of the software developer before downloading a freeware, shareware, or beta version of software. If it's a reliable developer whose software you are already familiar with, you can be more certain that a virus is not hiding in the software. However, downloading software from an unknown source could potentially put your system at risk for contracting a virus. (We discuss viruses in detail in Chapter 7. A good practice

to establish before installing any software on your system is to use the operating system's Restore feature and create a *restore point*. That way, if anything goes wrong during installation, you can always restore your system back to how it was before you started. (We discuss the System Restore utility in Chapter 5.) Also, make sure that your virus protection software is up-to-date.

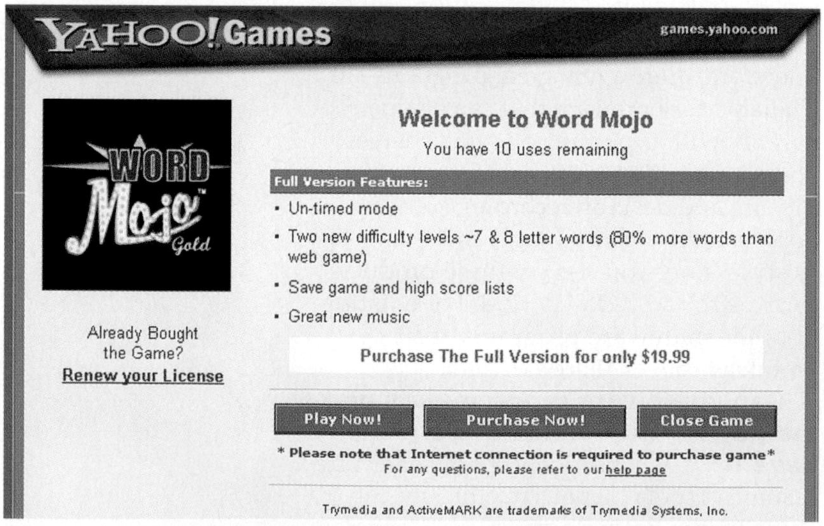

SOFTWARE VERSIONS AND SYSTEMS REQUIREMENTS

What do the numbers after software names indicate? Software developers sometimes change their software programs to repair problems (or bugs) or to add new or upgraded features. Generally, they keep the software program's name but add a number to it to indicate it is a different version. Originally, developers used numbers only to indicate different software versions (major upgrades) and releases (minor upgrades). Today, however, software developers also use years (such as Office 2003) and letters (Windows XP) to represent a version upgrade.

When is it worth it to buy a newer version? Although software developers suggest otherwise, there is no need to rush out and buy the latest version of a software program every time one is released. Depending on the software, some upgrades are not significantly different from the previous version to make it cost-effective for you to buy the new version. Unless the upgrade adds features that are important to you, you may be better off waiting to upgrade every other release. You should also consider how often you use the software to justify an upgrade, and whether your current system can handle the new system requirements of the upgraded version.

If I have an older version of software and someone sends me files from a newer version, can I still open them? Software vendors recognize that people work on different versions of the same software. Vendors therefore make the newest version backward compatible, meaning it can recognize (open) files created with older versions. However, many software programs are not forward compatible, meaning that older versions cannot recognize files created on newer versions.

FIGURE 4.28

Many software programs, such as some online games, are available as evaluation versions. With screens such as the one shown, they gently remind you that the product is not free by offering a limited number of trial uses and provide you with easy options for paying and legally registering the product.

How do I know whether the software I buy will work on my computer? Every software program has a set of **system requirements** that specify the minimum recommended standards for the operating system, processor, primary memory (RAM), and hard drive capacity. Sometimes there are other specifications for the video card, monitor, CD drive, and other peripherals. These requirements are generally printed on the software packaging or at the publisher's Web site. Before installing software on your computer, ensure your system setup meets the minimum requirements by having sufficient storage, memory capacity, and processing capabilities.

Installing/Uninstalling and Opening Software

Before you use your software, you must permanently place it, or install it, on your system. The installation process is slightly different depending on whether you've purchased the software from a retail outlet and have an installation CD or whether you are downloading it from the Internet. And deleting, or uninstalling, software from your system requires certain precautions to ensure you remove all associated programs from your system.

How do I install software? When you purchase software today, you insert the CD that contains the program files, and for most programs, an installation wizard automatically opens, as shown in Figure 4.29. By simply following the steps indicated by the wizard, you can install the software application on your system. If for some reason the wizard doesn't open automatically, the best way to install the software is to go to the Add/Remove Programs icon located in Control Panel on the Start menu. This feature locates and launches an installation wizard.

How is the installation process different for software I download off the Web? Obviously, when you download software from the Internet, you do not get an installation CD. Instead, everything you need to install and run the downloaded program is contained in one file that has been compressed (or zipped) to make the downloading process quicker. For the most part,

these downloaded files unzip themselves and automatically start or *launch* the setup program. During the installation and setup process, these programs select or create the folder on your computer's hard drive in which most of the program files will be

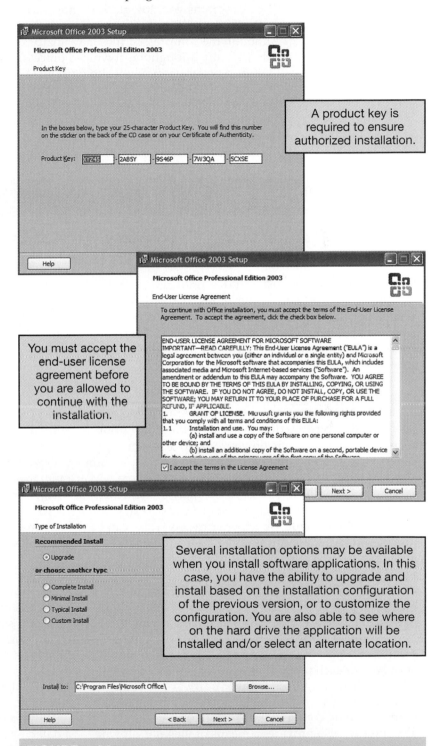

A product key is required to ensure authorized installation.

You must accept the end-user license agreement before you are allowed to continue with the installation.

Several installation options may be available when you install software applications. In this case, you have the ability to upgrade and install based on the installation configuration of the previous version, or to customize the configuration. You are also able to see where on the hard drive the application will be installed and/or select an alternate location.

FIGURE 4.29

Installation wizards guide you through the installation process and generally appear automatically when you install new software.

saved. You can also usually select a different location if you desire. Either way, note the name and location of the files, because you may need to access them later.

What do I do if the downloaded program doesn't install by itself? Some programs you download do not automatically install and run on your computer. Although the compressed files may unzip automatically through the download process, the setup program may not run without some help from you. In this case, you need to locate the files on the hard drive (this is why you must remember the location of the files) and find the *Setup.exe* program. (Files

ending with the .exe extension are executable files or applications. All other files in the folder are support, help, and data files.) Once the setup program begins, you will be prompted with the necessary actions to complete the installation.

What's the difference between a custom installation and a full installation? One of the first steps in the installation wizard is deciding between a full installation and a custom installation. A **full installation** will copy all the files and programs from the distribution CD to the computer's hard drive. By selecting **custom installation**, you can decide which features

TRENDS IN IT

Ethics: Can I Borrow Software That I Don't Own?

Most people don't understand that unlike other items they purchase, software applications they buy don't belong to them. The only thing they're actually purchasing is a license that gives them the right to use the software for their own purposes as the *only* user of that copy. The application is not theirs to lend or copy for installation on other computers, even if it's another one of their own.

Software licenses are agreements between you, the user, and the software developer that you accept prior to installing the software on your machine. It is a legal contract that outlines the acceptable uses of the program and any actions that violate the agreement. Generally, the agreement will state who the ultimate owner of the software is, under what circumstances copies of the software can be made, or whether the software can be installed on any other machine. Finally, the license agreements will state what, if any, warranty comes with the software.

A computer user who copies an application onto more than one computer, if the license agreement does not permit this, is participating in **software piracy**. Historically, the most common way software has been pirated among computer users has been when they supplement each other's software library by borrowing CDs and installing the borrowed software on their own computers. Larger-scale illegal duplication and distribution by counterfeiters is also quite common. The Internet also provides a means of illegally copying and distributing pirated software.

Is it really a big deal to copy a program or two? As reported by the Business Software Alliance, 40 percent of all software is pirated. Not only is pirating software

unethical and illegal, the practice also has financial impacts on all software application consumers. The reduced dollars from pirated software lessen the amount of money available for further software research and development while increasing the up-front cost to legitimate consumers.

To tell if you have a pirated copy of software installed on your computer at work or at home, you can download a free copy of GASP (a suite of programs designed to help identify and track licensed and unlicensed software and other files) from the Business Software Alliance Web site (**www.bsa.org/usa/freetools**). There is a similar program available at the Microsoft Web site (**www.microsoft .com/piracy/**). These programs check the serial numbers for the software installed on your computer against software manufacturer databases of official licensed copies and known fraudulent copies. Any suspicious software installations are flagged for your attention.

As of yet, there's no such thing as an official software police, but software piracy is so rampant that the U.S. government is taking steps to stop piracy worldwide. Efforts to stop groups that reproduce, modify, and distribute counterfeit software over the Internet are in full force. Software manufacturers also are becoming more aggressive in programming mechanisms into software to prevent repeated installations. For instance, with the launch of Microsoft Office 2003, installation requires the registration of the serial number of your software with a database maintained at Microsoft. Failure to register your serial number in this database or attempting to register a serial number that has been used previously results in the software failing to operate after the 50th time you use it.

you want installed on the hard drive. By doing so, you can save space on your hard drive, installing only those features you know you want.

Can I just delete a program to uninstall it? A software application contains many different files such as library files, help files, and other text files in addition to the main file you use to run the program. By just deleting the main file, you are not ridding your system of all the other ancillary programs. Although this is not harmful to your system, you end up with a lot of useless clutter on your hard drive.

Sometimes, programs have an Uninstall Program icon in the main program file. Using this icon will clear out most of the associated programs as well as the main program. If you can't locate the uninstall program for your particular software application, you can go to the Add/Remove Software icon in Control Panel on the Start menu. This feature will give you a list of software applications installed on your system, from which you choose the software application you would like to delete.

Is there a best way to open an application? The simplest way to open an application is by clicking its icon on the Start menu. Every program that you install on your system is listed on the Start menu. However, if you find you use only a few

BITS AND BYTES

Keeping Your Software Up-to-Date

Bugs in software occur all the time. Software developers are constantly testing their product, even after releasing the software to the retail market, and users report errors they find. In today's environment where security is a large concern, companies test their products for vulnerabilities against hackers and other malicious users. Once a fix or patch to a bug or vulnerability is created, most software developers will put the repair in downloadable form on the Internet, available at no charge. You should check periodically for any software updates or service packs to ensure your software is up-to-date.

programs most often, you can place a shortcut to that program either on the QuickLaunch toolbar on the taskbar or on your desktop. To place a program in the QuickLaunch toolbar on the taskbar, simply open the QuickLaunch toolbar (right-click the taskbar and select QuickLaunch), then drag the selected program from the Start menu to the QuickLaunch toolbar (see Figure 4.30a).

To create a shortcut on the desktop, simply right-click the icon of the desired program and select Create Shortcut (see Figure 4.30b). You can identify a shortcut icon by the little black arrow in the lower-left corner of the icon.

FIGURE 4.30

To quickly access an application you use often, you can place a shortcut in (a) the QuickLaunch toolbar or (b) on your desktop.

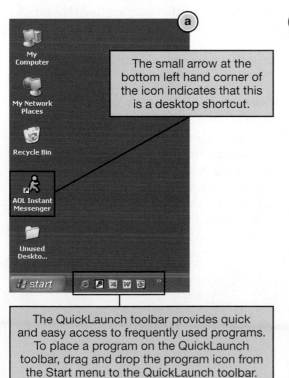

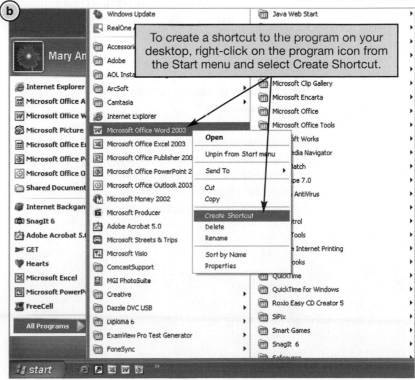

Summary

1. What's the difference between application software and system software?

System software is the software that helps run the computer and coordinates instructions between application software and the computer's hardware devices. System software includes the operating system and utility programs. Application software is the software you use to do everyday tasks at home, school, and work. Application software includes productivity, financial and business, graphics and multimedia, educational and reference, entertainment, and communications software programs.

2. What kinds of applications are included in productivity software?

Productivity software programs include word processing, spreadsheet, presentation, personal information manager (PIM), and database programs. You use word processing software to create and edit written documents. Spreadsheet software enables you to do calculations and numerical and what-if analyses easily. Presentation software enables you to create slide presentations. Personal information management (PIM) software helps keep you organized by putting a calendar, address book, notepad, and to-do lists within your computer. Database programs are electronic filing systems that allow you to filter, sort, and retrieve data easily.

3. What kinds of software do businesses use?

Many businesses, across a variety of industries, use general business software, such as Business Plan Pro and Marketing Plan Pro, to help them with tasks common to most businesses. In addition, businesses may use specialized business software that is designed for their specific industry. Individuals can also use software to help with business-like tasks such as preparing taxes or managing personal finances. These programs are called personal financial software programs.

4. What are the different kinds of graphics and multimedia software?

Graphics software encompasses a wide range of programs used to design and create attractive documents, images, illustrations, Web pages, and three-dimensional models and drawings. Graphics software is a part of a larger group of software called multimedia software. Multimedia software includes video and audio editing software, animation software, and other special software required to produce computer games.

5. What is educational and reference software?

Educational software refers to the variety of software applications on the market that offer some form of instruction or training. This ranges from simple tutorials to online course programs to complex simulation training programs. Software applications that act as sources for reference materials, such as the standard atlases, dictionaries, and thesauri, are referred to collectively as reference software. A lot of reference software on the market incorporates complex multimedia.

6. What are the different types of entertainment software?

Beyond the games that most of us are familiar with, entertainment software includes virtual reality programs that use special equipment to make users feel as though they are actually experiencing the program in a realistic 3-D environment. In addition, a wide variety of software programs are used to play, copy, record, edit, and organize MP3 files.

7. What kinds of software are available for communications?

E-mail and IM are two popular forms of electronic communications. Groupware, software that helps people who are in different locations work together, is also becoming popular. In addition, businesses use communications software such as telephony programs to add phone capabilities to computer systems and videoconferencing software to enable people to meet without being physically present in the same room.

8. Where can I go for help when I have a problem with my software?

Most software programs have a Help menu built into the program with which you can search through an index or subject directory to find answers. Some programs group those most commonly asked questions in a single frequently asked questions (FAQ) document. Additionally, there are vast resources of free or fee-based help and training available on the Internet or at booksellers.

9. How can I purchase software or get it for free?

Almost every new computer system comes with some form of software to help you accomplish basic tasks. All other software you need to purchase unless it is freeware, which you can download from the Internet for free. You can also find special software called shareware that lets you run it free of charge for a test period. Although you can find software in almost any store, as a student you can purchase the same software at a reduced price with an academic discount.

10. How do I install and uninstall software?

When installing and uninstalling software, it's best to use the specific Add/Remove Program feature that comes with the operating system. Most programs are installed using an installation wizard that steps you through the installation. Other software programs may require you to activate the setup program, which will begin the installation wizard. Using the Add/Remove Programs feature when uninstalling a program will help you ensure that all ancillary program files are removed from your computer.

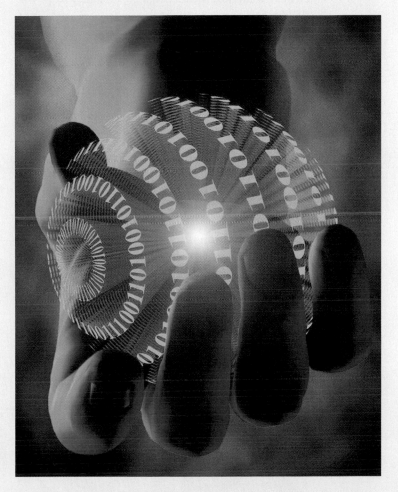

Key Terms

Buzz Words

Word Bank

- productivity software
- worksheet
- wizards
- system software
- application software
- field
- integrated software
- templates
- software suite
- word processing

- personal information management (PIM) software
- database
- applications
- speech-recognition software
- help
- utility program
- software piracy

- image-editing software
- illustration software
- virtual reality
- presentation software
- shareware
- system requirements
- spreadsheet
- freeware
- beta versions

Instructions: Fill in the blanks using the words from the Word Bank.

Roxanne is happy. Her aunt is upgrading to a newer computer and is giving Roxanne her old one. Roxanne has just enrolled in college and knows she's going to need at least a (1)_____ program to help her write papers and a (2)_____ program to help her keep track of expenses while at school. Because both these software applications are part of a larger group of applications called (3)_____, she knows she can buy them as a group. She's been told that it's cheaper to buy them as a(n) (4)_____ than to buy them individually. Because she knows she'll need the full versions, she cannot buy a(n) (5)_____ program.

Because she's not a great typist, Roxanne is interested in (6)_____ that will convert her dictated words into typed text. As a graduation present, Roxanne received a new digital camera. She needs to install the (7)_____ that came with her camera to edit and manage her digital pictures. Although she's used the software a couple of times on her parents' computer, she is still glad for the (8)_____ feature to assist her with specific feature questions and the (9)_____ that provide step-by-step guides to help her do things.

Roxanne especially likes the decorative preformatted (10)_____ she can use to insert pictures and make them seem professional. She also knows of some (11)_____ games she can download without cost from the Internet and other (12)_____ programs that she could try but eventually pay for. There are actually so many (13)_____ programs she'd like to install, she doesn't know what to pick first. It's tempting for her to borrow software from her friends, but she knows that it's considered (14)_____. She also knows before installing any of the programs she must check the (15)_____ to see if the software is compatible with her system as well as whether the system has enough resources to support the software.

Organizing Key Terms

Instructions: *This chapter introduces many new terms and concepts. In the following illustration, fill in each of the blanks with key terms or concepts from the chapter in order to show how categories of ideas fit together.*

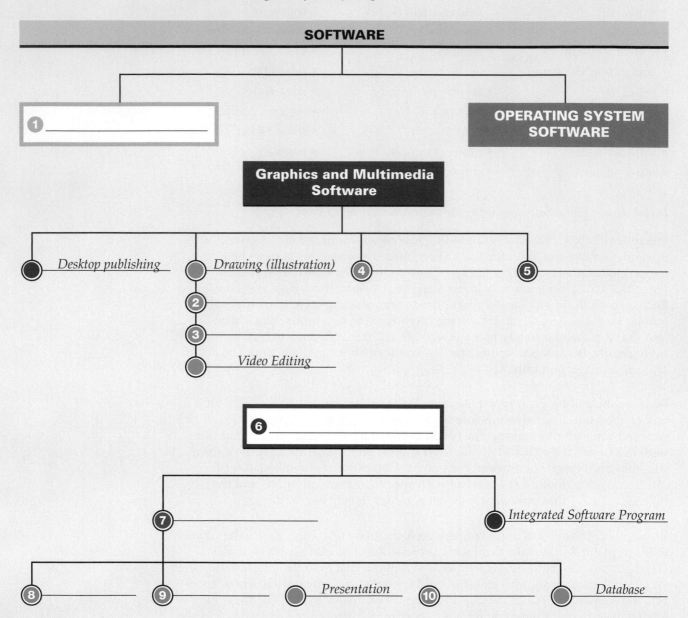

SOFTWARE

1. _____

OPERATING SYSTEM SOFTWARE

Graphics and Multimedia Software

- *Desktop publishing*
- *Drawing (illustration)*
  2. _____
  3. _____
- *Video Editing*
- 4. _____
- 5. _____

6. _____

7. _____

Integrated Software Program

8. _____
9. _____
- *Presentation*
10. _____
- *Database*

Making the Transition to . . . Next Semester

1. Software Training

You are most likely familiar with many software applications. Undoubtedly, you will use many more applications before your course work is done. Make two lists. In one list, itemize by category the software applications you are already familiar with. In the other list, identify at least three other software applications you think you may need, or would want to try, in the future. Research the types of on-campus or online training or help features that may be offered for those programs you have on your second list.

2. Installing Software

You have just spent $285 on a software package. You have a desktop you use at home and a laptop you use only at work.

a. Are you allowed to install the software on both computers? Should you be allowed to do that?

b. What if you wanted to install the software on two computers that you own and use exclusively at home?

c. Can you install the software on two computers if you use only one computer at a time?

d. Could you install the software package on your computer and also on a friend's computer if she is interested in buying her own copy but wanted to test it first?

3. Removing Software

You are trying to decide if you want to remove some software that you used this past semester from your system. How do the following items weigh into your decision to remove the software or to leave it on your system:

a. The amount of hard disk space available

b. How frequently you use the software

c. Licensing agreements

d. The amount of RAM installed on the system

4. More Than One Application?

Can you think of a situation that would make it useful for you to have multiple software applications for the same type of work? For example, two word processor packages or two tax software applications? What would the advantages and disadvantages be?

5. Choosing the Best Software

This past semester you spent a lot of time doodling and created a comic strip character that all your friends love. You've decided to start releasing a small newsletter, including some articles and a few comics each week. Which software applications would be the best fit for the following tasks:

a. Designing and laying out the newsletter

b. Creating the text articles

c. Creating the comic strip

After the first five issues it is clearly a smash, and you decide to expand it into a *zine*, an Internet-delivered magazine. Now which software applications are important to you for the same tasks?

Making the Transition to . . . The Workplace

1. Software Training Needs

When applying for a new position, whether in your current company or in a different one, it's always good to indicate your experience with products or processes you will be required to use on the job. Research the types of software applications you will be required to use in your next position or in the job you'd like to have. Do you have any experience with these applications? If not, what kinds of training can you seek to familiarize yourself quickly with these applications? Are there resources within the company you can take advantage of, training manuals you can read, or courses you can take?

2. Integrating Applications

Some software applications work well together and some do not. Certainly, all of the applications within a given suite such as Microsoft Office are well integrated. Give an example of a business office need that would benefit from the following:

a. Integrating Excel with Word
b. Integrating Access with Excel
c. Integrating Access with Word

3. Choosing the Best Software for the Job

For each of the following positions, describe the set of software applications you would expect to encounter if you were

a. A photographer opening a new business to sell your own photography
b. An administrative assistant to a college president
c. A graphic designer at a large publishing house
d. A director in charge of publicity for a new summer camp for children
e. A presenter to elementary students discussing your year living abroad
f. A Web page designer for a small not-for-profit organization
g. A construction site manager
h. A person in the career you are pursuing

Critical Thinking Questions

Instructions: Albert Einstein used "Gedanken experiments," or critical thinking questions, to develop his theory of relativity. Some ideas are best understood by experimenting with them in our own minds. The following critical thinking questions are designed to demand your full attention but require only a comfortable chair—no technology.

1. Software Ethics

The cost of new software applications can be prohibitively high. You need to do a project for school that requires the use of a software application you don't own, but your roommate has a copy that her dad gave her from his work. She is letting you install it on your machine.

a. Is it okay for you to borrow this software?

b. Would your answer to the preceding question be different if you uninstalled the application after you were finished using it?

c. Would the answer to the preceding question be different if the software was on the school's network and you could copy it from there?

2. Software Ethics 2

Currently, there is no true system to check for illegal installations of software programs. What kind of program/system do you think could be developed to do this type of checking? Who would pay to develop, run, and maintain the program: the developers or the software users?

3. Categories of Software

This chapter has organized the many software applications into a variety of categories. Which category (or categories) of software do you feel has the need for a new, breakthrough product? What needs are there in your work or hobbies that existing software applications do not yet address?

4. The Pros and Cons of Software

Over the past 10 years many tasks have moved from professional, expensive environments to home desktops. Image editing and video editing were once available only to expensive professional studios but now can be done at home. Résumés were once taken to professional typesetters, but popular word processors can now do the work at home. What are the positive and negative impacts of this pattern for consumers? Does it offer consumers more power, opportunity, and control, or impose more pressures to purchase software and learn new skills?

5. Software for the Hearing and Visually Impaired

The World Wide Web Consortium (W3C) currently has an initiative to ensure that all Web pages are accessible to everyone, including those with visual and hearing impairments. Currently, software such as the freeware program Bobby (**bobby.watchfire.com**) can test Web pages to determine whether alternatives to auditory and visual Web content is available, such as closed captioning for auditory files and auditory files for visual content. Bobby generates a report that identifies and prioritizes Web site areas that do not meet the guidelines.

a. Can you think of any other unique uses of software that might make the world a better place for those with visual and hearing impairments?

b. Pick a favorite Web site and see how it checks out using the Bobby software. What changes would be necessary for that Web site to conform to W3C standards?

Team Time   Assessing Software Needs

Problem:

Gizmos Inc. is a start-up company in the business of designing, building, and selling the latest gizmos. You have been hired as director of information systems. As such, one of your responsibilities is to ensure all necessary software applications are purchased and installed on the company's server.

Task:

Split your class into as many groups of four or five as possible. Each group is to perform the same activity and present and compare their results at the end of the project.

Process:

1. Identify a team leader who will coordinate the project and record and present results.
2. Each team is to identify the various kinds of software that Gizmos Inc. needs. Ensure that all activities and departments of the company have software to meet their needs. Consider communications software employees will need, software they can use to design the gizmos, productivity software they may need, and software the sales reps will need to help keep track of their clients. Also consider software that human resources personnel can use to keep track of employee data and that software product managers can use to track projects. In addition, think of other software that might be useful to Gizmos Inc.
3. Create a detailed and organized list of required software applications. If possible, include licensing fees, assuming the company has 50 users.

Conclusion:

Software applications help us do the simplest and most complex tasks every day. It's important to understand how dependent we are becoming on computers and technology. Compare your results with other team members. Were there software applications that you didn't think about that other members did? How expensive is it to ensure that even the smallest company has all the software to carry out daily activities?

Becoming Computer Fluent

Instructions: Using key terms from this chapter, write a letter to one of your friends or relatives about which software applications he or she may need to work more productively. Also include which software application(s) that individual may need to modify, review, and store the pictures from a digital camera he or she just purchased.

Materials on the Web

In addition to the review materials presented here, you'll find extra materials on the book's companion Web site (**www.prenhall.com/techinaction**) that will help reinforce your understanding of the chapter content. These materials include the following:

Sound Byte Lab Guides

For each Sound Byte mentioned in the chapter, there is a corresponding lab guide located on the book's companion Web site. These guides review the material presented in the Sound Byte and direct you to various Web resources that examine the material. The Sound Byte Lab Guides for this chapter include these:

- Speech-Recognition Software
- Enhancing Photos with Image-Editing Software

True/False and Multiple-Choice Quizzes

The book's Web site includes a true/false and a multiple-choice quiz for this chapter. You can take these quizzes, automatically check the results, and e-mail the results to your instructor.

Web Research Projects

The book's Web site also includes a number of Web research projects for this chapter. These projects ask you to search the Web for information on computer-related careers, milestones in computer history, important people and companies, emerging technologies, and the applications and implications of different technologies.

Technology in Action also features unique interactive Help Desk training, in which you'll assume the role of Help Desk operator taking calls about concepts learned in each chapter. The Help Desk calls for this chapter include:

- Choosing Software
- Buying and Installing Software

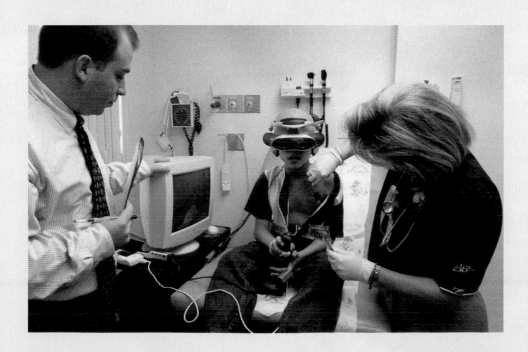

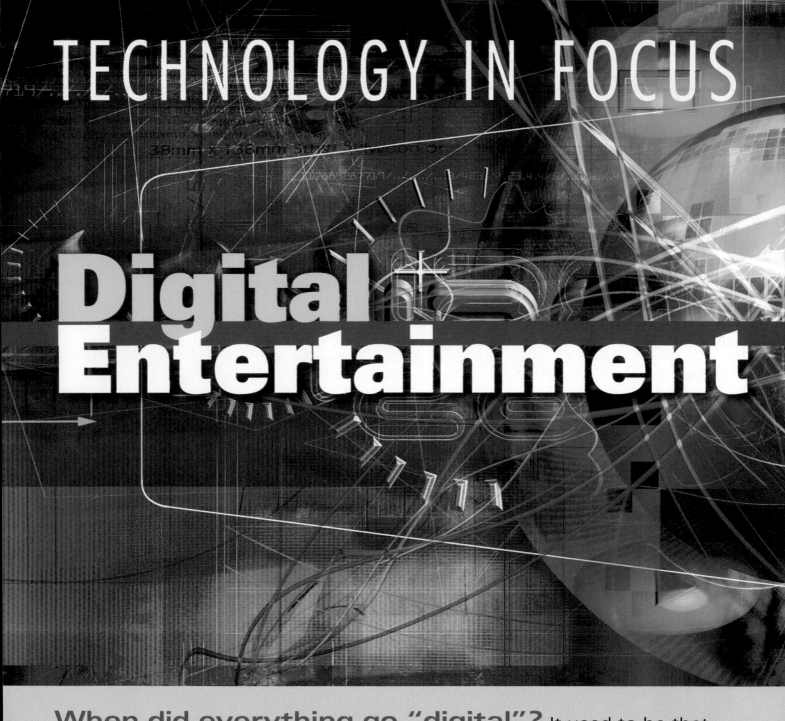

TECHNOLOGY IN FOCUS

Digital Entertainment

When did everything go "digital"? It used to be that you'd only find analog forms of entertainment. Today, no matter what you're interested in—music, movies, television, radio—a digital version exists (see Figure 1). MP3 files encode digital forms of music, while digital cameras and video camcorders are now commonplace. In Hollywood, feature films are being shot with digital equipment. For example, *Star Wars: Episode II Attack of the Clones* was filmed entirely in digital format and played in special digital release at digitally ready theaters.

FIGURE 1
Analog vs. Digital Entertainment

	ANALOG	DIGITAL
Music	Vinyl albums Cassette tapes	CDs MP3 files
Photography	35-mm single lens reflex (SLR) cameras Photos stored on film	Digital cameras Photos stored as digital files
Video	8-mm, Hi8, or VHS camcorders Film stored on VHS tapes	Digital video (DV) camcorders Film stored as digital files; often distributed on DVDs
Radio	AM/FM radio	HD radio XM radio
Television	Conventional broadcast TV	HDTV

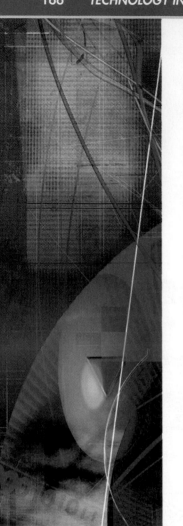

Satellite radio systems such as XM radio and HD radio are digital formats, and High-Definition Television (HDTV), a digital encoding of television signals, will become the national standard in 2006. In this Technology in Focus, we look at two popular forms of digital entertainment: digital photography and digital video. But first, let's consider what makes digital special.

What's So Special About Digital?

So, what *is* so special about digital? Think about the information captured in music and film: sounds and images. Sound is carried to your ears by sound waves, which are actually patterns of pressure changes in the air. Images are our interpretation of the changing intensity of light waves around us. These sound and light waves are called *analog* or continuous waves. They illustrate the loudness of the sound or the brightness of the colors in the image at a given moment in time. They are continuous signals because you would never have to lift your pencil off the page to draw them: they are just one long continuous line.

The first generation of recording devices (such as vinyl records and analog television shows) was designed to reproduce these sound and light waves. The needle in a groove of a vinyl record vibrates in the same pattern as the original sound wave. Television signals are actually waves that tell your TV how to display the same color and brightness as seen in the original studio. But it's difficult to describe a wave, even mathematically. Very simple sounds, like the C note of a piano, have a very simple shape, like that shown in Figure 2a. However, something like the word *hello* generates a very complex pattern, like that shown in Figure 2b.

Digital formats are descriptions of these signals as a long string of *numbers*. This is the main reason why digital recording has such an advantage over analog. Digital gives us a simple way to describe sound and light waves *exactly*, so sounds and images can be reproduced perfectly each time. We already have easy ways to distribute digital information (on CDs, DVDs, or using e-mail, for example). But how could a digital format, a sequence of numbers, act as a convenient way to express these complicated wave shapes?

The answer is provided by something called **analog-to-digital conversion**. In analog-to-digital conversion, the incoming analog signal is measured many times each second. The strength of the signal at each measurement is recorded as a simple number.

FIGURE 2

(a) This is an analog wave showing the simple, pure sound of a piano playing middle C. (b) This is the complex wave produced when a person says, "Hello."

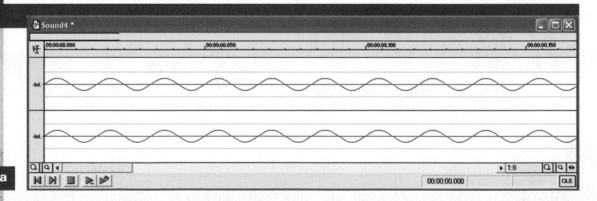

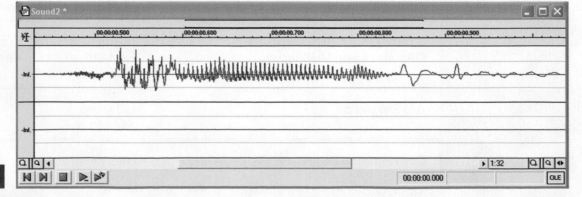

| a | Analog Sound Wave | b | Digitized Sound Wave | FIGURE 3 |

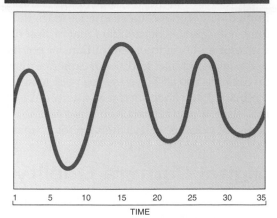
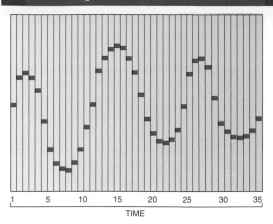

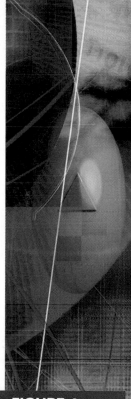

(a) Here you see a simple analog wave. (b) Here you see a digitized version of the same wave.

The series of numbers produced by the analog-to-digital conversion process gives us the digital form of the wave. Figure 3 shows an analog and digital version of the same wave. In Figure 3a, you see the original continuous analog wave. You could draw the wave in Figure 3a without lifting your pencil from the page. In Figure 3b, the wave has been digitized and now is not a single line but rather is represented as a series of points or numbers.

So, how does this all work? Let's take music as an example. Figure 4 shows how the process of creating digital entertainment begins with the physical act of playing music,

which creates analog waves. Next, a chip inside the recording device called an *analog-to-digital converter* (ADC) digitizes these waves into a series of numbers. This series of numbers can be recorded onto CDs, DVDs, or sent electronically. On the receiving end, a playback device, such as a CD or DVD player, is fed that series of numbers. There, a *digital-to-analog converter* (DAC), a chip that converts the digital numbers to a continuous wave, reproduces the original wave exactly.

Rather, the digital wave will be *close* to exact. How accurate it is, how close the digitized wave is in shape to the original analog wave, depends on the **sampling rate** of the

FIGURE 4

STEP 1: A singer plays music and sends complex analog sound waves into the air.

STEP 2: In the recording process, a microphone feeds these analog waves into an analog-to-digital converter (ADC).

STEP 3: The ADC digitizes the waves. They are now represented as a series of numbers.

During the complete recording process, information moves from analog form to digital data and then back again to analog sound waves.

Singer playing music

Analog wave

ADC

STEP 4: These numbers are easily recorded on a CD or DVD. They are the same each time you copy the disc.

Digital format
28,36,42,
84,120,126,
120,98,98...

Speaker

DAC

CD or DVD

28,36,42,
84,120,126,
120,98,98...

STEP 6: These analog waves tell your receiver how to move the speaker cones to duplicate the same sound waves as in the original music.

STEP 5: To play the CD, your CD player must have a digital-to-analog converter (DAC) to convert the numbers back to the analog wave.

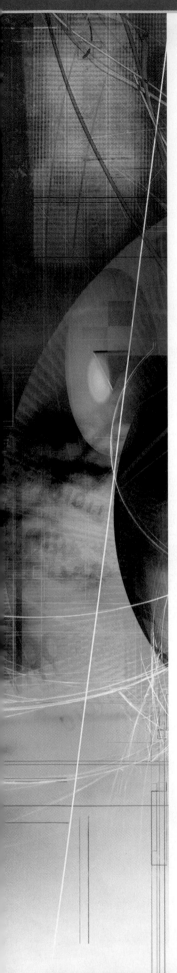

ADC. The sampling rate specifies the number of times the analog wave is measured each second. The higher the sampling rate, the more accurately the original wave can be re-created. However, higher sampling rates also produce much more data, and therefore result in bigger files. For example, sound waves on CDs are sampled at a rate of 44,000 times a second. This produces a huge list of numbers—44,000 of them each second!

So, when sounds or image waves are digitized, it means that analog data is changed into digital data—from a wave into a series of numbers. The digital data is perfectly reproducible and can be distributed easily on CDs, DVDs, or through the airwaves. It can also be easily processed by a computer.

These digital advantages have revolutionized photography, music, movies, television, and radio. For example, digital television has a sharper picture and superior sound quality. However, there is a cost in the shift from analog to digital technologies. The Federal Communications Commission (FCC) has mandated that all over-the-air broadcasters transmit in digital format by May 2006. Consumers will be forced to choose between upgrading to digital HDTV sets or purchasing a converter for older sets. The digital revolution in television will bring better quality and additional conveniences, but at a cost, as the older analog equipment is phased out.

The same tension exists in the migration from analog to digital technology in photography. Let's take a look at this form of entertainment and explore the advantages and investment required in migrating from an analog to a digital format.

Digital Photography

Before digital cameras hit the market, most people used some form of 35-mm single lens reflex (SLR) camera. When you take a picture using a traditional SLR camera, an aperture (a small window in the camera) opens, allowing light to hit the 35-mm film inside. Chemicals coating the film react when exposed to light. Later, additional chemicals develop the image on the film and it is printed on special light-sensitive paper. A variety of lenses and processing techniques, special equipment, and filters are needed to create printed photos from traditional SLR cameras.

Digital cameras, on the other hand, do not use film. Instead, they capture images and immediately convert those images to digital data, a long series of numbers that represents the color and brightness of millions of points in the image. Unlike traditional cameras, digital cameras also allow you to see your images the instant you shoot them. Many camera models now also can record limited amounts of digital video as well as digital photographs.

Digital Camera Quality

Part of what determines the quality of a digital camera is its **resolution**, or the sharpness of the images it records. A digital camera's resolution is measured in megapixels (MP). The prefix *mega* is short for millions. The word *pixel* is short for picture element, or a single dot in a digital image. The higher the number of megapixels, the higher the quality of the camera and the images it takes.

Popular camera models come in a range of resolutions. An inexpensive pocket-sized camera like the Nikon SQ is a 3.1-MP camera, which means that every photo it takes contains 3.1 megapixels, or 3.1 million picture elements. More expensive consumer cameras such as the Minolta Dimage S414 measure 4 MP. Professional photographers are moving to digital cameras as well. Professional digital cameras such as the Kodak DCS Pro 14 can take photos at resolutions up to 14 MP, but sell for over $4,500. Figure 5 shows some popular digital camera models and the number of pixels they record at their maximum resolution.

If you're interested in an inexpensive digital camera and plan to make only 5 x 7 or 8 x 10 prints, a 2-MP camera is fine. However, these cameras do not record enough pixels to print larger-size prints. If you did print an 11 x 14 enlargement from a 2-MP shot, the image would look grainy—you would see individual dots of color instead of a clear, sharp image.

Camera prices continue to drop as new models with higher resolutions are introduced, so 4-MP and 5-MP cameras are becoming affordable. With such resolutions, you can print larger photos (11 x 14 and up) and still have sharp, detailed images.

Digital Camera Storage

When a digital camera takes a photo, it stores the images on a flash memory card inside the camera, as shown in Figure 6. Flash memory

FIGURE 5

Digital Camera Resolutions

Nikon SQ
(highest resolution 3.1 MP)

Minolta Dimage S414
(highest resolution 4 MP)

Canon EOS Rebel 300D
(highest resolution 6.1 MP)

Kodak DCS Pro
(highest resolution 14 MP)

cards are very small and powerful and allow you to transfer digital information between your camera and your computer or printer. Flash memory therefore takes the place of film used in traditional cameras.

To fit more photos on the same size flash memory card, digital cameras allow you to choose from several different file types in order to *compress*, or squeeze, the image data into less space. When you choose to compress your images, you will lose some of the detail, but in return you'll be able to fit more images on your flash card. Figure 7 shows the most common file types supported by digital cameras: the RAW uncompressed data type and the Joint Photographic Experts Group (JPEG) type. RAW files record all of the original image information and so are

FIGURE 6

Flash memory slides into a digital camera and is used to store images.

larger than the compressed JPEG files. JPEG files can be compressed just a bit, keeping most of the details, or compressed a great deal, losing some detail. Most cameras allow you to select from a few different JPEG compression levels.

FIGURE 7
File Types Commonly Used in Digital Cameras

FILE TYPE	COMPRESSED	SAMPLE QUALITY	FILE SIZE	NUMBER OF IMAGES THAT FIT ON A 128-MB FLASH CARD
RAW	No	High: Contains all the original data	6.0 MB	21
JPEG (at highest camera resolution)	Yes	Medium: Moderate compression; some lost quality	3.1 MB	41
JPEG (at lowest camera resolution)	Yes	Low: More compression; more lost quality	0.9 MB	142

Note: The file sizes in this table refer to image storage on a Canon EOS Rebel 300D camera.

Preparing Your Camera and Taking Your Photos

Preparing your camera includes ensuring that your camera's batteries are charged and the settings are correct. Digital cameras consume a great deal of power, so you might want to carry a spare charged battery pack. Also make sure the flash card is installed and that it has enough space for the number of photos you plan to take.

Next, set the resolution on your camera. Most cameras offer two or three different resolution settings. For example, a 6-MP camera might be able to shoot images at 6 MP, 2.7 MP, or 1.5 MP. If you're taking a photo that will be enlarged and that needs to be at a very high quality, use the full power of your camera. Shoot the image at 6 MP and save the image as uncompressed data (a TIFF file) at the highest resolution. If you're planning to use the image for a Web page, where having a smaller file would be helpful, use a lower resolution and the space-saving compressed JPEG format. If you're unsure how you're going to use your images, use the maximum resolution and save them as TIFF files as long as you have enough space on your flash card.

Most cameras include an autofocus feature and automatically set the aperture and correct shutter speed. This makes taking a digital photo as simple as pressing a button. The great thing about digital cameras is that they let you instantly examine your photos in a liquid crystal display (LCD) window on the camera. If you don't like a certain photo, you can delete it immediately, freeing space on your flash card.

Transferring Your Photos to Your Computer

If you just want to print your photos, you may not need to transfer them to your computer. Many photo printers can make prints directly from your camera or from the flash memory card. However,

transferring the photos to your computer allows you to store them and frees your flash card for reuse. Once they're on your computer, you can transfer the images to CDs, e-mail them, use them in Web pages, or edit them.

Transferring your photos to your computer is simple. All digital cameras have a built-in universal serial bus (USB) port. Using a USB cable, you can connect the camera to your computer to store the converted images as uncompressed files or in a compressed format as JPEG files. Another option is to transfer the flash card from your camera to the computer. Some desktops have flash card slots on the front of the system unit. However, if yours does not, you can buy an external memory card reader like the one shown in Figure 8 and attach it to your computer using an available USB port.

When you connect your camera to your computer, with the Microsoft Windows XP operating system, the rest of the transfer is automatic. You'll hear a ding-dong sound, telling you the computer and camera are connected and can communicate. Next, a series of prompts appears, asking you which images you'd like to transfer and where you'd like to store them. You now have TIFF or JPEG image files on your computer. If you're satisfied with the photos, you can send them to your friends as e-mail attachments, for example. If you're not satisfied with them, you can process them further.

Processing Your Photos and Adding Special Effects

Once you're a seasoned digital photographer, you may want to process your photos, cropping them, for example, or adding special effects. Traditional photographers often invest in special equipment and chemicals needed to develop 35-mm film. The photographer can then resize or crop the photo, add different filtering effects, or combine photos. With digital photography, you can do all of this using inexpensive image-editing software.

There are hundreds of image-editing programs available, from freeware to very sophisticated suites. Adobe Photoshop and Jasc Paint Shop Pro are two popular packages. They allow you to remove flaws such as red-eye; crop images; correct poor color balance; apply filtering effects such as mosaics, charcoal, and impressionistic style; and merge

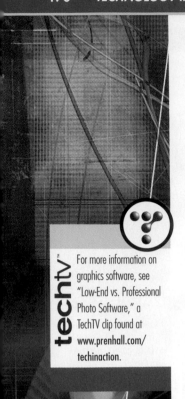

techtv™

For more information on graphics software, see "Low-End vs. Professional Photo Software," a TechTV clip found at www.prenhall.com/techinaction.

SanDisk
256
2.0 GB

FIGURE 8

If your computer does not have a built-in flash card reader, you can buy an external reader that attaches to your computer using a USB cable and port.

How Do My Old Photos Become Digital?

Obviously, not every document or image you have is in an electronic form. What about all the photographs you have already taken? Or an article from a magazine or a hand-drawn sketch? How can these be converted into digital format?

Digital scanners like the one shown in Figure 9 convert paper text and images into digital formats. You can place any flat material on the glass surface of the scanner and then convert it into a digital file. Most scanner software allows you to store the converted images as RAW files or in compressed form as JPEG files. And some scanners include optional hardware that allows you to scan film negatives or slides as well.

Scanner quality is measured by its resolution, which is given in dots per inch (dpi). Most modern scanners can digitize a document at 2,400 x 4,800 dpi, in either color or gray-scale modes. You can easily connect a scanner to your computer using USB 2.0 or FireWire ports. Scanners also typically come with software supporting optical character recognition (OCR). OCR software converts pages of handwritten or typed text into electronic files. You can then open and edit these converted documents with traditional word processing programs.

FIGURE 9

Scanners can convert paper documents, photo prints, or strips of film negatives into digital data.

components from multiple images. Figure 10 shows just a few examples of the filtering effects you can apply to an image. The exact set of filtering effects you will have depends on the software you're using.

Printing Your Photos (Optional)

Once you've processed your photos, you can print them using a professional service or your own printer. Most photo printing labs, including the film-processing departments at stores such as Wal-Mart and Target, offer digital printing services, as do many high-end online processing labs. These sites accept original or edited image files and print them on professional photo paper with high-quality inks. The paper and ink used at processing labs are higher quality than what is available for home use and produce heavier, glossier prints that won't fade. In addition, Kodak and Sony have kiosks in department stores and photography stores that you can use yourself. They accept image files directly from your flash cards,

FIGURE 10

Using image-editing software, you can add filtering effects such as color pencil, collage, and oil painting.

Original

Color Pencil

Collage

Oil Painting

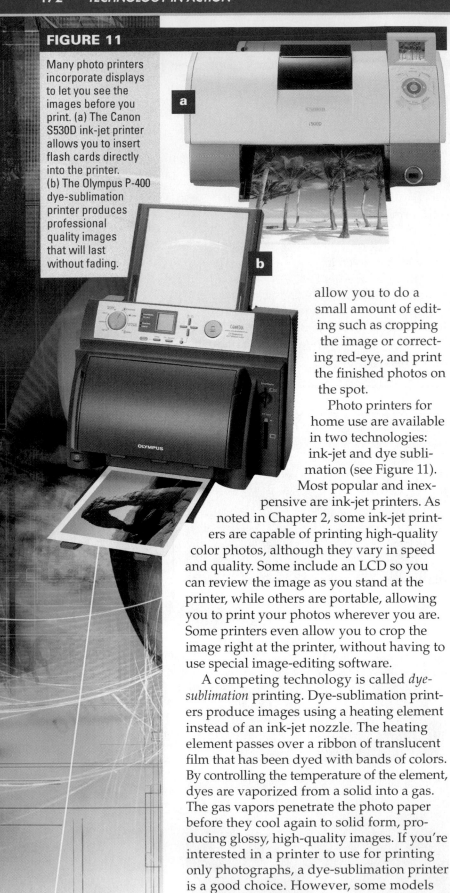

FIGURE 11

Many photo printers incorporate displays to let you see the images before you print. (a) The Canon S530D ink-jet printer allows you to insert flash cards directly into the printer. (b) The Olympus P-400 dye-sublimation printer produces professional quality images that will last without fading.

allow you to do a small amount of editing such as cropping the image or correcting red-eye, and print the finished photos on the spot.

Photo printers for home use are available in two technologies: ink-jet and dye sublimation (see Figure 11). Most popular and inexpensive are ink-jet printers. As noted in Chapter 2, some ink-jet printers are capable of printing high-quality color photos, although they vary in speed and quality. Some include an LCD so you can review the image as you stand at the printer, while others are portable, allowing you to print your photos wherever you are. Some printers even allow you to crop the image right at the printer, without having to use special image-editing software.

A competing technology is called *dye-sublimation* printing. Dye-sublimation printers produce images using a heating element instead of an ink-jet nozzle. The heating element passes over a ribbon of translucent film that has been dyed with bands of colors. By controlling the temperature of the element, dyes are vaporized from a solid into a gas. The gas vapors penetrate the photo paper before they cool again to solid form, producing glossy, high-quality images. If you're interested in a printer to use for printing only photographs, a dye-sublimation printer is a good choice. However, some models print only specific photo sizes, such as 4 x 6 prints, so be sure the printer you buy will fit your long-term needs.

Transferring your images to the printer is similar to transferring them to your computer. If you have a direct-connection camera, you can plug the camera directly into the printer with a cable. Some printers have slots that accept different types of flash memory cards. You can also transfer your images to the printer from your computer if you have stored them there.

Some printers support a system known as Digital Print Order Format (DPOF). Using a combination of a DPOF camera and a DPOF printer, you can review all the shots on your camera and build an order of how many copies and what sizes you would like to print. You then just insert the flash card into the printer and your entire order is printed automatically.

The Digital Advantage

Is a digital camera right for you? Figure 12, p. 173, lists just a few of the advantages digital cameras have over traditional cameras. Digital cameras give you the power to create images that only professional photographers with expensive processing studios could produce a few years ago.

Digital Video

Personal video cameras have been popular for a long time. The first camcorders were analog video cameras, like the one shown in Figure 13a. These were large, heavy units that held a full-size VHS tape. The push to produce smaller, lighter models led to the introduction of compact VHS tapes and then to 8-mm and Hi8 formats. Still, all of these are analog formats, and each records to its own specific type of tape.

The newest generation of video equipment for home use is the *digital video,* or DV, format shown in Figure 13b. Introduced in 1995, the digital video standard led to a new generation of recording equipment. Today, digital video cameras offer many advantages over their VHS counterparts. They are incredibly small and light and use tapes of a new format called MiniDV. These tapes can hold one to three hours of video but are just about 2 square inches in size, and they allow manufacturers to design stylish and sleek cameras.

In addition, by using digital video cameras, you can easily transfer video files to your

FIGURE 12
Digital Photography Advantages

	TRADITIONAL SLR CAMERA	DIGITAL ADVANTAGE
Developing	Send out or pay more for one-hour developing Forced to develop the entire roll Special equipment required for applying special effects before printing	Immediate processing Print only the shots you like Easy to apply filters and special effects using inexpensive software
Storage	Need to purchase and carry many rolls of film; temperature and x-ray sensitive Can be stored on hard drive, CD, or DVD only after scanning the negative or print Negatives must be protected in special sleeves	No need to purchase film; large flash memory cards provide room for many shots Can easily be stored on hard drive, CD, or DVD with no scanning necessary Images stored as data files; only need to back up these files to ensure they are protected
Distribution	Paper prints can be mailed; however, must be scanned into a digital format for electronic distribution	Images can be printed on home printers and professionally; easy to distribute image files as e-mail attachments or on CD; can also post images to Web easily
Quality	Sets the standard for quality	Excellent quality comparable to traditional photos

computer. Then, using simple video-editing software, you can edit the video at home, cutting out sections, resequencing segments, and adding titles. To do the same on analog videotape would require thousands of dollars of complex audio/video equipment available only in video production studios. And with digital video, you can save (or *write*) your final product on a CD or DVD and play it in your home DVD system or on your computer.

Although you have terrific convenience and control with digital video, there are costs in making the move from analog to digital. Digital video cameras come in a wide range of prices, but they are more expensive than the analog models still available. This is reasonable because digitizing video and audio requires a lot of processing power. Video for motion pictures is recorded as high-resolution images at a rate of 30 frames per second (fps). This means 1,800 images must be digitized for each minute of video. In addition to the video, the audio also must be digitized. Digital video cameras do the analog-to-digital conversion right in the camera. They are equipped with

FIGURE 13

(a) First-generation home video camcorders recorded on full-size VHS cassettes. (b) Modern digital video camcorders can be smaller and lighter.

FireWire ports so you can later send the digital data quickly from the camera directly to your computer.

For many people, the advantages of working with digital video are worth the extra cost. Let's look at how you would use a digital video camera and see if the investment would be worthwhile for you.

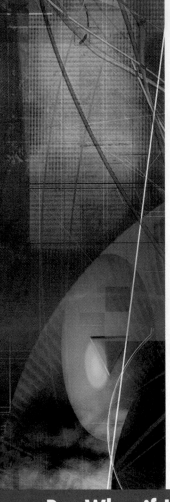

Preparing Your Camera and Shooting Your Video Footage

Preparing your digital video camera involves making sure you have enough battery power and tape capacity. Batteries for digital video cameras are rechargeable and can provide between one and nine hours of shooting time. Longer-lasting batteries cost and weigh more, so you'll want to think about how you use your camera before deciding which batteries to purchase. Most videographers recommend carrying two spare batteries, though having one spare is fine if you can recharge it while you're using the second.

Digital video cameras record on tape, so make sure you have enough tape to cover the event. Some models also let you record short segments onto a flash memory card. If you want to record a short clip that you can quickly transfer to your computer without having to hook up any cables, make sure you have a large enough flash memory card with you. Check the user guide for your particular camera to see how much flash memory you need to store video. For example, on the

Sony DCR-TRV80, you can store about 10 minutes of video on a 64-MB Memory Stick.

Shooting video with a digital video camera is similar to shooting video with an analog camera. Automated programs control the exposure settings for different environments (nighttime shots, action events, and so on), while automatic focusing and telephoto zoom lens features are common as well. Many cameras include an antishake feature that stabilizes the image when you're using the camera without a tripod. Using these features, you can capture great footage by just pointing and hitting Record.

Transferring Your Video to Your Computer

Digital video cameras already hold your video as digital data, so transferring the data to your computer is simple. All you need is a FireWire port on your computer and a FireWire cable. Although every FireWire port is the same, there are two different types of connectors used on FireWire cables: 4-pin and 6-pin. Digital video cameras usually have a port that matches the 4-pin connector, while desktop computers may have a port

But What if I Already Have an Analog Camcorder?

If you have an older analog video camera, you can still begin to play with digital video if you purchase a special unit called a *video capture device*. A video capture device digitizes and compresses analog video and then passes it on to your computer. To use one, you connect your analog video camera to the video capture unit, which in turn connects to your computer. Your camera then feeds its video signals to the capture device, which then sends the video to the computer in a digitized form. You can use this device to convert and send existing analog tapes into your computer or to process new videos you shoot with your analog camcorder into digital computer files. Figure 14a shows an example of an external video capture device. Note that video capture devices also are available as expansion (adapter) cards that you install in an unused expansion slot inside your computer.

There are some other options available as well. If you want the ultimate in simplicity, devices such as the Iomega Super DVD QuickTouch Burner, shown in Figure 14b, allow you to transfer video from an analog camera or old tapes directly to DVD discs with just one button. Or you may want to purchase a new video card. Some video cards have a video-in port built into the design. You can connect an older analog camera directly to the video card and digitize from your analog camera.

FIGURE 14

(a) You can still create digital video with an older analog camera by connecting your camera to a video capture device, which in turn connects to your computer. (b) Or, using a device such as the Iomega Super DVD QuikTouch Burner shown here, you can easily transfer your analog video to DVD. The burner plugs into your computer using a USB 2.0 port, and the burner has jacks that allow you to connect it to your analog camera.

matching either the 4- or 6-pin connectors. Be sure to check both your camera and computer and buy a cable with the matching connector on each end.

Once you connect your camera to your computer, Microsoft Windows XP automatically identifies it, recognizing its manufacturer and model. The Windows operating system then scans the software on your system and presents a list of all the programs you can use to import your video. Windows Movie Maker is one such program and is included with Windows XP Home Edition. Other digital video-editing programs such as Adobe Premiere and Pinnacle Studio DV can import video as well. These are more powerful, full-featured programs that you purchase separately. Figure 15a shows the list that pops up for a computer with Windows Movie Maker, Sonic Solutions, and Adobe Premiere installed.

The software allows you to fast-forward, pause, and rewind, moving to the segment you wish to transfer (or record) to your hard drive. In Figure 15b, both video and audio are chosen to record (transfer). You can use the digital video camera control arrows on the bottom right-hand side of the Record dialog box to locate the exact piece of footage you want to transfer. Click the Record button and the video file transfers to the hard drive.

One camcorder on the market today offers another option. Made by Sony, the DVD Handycam® Camcorder DCR-DVD101 writes its digital data directly onto 3-inch DVDs. It can record up to 20 minutes of video when using the highest quality setting. You can then drop the DVD into most DVD players and view it immediately.

Editing Your Video and Adding Special Effects

Once the digital video data is in a file on your hard drive, the fun really begins. Video-editing software presents a storyboard or time line with which you can manipulate your video file, as shown in Figure 16 (p. 176). Using this software, you can review your clips frame by frame or trim them at any point. You can order each segment on the time line in whichever sequence you like and correct segments for color balance, brightness, or contrast.

In addition, you can add transitions to your video such as those you're used to seeing on TV—fades to black, dissolves, and so on. Figure 16 shows how easy it is to add

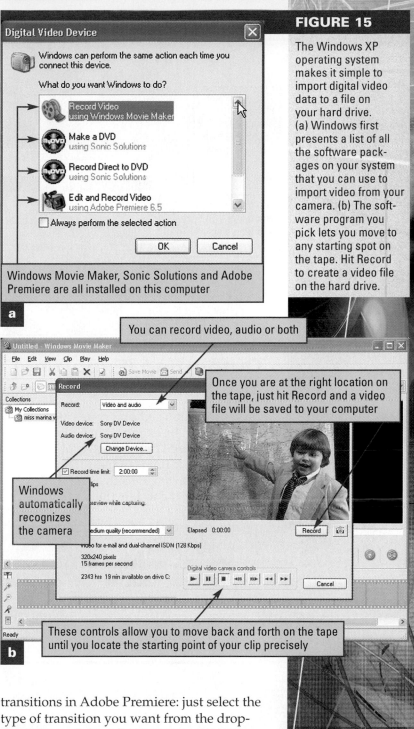

FIGURE 15

The Windows XP operating system makes it simple to import digital video data to a file on your hard drive. (a) Windows first presents a list of all the software packages on your system that you can use to import video from your camera. (b) The software program you pick lets you move to any starting spot on the tape. Hit Record to create a video file on the hard drive.

Windows Movie Maker, Sonic Solutions and Adobe Premiere are all installed on this computer

a

You can record video, audio or both

Once you are at the right location on the tape, just hit Record and a video file will be saved to your computer

Windows automatically recognizes the camera

These controls allow you to move back and forth on the tape until you locate the starting point of your clip precisely

b

transitions in Adobe Premiere: just select the type of transition you want from the drop-down list and drag that icon into the time line where you want the transition to occur.

Video-editing software also lets you add titles, animations, and audio tracks to your video, including background music, sound effects, and additional narration. In Figure 16 there are two audio tracks, the original voices on the video as well as an additional audio clip. You can adjust the volume of each audio track to switch from one to the other or have both playing together. Finally, you can preview all of these effects in real time.

FIGURE 16

Adobe Premiere allows you to build a movie from video clips and add soundtracks and special effects such as three-dimensional transitions between scenes.

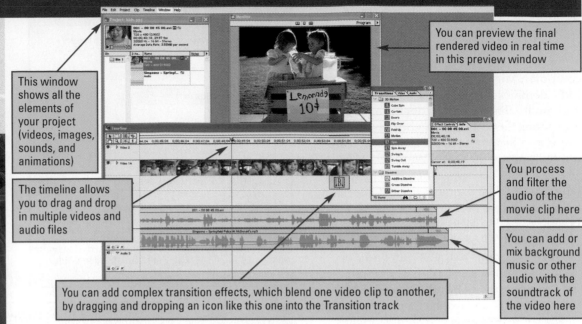

This window shows all the elements of your project (videos, images, sounds, and animations)

The timeline allows you to drag and drop in multiple videos and audio files

You can preview the final rendered video in real time in this preview window

You process and filter the audio of the movie clip here

You can add or mix background music or other audio with the soundtrack of the video here

You can add complex transition effects, which blend one video clip to another, by dragging and dropping an icon like this one into the Transition track

Outputting (Exporting) Your Video

Once you're done editing your video file, you can save (or export) it in a variety of formats. Figure 17 shows some of the popular video file formats in use today, along with the file extensions they use. (*File extensions* are the letters that follow the period in a file name, such as in Movie1.mpg. These extensions indicate the type of data inside the file.)

Your choice of file format for your finished video will depend on what you want to do with your video. For example, the RealMedia streaming file format is a great choice if your file is very large and you'll be posting it on the Web. The Microsoft

FIGURE 17
Typical File Formats for Digital Video

FORMAT	FILE EXTENSION	NOTES
QuickTime	.mov .qt	You can download QuickTime player for free from **www.apple.com/quicktime**. The pro version allows you to build your own QuickTime files.
Moving Picture Experts Group (MPEG)	.mpg .mpeg	MPEG-4 video standard adopted internationally in 2000; recognized by most video player software.
Windows Media Video	.wmv	Microsoft file format recognized by Windows Media Player (included with Windows operating system).
Microsoft Video for Windows	.avi	Microsoft file format recognized by Windows Media Player (included with Windows operating system).
RealMedia	.rm	Format from RealNetworks is popular for streaming video. You can download the player for free at **www.real.com**.

AVI format is a good choice if you're sending your file to a wide range of users because it's very popular and commonly accepted as the standard video format on Windows machines.

When you export your video, you have control over every aspect of the file you create, including its format, window size, frame rate, audio quality, and compression level. You can customize any of these if you have specific production goals, but most often just using the default values works well.

When would you want to customize some of the audio and video settings? If you're trying to make the file as small as possible so it will download quickly or so it can fit on a single CD, you would select values that trade off audio and video quality for file size. For example, you could drop the frame rate to 15 fps, shrink the window size to 320 x 240 pixels, and switch to mono audio instead of stereo.

You can also try different compression choices to see which one does a better job of compressing your particular file. **Codecs** (**co**mpression/**dec**ompression) are rules implemented in either software or hardware that squeeze the same audio/video information into less space. Some information will be lost using compression, and there is a variety of different codecs to choose from, each claiming better performance than its competitors. Commonly used codecs include MPEG, Indeo, and Cinepak. There is no one codec that is always superior—a codec that works well for a simple interview may not do a good job compressing a live-action scene.

If you'd like to save your video onto a DVD, you can use special DVD authoring software such as Ulead's DVD Workshop or Adobe's Encore DVD. These programs create final DVDs that have animated menu systems and easy navigation controls, allowing the viewer to move quickly from one movie or scene to another. Home DVD players as well as gaming systems such as Playstation 2 and Xbox can read these DVDs, so your potential audience is even greater!

The Digital Advantage

Is a digital video camera right for you? Figure 18 lists just a few of the advantages of digital video cameras over traditional analog camcorders. Analog video changed how we communicate. It became possible to make a video of a baby's first steps and send it to relatives all across the country. Digital video allows you even more creative control over the videos you produce, enabling you to edit them at home and share them with others even more easily.

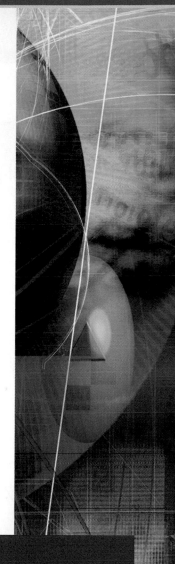

FIGURE 18
Digital Video Advantages

	ANALOG VIDEO CAMERA	DIGITAL ADVANTAGE
Editing	Home users cannot edit their videos without expensive equipment.	Editing video is easy using inexpensive software.
Storage	Film is stored on analog tapes (VHS, 8-mm, or Hi8 tapes). Tapes have a limited lifetime and are sensitive to heat, magnetic fields, water damage, and mechanical breakdown.	Video is stored on smaller MiniDV tapes. Short video clips can be saved directly to flash memory cards. You can easily transfer and store video files onto a computer hard drive, CD, or DVD. There is no loss of information over time.
Distribution	You can make copies of tapes but only if you own multiple VHS VCRs or Hi8 players. To make digital versions of analog tapes, you need a separate video capture device.	You can make DVD copies using a simple DVD-RW drive. You can also post videos to Web sites or attach them to e mail messages.
Quality	Excellent video and audio quality.	Excellent video quality and CD-quality audio.

CHAPTER 5

OBJECTIVES

After reading this chapter, you should be able to answer the following questions:

- What software is included in system software? (p. 180)

- What are the different kinds of operating systems? (pp. 180–182)

- What are the most common desktop operating systems? (pp. 182–186)

- How does the operating system provide a means for users to interact with the computer? (pp. 186–188)

- How does the operating system help manage the processor? (pp. 188–189)

- How does the operating system manage memory and storage? (p. 189)

- How does the operating system manage hardware and peripheral devices? (p. 190)

- How does the operating system interact with application software? (pp. 190–191)

- How does the operating system help the computer start up? (pp. 191–195)

- What are the main desktop and window features? (pp. 195–197)

- How does the operating system help me keep my computer organized? (pp. 197–202)

- What utility programs are included in system software and what do they do? (pp. 202–209)

SOUND BYTES

- Customizing Windows XP (p. 196)
- File Management (p. 199)
- File Compression (p. 205)

- Hard Disk Anatomy Interactive (p. 207)
- Letting Your Computer Clean Up After Itself (p. 208)

Using System Software:

The Operating System, Utility Programs, and File Management

TECHNOLOGY IN ACTION: WORKING WITH SYSTEM SOFTWARE

Franklin begins his workday as he does every morning, powering on his computer and watching it boot up. Once he sees the welcoming image of his desktop, he opens Microsoft Outlook to check his e-mail, Internet Explorer to access his company's Web site, and Microsoft Word to bring up the proposal he needs to finish. As he reads his e-mail, a warning pops up alerting him that one message may contain a file with a virus. He deletes the file without opening it, glad that his antivirus software had been automatically updated the night before.

Clicking back to Word, Franklin searches for a proposal he worked on last year. Fortunately, he knows where to look because he has been creating folders for his projects and diligently saving his files in their proper folder. He learned the hard way that keeping his files organized in folders is worth the effort it takes to create them. Last year, his desktop was a complete mess. He was constantly losing time trying to find files because he couldn't remember where he saved them and he gave them names he easily forgot. His organized folders now make finding his files a snap.

Later, at the end of the day, Franklin has one more thing to do. Recently, his computer has been running sluggishly, so he is hoping to improve its performance. Last night, he ran Disk Cleanup, a utility program that removes unneeded files from the hard drive, as well as ScanDisk, a utility program that checks for disk errors. Although he had seen an improvement in his computer's performance, he decides to use the defrag utility to defrag his hard drive, hoping it will give him more space. As he's leaving work, Franklin hears the clicking of the hard drive as the defrag utility goes to work.

Are you as familiar with your system as Franklin is? In this chapter, you'll learn all about system software and how vital it is to your computer. We'll start by examining the operating system (OS), looking at the different operating systems on the market as well as the tasks the OS manages. We'll then look at how you can use the OS to keep the files and folders on your desktop organized so that you can use your computer more efficiently. Finally, we'll look at the many utility programs included as system software on your computer. Using these utility programs, you'll be better able to take care of your system and extend its life.

System Software Basics

As you learned in the last chapter, there are two basic types of software on your computer: application software and system software. **Application software** is the software you use to do everyday tasks at home and at work. It includes programs such as Microsoft Word and Excel. **System software** is the set of software programs that helps run the computer and coordinates instructions between application software and the computer's hardware devices. From the moment you turn on your computer to the time you shut it down, you are interacting with system software.

System software consists of two primary types of programs: the operating system and utility programs. The **operating system (OS)** is the main program that controls how your computer system functions. It manages the computer's hardware, including the processor (also called the central processing unit, or CPU), memory, and storage devices, as well as peripheral devices such as the monitor and printer. The operating system also provides a consistent means for software applications to work with the CPU. Additionally, it is responsible for the management, scheduling, and interaction of tasks as well as system maintenance. Finally, the OS provides a *user interface* through which users can interact directly with the computer.

System software also includes **utility programs**. These are small programs that perform many of the general housekeeping tasks for the computer, such as system maintenance and file compression.

Do all computers have operating systems? Every computer, from the smallest notebook to the largest supercomputer, has an operating system. Even tiny personal digital assistants (PDAs) as well as some appliances have operating systems. The role of the OS is critical; the computer cannot operate without it.

Operating System Categories

Although most computer users can name only a few operating systems, hundreds exist. As Figure 5.1 illustrates, these operating systems can be classified into four categories, depending on the number of users they service and the tasks they perform. Some operating systems coordinate resources for many users on a network (multiuser operating system), whereas other operating systems, such as those found in some household appliances and car engines, don't

FIGURE 5.1   Operating System Categories

CATEGORY OF OPERATING SYSTEM	EXAMPLES OF OPERATING SYSTEM SOFTWARE	EXAMPLES OF DEVICES USING THE OPERATING SYSTEM
Real-Time Operating System (RTOS)	There are no commercially available RTOS programs. Non–commercially available programs include QNX Neutrino and Lynx.	Scientific instruments Automation and control machinery Video games
Single-User, Single-Task Operating System	Palm OS Pocket PC (Windows CE) Windows Mobile 2003 MS-DOS Symbian OS	PDAs Embedded computers in cell phones, cameras, appliances, and toys
Single-User, Multitask Operating System	Windows family (2003, XP, 2000, Me, 98, NT) Mac OS X Linux	Personal desktop computers Portable computers
Multiuser Operating System	UNIX Novell NetWare Windows Server 2003 OS/2	Networks Mainframes Supercomputers

require the intervention of any users at all (real-time operating system). Some operating systems are available commercially, for personal and business use (single-user, multitask operating system), whereas others are proprietary systems developed specifically for the devices they manage (single-user, single-task operating system).

REAL-TIME OPERATING SYSTEMS

Do machines with built-in computers need an operating system? Machinery that is required to perform a repetitive series of specific tasks in an exact amount of time requires a **real-time operating system (RTOS)**. This type of operating system is a program with a specific purpose and must guarantee certain response times for particular computing tasks, or the machine's application is useless. For example, instruments such as those found in the scientific, defense, and aerospace industries that must perform regimented tasks or record precise results require real-time operating systems.

Real-time operating systems are also found in many types of robotic equipment. Television stations use robotic cameras with real-time operating systems that glide within a suspended cable system to record sports events from many angles. You also encounter real-time operating systems in devices you use in your everyday life, such as fuel-injection systems in car engines, video game consoles, and many home appliances (see Figure 5.2).

Real-time operating systems require minimal user interaction. The programs are written specifically to the needs of the devices and their functions. Therefore, there are no commercially available standard RTOS software programs.

SINGLE-USER OPERATING SYSTEMS

What type of operating system controls my personal computer? Because your computer, whether it's a desktop, laptop, or even a tablet PC, can handle only one person working on it at a time, but can perform a variety of tasks simultaneously, it uses a **single-user, multitask operating system**. The Windows family of operating systems and the Macintosh operating system (Mac OS)

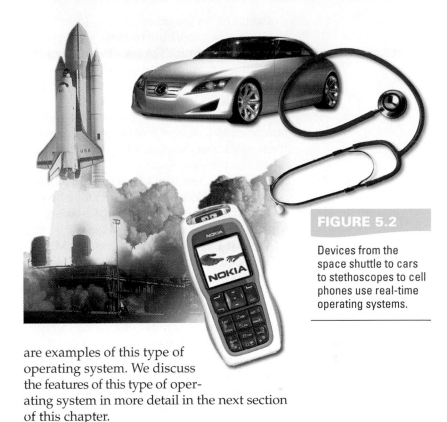

Devices from the space shuttle to cars to stethoscopes to cell phones use real-time operating systems.

are examples of this type of operating system. We discuss the features of this type of operating system in more detail in the next section of this chapter.

Usually, when you buy a desktop or laptop computer, its operating system software is already installed on the computer's hard disk. Sometimes you may need to install the OS yourself if you change or upgrade to a different version, or you might reinstall it in the case of a system problem.

Does the same kind of operating system also control my PDA? All computers on which one user is performing just one task at a time require a **single-user, single-task operating system**. PDAs currently can perform only one task at a time by a single user, so they require single-user, single-task operating system software such as Pocket PC or Palm OS.

Microsoft's Pocket PC is an application that includes both operating system software (Windows CE) and application components bundled specifically for PDAs (see Figure 5.3). Besides the address book, date book, memo pad, and to-do list that are standard with Windows CE, the bundled Pocket PC software also includes versions of Word, Excel, Outlook, and Internet Explorer that are designed specifically for PDAs. The latest version of Pocket PC, Windows Mobile 2003, comes with advanced wireless Internet connection capabilities.

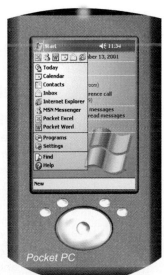

Although PDAs use a single-user, single-task operating system in which only one user can perform one task at a time, the operating system has a similar look to that of a traditional desktop operating system.

Palm OS, on the other hand, is found in a number of devices but is strictly an operating system. If your PDA uses Palm OS as its operating system, you must purchase and install any additional software you want to run on your PDA.

Cell phones also use a single-user, single-task operating system that not only manages the functions of the phone, but also provides other functionality, such as built-in phone directories, games, and calculators. Symbian is the leading OS software for mobile phones.

Are there any other single-user, single-task operating systems?
Microsoft Disk Operating System (MS-DOS) is another example of a single-user, single-task operating system. DOS was the first widely installed operating system in personal computers. Compared to the operating systems we are familiar with today, DOS was a highly user "unfriendly" OS. To use it, you needed to type in specific commands. For example, to copy a file named "letter" from the hard drive to a floppy disk, you would type in the following command after the C prompt:

```
C:\>copy letter.txt A:
```

Although DOS is infrequently used today as a primary operating system, Information Technology (IT) professionals still use it to edit and repair system files and programs.

MULTIUSER OPERATING SYSTEMS

What kind of operating system do networks use? A **multiuser operating system** (also known as a **network operating system**) enables more than one user to access the computer system at one time by efficiently juggling all the requests from multiple users. Networks require a multiuser operating system because many users access the server computer at the same time and share resources such as printers. A network operating system is installed on the server and manages all user requests, ensuring they do not interfere with each other. For example, on a network where users share a printer, the printer can produce only one document at a time. The OS is therefore responsible for managing all the printer requests and making sure they are processed one at a time. Examples of network operating systems include UNIX, Novell NetWare, and Windows Server 2003.

What other kinds of computers require a multiuser operating system?
Large corporations with hundreds or thousands of employees often use powerful computers known as mainframes. These computers are responsible for storing, managing, and simultaneously processing data from all users. Mainframe operating systems fall into the multiuser category. Examples include IBM's OS/2 and z/OS.

Supercomputers also use multiuser operating systems. Scientists and engineers use supercomputers to solve complex problems or to perform massive computations. Some supercomputers are single computers with multiple processors, whereas others consist of multiple computers that work together.

Desktop Operating Systems

As mentioned earlier, desktop computers (and laptops) use single-user, multitask operating systems, of which there are several on the market, including Windows and Mac OS. The type of processor in the computer determines which operating system a particular desktop computer uses. The combination of operating system and processor is referred to as a computer's **platform**.

For example, Microsoft Windows operating systems are designed to coordinate with a series of processors from Intel Corporation that share the same or similar sets of instructions, whereas Apple Macintosh operating systems work primarily with processors from the Motorola Corporation designed specifically for Apple computers. The two operating systems, as well as application programs designed for those operating systems, are not interchangeable. If you attempt to load a Windows OS on a Mac, for example, the Mac processor will not understand the operating system and will not function properly.

MICROSOFT WINDOWS

What is the most popular operating system for desktop computers?
Microsoft Windows is the market leader in operating system sales, maintaining an approximate 90 percent market share. Although Windows XP is the most recent version on the market, many computers still run earlier versions, such as Windows 95,

Windows 98, Windows Millennium Edition (Me), and Windows 2000. Windows XP comes in a number of versions to suit different users, including Windows XP Home Edition, Windows XP Professional, and Windows XP Tablet PC.

What is the difference between the various Windows operating systems? Figure 5.4 presents a time line of the evolution of Microsoft Windows. As you can see, with each new version, Microsoft made improvements. What was once only a single-user,

FIGURE 5.4   Windows Time Line

1985	WINDOWS 1.0	Introduces point-and-click commands with a mouse and includes modest multitasking capabilities and desktop applications.
87	WINDOWS 2.0	Includes better graphics capabilities and introduces keyboard shortcuts and the ability to overlap windows.
1990	WINDOWS 3.0	Added programs to manage applications, files, and print jobs as well as improved icons.
92	WINDOWS 3.1	First widely used PC graphical user interface (GUI) operating system. Improved point-and-click mouse operations and multitasking capabilities.
1993	WINDOWS NT 3.1	Fundamentally different operating system with increased security, power, performance, and multitasking scheduler.
1995	WINDOWS 95	Provides major enhancements over Windows 3.1. This operating system runs faster and more efficiently, introduces Plug and Play capabilities, long file names, short-cut right-click menus, and a cleaner desktop. Sells more than 1 million copies within 4 days.
96	WINDOWS NT 4.0	Has a similar feel to that of Windows 95 but with enhanced network support and security features.
97	WINDOWS CE	Released to compete with the Palm OS for Personal Digital Assistants (PDAs). It has the same look and features of Windows 95.
1998	WINDOWS 98	This upgrade to Windows 95 includes additional file protection features and incorporates Internet Explorer 4.0, a customizable taskbar, and desktop features that let you customize backgrounds as well as live Web content such as a stock ticker or weather map.
2000	WINDOWS 2000 PROFESSIONAL	This upgrade to Windows NT offers improvements to file security and Internet support.
2000	WINDOWS MILLENNIUM EDITION (ME)	This upgrade to Windows 95 and Windows 98 includes system backup and multimedia capabilities (such as Media Player).
2001	WINDOWS XP HOME AND PROFESSIONAL	Offers a new multiuser desktop as well as improved digital media features and Internet capabilities.
2001	WINDOWS XP MEDIA CENTER OS	Designed specifically for Media Center PCs, this operating system integrates digital entertainment (TV, movies, music, photos, and radio). For example, you can record live TV and radio programs, create your own DVDs, and edit and show photos.
2001	WINDOWS XP TABLET PC	Designed specifically for new Tablet PC notebooks, this operating system incorporates a digital pen that enables users to write directly on the Tablet screen and perform mouse functions. It also includes built-in wireless technologies.

single-task operating system is now a powerful multiuser operating system. Over time, Windows improvements have concentrated on increasing user functionality and friendliness, improving Internet capabilities, and enhancing file privacy and security.

MAC OS

How is Mac OS different from Windows?
Although Apple's **Mac OS** and the Windows operating systems are not compatible, they are very similar in terms of functionality. In 1984, Mac OS became the first operating system to incorporate the user-friendly point-and-click technology in a commercially affordable computer. Both operating systems now have similar window work areas on the desktop that house individual applications and support users working in more than one application at a time (see Figure 5.5).

Despite their similarities, there are many subtle and not-so-subtle differences that have created loyal fans of each product. Macs have long been recognized for their superior graphics display and processing capabilities. Users also attest to Mac's greater system reliability and better document recovery. Despite these advantages, there are fewer software applications available for the Mac platform and Mac systems tend to be a bit more expensive than Windows-based PCs.

The most recent version of the Mac operating system, Mac OS X, is based on the UNIX operating system. Previous Mac operating systems had been based on their own proprietary program. Mac OS X includes a new user interface and larger icons, among other features.

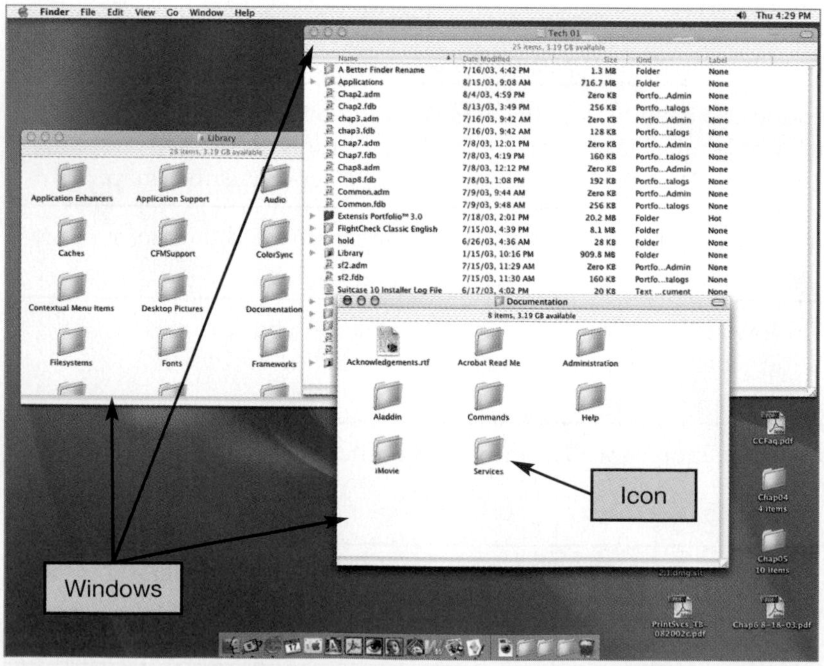

UNIX

What is UNIX?
UNIX is a multiuser, multitask operating system used primarily with mainframes as a network operating system, although it is also often found on PCs. Originally conceived in 1969 by Ken Thompson and Dennis Ritchie of AT&T's Bell Labs, the UNIX code was initially not proprietary—in other words, no company like Microsoft or Apple owned it. Rather, any programmer was allowed to use the code and modify it to meet his or her needs. Later, AT&T licensed the UNIX source code to the Santa Cruz Operation (SCO). UNIX is a brand that belongs to the company X/Open, but any vendor that meets testing requirements and pays a fee can use the UNIX name. Individual vendors then modify the UNIX code to run specifically on their hardware. HP/UX from Hewlett-Packard, Solaris from Sun, and AIX from IBM are some of the UNIX systems currently available in the marketplace.

LINUX

What is Linux?
Linux is an open-source operating system based on UNIX and designed primarily for use on personal computers (although some versions can also be used on networks). An **open-source program** is one that is available for developers to use or modify as they wish. Linux began in 1991 as a part-time project by a Finnish university student named Linus Torvalds, who wanted to create a free operating system to run on his home computer. He posted his operating system program code to the Web for others to use and modify. It has since been tweaked by scores of programmers as part of the Free Software Foundation GNU (or GNU's not UNIX) project.

FIGURE 5.5

The most recent version of the Mac operating system, Mac OS X, is based on the UNIX operating system. Despite not being compatible with Windows OS, Mac OS has very similar features to Windows.

TRENDS IN IT

EMERGING TECHNOLOGIES
Open-Source Software: Why Isn't Everyone Using Linux?

Proprietary software, such as Microsoft Windows, is developed by corporations and sold for profit. This means that the *source code*, the actual lines of instructional code that make the program work, is not accessible to the general public. Without being able to access the source code, it's difficult to modify the software or see exactly how the program author constructed various parts of the system.

Restricting access to the source code protects companies from having their programming ideas stolen, and prevents customers from using modified versions of the software. This benefits the companies that create the software because their software code can't be pirated (or stolen). However, in the late 1980s, computer specialists became concerned over the fact that large software companies (such as Microsoft) were controlling a large portion of market share and driving out competitors. They also felt that proprietary software was too expensive and contained too many bugs (errors).

These people felt that software should be developed without a profit motive and distributed with its source code free for all to see. The theory was that if many computer specialists examine, improve, and change the source code, a more full-featured, bug-free product would result. Hence the open-source movement was born.

Open-source software is freely distributed (no royalties accrue to the creators), contains the source code, and can in turn be redistributed freely to others. Most open-source products are created by teams of programmers and modified (updated) by hundreds of other programmers around the world. You can download the products for free off the Internet. Linux is probably the most widely recognized name in open-source software, but other products such as MySQL (a database program) and OpenOffice (a suite of productivity applications) are also gaining in popularity.

So, if an operating system such as Linux is free, why does Windows (which you must pay for) have such a huge market share? Corporations and individuals have grown accustomed to one thing that proprietary software makers can provide: technical support. It is almost impossible to provide technical support for open-source software because it can be freely modified, and there is no one specific developer to take responsibility for technical support (see Figure 5.6). Therefore, corporations have been reluctant to install open-source software extensively because of the cost of the internal staff of programmers that must support it.

Companies such as Red Hat have been combating this problem. Red Hat has been packaging and selling versions of Linux since 1994. The company provides a warranty and technical support for its version of Linux (which Red Hat programmers modified from the original source code). Packaging open source software in this manner has made using it much more attractive to businesses. Today, many Web servers are hosted on computers running Linux.

So, when will free versions of Linux (or another open-source operating system) be the dominant OS on home computers? The answer is maybe never. Most casual computer users won't feel comfortable without technical support; therefore, any open-source products for home use would probably need to be marketed the way Red Hat markets Linux. Also, many open-source products are not easy to install and maintain.

However, companies such as Linspire (**www.linspire.com**) are making operating systems with easy-to-use visual interfaces that work with the Linux operating system. If one of these companies can develop an easy-to-use product and has the marketing clout to challenge Microsoft, you may see more open-source software deployed in the home computer market in the future.

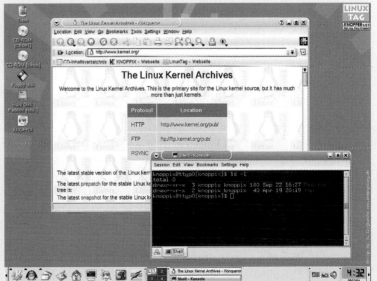

FIGURE 5.6

Although free Linux software, provided by companies like Knoppix, is available, a lack of technical support scares many companies away from wide scale adoption.

BITS AND BYTES

Why a Penguin?

If you've seen Linux products, you know Linux's logo is a penguin. Why would Linus Torvalds, the creator of Linux, choose a penguin? It's not exactly the image most people think of when considering operating systems. However, Torvalds liked the image of a penguin because he felt that it represented the idea that "the world is a good place to be." With regard to the penguin portraying the true appeal of Linux, Torvalds writes on the Linux Web site: "Some people have told me they don't think a fat penguin really embodies the grace of Linux, which just tells me they have never seen an angry penguin charging at them in excess of 100 miles per hour. They'd be a lot more careful about what they say if they had."

FIGURE 5.7

Chances are you'll be seeing more of this penguin image as Linux continues to make strides as a legitimate competitor to market leader Windows XP.

What the Operating System Does

As shown in Figure 5.8, the operating system is like a traffic cop that coordinates the flow of data and information through the computer system. In doing so, the OS performs several specific functions:

- It provides a way for the user to interact with the computer.
- It manages the processor, or central processing unit (CPU).
- It manages the memory and storage.
- It manages the computer system's hardware and peripheral devices.
- It provides a consistent means for software applications to work with the CPU.

In this section, we look at each of these functions in detail.

THE USER INTERFACE

How does the operating system control how I interact with software? The operating system provides a **user interface** that enables you to interact with the computer. As noted earlier, the first personal computers had a DOS operating system with a command-driven interface, as shown in Figure 5.9a. A **command-driven interface** is one in which you enter commands to communicate with the computer system. The commands were not always easy to understand and therefore the interface proved to be too complicated for the average user. Therefore, PCs were used primarily in business and by professional computer operators.

The command-driven interface was later improved by incorporating a menu-driven interface, as shown in Figure 5.9b. A **menu-driven interface** is one in which you choose a command from menus displayed on the screen. Menu-driven interfaces eliminated the need to know every command because you could select most of the commonly used commands from a menu. However, they were still not easy enough for most people to use.

What kind of interface do operating systems use today? Most operating systems today, such as Mac OS and Microsoft Windows, use a **graphical user interface**, or **GUI** (pronounced "gooey"). Unlike the command- and menu-driven interfaces used

Today, Linux is gaining a reputation as a stable operating system that is not subject to crashes and failures. Because the code is open and available to anyone, Linux is quickly tweaked to meet virtually any new operating system need. For example, when Palm PDAs emerged, the Linux OS was promptly modified to run on this new device. Similarly, only a few weeks were necessary to get the Linux OS ready for the new Intel Xeon processor, a feat unheard of in proprietary operating system development. Linux is also gaining popularity among computer manufacturers, which have begun to ship it with some of their latest PCs.

Where can I buy Linux? You can download the open-source versions of Linux for free off the Internet. However, there are several versions of Linux that are more proprietary in nature. These versions come with support and other products not generally associated with the open-source Linux. Red Hat has been packaging and selling versions of Linux since 1994 and is probably the most well-known Linux distributor. Red Hat Enterprise Linux is the current version on the market. Other Linux distributors include Mandrake, Debian GNU/Linux, and Gentoo Linux. For a full listing and explanation of all Linux distributors, visit **www.distrowatch.com**.

techtv

For information on running Linux, see "Review: Lindows 4.0," a TechTV clip found at www.prenhall.com/ techinaction.

Manages the computer system's hardware and peripheral devices

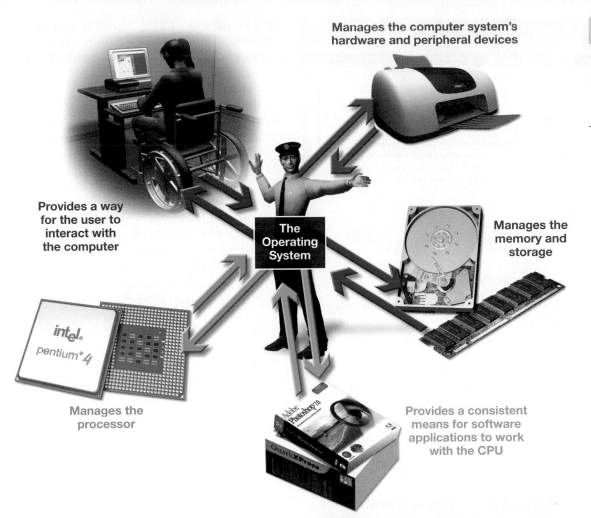

Provides a way for the user to interact with the computer

The Operating System

Manages the memory and storage

Manages the processor

Provides a consistent means for software applications to work with the CPU

FIGURE 5.8

The operating system is the traffic cop of your computer, coordinating its many activities and devices.

earlier, GUIs display graphics and use the point-and-click technology of the mouse and cursor, making them much more user friendly. As illustrated in Figure 5.10 (p. 188), a GUI uses **windows** (rectangular boxes that contain programs displayed on the screen), **menus** (lists of commands that appear on the screen), and **icons** (pictures that represent an object such as a software application or a file or folder). Because users no longer have to enter commands to interact with the computer, GUIs are a big reason why desktop computers are now such popular tools.

Unlike Windows or Mac OS, Linux does not have a built-in user interface. Instead, users are free to choose among many commercially available or free interfaces, such as GNOME, KDE, and Motif, each of which provides a different look and feel. For example, GNOME (pronounced "gah-NOHM") actually allows you to select which desktop appearance (Windows or Mac) you'd like your system to display. This means that if you're using Linux for the first time, you don't

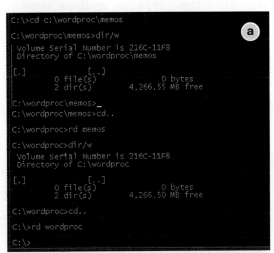

FIGURE 5.9

(a) Command-driven and (b) menu-driven interfaces were not user friendly.

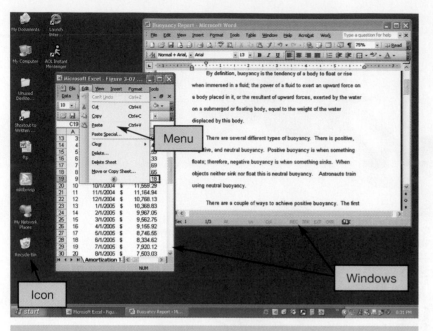

FIGURE 5.10

Today's operating systems include a graphical user interface (GUI). These user interfaces are much more user friendly than the DOS command-driven interfaces used previously.

have to learn a new interface: you just use the one you're most comfortable with already.

PROCESSOR MANAGEMENT

Why does the operating system need to manage the processor? When you use your computer, you are usually asking it to perform several tasks at once. For example, you might be printing a Word document, waiting for a file to download from the Internet, listening to a CD from your CD drive, and working on a PowerPoint presentation, all at the same time—or at least what *appears* to be at the same time. Although the processor is the powerful brains of the computer, processing all of its instructions and performing all of its calculations, it can perform only one action at a time. Therefore, it needs the operating system to arrange for the execution of all these activities in a systematic way to give the appearance that everything is happening simultaneously.

To do so, the operating system assigns a slice of its time to each activity requiring the processor's attention. The OS must then switch between different processes thousands of times a second to make it appear that everything is happening in a seamlessly fluid manner. Otherwise, you wouldn't be

able to listen to a CD and print at the same time without experiencing delays in the process. When the operating system allows you to perform more than one task at a time, it is said to be **multitasking**.

How exactly does the operating system coordinate all the activities? When you type and print a document in Word, for example, many different devices in the computer system are involved, including your keyboard, mouse, and printer. Every keystroke, every mouse click, and each signal to the printer creates an action, or **event**, in the respective device (keyboard, mouse, or printer) to which the operating system responds.

Sometimes these events occur sequentially (such as when you type characters one at a time), but other events require two devices working simultaneously (such as the printer printing while you continue to type). Although it *looks* as though the keyboard and printer are working at the same time, as mentioned earlier, the processor actually can handle only one event at a time and switches back and forth between processes. To do this, the operating system controls the timing of events the processor works on.

For example, assume you are typing and you want to print another document. When you tell your computer to print your document, the printer generates a unique signal called an **interrupt** that tells the operating system that it is in need of immediate attention. Every device has its own type of interrupt, which is associated with an *interrupt handler*, a special numerical code that prioritizes the requests. These requests are placed in the *interrupt table* in the computer's primary memory (or random access memory, RAM).

In our example, the operating system pauses the CPU from its typing activity when it receives the interrupt from the printer and puts a "memo" in a special location in RAM called a *stack*. The memo is a reminder of where the CPU was before it left off so that it can work on the printer request. The CPU then retrieves the printer request from the interrupt table and begins to process it. Upon completion of the printer request, the CPU goes back to the stack, retrieves the memo it placed about the keystroke activity, and returns to that task until it is interrupted again.

What happens if there is more than one document waiting to be printed? The operating system also coordinates multiple activities for peripheral devices such as printers. When the processor receives a request to send information to the printer, it first checks with the operating system to ensure that the printer is not already in use. If it is in use, the OS puts the request in another temporary storage area in RAM called the *buffer*. It will wait in the buffer until the *spooler*, a program that helps coordinate all print jobs currently being sent to the printer, indicates the printer is available. If more than one print job is waiting, a line, or *queue*, is formed so that the printer can process the requests in order.

MEMORY AND STORAGE MANAGEMENT

Why does the operating system have to manage the computer's memory?

As the operating system coordinates the activities of the processor, it uses RAM as a temporary storage area for instructions and data the processor needs. The processor then accesses these instructions and data from RAM when it is ready to process them. The OS is therefore responsible for coordinating the space allocations in RAM to ensure that there is enough space for all the waiting instructions and data. It then clears the items from RAM when the processor no longer needs them.

Can my system ever run out of RAM space?
RAM has limited capacity. The average computer system has anywhere from 128 megabytes (MB) to 2 gigabytes (GB) of memory in RAM. Although 2 GB of RAM seems like a lot of space, if you're running numerous multimedia-intensive applications at the same time, you can easily use up the RAM in your computer.

What happens if my computer runs out of RAM?
When there isn't enough room in RAM for the operating system to store the required data and instructions, the operating system borrows room from the more spacious hard drive. This process of optimizing RAM storage by borrowing hard drive space is called **virtual memory**. As shown in Figure 5.11, when more RAM space is needed, the operating system swaps out from RAM the data or instructions that have not been recently used and moves them to a temporary storage area on the hard drive called the **swap file** (or **page file**). If the data and/or instructions in the swap file are needed later, the operating system swaps them back into active RAM and replaces them in the hard drive's swap file with less-active data or instructions. This process of swapping is known as **paging**.

Can I ever run out of virtual memory?
Only a portion of the hard drive is allocated to virtual memory. You can manually change this setting to increase the amount of hard drive space allocated, but eventually your computer system will become sluggish as it is forced to page more and more often. This condition of excessive paging is called **thrashing**. The solution to this problem is to increase the amount of RAM in your system so that you can avoid it having to send data and instructions to virtual memory. You'll learn how to monitor your RAM and virtual memory requirements in Chapter 6.

How does the operating system manage storage?
If it weren't for the operating system, the files and applications you save to the hard drive and other storage locations would be a complete mess. Fortunately, the OS has a file management system that keeps track of the name and location of each file you save and programs you install. We talk more about file management later in the chapter.

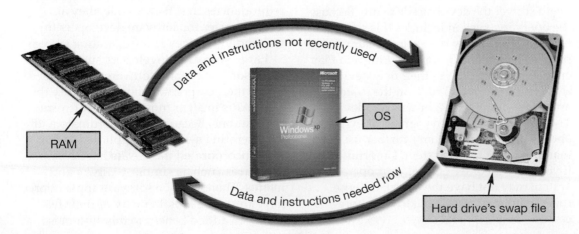

Virtual memory borrows excess storage capacity from the hard drive when there is not enough capacity in RAM.

HARDWARE AND PERIPHERAL DEVICE MANAGEMENT

How does the operating system manage the hardware and peripheral devices? Each device attached to your computer comes with a special program called a **device driver** that facilitates the communication between the hardware device and the operating system. Because the OS must be able to communicate with every device in the computer system, the device driver translates the specialized commands of the device to commands that the operating system can understand, and vice versa. Thus, devices will not function without the proper device driver, because the OS would not know how to communicate with them.

How can I get device drivers? Manufacturers preinstall device drivers for the original hardware that comes with your computer, such as your mouse, monitor, and CD-ROM drive. However, if you replace any of these devices or purchase additional devices, such as a scanner, printer, or DVD player, you must install separate device drivers. Hardware manufacturers generally include device drivers with their devices, but sometimes you have to download the driver from the manufacturer's Web site. Should you purchase a device secondhand and not receive the device driver, you can often contact the manufacturer for a copy. You can also check out Web sites such as **www.driverzone.com** or **www.driverguide.com** to locate drivers.

Is Plug and Play a device driver? Plug and Play (PnP) is not a driver. Instead, it is a software and hardware standard that Microsoft created with the Windows 95 operating system. This standard is designed to facilitate the installation of a new piece of hardware in personal computers by including the driver the device needs to run. Because the operating system includes this software, incorporating a new device into your computer system seems automatic. Plug and Play enables users to plug in their new device to a port on the system, turn on the system, and immediately play, or use, the device. The OS automatically recognizes the device and its driver without any further user manipulations to the system. Unfortunately, if you have an older device, your operating system may not have the driver. In those cases, you must install the driver before you can use the peripheral device.

Can I damage my system by installing a device driver? Occasionally, when you install a driver, your system may become unstable (that is, programs may stop responding, certain actions may cause a crash, or the device or the entire system may stop working). Although this is not common, it can happen. Fortunately, Windows XP has a Roll Back Driver feature (accessible through the Control Panel) that reinstalls the old driver and remedies the problem.

SOFTWARE APPLICATION COORDINATION

How does the operating system help software applications run on the computer? Software applications feed the CPU the instructions it needs to process data. These instructions take the form of computer code. Every software application, no matter what its type or manufacturer, needs to interact with the CPU. For programs to work with the CPU, they must contain code that the CPU recognizes. Rather than having the same blocks of code for similar procedures in each software application, the operating system includes the blocks of code that software applications need to interact with it. These blocks of code are called **application programming interfaces (APIs)**. Microsoft DirectX, for example, is a group of multimedia APIs built into the Windows operating system that improves graphics and sounds when you're playing games or watching video on your PC.

To create programs that can communicate with the operating system, software programmers need only *refer* to the API code blocks in their individual application programs, rather than including the entire code in the application itself. Not only do APIs avoid redundancies in software code, they also make it easier for software developers to respond to changes in the operating system.

Large software developers such as Microsoft have many software applications under their corporate umbrella and use the same APIs in all or most of their software applications. Because APIs coordinate with the operating system, all applications that have incorporated these APIs have common interfaces such as similar toolbars and menus. Therefore, the software applications have the same look to many of their features. An added benefit to this system is that applications sharing these same formats can also easily exchange data between different programs. As such, it's easy to create a chart in Microsoft Excel from data in Microsoft Access and incorporate the finished chart into a Microsoft Word document.

The Boot Process: Starting Your Computer

Although it only takes a minute or two, a lot of things happen very quickly between the time you turn on the computer and when it is ready for you to enter your first command. As you learned earlier, all data and instructions (including the operating system) are stored in RAM while your computer is on. When you turn your computer off, RAM is wiped clean of all its data (including the OS). So, how does the computer know what to do when you turn

it on if there is nothing in RAM? It runs through a special process, called the **boot process** (or start-up process), to load the operating system into RAM.

What are the steps involved in the boot process? The boot process, illustrated in Figure 5.12, consists of four basic steps:

1. The basic input/output system (BIOS) is activated by powering on the CPU.

2. The BIOS checks that all attached devices are in place (called a power-on self-test, or POST).

3. The operating system is loaded into RAM.

4. Configuration and customization settings are checked.

As the computer goes through the boot process in Windows operating systems, indicator lights on the keyboard and disk drives will illuminate and the system will emit various beeps. If you have a version of Windows earlier than XP, text like that

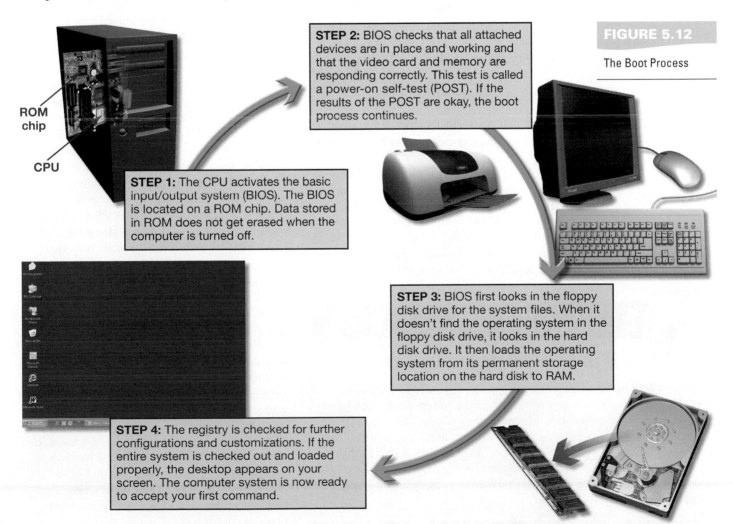

FIGURE 5.12

The Boot Process

STEP 1: The CPU activates the basic input/output system (BIOS). The BIOS is located on a ROM chip. Data stored in ROM does not get erased when the computer is turned off.

STEP 2: BIOS checks that all attached devices are in place and working and that the video card and memory are responding correctly. This test is called a power-on self-test (POST). If the results of the POST are okay, the boot process continues.

STEP 3: BIOS first looks in the floppy disk drive for the system files. When it doesn't find the operating system in the floppy disk drive, it looks in the hard disk drive. It then loads the operating system from its permanent storage location on the hard disk to RAM.

STEP 4: The registry is checked for further configurations and customizations. If the entire system is checked out and loaded properly, the desktop appears on your screen. The computer system is now ready to accept your first command.

ROM chip

CPU

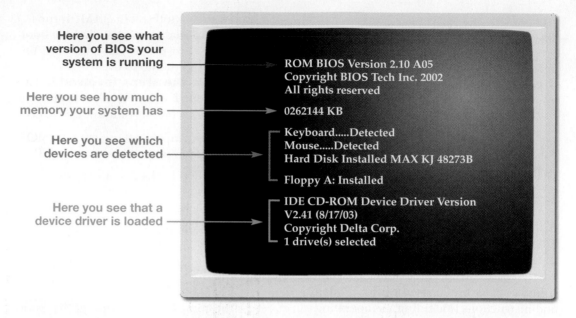

If you have a version of Windows earlier than XP, you'll see a screen similar to this one during the boot process.

Here you see what version of BIOS your system is running

Here you see how much memory your system has

Here you see which devices are detected

Here you see that a device driver is loaded

ROM BIOS Version 2.10 A05
Copyright BIOS Tech Inc. 2002
All rights reserved

0262144 KB

Keyboard.....Detected
Mouse.....Detected
Hard Disk Installed MAX KJ 48273B

Floppy A: Installed

IDE CD-ROM Device Driver Version
V2.41 (8/17/03)
Copyright Delta Corp.
1 drive(s) selected

shown in Figure 5.13 will scroll down the screen as well. When you boot up on a Mac, you won't hear any beeps or see any keyboard lights illuminate. Instead, a Welcome screen will appear, indicating the progress of the start-up process. Once the boot process has completed these steps, it is ready to accept commands and data. Let's look at each of these steps in more detail.

STEP 1: ACTIVATING BIOS

What's the first thing that happens after I turn on my computer? In the first step of the boot process, the CPU activates the BIOS. The **basic input/output system**, or **BIOS** (pronounced "bye-OSE"), is a program that manages the data between the operating system and all the input and output devices attached to the system, hence its name. BIOS is also responsible for loading the OS from its permanent location on the hard drive to RAM.

BITS AND BYTES

How Did "Boot" Get Its Name?

The term *boot*, used to describe the process of starting a computer, gets its name from the term *bootstrap*. In the olden days, men used straps of leather, called bootstraps, to help them pull on their boots. The use of bootstraps in this way created the expression to "pull oneself up by the bootstraps." In computing terms, the *bootstrap loader* is a very small program that begins the process of loading a much larger and more powerful program that then controls the rest of the system.

BIOS itself is stored on a special read-only memory (ROM) chip on the motherboard. Unlike data stored in RAM, data stored in ROM is permanent and does not get erased when the power is turned off.

STEP 2: PERFORMING THE POWER-ON SELF-TEST

How does the computer determine whether the hardware is working properly? The first job BIOS performs is to ensure that essential peripheral devices are attached and operational. This process is called the **power-on self-test**, or **POST**. The POST consists of a test on the video card and video memory, a BIOS identification process (during which the BIOS version, manufacturer, and data are displayed on the monitor), and a memory test to ensure memory chips are working properly.

The BIOS compares the results of the POST with the various hardware configurations that are permanently stored in CMOS (pronounced "see-moss"). CMOS, which stands for complementary metal-oxide semiconductor, is a special kind of memory that uses almost no power. A little battery provides enough power so its contents will not be lost after the computer is turned off. CMOS contains information about the system's memory, types of disk drives, and other essential input and output hardware components. If the results of the POST compare favorably to the hardware configurations stored in CMOS, the boot process continues.

STEP 3: LOADING THE OPERATING SYSTEM

How does the operating system get loaded into RAM? BIOS looks through the storage disks for the **system files**, the main files of the operating system. The first place it looks is the floppy disk drive. When it doesn't find the OS there, it looks in the hard disk drive. It then loads the operating system from its permanent storage location on the hard drive to RAM.

Once the system files are loaded into RAM, the **kernel** (or **supervisor program**) is loaded. The kernel is the essential component of the operating system. It is responsible for managing the processor and all other components of the computer system. Because it stays in RAM the entire time your computer is powered on, the kernel is called *memory resident*. To not take up all the RAM, other parts of the OS that are less critical stay on the hard drive and are copied over to RAM on an as-needed basis. These programs are called *nonresident*. Once the kernel is loaded, the operating system takes over the control of the computer's functions.

STEP 4: CHECKING FURTHER CONFIGURATIONS AND CUSTOMIZATIONS

When are the other components and configurations of the system checked? Although CMOS checks the configuration of memory and essential peripherals in the beginning of the boot process, the operating system continues to check the configuration of other system components in this last phase of the boot process. The **registry** contains all the different configurations (settings) used by the OS as well as by other applications. It contains the customized settings you put into place, such as mouse speed, the display settings for your monitor and desktop, as well as instructions as to which programs should be loaded first.

Why do I sometimes need to enter a password at the end of the boot process? In a networked environment, such as that found at most colleges, the operating system services many users. To determine whether a user is authorized to use the system (that is, whether a user is a paying student or college employee),

BITS AND BYTES

Are Booting and Installing the Same Thing?

Like most software programs, the operating system is saved to the hard disk, or *installed*, only once. Typically, computer manufacturers preinstall the operating system. However, booting is done every time you turn the computer on, either from an off position (called a *cold boot*) or when you restart the system after it's already on (called a *warm boot*). You might need to perform a warm boot if the operating system or other software application stops responding. You do a cold boot each time you start the computer after you've turned it off completely.

authorized users are given a login name and password. The verification of your login name and password at the end of the boot process is called **authentication**. The authentication process blocks unauthorized users from entering the system.

You may also need to insert a password following the boot process to log in to your account on your home computer. The newest version of the Windows operating system, Windows XP, is a multiuser system. Even in a home environment, all users with access to a Windows XP computer (such as family members or roommates) have their own user accounts. Users can set up a password to protect their account from being accessed by another user without permission.

How do I know if the boot process is successful? The entire boot process takes only a minute or two to complete. If the entire system is checked out and loaded properly, the process completes by displaying the desktop. The computer system is now ready to accept your first command.

HANDLING ERRORS IN THE BOOT PROCESS

What can go wrong during the boot process? During the boot process, if you come across a message like the following:

```
Non-system disk or disk error
Replace and strike any key when ready
```

check to see whether you've left a disk in the floppy disk drive. As explained earlier, when the BIOS is performing its system check, it first looks in the floppy drive for the operating system. With early computers, operating systems were not permanently stored on the hard drive but were instead loaded into the system from a floppy disk. (That's how DOS, or Disk Operating System, got its name.) If you have ever had a hard disk crash and needed to install the system repair disk, you understand why it's important for today's systems to still check the floppy disk drive first.

If BIOS doesn't find a floppy in the floppy drive, it proceeds to the hard drive. However, if it *does* find a floppy in the floppy drive, it will attempt to find the OS on that floppy. When it does not find the operating system software on the floppy, the boot process stops and displays the error message "Non-system disk or disk error." When this happens, simply remove the floppy disk and press any key to resume the boot process.

How can I tell if there are other errors during the boot process? During the boot process, a string of text scrolls down your monitor screen. This text contains a list of devices attached to your system as well as their settings. If there is a problem with loading a device during the POST, an error message (generally on a blue background) appears on your screen.

Sometimes, however, the problem occurs before the video (display) card that controls your monitor has been activated, making a display message impossible. In those instances, you will hear a series of beeps. (These beeps are in place of the single beep you would hear if everything was loading properly.) Each device in your computer system is assigned a specific beep code. Because different BIOS manufacturers have different beep codes, you can identify the error by listening to the number of beeps and then comparing them to the beep codes listed in your computer's user manual or on the BIOS manufacturer's Web site.

Figure 5.14 shows sample beep codes for the Phoenix BIOS. Being able to identify an "error beep" during the boot process will facilitate conversations you may later have with a technical assistant to diagnose the problem.

What should I do if my keyboard or other device doesn't work after I boot my computer? Sometimes during the boot process, BIOS skips a device (such as a keyboard) or improperly identifies it. You won't hear any beeps or see any error messages when this happens. Your only indication that this sort of problem has occurred is that the device won't respond after the system has been booted. When that happens, you can generally resolve the problem by rebooting. If the problem persists, you may want to check the operating system's Web site for any patches (or software fixes) that may resolve the issue. If there are no patches or the problem persists, you may want to get technical assistance.

What is Safe mode? Sometimes Windows does not boot properly and you end up with a screen with the words *Safe Mode* in the corners, as shown in Figure 5.15. **Safe mode** is a special diagnostic mode designed for troubleshooting errors that occur during the boot process. While in Safe mode, only the essential devices of the system (such as the mouse, keyboard, and monitor) function. Even the regular graphics device driver will not be activated in Safe mode. Instead, the system runs in the most basic graphics mode, resulting in a grayish-toned screen.

What should I do if my operating system boots into Safe mode? Sometimes, Safe mode indicates that there is a problem with the loading of a device or software application. Try rebooting the machine before doing anything else. If you still end up in Safe mode and if you have recently installed new software or a new hardware device, try uninstalling it. (Make sure you use the Add/Remove feature in Control Panel.) If the problem then goes away after rebooting, you have determined

FIGURE 5.14 Sample Phoenix BIOS Beep Codes	
SEQUENCE OF BEEPS YOU HEAR	**WHAT THE BEEPS INDICATE**
1-1-3	Your computer isn't able to read the configuration information stored in the CMOS chip
1-1-4	There is something wrong with BIOS
1-4-2	Some of the memory in your computer is not functioning correctly
4-2-2	Your computer is not able to communicate with the keyboard

the cause of the problem. You can then reinstall the device or software. If the problem
does not go away, you should consult a technical support person for further diagnosis.

The Desktop and Windows Features

The **desktop** is the first interaction you have
with the operating system and the first image
you see on your monitor. As its name implies,
your computer's desktop puts at your fingertips all of the elements necessary for a
productive work session that are typically
found on or near the top of a traditional
desk, such as files and folders.

**What are the main features of the
desktop?** The very nature of a desktop is
that it enables you to customize it to meet
your individual needs. As such, the desktop on your computer may be different
from the desktop on your friend's computer.
However, most desktops share common
features, some of which are illustrated in
Figure 5.16.

FIGURE 5.15

If your screen looks like this, your computer has booted into Safe mode.
This means that something did not function properly during the boot process.
Safe mode provides you with enough functionality so that you can accomplish
diagnostic testing.

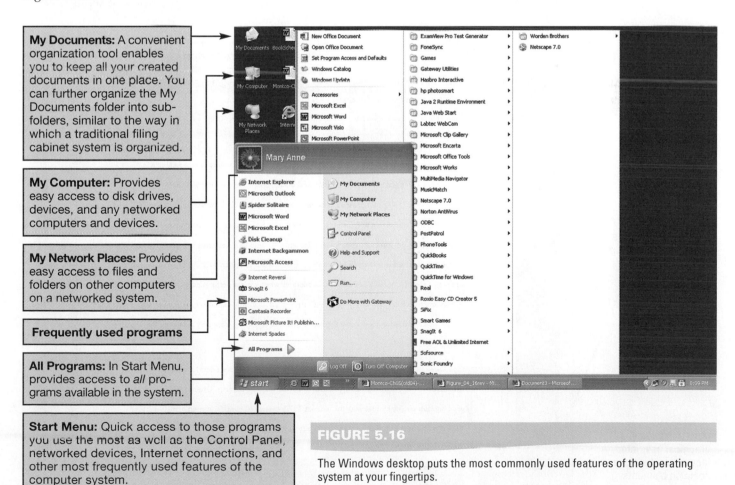

My Documents: A convenient
organization tool enables
you to keep all your created
documents in one place. You
can further organize the My
Documents folder into subfolders, similar to the way in
which a traditional filing
cabinet system is organized.

My Computer: Provides
easy access to disk drives,
devices, and any networked
computers and devices.

My Network Places: Provides
easy access to files and
folders on other computers
on a networked system.

Frequently used programs

All Programs: In Start Menu,
provides access to *all* programs available in the system.

Start Menu: Quick access to those programs
you use the most as well as the Control Panel,
networked devices, Internet connections, and
other most frequently used features of the
computer system.

FIGURE 5.16

The Windows desktop puts the most commonly used features of the operating
system at your fingertips.

What are common features of a window? As noted earlier, one feature introduced by the graphical user interface is windows (with a lowercase *w*), the rectangular panes on your computer screen that display applications running on your system. Windows provide for a flexible, user-friendly, multitasking environment. Figure 5.17 illustrates some of the features of windows, including **toolbars** (groups of icons collected together in a small box) and **scrollbars** (bars that appear at the side or bottom of the screen that control which part of the information is displayed on the screen). Using the Minimize, Maximize and Restore, and Close buttons, you can open, close, resize, and move windows anywhere on the desktop.

How can I see more than one window on my desktop at a time? You can easily arrange the windows on a desktop by tiling them, which means arranging separate windows so that they sit next to each other either horizontally or vertically. You can also arrange windows by cascading them so that they overlap one another, or simply resize two open windows so they appear on the screen at the same time.

SOUND BYTE
CUSTOMIZING WINDOWS XP

In this Sound Byte, you'll find out how to customize your desktop. You'll learn how to configure the desktop, set up a screen saver, change pointer options, customize the Start menu, and manage user accounts.

Tiling windows makes accessing two or more active windows more convenient. For example, as shown in Figure 5.18, you can input stock prices from a Web site into an Excel spreadsheet without clicking back and forth between the browser and Excel windows by tiling them horizontally. To untile the windows, or to bring a window back to its full size, click the Restore button in the top right corner of the window.

Can I move or resize the windows once they are tiled? Regardless of whether the windows are tiled, you can resize and move them around the desktop. You can reposition windows on the desktop by pointing to the title bar at the top of the window with your cursor, and while hold-

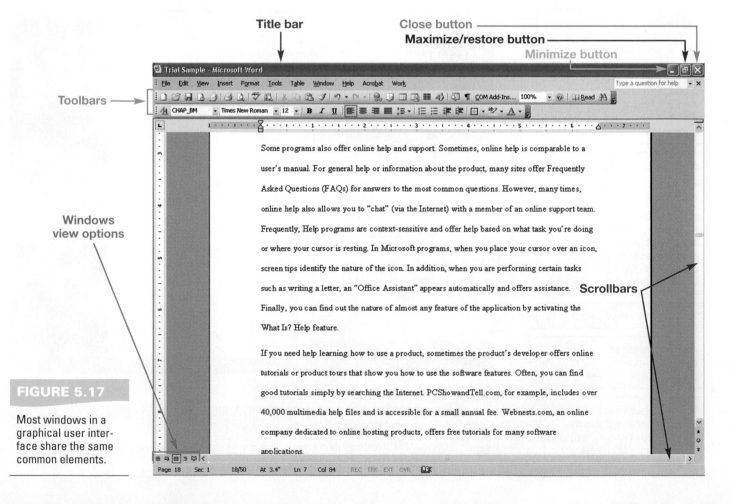

FIGURE 5.17

Most windows in a graphical user interface share the same common elements.

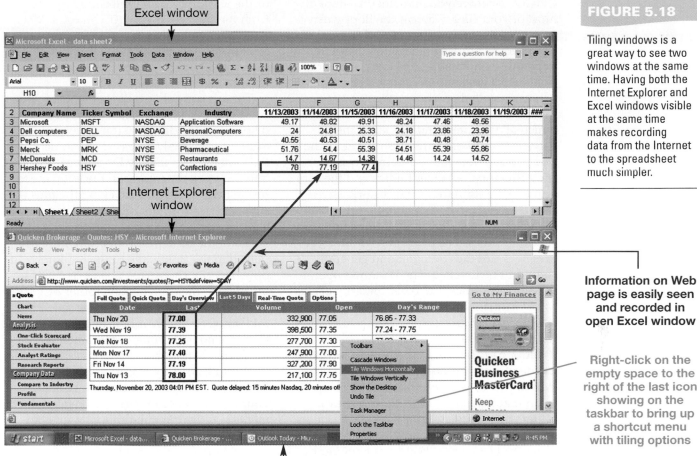

FIGURE 5.18

Tiling windows is a great way to see two windows at the same time. Having both the Internet Explorer and Excel windows visible at the same time makes recording data from the Internet to the spreadsheet much simpler.

Information on Web page is easily seen and recorded in open Excel window

Right-click on the empty space to the right of the last icon showing on the taskbar to bring up a shortcut menu with tiling options

ing down the left mouse button, drag them to a different location. To resize a window, place your cursor on any side or corner of a window until it changes to a double-headed arrow [↕]. You can then left-click and drag the window to the new desired size.

Organizing Your Computer: File Management

You have learned so far that the operating system is responsible for managing the processor, memory, storage, and devices, and that it provides a mechanism for applications and users to interact with the computer system. An additional function of an operating system is to enable **file management**, which entails providing organizational structure to the computer's contents. The OS allows you to organize the contents of your computer in a hierarchical structure of **directories** that includes *files*, *folders*, and *drives*. In

this section, we discuss how you can use this hierarchical structure to create a more organized and efficient computer.

ORGANIZING YOUR FILES

What exactly is a file? Technically, a **file** is a collection of related pieces of information stored together for easy reference. A file in an operating system is a collection of program instructions or data stored and treated as a single unit. Files can be generated from an application, such as a Word document or Excel spreadsheet. Additionally, files can represent an entire application, a Web page, an audio file, or an image file. Files are stored on the hard drive, a floppy disk, or other storage medium for permanent storage. As the number of files you save increases, it is important to keep them organized in **folders**, or collections of files.

How does the operating system organize files? Windows organizes the contents of the computer in a hierarchical structure with drives, folders, subfolders, and files. The hard drive, represented as the

C drive, is where you permanently store most of your files, whereas the floppy drive is the A drive. You may have additional drives (D, E, F, or any other letter designation) depending on whether you have any additional storage devices (Zip, CD, or DVD drives) installed on your computer.

The C drive is like a large filing cabinet in which all files are stored. As such, the C drive is the top of the filing structure of the computer system and is referred to as the **root directory**. All other folders and files are organized within the root directory. There are areas in the root directory that the operating system has filled with folders holding special OS files. The programs within these files help run the computer and generally shouldn't be touched. The Windows operating system also creates other folders, such as My Documents and My Pictures, which are available for you to begin to store and organize your text and image files, respectively.

How can I easily locate and see the contents of my computer? If you use a Windows PC, **Windows Explorer** is the program that helps you manage your files and folders by showing the location and contents of every drive, folder, and file on your computer. You can access Windows Explorer by right-clicking the My Computer desktop icon or the Start button and selecting Explore from the shortcut menu. (If you use a Mac, the Finder is the program that enables you to manage your files and folders.) As illustrated in Figure 5.19, Windows Explorer is divided into two sections.

The left pane shows the contents of your computer in a hierarchical tree structure. It displays all the drives of the system as well as other commonly accessed areas such as the Desktop and the My Documents folder. You can open the folders in the left pane to reveal their contents by clicking the plus (+) sign next to the folder name. Once you open a folder, the plus sign changes to a minus (–) sign and the contents of that folder are displayed in the right pane of the Explorer window. You can choose to expand or collapse the view of the contents of a folder by clicking the plus or minus sign, respectively. If a folder does not have a plus or minus sign, there are no other folders contained within the folder, although it may contain files.

How should I organize my files? Creating **folders** is the key to organizing your files, because folders keep related documents together. Again, think of your computer as a big filing cabinet to which you can add many separate filing drawers, or subfolders. Those drawers, or subfolders,

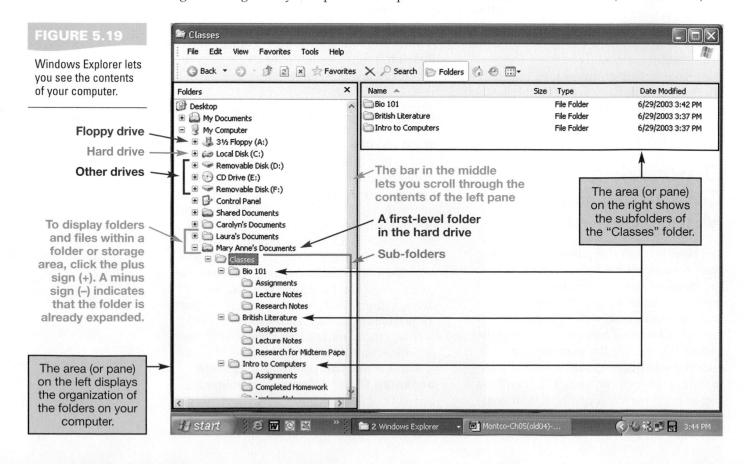

FIGURE 5.19

Windows Explorer lets you see the contents of your computer.

Floppy drive

Hard drive

Other drives

To display folders and files within a folder or storage area, click the plus sign (+). A minus sign (–) indicates that the folder is already expanded.

The area (or pane) on the left displays the organization of the folders on your computer.

The bar in the middle lets you scroll through the contents of the left pane

A first-level folder in the hard drive

Sub-folders

The area (or pane) on the right shows the subfolders of the "Classes" folder.

SOUND BYTE

FILE MANAGEMENT

In this Sound Byte, you'll examine the features of file management and maintenance. You'll learn the various methods of creating folders, how to turn a jumble of unorganized files into an organized system of folders, and how to maintain your file system.

have the capacity to hold even more folders, which can hold other folders or individual files. For example, you can create one folder for your class work called Classes. Inside the Classes folder, you can create folders for each of your classes (such as Intro to Computers, Bio 101, and British Literature). Inside each of those folders, you can create subfolders for each class's assignments, completed homework, research, notes, and so on.

Grouping related files together in folders allows you to more easily identify and find files. Which would be easier, going to the Bio 101 folder to find a file or searching through the 143 individual files in My Documents hoping to find the right one? Grouping files in a folder also allows you to move them more efficiently, so you can quickly transfer critical files needing frequent backup to a floppy disk, for instance.

VIEWING AND SORTING FILES AND FOLDERS

Are there different ways I can view and sort my files and folders? In Windows XP, when you are in a folder, such as My Documents, you can use any of the viewing options located on the View menu to arrange and view your files and folders:

- **Tiles view** displays files and folders as icons in list form. Each icon includes the filename, the application associated with the file, and the file size. The display information is customizable. The Tiles view also displays picture dimensions, a handy feature for Web-page developers.

- **Icon view** also displays files and folders as icons in list form, but the icons are smaller and no other file information beside the filename is listed. However, file information is displayed when you place your cursor over the file icon.

- **List view** is another display of even smaller icons and filenames. This is a good view if you have a lot of content in the folder and need to see most or all of it at once.

- **Thumbnails view**, illustrated in Figure 5.20, shows the contents of folders as

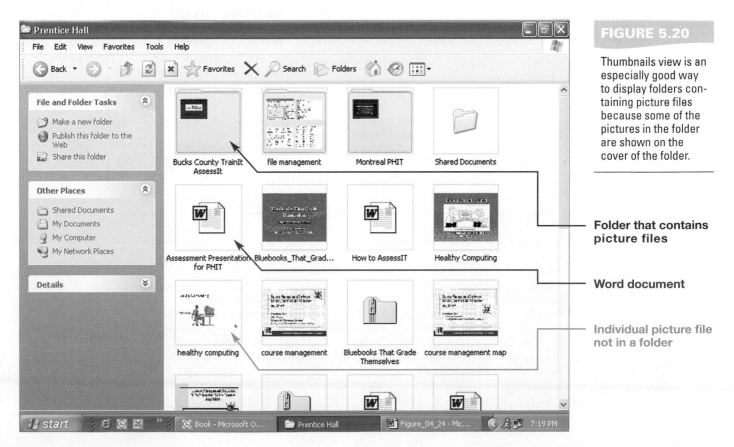

FIGURE 5.20

Thumbnails view is an especially good way to display folders containing picture files because some of the pictures in the folder are shown on the cover of the folder.

Folder that contains picture files

Word document

Individual picture file not in a folder

small images. Thumbnails view is therefore the best view to use if your folder contains picture files. For those folders that contain collections of MP3 files, you can download the cover of the CD or an image of the artist to display on any folder to further identify that collection.

• **Details view** is the most interactive view. As shown in Figure 5.21, the files and folders are displayed in list form, but the

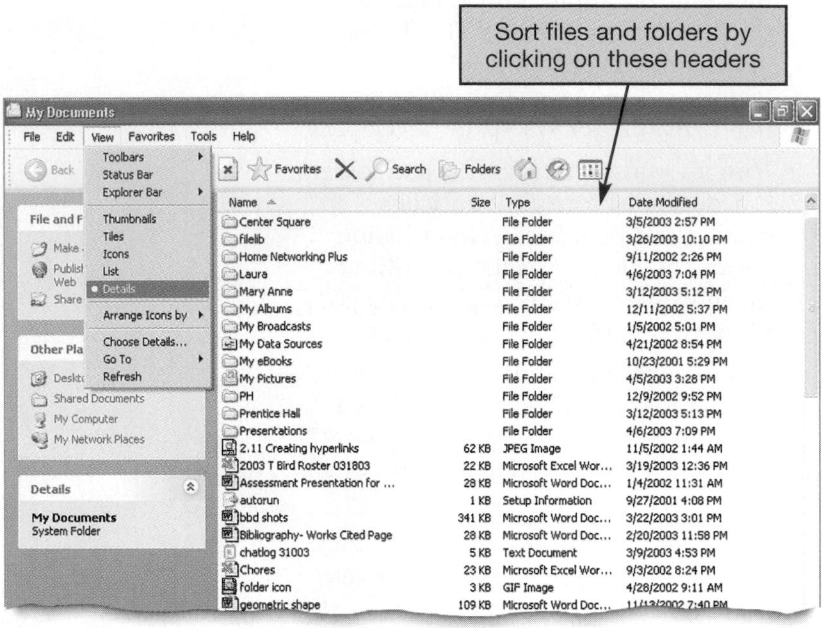

FIGURE 5.21

Details view enables you to sort and list your files in a variety of ways to further assist you in quickly finding the correct file.

additional file information is displayed in columns alongside the filename. You can sort and display the contents of the folder by any of the column headings, so you may sort the contents alphabetically by filename or type, or hierarchically by date last modified or by file size.

What's the best way to search for a file? You've no doubt saved a file and forgotten where you saved it, or have downloaded a file from the Internet and were not sure where it was saved. What's the quickest way to find a file? Looking through every file stored on your computer could take hours, even with a well-organized file management system. Fortunately, Windows includes a Search feature, found on the Start menu, that searches through your hard drive or other storage device (CD, floppy, or flash memory) to locate files that match criteria you provide. Your search can be based on a part of the filename or just a word or phrase in the file. Advanced features let you narrow down your search by providing information about the type of file, which application was used to create the file, or even how long ago the file was saved. (Mac OS has a similar feature called Sherlock.)

NAMING FILES

Are there special rules I have to follow when I name files? Files have names just like people. The first part of a file, or the **filename**, is similar to our first names and

FIGURE 5.22	Filename Extensions	
EXTENSION	**TYPE OF DOCUMENT**	**APPLICATION THAT USES THE EXTENSION**
.doc	Word processing document	Microsoft Word; Corel Word Perfect
.xls	Workbook	Microsoft Excel
.ppt	PowerPoint presentation	Microsoft PowerPoint
.mdb	Database	Microsoft Access
.bmp	Bitmap image	Windows
.zip	Compressed file	WinZip
.pdf	Portable Document Format	Adobe Acrobat
.htm or .html	Web page	Hypertext Markup Language

is generally the name you assign to the file when you save it. For example, "bioreport" may be the name you assign a report you have completed for biology. In a Windows application, following the filename and after the dot (.) comes a three- or four-letter **extension**, or **file type**. Like our last name, this extension identifies what kind of family of files the file belongs to or which application should be used to read the file. For example, if the bioreport file is a Word document, it has a .doc extension and is named bioreport.doc. Figure 5.22 lists the common file extensions and the types of documents they indicate.

Do I need to know the extensions of all files to save them? As shown in Figure 5.23, when you save a file created in a Windows operating system, you do not need to add the extension to the filename; it is automatically added for you. With Mac and Linux operating systems, you are not required to use file extensions when saving files. This is because the information as to the type of application the computer should use to open the file is stored inside the file. However, if you're using these operating systems and will be sending files to Windows users, you should add an extension to your filename so that they can more easily open your files.

Are there things I shouldn't do when naming my file? Each operating system has its own naming conventions, or rules, which are listed in Figure 5.24. Beyond those conventions, it's important that you name your files so that you can easily identify them. A filename like research.doc may be descriptive to you if you're only working on one research paper. However, if you create other research reports later and need to identify the contents of these files quickly, you'll soon wish you had been more descriptive. Giving your files more descriptive names, such as bioresearch.doc or, better yet, bio101research.doc, is a good idea.

Keep in mind, however, every file in the same folder or storage device (hard disk, floppy disk, CD, and so on) must be *uniquely* identified. Therefore, files may share the same filename (such as *bioreport*.doc or *bioreport*.xls), or they may share the same extension (*bioreport.xls* or *budget.xls*); however, no two files stored on the same device or folder can share both the same filename *and* the same extension.

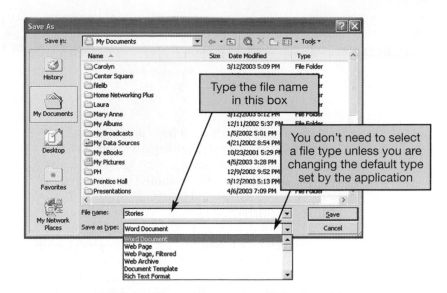

FIGURE 5.23

When you save a file in Windows, you type the filename in the Save As dialog box. The extension is added automatically, though you can change it if necessary.

FIGURE 5.24   File Naming Conventions

	MACINTOSH	WINDOWS
FILE AND FOLDER NAME LENGTH	Up to 31 characters	Up to 255 characters
CASE SENSITIVE?	Yes	No
FORBIDDEN CHARACTERS	The colon (:)	" / \ * ? < >	:
SPACES ALLOWED?	Yes	Yes
THREE-LETTER FILE EXTENSIONS NEEDED?	No	Yes
PATH SEPARATOR	:	\

How can I tell where my files are saved? When you save a file for the first time, you give the file a name and designate where you want to save it. The operating system has default folders where files are saved. In Windows, the default folders are "My Documents" for files, "My Music" for audio files, and "My Pictures" for graphic files. The location of the file is defined by a **file path** that identifies the exact location of the file, starting with the drive in which the file is located, and including all folders, subfolders (if any), the filename, and extension. For example, if you were saving a picture of

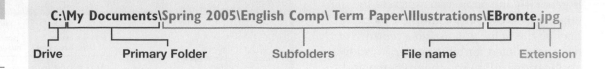

FIGURE 5.25

Understanding
File Paths

C:\My Documents\Spring 2005\English Comp\ Term Paper\Illustrations\EBronte.jpg

Drive   Primary Folder   Subfolders   File name   Extension

Emily Brontë for a term paper for an English Comp course, the file path might be C:\My Documents\Spring 2005\English Comp\ Term Paper\Illustrations\EBronte.jpg.

As shown in Figure 5.25, the C indicates the drive the file is stored on (in this case, the hard drive), and My Documents is the file's primary folder. Spring 2005, English Comp, Term Paper, and Illustrations are successive subfolders within the My Documents main folder. Last is the filename, EBronte, separated from the file extension (in this case, .jpg) by a period. Notice that in between the drive, primary folder, subfolders, and filename are backslash characters (\). These backslash characters, used by Windows and DOS, are referred to as **path separators**. Mac files use a colon (:) and UNIX and Linux use the forward slash (/) as the path separator.

WORKING WITH FILES

How can I rename and delete files?
Once you've located your file with Windows Explorer, you can perform many other file management actions, such as opening, copying, moving, renaming, and deleting

files. You open a file by double clicking the file in its storage location. The operating system then determines which application needs to be loaded to open the requested file and opens the file within the correct application automatically. You can copy a file to another location using the Copy command. When you copy a file, a duplicate file is created and the original file remains in its original location. To move a file from one location to another, you use the Move command. When you move a file, the original file is deleted from its original location.

Where do deleted files go? One of the improvements made to Windows 95 is the **Recycle Bin**, which is a folder on the desktop where files deleted *from the hard drive* reside until you permanently purge them from your system. Unfortunately, files deleted from other drives, such as the floppy drive, CD, or network drive, do not go to the Recycle Bin, but are deleted from the system immediately. (Mac systems have something similar to the Recycle Bin, called the Trash Can. To delete files on a Mac system, you simply drag the file to the Trash Can on the desktop. Then select Empty Trash from the Finder menu in OS X, or from the Special menu in earlier versions.)

Is it possible to retrieve a file that I've accidentally deleted? The benefit of the Recycle Bin is that you can restore the files you place there. To do so, open the Recycle Bin, locate the file, and select Restore. To delete your files from the Recycle Bin permanently, select Empty the Recycle Bin after clicking the desktop icon.

Utility Programs

You have learned that the operating system is the single most essential piece of software in your computer system because it coordinates all the system's activities and provides a means by which other software applications and users can interact with the system. However, there is another set of programs included in system software.

BITS AND BYTES

Need to Recover a Deleted Recycle Bin File?

Once you empty the Recycle Bin, because you don't see the file-name anymore, it looks as if the file has been erased from the hard drive. However, only the *reference* to the deleted file is deleted permanently, so the operating system has no easy way to find the file. The file data actually remains on the hard drive, until otherwise written over. Should you delete a file from the Recycle Bin in error, you can immediately restore the deleted file by clicking the undo arrow on the toolbar. Programs such as RestoreIT! or Roxio's GoBack allow you to recover longer-term deleted files—but the longer you wait to recover a deleted file, the chances of a full recovery decrease. That's because the probability that your file has been overwritten increases.

Utility programs are small applications that perform special functions. Some utility programs help manage system resources (such as disk defragmenter utilities), others help make your time and work on the computer more pleasant (such as screen savers), and still others improve efficiency (such as file compression utilities).

Some of these utility programs are incorporated into the operating system. Other utility programs, such as antivirus programs, have become so large and require such frequent updating that they are sold as stand-alone off-the-shelf programs in stores or as Web-based services available for an annual fee. Sometimes utility programs are offered as software suites, bundled together with other useful maintenance and performance-boosting utilities. Still other utilities are offered as shareware programs and are available as free downloads from the Web. Figure 5.26 illustrates some of the types of utility programs available within the Windows operating system as well as those available as off-the-shelf programs in stores.

In this section, we explore many of the utility programs you'll find installed on a Windows operating system. Unless otherwise noted, you can find these utilities in Control Panel or on the Start menu by selecting Programs, Accessories, and then System Tools. (We also take a brief look at some Mac utilities.) We discuss antivirus and personal firewall utility programs in Chapter 7.

DISPLAY UTILITIES

How can I change the appearance of my desktop? The Display folder in the Control Panel has all the features required to change the appearance of your desktop, providing different options for the desktop background, screen savers, windows colors, font sizes, and screen resolution. Although Windows has many different background themes and screen saver options available, there are hundreds of downloadable options available on the Web. Just search for backgrounds or screen savers on your favorite search engine to customize your desktop. To access the background and screen saver options and all display utilities, choose Control Panel from the Start menu, then select the Display folder. (Note: If you have Windows XP and are showing the Categories view, the Display folder is in the Appearance and Themes category.)

Can I make the display on my LCD monitor clearer? If you use a portable computer or have a flat-panel liquid crystal display (LCD) monitor, you may be interested in the Clear Type feature Windows XP

FIGURE 5.26 Utility Programs Available within Windows and as Stand-Alone Programs

WINDOWS UTILITY PROGRAM	OFF-THE-SHELF (STAND-ALONE) UTILITY PROGRAM	FUNCTION
FILE MANAGEMENT		
Add/Remove Programs	Aladdin Systems Easy Uninstall	Properly installs/uninstalls software
Windows Explorer File Compression	WinZip	Reduces file size
WINDOWS SYSTEM MAINTENANCE AND DIAGNOSTICS		
Backup	Norton Ghost	Backs up important information
Disk Cleanup	Ontrack System Suite	Removes unnecessary files from hard drive
Disk Defragmenter	Norton SystemWorks	Arranges files on hard drive in sequential order
ScanDisk	Norton CleanSweep	Checks hard drive for unnecessary or damaged files
System Restore	FarStone RestoreIT!	Restores system to a previously established set point

offers. Turning this feature on smoothes the edges of screen fonts to make words easier to read. Note that Clear Type is not very effective with cathode-ray tube (CRT) monitors.

Do I really need to use a screen saver? Screen savers are animated images that appear on a computer monitor when no user activity has been sensed for a certain time. Originally, screen savers were used to prevent *burn-in*, the result of the same image being rescanned into the phosphor inside the monitor's cathode-ray tube. In the early days of personal computers when the cursor was left blinking in the same spot for hours, burn-in was a concern. However, today's CRT display technology has changed; thus, burn-in is not probable. Screen savers are now used almost exclusively for decoration.

You can also control how long your computer sits idle before the screen saver starts. For example, if you don't want people looking at what's on your screen when you leave your computer unexpectedly for a time, you may want to program your screen saver to run after only a minute or two of inactivity. However, if you find that you let your computer sit inactive for a while but need to look at the screen image (while you study or read a screen image, for example), you may want to extend the period of inactivity a bit.

THE ADD OR REMOVE PROGRAMS UTILITY

What is the correct way to add new programs to the system? These days, when you install a new program to your system, the program automatically runs a wizard that walks you through the installation process. If a wizard does not initialize

automatically, however, you should go to the Add or Remove Programs folder in the Control Panel. This prompts the operating system to look in the CD or floppy disk drive for the setup program of the new software and starts the installation wizard.

What is the correct way to remove unwanted programs from my system? Some people think that deleting a program from the Program Files folder on the C drive is the best way to remove a program from your system. However, most programs include support files such as a help file, dictionaries, and graphics files that are not located in the main program folder found in Program Files. Depending on the supporting file's function, support files can be scattered throughout various folders within the system. You would normally miss these files by just deleting the main program file from the system. By selecting the Add or Remove Programs icon in the Control Panel, you not only delete the main program file, you also delete all supporting files as well.

FILE COMPRESSION UTILITIES

What is file compression? A file compression utility is a program that takes out redundancies in a file to reduce the file size. File compression is helpful because it makes a large file more compact, making it easier and faster to send over the Internet, upload to a Web page, or save onto a disk. As shown in Figure 5.27, Windows XP has built-in compression (or zip) file support. There are also several stand-alone freeware and shareware programs, such as WinZip (for Windows) and StuffIt (for Windows or Mac) that you can obtain to compress your files.

How does file compression work? Compression programs look for repeated patterns of letters and replace these patterns with a shorter placeholder. The repeated patterns and the associated placeholder are cataloged and stored temporarily in a separate file, called the dictionary. For example, in the following sentence, you can easily see the repeated patterns of letters:

The rain in spain falls mainly on the plain.

Although in this example there are obvious repeated patterns (ain and the), in a large document, the repeated patterns may

---

BITS AND BYTES

Putting Pictures on Your Desktop

You can have most any picture displayed as your desktop background with only a few clicks of your mouse. If you have a digital photograph or an image that you want displayed as your desktop background, simply right-click the image, select Set as Background, and you're done. Your image will appear immediately as the desktop background. On a Mac, you select the Apple Menu, Control Panels, Appearance, and then select the Desktop tab. Click the Place Picture button, select the image you want to display on your desktop, click Open, then click Set Desktop.

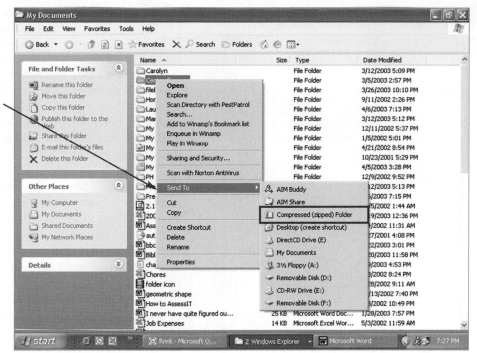

Clicking on the "Send To" option brings you to the file compression utility

be more complex. The compression program's algorithm therefore runs through the file several times to determine the optimal repeated patterns to obtain the greatest compression.

How effective are file compression programs? The effectiveness of file compression—that is, how much a file's size is reduced—depends on several factors, including the type and size of the individual file and the compression method used. Current compression programs can reduce text files by as much as 50 percent. However, some files, such as database files, already contain a form of compression and therefore do not compress further. Other file types, especially graphics and audio formats, have gone through a compression process that reduces file size by permanently discarding "unnecessary" data. For example, image files such as Joint Photographic Experts Group (JPEG), Graphics Interchange Format (GIF), and Portable Network Graphics (PNG) files discard small variations in colors that the human eye may not pick up. Likewise, MP3 files permanently discard sounds that the human ear cannot hear.

How do I decompress a file I've compressed? When you want to restore the file to its original state, you simply decompress the file and the pieces of file that the compression process temporarily removed are restored to the document. Generally, the same program you used to

SOUND BYTE

FILE COMPRESSION

In this Sound Byte, you'll learn about the advantages of file compression and how to use Windows XP to compress and decompress files. If you own an earlier operating system, this Sound Byte will teach you how to find and install file compression shareware software programs.

compress the file has the capability to decompress the file as well.

SYSTEM MAINTENANCE UTILITIES

Are there any utilities that make my system work faster? Disk Cleanup is a Windows utility that cleans unnecessary files off your hard drive. These files include files that have accumulated in the Recycle Bin as well as temporary files, which are files created by Windows to store data temporarily while a program is running. Windows usually deletes these temporary files when you exit the program, but sometimes it forgets or doesn't have time if your system freezes up or incurs a problem preventing you from properly exiting a program. Disk Cleanup also removes temporary Internet files (Web pages stored on your hard drive for quick viewing) as well as offline Web pages (pages that are stored on your

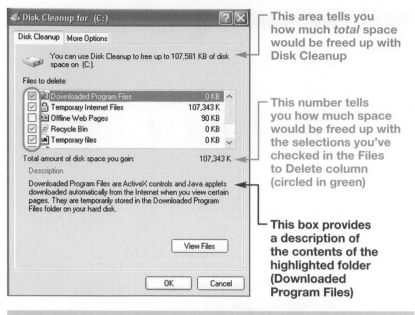

This area tells you how much *total* space would be freed up with Disk Cleanup

This number tells you how much space would be freed up with the selections you've checked in the Files to Delete column (circled in green)

This box provides a description of the contents of the highlighted folder (Downloaded Program Files)

FIGURE 5.28

Using Disk Cleanup will help free space on your hard drive.

computer so you can view them without being connected to the Internet). If not deleted periodically, these unnecessary files can deter efficient operating performance.

How can I control which files Disk Cleanup deletes? When you run Disk Cleanup, the program scans your hard drive to determine which folders have files that can be deleted and calculates the amount of hard drive space that would be freed by doing so. You check off which type of files you would like to delete, as shown in Figure 5.28.

What else can I do if my system runs slowly? Over time, as you add or delete information to a file, the file pieces are saved in scattered locations on the hard disk. Locating all the pieces of the file takes extra time, making the operating system less efficient. **Disk defragmenter utilities** regroup related pieces of files together on the hard disk, allowing the OS to work more efficiently. You can find the Windows Disk Defragmenter utility under System Tools in the Accessories folder of the

DIG DEEPER

How Disk Defragmenter Utilities Work

To understand how disk defragmenter utilities work, you must first understand the basics of how a hard disk drive stores files. A hard disk drive is composed of several platters, or round thin plates of metal, that are covered with a special magnetic coating that records the data. The platters are about 3.5 inches in diameter (approximately the width of a floppy disk) and are stacked onto a spindle. There are usually two or three *platters* in any hard disk drive, with data being stored on one or both sides. Data is recorded on hard disks in concentric circles, called *tracks*, which are further broken down into pie-shaped wedges called *sectors* (see Figure 5.29). The data is further identified by clusters, which are the smallest segments within the sectors.

When you want to save (or *write*) a file, the bits that make up your file are recorded onto one or more sectors of the drive. To keep track of which sectors hold which files, the drive also stores an index of all sector numbers in a table called the **File Allocation Table (FAT)**. To save a file, the computer will look in the FAT for sectors that are not already being used and will then record the file information on those sectors. When you open (or *read*) a file, the computer searches through the FAT for the sectors that hold the desired file and reads that file. Similarly, when you delete a computer file, you are actually not deleting the file itself, but rather the reference in the FAT to the file.

Windows XP offers a different file system than the FAT, called the **New Technology File System (NTFS)**. NTFS was developed with the Windows NT version and has been used in Windows 2000 and Windows XP. When you install Windows XP, you may choose whether to use FAT32 (FAT32 is the latest version of FAT and supports larger cluster sizes than the original FAT) or NTFS as the file system, unless the manufacturer has already preinstalled NTFS.

Most system manufacturers are choosing to use the NTFS file system as a default system, but some have continued to preinstall FAT32. The benefits of NTFS over FAT32 are that NTFS supports hard drive capacities larger than 32 GB and files sizes larger than 4 GB. Most of today's hard drives have capacities that exceed 32 GB, and with multimedia capabilities, it's not uncommon to see a file size greater than 4 GB. Additionally, NTFS was designed to be more secure

Track

Sector

Cluster

FIGURE 5.29

On a hard disk platter, data is recorded onto tracks, which are further broken down into sectors and clusters.

SOUND BYTE

HARD DISK ANATOMY
INTERACTIVE

In this Sound Byte, you'll watch a series of animations that show various aspects of a hard drive, including the anatomy of a hard drive, how to read and write data to a hard drive, and the fragmenting/defragmenting of a hard drive.

Start menu. On Macs, you can defrag your hard drive with Norton Utilities or Mac Tools. Depending on your usage, you should defrag your hard drive at least once a month.

How do I diagnose potential errors or damage on my storage devices? **ScanDisk** is a Windows utility that checks for lost files and fragments as well as physical errors on your hard drive. Lost files and fragments of files occur as you save, resave, move, delete, and copy files on your hard drive. Sometimes the system becomes con-

fused, leaving references on the file allocation table to files that no longer exist or have been moved. Physical errors on the hard drive occur when the mechanism that reads the hard drive's data (which is stored as 1s or 0s) can no longer determine whether the area holds a 1 or a 0. These areas are called *bad sectors*. Sometimes ScanDisk can recover the lost data, but more often, it deletes the files that are taking up space unnecessarily. ScanDisk also makes a note of any bad sectors so the system will not use them again to store data.

Where can I find ScanDisk? Windows XP has moved the ScanDisk utility from System Tools (where it is located in previous versions of Windows) to Disk Properties. Right-click the disk you want to diagnose, select Properties, then select Tools. It is now listed as Error Checking. Norton Disk Doctor is a stand-alone product included in Norton Utilities that performs the same check-and-repair routine. On Macs, you use the Disk First Aid utility to

and more efficient and will ultimately nudge out FAT structure with subsequent operating system versions.

So, how does a disk become fragmented? When only part of an older file is deleted, the deleted section of the file creates a gap in the sector of the disk where the data was originally stored. In the same way, when new information is added to an older file, there may not be space sequentially near where the file was originally saved to save the new information. In that case, the system writes the added part of the file to the next available location on the disk, and a reference is made in the FAT or NTFS table as to the location of this file fragment. Over time, as files are saved, deleted, and modified, the bits of information for various files fall out of sequential order and the disk becomes fragmented.

Disk fragmentation is a problem because when a disk is fragmented, the operating system is not as efficient. It takes longer to locate a whole file because more of the disk must be searched for the various pieces. A fragmented hard drive can greatly slow down the performance of your computer.

How can you make the files line up more efficiently on the disk? At this stage, the disk defragmenter utility

enters the picture. The defragmenter tool takes the hard drive through a defragmentation process in which pieces of files that are scattered over the disk are placed together and arranged sequentially on the hard disk. Also, any unused portions of clusters that were too small in which to save data before are grouped together, increasing the available storage space on the disk.

Figure 5.30 shows before and after shots of a fragmented disk having gone through the defragmentation process.

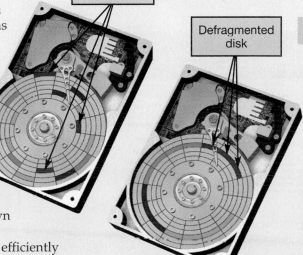

Fragmented disk

Defragmented disk

FIGURE 5.30

Over time, as files are saved, deleted, and modified, the fragments of information for various files fall out of sequential order on the hard disk and the disk becomes fragmented. Defragmenting the hard drive arranges file fragments so that they are located next to each other. This makes the hard drive run more efficiently.

test and repair disks. You find this utility in the Utilities folder on your hard drive.

How can I check on a program that has stopped running? If a program on your system has stopped working, you can use the Windows **Task Manager utility** to check on the program or to exit the nonresponding program. Although you can access Task Manager from the Control Panel, it is more easily accessible by pressing Ctrl + Alt + Del at the same time, or by right-clicking an empty space on the taskbar at the bottom of your screen. The Applications tab of Task Manager lists all programs that you are using and indicates whether they are working properly (running) or have stopped improperly (not responding). You can terminate programs that are not responding by clicking the End Task button in the dialog box.

SYSTEM RESTORE AND BACKUP UTILITIES

Is there an undo command for the system? Say you have just installed a new software program and your computer freezes. After rebooting the computer, when you try to start the application, the system freezes once again. You uninstall the new program, but your computer continues to freeze after rebooting. What can you do now?

Windows XP has a new utility called **System Restore** that lets you restore your system settings back to a specific date when everything was working properly. You can find the System Restore Wizard under System Tools on the Accessories menu. In this case, because the computer was running just fine before you installed the software, you would restore your computer to a date before the software installation, such as a day or two earlier. System Restore does not affect your personal data files (such as Microsoft Word documents, browsing history, drawings, favorites, or e-mail), so you won't lose changes made to these files when you use System Restore.

How does the computer remember its previous settings? Every time you start your computer, or when a new application or driver is installed, Windows XP automatically creates a snapshot of your entire system's settings. This snapshot is called a **restore point**. You can also create and name your own restore points at any time. Creating a restore point is a good idea before making changes to your computer such as installing hardware or software. If something goes wrong with the installation process, Windows XP can reset your system to the restore point. As shown in Figure 5.31, Windows includes a Restore Point Wizard that walks you through the process of setting restore points.

How can I protect my data in the event something goes awry with my system? When you use the Windows **Backup utility**, you create a duplicate copy of all the data on your hard disk and copy it to another storage device, such as a Zip disk. A backup copy protects your data in the event your hard disk fails or files are accidentally erased. Although you may not need to back up every file on your computer, you should back up the files that are most important to you and keep the backup copy in a safe location. Note that in Windows XP Home Edition, you must manually install the Backup utility from the ValueAdd folder on the CD-ROM. (For more information on backing up your files, see the Technology in Focus "Protecting Your Computer and Backing Up Your Data.")

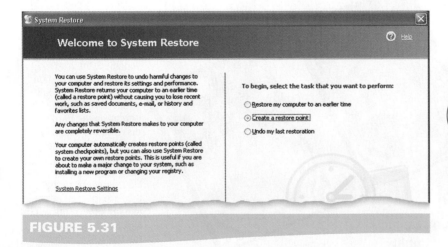

FIGURE 5.31

Setting a restore point is good practice before installing any hardware or software.

THE TASK SCHEDULER UTILITY

How can I remember to perform all these maintenance procedures? To keep your computer system in top shape, it is important to run some of the utilities described here routinely. For example, depending on your usage, you may want to defrag your hard drive every month or so and clean out temporary Internet files once a week. However, many computer users forget to initiate these tasks. Luckily, the Windows **Task Scheduler utility**, shown in Figure 5.32, allows you to schedule tasks to run automatically at predetermined times, with no interaction necessary on your part.

ACCESSIBILITY UTILITIES

Are there utilities designed for accessibility? **Utility Manager** is a utility found in the Accessories folder of Windows XP. Through the Utility Manager, you can magnify the screen image, have screen contents read to you, and display an on-screen keyboard. The accessibility features include the following:

- The Magnifier is a display utility that creates a separate window that displays a magnified portion of your screen. This feature makes the screen more readable for users who have impaired vision. Additionally, you can change the color scheme of the window with the Magnifier so that the screen colors are inverted. Some visually impaired individuals find it easier to see white text on a dark background.

- The Narrator utility is a very basic speech program that reads what is on-screen, whether it's the contents of a window, menu options, or text you have typed. The Narrator coordinates with text utilities, such as Notepad and WordPad, as well as Internet Explorer, but may not work correctly with other programs. For this reason, Narrator is not meant for individuals who must rely solely on a text-to-speech utility to operate the computer.

- The Onscreen Keyboard displays a keyboard on the screen. You type by clicking on or hovering over the keys with a pointing device (mouse or trackball) or joystick. Similar to the Narrator, this utility is not meant for everyday use for individuals with severe disabilities. A separate program with more functionality is better in those circumstances.

BITS AND BYTES

Need a System Software Update?

Bugs in software occur all the time. Software developers are constantly testing their products, even after releasing the software to the retail market, and users report errors they find. Windows Update is Microsoft's service for updating desktop operating system software. For Windows XP users, Windows Update automatically notifies you when updates are available for download. Non–Windows XP users should regularly check **windowsupdate.microsoft.com** to keep their system current.

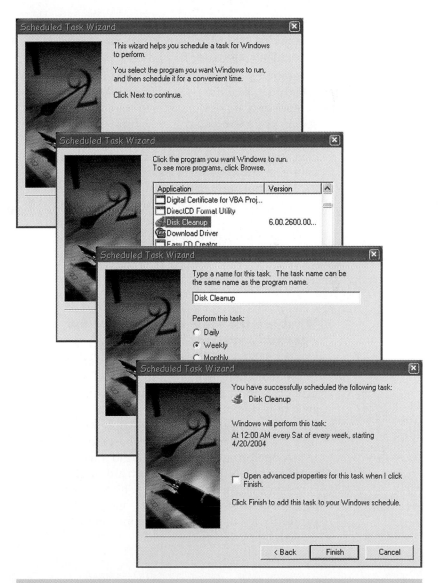

FIGURE 5.32

To keep your machine running in top shape, schedule a maintenance routine to run automatically at convenient times. Task Scheduler (listed as Scheduled Tasks), found in the Accessories folder on the All Programs menu, has a convenient wizard that guides you to select the program and assign the time you want it to run.

Summary

1. What software is included in system software?

System software is the set of software programs that helps run the computer and coordinates instructions between application software and hardware devices. It consists of the operating system (OS) and utility programs. The operating system controls how your computer system functions. Utility programs are programs that perform general housekeeping tasks for the computer, such as system maintenance and file compression.

2. What are the different kinds of operating systems?

Operating systems can be classified into four categories. Real-time OSs require no user intervention and are designed for systems with a specific purpose and response time (such as robotic machinery). Single-user, single-task OSs are designed for computers on which one user is performing one task at a time (such as PDAs). Single-user, multitask OSs are designed for computers on which one user is performing more than one task at a time (such as desktop computers). Multiuser OSs are designed for systems in which multiple users are working on more than one task at a time (such as networks).

3. What are the most common desktop operating systems?

Microsoft Windows is the most popular OS. It has evolved from being a single-user, single-task OS into a powerful multiuser operating system. Another popular OS is the Mac OS, which is designed to work on Apple Macs. Its most recent release, OS X, is based on the UNIX operating system. You'll find various versions of UNIX on the market, although it is most often used on networks. Linux is an open-source OS based on UNIX and designed primarily for use on personal computers.

4. How does the operating system provide a means for users to interact with the computer?

The operating system provides a user interface that enables you to interact with the computer. Most OSs today use a graphical user interface (GUI). Unlike the command- and menu-driven interfaces used earlier, GUIs display graphics and use the point-and-click technology of the mouse and cursor, making the OS more user friendly. Common features of GUIs include windows, menus, and icons.

5. How does the operating system help manage the processor?

When you use your computer, you are usually asking it to perform several tasks at the same time. When the OS allows you to perform more than one task at a time, it is multitasking. To provide for seamless multitasking, the OS controls the timing of events the processor works on.

6. How does the operating system manage memory and storage?

As the OS coordinates the activities of the processor, it uses RAM as a temporary storage area for instructions and data the processor needs. The OS is therefore responsible for coordinating the space allocations in RAM to ensure that there is enough space for the waiting instructions and data. If there isn't sufficient space in RAM for all the data and instructions, the OS allocates the least necessary files to temporary storage on the hard drive called virtual memory. The OS manages storage by providing a file management system that keeps track of the names and locations of files and programs.

7. How does the operating system manage hardware and peripheral devices?

Programs called device drivers facilitate the communication between devices attached to the computer and the OS. Device drivers translate the specialized commands of devices to commands that the OS can understand, and vice versa, enabling the OS to communicate with every device in the computer system. Device drivers for common devices are included in the OS software, whereas other devices come with a device driver you have to install or download off the Web.

8. How does the operating system interact with application software?

All software applications need to interact with the CPU. For programs to work with the CPU, they must contain code the CPU recognizes. Rather than having the same blocks of code appear in each software application, the OS includes the blocks of code to which software applications refer. These blocks of code are called application programming interfaces (APIs).

9. How does the operating system help the computer start up?

When you start your computer, it runs through a special process, called the boot process. The boot process consists of four basic steps: (1) the basic input/output system (BIOS) is activated by powering on the CPU; (2) in the POST test, the BIOS checks that all attached devices are in place; (3) the operating system is loaded into RAM; and (4) configuration and customization settings are checked.

10. What are the main desktop and windows features?

The desktop is the first interaction you have with the OS and the first image you see on your monitor once the system has booted up. It provides you with access to your computer's files, folders, and commonly used tools and applications. Windows are the rectangular panes on your screen that display applications running on your system. Common features of windows include toolbars and scrollbars.

11. How does the operating system help me keep my computer organized?

The OS allows you to organize the contents of your computer in a hierarchical structure of directories that includes files, folders, and drives. Windows Explorer helps you manage your files and folders by showing the location and contents of every drive, folder, and file on your computer. Creating folders is the key to organizing files, because folders keep related documents together. Following naming conventions and using proper file extensions are also important aspects of file management.

12. What utility programs are included in system software and what do they do?

Some utility programs are incorporated into the OS; others are sold as stand-alone off-the-shelf programs. Common Windows utilities include those that enable you to adjust your display, add or remove programs, compress files, defrag your hard drive, clean unnecessary files off your system, check for lost files and errors, restore your system to an earlier setting, back up your files, schedule automatic tasks, and check on programs that have quit running.

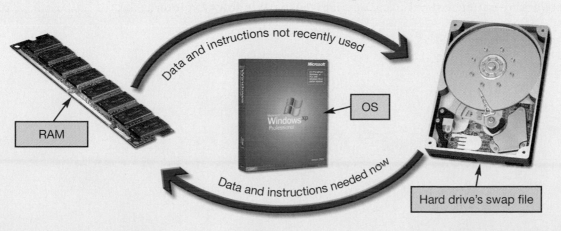

Key Terms

Buzz Words

Word Bank

- system software
- Windows Explorer
- utility programs
- real-time operating system
- single-user, multitask operating system
- single-user, single-task operating system
- platform

- defrag
- files
- Windows XP
- Linux
- Task Scheduler
- Mac OS
- Windows
- boot
- cold boot

- Task Manager
- Safe mode
- window
- folders
- file management
- file compression
- tracks
- sectors
- FAT

Instructions: Fill in the blanks using the words from the Word Bank above.

Veena was looking into buying a new computer and was trying to decide what (1)_____ to buy, a PC or a Mac. She had used PCs all her life, so she was more familiar with the (2)_____ operating system. Still, she liked the way the (3)_____ looked and was considering switching. Her brother didn't like either operating system so used (4)_____, a free operating system, instead.

After a little research, Veena decided to buy a PC. With it, she got the most recent version of Windows, (5)_____. She vowed that with this computer, she'd practice better (6)_____, because she often had a hard time finding files on her old computer. To view all of the folders on her computer, she opened (7)_____. She made sure that she gave descriptive names to her (8)_____ and placed them in organized (9)_____.

Veena also decided that with her new computer, she'd pay more attention to the (10)_____, those little special-function programs that help with maintenance and repairs. These special function programs, in addition to the OS, make up the (11)_____. Veena looked into some of the more frequently used utilities. She thought it would be a good idea to (12)_____ her hard drive regularly so that all the files lined up in contiguous (13)_____ and so that it was more efficient. She also looked into (14)_____ utilities, which would help her reduce the size of her files when she sent them to others over the Internet. Finally, she decided to use the Windows (15)_____ utility to schedule tasks automatically so that she wouldn't forget.

Organizing Key Terms

Instructions: This chapter introduces many new terms and concepts. In the following illustration, fill in each of the blanks with key terms or concepts from the chapter in order to show how categories of ideas fit together.

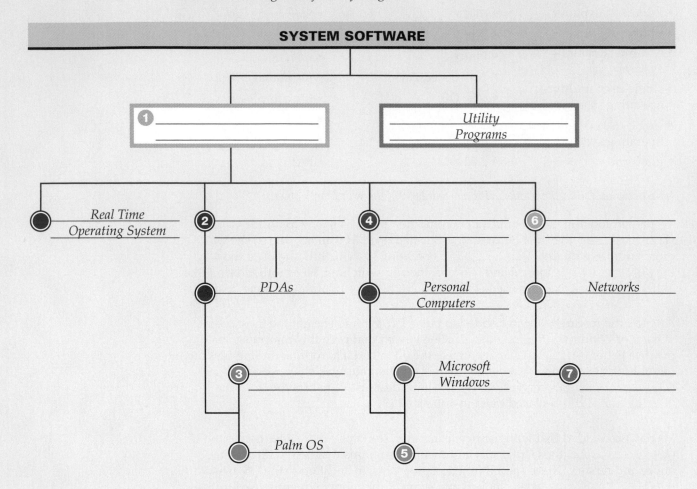

SYSTEM SOFTWARE

1 _____
_____

Utility
Programs

● Real Time
Operating System

2 _____

● PDAs

3 _____
_____

● Palm OS

4 _____

● Personal
Computers

● Microsoft
Windows

5 _____
_____

6 _____

● Networks

7 _____
_____

Making the Transition to . . . Next Semester

1. Organizing Files and Folders

It's the beginning of a new semester, and you promise yourself that you are going to keep all files related to your schoolwork more organized this semester. Develop a plan that outlines how you'll set up folders and subfolders for each subject. Identify at least three different folders for each class. If time and schedule permit, discuss your organization scheme with your instructor.

2. OS Compatibility Issues

Your school requires that you purchase a laptop to run on the school's system. The required machine runs on the Windows operating system. You have a reasonably new Apple computer at home.

a. Research the compatibility issues between the two computers.

b. How does a PDA running with Palm OS fit into the equation?

c. Can you synch the PDA with either or both machines?

d. Explore the application Virtual PC. What does it do? Would it be helpful in this situation?

3. Understanding Safe Mode

It is the night before the major term paper for your philosophy class is due. Your best friend comes screaming down the hall, begging for help. His only copy of his draft paper is on his desktop computer and it is suddenly booting up with the words *Safe Mode* in the corners of the screen. What would be the most useful questions to ask him? What steps would you take to debug the problem? If you cannot get the computer to come out of Safe mode, is there a way to retrieve the draft? How many times will you say, "Make backups!" that evening?

4. Software Requirements

This semester you have added six new applications to your laptop. You know which courses you will be taking next semester and realize they will require an additional eight major software applications. A friend who is in a similar position tells you she's not worried about putting that much software on her computer because she has a really big hard drive.

a. Is hard disk storage your only concern? Should it be your main concern or should you worry more about having sufficient RAM? How does your use of the programs impact your answer?

b. Does virtual memory management by your operating system allow you to ignore RAM requirements?

5. Connecting Peripherals

You decide to buy a new keyboard for next semester, a very fancy one that is wireless and that features integrated volume and CD player controls, and an integrated trackball. You are also planning to upgrade your printer. Do you have to worry about having the correct device drivers for these peripherals if:

a. You are using a Plug and Play operating system?

b. You have an older PC but are using the latest version of the Windows operating system?

c. You have an older PC and its original operating system, Windows 95?

Making the Transition to . . . The Workplace

1. Organizing Files and Folders

You started a new job and are given a new computer. You never kept your files and folders organized on the computer you used while in college, but now you are determined to do a better job at keeping your files organized. You know you need folders for the several clients with whom you will be working. For each client, you'll need to have folders for billing information, client documents, and account information. In addition, you need folders for the MP3 files you will listen to when you're not working, as well as a folder for the digital pictures you'll take for personal and company reasons. Last, you're working toward an advanced degree and will be taking business finance and introduction to marketing courses at night, so you'll need folders for all the homework assignments for both courses. Determine the file structure you would need to create to accommodate your needs. Start with the C drive and assume that My Documents, My Pictures, and My Music are the default folders for documents, pictures, and music files, respectively.

2. Using Mac Utility Programs

Your company has been having trouble with some of its Macintosh computers running inefficiently. Your boss asks you to research the utility programs your company could use on its Macs to make them run better. In particular, your boss would like you to find a disk defrag utility, a file compression utility, and a diagnostic utility you could run to check the hard drive for errors. Using the Internet, what utilities can you find? Will they run on all versions of the Mac OS?

3. Monitoring Activities with the OS

The company that you work for has just announced a new internal accounting structure. From now on, each department will be charged individually for the costs associated with computer usage, such as backup storage space, Internet usage, and so on.

a. Research how the operating system may be set up to monitor such activity by department.
b. What other activities do you think the operating system can be set up to monitor?

4. Choosing the Best OS

Your new boss is considering moving some of the department operations to UNIX-based computer systems. He asks you to research the advantages and disadvantages of moving to UNIX, Linux, or Mac OS X. How would these choices impact his department in the following areas?

a. Budget for technical support for the systems
b. Choice and budget for hardware for the systems
c. Costs of implementation
d. Possibility for future upgrades

Critical Thinking Questions

Instructions: *Albert Einstein used "Gedanken experiments," or critical thinking questions, to develop his theory of relativity. Some ideas are best understood by experimenting with them in our own minds. The following critical thinking questions are designed to demand your full attention but require only a comfortable chair—no technology.*

1. Open-Source Pros and Cons

Open-source programming embraces a philosophy that states programmers should make their code available to everyone rather than keeping it proprietary. The operating system Linux has had much success as an open-source code. The chapter mentions some of the advantages of open-source code, such as quicker code updates in response to technological advances and changes.

a. What are other advantages of open-source code?

b. Can you think of disadvantages to open-source code?

c. Why do you think that companies such as Microsoft maintain proprietary restrictions on their code?

d. Are there disadvantages to maintaining proprietary code?

2. The OS of the Future

Operating system interfaces have evolved from a text-based console format to the current graphical user interface. What direction do you think they will move toward next? How could operating systems be organized and used in a manner that is more responsive to humans and better suited to how we think? Are there alternatives to hierarchical file structures for storage? Can you think of ways in which operating systems could be able to adapt and customize themselves based on your usage?

3. Which OS Would You Choose?

Suppose you are building a computer system from scratch and have complete discretion as to your choice of operating system. Which one would you install and why?

4. The OS: With or Without Utilities?

Which environment do you think is better for consumers: to have companies develop smaller, more inexpensive operating systems and then allow competing companies to develop and market utility programs, or to have very large full-featured operating systems that include most utilities as part of the operating system itself? Do you think that including utility programs with the operating system makes the cost of the operating system higher?

Team Time   Choosing the Best OS

Problem:

You have been hired to help set up the technology requirements for a small advertising company. The company is holding off buying anything until the decision has been made as to which platform the computers should run on. Obviously, one of the critical decisions is the operating system.

Task:

Recommend the appropriate operating system for the company.

Process:

1. Break up into three teams. Each team will represent one of the three primary operating systems today: Windows, Mac, and Linux.
2. As a team, research the pros and cons of your operating system. What features does it have that would benefit your company? What features does it not have that your company would need? Why (or why not) would your operating system be the appropriate choice? Why is your OS better (or worse) than either of the other two options?
3. Develop a presentation that states your position with regard to your operating system. Your presentation should have a recommendation, with facts to back it up.
4. As a class, decide which operating system would be the best choice for the company.

Conclusion:

Because the operating system is the critical piece of software in the computer system, the selection should not be taken lightly. The OS that is best for an advertising agency may not be best for an accounting firm. It is important to make sure you consider all aspects of the work environment and the type of work that is being done to ensure a good fit.

Becoming Computer Fluent

Using key terms from the chapter, write a letter to your computer-illiterate aunt explaining the benefits of simple computer maintenance. First, explain any symptoms her computer may be experiencing (such as a sluggish Internet connection), then include a set of steps she can follow in setting up a regimen to remedy the problems. Make sure you explain some of the system utilities described in this chapter, including, but not limited to, defrag, Disk Cleanup, and Task Scheduler. Include any other utilities she might need and explain why she should have them.

Materials on the Web

In addition to the review materials presented here, you'll find extra materials on the book's companion Web site (**www.prenhall.com/techinaction**) that will help reinforce your understanding of the chapter content. These materials include the following:

Sound Byte Lab Guides

For each Sound Byte mentioned in the chapter, there is a corresponding lab guide located on the book's companion Web site. These guides review the material presented in the Sound Byte and direct you to various Web resources that examine the material. The Sound Byte Lab Guides for this chapter include these:

- Customizing Windows XP
- File Management
- File Compression
- Hard Disk Anatomy Interactive
- Letting Your Computer Clean Up After Itself

True/False and Multiple-Choice Quizzes

The book's Web site includes a true/false and a multiple-choice quiz for this chapter. You can take these quizzes, automatically check the results, and e-mail the results to your instructor.

Web Research Projects

The book's Web site also includes a number of Web research projects for this chapter. These projects ask you to search the Web for information on computer-related careers, milestones in computer history, important people and companies, emerging technologies, and the applications and implications of different technologies.

Technology in Action also features unique interactive Help Desk training, in which you'll assume the role of Help Desk operator taking calls about concepts learned in each chapter. The Help Desk calls for this chapter include:

- Managing Hardware and Peripheral Devices: The OS
- Starting the Computer: The Boot Process
- Organizing Your Computer: File Management
- Using Utility Programs

CHAPTER 6

OBJECTIVES

After reading this chapter, you should be able to answer the following questions:

- How can I determine whether I should upgrade my existing computer or buy a new one? (pp. 222–224)

- What does the CPU do and how can I evaluate its performance? (pp. 224–227)

- How does memory work in my computer and how can I evaluate how much memory I need? (pp. 227–231)

- What are the computer's main storage devices and how can I evaluate whether they match my needs? (pp. 231–237)

- What components affect the output of video on my computer and how can I evaluate whether they meet my needs? (pp. 238–240)

- What components affect my computer's sound quality and how can I evaluate whether they meet my needs? (pp. 240–242)

- What are the ports available on desktop computers and how can I determine what ports I need? (pp. 242–246)

- How can I ensure the reliability of my system? (pp. 246–247)

SOUND BYTES

- Using Windows XP to Evaluate CPU Performance (p. 225)
- Installing RAM (p. 229)
- Hard Disk Anatomy Interactive (p. 233)
- CD and DVD Reading & Writing Interactive (p. 235)
- Installing a CDRW Drive (p. 236)
- Port Tour (p. 245)
- Letting Your Computer Clean Up After Itself (p. 247)

Evaluating Your System:

Understanding and Assessing Hardware

TECHNOLOGY IN ACTION:
TO UPGRADE OR NOT TO UPGRADE?

After saving up for a computer, Natalie took the leap a few years ago and bought a new desktop PC. Now she is wondering what to do. Her friends with newer computers are burning CDs and DVDs, and they're able to hook their digital cameras right up to their computers and create multimedia. They seem to be able to do a hundred things at once without their computers slowing down at all.

Natalie's computer can't do any of these things—or at least she doesn't think it can. And lately it seems to take longer to open files and scroll through Web pages. Making matters worse, her computer freezes three or four times a day and takes a long time to reboot. Now she's wondering whether she should buy a new computer, but the thought of spending all that money again makes her think twice. As she looks at ads for new computers, she realizes she doesn't know what such things as "CPU" and "RAM" really are, or how they affect her system. Meanwhile, she's heard it's possible to upgrade her computer, but the task seems daunting. How will she know what she needs to do to upgrade, or whether it's even worth it?

How well is your computer meeting your needs? Are you unsure whether it's best to buy a new computer or upgrade your existing system? If you don't have a computer, do you fear purchasing one because computers are changing all the time? Do you know what all the terms in computer ads mean and how the different parts affect your computer's performance?

In this chapter, you'll learn how to evaluate your computer system to determine whether it is meeting your needs. You'll start by figuring out what you want your ideal computer to be able to do. You'll then learn about important components of your computer system (its CPU, memory, storage devices, audio and video devices, and ports) and how these components affect your system. Along the way, worksheets will help you conduct a system evaluation, and multimedia Sound Bytes will show you how to install various components in your system and how to increase its reliability. You'll also learn about the various utilities available to help speed up and clean up your system. If you don't have a computer, this chapter will provide you with important information you need about computer hardware to make an informed purchasing decision.

To Buy or To Upgrade: That Is the Question

There never seems to be a good time to buy a new computer. It seems that if you can just wait a year, computers will inevitably be faster and cost less. But is this actually true?

As it turns out, it is true. In fact, a rule of thumb often cited in the computer industry, called **Moore's Law**, describes the pace at which CPUs (the central processing unit)—the small chip that can be thought of as the "brains" of the computer—improve. This mathematical rule, named after Gordon Moore, the cofounder of the CPU chip manufacturer Intel, predicts that the number of transistors inside a CPU will increase so fast that CPU capacity will double every 18 months. (The number of transistors on a CPU chip helps determine how fast it can process data.)

As you can see in Figure 6.1, this rule of thumb has held true since 1965, when Moore first published his theory. Imagine if you could find a bank that would agree to treat your money this way. If you had put 10 cents in a savings account in 1965, you would have a balance of more than $3.3 million today!

In addition to the CPU becoming faster, other system components also improve dramatically. For example, the capacity of memory chips such as dynamic random access memory (DRAM)—the most common form of memory found on personal computers—increases about 60 percent every year, as shown in Figure 6.2. Meanwhile, hard disk

FIGURE 6.2   The Growing Capacity of Memory Chips

YEAR	CAPACITY OF MEMORY (DRAM) CHIP
1977	16 KB
1980	64 KB
1983	256 KB
1985	1,000 KB
1989	4,000 KB
1992	16,000 KB
1996	64,000 KB
2001	256,000 KB
2002	1,000,000 KB (1 GB)
2004	2,000,000 KB (2 GB)

Source: Adapted from David Patterson and John Hennesey, *Computer Architecture: A Quantitative Approach,* 3rd ed. (San Francisco, Calif.: Morgan Kaufmann, 2002), p. 22.

drives have been growing in storage capacity by about 50 percent each year.

So, with technology advancing so quickly, which is better: upgrading a current computer or buying a new one? Certainly, no one wants to buy a new computer every year just to keep up with

FIGURE 6.1

Moore's Law predicts that CPUs will continue to get faster. The number of transistors on these Intel CPU chips helps determine how quickly they can process data.

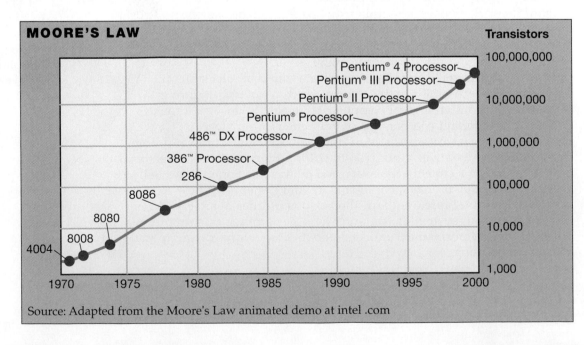

Source: Adapted from the Moore's Law animated demo at intel .com

technology. Even if money weren't a consideration, the time it would take to transfer all of your files and to reinstall and reconfigure your software would make buying a new computer every year terribly inefficient.

Of course, no one wants to keep doing costly upgrades that won't significantly extend the life of a system, either. So how can you determine if your system is suitable or needs upgrading? And how can you know which is the better option: upgrading or buying a new computer? In this chapter, you'll determine how to answer these questions by learning useful information about computer systems. The first step is figuring out what you want your computer to do for you.

What Is Your Ideal Computer?

As you decide whether you should upgrade or buy a new computer, it's important to know exactly what you want your ideal computer system to be able to do. Later, as you perform a system evaluation, you can compare your existing system to your ideal system. This will help you determine whether you should purchase hardware components to add to your system or buy a new system.

But what if I don't have a computer? Even if you're a new computer user, being able to understand and evaluate computer systems will make you a more informed buyer. What is a CPU and how does it affect your system? How much RAM do you need and what role does it play in your system? It's important that you're able to answer questions such as these before you buy a computer.

How do I know what my ideal system is? To determine your ideal system, consider what you want to be able to do with your computer. For example, do you want to be able to edit digital photos? Do you want to watch and record DVDs? Or are you just using your computer for word processing? The worksheet in Figure 6.3 lists a number of ways in which you may want to use your computer. In the second column, place a check next to those computer uses that apply to you.

Next, look at the list of desired uses for your computer and determine whether your current system can perform these activities. If there are things you can't do, you may need to purchase additional hardware or a better computer. For example, if you want to play CDs, all you need is a CD-ROM drive.

FIGURE 6.3   What Should Your Ideal Computer System Be Able to Do?

COMPUTER USES	DO YOU WANT YOUR SYSTEM TO DO THIS?	CAN YOUR SYSTEM DO THIS NOW?
ENTERTAINMENT USES		
Access the Internet/Send E-Mail		
Play CDs and DVDs		
Record (Burn) CDs and DVDs		
Produce Digital Videos		
Record and Edit Digital Music		
Edit Digital Photos		
Play Graphics-Intensive Games		
Transfer Digital Photos (or Other Files) to Your Computer Using Flash Memory Cards		
Connect All Your Peripheral Devices to Your Computer at the Same Time		
Download Music from the Internet		
Other		
EDUCATIONAL USES		
Perform Word Processing Tasks		
Use Other Educational Software		
Create CD or Zip Disk Backups of All Your Files		
Access Library and Newspaper Archives		
Create Multimedia Presentations		
Other		
BUSINESS USES		
Create Spreadsheets		
Create Databases		
Work on Multiple Software Applications Quickly and Simultaneously		
Conduct Online Banking/Pay Bills Online		
Conduct Online Job Searches/ Post Résumé		
"Synchronize" Your PDA and Desktop Computer		
Other		

However, you need a CD-R drive if you want to burn (record) CDs. Likewise, if you're going to edit digital video files or play games that include a lot of sounds and graphics, you may want to add more memory, buy a better set of speakers, and possibly invest in a new monitor. In this chapter, you'll learn about the hardware you may need to achieve your ideal system.

Note that you may also need new software and training to use new system components. Many computer users forget to consider the training they'll need when they upgrade their computer. Missing any one of these pieces might be the difference between your computer enriching your life or it becoming another source of stress.

How do I know if I need training? Although computers are becoming increasingly user friendly, you still need to learn how to use them to your best advantage. Say you want to edit digital photos. You know image-editing software exists, but how do you know if your computer's hardware can support the software? What will happen if you can't get it installed or don't know how to use it? If you have questions like these, you know you need training. Training shouldn't be an afterthought. Consider the time and effort involved in learning about what you want your computer to do before you buy hardware or software. If you don't, you may have a wonderful computer system but lack the skills necessary to take full advantage of it.

Assessing Your Hardware: Evaluating Your System

With a better picture of your ideal computer system in mind, you can make a more informed assessment of your current computer. To determine whether your computer system has the right hardware components to do what you ultimately want it to do, you need to conduct a **system evaluation**. To do so, you look at your computer's subsystems, what they do, and how they perform. These subsystems include the following:

- The CPU subsystem
- The memory subsystem (your computer's random access memory, or RAM)
- The storage subsystem (your hard drive and other drives)

- The video subsystem (your video card and monitor)
- The audio subsystem (your sound card and speakers)
- Your computer's ports

In the rest of this chapter, we examine each of these subsystems. At the end of each section, you'll find a small worksheet you can use to evaluate each subsystem on your computer.

Evaluating the CPU Subsystem

As mentioned earlier, your computer's **central processing unit (CPU** or **processor)** is very important because it is the "brains" of the computer. The CPU processes instructions, performs calculations, manages the flow of information through a computer system, and is responsible for processing the data you input into information. The CPU, as shown in Figure 6.4, is located on the **motherboard**, the primary circuit board of the computer system. There are several types of processors on the market: Intel processors (such as the Pentium family) and AMD processors (such as the Athlon and Duron), both of which are used on PCs, and Motorola processors (such as the G5), which are used on Macintosh computers.

How does the CPU work? The CPU is composed of two units: the **control unit** and the **arithmetic logic unit (ALU)**. The control unit coordinates the activities of all the other computer components. The ALU is responsible for performing all the arithmetic calculations (addition, subtraction, multiplication, and

FIGURE 6.4

The CPU is a small chip that sits on the motherboard inside your system unit.

division). Additionally, the ALU makes logic and comparison decisions, such as comparing items to determine if one is greater than, less than, equal to, or not equal to another.

Every time the CPU performs a program instruction, it goes through the same series of steps: First, it fetches the required piece of data or instruction from RAM, the temporary storage location for all the data and instructions the computer needs while it is running. Next, it decodes the instruction into something the computer can understand. Once the CPU has decoded the instruction, it executes the instruction and stores the result to RAM before fetching the next instruction. This process is called a **machine cycle**. (We discuss the machine cycle in more detail in Chapter 9.)

How is CPU speed measured? The computer goes through these machine cycles at a steady and constant pace. This pace, known as **clock speed**, is controlled by the system clock, which works like a metronome in music. The system clock keeps a steady beat, regulating the speed at which the processor goes through machine cycles. Processors work incredibly fast, going through millions or billions of machine cycles *each second*. Processor speed is measured in units of **megahertz (MHz)**, or 1 million hertz, and **gigahertz (GHz)**, or 1 billion hertz. Hertz (Hz) here means "machine cycles per second," so a 3.0-GHz processor performs work at a rate of 3 billion machine cycles per second.

However, it's important to realize that CPU speed alone doesn't determine the performance of the CPU. We discuss more of the factors that control CPU speed in Chapter 9.

How can I tell how fast my CPU is? You can easily identify the speed of your current system's CPU. To do so, locate the My Computer icon on your desktop, right-click it, and select Properties. As shown in Figure 6.5, the General tab of the System Properties dialog box shows you which CPU is installed in your system as well as its speed.

How fast should my CPU be? At a minimum, your CPU should meet the requirements of your system's software and hardware. If your system is older and you are buying new software and peripheral devices, your CPU may not be able to handle the load.

For example, say your computer is three years old. For the past three years, you've been using it primarily for word processing and to surf the Internet. You recently

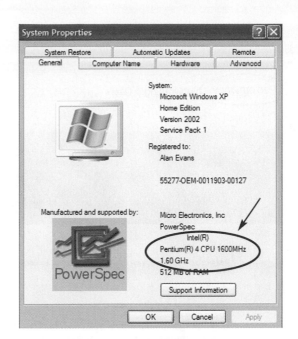

SOUND BYTE

USING WINDOWS XP TO EVALUATE CPU PERFORMANCE

In this Sound Byte, you'll learn how to use the utilities provided by Windows XP to evaluate your CPU's performance. You'll also learn about shareware utilities (software that you can install and try before you purchase it) that expand on the information the Task Manager provides.

purchased a digital camera. Now you want to edit your digital photos, but your system doesn't seem to be able to handle this. You check the system requirements on the photo-editing software you just installed and realize that the software runs best with a more powerful processor. In this case, if everything else in your system is running properly, a faster CPU would help improve the software's performance. Pentium III processors running at 700 MHz or higher and Pentium 4 processors running at any speed are good processors for the average user, enabling you to run most programs at a decent speed.

How can I tell whether my CPU is fast enough? The workload your CPU experiences varies considerably depending on what you're doing. Even though your CPU meets the minimum requirements specified for a particular software application, if you're running other software (in addition to the operating system, which is always running), you'll need to check to see how well

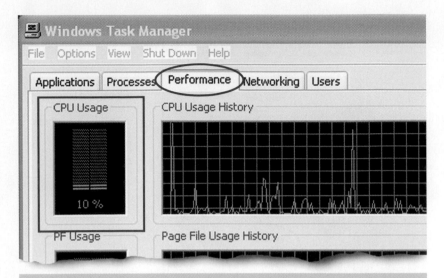

FIGURE 6.6

The Performance tab of the Windows Task Manager utility shows you how busy your CPU actually is when you're using your computer. In this case, current CPU usage level is at 10 percent. If CPU usage levels are above 90 percent for long periods of time, you may want to consider getting a faster, more powerful processor.

the CPU is handling the entire load. You can tell whether your CPU speed is limiting your system performance if you periodically watch how busy it is as you work on your computer. The percentage of time that your CPU is working is referred to as **CPU usage**.

To view information on your CPU usage, right-click an open area of the System toolbar, select Task Manager (a utility program that comes with Windows XP), and click the Performance tab, shown in Figure 6.6. The CPU Usage graph records your CPU usage for the past several seconds. Of course, there will be periodic peaks of high CPU usage, but if you see that your CPU usage levels are greater than 90 percent during most of your work session, a new CPU would contribute a great deal to your system performance.

UPGRADING YOUR CPU

Is it expensive or difficult to upgrade a CPU? Replacement CPUs are expensive. In addition, although it is reasonably easy to install a CPU, it can be difficult to determine which CPU to install. Not all CPUs are interchangeable, and the replacement CPU must be compatible with the motherboard. Some people opt to upgrade the entire motherboard, but motherboards are a lot more difficult to install. As we discuss at the end of this chapter, if you plan on upgrading your computer in other ways in addition to upgrading the CPU, you may just want to consider buying a new computer.

Are the fastest CPUs the best to use? If you decide to upgrade your CPU, consider buying one that is not the most recently released with the fastest speed, but rather a slightly slower one of the same type. For example, if the Intel Pentium 4 family has just released a 3.4-GHz CPU, you will pay a premium to buy this newest processor. However, its release will drive down the prices on the earlier Pentium 4 chips running at speeds of 3.0 GHz, 2.8 GHz, and 2.6 GHz. Buying a slightly slower CPU and investing the savings in other system components (such as additional RAM) will often result in a better-performing system. (The same is true if you're buying a new computer: often, you'll save money without losing a great deal of performance by buying a computer with a CPU slightly slower than the fastest one on the market.)

What else do I need to consider if I want to upgrade my CPU? You first need to determine whether a new CPU is compatible with your system's motherboard. (**www.powerleap.com** has a great tool

BITS AND BYTES

Feeling Hot Hot Hot

Heat isn't good for a computer system. However, computer chips, especially the CPU, produce heat, and if that heat isn't dissipated, the chips will have a shorter life. System cases are always designed with one internal fan, but if you're upgrading, you may want to consider a case that pays more attention to keeping your system cool. **www.highspeedpc.com** and **www.tigerdirect.com** are suppliers that offer cases featuring special venting

designs and dual exhaust fans. You can also buy high-quality fans that sit directly on top of the CPU, dissipating heat directly off the chip. And if you want a more extreme solution, water cooling systems can replace the fans altogether. The Corsair Hydrocool unit sits next to your computer and pumps coolant through hoses and past the CPU chip to remove heat more efficiently and quietly than airflow. Very cool indeed!

FIGURE 6.7

It can be fairly simple to replace a CPU: you line up the slots and drop it in. However, because it's important that you pick the right replacement part and process, many computer owners seek the help of professionals when upgrading their CPU.

Does your CPU subsystem need to be upgraded?		
	CURRENT SYSTEM	**UPGRADE REQUIRED?**
CPU Speed (in MHz or GHz)		
CPU Usage at Appropriate Level?		

to walk you through CPU and motherboard compatibility.) Check your computer's manual for the make and model of the components on your motherboard.

In addition, because the CPU generates a lot of heat, a small cooling device called a *heat sink* sits directly on top of the CPU to absorb excess heat. If you upgrade your CPU, you need to make sure you purchase the correct heat sink for your processor (although often heat sinks come in a kit with the replacement CPU).

Be mindful that while replacing the CPU is not terribly difficult (as shown in Figure 6.7), it is important that you pick the right replacement part and process. It may be best to get the help of a professional should you decide to upgrade your CPU.

Will replacing the CPU be enough to improve my computer's performance? You may think that if you have the fastest processor, you will have a system with the best performance. However, upgrading your CPU will only affect the *processing* portion of the system performance, not how quickly data can move to or from the CPU. Your system's overall performance depends on many other factors, including the amount of RAM installed as well as hard disk speed. Therefore, replacing or upgrading the CPU may not offer significant improvements to your system's performance if there is insufficient RAM or hard drive capacity.

Evaluating RAM: The Memory Subsystem

Random access memory (RAM) is your computer's temporary storage space. Although we refer to RAM as a form of storage, RAM is really the computer's short-term memory. As such, it remembers everything that the computer needs to process the data into information, such as inputted data and software instructions, but only while the computer is on. This means that RAM is an example of **volatile storage**. When the power is off, the data stored in RAM is cleared out. This is why, in addition to RAM, systems always include **nonvolatile storage** devices for permanent storage of instructions and data when the computer is powered off. Hard disks provide the greatest nonvolatile storage capacity in the computer system.

Why not use a hard drive to store the data and instructions? It's about one million times faster for the CPU to retrieve a piece of data from RAM than from a hard disk drive. The time it takes the CPU to retrieve data from RAM is measured in *nanoseconds* (billionths of seconds), whereas retrieving data from a fast hard drive takes an average of 10 *milliseconds* (or ms, thousandths of seconds). This difference is influential in designing a balanced computer system and can have a tremendous impact on system performance. Therefore, it's critical that your computer has more than enough RAM.

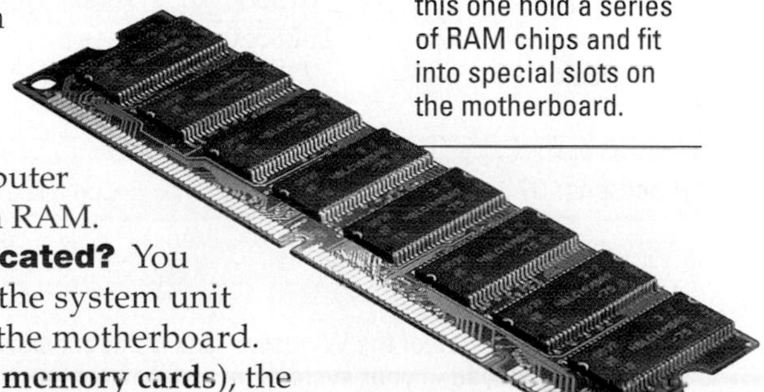

Where is RAM located? You can find RAM inside the system unit of your computer on the motherboard. **Memory modules** (or **memory cards**), the small circuit boards that hold a series of RAM chips (see Figure 6.8), fit into special

FIGURE 6.8

Memory modules like this one hold a series of RAM chips and fit into special slots on the motherboard.

slots on the motherboard. There are three different types of memory modules: single inline memory modules (SIMMs), dual inline memory modules (DIMMs), and Rambus inline memory modules (RIMMs). Most computers today either have DIMM or RIMM modules. As a consumer, you need to know this information only if you are upgrading your RAM (you need to stay with the same kind of module when you upgrade).

Are there different types of RAM?
To add to the confusion new computer users face, several different types of RAM are available. DRAM, static RAM (SRAM), and synchronous DRAM (SDRAM) are all

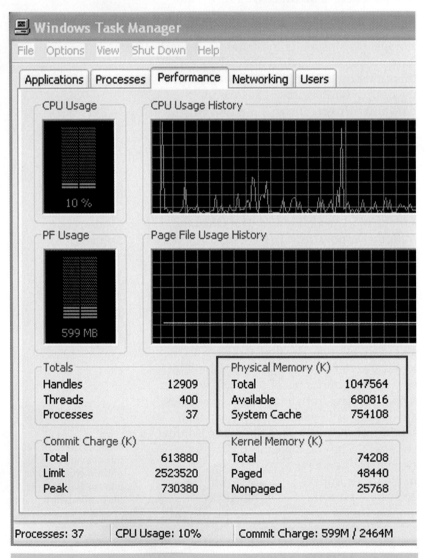

FIGURE 6.9

The Performance tab of the Windows Task Manager shows you how much physical memory is installed in your system, as well as how much is currently being used and how much is available. The computer shown here has approximately 680 MB of memory still available from a total of 1,047 MB.

slightly different in how they function and in the speed at which memory can be accessed. If you're purchasing a new system, most manufacturers use the same type of RAM (SDRAM) on all models. But if you're adding RAM to an older system, you must determine what type your system needs. Consult your user's manual or the manufacturer's Web site. In addition, many online RAM resellers (such as **www.crucial.com**) can help you determine the type of RAM your system needs based on the model number and brand of your computer. We discuss the different kinds of RAM in more detail in Chapter 9.

How can I tell how much RAM I have installed in my computer? The amount of RAM that is actually sitting on memory modules in your computer is your computer's **physical memory**. The easiest way to see how much RAM you have is to look in the General tab of the System Properties dialog box. This is the same tab you looked in to determine your system's CPU type and speed and is shown in Figure 6.5. RAM capacity is measured in megabytes (MB) or gigabytes (GB). The computer in Figure 6.5 has 512 MB of RAM installed.

More detailed information on physical memory is displayed in the Physical Memory table in the Performance tab of Windows Task Manager, shown in Figure 6.9. The Physical Memory table shows both the total amount of physical memory you have installed as well as the *available* physical memory you have at this moment. You can see this computer has approximately 1,047 MB (1,047,564 kilobytes, or KB) of total memory installed, and approximately 680 MB is available (which means 367 MB is being used). The amount of available memory will always be less than the amount of total memory because a certain portion of the physical memory is always tied up running the operating system.

How much memory does the operating system need to run? The memory that your operating system uses is referred to as **kernel memory**. This memory is listed in a separate Kernel Memory table in the Performance tab. In Figure 6.9, the Kernel Memory table tells you that approximately 74 MB (74,208 KB) of the total 1,047 MB of RAM is being used to run Windows XP.

As you know from Chapter 5, the operating system is the main software application that runs the computer. Without it the computer would not work. At a minimum, the system needs enough RAM to run the operating system. Therefore, the amount of kernel memory that the system is using is the *absolute minimum* amount of RAM that your computer can run on. However, because you are running additional applications, you need to have more RAM than the minimum.

How much RAM do I need? Since RAM is the temporary holding space for all the data and instructions that the computer uses while it is on, most computer users need quite a bit of RAM. In fact, it's not unusual to have 1 GB of RAM on a newer home system. The amount of RAM your system needs depends on how you use it. At a minimum, you need enough RAM to run the operating system (as explained earlier), plus whatever other software applications you're using, then a bit of additional RAM to hold the data you're inputting.

To determine how much RAM you need, list all the software applications you might be running at one time. Figure 6.10 shows an example of RAM requirements. In this example, if you are running your operating system, word processing and spreadsheet programs, a Web browser, a music player, and photo-editing software simultaneously, you would need a *minimum* of 460 MB RAM.

However, it's a good idea to have more than the minimum amount of RAM, so you can use more programs in the future. When upgrading RAM, the rule of thumb is to buy as much as you can afford but no more than your system will handle.

VIRTUAL MEMORY

Would adding more RAM also improve my system performance? If your system is **memory bound**—that is, limited in how fast it can send data to the CPU because there's not enough RAM installed—it will become sluggish, freeze more often, or just shut down during the day. If this is the case, adding more RAM to your system will have an immediate impact on performance.

How do I know whether my system is memory bound? You learned in Chapter 5 that if you don't have enough RAM to hold all of the programs you're currently trying to run, the operating system will begin to store the data that doesn't fit in RAM into a space on the hard disk called

FIGURE 6.10 Sample RAM Requirements

APPLICATION	MINIMUM RAM REQUIRED
Windows XP	128 MB
MS Office Pro 2003	128 MB
Internet Explorer	12 MB
Windows Media Player	64 MB
Microsoft Picture It!	128 MB
Total RAM Required if Running All Programs Simultaneously	460 MB RAM

virtual memory. When it is using virtual memory, your operating system builds a file called the **page file** on the hard drive to allow processing to continue. This enables the system to run more applications than can actually fit in your computer's RAM.

So far, this system of memory management sounds like a good idea, especially because hard disk drives are much cheaper than RAM per megabyte of storage. The drawback is speed. Remember that accessing data from the hard drive to send it to the CPU is more than one million times slower than accessing data from RAM. Another drawback is that some applications do not run well on virtual memory. So, using virtual memory is a method of last resort. If your system is running with a large page file (that is, if it is using a large amount of virtual memory), adding more RAM will dramatically increase performance.

How do I determine how much virtual memory I'm using? As shown in Figure 6.11 (p. 230), the Performance tab of the Task Manager provides information about your computer's virtual memory (referred to as the *PF Usage*). By watching the information displayed in the PF Usage section, you can determine how much virtual memory is being

SOUND BYTE
INSTALLING RAM

In this Sound Byte, you'll learn how to select the appropriate type of memory to purchase, how to order memory online, and how to install it yourself. As you'll discover, the procedure is a simple one and can add great performance benefits to your system.

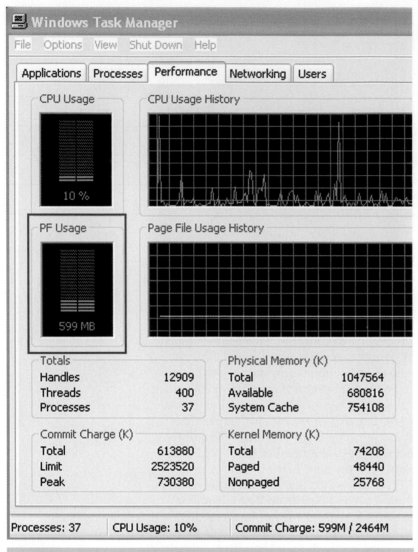

FIGURE 6.11

You can see how much page file (virtual memory) is being used at any given point in time by looking at the PF Usage chart in the Performance tab of the Windows Task Manager (in this case, 599 MB is being used).

used. If you consistently have a large page file in use (that is, more than 1.5 percent of the amount of RAM installed in your system) and very little physical memory available, adding more RAM will significantly improve your system performance.

ADDING RAM

Is there a limit to how much RAM I can add to my computer? Every computer is designed with a maximum limit on the amount of RAM it can support. In addition, each computer is designed with a specific number of slots on the memory board in which the memory cards fit, and each slot may have a limitation on the amount of RAM it can support. To determine these limitations, check your owner's manual or the manufacturer's Web site.

Once you know how much RAM your computer can support, you can determine the best configuration of memory cards to achieve the greatest amount of RAM. For example, say you have a total of four memory card slots: two are already filled with 128-MB RAM cards and the other two are empty. Maximum RAM allowed for your system is 512 MB. This means you can buy two more 128-MB RAM modules for the two empty slots, for a total of 512 MB (4 x 128 MB) of RAM. If all the memory card slots are already filled, you may be able to replace the old modules with greater-capacity RAM modules, depending on your maximum allowed RAM.

Is it hard to add RAM? Adding RAM to a computer is fairly easy (see Figure 6.12). RAM comes with installation instructions,

FIGURE 6.12

Adding RAM to a personal computer is quite simple and relatively inexpensive. You simply line up the notches and push in the memory module. Just be sure that you're adding a compatible memory module to your computer.

which you should follow carefully. RAM is also relatively inexpensive compared with other system upgrade options. Still, the cost of RAM fluctuates in the marketplace as much as 400 percent over time, so if you're considering adding RAM, you should watch the prices of memory in online or print advertisements.

Evaluating the Storage Subsystem

As you've learned, there are two ways data is saved on your computer: temporary storage and permanent storage. RAM is a form of *temporary* (or *volatile*) storage—thus, anything residing in RAM is not permanently saved. Therefore, it's critical to have means to store data and software applications *permanently*.

Fortunately, several storage options exist within every computer system. Storage devices for a typical personal computer include the hard disk drive, floppy disk drive, Zip disk drive, and CD and DVD drives. When you turn off your computer, the data stored to these devices is saved. These devices are therefore referred to as *nonvolatile storage* devices. Of all the nonvolatile storage devices, the hard disk drive is used the most.

THE HARD DISK DRIVE

What makes the hard disk drive the most popular storage device? With storage capacities of up to 400 GB, **hard disk drives** (or just **hard drives**), shown in Figure 6.13, have the largest storage capacity of any storage device. The hard disk drive is also a much more economical device than floppy, Zip, or CD/DVD drives because it offers the most megabytes of storage per dollar.

Second, the hard drive's **access time**, or the time it takes a storage device to locate its stored data and make it available for processing, is also the fastest of all permanent storage devices. Hard drive access times are measured in milliseconds, or thousandths of seconds. For large-capacity disk drives, access times of approximately 9.5 milliseconds—that's less than one-hundredth of a second—are not unusual. This is much faster than the access times of other popular storage devices, such as floppy and Zip disk drives.

Another reason hard drives are popular is that they transfer data to other computer

Do you need more memory?		
	CURRENT SYSTEM	**UPGRADE REQUIRED?**
Amount of RAM		
Type of RAM		
Maximum Amount of RAM You Need		
Total RAM You Can Add to Your Computer		
Total Number of Memory Slots		
Number of Open Memory Slots		

components (such as RAM) much faster than the other storage devices do. This speed of transfer is referred to as **data transfer rate** and depending on the manufacturer is expressed in either mega*bits* or mega*bytes* per second.

How is data stored on hard drives? As you learned in Chapter 5, a hard disk drive is composed of several coated **platters** (round, thin plates of metal) stacked onto a spindle. When data is saved to a hard disk, a pattern of magnetized spots is created on the iron oxide coating each platter. Each of these spots represents a 1, whereas the spaces not "spotted" represent a 0. These 0s and 1s are bits (or binary digits) and are the smallest pieces of data that computers can

Hard drive inside the system unit

FIGURE 6.13

Hard disk drives are the most popular storage device for personal computers. The hard disk drive is installed permanently inside the system unit.

DIG DEEPER

How a Hard Disk Drive Works

The thin metal platters that make up a hard drive are covered with a special magnetic coating that enables the data to be recorded onto one or both sides of the platter. Hard disk manufacturers prepare the disks to hold data through a process called low-level formatting. In this process, **tracks** (concentric circles) and **sectors** (pie-shaped wedges) are created in the magnetized surface of each platter, setting up a gridlike pattern used to identify file locations on the hard drive. A separate process, called high-level formatting, establishes the catalog that the computer uses to keep track of where each file is located on the hard drive. As you learned in Chapter 5, this catalog is called the **File Allocation Table (FAT)**.

Hard drive platters spin at a high rate of speed, some as fast as 15,000 revolutions per minute (rpm). Sitting between each platter are special "arms" that contain **read/write heads** (see Figure 6.14). The read/write heads move from the outer edge of the spinning platters to the center, up to 50 times per second, to retrieve (read) and record (write) the magnetic data to and from the hard disk. As noted earlier, the average total time it takes for the read/write head to locate the data on the platter and return it to the CPU for processing is the access time. A new hard drive should have an average access time of about 10 ms.

Access time is mostly the sum of two factors, seek time and latency. The time it takes for the read/write heads to move over the surface of the disk, between tracks, to the correct track is called the **seek time** (sometimes people incorrectly refer to this as access time). Once the read/write head locates the correct track, it may need to wait for the correct sector to spin to the read/write head. This waiting time is called **latency** (or rotational delay). The faster the platters spin (or the faster the rpm), the less time you'll have to wait for your data to be accessed. Currently, you can find new hard drives that spin between 5,400 and 7,200 rpm.

The read/write heads do not touch the platters of the hard drive; rather, they float above them on a thin cushion of air at a height of 0.5 microinches. As a matter of comparison, a human hair is 2,000 microinches thick and a particle of dust is larger than a human hair. Therefore, it's critical to keep your hard disk drive free from all dust and dirt, as even the smallest particle could find its way between the read/write head and the disk platter, causing a **head crash**—a stoppage of the hard disk drive that often results in data loss.

Capacities for hard disk drives in personal computers exceed 400 GB. Increasing the amount of data stored in a hard disk drive is achieved by either adding more platters and/or by increasing the amount of data stored on each platter. How tightly the tracks are placed next to each other, how tightly spaced the sectors are, and how closely the bits of data are placed affect the measurement of the amount of data that can be stored in a specific area of a hard disk. Modern technology continues to increase the standards on all three levels, enabling massive quantities of data to be stored in small places.

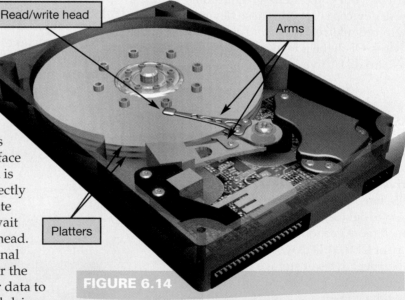

Read/write head

Arms

Platters

FIGURE 6.14

The hard drive is a stack of platters enclosed in a sealed case. Special arms fit in between each platter. The read/write heads at the end of each arm read from and save data to the platters.

understand. When data stored on the hard disk is retrieved (or read), your computer translates these patterns of magnetized spots into the data you have saved.

How do I know how much capacity my hard drive has? Hard drive capacity is measured in MB or GB. To check how much total capacity your hard drive has, as well as how much is being used, simply double-click the My Computer icon, right-click the C drive icon, and select Properties from the shortcut menu. The Properties dia-

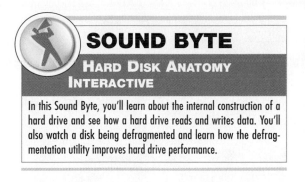

SOUND BYTE

HARD DISK ANATOMY
INTERACTIVE

In this Sound Byte, you'll learn about the internal construction of a hard drive and see how a hard drive reads and writes data. You'll also watch a disk being defragmented and learn how the defragmentation utility improves hard drive performance.

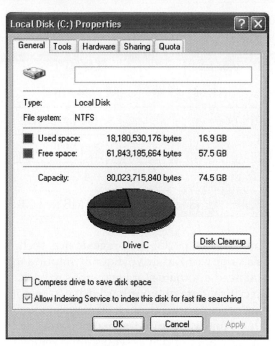

FIGURE 6.15

Using the pie chart in the General tab of the Properties dialog box, you can determine the capacity of your hard drive. This hard drive has 74.5 GB of space, with 57.5 GB of free space.

log box displays a pie chart that indicates the total capacity of your hard drive as well as the capacity being used, as shown in Figure 6.15.

How do I know how much storage capacity I need? To determine the storage capacity your system needs, calculate the amount of storage capacity basic computer programs need to reside on your computer. Because the operating system is the most critical piece of software, your hard drive needs enough space to store that program. The demands on system requirements have grown with new versions of operating systems. Windows XP, the latest Microsoft operating system, requires a whopping 1.5 GB of hard drive capacity. Five years ago, such software wouldn't have fit on most hard drives.

In addition to having space for the operating system, you need enough space to store software applications you use, such as Microsoft Office, a Web browser, and games. It's always best to check the system requirements of any software program before you purchase it to make sure your system can handle it. Storage requirements are found on the software package or on the manufacturer's Web site. Figure 6.16 shows an example of hard drive requirements for someone storing a few programs on a hard drive.

Are some hard drives faster than others? There are two basic types of hard drives: Integrated Drive Electronics (IDE) and Small Computer System Interface (SCSI). (Note that SCSI is pronounced as "scuzzy.") IDE drives have data transfer rates ranging from 16 to 66 MB per second. IDE drives are best if you use your computer primarily for word processing, spreadsheets, e-mail, and the Internet. However, "power users," such as graphic designers and software developers, may need to consider a faster SCSI hard drive. Data transfer rates for SCSI hard drives range from 40 to 80 MB per second.

Another factor affecting a hard disk's speed is access time (or the speed with which

FIGURE 6.16 Sample Hard Drive Requirements

APPLICATION	HARD DISK SPACE REQUIRED
Windows XP	1.5 GB
MS Office Pro 2003	690 MB
Internet Explorer	75 MB
Windows Media Player	521 MB
Microsoft Picture It!	150 MB
Total Required	2.94 GB

it locates data for processing). As noted earlier, access time is measured in milliseconds (ms). The faster the access time the better, although most hard drives will have similar access times.

PORTABLE STORAGE OPTIONS: THE FLOPPY AND BEYOND

If my hard drive is so powerful, why do I need other forms of storage? Despite all the advantages that the hard drive has as a storage device, one drawback is that data stored on it is not portable. To get data from one computer to another (assuming the computers aren't networked),

FIGURE 6.17 Portable Storage Capacities	
STORAGE MEDIA	**CAPACITY**
Floppy Disk	1.44 MB
Zip Disk	100 to 750 MB
CD	700 MB
DVD	9.4 GB
Flash Memory	16 MB to 2 GB

FIGURE 6.18

Flash drives, also known as thumb drives or jump drives, allow you to carry 256 MB or more on your key chain.

you'll need a portable storage device, such as a floppy or Zip drive. Equally important, you need alternate storage options to back up critical data on your hard drive in case it experiences a head crash or other system problems. Finally, despite the massive storage capacity of hard drives, you should remove infrequently used files from your hard drive to maintain optimal storage capacity.

What forms of portable storage are best? Several portable storage formats (or media) are popular now, with varying ranges of storage capacity (see Figure 6.17). The **floppy disk**, with a storage capacity of 1.44 MB, holds the least amount of data but has been the primary form of convenient, portable data storage. However, today's average user is generating much larger files because of the incorporation of multimedia. Floppy disks are too small to hold even one file that has been bulked up with multimedia. For this reason, floppy disks will eventually

become obsolete. **Zip disks**, with storage capacities ranging from 100 MB to 750 MB, and CD-R, CD-RW, DVD-R, and DVD-RW discs, with storage capacities ranging from 700 MB to 9.4 GB, have become increasingly popular to store larger files.

Flash memory cards are another form of portable storage. These tiny removable memory cards are often used in digital cameras, MP3 players, and personal digital assistants (PDAs). Some newer flash cards can hold as much as 2 GB of data. As the technology becomes more popular, capacities will continue to increase.

This same technology is also packaged as **flash drives** (sometimes called *thumb drives* or *jump drives*). Small enough to fit on your key chain, a flash drive can hold between 32 MB and 1 GB of data and can be plugged into any universal serial bus (USB) port (see Figure 6.18). Windows XP instantly recognizes flash drives when they are plugged into a USB port and treats them as another hard drive on the system. For $20 you can carry 128 MB with you easily and have enough room to store a huge PowerPoint presentation, several images, and even a few MP3 songs.

Floppy and Zip Disks
How is data stored on floppy and Zip disks? Inside the plastic cases of both floppy and Zip disks you'll find a round piece of plastic film. This film is covered with a magnetized coating of iron oxide. As is the case with hard drives, when data is saved to the disk, a pattern of magnetized spots is created on

BITS AND BYTES

Taking Care of Floppy and Zip Disks

The following guidelines will help you keep your floppy and Zip disks safe:

- Place disks in a protective case when carrying or mailing them.
- Keep disks away from devices that generate a magnetic field, such as speakers, televisions, and mobile phones.
- Use a felt-tip marker (not a pen or pencil) when labeling disks. Better yet, create a label and place it on the disk.
- Don't expose your disk to excessive heat or cold.
- Don't move the metal shutter that protects the disk. Dirt and dust that get into the disk can harm your data. If the metal shutter comes off the floppy, transfer the data immediately to the hard drive, because dust and dirt will corrupt the data on the exposed part of the floppy.

the iron oxide coating within established tracks and sectors. Each of these spots represents either a 0 or a 1, or a bit. When data stored on the disk is retrieved (read), your computer translates these patterns of magnetized spots into information. Because floppies and Zip disks use a magnetized film to store data, they are referred to as **magnetic media**.

CDs and DVDs
How is data saved onto a CD or DVD?
Like the hard drive and floppy and Zip disks, data is saved to CDs and DVDs within established tracks and sectors. However, unlike floppy and Zip disks, which store their data on a piece of magnetized film, CDs and DVDs store data as tiny pits that are burned into a disk by a high-speed laser. These pits are extremely small, less than 1 micron in diameter, so that nearly 1,500 pits fit across the top of a pinhead. As you can see in Figure 6.19, data is read off the CD by a laser beam, with the pits and nonpits translating into the 1s and 0s of the binary code computers understand. Because CDs and DVDs use a laser to read and write data, they are referred to as **optical media**.

Why can I store data on some CDs but not others? CD-ROMs are read-only optical disks, meaning you can't save any data onto them. To play a CD-ROM, you use a CD-ROM drive. However, most computers today are equipped with special CD drives that allow you to save, or "burn," data onto specially designed CDs. **Compact Disc–Read/ Writable (CD-RW) discs**, which use a CD-RW drive, can be written to hundreds of times. **Compact Disc–Recordable (CD-R) discs** can be written to once and can be used with either a CD-R drive or a CD-RW drive. If your computer isn't equipped with a CD-R or CD-RW drive, you can buy one at a reasonable cost, and they're quite simple to install.

What's the difference between CDs and DVDs? DVDs use the same optical technology to store data as CDs. The difference is

To read information stored on a disk, a laser inside the disk drive sends a beam of light through the spinning disk

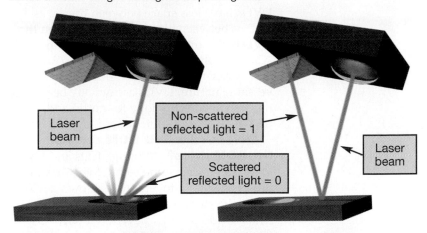

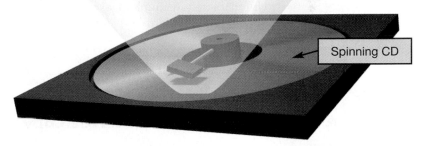

If the light reflected back is scattered in all directions (which happens when the laser hits a pit), the laser translates this into the binary digit 0

If non-scattered light is reflected back to the laser (which happens when the laser hits an area in which there is no pit), the laser translates this into the binary digit 1

In this way, the laser reads the pits and non-pits as a series of bits (0s and 1s), which the computer can then process

FIGURE 6.19

Data is read from a CD using focused laser light.

SOUND BYTE
CD AND DVD READING & WRITING INTERACTIVE

In this Sound Byte, you'll learn about the process of storing and retrieving data from CD-R, CD-RW, and DVD discs. You'll be amazed to see how much precision engineering is required to burn MP3 files onto a disc.

BITS AND BYTES
Taking Care of CDs and DVDs

The following guidelines will help you keep your CDs and DVDs safe:

- Exercise care in handling your CDs and DVDs. Dirt or oil on CDs/DVDs can keep data from being read properly, while large scratches can interrupt data completely.
- To keep CDs/DVDs from warping, avoid placing them near heat sources and store them at room temperature.
- Clean CDs/DVDs by taking a bit of rubbing alcohol on a cotton ball and wiping them from the center to the edge of the disk in long swipes. Don't rub the CD/DVD circularly, because you may cause more scratches.
- Use a felt-tip marker to label CDs/DVDs and write on the area provided for the label. Don't put stickers or labels on CDs/DVDs, unless they're specifically designed for that purpose.

that a DVD's storage capacity is much greater than a CD's. To hold more data than CDs, DVDs have less space between tracks, as well as between bits. The size of pits on the DVD is also much smaller than those on a CD. Additionally, DVD audio and video quality is superior to that of a CD. Because of their versatile nature, DVDs are quickly becoming the standard technology for audio and video files as well as graphics and data files.

Do I need a DVD-ROM drive *and* a CD-ROM drive? Although CDs and DVDs are based on the same technology, they are different enough to require their own devices. If your system has only a CD drive, you need to add a DVD drive to view DVDs. However, because DVD drives can read CDs, if your system has a DVD drive, you do not need to add a CD drive.

To record data to DVDs, you need recordable DVD discs and a read/write DVD drive. Unfortunately, technology experts have not agreed on a standard DVD format. Currently,

SOUND BYTE
INSTALLING A CDRW DRIVE

In this Sound Byte, you'll learn how to install a CDRW drive in your computer.

there are two recognized formats, **DVD-R/RW** (pronounced "DVD dash") and **DVD+R/RW** (pronounced "DVD plus"). You can purchase a DVD-RW drive or a DVD+RW drive or even a "super drive" DVD-/+RW that can read and write both formats. Either the plus or dash format discs you write will be compatible in about 85 percent of all DVD players. However, you must make sure you purchase blank DVD discs that match the type of drive you own. Any DVD drive can burn CDs, however— the wars fought over the CD standard have been settled for several years now.

Are some CD and DVD drives faster than others? When you buy a CD or

TRENDS IN IT

Ethics: CD and DVD Technology: A Free Lunch—or at Least a Free Copy

Years ago, when the electronic photocopier made its debut, book publishers and others who distributed the printed word feared they would be put out of business. They were worried that people would no longer buy books and other printed matter if they could simply copy someone else's original. Years later, when the cassette player/recorder and VCR player/recorder arrived on the market, those who felt they would be negatively affected by these new technologies expressed similar reactions. Now, with the arrival of DVD-RW and CD-RW technology, which allows users to copy DVDs and CDs in a matter of minutes, the music and entertainment industries are up in arms.

Although copy machines and VCRs certainly didn't put an end to the industries they affected, some still say the music and entertainment industries will take a significant hit with CD-RW/DVD-RW technology. Already, CD and DVD sales are plummeting. Industry insiders are claiming that these new technologies are unethical, and they're pressing for increased federal legislation against such copying. And it's not just the CD-RW/DVD-RW technology that's causing problems— "copies" are not necessarily of the physical sort. Thanks to the Internet, *file transferring* copyrighted works— particularly music and films—is now commonplace. Viant, a company known for its studies on Internet

piracy, reported recently that, on average, between 300,000 and 500,000 films per day are being transferred over the Internet.

In a separate survey, the Recording Industry Association of America (RIAA), a trade organization that represents the interests of recording giants such as Sony, Capitol Records, and other major producers of musical entertainment, reported that 23 percent of music fans revealed they were buying less music because they could download it or copy a CD-ROM from a friend.

As you would expect, the music and entertainment industries want to be fairly compensated for their creative output. They blame the technology industry for the creation of means by which artists, studios, and the entertainment industry in general are being "robbed." Although the technology exists that readily allows consumers to transfer and copy music and videos, the artists who produce these works do not want to be taken advantage of. However, others claim that the technology industry should not bear the complete burden of protecting entertainment copyrights. The RIAA sums up the future of this debate nicely: "Goals for the new millennium are to work with [the recording] industry and others to enable technologies that open up new opportunities but at the same time to protect the rights of artists and copyright owners."

DVD drive, knowing the drive speed is important. Speeds are listed on the device's packaging. Record (write) speed is always listed first, rewrite speed is listed second (except for CD-R drives, which cannot rewrite data), and playback speed is listed last. For example, a CD-RW drive may have speeds of 48x12x48x, meaning that the device can record data at 48x speed, rewrite data at 12x speed, and play back data at 48x speed. For CDs, the x in between each number represents the transfer of 150 KB of data per second. So, for example, a CD-RW drive with a 48x12x48x rating records data at 48 x 150 KB per second, or 7,200 KB per second.

DVD drives are much faster than CD drives. For example, a 1x DVD-ROM drive provides a data transfer rate of approximately 1.3 MB of data per second, which is roughly equivalent to a CD-ROM speed of 9x. CD and DVD drives are constantly getting faster. If you're in the market for a new CD-RW, you'll want to investigate the drive speeds on the market and make sure you get the fastest one you can.

UPGRADING YOUR STORAGE SUBSYSTEM

How can I upgrade my storage devices?
There are several ways in which you can increase your storage capacity or add extra drives to your computer.

If you find your hard drive is running out of space, or you want a place to back up or move files to create more room on your hard drive, you have several options. You can replace the hard drive installed in your system unit with a bigger one. However, replacing your internal hard drive requires backing up your entire hard drive and reloading all the data onto your new hard drive. Instead, you may want to install an additional hard drive in your current system if you have an extra drive bay (the space reserved on the inside of your system unit for hard disk drives). In lieu of installing a bigger hard drive, there are now external hard drives you can plug directly into a free USB 2.0 or FireWire port. Figure 6.20 shows an example of such an external hard drive.

You can also upgrade your storage subsystem by adding a new Zip drive or other drive to your system. If your computer did not come with an internal Zip, CD-RW, or DVD-RW drive, and if you have an open

This external hard disk drive offers you extra storage and plugs into your computer through a FireWire port.

(unused) drive bay in your system, you can easily install a drive there. Most people upgrade to a CD-RW and DVD-RW not for more storage, but because they want additional multimedia capabilities (such as the ability to burn CDs). If you don't have open bays in your system, you can still add Zip and CD/DVD drives. As is the case with hard drives, these drives are available as external units you attach to your computer through an open port.

What if I want to use flash memory? As flash memory becomes more popular, you may want your computer to be able to read flash memory cards. Although most desktop computers don't include internal **memory card readers**, you can purchase external memory card readers like the one shown in Figure 6.21 that connect to your system through an open USB port. Some flash memory comes in "sticks" that just plug directly into a USB port.

Flash card readers hook up to your computer through a USB port.

Do you need to upgrade your storage subsystem?		
	CURRENT SYSTEM	**UPGRADE REQUIRED?**
Hard Disk Drive Capacity		
Floppy Disk Drive		
Zip Disk Drive		
CD-ROM Drive		
CD-RW Drive		
DVD-ROM Drive		
DVD-RW Drive		
Other Storage Devices Needed?		

Evaluating the Video Subsystem

How video is displayed depends on two components: your video card and your monitor. It's important that your system have the correct monitor and video card to meet your needs. If you use your computer system to display files that have complex graphics, such as videos on DVD or from your camcorder, or even play graphics-rich games with a lot of fast action, you may want to consider upgrading your video subsystem.

VIDEO CARDS

What is a video card? A **video card** (or **video adapter**) is an expansion card that is installed inside your system unit to translate binary data (the 1s and 0s your computer uses) into the images you view on your monitor. Today, almost all computers ship with a video card installed. Modern video cards, like the one shown in Figure 6.22, are very sophisticated. They include ports allowing you to connect to different video equipment as well as their own RAM, called **video RAM (VRAM)**. Because displaying graphics demands a lot of the CPU, video cards also come with their own processors. Calls to the CPU for graphics processing are redirected to the processor on the video card, significantly speeding up graphics processing.

How can I tell how much VRAM my video card has? The Display Properties dialog box in Windows XP displays the *type* of video card in use on your computer. Unfortunately, it does not display the *amount* of VRAM that the card has. However, the documentation that came with your computer should contain specifications for the video card, including the amount of VRAM it has installed. If you can't find this documentation, check the Web site of your computer's manufacturer or the manufacturer of the video card.

How much VRAM does my video card need? The amount of VRAM your video card needs depends on what you want to display on your monitor. If you only work in Microsoft Word and conduct general Web searching, 16 MB is a realistic minimum. For the serious gamer, a 128-MB or 256-MB video card is essential, allowing games to generate smoother animations. Before purchasing new software, check the specifications to ensure your video card has enough VRAM to handle the load.

What else does the video card do? The video card also controls the number of colors your monitor can display. The number of bits the video card uses to represent each pixel on the monitor (referred to as **bit depth**) determines the color quality of the image displayed. The more bits, the better the color detail of the image. A 4-bit video card displays 16 colors, the minimum number of colors your system works with

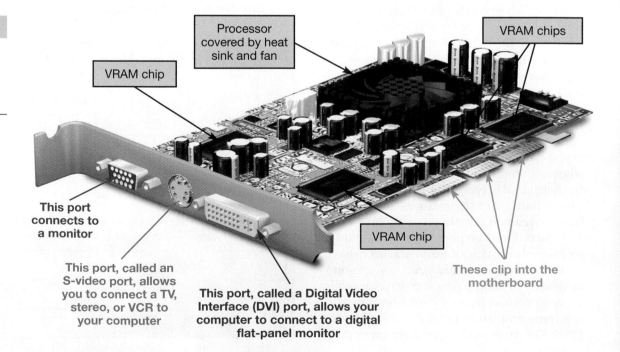

FIGURE 6.22

Video cards have grown to be very specialized subsystems.

Processor covered by heat sink and fan

VRAM chips

VRAM chip

This port connects to a monitor

This port, called an S-video port, allows you to connect a TV, stereo, or VCR to your computer

This port, called a Digital Video Interface (DVI) port, allows your computer to connect to a digital flat-panel monitor

VRAM chip

These clip into the motherboard

(referred to as *Standard* VGA). Most video cards today are 24-bit cards, displaying over 16 million colors. This mode is called *true color mode* (see Figure 6.23).

The most recent generation of video cards can add some great features to your computer if you are a TV fan. Such cards as the ATI All-In-Wonder 9800 Pro can pop open a live TV window on your screen, including features such as picture-in-picture. Using this video card, you can record programs to your hard drive or pause live TV. The card even comes with a wireless remote control unit.

There are also video cards that allow you to import video. These models have a special video-in port that you can connect to a VHS tape player or an analog video camera. The video is then digitized into a file that is stored on your hard drive. Video editing software, often included with these video cards, enables you to edit, add effects or titles to your original clips, and produce polished versions of your favorite home movies. For more information on digital video editing, see the Technology in Focus feature, "Digital Entertainment."

So how do I know if I need a new video card? If your monitor takes a while to refresh when editing photos, surfing the Web, or playing a graphics-rich game, the video card could be short on memory. You also may want to upgrade if added features such as television viewing or importing analog video are important to you. Replacing a video card with one with more memory and/or bit depth is fairly simple: you simply insert the new video card in the correct expansion slot.

MONITORS

How do I evaluate my monitor? You've evaluated your video card to ensure the best display. However, if the monitor is no good, you're still out of luck. As you learned in Chapter 2, there are two types of monitors: cathode-ray tube (CRT) and liquid crystal display (LCD). We discussed in that chapter the factors you need to think about when deciding whether you should buy a CRT or an LCD. If you currently have a CRT monitor and believe the advantages of the LCD are worth the extra money, you may want to upgrade.

Another factor you need to consider in evaluating your monitor is its size. The most

FIGURE 6.23 Bit Depth and Color Quality

BIT DEPTH	COLOR QUALITY DESCRIPTION	NUMBER OF COLORS DISPLAYED
4-bit	Standard VGA	16
8-bit	256-Color Mode	256
16-bit	High Color	65,536
24-bit	True Color	16,777,216

common monitor sizes are 15, 17, 19, and 21 inches. If your monitor is 15 inches or smaller, you may need to scroll horizontally and vertically to see an entire Web page, for example. Note that monitor size listed for CRT monitors is the diagonal measurement of the tube before it's placed in the screen case. The actual viewing size is less. LCD monitors are also measured diagonally, but the measurement is equal to the viewing size. Therefore, the viewable area of a 17-inch LCD is approximately equal to the viewable area of a 19-inch CRT. If you have a CRT monitor and want to increase the size of your monitor but can't afford giving up desktop space, you may want to consider buying the same size LCD monitor. If you can't afford to buy a larger screen but want to see more on the screen itself, you can try adjusting the resolution of your monitor.

How would changing my screen resolution help me see more on my screen? Most monitors can display different resolutions. Changing the screen resolution can make a difference in what is displayed. In Figure 6.24 (p. 240), the screen resolution on a 15-inch monitor is set to 800 x 600. Notice that it's difficult to see large portions of Word and Excel when they're both on-screen. In Figure 6.25 (p. 240), the screen resolution on the same monitor has been increased to 1,024 x 768. More of the Word and Excel screens are now visible, making it much easier to simultaneously view both documents. However, while increasing the screen resolution allows more to be displayed on the monitor, it also makes the images on the screen smaller and perhaps more difficult to read.

How do I change my screen resolution? To change your screen resolution,

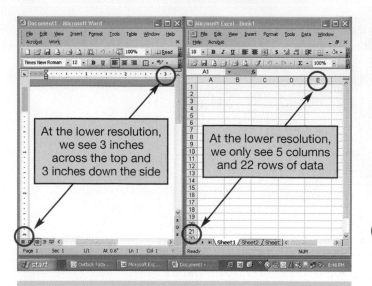

FIGURE 6.24

Here you see the screen display of a 15-inch flat-panel monitor with the resolution set to 800 x 600.

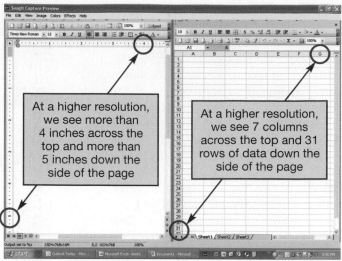

FIGURE 6.25

Here you see the same monitor and same screen display, but the screen resolution has been increased to 1,024 x 768. Notice you can see more of each application.

right-click anywhere on the desktop to display the Display Properties dialog box. Next, left-click the Settings tab. The Screen Resolution section of this dialog box shows your current screen resolution. Left-click the slider bar and drag it to adjust the resolution. Finally, click the Apply button and the monitor resolution will reset itself.

What other features should I look for in a monitor? In Chapter 2 we discussed a number of factors that affect monitor quality, including *refresh rate* (the number of times per second the illumination of each pixel on the monitor is recharged) and *dot pitch* (the diagonal distance between pixels of the same color on the screen). For a clearer, brighter image, look for a monitor with a refresh rate of around 75 Hz and a low dot pitch (no

more than 0.28 mm for a 17-inch screen or 0.31 mm for a 21-inch screen).

Is it easy to install a new monitor? Virtually all monitors sold today support the *Plug and Play* technology that Microsoft introduced in Windows 95. **Plug and Play** means that once you've connected the new monitor to your computer and have booted up the system, Windows will automatically recognize the monitor and configure it to work with your system.

Evaluating the Audio Subsystem

Computers output sound by means of speakers and a sound card. For many users, the preinstalled speakers and sound card are adequate for the sounds produced by the computer itself—the beeps and so on that the computer makes. However, if you're listening to music, viewing DVDs, hooking into a household stereo system, or playing games with sophisticated sound tracks, you may want to upgrade your speakers and/or your sound card.

SPEAKERS

What kinds of computer speakers are available? Two types of speakers ship

Do you need to upgrade your video subsystem?		
	CURRENT SYSTEM	**UPGRADE REQUIRED?**
Video Card VRAM		
Monitor Type (CRT or LCD)		
Monitor Size (Viewable Area)		
Monitor Refresh Rate		
Monitor Dot Pitch		

with most personal computers: amplified speakers (which use external power) or unamplified speakers (which use internal power). Amplified speakers are easy to identify: they come with a separate power transformer and must be plugged into an electrical outlet before they'll function. Unamplified speakers merely plug into the speaker jack on your sound card and require no extra outside power.

Which type of speaker is better? Amplified speakers generally produce better quality sound. However, they usually do not adequately reproduce the low-frequency bass sounds that make gaming and musical scores sound richer and fuller. For better bass sounds, consider purchasing a speaker system that includes a **subwoofer**, a special type of speaker designed to more faithfully reproduce low-frequency sounds (see Figure 6.26).

SOUND CARDS

What does the sound card do? Sound **cards**, like video cards, are expansion cards that attach to the motherboard inside your system unit. Like the video card that enables your computer to produce images on the monitor, sound cards enable the computer to produce sounds.

Can I hook up a surround-sound system to my computer? Most computers ship with a basic sound card, most of which are **3D sound cards**. 3D sound is a technology that advances sound reproduction beyond traditional stereo sound (where the human ear perceives sounds as coming from the left or the right of the performance area). 3D sound is better at convincing the human ear that sound is omnidirectional, meaning you can't tell from which direction the sound is coming. This tends to produce a fuller, richer sound than stereo sound. However, 3D sound is not surround sound.

What is surround sound then? The current surround-sound standard is Dolby Digital 5.1. The 5.1 format takes digital sound from a medium (such as a DVD-ROM) and reproduces it in six channels. Five channels cover the listening field with placement to the left front, right front, and center of the audio stage, as well as the left rear and right rear, as shown in Figure 6.27. The sixth channel holds very low-frequency sound data and is sent to a subwoofer, which can be placed anywhere in the room. To set up surround sound on your computer, you need two things: a set

FIGURE 6.26

Speaker systems that include a subwoofer have a wider dynamic range that features more bass.

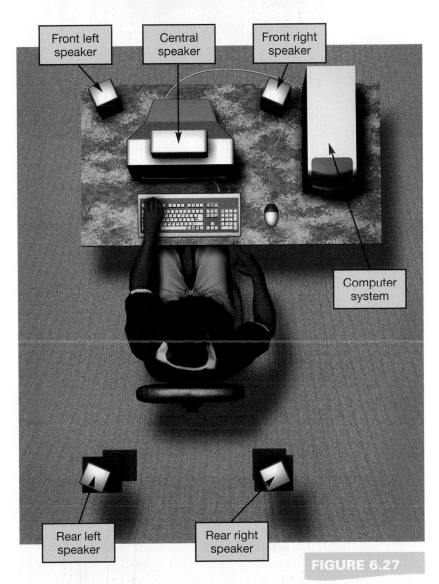

Front left speaker

Central speaker

Front right speaker

Computer system

Rear left speaker

Rear right speaker

FIGURE 6.27

Dolby Digital 5.1 surround sound gives you better quality audio output.

of surround-sound speakers and a sound card that is Dolby 5.1 compatible.

How can I tell if the sound card in my computer is Dolby 5.1 compatible? Unfortunately, the device manager in Windows XP does not show the model of sound card installed in your system. To identify your sound card, you'll need to once again consult the documentation that came with your computer or open your

FIGURE 6.28

In addition to improving sound quality, upgrading sound cards can provide additional jacks for your audio equipment.

computer and search for a name and model number on the sound card. Manufacturers' Web sites usually provide specifications for the various models of sound cards.

I don't need surround sound on my computer. Why else might I need to buy an upgraded sound card? Most basic sound cards contain the following input and output jacks (or ports): microphone in, speaker out, line in, and a gaming port. This allows you to hook up a set of stereo speakers, a microphone, and a joystick. However, what if you want to hook up a right and left speaker individually or attach other audio devices to your computer? To do so, you need more jacks, which are provided on upgraded sound cards like the one shown in Figure 6.28.

With an upgraded sound card, you can connect portable minidisc players, MP3 players, portable jukeboxes, headphones, and CD players to your computer. Musicians also create music on their computers by

connecting special devices (such as keyboards) directly to sound card ports.

Evaluating Port Connectivity

New computer devices are being introduced all the time, and the system you purchased last year may not support the hardware you're interested in today. A **port** is an interface through which external devices are connected to your computer. To evaluate your system's port connectivity, check the camera, camcorder, printer, scanner, and other devices you'd like to be able to connect to your computer and look for what type of port connection they require. Does your system have the ports necessary to connect to all of these devices?

What types of ports are there? The most common types of ports include serial, parallel, universal serial bus (USB), FireWire, and Ethernet. Each type of port operates at a certain speed, measured in either kilobits per second (Kbps) or megabits per second (Mbps). Figure 6.29 lists the basic characteristics of these ports.

The **serial port** allows the transfer of data, one bit at a time, over a single wire at speeds of up to 56 Kbps. Typical devices that still connect to serial ports include external modems and personal digital assistant (PDA) cradles. Serial ports are slowly being phased out by faster ports, such as the USB port.

A **parallel port** sends data between devices in *groups* of bits and is therefore much faster than a serial port. Parallel ports have traditionally been used to connect printers and scanners to computers. Today, most parallel ports achieve data transfer rates of 12 Mbps, much faster than the serial port. Despite this speed increase, parallel ports are becoming less popular now in favor of even higher speed ports.

The **universal serial bus (USB) port** is fast becoming the most common port on computers today. The original USB (version 1.1) port could transfer data at only 12 Mbps. However, in 2002, USB version 2 (USB 2.0) was released, increasing throughput to 480 Mbps. Printers, scanners, digital cameras, keyboards, and mice can all be connected to the computer using USB ports.

The **FireWire port** (previously called the **IEEE 1394 port**) is based on a standard

Do you need to upgrade your audio subsystem?		
	CURRENT SYSTEM	**UPGRADE REQUIRED?**
Speakers (Amplified or Unamplified)		
3D Sound Card		
Dolby Digital 5.1		
Sufficient Ports?		

FIGURE 6.29 Ports and Their Uses

PORT NAME	PORT SHAPE	CONNECTOR SHAPE	DATA TRANSFER SPEED	TYPICAL DEVICES ATTACHED TO PORT
Serial	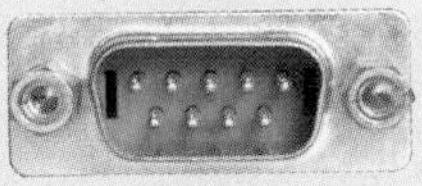	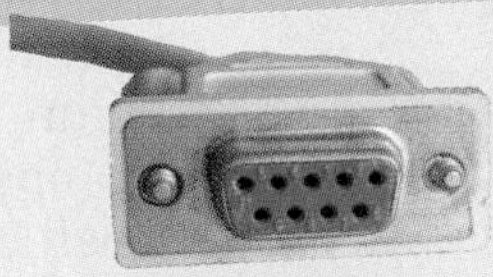	56 Kbps	Mice External modems
Parallel		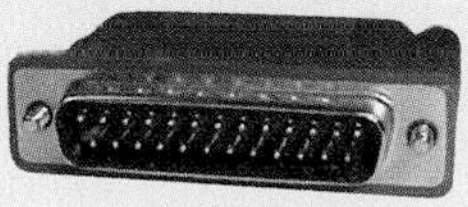	12 Mbps (12,000 Kbps)	Printers External Zip drives
NEW TECHNOLOGY				
USB 1.1			12 Mbps	Mice Keyboards External Zip drives Printers Scanners Game controllers
USB 2.0			480 Mbps	Same as USB 1.1, but at faster transfer rates Also suitable for camcorders and digital cameras Maintains backward compatibility with USB
FireWire			400 Mbps	Digital video camcorders Digital cameras
Ethernet			Up to 100 Mbps	Network connections Cable modems

developed by the Institute of Electrical and Electronics Engineers (IEEE). Until the introduction of USB 2.0, FireWire was the fastest port available, with a transfer rate of 400 Mbps. Today, it is most commonly used to connect digital video devices such as digital cameras to the computer.

The **Ethernet port** (technically called an RJ-45 jack) is used to connect your computer to a local network or cable modem. Because one of the most common uses of RJ-45 jacks is for connecting Ethernet networks, it is often referred to simply as an Ethernet jack. Ethernet originally offered a transfer rate of 10 Mbps. Fast Ethernet (called

100Base-T), with a transfer rate of 100 Mbps, is the standard used in most personal computers today.

Are there any other kinds of ports? In addition to the more common ports, you may also need more specialized ports, such as IrDA, Bluetooth, and MIDI.

The **IrDA port** (shown in Figure 6.30, p. 244) is based on a standard developed by the Infrared Data Association for transmitting data. IrDA ports allow you to transmit data between two devices by using infrared light waves. IrDA ports have a maximum throughput of 4 Mbps and require that a line of sight be maintained between the two ports. Many

FIGURE 6.30

IrDA ports enable you to transmit data between devices without using wires.

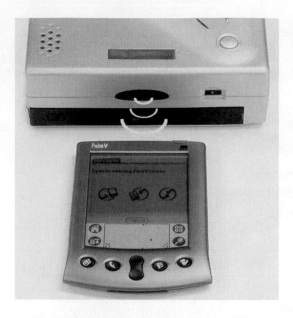

printers, laptops, and PDAs include IrDA ports. If a printer and a laptop both have IrDA ports, the laptop can send a file to the printer without being physically connected to it.

Bluetooth technology uses radio waves to send data over short distances (see Figure 6.31). The maximum transfer rate is 1 Mbps. Many laptops and PDAs include a small Bluetooth chip that allows them to transfer data wirelessly to any other device with a Bluetooth chip. Just like IrDA, the main advantage is that Bluetooth devices don't need to be connected by wires to exchange data. Because it uses radio waves, Bluetooth transmission doesn't require that a line of sight exist between the two devices. However, transmission distance is limited to approximately 30 feet.

FIGURE 6.31

Bluetooth-equipped devices communicate wirelessly with one another using radio waves.

A **MIDI port** (see Figure 6.32) is a port that allows you to connect electronic musical instruments (such as synthesizers) to your computer. Musical Instrument Digital Interface (MIDI) is a standard adopted by the music industry that provides for capturing specific data about a sound such as pitch, duration, and volume. That data is transferred between the computer and the MIDI device at a rate of 31.5 Kbps. In addition to synthesizers, MIDI ports also work with electronic drum machines and other electronically adapted instruments.

ADDING PORTS: EXPANSION CARDS AND HUBS

What if I don't have all the ports I need? New port standards are developed every few years, and special expansion cards are usually the only way to add the newest ports to an older computer or to expand the number of ports on your computer. For example, your computer may have only one USB port, but you may have several devices that connect to the computer with USB connectors. Just as sound cards and video cards provide ports for sound and video equipment to connect to the computer, there are also expansion cards that you can install in your system unit to provide you with additional ports (such as USB and FireWire). Like the other expansion cards, these cards clip into an open expansion slot on the motherboard. Figure 6.33 shows an example of such an expansion card.

What if there are no open slots on the motherboard for me to insert an expansion card? If there are no open slots on the motherboard and you still need extra ports, you can add an *expansion hub* (shown in Figure 6.34). An **expansion hub** is a device that connects to one port, such as a USB port, to provide four or eight new ports, similar to a multi-plug extension cord you use with electrical appliances.

You can also connect multiple USB devices through a single USB port by connecting the devices together in a *daisy chain*. In a daisy chain, you attach one

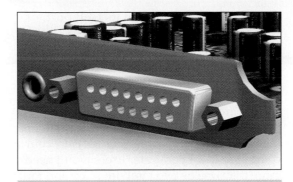

FIGURE 6.32

MIDI ports enable you to connect your computer to musical devices such as synthesizers.

SOUND BYTE

PORT TOUR

In this Sound Byte, you'll take a tour of a desktop system and a laptop system to compare the number and variety of available ports. You'll also learn about the different types of ports and compare their speed and expandability.

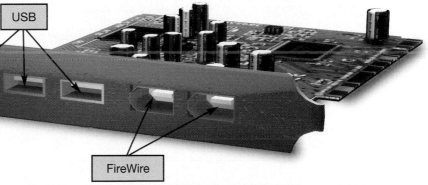

USB

FireWire

FIGURE 6.33

This expansion card provides your computer with additional ports.

FIGURE 6.34

If you don't have enough USB ports to support your USB devices, consider getting an expansion hub, which can add four or eight USB ports to your system.

techtv

For more information on maintaining your PC, see "Cat's Clicks: Tips for Healthy Computing," a TechTV chip found at www.prenhall.com/techinaction.

device to another through its USB port, with the last device connecting to a USB port on the computer.

Is there a limit to the number of ports I can add? Using expansion hubs, you can expand your computer so that it can handle more USB and FireWire devices. For installation of other ports, you're limited by the number of open expansion slots in your computer. Most computer users won't need more than one or two FireWire ports and four USB ports, a number that you can easily achieve using expansion hubs and cards.

You can also add ports to an empty drive bay, giving you easy-to-reach new ports. The Koutech 10-in-1, shown in Figure 6.35, fits into a regular drive bay and adds front-panel

access to two USB 2.0 ports, two FireWire ports, three audio jacks, and a 6-in-1 digital media card reader.

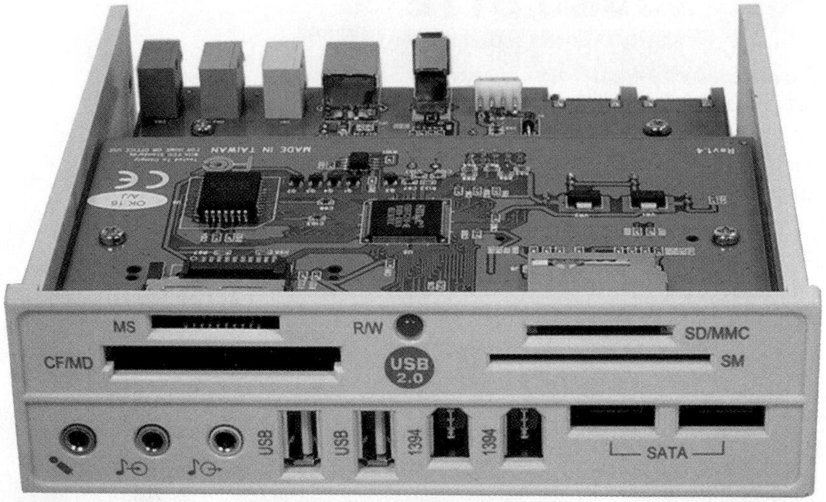

Which port should I use when I have a choice? Obviously, the fastest port is preferable but may not always be possible or cost effective. For example, most currently produced ink-jet printers offer the option of connecting by a parallel port or USB port. Because USB ports are faster, your printer will perform better if you connect it to a USB port. However, if you don't have an available USB port and you don't want to buy an expansion hub or card, you can connect the printer to a parallel port instead.

Which devices benefit most from high-speed ports? Any device that requires the transfer of large amounts of data significantly benefits from using a high-speed port such as a FireWire or USB 2.0 port. For example, digital video cameras produce large files that need to be transferred to a computer. If your video camera has a FireWire port but your computer doesn't, investing in a FireWire expansion port would definitely be worth the cost (about $40) based on the time you'll save during downloads.

Evaluating System Reliability

Many computer users decide to buy a new system not necessarily because they need a faster CPU, more RAM, or a bigger hard drive, but because they are experiencing problems, such as slow performance, freezes, and crashes. Over time, your computer builds up excess files and becomes internally disorganized just from normal everyday use. This excess clutter and disorganization can lead to failing performance, or worse, system failure. Therefore, before you buy a new system because you think yours may be unreliable, make sure the problem is not one you can fix. Proper upkeep and maintenance may also postpone an expensive system upgrade or replacement.

What can I do to ensure my system performs reliably? There are several procedures you can follow to ensure your system performs reliably:

1. Run the Disk Defragmenter utility on your hard drive. When your hard drive

FIGURE 6.35

You can also use an empty drive bay to add additional ports and even a flash card reader to the front panel of the system unit.

Do you need more ports?

	CURRENT SYSTEM	UPGRADE REQUIRED?
Number of USB (1.1 or 2.0) Ports		
Number of FireWire Ports		
Number of Ethernet Ports		
IrDA Port Included?		
Bluetooth Included?		
MIDI Port Included?		

becomes fragmented, its storage capacity is negatively impacted. When you defrag your hard drive, files are reorganized, making the hard drive work more efficiently. For more complete coverage of the Disk Defragmenter, refer to Chapter 5.

2. Clean out your Startup folder. Some programs install themselves into your Startup folder and are automatically run each time the computer reboots, whether you are using them or not. This unnecessary load causes extra stress on RAM. Check your Startup folder and make sure all the programs listed are important to you. Right-click on any unnecessary program and select Delete to remove it from the Startup folder. Make sure you delete *only* programs you know for sure are unnecessary.

3. Clear out unnecessary files. Temporary Internet files can accumulate very quickly on your hard drive, taking up unnecessary space. Running the Disk Cleanup utility is a quick and easy way to ensure your temporary Internet files don't take up precious hard drive space. Likewise, you should delete any unnecessary files from your hard drive regularly, because they can make your hard drive run slower.

My system crashes often during the day. What can I do? Computer systems are complex. It's not unusual to have your system stop responding occasionally. If rebooting the computer doesn't help, you'll need to begin troubleshooting:

1. Make sure you have installed any new software or hardware properly. If you are using a PC, use the System Restore utility in Windows XP to "roll back" to a time when the system worked more reliably.

2. If you see an error code in Windows, visit the Microsoft Knowledge Base (**http://support.microsoft.com**), an online resource for resolving problems with Microsoft products. This may help you determine what the error code indicates and how you may be able to solve the problem.

3. Check that you have enough RAM. Often systems will crash because of insufficient RAM.

Can my software affect my system reliability? Having the latest version of software products makes your system much more reliable. You should upgrade or update your operating system, browser software, and application software as often as new *patches* (or fixes) are reported for resolving errors. Sometimes these errors are performance related; sometimes they're tied to maintaining better security for your system.

How do I know whether updates are available for my software? You can configure Windows XP so that it automatically checks for, downloads, and installs any available updates for itself and for Internet Explorer. In addition, products such as Oil Change by McAfee enable you to sort through numerous Web sites and quickly find the bug fixes for most application software.

What if none of this helps? Is buying a new system my only option? If your system is still unreliable after these changes, you have two options:

1. Reinstall the operating system. To do so, you'll want to back up all of your data files before the installation and be prepared to reinstall your software programs after the installation. Make sure you have all of the original disks and CDs for the software installed on your system, along with the product keys, serial numbers, or other activation codes so that you can reinstall them.

2. Upgrade your operating system to the latest version. There are substantial increases in reliability with each major release of a new operating system. However, upgrading the operating system may require hardware upgrades. Be sure to examine the *recommended* (not required) specifications of the new operating system.

SOUND BYTE

LETTING YOUR COMPUTER CLEAN UP AFTER ITSELF

In this Sound Byte, you'll learn how to use the various maintenance utilities within the operating system. In addition, you'll learn how to use Task Scheduler to clean up your hard disk automatically. You'll also learn the best times of the day to schedule these maintenance tasks and why they should be done on a routine basis to make your system more stable.

TRENDS IN IT

Computers in Society: Is It Safe to Donate Your Old Computer?

What happened to your last computer? If you threw it away hoping it would be safely recycled with your empty Coke cans, think again. Mercury in screens, cadmium in batteries and circuit boards, and flame retardant in plastic housing are all toxic, as are the four to eight pounds of lead in the cathode-ray tube of nearly every monitor. Discarded machines are beginning to create an e-waste crisis.

Instead of throwing your computer away, you may be able to donate it to a nonprofit organization. If no one wants your computer, take it to an authorized computer recycling center in your area (find a local one at **www.used computer.com**). You may have to pay a small recycling fee, but it is worth it because you are helping protect the environment. However, before donating or recycling a computer, make sure you carefully remove all data from your hard drive, or you may end up having your good deed turn bad, making you the victim of identity theft.

What type of information is stored on a hard drive that could cause you troubles? Credit card numbers, bank information, social security numbers, tax records, passwords, and PIN numbers are just a few of the pieces of sensitive information that we casually record to our computer's hard drive. Most people know that when they get rid of their computers, just deleting their files is not protection enough. But did you know that even if you reformat your hard drive it's still not totally wiped clean? That's because when data is deleted from the hard drive—even through the reformatting process—only the *link* to the data is removed. The data remains on the hard drive until it is written over by more data.

In early 2003, two MIT graduate students proved how much personal financial data is left on hard drives that are on the secondary sale market. They bought over 150 used hard drives from various sources. Although some of the hard drives were reformatted or damaged so the data was supposedly irrecoverable, the two students were able to retrieve medical records, financial information, pornography, personal e-mails, and over 5,000 credit card numbers!

What can you do to protect yourself without putting your hard disk drive through a metal shredder? The United States Department of Defense suggests a seven-layer overwrite for a "secure erase." That is, they suggest that you fill your hard drive *seven times over* with a random series of ones and zeros. Fortunately, several software programs are available that provide secure hard drive erasures, either of specific files on your hard drive or of the entire hard drive. Examples of these programs include Active @ KillDisk, Eraser, CyberScrub, Wipe for Linux, and Shredit X for OS X.

Keep in mind that even these data erasure software programs can't provide the ultimate level in security. Computer forensic specialists or super cyber criminals can still manage to retrieve some data from your hard drive with the right tools. The ultimate level of protection is to destroy the hard drive altogether. Suggested methods include drilling holes in the hard drive, burning/melting the hard drive, or just taking an old-fashioned sledgehammer to it! Still, with a bit of common sense and some careful use of software, you can make your computer safe enough to donate.

Making the Final Decision

Now that you have evaluated your computer system, you need to shift to questions of *value*. How closely does your system come to meeting your needs? How much would it cost to upgrade the system you have to match what you'd ideally like your computer to do? How much would it cost to purchase a new system that meets these specifications?

To decide which option (upgrading or buying a new system) has better value for you, you need to price both scenarios. Figure 6.36 provides an upgrade worksheet you can use to evaluate both the upgrade path and the new purchase path. Be sure to consider what benefit you might obtain by having two systems, if you were to buy a new computer. Would you have a use for the older system? Would you donate it to a charitable organization? Would you be able to give it to a family member? Purchasing a new system is an important investment of your resources and you want to make a well-reasoned, well-supported decision.

FIGURE 6.36 Upgrade vs. New Purchase Comparison Worksheet

NEEDS	HARDWARE UPGRADE COST	INCLUDED ON A NEW SYSTEM?	ADDITIONAL EXPENSE FOR ITEM IF IT IS NOT INCLUDED ON A NEW SYSTEM
CPU AND MEMORY SUBSYSTEMS			
CPU Upgrade			
RAM Upgrade			
STORAGE SUBSYSTEM			
Hard Disk Upgrade			
Zip Drive			
CD-RW/CD-R Drive			
DVD-ROM Drive			
DVD-RW Drive			
Flash Card Reader			
Other Storage Device			
VIDEO AND AUDIO SUBSYSTEMS			
New Monitor			
Video Card Upgrade			
Speaker Upgrade			
Sound Card Upgrade			
PORT CONNECTIVITY			
USB 1.1 or 2.0 Ports			
FireWire Port			
Ethernet Port			
IrDA Port			
Bluetooth Port			
MIDI Port			

Summary

1. How can I determine whether I should upgrade my existing computer or buy a new one?

To determine whether you need to upgrade or purchase a new system, you need to define your ideal system and what it can do. Then, you need to perform a system evaluation to assess the subsystems in your computer, including the CPU, memory, storage, video, audio, and ports. Last, you need to determine if it's economically practical to upgrade or whether buying a new computer would be best.

2. What does the CPU do and how can I evaluate its performance?

Your computer's CPU processes instructions, performs calculations, manages the flow of information through a computer system, and is responsible for processing into information the data you input. It is composed of two units: the arithmetic logic unit and the control unit. CPU speed is measured in megahertz or gigahertz, or millions or billions of machine cycles a second. A machine cycle is the process the CPU goes through to fetch, decode, execute, and store data. You can tell whether your CPU is limiting your system performance by watching how busy it is as you work on your computer. The percentage of time that your CPU is working is referred to as CPU usage, which you can determine by checking the Task Manager.

3. How does memory work in my computer and how can I evaluate how much memory I need?

RAM is your computer's short-term memory. It remembers everything that the computer needs to process data into information. However, it is an example of volatile storage. When the power is off, the data stored in RAM is cleared out. The amount of RAM sitting on memory modules in your computer is your computer's physical memory. The memory your OS uses is kernel memory. At a minimum, you need enough RAM to run the OS plus the software applications you're using, plus a bit more to hold the data you're inputting.

4. What are the computer's main storage devices and how can I evaluate whether they match my needs?

Storage devices for a typical computer system include a hard disk drive, floppy drive, Zip drive, and CD/DVD drives. When you turn off your computer, the data stored in these devices is saved. These devices are therefore referred to as nonvolatile storage devices. Hard drives have the largest storage capacity of any storage device and the fastest access time and data transfer rate of all nonvolatile storage options. Floppy disks have a storage capacity of 1.44 MB, Zip disks have capacities up to 750 MB, and CDs and DVDs have capacities from 700 MB to 9.4 GB. To determine the storage capacity your system needs, calculate the amount of storage your software needs to reside on your computer. To add more storage, or to provide more functionality for your system, you can install additional drives, either internally or externally.

Read/write head

Arms

Platters

5. What components affect the output of video on my computer and how can I evaluate whether they are meeting my needs?

How video is displayed depends on two components: your video card and monitor. A video card translates binary data into the images you see. These cards include their own RAM (VRAM) as well as ports that allow you to connect to video equipment. The amount of VRAM you need depends on what you want to display on the monitor. If you only work in Microsoft Word and surf the Web, 16 MB is enough. More powerful cards allow you to play graphics-intense games and multimedia. Your monitor's size, resolution, refresh rate, and dot pitch all affect how well the monitor performs. For a clearer, brighter image, buy a monitor with a high refresh rate and a low dot pitch.

6. What components affect the quality of sound on my computer and how can I evaluate whether they are meeting my needs?

Your computer's sound depends on your speakers and sound card. Two types of speakers ship with most computers: amplified speakers and unamplified speakers. If you're listening to music, viewing DVDs, or playing games, you may want to have speakers with a subwoofer. Sound cards enable the computer to produce sounds. Users upgrade their sound cards to provide for 3D sound, surround sound, as well as additional ports for audio equipment.

7. What are the ports available on desktop computers and how can I determine what ports I need?

A port is an interface through which external devices connect to the computer. Common ports include serial, parallel, universal serial bus (USB), FireWire, and Ethernet, while specialized ports include IrDA, Bluetooth, and MIDI. To evaluate your port connectivity, check the devices you'd like to connect to your computer and look for what type of port they require. If your system doesn't have enough ports, you can add ports through expansion cards (which you install in your system unit) and expansion hubs (which connect to your system through a port).

8. How can I ensure the reliability of my system?

Many computer users decide to buy a new system because they are experiencing problems with their computer. However, before you buy a new system because you think yours may be unreliable, make sure the problem is not one you can fix. Run system utilities such as Disk Defragmenter and Disk Cleanup, clean out your Startup folder, remove unnecessary files from your system, and keep your software updated with patches. If you continue to have troubles with your system, reinstall or upgrade your OS, and, of course, seek technical assistance.

Key Terms

Buzz Words

Word Bank

- system evaluation
- floppy disk
- volatile storage
- LCD
- serial
- Zip disk
- expansion card
- subwoofer
- Bluetooth
- access time

- CPU
- motherboard
- USB
- RAM
- cache
- Zip drive
- expansion hub
- CD/DVD
- upgrading
- hard drive

- monitor
- CD-RW drive
- sound card
- port
- magnetic media
- parallel
- FireWire
- Ethernet

Instructions: Fill in the blanks using the words from the Word Bank above.

Joe already has a computer but just found out about a great deal on a new one. He decides to perform a (1)_____ on his computer to see whether he should keep it or buy the new one. First, he right-clicks the My Computer icon to check his System Properties. By doing so, he can check what (2)_____ is in his computer. He sees he has a Pentium 4 processor running at 2.8 GHz. Next, he decides to check his computer's internal memory, or its (3)_____. He then turns to the Task Manager to evaluate his computer's CPU and RAM usage and confirms his suspicions that he needs to add more RAM should he decide to keep his system.

He continues to evaluate his current system by checking out what components he has and what he'll need. He notes the storage capacity of the (4)_____. Recently, Joe has been using a (5)_____ to store some frequently used files because his hard drive is nearing capacity. But the (6)_____, or the amount of time it takes for the disk to find the right data, is so slow that the larger hard drive of a new computer is appealing.

Joe notes he is unable to download large music and video files from the Internet and save them onto a CD like his friends do. His current system does not have a (7)_____ with which to burn CDs, but the new system would. The new system would also include a great set of speakers with a (8)_____ to improve the quality of sound. He also sees that it would include a better (9)_____ that would allow him to connect more of his audio equipment to his computer.

Joe's 15-inch (10)_____ doesn't fit well on his desktop, and having an (11)_____ monitor would be helpful to conserve space. He is also concerned that if he wants to attach more devices to his computer than his keyboard, mouse, or printer in the future, he will need additional (12)_____ ports, because his current system has only a few of these faster ports. He notes, however, that it may be just as easy and cost effective to install an (13)_____ in his system to give it more ports or to buy an (14)_____ he could attach to his system unit to add more ports.

Finally, Joe considers the cost of buying the new computer versus (15)_____ his current system. Joe realizes it's more economical right now to keep his current system.

Organizing Key Terms

Instructions: *This chapter introduces many new terms and concepts. In the following illustration, fill in each of the blanks with key terms or concepts from the chapter in order to show how categories of ideas fit together.*

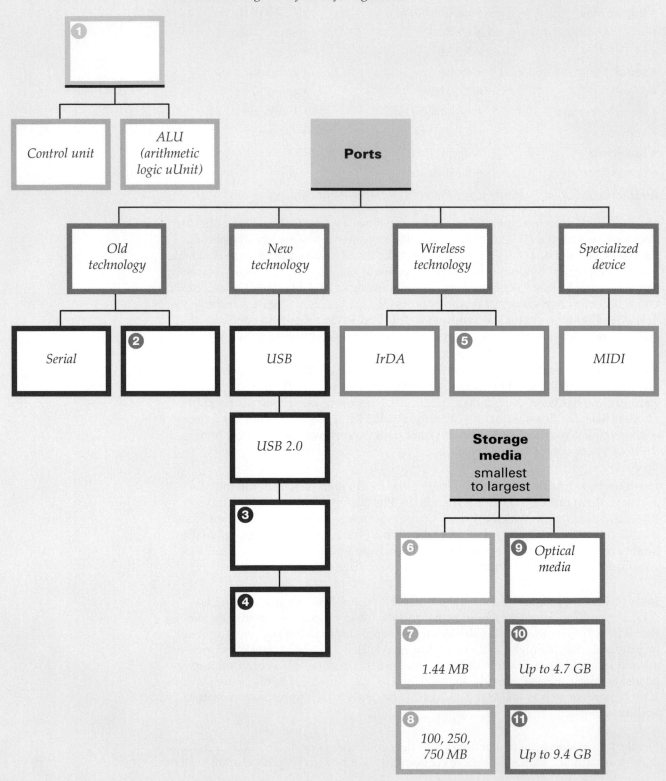

Making the Transition to . . . Next Semester

1. Evaluating Your System

A small worksheet follows the end of each section in this chapter to guide you as you evaluate your own system. These smaller worksheets have been combined into one complete worksheet that is on the book's companion Web site (**www.prenhall.com/techinaction**). Download the worksheet and fill it in based on the computer you are currently using while taking this class.

a. Research the costs of replacement parts for those components you feel should be upgraded.

b. Research the cost of a new system that would be roughly equivalent to your current computer *after* upgrades.

c. Determine whether it would be more cost effective to upgrade your computer or buy a new one.

2. Your Software Needs

What software do you need for the courses you're taking this semester? Will you need any different software for next semester? How many of these software applications do you run at one time? Examine the specs for those software packages. Prepare a table that lists the software applications you are currently using as well as any you may need to use in the future. For each, list the minimum RAM and hard disk space requirements. How does your system measure up against those requirements?

3. Campus Computer Use

What kinds of computers do students use in college and how do different people budget for their computer needs? To find an answer to these questions, interview several college students in different years of school. Ask them the following questions:

a. Did you need your own computing equipment or did you use your college's equipment when you first started school? Would you recommend I do the same?

b. Did you need to upgrade your computer *before* you came to college? How did you do this?

c. Was the computer you used in your first year of college able to handle your workload in later years?

d. If you used one computer, what upgrades did you need to perform?

e. If you had to buy a new computer, how much money did you budget and how much did you spend? What did you do with your old computer?

4. Buying Computers Online

Visit an online seller of computer systems and components (such as **www.coolcomputing.com**, **www.pricewatch.com**, **www.zdnet.com**, **www.tigerdirect.com**, or **www.campusdirect.com**) and answer the following questions:

a. What is the current cost of RAM?

b. How much additional RAM could you add to your system?

c. What are the prices of the most popular CPU upgrades?

d. How much would you need to spend to upgrade to a new operating system?

e. How would each of these help you in your work?

Making the Transition to . . . The Workplace

1. Using Your Computer for Education and Business

As you move from an educational environment to a business environment, how you use your computer will inevitably change. Write a paragraph or two describing what your computer system is like now. Then write a paragraph or two describing what your ideal computer system would be like after you've graduated and have entered the workforce. What different components, if any, would your system need? Could you upgrade your current system to incorporate these new components, or would you need to buy a new system? Make sure you defend either position you take with information covered in this chapter. Fill out the worksheet similar to Figure 6.3 that is available on the book's companion Web site (**www.prenhall.com/techinaction**) to help you in your decision.

2. Assessing Memory Use

Your home office computer is running a bit sluggish, and you want to determine which application is the memory hog so you can either avoid using it or use it without any other programs running to preserve RAM. You've been told you can do this in the Processes tab in the Task Manager utility. On your computer, open the Task Manager utility and determine which application currently running is using the most memory. Can you tell how much it is using? Note that because the names of the programs have been shortened (for example, Microsoft Word is referred to as winword.exe), you may not immediately recognize the program names.

3. IT Support at Work

When you are evaluating potential employers, one consideration will be how well they support you as an employee and provide the environment you need to do productive work. What questions would you ask in an interview to determine what kind of Information Technology (IT) support you can expect in your new position?

4. Web Programming Software at Home

You are a Web programmer and you often work from home. You need to investigate whether your home computer would be able to run three programs you use most frequently at work: Adobe PhotoShop, Microsoft Visual Basic, and Microsoft Word. Use the Web to research RAM and hard disk requirements for these programs. Will your computer be able to handle the load?

5. Build an Ideal System

Imagine that a client tells you she wants a system that has at least 512 MB of RAM, the fastest processor on the market, and enough storage space to edit hours of video and music files. Price three systems that would meet the client's needs by visiting manufacturer Web sites such as **www.dell.com**, **www.gateway.com**, and **www.alienware.com**. Make a final selection and justify why this is the best solution.

Critical Thinking Questions

Instructions: *Albert Einstein used "Gedanken experiments," or critical thinking questions, to develop his theory of relativity. Some ideas are best understood by experimenting with them in our own minds. The following critical thinking questions are designed to demand your full attention but require only a comfortable chair—no technology.*

1. Your Ideal System

If you could buy any new system on the market, not worrying about the price, what would you buy? What kind of monitor would you have? How much RAM and CPU? Would you know how to use your ideal system?

2. Future Systems

Given current trends in technology, what kind of system can you imagine upgrading to or buying new in 10 years? Which components would change the most? Which components would need to stay the same, if any? What do you imagine the entire system would look like?

3. Portable Storage Solutions

Some newer computers do not include a floppy disk drive as standard. This is in response to many users requiring portable storage media to hold larger files that cannot fit on a floppy. What other solutions are possible? Are there reasons why floppy disks are still a viable means of portable storage?

4. Impacts of New Technology

We are constantly being bombarded with new technology. We hear of new tools and system improvements from our friends, relatives, and advertisements almost daily. This chapter talks about upgrading current systems so that we can take advantage of some of the newer technology. Some improvements we absolutely need (more RAM, perhaps), others we may just really want (such as an LCD monitor). What do you think are the societal, economic, and environmental impacts of our wanting to have the latest and greatest computers? Do you think the push toward faster and more powerful machines is a good thing?

5. New Technologies: Putting Industries at Risk?

The Trends in IT feature in this chapter discusses the impact DVD and CD technology has had on the music and entertainment industries. Can you think of other industries that might be at risk because of these new technologies?

6. Recycling Computers

Mercury in screens and switches, cadmium in batteries and circuit boards, and the four to eight pounds of lead in CRT monitors are all toxic. Discarded machines are beginning to create an e-waste crisis. Who do you think should assume the cost of recycling computers? The consumer, the government, the industry? What other options are there besides just throwing older computers away?

7. System Longevity

If you purchase a computer system for business purposes, the IRS allows you to depreciate its cost over three years. The IRS considers this a reasonable estimate of the useful lifetime of a computer system. What do you think most home users expect in terms of how long their computer systems should last? How does the purchase of a computer system compare with other major household appliances in terms of cost, value, benefit, life span, and upgrade potential?

Team Time   Meeting a Corporation's Computing Need

Problem:

In a large organization, whether it is a company or a college, the IT department often has to install several different types of computing systems. There certainly would be advantages to having every computer be identical, but because different departments have different needs, and items are purchased at different times, it is typical for there to be significant differences between two computers in the same corporation.

Process:

Split your class into teams.

1. Select a department or computer lab on campus (or within your company, at the public library, and so on). Note: If you physically cannot go to the various labs, describe the type of components that would be needed by that particular department. (For example, if you choose the computer art department, you know you would need good graphics software. You also know you would need certain levels of RAM, and so forth, to accommodate that graphics software.)
2. Following the worksheet in Figure 6.3, analyze the computing needs of that particular department.
3. Using the System Evaluation worksheet (found on the book's companion Web site at **www.prenhall.com/techinaction**), develop a complete systems evaluation of the computers at the lab.
4. Consider possible upgrades in hardware, software, and peripherals that would make this lab better able to meet the needs of its users.
5. Write a report that summarizes your findings. If purchasing a new system is more economical, recommend which system the lab should buy.

Conclusion:

The pace of technological change can make computer science an uncomfortable field for some. For others, it is precisely the pace of change that is exciting. Being able to evaluate a computer system and match it to the current needs of its users is an important skill.

Becoming Computer Fluent

Gerri lives across the hall from you. She heard you worry all last semester that your computer wasn't fast enough to handle your course workload. Between the simulation program for math, the reports and research you did for English, and the programming class you tried, your computer was running too slowly and you were out of storage space. She's offered to do a complete system upgrade for you but has asked you to write a letter telling her exactly what you want upgraded and why.

Instructions: Using the preceding scenario, write a letter using as many of the terms from the chapter as you can. Be sure your sentences are grammatically correct and technically meaningful.

Materials on the Web

In addition to the review materials presented here, you'll find extra materials on the book's companion Web site (**www.prenhall.com/techinaction**) that will help reinforce your understanding of the chapter content. These materials include the following:

Sound Byte Lab Guides

For each Sound Byte mentioned in the chapter, there is a corresponding lab guide located on the book's companion Web site. These guides review the material presented in the Sound Byte and direct you to various Web resources that examine the material. The Sound Byte Lab Guides for this chapter include these:

- Using Windows XP to Evaluate CPU Performance
- Installing RAM
- Hard Drive Anatomy Interactive
- CD/DVD Reading and Writing
- Installing a CD-RW Drive
- Port Tour
- Letting Your Computer Clean Up After Itself

True/False and Multiple-Choice Quizzes

The book's Web site includes a true/false and a multiple-choice quiz for this chapter. You can take these quizzes, automatically check the results, and e-mail the results to your instructor.

Web Research Projects

The book's Web site also includes a number of Web research projects for this chapter. These projects ask you to search the Web for information on computer-related careers, milestones in computer history, important people and companies, emerging technologies, and the applications and implications of different technologies.

Technology in Action also features unique interactive Help Desk training, in which you'll assume the role of Help Desk operator taking calls about concepts learned in each chapter. The Help Desk calls for this chapter include:

- Evaluating Your CPU and RAM
- Evaluating Your Storage Subsystem and Ports

CHAPTER 7

OBJECTIVES

After reading this chapter, you should be able to answer the following questions:

- What is a network and what are the advantages of setting up one? (p. 262)

- What is the difference between a client/server network and a peer-to-peer network? (pp. 263–264)

- What are the main components of every network? (pp. 264–266)

- What are the most common home networks? (p. 266)

- What are power line networks and how are they created? (pp. 266–267)

- What are phoneline networks and how are they created? (pp. 267–268)

- What are Ethernet networks and how are they created? (pp. 268–271)

- What are wireless networks and how are they created? (pp. 272–274)

- How can hackers attack a network and what harm can they cause? (pp. 278–283)

- What is a firewall and how does it keep my computer safe from hackers? (pp. 284–286)

- From which types of viruses do I need to protect my computer? (pp. 287–289)

- What can I do to protect my computer from viruses? (pp. 289–291)

SOUND BYTES

- Installing a Computer Network (p. 266)
- Securing Your Wireless Networks (p. 274)
- Installing a Personal Firewall (p. 285)
- Protecting Your Computer (p. 290)

Networking and Security:

Connecting Computers and Keeping Them Safe from Hackers and Viruses

TECHNOLOGY IN ACTION: THE PROBLEMS OF SHARING

The Williams family is facing computer-sharing problems. Derrick and Vanessa realized that they both needed computers, and they bought their children, Stephanie and Jake, their own computers too. Still, there is trouble in this "paradise."

Scarce Resources: Jake was using his computer to scan photos for a school Web site project. Just then, his sister Stephanie burst into his room and demanded to use his scanner because she didn't have one and needed to scan images for an art project. Jake wouldn't budge. The ensuing shouting match brought their mother Vanessa to the room. Because both projects were due the next day, Vanessa told Jake he would have to let Stephanie use the scanner at some point. In exchange, Stephanie would have to let Jake use her computer so he could print from the color printer attached to it. Neither was happy, but it was the best Vanessa could do.

Internet Logjam: Derrick frowned at his e-mail inbox. He was on vacation, but his boss had e-mailed him asking him to look over a marketing plan. Meanwhile, Vanessa needed to get online to confirm the family's reservations at Disney World. Because they had only one phone line, they constantly had to take turns getting online, and with Stephanie and Jake wanting to check their e-mail too, the phone line was almost always tied up.

Virus Attack: Later that night, Derrick booted up his computer to make some changes to the marketing plan. Right away, he noticed that many of his icons had disappeared from his desktop. As he launched Microsoft Word, a message flashed on the screen that read, "The Hacker of Death Was Here!" Suddenly, his screen went black. When he rebooted his computer, it was unable to recognize the hard drive. The next day, Derrick called the computer support technician at work and learned he had caught the "Death Squad" virus, which had erased the contents of his hard drive. Derrick mused that he should have bought an antivirus program instead of Mech Warrior 5.

If this scenario doesn't reflect the situation in your home, it may in the future. As the price of computers continues to drop, more families will have multiple home computers. To avoid inconvenience and the expense of redundant equipment, computers need to be able to communicate with each other and to share peripherals (such as scanners and printers) and resources (such as Internet connections). Thus, this chapter explores how you can network computers. In addition, you'll learn strategies for keeping unauthorized outsiders from prying into your computer when you're sharing resources with the outside world, as well as how to keep your computer safe from viruses.

Networking Fundamentals

Although you may not yet have a home network, you use and interact with networks all the time. In fact, every time you use the Internet you're interacting with the world's largest network. But what exactly *is* a network? A **computer network** is simply two or more computers that are connected together via software and hardware so they can communicate. Devices connected to a network are referred to as **nodes**. A node can be a computer, a peripheral (such as a printer), or a communications device (such as a modem). The main function for most networks is to facilitate information sharing, but networks provide other benefits as well.

What are the benefits of networks? One benefit of networks is that they allow users to share peripherals. For example, in Figure 7.1a, the computers are not networked; Computer 1 is connected to the printer, but Computer 2 is not. To print files from Computer 2, users have to transfer them using a floppy disk or another storage medium to Computer 1, or they have to disconnect the printer from Computer 1 and connect it to Computer 2. By networking Computer 1 and Computer 2, as shown in Figure 7.1b, both computers can print from the printer attached to Computer 1 without transferring files or moving the printer.

By networking computers, you can also transfer files from one computer to another without using external storage media such as Zip disks. And you can set up shared directories in Windows that allow the user of each computer on the network to store files that other computers on the network may need to access, as shown in Figure 7.2.

Can I use a network to share an Internet connection? Sharing Internet connections is a significant benefit of setting up a home network. Without a network, only one user at a time can use an Internet connection. Although dial-up connections don't have sufficient bandwidth to support sharing a connection, broadband connections (such as cable and DSL) have more than enough bandwidth to allow users to share the connection.

FIGURE 7.1

(a) Computer 1 and Computer 2 are not networked. Only Computer 1 can use the printer unless the printer is disconnected from Computer 1 and reconnected to Computer 2.
(b) Computer 1 and Computer 2 are networked. Both computers can use the printer without having to move it.

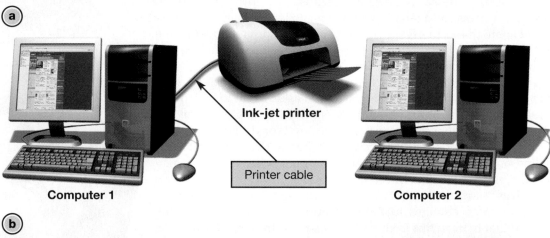

(a) Ink-jet printer

Printer cable

Computer 1   Computer 2

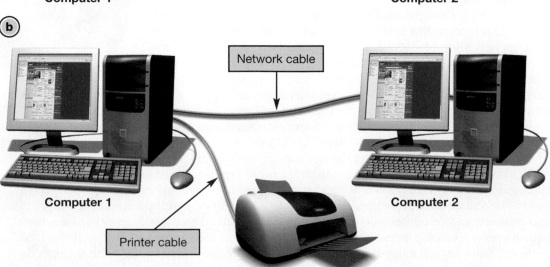

(b) Network cable

Computer 1   Computer 2

Printer cable

Ink-jet printer

Network Architectures

The architecture of a building refers to its design and how it fits into its surroundings. The term **network architecture** refers to the design of a network. Network architectures are classified according to the way in which they are controlled and the distance between their nodes.

DESCRIBING NETWORKS BASED ON NETWORK CONTROL

What do we mean by networks being "controlled"? There are two main ways a network can be controlled: locally or centrally. A *peer-to-peer network* is the most common example of a locally controlled network. The most common type of centrally controlled network is a *client/server network*.

What are peer-to-peer networks? In **peer-to-peer (P2P) networks**, each node connected to the network can communicate directly with every other node on the network, instead of having a separate device exercise central control over the network. Thus, all nodes on this type of network are in a sense *peers*. When printing, for example, a computer on a P2P network doesn't have to go through the computer that's connected to the printer. Instead, it can communicate directly with the printer. Figure 7.1b shows a very small peer-to-peer network.

Because they are simple to set up, P2P networks are the most common type of home network. We discuss different types of peer-to-peer networks that are popular in homes later in this chapter.

What are client/server networks? Very small schools and offices may have P2P networks. However, most networks that comprise 10 or more nodes are **client/server networks**. A client/server network contains two different types of computers: clients and servers. The **client** is the computer on which users accomplish specific tasks (such as construct spreadsheets). The **server** is the computer that provides information or resources to the client computers on the network. The server also provides central control for functions on the network (such as printing). Figure 7.3 illustrates a client/server network in action.

As you learned in Chapter 3, the Internet is an example of a client/server network.

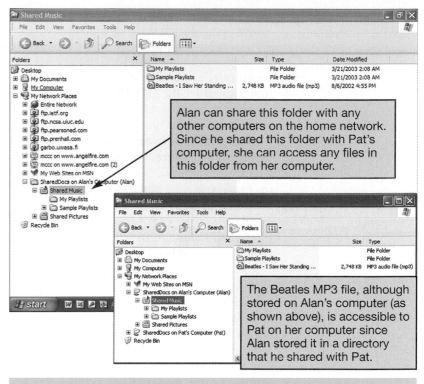

Alan can share this folder with any other computers on the home network. Since he shared this folder with Pat's computer, she can access any files in this folder from her computer.

The Beatles MP3 file, although stored on Alan's computer (as shown above), is accessible to Pat on her computer since Alan stored it in a directory that he shared with Pat.

FIGURE 7.2

This Windows XP network has two computers attached to it: Alan (a) and Pat (b). Shared directories (the SharedDocs folders) have been set up so that Alan and Pat can share files. When Pat is working on her computer, she can easily access the files located in the shared directory on Alan's computer, such as the folder called Shared Music.

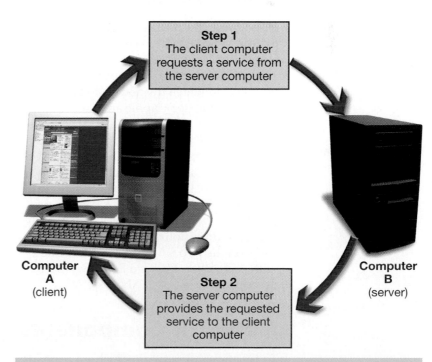

Step 1
The client computer requests a service from the server computer

Step 2
The server computer provides the requested service to the client computer

Computer A (client)

Computer B (server)

FIGURE 7.3

In a client/server network, a computer acts as a client, making requests for resources, or as a server, providing resources.

When your computer is connected to the Internet, it is functioning as a *client computer*. When connecting to the Internet through an Internet service provider (ISP), your computer connects to a *server computer* maintained by the ISP. The server "serves up" resources to your computer so that you can interact with the Internet.

Are client/server networks ever used as home networks? Although client/server networks *can* be configured for home use, P2P networks are more often used in the home because they cost less than client/server networks and are easier to configure and maintain. To set up a client/server network in your home, you have to buy an extra computer to act as the server. (Although an existing computer could function as a server, its performance would be significantly degraded, making it impractical to use as both a client and a server.) In addition, you need extensive training to install and maintain the special software client/server networks require. Finally, the major benefits a client/server network provides (such as centralized security and administration) are not necessary in most home networks.

DESCRIBING NETWORKS BASED ON DISTANCE

How does the distance between nodes define a network? The proximity of network nodes to each other can help describe a network. **Local area networks (LANs)** are networks in which the nodes are located within a small geographic area. A network in your home or a computer lab at school is an example of a LAN. **Wide area networks (WANs)** are made up of LANs connected over long distances. Say a school has two campuses (east and west) located in different towns. Connecting the LAN at the east campus to the LAN at the west campus (by telecommunications lines) would allow the users on the two LANs to communicate with each other. The two LANs would be described as a single WAN.

Network Components

To function, all networks include a means of connecting the nodes on the network (by cables or wireless technology), special devices that allow the nodes to communicate with each other and to send data, and

software that allows the network to run. We discuss each of these components, shown in Figure 7.4, next.

TRANSMISSION MEDIA

How are nodes on a network connected? All network nodes (computers and peripherals) are connected to each other and to the network by **transmission media**. A transmission medium establishes a communications channel between the nodes on a network and can take several forms:

1. Networks can use existing wiring (such as phone lines or power lines) to connect nodes.

2. Networks can use additional cable to connect nodes, such as twisted pair cable, coaxial cable, or fiber-optic cable. You have probably seen twisted pair and coaxial cable. Normal telephone wire is **twisted pair cable** and is made up of copper wires that are twisted around each other and surrounded by a plastic jacket. If you have cable TV, the cable running into your TV or cable box is **coaxial cable**. Coaxial cable consists of a single copper wire surrounded by layers of plastic. **Fiber-optic cable** is made up of plastic or glass fibers that transmit data at very fast speeds.

3. Wireless networks use radio waves instead of wires or cable to connect nodes.

Different types of transmission media transmit data at different speeds. **Data transfer rate** (also called **bandwidth** or **throughput**) is the speed at which data can be transmitted between two nodes on a network. Data transfer rate is usually measured in megabits per second (Mbps). A megabit, when applied to data transfer rates, represents 1 million bits. (As you'll recall, a *bit* is the smallest measure of data a computer can process.) Twisted pair cable, coaxial cable, and wireless media provide enough bandwidth for most home networks, whereas fiber-optic cable is used mostly in client/server networks.

NETWORK ADAPTERS

How do the different nodes on the network communicate? Network **adapters** are devices connected to or installed in network nodes that enable the nodes to communicate with each other and to access

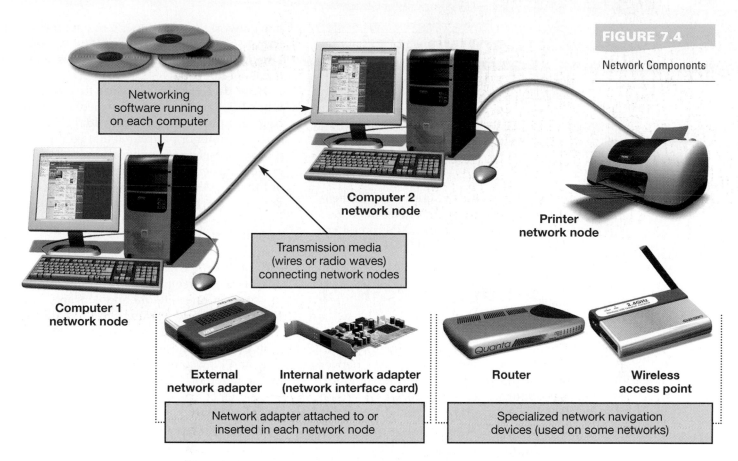

FIGURE 7.4

Network Components

Networking software running on each computer

Computer 2 network node

Printer network node

Transmission media (wires or radio waves) connecting network nodes

Computer 1 network node

External network adapter

Internal network adapter (network interface card)

Router

Wireless access point

Network adapter attached to or inserted in each network node

Specialized network navigation devices (used on some networks)

the network. Some network adapters take the form of external devices that plug into an available universal serial bus (USB) port. Other network adapters are installed *inside* computers and peripherals as expansion cards. These adapters are referred to as **network interface cards (NICs)**. Specialized network adapters are created for the various types of networks. We discuss network adapters in more detail throughout the chapter.

NETWORK NAVIGATION DEVICES

How is data sent through a network?
Data is sent over transmission media in bundles called **packets**. For computers to communicate, these packets of data must be able to flow freely between computers. **Network navigation devices** help to make this data flow possible. These devices, which are attached to the network, enable the transmission of data. In simple networks, navigation devices are built right into network adapters. More sophisticated networks need specialized navigation devices.

The two most common specialized navigation devices are routers and hubs. **Routers** route packets of data between two or more networks. For example, if a home network

is connected to the Internet, a router is required to send data between the two networks (the home network and the Internet). **Hubs** are simple amplification devices. They receive data packets and retransmit them to all nodes on the same network (not between different networks). We discuss routers and hubs in more detail later in the chapter.

NETWORKING SOFTWARE

What software do networks require?
Home networks need operating system (OS) software that supports peer-to-peer networking. The most common versions of Windows used in the home (XP, Millennium Edition, and 98) support P2P networking. You can connect computers running any of these OSs to the same network. You can also add computers that use the Windows 95 or 2000 OS to the same network, but you may need to install additional software to enable file or peripheral device sharing. The latest versions of the Mac OS also support P2P networking.

Client/server networks, on the other hand, are controlled by a central server that has specialized **network operating system (NOS)** software installed on it. This software handles requests for information, Internet

SOUND BYTE

INSTALLING A COMPUTER NETWORK

Installing a network is relatively easy if you've seen someone else do it. In this Sound Byte, you'll learn how to install the hardware and configure Windows for a wired or wireless home network.

access, and the use of peripherals for the rest of the network nodes. Examples of NOS software include Windows XP Professional, Windows Server 2003, and Novell Netware.

Types of Peer-to-Peer Networks

The most common type of network you will probably encounter is a peer-to-peer network, because this is the network you would set up in your home. Therefore, we'll focus on P2P networks in this chapter. There are four main types of P2P networks:

1. Power line networks
2. Phoneline networks
3. Ethernet networks
4. Wireless networks

The major differences in these networks are the transmission media by which the nodes are connected. We will look at these networks and how each one is set up next.

POWER LINE NETWORKS

What are power line networks? Power line networks use the electrical wiring in your home to connect the nodes in the network. Thus, in a power line network, any electrical outlet provides a network connection. Power

line networks have a maximum data transfer rate of 14 Mbps. The HomePlug Power Line Alliance (**www.homeplug.org**) sets standards for home power line networking.

How do I create a power line network? To create a power line network, you connect a **power line network adapter** to each computer or peripheral that you're going to attach to the network. You can buy power line network adapters in either USB or Ethernet versions, as shown in Figure 7.5. Both are easy to install, because they plug into either a USB or Ethernet port on your computer or peripheral.

After you attach a network adapter to each node on the network, you plug the adapters into an electrical outlet. Because most power line network adapters are Plug and Play compatible, your OS automatically recognizes them and knows how to interact with them. For those adapters that are not Plug and Play compatible, device drivers are provided on CD-ROMs. As you learned in Chapter 5, a **device driver** is software you install on your computer; when you attach new devices to your computer, the device driver allows your OS to interact with the device.

In addition, each computer attached to a power line network needs to have its OS configured for networking. (We discuss how to configure the OS later in the chapter.) Once you've set up the network, adding computers or peripherals is relatively easy. You simply attach a power line adapter to the computer or peripheral you wish to add and plug it into another electrical outlet. Figure 7.6 shows a power line network installed in a home.

Are routers and hubs used on power line networks? When functioning only to allow computers to communicate with each other (not with other networks), power line networks do *not* require routers or hubs. However, if you want computers connected on a power line network to share an Internet connection, you need a router.

Will using electrical appliances interfere with a power line network? Using existing wiring doesn't interfere with the flow of electricity, so you

FIGURE 7.5

This Ethernet power line network adapter is ready for installation. USB power line adapters look very similar to this Ethernet adapter.

Connect with a cable to an Ethernet port on the system unit

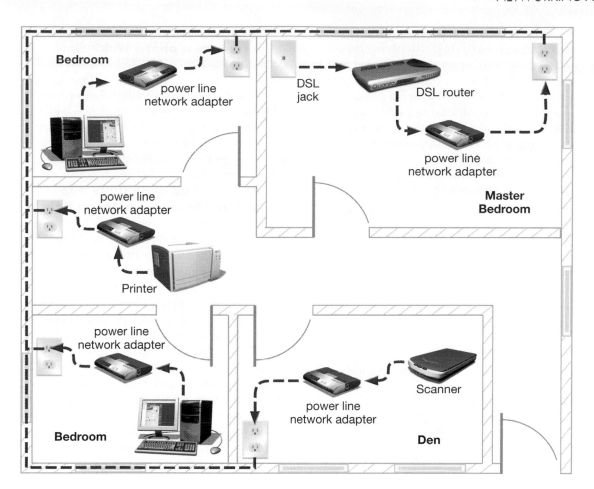

FIGURE 7.6

Example of a power line network. A power line network uses existing electrical wiring as its transmission media. Any electrical outlet in a house can therefore provide a network connection. In this power line network, the computers in the spare bedrooms can both use the scanner, printer, and DSL connection.

can use electrical appliances at the same time as you're using your power line network.

PHONELINE NETWORKS

What are phoneline networks?

Phoneline networks move data through the network using conventional phone lines rather than power lines. Thus, with a phoneline network, any phone jack in a house provides a network connection. Phoneline networks have a maximum data transfer rate of 10 Mbps. The Home Phone Line Networking Alliance (HPNA) (**www.homepna.org**) sets the standards for phoneline networking.

How do I create a phoneline network? To create a phoneline network, you need to attach or install a **home phoneline network adapter** (also called an **HPNA adapter**) to all computers and peripherals you want to attach to the network, as shown in Figure 7.7. You then attach the adapter to a phone jack on the wall with standard

phone cord. Most phoneline adapters are Plug and Play compatible, but if your OS doesn't recognize the adapter, manufacturers provide device drivers you can install on your computer.

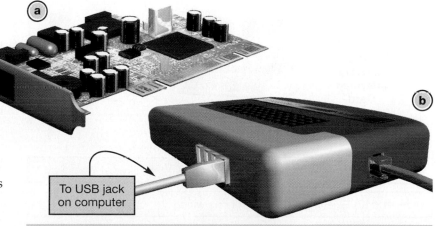

To USB jack on computer

FIGURE 7.7

To create a phoneline network, you (a) install a home phoneline network interface card (NIC) or (b) connect a USB home phoneline network adapter to each computer or peripheral attached to your network. NICs are installed in the system unit, whereas USB adapters plug into an available USB port. You then connect the NICs or adapters to phone jacks with phone cord.

As is the case with power line networks, each computer attached to a phoneline network needs to have its OS configured for networking. To add computers or peripherals to the network, you attach a phoneline adapter to the computer or peripheral you wish to add and plug it into another phone jack. Figure 7.8 shows an example of a phoneline network.

Are routers and hubs used on phoneline networks? As is the case with power line networks, when functioning only to allow computers to communicate with each other (not with other networks), phoneline networks do *not* require routers or hubs. You need a router only if you want networked computers to share an Internet connection.

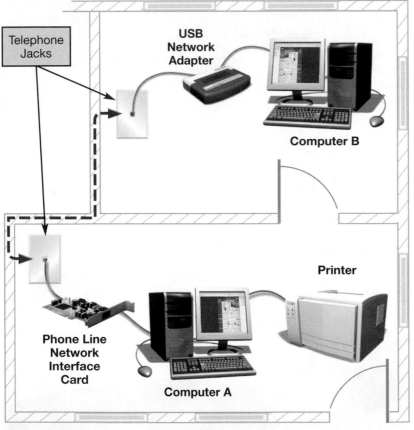

| Telephone cord |
| Existing internal telephone wiring |

FIGURE 7.8

Example of a phoneline network. In this example, Computer A and Computer B are networked. Computer B can share the printer attached to Computer A. Both network interface cards (NICs) and USB network adapters can be used in phoneline networks. NICs are installed inside the system unit, whereas USB network adapters plug into an available USB port.

Can a telephone and a network device share a phone jack? Some phoneline network adapters come with pass-through connections that allow you to plug your telephone into the adapter. For adapters *without* a pass-through connection, you can obtain a phone jack splitter, which turns one wall jack into two. This allows you to plug the network adapter and your phone into the same wall jack.

Can I hook up computers and peripherals to separate phone lines? There is no reason why you can't hook up phoneline network devices to separate phone lines in the same house. However, because the phone lines are separate, devices hooked up to the first phone line can't communicate with devices hooked up to the second line. Therefore, unless you want to create two separate networks, hook up your computers to phone jacks on the same phone line.

Can I use an unused phone line (one that has no dial tone) to create a phoneline network? Having a live phone line is not necessary for creating a phoneline network. The only requirement for a phoneline network is the phone cable itself.

ETHERNET NETWORKS

What are Ethernet networks? Ethernet networks differ from power line and phoneline networks in that they use the Ethernet protocol as the means (or standard) by which the nodes on the network communicate. This protocol makes Ethernet networks extremely efficient at moving information. However, to achieve this efficiency, the algorithms for moving data through an Ethernet network are more complex than on the other peer-to-peer networks. Because of this complexity, Ethernet networks require additional devices (such as hubs and routers).

Although Ethernet networks are slightly more complicated to set up than phoneline or power line networks, they are faster and more reliable. In fact, Ethernet networks are the most popular choice for home networks. Although you can install a 1-gigabit-per-second (Gbps) Ethernet network in your home, such networks tend to be prohibitively expensive and are often unnecessarily powerful in terms of bandwidth for most home users. Thus, 100-Mbps Ethernet networks are more commonly installed in the home.

How do I create an Ethernet network? Much like phoneline and power line networks, an Ethernet network requires that you install or attach network adapters to each computer or peripheral you want to connect to the network. Because Ethernet networks are so common, most computers come with Ethernet adapters preinstalled. As noted earlier, such internal network adapters are referred to as network interface cards (NICs). Modern Ethernet NICs are usually 10/100-Mbps cards. This means they can handle the old 10-Mbps Ethernet throughput traffic as well as the newer 100-Mbps throughput.

If your computer doesn't have a NIC, you can buy one and install it, or you can use a USB adapter, which you plug into any open USB port on the system unit. Although you can use USB versions in laptops, PC Card versions of Ethernet NICs are made especially for laptops. PC Cards are about the size of a credit card and fit into specially designed slots on a laptop. Figure 7.9 shows these different Ethernet network adapter options.

How are nodes connected on Ethernet networks? The most popular transmission media option for Ethernet networks is **unshielded twisted pair (UTP) cable**. UTP cable is composed of four pairs of wires that are twisted around each other to reduce electrical interference. You can buy UTP cable in varying lengths with RJ-45 jacks already attached. RJ-45 jacks resemble standard phone connectors (called RJ-11 jacks) but are slightly larger, as shown in Figure 7.10.

Do all Ethernet networks use the same kind of UTP cable? Figure 7.11 lists the three main types of UTP cable used in home Ethernet networks—Cat 5, Cat 5E, and Cat 6—and their data transfer rates. In general, it's better to install Cat 5E cable than Cat 5 because they're about the same price, and installing Cat 5E cable will enable you to take advantage of higher-bandwidth Ethernet systems when they become cost effective for home use. Cat 6 cable is faster but not necessary for most home networks.

Is UTP cable difficult to install? UTP cable is no more difficult to install than normal phone cable, you just need to take a few precautions: avoid putting sharp bends

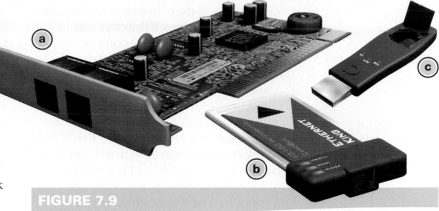

FIGURE 7.9

Ethernet network adapters come in a variety of versions, including (a) a 10/100 NIC, which is installed in an expansion slot inside the system unit; (b) a PC Card, which you slide into a specially designed slot on a laptop; and (c) a USB adapter, which you plug into an open USB port.

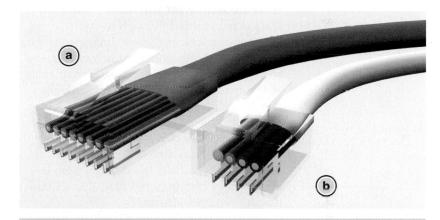

FIGURE 7.10

(a) An RJ-45 connector, used on UTP cable, and (b) a typical RJ-11 connector, used on standard phone cord. Note the RJ-45 is larger and has contacts for eight wires (four pairs) instead of four wires. You must use UTP cable with RJ-45 connectors on an Ethernet network because phone cable will not work.

FIGURE 7.11 Data Transfer Rates for Popular Network Cable Types

UTP CABLE CATEGORY	MAXIMUM DATA TRANSFER RATE
Category 5 (Cat 5)	100 Mbps
Category 5E (Cat 5E)	200 Mbps
Category 6 (Cat 6)	1,000 Mbps (1 Gbps)

into the cable when running it around corners, because this can damage the copper wires inside and lead to breakage. Also, run the cable around the perimeter of the room (instead of under a rug, for example) to avoid damaging the wires from foot traffic.

How long can an Ethernet cable run be? Cable runs for Ethernet networks can't exceed 328 feet or else the signal starts to degrade. For cable runs over 328 feet, you can use **repeaters**, devices that are installed on long cable runs to amplify the signal. In effect, repeaters act as signal boosters. Repeaters can extend run lengths to 600 feet, but they can add up to $200 to the cost of a network. When possible, you should use continuous lengths of cable. Although you can splice two cables together with a connecting jack, this presents a source of failure for the cable, because connectors can loosen up in the connecting jack and moisture or dust can accumulate on the contacts.

Ethernet Hubs
How do Ethernet networks use hubs?
Data is transmitted through the wires of an Ethernet network in packets. Imagine the data packets on an Ethernet network as cars on a road. If there were no traffic signals or rules of the road (such as driving on the right-hand side), we'd see a lot more collisions between vehicles, and people wouldn't get where they were going as readily (or at all). Data packets can also suffer collisions. If data packets collide, the data in them is damaged or lost. In either case, the network doesn't function efficiently.

As shown in Figure 7.12, a hub in an Ethernet network acts like a traffic signal by enforcing the rules of the data road on the transmission media. The hub keeps track of the data packets and helps them find their destination without running into each other.

The hub also amplifies signals and retransmits them across the network. This keeps the network running efficiently.

How many computers and peripherals can be connected to a hub? Hubs are differentiated by the number of ports they have for connecting network devices. Four- and eight-port hubs are often used in home networks. A four-port hub can connect up to four devices to the network, whereas an eight-port hub can handle eight devices. Obviously, you should buy a hub that has enough ports for all the devices you want to connect to the network. Many people buy hubs with more ports than they currently need so that they can expand their network in the future.

A wonderful feature of hubs is that you can chain them together. Usually, one port on a hub is designated for plugging into a second hub. As shown in Figure 7.13, you can chain two four-port hubs together to provide connections for a total of six devices. Most hubs can be chained together to provide hundreds of ports, which would far exceed the needs of most home networks.

Ethernet Routers
How does data from an Ethernet network get shared with the Internet or another network? As mentioned earlier, *routers* are devices that route packets of data between two or more networks. If a home network is connected to the Internet, you need a router to send data between the home network and the Internet.

Because so many people are sharing Internet access in home networks, manufacturers are making devices that combine hubs and routers and are specifically designed

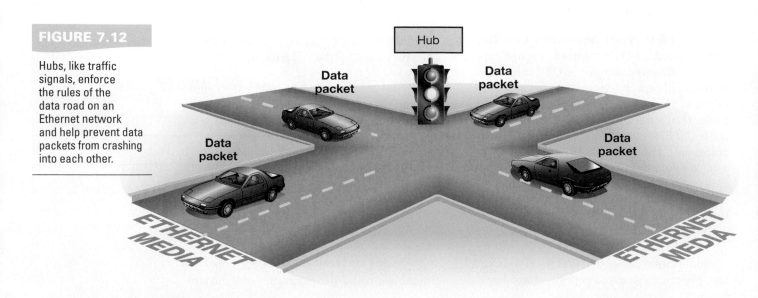

FIGURE 7.12

Hubs, like traffic signals, enforce the rules of the data road on an Ethernet network and help prevent data packets from crashing into each other.

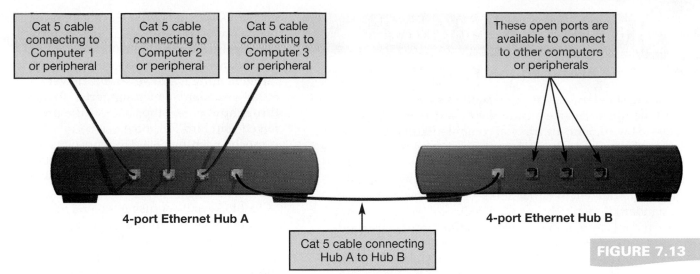

Cat 5 cable connecting to Computer 1 or peripheral

Cat 5 cable connecting to Computer 2 or peripheral

Cat 5 cable connecting to Computer 3 or peripheral

These open ports are available to connect to other computers or peripherals

4-port Ethernet Hub A

4-port Ethernet Hub B

Cat 5 cable connecting Hub A to Hub B

to connect to Digital Subscriber Line (DSL) or cable modems. These are often referred to as **DSL/cable routers**. If you want your Ethernet network to connect to the Internet through a DSL or cable modem, obtaining a DSL/cable router is a good idea. Although

you could share an Internet connection without one, a DSL/cable router provides increased throughput and is easier to configure than other methods. Figure 7.14 shows an example of an Ethernet network configured using a DSL/cable router.

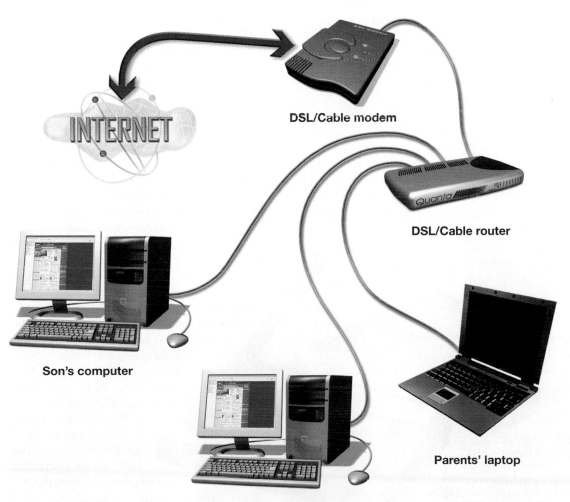

DSL/Cable modem

DSL/Cable router

Son's computer

Parents' laptop

Daughter's computer

BITS AND BYTES

One Brand Equals Fewer Headaches

Networking standards set by organizations such as the HomePlug Power Line Alliance make it easier for manufacturers to produce devices that work with a variety of computers and peripherals. In theory, such standards should benefit consumers as well because equipment from different manufacturers should work together when placed on the same network. The reality, however, is that devices from different manufacturers—even if they follow the same standards—don't always work together perfectly. This is because manufacturers sometimes introduce proprietary hardware and software that deviate from the standards (such as in the case of Super G wireless). This means that an Ethernet NIC from Manufacturer A might not work with a DSL/cable router from Manufacturer B. The safe course of action is to use equipment manufactured by the same company.

WIRELESS NETWORKS

What is a wireless network? As its name implies, a **wireless network** uses radio waves instead of wires or cable as its transmission media. For wireless network devices to work with other networks and devices, standards were established. Current wireless networks in the United States are based on the **802.11 standard** established in 1997 by the Institute of Electrical and Electronics Engineers (IEEE, pronounced "I-triple-E"). The 802.11 standard is also known as **Wi-Fi** (short for Wireless Fidelity). Three standards are currently defined under 802.11: 802.11a, 802.11b, and 802.11g. The main difference between these standards is their maximum data transfer rate. For home networking, 802.11b and 802.11g are the standards used.

The 802.11b standard, which supports a maximum bandwidth of 11 Mbps, quickly became the accepted industry standard for home networks because of the low cost of implementing it. However, the newer 802.11g standard, which supports a higher throughput of 54 Mbps, is now the preferred standard for home use because it is much faster than 802.11b. Fortunately, 802.11g devices can be used together (that is, they have backward compatibility) with 802.11b devices.

Just to keep it confusing, several manufacturers have recently introduced products in a new Super G (also called Extreme G) category. These devices are still based on the 802.11g standard but use proprietary hardware and software tweaks to increase throughput to a blistering 108 Mbps. Super G devices are designed to be backward compatible with 802.11b and regular 802.11g devices. However, because Super G is not standards based (i.e., it is not based on its own IEEE standard), Super G devices from one manufacturer might not work with those of another manufacturer.

What do I need to set up a wireless network? Wireless networks are basically Ethernet networks configured to use radio waves instead of wires. Just like other networks, each node on a wireless network requires a **wireless network adapter**. These adapters are available as NICs that are inserted into expansion slots on the computer or as USB devices that plug into an open USB port.

Wireless network adapters differ from other network adapters in that they contain *transceivers*. A **transceiver** is a device that translates the electronic data that needs to be sent along the network into radio waves and then broadcasts these radio waves to other network nodes. Transceivers serve a dual function because they also receive the signals from other network nodes. As shown in Figure 7.15, wireless network adapters have antennas poking out of them, which are necessary for the transmission and reception of these radio waves.

What types of problems can I run into when installing wireless networks? The maximum range of wireless devices is about 250 feet. However, as the

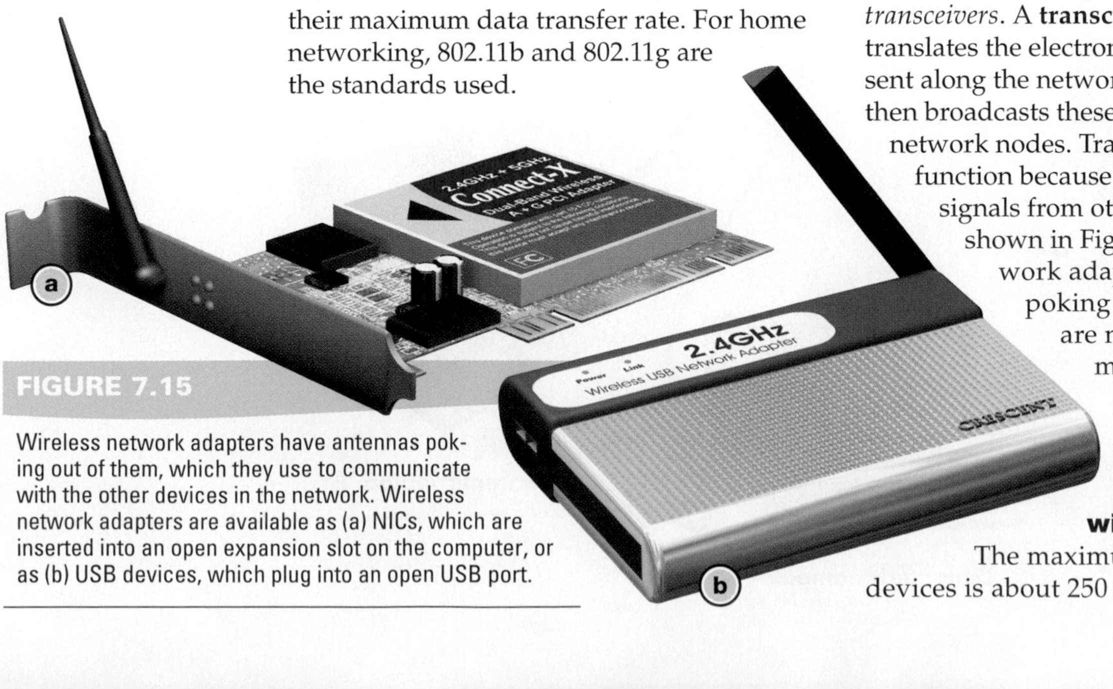

FIGURE 7.15

Wireless network adapters have antennas poking out of them, which they use to communicate with the other devices in the network. Wireless network adapters are available as (a) NICs, which are inserted into an open expansion slot on the computer, or as (b) USB devices, which plug into an open USB port.

distance between nodes increases, throughput decreases markedly. Also, 802.11b and 802.11 devices work on a bandwidth of 2.4GHz. This is the same band that many cordless phones use and therefore, your phone and wireless network may interfere with each other. The best solution is to purchase a new cordless phone that uses a bandwidth of 5.8GHz. These phones are now readily available.

Obstacles between wireless nodes also decrease throughput. Walls and large metal objects are the most common sources of interference with wireless signals. For example, placing a computer with a wireless network adapter next to a refrigerator may prevent the signals from reaching the rest of the network. And a node that has four walls between it and the Internet connection will most likely have lower than the maximum throughput.

What if the nodes can't communicate? Repositioning your computer or the wireless network adapter within the same room (sometimes even just a few inches from the original position) can often affect communication between the nodes. If this doesn't work, try moving the computers closer together or to other rooms in your house.

If these solutions don't work, you may need to add a wireless access point to your network, as shown in Figure 7.16. A **wireless access point** is a device similar to a hub in an Ethernet network. It takes the place of a wireless network adapter and helps to relay data between network nodes.

For example, as you can see in Figure 7.17, Laptop C on the back porch and Computer A in the bedroom can't connect with each other,

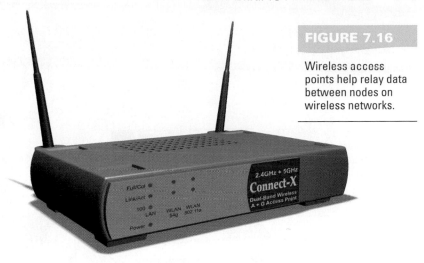

FIGURE 7.16

Wireless access points help relay data between nodes on wireless networks.

but they can connect to Computer B in the den. By connecting a wireless access point to Computer B (instead of a wireless network adapter), all traffic from Computer A is relayed to Laptop C through the access point on Computer B.

How do I share an Internet connection on a wireless network? A *gateway* is a specialized device that enables wireless networks to share broadband connections. It is basically the router for a wireless network.

Can I have wired and wireless nodes on one network? Many users want to create a network in which some computers (such as desktops) connect to the network with wires while other computers (such as laptops) connect to the network wirelessly. **Wireless DSL/cable routers** allow you to connect wireless and wired nodes to the same network. This type of router contains both a wireless access point

FIGURE 7.17

With a wireless access point installed on Computer B, data can travel from Computer A (in the bedroom) to Laptop C (on the back porch).

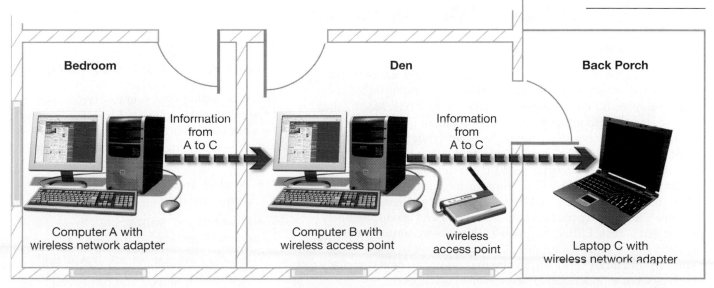

Bedroom — Computer A with wireless network adapter

Information from A to C

Den — Computer B with wireless access point — wireless access point

Information from A to C

Back Porch — Laptop C with wireless network adapter

Using a wireless DSL/cable router, the computers in the den and bedroom still maintain a high-speed wired Ethernet connection. However, the laptop can connect to the network wirelessly and be used in many areas of the home.

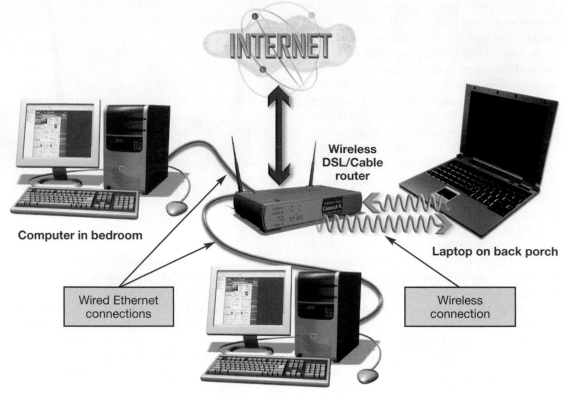

Computer in bedroom

Wireless DSL/Cable router

Laptop on back porch

Wired Ethernet connections

Wireless connection

Computer in den

SOUND BYTE

SECURING YOUR WIRELESS NETWORKS

In this Sound Byte, you'll learn what "war drivers" are and why they could potentially be a threat to your wireless network. You'll also learn the simple steps to secure your wireless network against intruders.

BITS AND BYTES

Wireless Hot Spots

The rise of mobile computing is driving demand for wireless networks. To meet that demand, Starbucks, for example, offers wireless access to its customers in many of its shops. Many other businesses are also jumping on the bandwagon. Public places at which you can wirelessly connect to the Internet are known as "hot spots." Sometimes the service is free, other times there is a small charge. How can you tell? Just fire up your wireless-equipped laptop or PDA, start your browser, and try to access a Web site. If the service is not free, the store's "wireless gateway sentinel" software provides you with rates and an opportunity to pay for access. Either way, you are surfing in minutes while enjoying your latte. Going out of town and need to know where you can find a hot spot? Visit a site that offers hot spot directories, such as **www.wifinder.com** or **www.wi-fihotspotlist.com**.

as well as ports that allow you to connect wired nodes to the router. Figure 7.18 shows an example of a network with a wireless DSL/cable router attached to it. As you can see, the laptop maintains a wireless connection to the router while the other two computers are connected by wires. Using this type of router is a cost-effective way to have some wireless connections while still preserving the high-speed attributes of Ethernet where needed.

Choosing a Peer-to-Peer Network

If you're setting up a home network, the type of network you should choose depends on your particular needs. In general, consider the following factors in determining your network type:

- Whether you want wireless communications
- How fast you want your network connection to be
- Whether existing wiring is available
- How much money you can spend on your network

Figure 7.19 provides a flowchart that can help you decide which network to use in your home.

What if I want to use existing wiring for my home network? As noted earlier, you can use both phone lines and power lines (electrical wiring) as media for a home network. For phoneline networks, you need a phone jack in each room where you want to connect a node to the network. Likewise, for power line networks, you

need an electrical outlet available in each room where you want to connect a node to the network. Because you have to plug most nodes (computers, printers, and so on) into an electrical outlet to operate them anyway, connecting a power line network is usually convenient.

What are the pros and cons of wireless networks? Wireless networks free you from having to run wires in your home. In addition, you can use any flat surface as a

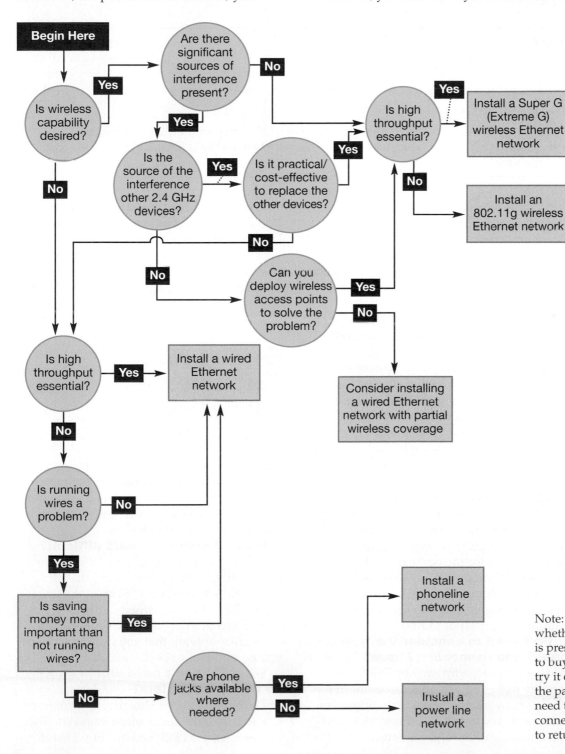

FIGURE 7.19

How to Choose a Home Network

Note: The only way to determine whether significant interference is present in your home may be to buy wireless equipment and try it out. Make sure you keep the packaging because you'll need to have it if you discover connectivity problems and need to return the equipment.

FIGURE 7.20 Comparing the Major Types of Home Networks

	POWER LINE	PHONELINE	ETHERNET	WIRELESS[2]
Maximum data transfer rate (throughput)	14 Mbps	10 Mbps	100 to 1,000 Mbps (1 Gbps)[1]	11 to 108 Mbps
Approximate cost to network two computers (adapters and wiring only)	$100	$70	$80	$75[2]
Additional cost for adding Internet connection sharing	$80	$65	$0[3]	$0[3]
Approximate cost to add an additional computer to network	$50	$35	$20	$20

[1]Costs shown are for a 100-Mbps network because 1,000-Mbps networks are too expensive for most home networks.

[2]Prices shown are for 802.11g accelerated hardware (Super G or Extreme G).

[3]A router (a device used to route packets of data between different networks) is required for a basic Ethernet (wired or wireless) setup and is assumed to be a cable/DSL router. The cost of the router is included in the base cost for networking two computers above.

workstation. However, wireless networks may not work effectively in every home. Therefore, you need to install and test the wireless network to figure out if it will work. To avoid unnecessary expenses, make sure you can return equipment for a refund if it doesn't work.

What network provides the best throughput for video and gaming? For the majority of tasks undertaken on a home network (such as Web browsing and e-mailing), 1- or 2-Mbps throughput is sufficient. However, if high-speed data transmission is important to you (for example, if you play computer games or exchange large files), you may want a network with high throughput. Without high throughput, streaming video can appear choppy, games can respond slowly, and files can take a long time to transfer. With data transfer rates up to 1,000 Mbps, Ethernet networks are the fastest home networks. Although 1,000-Mbps equipment is now available for the home market, it is at least twice as expensive as 100-Mbps Ethernet equipment. But you may want to consider this if you engage in a lot of multiplayer gaming or transfer of video.

Do I need to consider the type of broadband connection I have? Whether you connect to the Internet by DSL, cable, or satellite makes no difference in terms of the type of network you select. The differences occur with your particular network's hardware and software requirements.

What cost factors do I need to consider in choosing a network? Unfortunately, you may need to consider your budget when deciding what type of network to install. Figure 7.20 lists the approximate costs of installing the various types of peer-to-peer networks and their throughput.

Configuring Software for Your Home Network

Once you install the hardware for your network, you need to configure the software necessary for networking on your computers. In this section, you'll learn how to do just that using special Windows tools.

Is configuring software difficult? Windows XP makes configuring software relatively simple by providing the XP Network Setup Wizard, as shown in Figure 7.21. As you learned in Chapter 4, a wizard is a utility program included with Microsoft software that you can use to help you accomplish a specific task.

What if I don't have Windows XP on all my computers? Windows 98 and Millennium Edition (Me), the most common OSs found in the home other than Windows XP, both support P2P networking. Therefore,

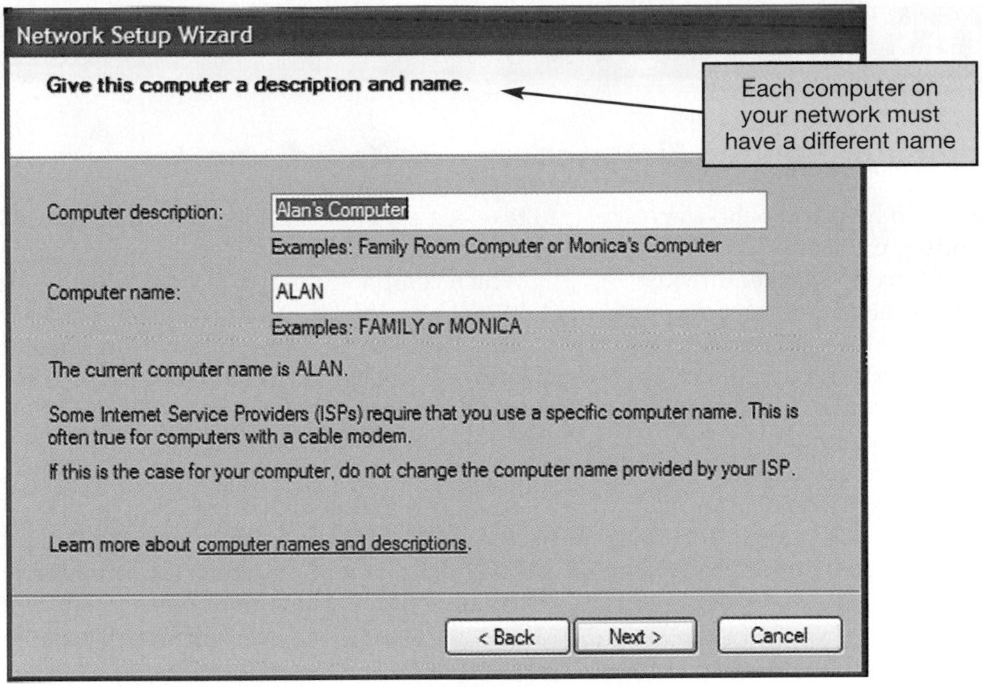

Network Setup Wizard

Give this computer a description and name.

Computer description: Alan's Computer

Examples: Family Room Computer or Monica's Computer

Computer name: ALAN

Examples: FAMILY or MONICA

The current computer name is ALAN.

Some Internet Service Providers (ISPs) require that you use a specific computer name. This is often true for computers with a cable modem.

If this is the case for your computer, do not change the computer name provided by your ISP.

Learn more about computer names and descriptions.

[< Back]   [Next >]   [Cancel]

FIGURE 7.21

The Windows XP Network Setup Wizard helps you configure your software for your network. On this screen, you give the computer a unique name (on your network) so that the software can keep track of it.

you can network these computers with other computers using Windows XP.

Where do I start? First, switch on all the computers and peripherals that are connected to your network. The wizard needs to check for other devices on the network, and it can't detect them if they're not turned on. If you have one computer with Windows XP but your other computers run on other versions of the Windows operating system, you should set up your Windows XP computer first with the Windows XP Network Setup Wizard. One step of the wizard gives you an option to create an installation disk you can use to set up non–Windows XP computers. Create the installation disk and then take the disk to your Windows 98 or Windows Me computers and follow the on-screen instructions.

What if I don't have Windows XP on any of my computers? Windows Me contains a similar wizard to Windows XP. (However, if you're mixing Windows XP and Windows Me computers, Microsoft recommends using the Windows XP wizard and an installation disk for the Windows Me computers.) If you're networking all Windows 98 machines, there is no wizard available, so you have to set up your computers manually. Various resources on the Internet can assist you in setting up Windows 98 networks. Not surprisingly, one of the best resources is the Microsoft Web site (**www.microsoft.com**).

Why does the wizard ask me to name my computer? Each computer on the network needs a unique name so that the network can identify it. This unique name ensures that the network knows which computer is requesting services and data (such as Web page requests) so the data can be delivered to the correct computer.

Is that it? Assuming you installed and configured everything properly, your home network should be up and running and allowing you to share files, Internet connections, and peripherals. In the next section, we explore how you can protect your computers from intruders.

Keeping Your Home Computer Safe

The media is full of stories about computer viruses damaging computers, and attacks on corporate Web sites have brought major corporations to a standstill. These are examples of a type of criminal mischief called **cybercrime**, which is formally defined as any criminal action perpetrated primarily through the use of a computer. The existence of cybercrime doesn't mean we should fear conducting business, research, and recreation over the Internet. It does mean that computer users must maintain

TRENDS IN IT

EMERGING TECHNOLOGIES:
Grid Computing: Fighting Bioterrorism with Your Computer

Want to use your computer to help wage the war against bioterrorists? Finding more effective drugs to fight diseases such as smallpox doesn't require just laboratory research. Scientists also need huge amounts of computing power to analyze the data they amass in the lab. Strike a blow against terrorism and enlist your computer in the PatriotGrid, a network of computers working together to fight bioterrorism.

So, when does your computer have time to work on this project? Although you may use your computer many hours each day, even at peak times, your CPU rarely exceeds 20 percent of its maximum processing capability. Computers perform calculations in bursts. In between the bursts of activity (even between keystrokes), there are periods of inactivity, which amounts to wasted computing resources. This doesn't mean your computer is inefficient, it just means that the power of today's computers is so great that you can't fully use it. Turning these periods of inactivity into productive time periods is the aim of **grid computing**, a technology being used to provide huge increases in computational power for a reasonable price. Using specialized software, a company can create a computer grid that can effectively link millions of computers to perform complex calculations during lulls in their processing cycles.

To become involved in the PatriotGrid project, go to **www.grid.org** (sponsored by United Devices) and download the PatriotGrid software. This software uses your computer during idle times to run chemical analyses on agents that may be effective in fighting smallpox. When you're on the Internet, the software sends the results of its calculations back to the lab and retrieves more data to analyze. Your computer is now joining millions of other computers in the PatriotGrid project. Without the PatriotGrid, the smallpox analysis project was estimated to take 45 years to complete. With the PatriotGrid, the processing time is shortened to a matter of months.

Which companies use grid computing besides those fighting bioterrorism? Aircraft and spacecraft manufacturers need to perform complex design calculations, whereas pharmaceutical companies need to run complex tests to determine how chemical compounds will react in the human body. By using grid software, these companies can link their employees' computers to take advantage of their computing power during periods of relative inactivity (especially at night). As opposed to leasing time on a supercomputer, using their employees' computers allows these companies to cut costs. Meanwhile, online games in which massive numbers of players play simultaneously require a lot of computing power. Companies such as Butterfly.net are creating grid computing programs to harness the power of multiple computers specifically to host large gaming networks.

However, do your homework before joining any grid project. Although it hasn't happened yet, there is no telling when scam artists may use a fake grid project to gather sensitive information about you. Make sure to research the grid project and the company supporting it. Chances are if the project has been reported on in multiple legitimate media sources (*New York Times, Wired Magazine, PC Magazine*, etc.), it is a bona fide project and not a con game.

Grid computing today is mostly confined to grids constructed at single organizations or to volunteer organizations such as the PatriotGrid. However, as network bandwidth continues to increase, third-party companies will construct grids and lease time to corporations. These third-party companies could very well pay consumers for the use of their home computers as part of these grids. Someday, your computer could pay for itself by working during its otherwise "off" hours.

---

an awareness of computer crime and take precautions to protect themselves.

Who perpetrates computer crimes? **Cybercriminals** are individuals who use computers, networks, and the Internet to perpetrate crime. Anyone with a computer and the wherewithal to arm themselves with the appropriate knowledge can be a cybercriminal. In the next sections, we discuss cybercriminals and the damage they can wreak on your computer. We also discuss methods for protecting your computer from attacks.

Computer Threats: Hackers

Although there is a great deal of dissension (especially among hackers themselves) as to what a hacker actually is, a **hacker** (also called a **cracker**) is defined as anyone who breaks into a computer system (whether an individual computer or a network) unlawfully.

Are there different kinds of hackers? Some hackers are offended by being labeled

BRINGING CIVILIZATION TO ITS KNEES...
Goths — Vandals — Huns — Geeks

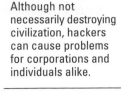

FIGURE 7.22

Although not necessarily destroying civilization, hackers can cause problems for corporations and individuals alike.

criminals and therefore attempt to divide hackers into classes. Many hackers who break into systems just for the challenge of it (and who don't wish to steal or wreak havoc on the systems) refer to themselves as **white-hat hackers**. They tout themselves as experts who are performing a needed service for society by helping companies realize the vulnerabilities that exist in their systems.

These white-hat hackers look down on those hackers who use their knowledge to destroy information or for illegal gain. White-hat hackers refer to these other hackers as **black-hat hackers**. The terms *white hat* and *black hat* are references to old Western movies in which the heroes wore white hats and the outlaws wore black hats. Irrespective of the opinions of the hackers, the laws in the United States (and in many foreign countries) consider any unauthorized access to computer systems a crime.

What about the teenage hackers who get caught every so often?
Although some of these teenagers are brilliant hackers, the majority are amateurs without sophisticated computer skills. These amateur hackers are referred to as **script kiddies**. Script kiddies don't create programs used to hack into computer systems; instead, they use tools created by skilled hackers that enable unskilled novices to wreak the same

BITS AND BYTES

Be Careful When Joining Social Networking Sites

Making contacts and meeting friends online has never been easier. Social networking services such as the well-established Friendster (**www.friendster.com**) and recent entries such as Friendzy (**www.friendzy.com**) and Tribe Networks (**www.tribe.net**) are signing up users at a rapid pace. These services have you list personal information about yourself (age, marital status, interests, hobbies, etc.) and encourage you to list connections to your friends. When your friends log on and view your profile, they can see themselves and long chains of other acquaintances. The idea is that everyone knows someone else and your friends can see who else you know and get you to make appropriate introductions (or do it themselves).

Although the sites offer fairly tight protection of personal information (such as not revealing last names), you should think carefully about personal information that is visible on the site and be wary of disclosing additional information to people you meet online. Given the vast problems with identity theft, you should be wary of giving out your full name, address, social security number, and any type of financial information. Also, be wary of accepting computer files from people you've met online because they could contain viruses or spyware. Just because you meet someone that is a friend of a friend of your second cousin in Idaho doesn't mean that person isn't a hacker or a scam artist. So, enjoy meeting new people, but exercise the appropriate amount of caution that you would elsewhere on the Internet.

havoc as professional hackers. Unfortunately, a search on any search engine will produce links to Web sites that feature hacking tools, complete with instructions, allowing anyone to become an amateur hacker.

Fortunately, because the users of these programs are amateurs, they're usually not proficient at covering their electronic tracks. Therefore, it's relatively easy for law enforcement officials to track them down and prosecute them. Still, script kiddies can cause a lot of disruption and damage to computers, networks, and Web sites before they're caught.

Why would a hacker be interested in breaking into my home computer? Some hackers just like to snoop. They enjoy the challenge of breaking into systems and seeing what information they can find. Other hackers are hobbyists seeking information about a particular topic wherever they can find it. Because many people keep proprietary business information on their home computers, hackers bent on industrial espionage may break into home computers. For other hackers, hacking is a way to pass time.

WHAT HACKERS STEAL

Could a hacker steal my credit card number? If you perform financial transactions online, such as banking or buying goods and services, you probably do so using a credit card. Credit card and bank account information can thus reside on your hard drive and may be detectable by a hacker. Even if this information is not stored on your computer, a hacker may be able to capture this information when you're online by using a *packet sniffer*.

What's a packet sniffer? As you learned earlier, data travels through the Internet in small pieces called *packets*. The packets are identified with a string of numbers, in part to help identify on which computer they should end up. Once the packets reach their destination, they are reassembled into cohesive messages. A **packet sniffer** is a program that looks at (or sniffs) each packet as it travels on the Internet—not just those that are addressed to a particular computer, but *all* packets. Some packet sniffers are configured to capture all the packets into memory, whereas others capture only certain packets that contain specific content (such as credit card numbers).

What do hackers do with the information they "sniff"? Once a hacker has your credit card information, he or she can either use it to purchase items illegally or sell the number to someone who will. If hackers can gather enough information in conjunction with your credit card information, they may be able to commit **identity theft**. Identity theft is characterized by someone using personal information about you (such as your name, address, and social security number) to assume your identity for the purpose of defrauding others.

Although this sounds scary, you can protect yourself from packet sniffers by simply installing a firewall, which we discuss later in this chapter.

TROJAN HORSES

Is there anything else hackers can do if they break into my computer? Hackers often use individuals' computers as a staging area to do mischief. To perpetrate widespread computer attacks, for example, hackers need to control many computers at the same time. To this end, hackers often use Trojan horses to install other programs on computers. A **Trojan horse** is a program that appears to be something useful or desirable (like a game or a screen saver), but at the

BITS AND BYTES

Terrorists Using the Internet?

Cyberterrorists are terrorists who use computers to accomplish their goals. Although there have been no major outbreaks of cyberterrorism yet, it is a concern of law enforcement agencies, ISPs, and major corporations. A cyberterrorist would attempt to disrupt the flow of information by attacking major networks, Web sites, or communications equipment. Bombing or otherwise disabling major ISPs could cripple network communications or the Internet. Disabling or corrupting the computer systems that control the New York Stock Exchange, for example, could undermine confidence in the financial markets, causing the economy to nosedive. Any action that would cause a disruption to the normal flow of information could potentially cause panic, which is the cyberterrorist's goal.

But the U.S. Government Office of Homeland Security has partnered with Dartmouth College's Institute for Security Technology Studies in an effort to head off potential threats. A project code named Livewire has been launched that simulates cyberattacks against large networks in both the public and private sectors. The results of these attacks are analyzed to assist in the development of a national cyber-response system.

TRENDS IN IT

COMPUTERS IN SOCIETY:
Identity Theft: Is There More Than One You Out There?

You've no doubt heard of identity theft: a thief steals your name, address, social security number, and bank account and credit card information and runs up debts in your name. This leaves you holding the bag as you're hounded by creditors collecting on the fraudulent debts. It sounds horrible, and it is. Many victims of identity theft spend months trying to reestablish their credit.

Stories of identity theft abound in the media, such as the Long Island, New York, man accused of stealing over 30,000 identities, and should serve to make the public wary. However, many media pundits would have you believe that the only way your identity can be stolen is by a computer. This is simply not true. The U.S. Federal Trade Commission (**www.ftc.gov**) has identified the following as methods thieves use to obtain others' personal information:

1. Identity thieves steal purses and wallets, where people often keep unnecessary valuable personal information (such as their ATM PIN codes).
2. Identity thieves steal mail or look through trash for bank statements and credit card bills, which provide valuable personal information.
3. Identity thieves may pose as bank or credit card company representatives and trick people into revealing sensitive information over the phone.

Notice that none of these methods involve using a computer. Of course, you're at risk from online attacks, too. You can give personal information to crooks by responding to bogus e-mail purportedly from your bank or ISP, for example. Once identity thieves have obtained your personal information, they can use it in a number of different ways:

Identity thieves can request a change of address for your credit card bill. By the time you realize that you aren't receiving your credit card statements, the thieves have rung up bogus charges on your account.

Identity thieves may open new credit card accounts in your name.

Identity thieves can open bank accounts in your name and write bad checks, ruining your credit rating. They can also counterfeit bank cards or checks for your legitimate accounts.

Although foolproof protection methods don't exist, the following precautions will help you minimize your risk:

1. Never reveal your password or PIN code to anyone or place it in an easy-to-find location.
2. Never reveal personal information unless you're sure that a legitimate reason exists for a business to know the information and you can confirm you're actually dealing with a legitimate representative. Banks and credit card companies usually request information by standard mail, not over the phone or online. If someone calls or e-mails asking you for personal information, decline and call the company where you opened your account.
3. Create hard-to-guess passwords for your accounts. Use a combination of letters and numbers and avoid using obvious passwords such as first or last names, birth dates, and so on.
4. When shopping online, be wary of unfamiliar merchants whom you can't contact through a mailing address or phone number or businesses whose prices are too good to be true. These can be attempts to collect your personal information for use in fraudulent schemes.

Using common sense and keeping personal information in the hands of as few people as possible are the best defenses against identity theft. For additional tips on preventing identity theft or for procedures to follow if you are a victim, check out the U.S. federal government site on identity theft at **www.consumer.gov/idtheft**.

same time does something malicious in the background without your knowledge.

Why is it called a "Trojan horse"? The term *Trojan horse* derives from Greek mythology and refers to a wooden horse that the Greeks used to sneak into the city of Troy. According to mythology, sometime between 1200 and 1500 B.C.E., the Greeks had the city of Troy under siege. Unable to break through the Trojan defenses, the Greeks withdrew from the battlefield one evening and left behind a large wooden horse. In the morning, the citizens of Troy thought that the horse was a gift from the gods and brought it into the city. That night, a group of Greek soldiers who were hiding in the belly of the horse snuck out and opened the gates of the city so the Greek army could march in and destroy Troy. Therefore, computer programs that contain a hidden "surprise" are referred to as Trojan horses.

What damage can Trojan horses do? Often, the malicious activity perpetrated by a Trojan horse program is the installation of **backdoor programs**, which allow hackers to take almost complete control of your computer without your knowledge. Using a backdoor program, hackers can access and delete all files on your computer, send e-mail, run programs, and do just about anything else you can do with your computer. Computers that hackers control in this manner are referred to as **zombies**.

DENIAL OF SERVICE ATTACKS

What else can hackers do? Hackers can also launch an attack from your computer called a **denial of service (DoS) attack**. In a denial of service attack, legitimate users are denied access to a computer system because a hacker is repeatedly making requests of that computer system through a computer

he or she has taken over as a zombie. Computers can handle only a certain number of requests for information at one time. When they are flooded with requests in a denial of service attack, they shut down and refuse to answer any requests for information, even if the requests are from legitimate users. Thus, the computer is so tied up responding to the bogus requests for information that authorized users can't gain access.

Launching a DoS attack on a computer system from one computer is easy to trace. Therefore, most savvy hackers use a distributed denial of service attack. **Distributed denial of service (DDoS) attacks** are automated attacks that are launched from more than one zombie at the same time. Figure 7.23 illustrates how a DDoS attack

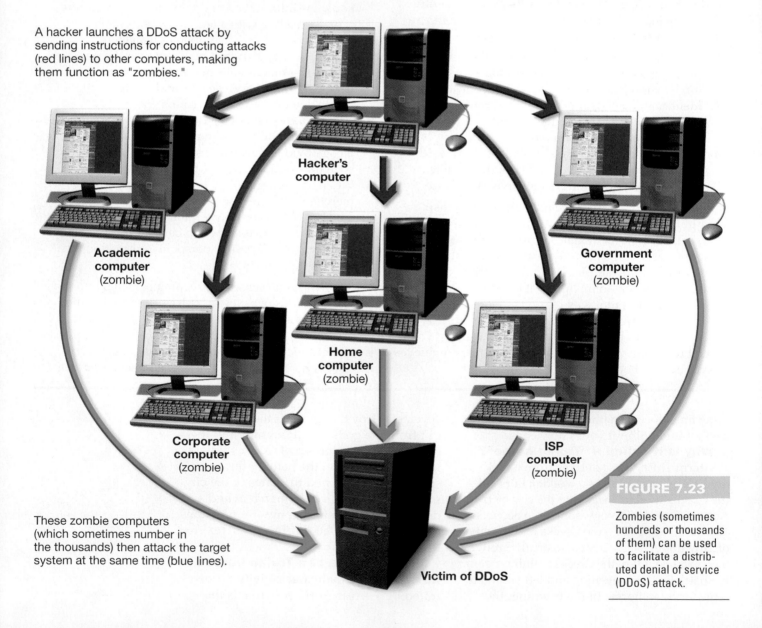

A hacker launches a DDoS attack by sending instructions for conducting attacks (red lines) to other computers, making them function as "zombies."

Hacker's computer

Academic computer (zombie)

Government computer (zombie)

Home computer (zombie)

Corporate computer (zombie)

ISP computer (zombie)

These zombie computers (which sometimes number in the thousands) then attack the target system at the same time (blue lines).

Victim of DDoS

FIGURE 7.23

Zombies (sometimes hundreds or thousands of them) can be used to facilitate a distributed denial of service (DDoS) attack.

works. A hacker creates many zombies (sometimes hundreds or thousands) and coordinates them so they begin sending bogus information requests to the same computer at the same time. Administrators of the victim computer often have a great deal of difficulty stopping the attack because it comes from hundreds of computers.

Distributed denial of service attacks are a serious problem. In February 2000, many high-profile Web sites were subjected to DDoS attacks that succeeded in locking out authorized users. Yahoo! was the first victim on February 7. In subsequent days, eBay, Amazon, CNN, E*Trade, Excite, and Buy.com suffered interruptions in service caused by DDoS attacks. Business losses were estimated to be in the millions of dollars.

HOW HACKERS GAIN ACCESS

How exactly does a hacker gain access to a computer? Hackers can gain access to computers directly or indirectly. Direct access involves sitting down at a computer and installing hacking software. This rarely occurs in your home. However, to deter unauthorized use, you may want to lock the room that your computer is in or remove key components (such as the power cord) when strangers (construction workers and so on) are in your house and may be unobserved for periods of time.

The most likely method a hacker will take to access a computer is indirectly through its Internet connection. When connected to the Internet, your computer is potentially open to attack by hackers. Many people forget that their Internet connection is a two-way street. Not only can you access the Internet, but people on the Internet can access your computer as well.

Think of the computer as a house. Common sense tells you to lock your doors and windows when you aren't home to deter theft. Hooking your computer up to the Internet is like leaving the front door to your house wide open when you're not home. Anyone passing by can access your computer and poke around for valuables. Your computer obviously doesn't have doors and windows like a house; instead, it has logical ports.

What are logical ports? Logical **ports** are virtual (that is, *not* physical) communications gateways or paths that allow a computer to organize requests for information (such as Web page downloads, e-mail routing, and so on) from other networks or computers. Unlike the physical ports (USB, FireWire, and so on) we discussed in Chapter 6, you can't see or touch a logical port. It is part of a computer's internal organization.

Logical ports are numbered and assigned to specific services. For instance, logical port 80 is designated for Hypertext Transfer Protocol (HTTP), the main communications protocol (or standard) for the Internet. Thus, all requests for information from your browser to the Web flow through logical port 80. E-mail messages sent by Simple Mail Transfer Protocol (SMTP), the protocol used for sending e-mail on the Internet, are routed through logical port 25. Open logical ports, like open windows in a home, invite intruders, as illustrated in Figure 7.24. Unless you take precautions to restrict access to your logical ports, other people on the Internet may be able to access your computer through them.

Fortunately, you can thwart most hacking problems by installing a firewall.

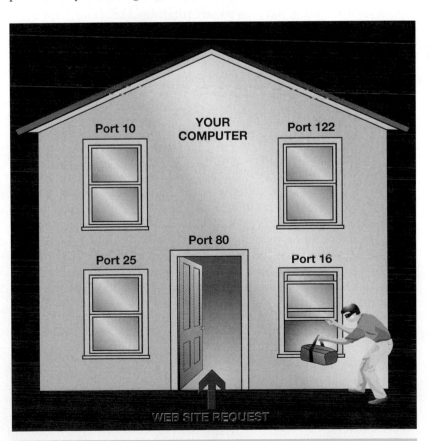

FIGURE 7.24

Open logical ports are an invitation to hackers.

Computer Safeguards: Firewalls

Firewalls are software programs or hardware devices designed to keep computers safe from hackers. Firewalls specifically designed for home networks are called **personal firewalls** and are made to be easy to install. By using a personal firewall, you can close off open logical ports to invaders and potentially make your computer invisible to other computers on the Internet.

Why are they called firewalls?
When houses were first being packed densely into cities (attached to each other with common walls), fire was a huge hazard because wood (the major construction component for houses) burns readily. An entire neighborhood could be lost in a single fire.

DIG DEEPER

How Firewalls Work

Firewalls are designed to restrict access to a network and the computers on it. Firewalls protect you in two major ways: by blocking access to logical ports, and by keeping your computer's network address secure.

To block access to logical ports, firewalls examine data packets that your computer sends and receives. Data packets contain information such as the address of the sending and receiving computers and the logical port that the packet will use. Firewalls can be configured so that they filter out packets sent to specific logical ports (a process referred to as **packet filtering**). For example, File Transfer Protocol (FTP) programs are a typical way in which hackers access a computer. If a firewall is configured to ignore *all* incoming packets that request access to port 25 (the port designated for FTP traffic), no FTP requests will get through to your computer (a process referred to as **logical port blocking**). If port 25 were a window on your home, you would have effectively locked it so a burglar couldn't get in. If you need port 25 for a legitimate purpose, you could instruct the firewall to allow access to that port for a specified period of time or by a certain user.

For the Internet to share information seamlessly, data packets must have a way of getting to their correct location. Therefore, all computers connected to the Internet have a unique address. These addresses are called **Internet Protocol addresses** (**IP addresses** for short). As noted earlier, data packets contain the IP address of the computer to which they are being sent. Routing servers on the Internet make sure the packets get to the correct address. This is similar to the way addresses work on a conventional letter. A unique street address (such as 123 Main St., Anywhere, CA 99999) is placed on the envelope and the postal service routes it to its correct destination. Without such addressing, data packets, like letters, would not reach the intended recipients.

IP addresses are assigned when users log on to their Internet service provider (ISP) in a procedure known as **dynamic addressing**, illustrated in Figure 7.25. IP addresses are assigned out of a pool of available IP

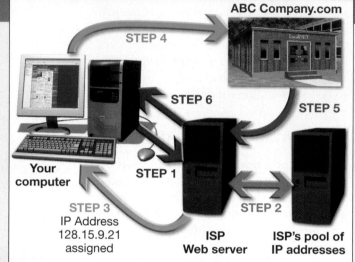

STEP 1: When you connect to your ISP, your computer requests an IP address.

STEP 2: The ISP's Web server consults its list of available IP addresses and selects one.

STEP 3: The selected IP address is communicated to your computer. The address remains in force for as long as you are connected to the ISP.

STEP 4: Once on the Internet, your Web browser requests access to ABC Company's Web site.

STEP 5: The ABC Company server consults an IP address listing and determines that the IP address of your computer is assigned to your ISP. It then forwards the requested information to the ISP's Web server.

STEP 6: The ISP's Web server knows to whom it assigned the IP address and therefore forwards the requested information on to your computer.

FIGURE 7.25

How Dynamic IP Addressing Works

addresses licensed to the ISP. Because hackers use IP addresses to find victims and come back to their computers for more mischief, frequently switching IP addresses helps make users less vulnerable to attacks. However, because many broadband (cable and DSL) users leave their modems on for long periods of time (consecutive days or weeks), their IP addresses tend to change less frequently than those of dial-up users. Such

Thus, builders started building common walls of nonflammable or slow-burning material to stop (or at least slow) the spread of fire. These came to be known as *firewalls*.

TYPES OF FIREWALLS

What kinds of firewalls are there? As noted previously, firewalls can be configured

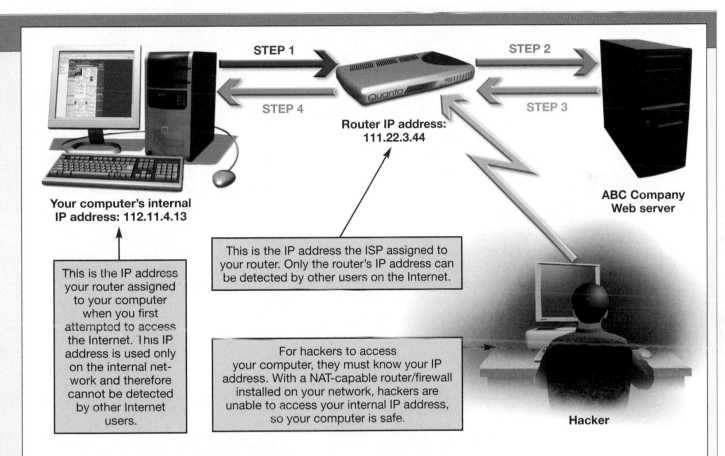

Your computer's internal IP address: 112.11.4.13

Router IP address: 111.22.3.44

ABC Company Web server

This is the IP address your router assigned to your computer when you first attempted to access the Internet. This IP address is used only on the internal network and therefore cannot be detected by other Internet users.

This is the IP address the ISP assigned to your router. Only the router's IP address can be detected by other users on the Internet.

For hackers to access your computer, they must know your IP address. With a NAT-capable router/firewall installed on your network, hackers are unable to access your internal IP address, so your computer is safe.

Hacker

STEP 1: Your computer's Web browser requests access to the ABC Company's Web site. This request travels through the router (which is configured as a firewall).

STEP 2: The router forwards your request to the ABC Company Web server. It directs the server to send the data back to the router IP address (111.22.3.44). The internal IP address of your computer (assigned by NAT) is not revealed to other computers outside your network.

STEP 3: The ABC Company Web server processes the request and sends the data back to the router IP address (111.22.3.44).

STEP 4: The router then passes the requested information on to the IP address of the computer that requested it (112.11.4.13).

FIGURE 7.26

Network Address Translation in Action

static addressing (retaining the same IP address for a period of time) makes broadband users more vulnerable to hackers because the hackers have a more permanent IP address with which to locate the computer. It also makes it easier for a hacker to go back to a computer repeatedly.

To combat the problems associated with static addressing, firewalls use a process called **Network**

Address Translation (NAT) to assign internal IP addresses on a network. These internal IP addresses are not shared with other devices that aren't part of the network, so the addresses are safe from hackers. Figure 7.26 shows how NAT works. You can use NAT in your home by purchasing a firewall with NAT capabilities. As noted earlier, many routers sold for home use are also configured as firewalls, and many feature NAT as well.

using software or hardware devices. Although installing either a software or a hardware firewall on your home network is probably sufficient, you should consider installing both for maximum protection.

What software firewalls are there? The most popular software firewalls for the home include Norton Personal Firewall, McAfee Firewall, ZoneAlarm, and BlackICE PC Protection. These products are easy to set up and include options that allow the software to make security decisions for you based on the level of security you request. These programs also come with monitoring systems that alert you if your computer is under attack. The newest versions of these programs have "smart agents" that automatically stop attacks as they are detected by closing the appropriate logical ports or disallowing the suspicious activity.

What are hardware firewalls? You can also buy and configure hardware firewall devices. For example, when buying a router for your network, make sure to buy one that also acts as a firewall. Manufacturers such as Linksys, D-Link, and Netgear make routers that double as firewalls. Just like software firewalls, the setup in hardware firewalls is designed for novices, and the default configuration is to keep unnecessary logical ports closed. Documentation accompanying the firewalls can assist more experienced users in adjusting the settings to allow access to specific ports if needed.

IS YOUR COMPUTER SECURE?

How can I tell if my computer is at risk? For peace of mind (and to ensure your firewall setup was successful), you can visit several Web sites that offer free services that test your computer's vulnerability. A popular site is Gibson Research (**www.grc.com**). The company's ShieldsUP and LeakTest programs are free and easy to run and can pinpoint security vulnerabilities in a system connected to the Internet. If you get a clean report from these programs, your system is probably not vulnerable to attack. Figure 7.27 shows the results screen from a ShieldsUP port probe test, which checks which logical ports in your computer are vulnerable.

What if I don't get a clean report from the testing program? If the testing program detects potential vulnerabilities and you don't have a firewall, you should install one as soon as possible. If the firewall is already configured and specific ports are shown as being vulnerable, consult your firewall documentation for instructions on how to close or restrict access to those ports.

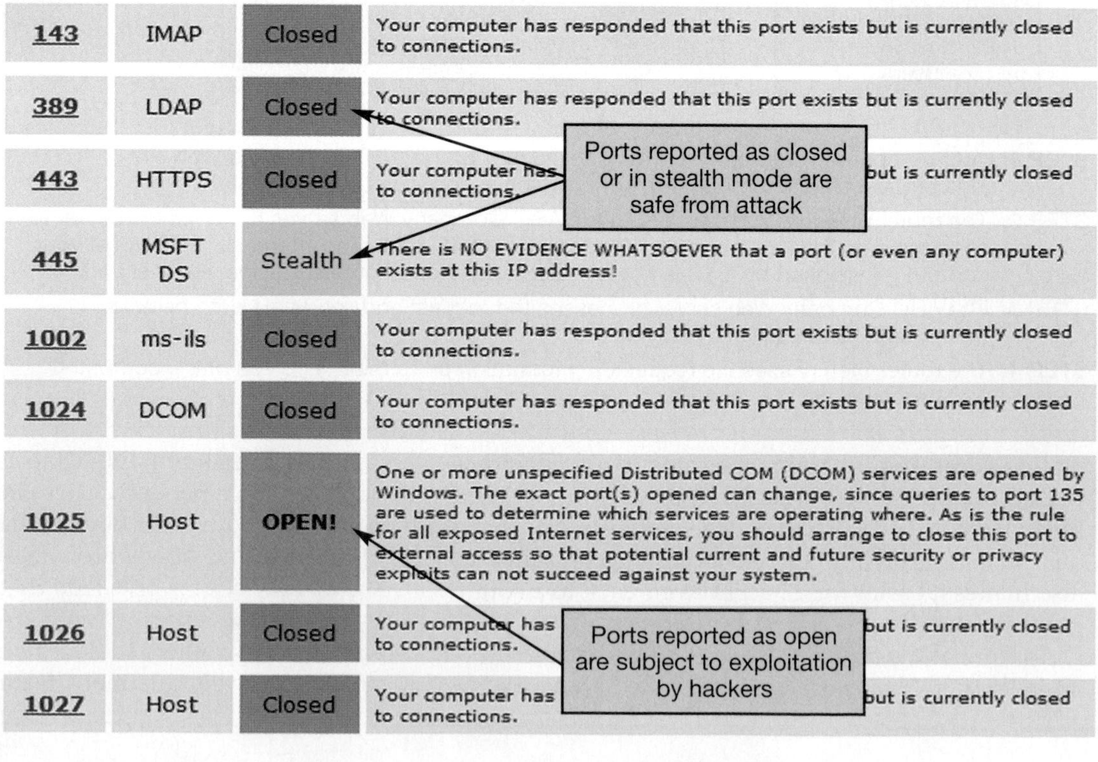

FIGURE 7.27

This screen shows results from a ShieldsUP port probe test. This test was run on a computer connected to the Internet with no firewall installed. Any ports that are reported as open (such as port 1025) by this test represent vulnerabilities that could be exploited by hackers. Installation of a hardware or software firewall should close any open ports.

Port	Service	Status	Description
143	IMAP	Closed	Your computer has responded that this port exists but is currently closed to connections.
389	LDAP	Closed	Your computer has responded that this port exists but is currently closed to connections.
443	HTTPS	Closed	Your computer has responded that this port exists but is currently closed to connections.
445	MSFT DS	Stealth	There is NO EVIDENCE WHATSOEVER that a port (or even any computer) exists at this IP address!
1002	ms-ils	Closed	Your computer has responded that this port exists but is currently closed to connections.
1024	DCOM	Closed	Your computer has responded that this port exists but is currently closed to connections.
1025	Host	OPEN!	One or more unspecified Distributed COM (DCOM) services are opened by Windows. The exact port(s) opened can change, since queries to port 135 are used to determine which services are operating where. As is the rule for all exposed Internet services, you should arrange to close this port to external access so that potential current and future security or privacy exploits can not succeed against your system.
1026	Host	Closed	Your computer has responded that this port exists but is currently closed to connections.
1027	Host	Closed	Your computer has responded that this port exists but is currently closed to connections.

Ports reported as closed or in stealth mode are safe from attack

Ports reported as open are subject to exploitation by hackers

Computer Threats: Computer Viruses

Keeping your computer safe entails keeping it safe from more than just hackers. You must also guard against computer viruses. A **computer virus** is a computer program that attaches itself to another computer program (known as the host program) and attempts to spread itself to other computers when files are exchanged. Viruses normally attempt to hide within the code of a host program to avoid detection.

What do computer viruses do? A computer virus's main purpose is to replicate itself and copy its code into as many other files as possible. Although virus replication can slow down networks, it is not usually the main threat. The majority of viruses have secondary objectives or side effects, ranging from displaying annoying messages on the computer screen to the destruction of files or the contents of entire hard drives. Because computer viruses do cause disruption to computer systems, including data destruction and information theft, virus creation is a form of cybercrime.

How does my computer catch a virus? If your computer is exposed to a file infected with a virus, the virus will try to copy itself and infect a file on your computer. If you never expose your computer to new files, it will not become infected. However, this would be the equivalent of a human being living in a bubble to avoid catching viruses from other people—quite unpractical, to say the least.

Sharing disks is a common source of virus infection, as is e-mail, although many people have misconceptions about how e-mail infection occurs. Just opening an e-mail message will not infect your computer with a virus. Downloading or running a file that is attached to the e-mail is how your computer becomes infected. Thus, be extremely wary of e-mail attachments, especially if you don't know the sender. Figure 7.28 shows how computer viruses are often passed from one computer to the next.

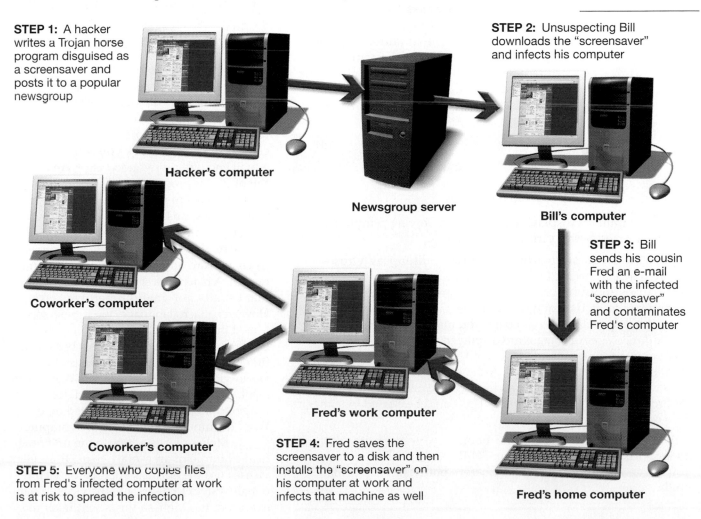

STEP 1: A hacker writes a Trojan horse program disguised as a screensaver and posts it to a popular newsgroup

Hacker's computer

Newsgroup server

STEP 2: Unsuspecting Bill downloads the "screensaver" and infects his computer

Bill's computer

STEP 3: Bill sends his cousin Fred an e-mail with the infected "screensaver" and contaminates Fred's computer

Coworker's computer

Coworker's computer

Fred's work computer

Fred's home computer

STEP 5: Everyone who copies files from Fred's infected computer at work is at risk to spread the infection

STEP 4: Fred saves the screensaver to a disk and then installs the "screensaver" on his computer at work and infects that machine as well

TYPES OF VIRUSES

What are the different kinds of viruses?
Although thousands of computer viruses and variants exist, they can be grouped into five broad categories based on their behavior and method of transmission.

Boot-Sector Viruses
What are boot-sector viruses? Boot-sector viruses replicate themselves into the Master Boot Record of a hard drive. The **Master Boot Record** is a program that executes whenever a computer boots up, ensuring that the virus will be loaded into memory immediately, even before some virus protection programs. Boot-sector viruses are often transmitted by a floppy disk left in a floppy drive. When the computer boots up with the disk in the drive, it tries to launch a Master Boot Record from the floppy, which is usually the trigger for the virus to infect the hard drive. Boot-sector viruses can be very destructive: they can erase your entire hard drive.

Logic Bombs
What are logic bombs? **Logic bombs** are viruses that execute when a certain set of conditions is met. The conditions are often specific dates keyed off of the computer's internal clock. The Michelangelo virus, first launched in 1992, is a famous logic bomb that is set to trigger every year on March 6,

Michelangelo's birthday. The effects of logic bombs range from annoying messages being displayed on the screen to reformatting of the hard drive, causing complete data loss.

Worms
What are worms? Worms are slightly different from viruses in that they attempt to travel between systems through network connections to spread their infections. Viruses infect a host file and wait for that file to be executed on another computer to replicate. Worms can run independently of host file execution and are much more active in spreading themselves. The Sasser worm broke out in April 2004, infecting millions of individual computers and servers. This worm exploits a weakness in the Windows operating system and therefore antivirus software doesn't protect against this worm. However, having a firewall installed and applying software patches as they are issued can protect you from most worms.

Script and Macro Viruses
What are script and macro viruses? Some viruses are hidden on Web sites in the form of **scripts**. Scripts are lists of commands, actually mini programs, that are executed without your knowledge. Scripts are often used to perform useful, legitimate functions on Web sites, such as collecting name and address information from customers. However, some scripts are malicious. For example, say you receive an e-mail encouraging you to visit a Web site full of useful programs and information. Unbeknownst to you, clicking a link to display a video runs a script that infects your computer with a virus.

Macro viruses are attached to documents (such as Word and Excel documents) that use macros. A **macro** is a short series of commands that usually automates repetitive tasks. However, macro languages are now so sophisticated that viruses can be written with them. In March 1999, the Melissa virus became the first major macro virus to cause problems worldwide. It attached itself to a Word document. Anyone opening an infected document triggered the virus, which infected other Word documents on the victim's computer.

The Melissa virus was also the first practical example of an **e-mail virus**. E-mail viruses use the address book in the victim's e-mail system to distribute the virus. When executed, the Melissa virus sent itself to

BITS AND BYTES

Virus Symptoms

If your computer is displaying any of the following symptoms, it may be infected with a virus:

1. Existing program icons or files suddenly disappear. Viruses often delete specific file types or programs.
2. Changes appear in your browser. If you fire up your browser and it takes you to an unusual home page (one you didn't set) or it has sprouted new toolbars, you may have a virus.
3. Odd messages or images are displayed on the screen or strange music or sounds play.
4. Data files become corrupted. Although there are many reasons why files become corrupt, a virus is one cause.
5. Programs don't work properly. This could be caused by either a corrupted file or a virus.

If you think you have a virus, boot up your computer with an antivirus software CD in your CD-ROM drive. This allows you to run the antivirus software before potential viruses load on the computer.

the first 50 people in the address book on the infected computer. This helped ensure that Melissa became one of the most widely distributed viruses ever released.

Trojan Horses

Are Trojan horses viruses? We discussed Trojan horses earlier in the chapter. Trojan horses, although not technically viruses, behave similarly to viruses and are detected by most antivirus programs. Trojan horses do something unintended to the victim's computer (such as recording keystrokes to gather passwords) while pretending to do something else (such as acting as a screen saver). Once executed, they perform their malicious duties in the background, often invisible to the user. Trojan horses are generally deployed by hackers in attempts to control remote computers.

VIRUS CLASSIFICATIONS

How else are viruses classified? Viruses can also be classified by the methods they take to avoid detection by antivirus software:

- **Polymorphic viruses** change their own code (or periodically rewrite themselves) to avoid detection. Most polymorphic viruses infect one certain type of file (.exe files, for example).

- **Multipartite viruses** are designed to infect multiple file types in an effort to fool the antivirus software that is looking for them.

- **Stealth viruses** temporarily erase their code from the files where they reside and hide in the active memory of the computer. This helps them avoid detection if only the hard drive is being searched for viruses. Fortunately, antivirus software developers are aware of these tricks and have designed software to watch for them.

Computer Safeguards: Antivirus Software

Certain viruses merely present minor annoyances, such as randomly sending an ambulance graphic across the bottom of the screen, as is the case with the Red Cross virus. Other viruses can significantly slow down a computer or network or destroy key files or the contents of entire hard drives.

The best defense against viruses is to install **antivirus software**, which is specifically designed to detect viruses and protect your computer and files from harm.

How often do I need to run antivirus software? You should run a virus check on your entire system at least once a week. By doing so, all files on your computer are checked for undetected viruses. Because these checks take time, you can configure the software to run these checks automatically when you aren't using your system, such as late at night (see Figure 7.29).

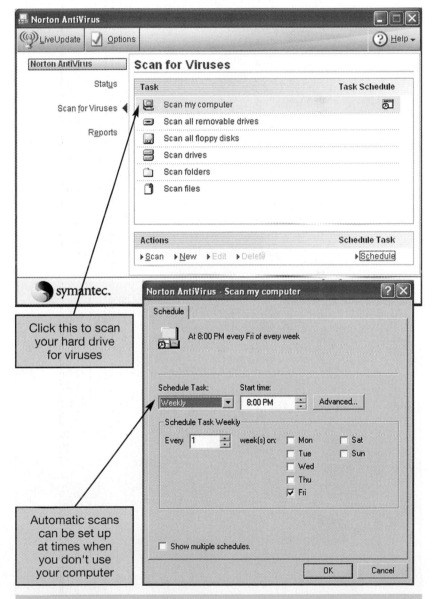

Click this to scan your hard drive for viruses

Automatic scans can be set up at times when you don't use your computer

FIGURE 7.29

Through the Schedule Task option (found in the lower right-hand corner of the Scan for Viruses option screen), a complete virus scan will be performed on this computer every Friday night at 8:00 p.m.

How does antivirus software work?

Most antivirus software looks for **virus signatures** in files. Signatures are portions of the virus code that are unique to a particular computer virus. Antivirus software scans files for these signatures and thereby identifies infected files and the type of virus that is infecting them.

The antivirus software scans files when they're opened or executed. If it detects a virus signature or suspicious activity (such as launching an unknown macro), it stops the execution of the file and virus and notifies you it has detected a virus. Usually it gives you the choice of deleting or repairing the infected file. Unfortunately, antivirus programs can't always fix infected files so that the files are usable again. You should keep backup copies of critical files so you can restore them in case a virus damages them irreparably.

Does antivirus software always stop viruses?

Antivirus software catches *known* viruses effectively. Unfortunately, new viruses are written all the time. To combat unknown viruses, modern antivirus programs search for suspicious virus-like activities as well as virus signatures. However, virus authors know how antivirus software works. They take special measures to disguise their virus code and hide the effects

SOUND BYTE

PROTECTING YOUR COMPUTER

In this Sound Byte, you'll learn how to use a variety of tools to protect your computer, including antivirus software and Windows utilities.

of a virus until just the right moment. This helps ensure the virus spreads faster and farther. Thus, your computer can still be attacked by a virus that your antivirus software doesn't recognize. To minimize this risk, you should keep your antivirus software up-to-date.

How do I make sure my antivirus software is up-to-date?

Most antivirus programs have an automatic updates feature that downloads a list of upgrades you can install on your computer while you're online (see Figure 7.30). Automatic updates ensure your programs are up-to-date.

What should I do if I think my computer is infected with a virus?

Boot up your computer with the antivirus CD that came with your antivirus software in your CD drive. This should prevent most virus programs from loading and will allow you to run the antivirus directly from the CD drive. If viruses are detected, you may want to research them further to determine whether your antivirus software will eradicate them completely or if you need to take additional manual steps to eliminate the virus. Most antivirus company Web sites (such as **www.symantec.com**) contain archives of information on viruses and provide step-by-step solutions for removing viruses.

OTHER SECURITY MEASURES

Is there anything else I should do to protect my system?

Many viruses exploit weaknesses in operating systems. To combat these threats, make sure your operating system is up-to-date and contains the latest security patches (or fixes). Windows XP makes this easy by providing automatic updates. When you enable automatic updates, your computer searches for Windows updates on the Microsoft Web site every time it connects to the Internet.

How do I enable automatic updates?

To enable automatic updates,

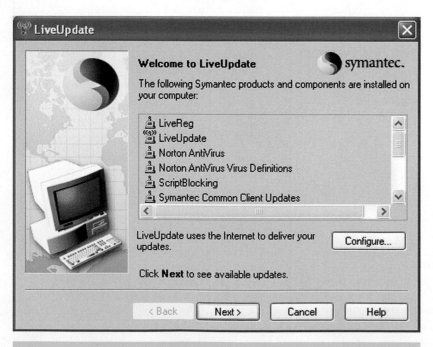

FIGURE 7.30

Norton's LiveUpdate provides automatic updates on all virus and security products installed on the computer.

click the Start button, select Control Panel, and double-click the System icon. Select the Automatic Updates tab, as shown in Figure 7.31. Select the Keep my computer up to date check box, and select one of the three options in the Settings section. The first option notifies you before downloading and installing updates. Choose this option if you have a dial-up connection to the Internet because it allows you to decide when your Internet connection will be tied up performing down-loads. The second option downloads the updates automatically but notifies you when they're ready to be installed. The third option downloads and installs updates without asking you for permission.

For more information on how you can protect your computer, see the Technology in Focus feature "Protecting Your Computer and Backing Up Your Data."

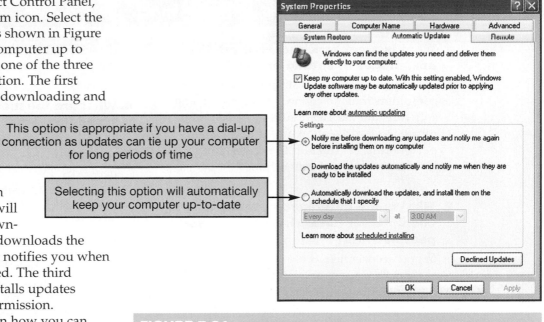

FIGURE 7.31

The Windows XP Automatic Updates screen makes it easy for users to configure Windows to update itself.

TRENDS IN IT

CAREERS:
Cybercops on the Beat: Computer Security Careers

With billions being spent on e-commerce initiatives every year, companies have a vested interest in keeping their Information Technology (IT) infrastructures humming along. The rise in terrorism has shifted the focus slightly from protecting just virtual assets and access to protecting physical assets and access points as well. The increased need for virtual and physical security measures means there should be a robust job market ahead for computer security experts.

What skill sets will be most in demand for security professionals? Obviously, strong technical skills with an emphasis on network engineering and data communications are essential. Security certifications certainly provide evidence of appropriate training and skills mastery. However, just as necessary are broad-based business experience and skills. IT security professionals need to understand the key issues of e-commerce and the core areas of their company's business (such as marketing, sales, and finance). Understanding how a business works is essential to pinpointing and correcting the security risks that could be detrimental to a company's bottom line. And because of the large number of attacks by hackers, security forensic skills and

certifications are in high demand. Working closely with law enforcement officials is essential to rapidly solving and stopping cybercrime.

Another important attribute of security professionals is the ability to lead and motivate teams. Security experts need to work with diverse members of the business community, including customers, to forge relationships and understanding among diverse groups. Security professionals must conduct skillful negotiations to ensure that large project implementations are not unduly delayed by security initiatives, or pushed through with inadequate security precautions. Diplomacy is therefore a sought-after skill.

Look for more colleges and universities to roll out security-based degrees and certificate programs as the demand for security professionals increases. These programs will most likely be appropriate for experienced networking professionals who are ready to make the move into the IT security field. If you're just preparing for a career, consider a degree in network engineering, followed by network security training while you're working at your first job. This should ensure a smooth transition into the exciting world of cybersecurity.

Summary

1. What is a network and what are the advantages of setting up one?

A computer network is simply two or more computers that are connected together using software and hardware so they can communicate. Networks allow users to (1) share peripherals, (2) transfer files easily, and (3) share an Internet connection.

2. What is the difference between a client/server network and a peer-to-peer network?

In peer-to-peer networks, each node connected to the network can communicate directly with every other node instead of having a separate device exercise central control over the network. Peer-to-peer networks are the most common type of network installed in homes. Most networks that have 10 or more nodes are client/server networks. A client/server network contains two types of computers: a client computer on which users accomplish specific tasks, and a server computer that provides resources to the clients and central control for the network.

3. What are the main components of every network?

To function, all networks contain four components: (1) transmission media (cables or radio waves) to connect and establish communication between nodes; (2) network adapters that allow the nodes on the network to communicate; (3) network navigation devices (such as routers and hubs) that move data around the network; and (4) software that allows the network to run.

4. What are the most common home networks?

The four most common home networks are power line, phoneline, Ethernet, and wireless networks. The major difference in these networks is the transmission media by which the nodes are connected.

5. What are power line networks and how are they created?

Power line networks use the electrical wiring in your home to connect the nodes in the network. To create a power line network, you connect power line network adapters to each node on the network. These adapters are then plugged into an electrical outlet, and data is transmitted through the electrical wires. Power line networks have a maximum data transfer rate of 14 Mbps.

6. What are phoneline networks and how are they created?

Phoneline networks move data through the network using conventional phone lines. To create a phoneline network, you connect phoneline network adapters to each node on the network. These adapters are then connected to phone line wall jacks with standard phone cord, and the phone line sends the data to and from the network nodes. Phoneline networks have a maximum data transfer rate of 10 Mbps.

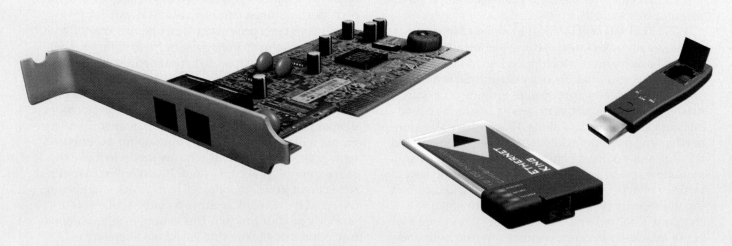

Materials on the Web

In addition to the review materials presented here, you'll find extra materials on the book's companion Web site (**www.prenhall.com/techinaction**) that will help reinforce your understanding of the chapter content. These materials include the following:

Sound Byte Lab Guides

For each Sound Byte mentioned in the chapter, there is a corresponding lab guide located on the book's companion Web site. These guides review the material presented in the Sound Byte and direct you to various Web resources that examine the material. The Sound Byte Lab Guides for this chapter include these:

- Installing a Network
- Securing Wireless Networks
- Installing a Personal Firewall
- Protecting Your Computer

True/False and Multiple-Choice Quizzes

The book's Web site includes a true/false and a multiple-choice quiz for this chapter. You can take these quizzes, automatically check the results, and e-mail the results to your instructor.

Web Research Projects

The book's Web site also includes a number of Web research projects for this chapter. These projects ask you to search the Web for information on computer-related careers, milestones in computer history, important people and companies, emerging technologies, and the applications and implications of different technologies.

Technology in Action also features unique interactive Help Desk training, in which you'll assume the role of Help Desk operator taking calls about concepts learned in each chapter. The Help Desk calls for this chapter include:

- Understanding Networking
- Understanding Firewalls
- Avoiding Computer Viruses

PROTECTING YOUR COMPUTER AND BACKING UP YOUR DATA

Just like any other valuable asset, computers and the data they contain require protection from damage, thieves, and unauthorized users. Although it's impossible to protect your computer and data completely, following the suggestions outlined in this Technology in Focus will provide you with peace of mind that you have done all you can to protect your computer from theft and keep it in working order.

PHYSICALLY PROTECTING YOUR COMPUTER

Your computer obviously isn't useful to you if it is damaged. Therefore, it's essential to select and ensure a safe environment for your computer. This includes protecting it from environmental factors, power surges, and power outages.

Environmental Factors

There are a number of environmental factors you need to consider to protect your computer.

1 Sudden movements (such as a fall) can damage your computer or mobile device's internal components, causing them to operate erratically. Therefore, take special care in setting up your computer. Make sure that the computer sits on a flat, level surface, and carry your laptop in a padded case to protect it should you drop it. If you do drop your computer or laptop, have it professionally tested by a computer repair facility to uncover any hidden damage.

2 Electronic components do not like excessive heat. Unfortunately, computers generate a lot of heat. This is why they contain a fan to cool their internal components. Make sure that you place your computer so that the fan's input vents (usually found on the rear of the system unit) are unblocked so that air can flow inside. Naturally, a fan drawing air into a computer also draws in dust and other particles, which can wreak havoc on your system. Therefore, keep the room in which your computer is located as clean as possible. Placing your computer in the workshop where you do woodworking and generate sawdust would obviously be a poor choice!

3 Because food crumbs and liquid can damage keyboards and other computer components, consume food and beverages far away from your computer to avoid food-related damage.

Power Surges

Power surges occur when electrical current is supplied in excess of normal voltage (120 volts in the United States). Old or faulty wiring, downed power lines, malfunctions at electric company substations, and lightning strikes can all cause power surges. **Surge protectors** are devices that protect your computer against power surges (see Figure 1). To use a surge protector, you simply plug all your electrical devices into the outlets of the surge protector, which in turn plugs into the wall.

FIGURE 1
How Surge Protectors Work

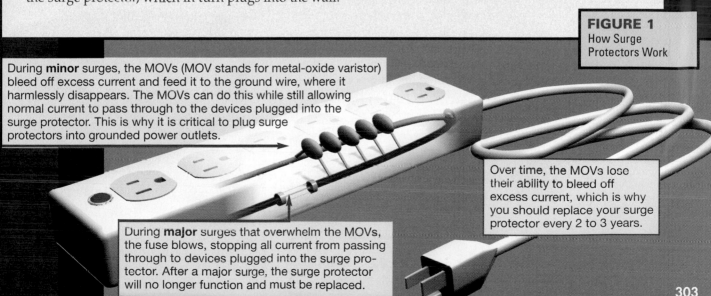

During **minor** surges, the MOVs (MOV stands for metal-oxide varistor) bleed off excess current and feed it to the ground wire, where it harmlessly disappears. The MOVs can do this while still allowing normal current to pass through to the devices plugged into the surge protector. This is why it is critical to plug surge protectors into grounded power outlets.

During **major** surges that overwhelm the MOVs, the fuse blows, stopping all current from passing through to devices plugged into the surge protector. After a major surge, the surge protector will no longer function and must be replaced.

Over time, the MOVs lose their ability to bleed off excess current, which is why you should replace your surge protector every 2 to 3 years.

Surge protectors wear out over time (usually in less than five years), so buy a surge protector that includes indicator lights. Indicator lights illuminate when the surge protector is no longer functioning properly, letting you know you need to replace it. Note that old surge protectors can still function as multiple-outlet power strips, delivering power to your equipment without protecting it. A power surge could ruin your computer and other devices if you don't protect them. Thus, at around $20, a surge protector is an excellent investment.

It's important to protect *all* your electronic devices, not just computers, from surges. TVs, printers, and other computer peripherals all require protection. However, it can be expensive to use individual surge protectors on everything. A more practical method is to install a **whole-house surge protector**, shown in Figure 2. Whole-house surge protectors function like other surge protectors but they protect all electrical devices in the house. Electricians usually install whole-house surge protectors, which cost $200 to $300 installed.

Data lines (transmission media), such as the coaxial cable or phone wires that attach to your modem, can also carry surges. Installing a **data line surge suppressor** for each data line connected to your computer through another device (such as a modem) provides you with additional protection (see Figure 3). A data line surge suppressor is connected to the data line at a point before it reaches the modem

or other device. In this way, it intercepts surges on the data line before they reach sensitive equipment.

Surge protectors won't necessarily guard against all surges. Lightning strikes can generate such high amounts of voltage that they can overwhelm a surge protector. As tedious as it sounds, unplugging computers and peripherals during an electrical storm is the only way to achieve absolute protection.

Power Outages

Like power surges, power outages can wreak havoc on a system. Mission-critical computers such as Web servers are often protected by **uninterruptible power supplies (UPSs)**, shown in Figure 4. A UPS is a device that contains surge protection equipment and a large battery. When power is interrupted (such as during a blackout), the UPS continues to send power to the attached computer from its battery. Depending on the battery capacity, you have between about 20 minutes and 3 hours to save your work and shut down your computer properly.

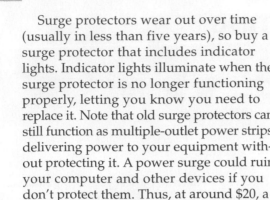

FIGURE 2
A whole-house surge protector is usually installed at the breaker panel or near the electric meter. It protects all appliances in the home from electrical surges.

Surge protector

SOUND BYTE
SURGE PROTECTORS

In this Sound Byte, you'll learn about the major features of surge protectors and how they work. You'll also learn about the key factors you need to consider before buying a surge protector, and you'll see how easy it is to install one.

FIGURE 3
APC, a large manufacturer of surge protection devices, makes a wide range of data line surge suppressors to accommodate almost any type of data line.

FIGURE 4
UPS devices contain a large battery that kicks in during power outages. If your computer is plugged into such a device, you'll have time to save your work before losing power.

DETERRING THEFT

Because they are portable, laptops and personal digital assistants (PDAs) are easy targets for thieves. Common sense dictates that you don't leave your laptop or PDA unattended or in places where it can be easily stolen. Three additional approaches to deterring computer theft include alarming them, locking them down, or allowing the devices to tell you when they are stolen.

FIGURE 5
A laptop alarm sends out an ear-piercing sound if your laptop is moved before you deactivate the alarm.

Alarms

To prevent your laptop from being stolen, you can attach a motion alarm to it, shown in Figure 5. When you leave your laptop, you use a small device called a "key fob activator" to activate the alarm. If your laptop is moved while the alarm is activated, it emits a wailing 85-decibel sound. The fact that the alarm is visible acts as an additional theft deterrent, just like a "beware of dog" sign in a front yard.

Locks and Surrounds

Chaining a laptop to your work surface can be an effective way to prevent theft. As shown in Figure 6, a special locking mechanism is attached to the laptop (some laptops are even manufactured with locking ports), and a hardened steel cable is connected to the locking mechanism. The other end of the cable is looped around something large and heavy, such as a desk. The cable lock obviously requires that you use a key to free the laptop from its mooring.

FIGURE 6
Cable locks are an effective deterrent to theft. New models have combination locks that alleviate keeping track of your keys.

Many people associate computer theft only with laptops or PDAs. But desktop computers are vulnerable to theft also, especially theft of internal components such as random access memory (RAM). Cable locks are available that connect through special fasteners on the back of desktop computers, but components can still be stolen because these cables often don't prevent the system unit case from being opened. A more effective theft deterrent for desktops is a **surround** (or **cage**), shown in Figure 7. A surround is a metal box that encloses the system unit and makes it impossible to remove the case, while still allowing access to ports and devices such as CD players.

FIGURE 7
Computer surrounds deter theft by making access to the internal components of the computer difficult while still allowing access to ports and drives.

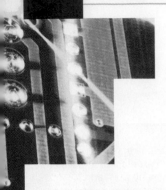

Computers that "Phone Home"

You've probably heard of LoJack, the popular theft-tracking device used in cars. Car owners install a LoJack transmitter somewhere in their vehicle. Then, if the vehicle is stolen, police activate the transmitter and use its signal to locate the car. Similar systems now exist for computers. Tracking software, such as Computrace (**www.computrace.com**) and zTrace Gold (**www.ztrace.com**), enables the computer it is installed on to alert authorities as to its location if it is stolen.

To use this computer version of LoJack, you install the tracking software on your computer's hard drive. Once you install the software, it contacts a server at the software manufacturer's Web site each time you connect to the Internet. If your computer is stolen, you notify the software manufacturer, who then instructs your computer to transmit tracking information (such as an Internet Protocol, or IP, address) that will assist authorities in locating and retrieving the stolen computer.

The files and directories holding the software are not visible to thieves looking for such software. What if the thieves reformat the hard drive in an attempt to destroy all files on the computer? The tracking software is written in such a way that it detects a reformat and hides the software code in a safe place in memory or on the hard drive (some sectors of a hard drive are not rewritten during most formats). That way, it can reinstall itself after the reformatting is completed.

PROTECTING YOUR COMPUTER FROM UNAUTHORIZED ACCESS

To protect yourself even further, you may want to restrict access to the sensitive data on your computer. Both software and hardware solutions exist to restrict others from accessing your computer, helping you keep its content safe.

Password Protection and Access Privileges

Windows XP has built-in password protection of files as well as the entire desktop. If your computer has been set up for multiple users with password protection, the Windows logon screen requires users to enter a password to gain access to the desktop. The computer can be set to default back to the Welcome screen after it is idle for a set period of time. This forces users to reenter a password to regain access to the computer. If someone attempts to log on to your computer without your password, that person won't be able to gain access.

Setting up a password also forces users to decide whether to share their files with other users. Figure 8 shows the dialog box that appears in Windows XP asking you to make this choice when you set up a user account password. Files not shared remain safe from the prying eyes of other users unless they know your password.

FIGURE 8
This dialog box appears whenever a password is assigned to a user account in Windows XP. Selecting Yes, Make Private ensures that other users can't access your files.

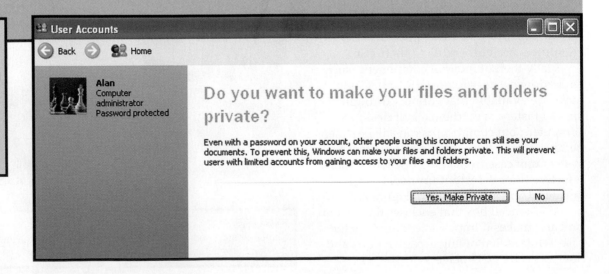

Of course, password protection works only as well as your password does. Creating a secure password is therefore very important. To do so, follow the basic guidelines shown here:

- Your password should be five to eight characters long and contain both numbers and letters.

- Your password should not be a word found in the dictionary.

- Your password should not be easily associated with you (such as your birth date, the name of your pet, or your nickname).

- Secure passwords take the first letters of a group of unrelated words or words in a particular phrase. It is also good to insert special characters such as the ampersand sign (&) or dollar sign ($) in your password.

- You should never tell anyone your password or write it down in a place where others might see it.

- You should change your password if you think someone may know it.

Figure 9 shows some possible passwords and explains why they make good or bad candidates.

PDA Bomb Software

PDAs can be vulnerable to unauthorized access if they are left unattended or are stolen. **PDA bomb software** features data and password protection for your PDA in an attempt to combat this problem. If you have PDA bomb software, a thief who steals your PDA is forced to crack your password to gain access. When a thief launches a brute force attack (repetitive tries to guess a password) on the PDA, the software's bomb feature kicks in after a certain number of failed password attempts. The "bomb" erases all data contained on the PDA, thereby protecting your sensitive information. PDA Defense, found at **www.pdadefense.com**, is a popular example of PDA bomb software.

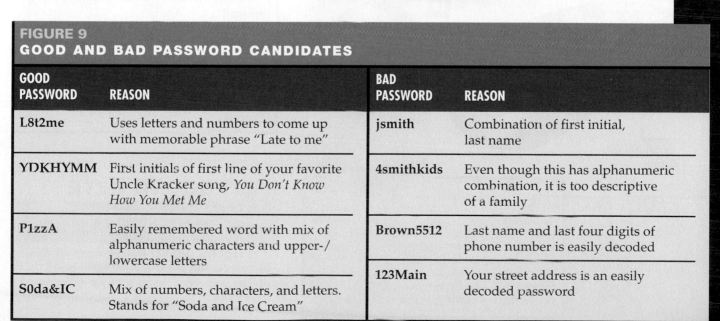

ARE KLINGONESE PASSWORDS SAFE?

Many computer users are diehard science fiction fans. Growing up watching *Star Trek*, *Babylon 5*, and *Battlestar Galactica* has provided computer users with loads of planet names, alien races, alien vocabulary (Klingon words from the Star Trek series are very popular), and starship names to use as passwords. Unfortunately, hackers are on to this ploy. Recently developed hacking programs use dictionaries of "geek-speak" to attempt to break passwords. Although "Qapla" (Klingonese for "success" and also used as "goodbye") might seem like an unbreakable password, don't bet your data on it!

FIGURE 9
GOOD AND BAD PASSWORD CANDIDATES

GOOD PASSWORD	REASON	BAD PASSWORD	REASON
L8t2me	Uses letters and numbers to come up with memorable phrase "Late to me"	jsmith	Combination of first initial, last name
YDKHYMM	First initials of first line of your favorite Uncle Kracker song, *You Don't Know How You Met Me*	4smithkids	Even though this has alphanumeric combination, it is too descriptive of a family
P1zzA	Easily remembered word with mix of alphanumeric characters and upper-/lowercase letters	Brown5512	Last name and last four digits of phone number is easily decoded
S0da&IC	Mix of numbers, characters, and letters. Stands for "Soda and Ice Cream"	123Main	Your street address is an easily decoded password

Biometric Authentication Devices

Biometric authentication devices are devices you can attach to your computer or PDA that read a unique personal characteristic, such as a fingerprint or the iris pattern in your eye, and convert that pattern to a digital code. When you use the biometric device, your pattern is read and compared to the pattern stored on the computer. Only users having an exact fingerprint or iris pattern match are allowed to access the computer.

Because no two people have the same biometric characteristics (fingerprints and iris patterns are unique), these devices provide a high level of security. They also eliminate the human error that can occur in password protection. You might forget your password, but you won't forget to bring your fingerprint to the computer! Some newer PDAs feature built-in fingerprint readers and Figure 10a shows a mouse that includes a fingerprint reader. An even more useful device is the APC Biometric Password Manager (shown in Figure 10b), which after it identifies you by your fingerprint, provides logon information to password-protected Web sites you need to access. Other biometric devices include voice authentication and face pattern recognition systems, but these are usually not cost effective for home use.

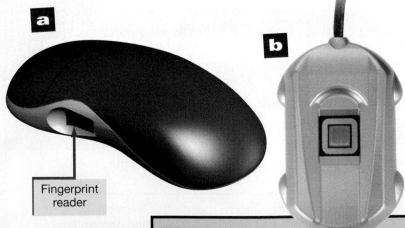

Fingerprint reader

FIGURE 10
(a) The BioLink U-Match Mouse is a conventional two-button mouse that includes a digital fingerprint reader. (b) The APC Biometric Password Manager shown here uses a fingerprint reader to recognize authorized users. The device stores all your logon names and passwords so you don't have to keep track of them. Up to 20 users can use the same device, making it perfect for shared computers.

Firewalls

As we noted in Chapter 7, unauthorized access often occurs when your computer is connected to the Internet. You can best prevent such cases of unauthorized access by using either hardware or software **personal firewalls**. Hardware firewalls are often built into a router. Figure 11 lists popular software firewall programs. Setting up either a hardware or software firewall should adequately protect you from unauthorized access related to being connected to the Internet.

DEALING WITH ONLINE ANNOYANCES

As you learned in Chapter 7, **computer viruses** can damage files and data on your computer. This type of destruction obviously impacts your productivity. As we noted in Chapter 7, you can eliminate this threat fairly easily by installing **antivirus software**, such as Norton AntiVirus or McAfee VirusScan. However, other problems can affect your ability to complete your work

FIGURE 11
POPULAR PERSONAL FIREWALL SOFTWARE

FIREWALL	URL
Norton Personal Firewall	**www.norton.com**
McAfee Firewall	**www.mcafee.com**
Zone Alarm	**www.zonelabs.com**
BlackICE PC Protection	**http://blackice.iss.net**

SOUND BYTE
SECURING WIRELESS NETWORKS

In this Sound Byte, you'll learn what "war drivers" are and why they could potentially be a threat to your wireless network. You'll also learn simple steps to take to secure your wireless network against intruders.

and can violate your privacy. In this section, we discuss how to deal with such problems as spam, pop-ups, and spyware.

Spam

As we noted in Chapter 3, **spam** is unwanted e-mail that is sent out by companies in an attempt to solicit business. Although not damaging to your computer, it can be annoying as your inbox fills up with useless messages. It was recently estimated that 60 percent of e-mail is now spam. That's a lot of junk mail!

Most Internet-based mail services, such as Yahoo! Mail, offer **spam filters** that filter spam out of your e-mail (see Figure 12). A spam filter is an option you can select in your e-mail account that places known spam messages into a folder other than your inbox. Outlook 2003 features a spam filter, but what if you are still using previous version of Outlook to manage your e-mail? Then you need to obtain **spam filtering**

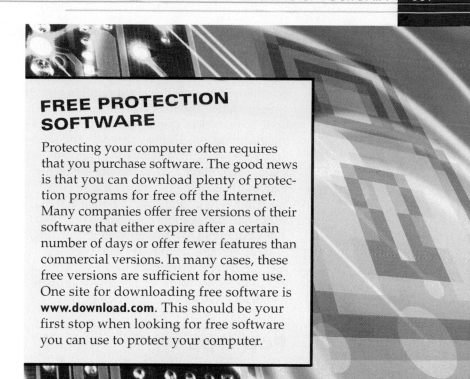

FREE PROTECTION SOFTWARE

Protecting your computer often requires that you purchase software. The good news is that you can download plenty of protection programs for free off the Internet. Many companies offer free versions of their software that either expire after a certain number of days or offer fewer features than commercial versions. In many cases, these free versions are sufficient for home use. One site for downloading free software is **www.download.com**. This should be your first stop when looking for free software you can use to protect your computer.

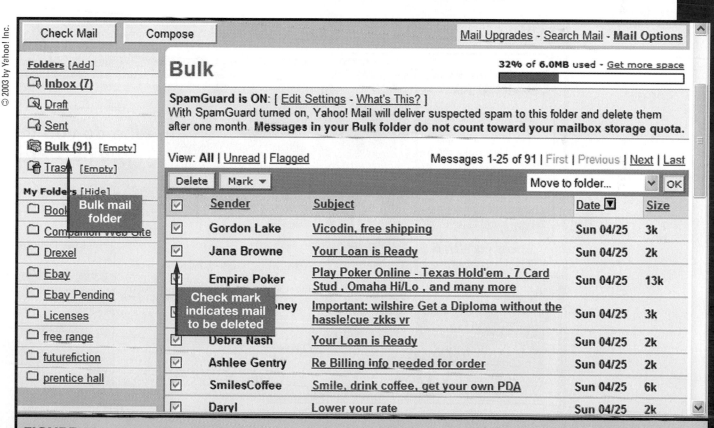

FIGURE 12

In Yahoo! Mail, turning on the SpamGuard feature alerts the Yahoo! Mail server to screen your incoming mail for obvious or suspected spam. This mail is then directed into a folder called "Bulk" where you can review the mail (to ensure it is really spam) and delete it. Click the check box next to the mail to flag it for deletion, or click the check box next to the word *Sender* at the top of the mail list to flag all the messages shown on the screen. Or just click the "Empty" link (next to the Bulk mail folder) and dump all the spam at once!

software and install it on your computer. Programs that provide you with some control over spam include MailWasher Pro, Spam Alarm, and SpamButcher, all of which can be obtained at **www.download.com**.

Spam filters and filtering software can catch up to 95 percent of spam. They work by checking incoming e-mail subject headers and sending addresses against databases of known spam. Spam filters also check your e-mail for frequently used spam patterns and keywords (such as "Viagra" and "free"). E-mail that the filter identifies as spam does not go into your inbox but rather to a folder called Spam, Junk, or Bulk. Because spam filters aren't perfect, you should check the Spam folder rather than just deleting its contents, because legitimate e-mail might occasionally end up there.

Pop-Ups

Pop-up windows are the unsightly billboards of the Internet (see Figure 13). These windows pop up when you enter Web sites, sporting

"useful" information or touting products. Although some sites use pop-ups to increase the functionality of their site (your account balance may pop up at your bank's Web site, for example), most pop-ups are just plain annoying.

To stop pop-ups from appearing, you need **anti-pop-up software**. Two free anti-pop-up programs are Pop-Up Stopper and Pop-Up Defender, both of which are available at **www.download.com**. When a site attempts to launch a pop-up, these programs either prevent it from being launched or close it immediately. The software also includes options that enable you to allow pop-ups that you do want to appear.

Spyware

If you ever install software from a Web site, you may be installing something on your computer together with the software. Called **spyware** (or **adware**), these unwanted piggy-back programs run in the background of

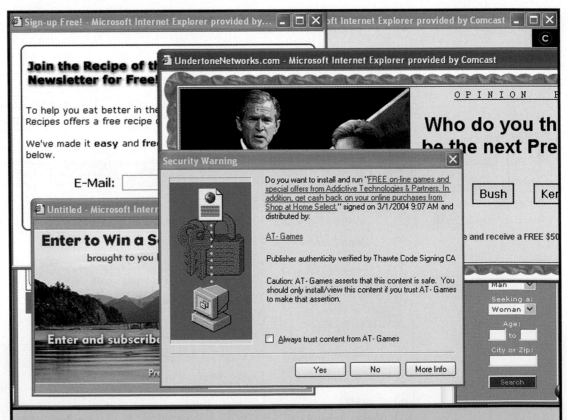

FIGURE 13
Although pop-ups are often used for useful purposes (such as displaying your address book in Yahoo! Mail), unwanted pop-ups can easily obliterate the Web page you are trying to view. Most worrisome are the pop-ups that try to get you to install software on your computer such as the one shown in the middle of this screen. You may wish to install anti-pop-up software on your computer to thwart their appearance altogether.

your system and gather information about you, usually your Internet surfing habits, without your knowledge. They then periodically transmit this information to the owner of the spyware program so that the information can be used for marketing purposes.

Many spyware programs use **cookies** to collect information. As you learned in Chapter 3, cookies are small pieces of text that are stored on your hard drive that have many legitimate uses. For instance, when you customize the look and feel of a Web site such as Amazon.com, that customization information is stored in a cookie file on your hard drive. However, cookies can also be used to help spyware track your movements.

Most antivirus software doesn't detect spyware or prevent spyware cookies from being placed on your hard drive. However, you can obtain **spyware removal software**

and run it on your computer to delete unwanted spyware. Because new spyware is created all the time, you should update your spyware removal software regularly. Ad-aware (which is available for free at **www.download.com**) and PestPatrol (available at **www.pestpatrol.com**) are programs that are easy to install and update. Figure 14 shows an example of PestPatrol in action.

BACKING UP YOUR DATA

The data on your computer faces three major threats: unauthorized access, tampering, and destruction. As we noted in Chapter 7, a hacker can gain access to your computer and steal or alter your data. However, a more likely scenario is that you will lose

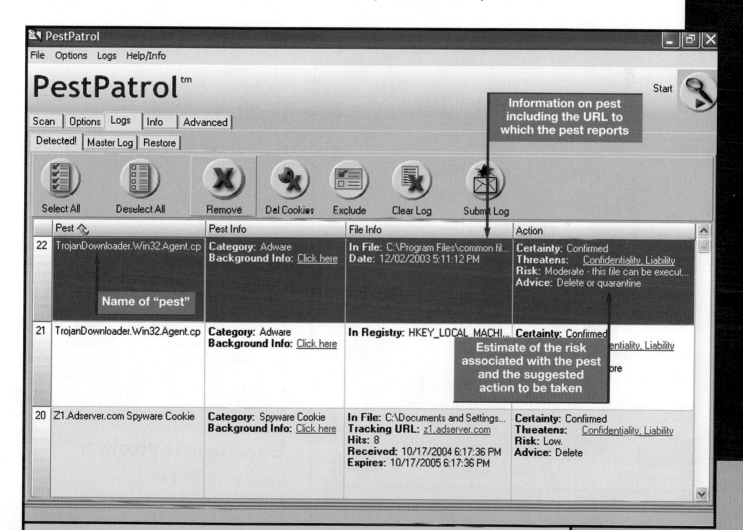

FIGURE 14
A PestPatrol log screen showing pests detected on a computer after a routine scan. PestPatrol allows you to easily detect and delete unwanted "pests" from your computer.

your data unintentionally. You may accidentally delete files; your hard drive may break down, resulting in complete data loss; a virus may destroy your original file; or a fire may destroy the room that houses your computer. Because many of these factors are beyond your control, you should have a strategy for backing up your files.

A file **backup** is merely a copy of that file that you can use to replace the original if it is lost or damaged. When you make a backup of your files, it's important that you store the copy in a different place than the original. Having two copies of the same file on the same hard drive does you little good when the hard drive breaks down. Likewise, storing your backup copies in the same room as your computer would not work well if there were a fire in the room. Removable storage media such as Zip disks, DVDs, CDs, and universal serial bus (USB) drives

are popular choices for backing up files because they hold a lot of data and can be easily transported.

Two types of files need backups, program files and data files:

- **Program files** are those files you use to install software. They should be on the CDs or DVDs that they originally came on. If any programs came preinstalled in your computer, you should still have received a CD or DVD that contains them. As long as you have the original media in a safe place, you shouldn't need to back up these files.

- **Data files** are those files you create (such as spreadsheets, letters, and so on), as well as contact lists, address books, e-mail archives, and your Favorites list from your browser.

You should back up your files (especially important ones) frequently, depending on how much work you can afford to lose. You should always back up data files when you make changes to them, especially if those changes involve hours of work. It may not seem important to back up your history term paper file when you finish it, but do you really want to do all that work again if your computer crashes before you have a chance to turn your paper in?

To make backups easier, store all your data files in one folder on your hard drive. For example, you can create a folder on your hard drive called Data Files. You can then create subfolders (such as History Homework, Music Files, and so on) within the Data Files folder. If you store all your data files in one place, to back up your files, you simply copy the Data Files folder and all of its subfolders onto an alternate storage media. If you have a DVD/CD-RW drive in your computer, open Windows Explorer (as shown in Figure 15) and right-click the Data Files folder. You can then copy the contents of the folder to the appropriate media.

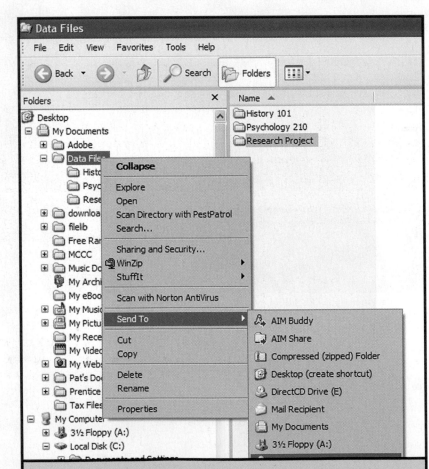

FIGURE 15
All of the data files on this computer are located in subfolders under the main Data Files folder. Right-clicking the Data Files folder brings up a menu that allows the user to send (or copy) the files to the CD-RW drive installed on this computer. Assuming a blank CD was inserted in the drive, this creates a backup CD containing a copy of all the data files.

Backup Software

Of course, the backup method described earlier assumes that you will take the initiative to back up your files on a regular basis. However, many people forget to do so, and only learn when it's too late that they should have been performing a systematic backup routine. The good news is that

backup software, such as Norton Ghost, allows you to schedule regular backups that occur automatically, with no intervention on your part. These products can back up individual files, folders, or an entire hard drive to another hard drive, such as an external drive connected to your computer by a USB port.

Backing up your entire hard drive greatly speeds up the recovery process should you experience a hard drive failure. With a backup of your entire hard drive, you won't need to reinstall all of the program software from the original CDs. Instead, you just replace the broken hard drive with the backup hard drive (or copy the entire contents of the backup drive to a new drive). This can save you time and may be worth the expense of an additional hard drive.

Online Backups

A final backup solution is to store backups of your files online. For a fee, companies such as NetMass (**www.systemrestore.com**) can provide you with such online storage. If you store a backup of your entire system on the Internet, you don't need to buy an additional hard drive for backups. This method also takes the worry out of keeping your backups in a safe place because they're always stored in an area far away from your computer (such as on the NetMass sever). However, if you would like to store your backups online, make sure you have high-speed Internet access such as cable or DSL; otherwise, your computer could be tied up as you transfer files.

ADDITIONAL RESOURCES

Hackers, spammers, and advertisers are constantly developing new methods for circumventing the protection that security software provides. Although the manufacturers of such software are constantly updating and improving it, you should keep abreast of new techniques being employed that could threaten your privacy and security. *SC Magazine* is a security magazine available in a free online version at **www.scmagazine.com**. Take a few minutes each month and scan the articles to make sure you have taken the appropriate protective measures on your computer to keep it safe and secure.

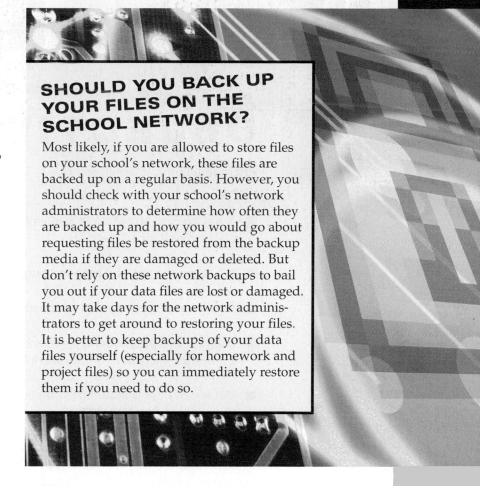

SHOULD YOU BACK UP YOUR FILES ON THE SCHOOL NETWORK?

Most likely, if you are allowed to store files on your school's network, these files are backed up on a regular basis. However, you should check with your school's network administrators to determine how often they are backed up and how you would go about requesting files be restored from the backup media if they are damaged or deleted. But don't rely on these network backups to bail you out if your data files are lost or damaged. It may take days for the network administrators to get around to restoring your files. It is better to keep backups of your data files yourself (especially for homework and project files) so you can immediately restore them if you need to do so.

SOUND BYTE
PROTECTING YOUR COMPUTER

In this Sound Byte, you'll learn how to use a variety of tools to protect your computer, including antivirus software and Windows utilities.

OBJECTIVES

After reading this chapter, you should be able to answer the following questions:

■ What are the advantages and limitations of mobile computing? (pp. 316–317)

■ What are the various mobile computing devices? (p. 318)

■ What can pagers do and who uses them? (pp. 318–319)

■ How do cell phone components resemble a traditional computer and how do they work? (pp. 319–322)

■ What can I carry in an MP3 player and how does it store data? (pp. 323–327)

■ What can I use a PDA for and what internal components and features does it have? (pp. 327–333)

■ How can I synchronize my PDA with my desktop computer? (p. 331)

■ What is a tablet PC and why would I want to use one? (pp. 333–337)

■ How powerful are laptops and how do they compare to desktop computers? (pp. 338–342)

SOUND BYTES

• Connecting with Bluetooth (p. 320)
• PDA on the Road and at Home (p. 332)
• Tablet and Laptop Tour (p. 341)

Mobile Computing:
Keeping Your Data on Hand

TECHNOLOGY IN ACTION:
USING MOBILE COMPUTING DEVICES

Kendra wakes up at 5:00 A.M. to get an early start to what will be a long day. She's taking a business trip for her new job, and it's a long flight from Boston to Los Angeles. She has packed her cell phone, her laptop, and her personal digital assistant (PDA) and has updated her contact information for all her LA contacts. Despite her preparation, when she arrives at the airport terminal, she finds her flight has been canceled. Trying not to get upset, she pulls out her PDA, accesses her wireless Internet account, and quickly rebooks a ticket on a competing airline while fellow passengers are racing off to the ticket counter. With an e-mail to her LA hotel and her business contacts there letting them know she'll be late, she smoothes the first wrinkle in her trip.

As Kendra waits for her new flight, she checks her work schedule on her PDA and e-mails a few of her clients. Because she'll be driving from the airport to the hotel on unfamiliar streets, she has purchased map software for her PDA that shows her the best route. She calls the rental car agency on her cell phone and tells them she'll be picking up the car later than planned, then checks out some of the LA restaurant reviews she found on the Internet the night before. With an hour left before her plane takes off, she does some work for the office on her laptop. She updates her expense report file, including the new flight information. Although canceled flights are never convenient, at least she's had a few hours to take care of some work before arriving in LA.

As this scenario indicates, mobile devices can offer you a great deal of convenience and can increase your productivity when you're away from the office. And going mobile is increasingly becoming the norm, as more and more people are buying cell phones and other mobile devices. In fact, more than 150 million Americans currently own cell phones, and that number is expected to rise in the next five years. In this chapter, we discuss the advantages and disadvantages of going mobile and look at the range of mobile computing devices you can choose from, discussing their components, features, and capabilities. Along the way, you'll learn how you can synchronize your mobile devices to make even better use of them. Whether you have already gone mobile or are still considering your options, this chapter will help you become a savvy consumer, taking full advantage of the world of mobile computing.

Mobile Computing: Is It Right for You?

Just 30 years ago, the idea of a powerful personal computer that could fit on a desktop was a dream. Today, you can carry computers around in your backpack, fit them in your pocket, and even incorporate them into your clothes. **Mobile computing devices**—portable electronic tools such as cell phones, personal digital assistants (PDAs), and laptops—are dramatically changing our day-to-day lives, allowing us to communicate with others, remain productive, and access a wide array of information no matter where we are.

Still, going mobile isn't for everyone. Although having instant access to your e-mail, schedule, and the Internet wherever you are during the day can be convenient and boost your productivity, there is a downside associated with mobile computing: because mobile devices have been miniaturized, they're more expensive and less rugged than stationary desktop equipment. It's therefore important that you balance the advantages of going mobile with how well doing so fits your lifestyle.

How do I know whether mobile devices are right for me? Before you purchase any mobile device, consider whether your needs match what mobile devices can offer. To do so, ask yourself these questions:

- **Do I need to communicate with others when I'm away from my desk?** Whether it means talking over the phone, getting an important page to call home, or checking your e-mail, if you need to communicate no matter where you are, mobile devices may be right for you.

- **Do I need to access my electronic information when I'm away from my desk?** If you need to access and make changes to electronic information (such as an Outlook schedule or Excel report) while you're out and about, mobile devices such as PDAs and laptops would be valuable tools for you. However, if it's as efficient for you to keep paper records when you're away from your computer and later enter that data into your computer system, you may not need mobile devices.

- **Do I need to access the Internet when I'm away from my desk?** Mobile devices that are **Web-enabled**—that is, set up so that they can access the Internet through a wireless network—allow you to have constant access to the Internet wherever you are. Of course, you'll access the Internet at greater speeds and for less cost when you're at home or in the office. However, if you need quickly changing information when you're away from your desk, Web-enabled mobile devices may be right for you.

- **Are the convenience and productivity mobile devices offer important to me?** Mobile devices can provide you with a great deal of convenience and help you to be more productive. For example, a nursing student would have an easier time performing a diagnostic interview with a patient if the reference codes she needed were available in her PDA rather than in a huge stack of books. Likewise, students who take online classes with such products as Blackboard can download their course and carry it on a PDA so they can work on their assignments anywhere, with or without Internet access.

- **Is the information I need to carry already in an electronic format?** Do you currently use personal information management (PIM) software such as Microsoft Outlook to store your daily schedule and contact list? Or are your schedule and contact list currently in paper form? Converting information to an electronic format and learning how to use mobile devices are hidden costs of going mobile.

MOBILE DEVICE LIMITATIONS

What are the limitations of mobile devices? In addition to the questions previously discussed, it's important that you consider whether your needs match the limitations mobile devices have:

- Battery life limits the usefulness of mobile devices.

- The screen display area is small on most devices (making the Internet experience very different).

- The speed of Internet connection available to mobile devices is currently very low.

The benefits of Internet connectivity are also dependent on the wireless Internet

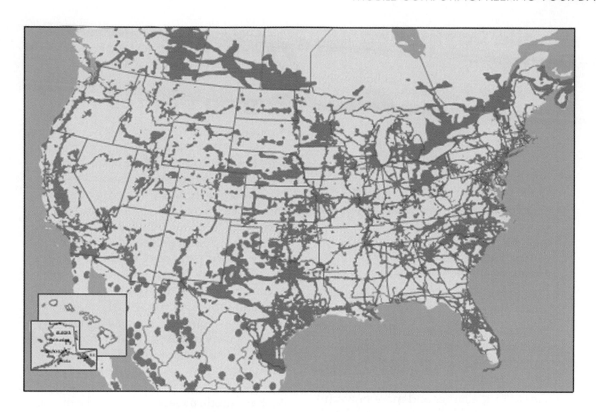

FIGURE 8.1

This map shows the wireless Internet coverage for wireless Internet provider T-Mobile in the United States and Canada. As you can see, many rural areas are not covered.

coverage in your area. For example, if you travel in rural areas, it may be impossible to take advantage of wireless Internet connectivity. Figure 8.1 shows the national coverage for one wireless Internet provider, T-Mobile.

As a student, you should consider how much of your campus is covered by wireless connectivity. Is your residence hall covered? Your classrooms? The library? Some schools create "wireless clouds" that enable you to be covered no matter where you are on campus. Other schools offer little coverage, making wireless connectivity to the Internet more difficult.

Finally, you must decide whether the extra cost of going mobile is worth the value and convenience. As mentioned earlier, mobile computing devices are more expensive and less rugged than desktop systems. Vibration, falls, dust, and liquids can all destroy your laptop, PDA, or cell phone. If the environment you live in or travel through is dusty or bumpy, for example, you should be prepared to spend money on additional warranty coverage or on repair and replacement costs. Finally, desktop systems always boast more expandability and better performance for the same cost when compared with mobile computers.

So, is mobile computing right for me? Figure 8.2 presents a checklist of the factors you need to consider when deciding

whether to go mobile. Do your needs to communicate and access electronic information and the Internet while you're away from your desk make mobile devices a good investment?

FIGURE 8.2 Are Mobile Devices Right for You?		
CONSIDERATION	**YES**	**NO**
I need to be able to communicate with others when I'm away from my desk.		
I need to access my electronic information wherever I am.		
I need to access the Internet when I'm away from my desk.		
The added convenience and productivity mobile devices offer is important to me.		
The information I need to carry with me is already in an electronic format.		
My needs match the limitations of mobile devices (such as short battery life, small display screen on some devices, and low Internet connection speeds).		
Most of my living and travel locations are covered by wireless Internet access.		
It is worth the added expense for me to go mobile.		

Mobile Computing Devices

If you do decide to go mobile, there is a wide range of mobile computing devices on the market today:

- *Paging devices* provide you with limited communication capabilities but are inexpensive options if you want some of the features of mobile computing.

- *Cellular phones* feature traditional phone services such as call waiting and voice mail. Many now come with calendars, contact databases, text messaging, and e-mail capabilities.

- *MP3 players* allow you to carry digital music files.

- *Personal digital assistants (PDAs)* are handheld devices that allow you to carry much of the same digital information as desktop systems.

- *Tablet PCs* are larger and more powerful than PDAs and incorporate specialized handwriting-recognition software.

- *Laptop computers* are expensive and powerful tools for carrying electronic information.

Figure 8.3 lists the main features of these mobile devices. In the next sections, we look at each of these devices in detail.

Paging Devices

A **paging device** (or a **pager**) is a small wireless device that allows you to receive and sometimes send numeric (and sometimes text) messages on a small display screen. Pagers have very low power consumption, which means long battery lives, and are very compact. They're also the most inexpensive mobile computing device you can carry.

Are there different kinds of pagers? **Numeric pagers** display only numbers on their screens, telling you that you have received a page and providing you with the number you should call. Numeric pagers do not allow you to send a response. A somewhat more sophisticated style of pager is the **voice pager**, which offers all the features of a numeric pager but also allows you to receive voice messages. **Alphanumeric pagers** are much like numeric pagers, but they also can display text messages. Like numeric pagers, alphanumeric pagers do not allow you to send messages.

More useful are **two-way pagers**, which support both receiving and sending text

DEVICE	APPROXIMATE PRICE	APPROXIMATE SIZE	APPROXIMATE WEIGHT	STANDARD CAPABILITIES
PAGING DEVICE	$35+ for the pager plus $10+/month for a service plan	2" x 2" x 0.5"	0.2 lbs.	Provides numeric and/or text messaging in one or two directions
CELLULAR PHONE	$50+ for the phone plus $30+/month for a monthly plan plus $10+/month for Internet access	5" x 2" x 0.5"	0.25 lbs.	Provides voice and e-mail connectivity
MP3 PLAYER	$70+	3" x 2" x 1"	0.25 lbs.	Provides storage of digital music files and other data
PDA	$100+	5" x 3" x 1"	0.5 lbs.	Provides PIM capabilities, access to application software, and access to the Internet
TABLET PC	$1,700+	10" x 8" x 1"	3 lbs.	Provides PIM capabilities, access to application software, access to the Internet, and special handwriting- and speech-recognition capabilities
LAPTOP	$900+	10" x 13" x 2"	5 to 8 lbs.	Provides all the capabilities of a desktop computer while also being portable

FIGURE 8.3   Mobile Devices: Price, Size, Weight, and Capabilities

messages. Two-way pagers have a small built-in keyboard so you can compose text messages, as shown in Figure 8.4. More advanced two-way pagers support preprogrammed replies. Instead of having to type out an entire reply, you can insert a standard phrase (such as "I'll meet you at") from a list, using just one keystroke. Advanced pagers also include an address book that stores the phone numbers and e-mail addresses of your contacts. In addition, two-way pagers can notify you of e-mail and allow you to check it and send replies.

How do pagers work? Pagers are radio devices. This means that all pagers have receivers that receive radio waves and then translate those waves into the signals needed to display numbers or characters on the display screen. In addition, every pager is assigned a unique code. When a message is sent to a pager, it is sent together with the unique code on a special channel, or frequency. This unique code ensures that the correct pager receives the message. Two-way pagers also have a transmitter that allows you to send messages.

With all the new devices on the market, does anyone still use pagers? People who need to be reachable but want an inexpensive and lightweight device are the primary market for pagers. Staff who are on call (such as doctors), expectant fathers, and teenagers are typical pager owners. Pagers cost less than a cell phone (they currently sell for about $35), and with monthly fees of around $10, they provide an inexpensive alternative to cell phones. However, as other devices such as cell phones continue to drop in price and shrink in size, pagers will have a difficult time finding a market. We may see pagers phased out completely within the next few years.

Cellular Phones

Cellular phones have evolved from their early days as large, clunky, boxlike devices to become the compact, full-featured communication and information storage devices they are today. Cell phones offer all of the features available on a home telephone system, including auto-redial, call timers, and voice-mail capabilities. Some cell phones also feature voice-activated dialing, which is important for hands-free operation. In addition to these services, cell phones offer

FIGURE 8.4

The Motorola Talkabout T900 is an example of a two-way pager. It displays four large lines of text and supports preprogrammed replies and an address book.

Internet access, text messaging, personal information management (PIM) features, and more, all within the palm of your hand.

CELL PHONE HARDWARE

Is a cell phone considered a computer? Cell phones are so advanced that they have the same components as a computer: a processor (central processing unit, or CPU), memory, and input and output devices, as shown in Figure 8.5. A cell phone also

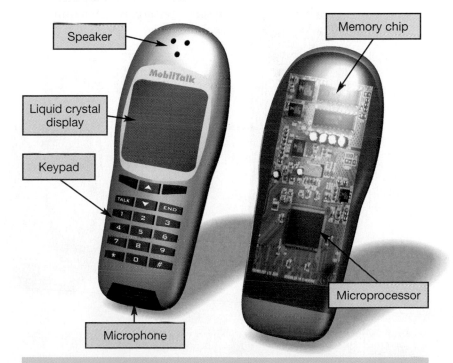

FIGURE 8.5

Inside your cell phone, you'll find some familiar components, including a processor (CPU), a memory chip, input devices such as a microphone and a keypad, and output devices such as a display screen and a speaker.

requires software and has its own operating system (OS). One popular operating system for full-featured cell phones is the **Symbian OS**. As cell phones begin to handle e-mail, images, and even video, more complex operating systems such as Symbian are required to translate the user's commands into instructions for the processor.

What does the processor inside a cell phone do? Although the processor inside a cell phone is obviously not as fast or as high powered as a processor in a desktop computer, it is still responsible for a great number of tasks. The processor coordinates sending all of the data between the other electronic components inside the phone. It also runs the cell phone's operating system, which provides a user interface so that you can change phone settings, store information, play games, and so on.

What does the memory chip inside a cell phone do? The operating system and the information you save into your phone (such as phone numbers and addresses) need to be stored in memory. The operating system is stored in read-only memory (ROM) because the phone would be useless without that key piece of software. As you learned earlier in this text, there are two kinds of memory used in computers: *volatile memory*, which requires

power to save data, and *nonvolatile memory*, which can store data even when the power is turned off. ROM is nonvolatile, or permanent, memory. This means that when you turn off your cell phone, the data you have saved to ROM (including the operating system) does not get lost.

The phone contact data is stored in separate internal memory chips. Full-featured phones have as much as 750 kilobytes (KB) of memory that can be used to store contact data, ring tones, images, and even small software applications such as currency converters or a world clock.

What input and output devices do cell phones use? The input devices for a cell phone are primarily the microphone, which converts your voice into electronic signals that the processor can understand, and a keypad, which is used for numeric or text entry. Newer phones such as the Kyocera 7135 Smartphone (shown in Figure 8.6a) feature the ubiquitous Palm Graffiti pad as well as touch-sensitive screens that allow you to input data. In addition, more and more cell phones include digital cameras. The Nokia 3650 (shown in Figure 8.6b) offers a built-in camera that can input photographs or even eight seconds of video to your phone.

Cell phone output devices include a speaker and a liquid crystal display (LCD) display. Higher-end models include full-color, high-resolution plasma displays. Such displays are becoming increasingly popular as more people are using their cell phones to send and receive the digital

FIGURE 8.6

(a) The Kyocera 7135 Smartphone includes a built-in keyboard and touch-sensitive color screen. (b) The Nokia 3650 weighs less than 4.5 ounces including the battery and is just 5 inches by 2 inches. Its camera can input both still photographs and video to your phone. (c) The Motorola T720 includes an outside LCD display as well as an inside color display.

images included in multimedia text messages and e-mail. Certain cell phones (such as the Motorola T720, shown in Figure 8.6c) include two displays: an outside LCD display you can see when the phone is folded and a separate color display inside.

HOW CELL PHONES WORK

How do cell phones work? When you speak into a cell phone, the sound enters the microphone as a sound wave. Because analog sound waves need to be digitized (that is, converted into a sequence of 1s and 0s that the cell phone's processor can understand), an **analog-to-digital converter chip** converts your voice's sound waves into digital signals. Next, the digital data must be compressed, or squeezed, into the smallest possible space so that it will transmit more quickly to another phone. The processor cannot perform the mathematical operations required at this stage quickly enough, so a specialized chip, called the **digital signal processor**, is included in a cell phone to handle the compression work. Finally, the digital data is transmitted as a radio wave through the cellular network to the destination phone.

When you receive an incoming call, the digital signal processor *decompresses* the incoming message. An amplifier boosts the signal to make it loud enough, and it is then passed on to the speaker, from which you hear the sound.

What's "cellular" about a cell phone? A set of connected "cells" makes up a cellular network. Each cell is a geographic area centered on a **base transceiver station**, which is a large communications tower with antennas, amplifiers, and receivers/transmitters. When you place a call on a cell phone, a base station picks up the request for service. The station then passes the request on to a central location, called a **mobile switching center**. (The reverse process occurs when you receive an incoming call on a cell phone.) A telecommunications company builds its network by constructing a series of cells that overlap, in an attempt to guarantee that its cell phone customers have coverage no matter where they are.

As you move during your phone call, the mobile switching center monitors the strength of the signal between your cell phone and the closest base station. When the signal is no longer strong enough between your cell phone and the base station, the mobile switching center orders the next base station

BITS AND BYTES

Are Cell Phones Bad for Your Health?

Cell phones work by sending electromagnetic waves into the air from an antenna. Depending on the phone's design—that is, whether there is a shield between the antenna and the user's head—up to 60 percent of the radiation emitted penetrates the area around the head. It is not yet clear whether there are long-term health consequences of using cell phones because of the electromagnetic waves they emit. What is clear is that using a cell phone while driving is dangerous. Studies show that motorists are four to nine times more likely to crash when talking on a cell phone while driving, a risk similar to the effects of driving drunk. In many states, hands-free cell phone use is mandatory. For more information on laws in your state as well as links to sites with accident data, visit the Governors Highway Safety Association (GHSA) Web site at **http://www.statehighwaysafety.org/html/state_info/laws/cellphone_laws.html**.

to take charge of your call. When your cell phone "drops out," it sometimes does so because the distance between base stations was too great to provide an adequate signal.

CELL PHONE FEATURES: TEXT MESSAGING

What is text messaging? Short Message Service (SMS) (often just called **text messaging**) is a technology that allows you to send short text messages (up to 160 characters) over mobile networks. To send SMS messages from your cell phone, you simply use the numeric keypad or a presaved template and type in your message. You can send SMS messages to other mobile devices (such as cell phones or pagers) or to any e-mail address. You can also use SMS to send short text messages from your home computer to mobile devices, such as your friend's phone.

How does SMS work? Unlike the text messages you send with a pager, which use radio waves, SMS uses the cell phone network to transmit messages. When you send an SMS message, an SMS calling center receives the message and delivers it to the appropriate mobile device using something called "store-and-forward" technology. This technology allows users to send SMS messages to any other SMS device in the world.

Many SMS fans like text messaging because it can be cheaper than a phone call and it allows the receivers to read messages when it is convenient for them. In fact in some countries, such as Japan, text messaging is more popular than voice messaging. However, entering text using your cell phone keypad can be time-consuming and hard on your thumbs. Frequent SMS users save typing

time by using a number of abbreviations, some of which are shown in Figure 8.7.

Can I send and receive multimedia files over a cell phone? SMS technology allows you to send only text messages. However, an extension of SMS called **Multimedia Message Service (MMS)** allows you to send messages that include text, sound, images, and video clips to other phones or e-mail addresses. MMS messages actually arrive as a series of messages; you view the text and then the image and then the sound, and so on. You can then choose to save just one part of the message (such as the image), all of it, or none of it. MMS users can subscribe to financial, sports, and weather services that will "push" information to them, sending it automatically to their phones in MMS format.

CELL PHONE INTERNET CONNECTIVITY

How do I get Internet service for my phone? Just as you pay an Internet service provider (ISP) for Internet access for your desktop computer, connecting your cell phone to the Internet requires that you have a **wireless Internet service provider**. Phone companies that provide cell phone calling plans (such as Verizon or T-Mobile) usually double as wireless ISPs. As noted earlier, accessing the Internet on a mobile device comes with limitations. For one, the connection is often very slow. Although you may be able to connect to the Internet at speeds ranging from 44 to 3,300 kilobits per second (Kbps) at home, your cell phone will connect at a maximum speed of just 14.4 Kbps.

In addition, because cell phones have a very limited amount of screen space and low screen resolution, the Internet experience is quite different. To make it possible for you to access the Internet, special **microbrowser** software runs on your cell phone. Figure 8.8 shows a typical microbrowser screen. As you can see, the Internet experience is not as enjoyable as on your home desktop computer.

Web sites are beginning to create content specifically designed for wireless devices to make such Internet connections worthwhile. This specially designed content, which is text-based and contains no graphics, is written in a format called **Wireless Markup Language (WML)**. Content is designed so it fits the tiny display screens of cell phones and PDAs.

FIGURE 8.7	Popular Text Messaging Abbreviations
AFAIK	As far as I know
B4N	Bye for now
BRB	Be right back
CUL	See you later
FBM	Fine by me
F2T	Free to talk
G2G	Got to go
HRU	How are you?
IDK	I don't know
JAS	Just a sec
LOL	Laughing out loud
QPSA	¿Qué pasa?
T+	Think positive
TTYL	Talk to you later
WUWH	Wish you were here
YBS	You'll be sorry

BITS AND BYTES

Using Text Messaging to Meet Mr. or Ms Right?

In Britain's pubs, Time2Flirt text messaging events are all the rage. When you arrive at the pub, you register your cell phone with a central server and receive a badge with a number that you stick on your clothing. Anyone in the bar can send an SMS message to anyone else's cell phone just by using their badge number (#12 u look beautiful). In this way, your cell phone number (and even your name) is never revealed to anyone unless you choose to do so. Sending text messages is a clever way to break the ice. Because of the popularity of these events in the United Kingdom, expect to see these SMS events arriving at a bar near you.

FIGURE 8.8

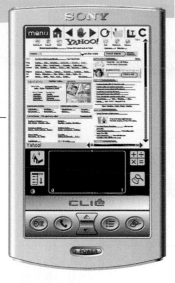

Microbrowser software helps you access the Internet from your cell phone or PDA.

BITS AND BYTES

Your Phone Called . . . It Needs a Tequila Shooter!

Someday soon, you may be sitting in a bar and instead of finishing that last shot of Jack Daniels, you may instead pour it into your cell phone! Researchers are currently working on a technology called a "biofuel cell" that could power mobile devices using alcohol. A standard fuel cell (that is, a battery) derives its power from chemical reactions between its elements (such as zinc and manganese oxide). A biofuel cell would use biological molecules (in this case, alcohol enzymes) to generate power. The advantage would be that the batteries are easily rechargeable—just add beer! Once the battery is charged, you would probably need to add only a few drops of alcohol to keep it running for a month or longer. More research is needed to develop these fuel cells before they can become commercially viable, but in the future you may hear someone say, "Bartender, another round for me and my cell phone!"

MP3 Players

MP3 is a format for efficiently storing music as digital files, or a series of bits. An **MP3 player** is a small portable device that enables you to carry your MP3 files around with you. Depending on the player, you can carry several hours of music or your entire CD collection in an incredibly small device. For example, the Apple iPod is 4 inches by 2.4 inches and can hold over 10,000 songs. The most compact players are the size of a cigarette lighter (although they hold far less music than the iPod). Figure 8.9 (p. 324) shows several popular models of MP3 players.

MP3 HARDWARE

How do I know how much music an MP3 player can hold? The number of songs an MP3 player can hold depends on how much storage space it has. MP3 players use memory chips and hard disk drives to store music files. Inexpensive players use memory chips (ranging from 64 megabytes, or MB, to 256 MB), whereas expensive models use a built-in hard drive, which provides up to 40 gigabytes (GB) of storage. Some MP3 players allow you to add storage capacity by purchasing removable memory cards.

Another factor that determines how much music a player can hold is the quality of the MP3 music files. The size of an MP3 file depends on the digital sampling of the song. The **sampling rate** is the number of times per second the music is measured and converted to a digital value. Sampling rates are measured in kilobits per second (Kbps). The same

song could be sampled at 192 Kbps or 64 Kbps. The size of the song file will be three times larger if it is sampled at 192 Kbps instead of the lower sampling rate of 64 Kbps. The higher the sampling rate, the better quality the sound, but the larger the file size.

If you are "ripping," or converting, a song from a CD into a digital MP3 file, you can select the sampling rate yourself. You decide by considering what quality sound you want as well as how many songs you want to fit onto your MP3 player. For example, if your player has 64 MB of storage and you have ripped songs at 192 Kbps, you can fit about 45 minutes of music onto the player. The same 64 MB could store 133 minutes of music if it were sampled at 64 Kbps. Whenever you are near your computer, you can connect your player and download a different set of songs, but you are always limited by the amount of storage your player has.

MP3 FLASH MEMORY AND FILE TRANSFER

What if I want to store more music than what my MP3 player's memory allows? Some MP3 players allow you to add additional, removable memory. The removable memory MP3 players use is a type of portable, nonvolatile memory called **flash memory**. Flash memory cards are noiseless, very light, use very little power, and slide into a special slot in the player. If

FIGURE 8.9 **Popular MP3 Players and Their Characteristics**

MP3 PLAYER	APPROXIMATE NUMBER OF MP3 SONGS	EXPANDABLE MEMORY	HARD DISK DRIVE CAPACITY	CONNECTION TO COMPUTER	OTHER FEATURES
CREATIVE LABS' NOMAD MUVO	About 30 songs	128 MB	None	USB 1.0 port	Size of a cigarette lighter
VERGE DFP200	About 60 songs	256 MB	None	USB 1.0 port	Includes voice recorder, FM tuner, six backlit display colors, and six equalizer settings
APPLE IPOD	About 5,000 songs (for 20 GB) to 10,000 songs (for 40 GB)	None	20 GB or 40 GB	FireWire or USB 2.0 port	Latest version includes a calendar, contact database, and can store images, corporate logos, and live URLs
APPLE IPOD MINI	1,000 songs	None	4 GB	FireWire or USB 2.0 port	Weighs only half what the largest iPod does and can be worn on armband
ARCHOS MULTIMEDIA ENTERTAINMENT CENTER	About 5,000 songs or 1,000 hours of voice recordings or 40 hours of video	None	20 GB	USB 2.0 port	Includes an MPEG4 video player/recorder, photo wallet and viewer, and acts as a 20-GB hard drive to store data and files

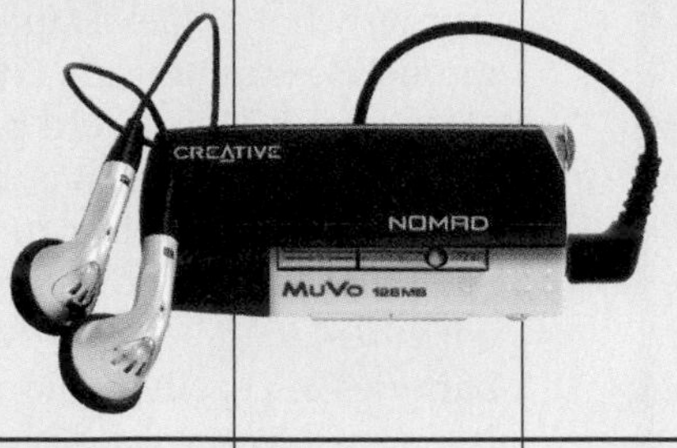

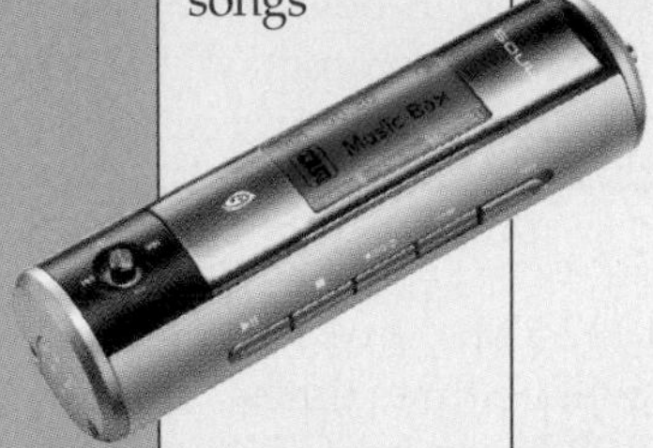

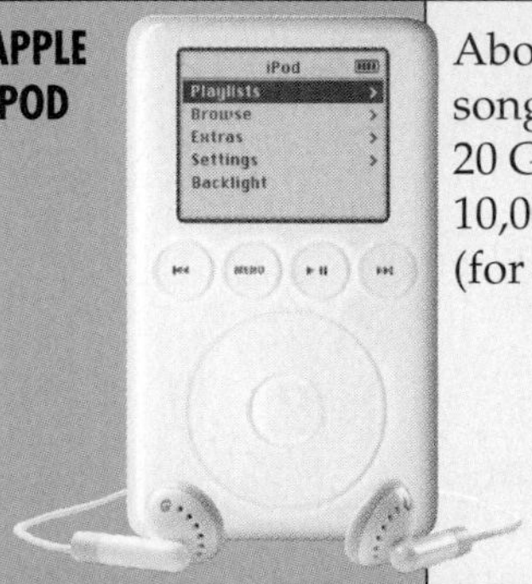

you've ever played a video game on PlayStation 2 or Nintendo and saved your progress to a memory card, you have used flash memory. Because flash memory is nonvolatile, when you store data on a flash memory card, you won't lose it when you turn off the player. In addition, flash memory can be erased and rewritten with new data.

What types of flash memory cards do MP3 players use? You can use several different types of flash cards with MP3 players, as shown in Figure 8.10. One popular type is **Compact Flash** cards. These are about the size of a matchbook and can hold between 64 MB and 1 GB of data. They are very durable, so the data you store on them is safer than it would be on a floppy disk, for example. **Multimedia cards (MMCs)** and **SmartMedia** cards are about the same size as CompactFlash cards but are thinner and less rugged. They can hold up to 128 MB of data. A newer type of memory card called **Secure Digital** is faster and offers encryption capabilities so your data is secure even if you lose the card. The stamp-sized Secure Digital cards can hold up to 512 MB of data.

Sony has its own brand of flash memory called the **Memory Stick**. These tiny cards—measuring just 2 inches by 1 inch and weighing a fraction of an ounce—are currently found only on Sony devices but are becoming more widely accepted. Particular models of MP3 players can support only certain types of flash cards, so check your manual to be sure you buy compatible memory cards.

How do I transfer MP3 files to my MP3 player? All MP3 players come with software that enables you to transfer your MP3 files from your computer onto the player. As noted earlier, players that hold thousands of songs use internal hard drives to store music. For example, the Apple iPod is available with a 20-GB or 40-GB hard drive (the iPod Mini has a 4-GB drive). To move that volume of data between your computer and MP3 player, you need a high-speed port. The iPod uses a FireWire port or the even faster Universal Serial Bus (USB) 2.0 port, whereas some other MP3 players use the slower USB 1.0 port. Using a FireWire port, you can transfer a complete CD to the iPod in less than 10 seconds.

Can MP3 players carry more than just music? MP3 players have become so popular that some manufacturers are redesigning their software and operating systems to support the transfer and storage of nonmusical

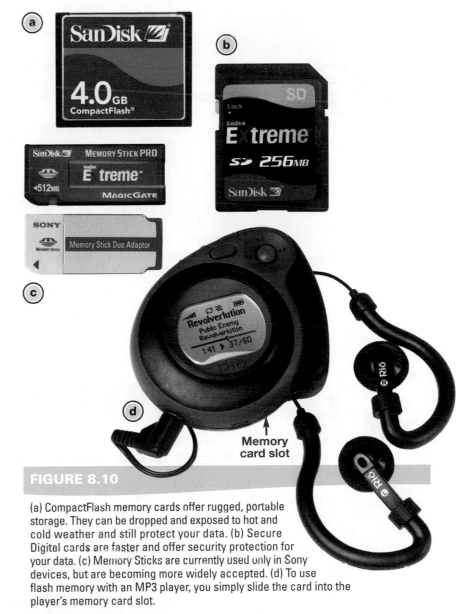

FIGURE 8.10

(a) CompactFlash memory cards offer rugged, portable storage. They can be dropped and exposed to hot and cold weather and still protect your data. (b) Secure Digital cards are faster and offer security protection for your data. (c) Memory Sticks are currently used only in Sony devices, but are becoming more widely accepted. (d) To use flash memory with an MP3 player, you simply slide the card into the player's memory card slot.

data as well. The latest version of the iPod sports a calendar and a contact database and can store images, corporate logos, and live URLs in addition to music files. Other high-end MP3 devices, such as the Archos Multimedia Entertainment Center, shown in Figure 8.9, offer you the ability to transfer and store music, video, and image files.

MP3 ETHICAL ISSUES: NAPSTER AND BEYOND

Is it illegal to download MP3 files? The initial MP3 craze was fueled by sites such as MP3.com. MP3.com differs from controversial sites such as the old version of Napster

TechTV

For more information on new portable gear see CES (Consumer Electronics Show) Favorites from the Giz Wiz—a TechTV clip found at www.prenhall.com/techninaction

because its files are on a public server, the songs are placed on the server with the permission of the original artist or recording company, and often you pay a fee for the right to download the song. Therefore, you are not infringing on a copyright by downloading songs from legal MP3 sites.

What was Napster all about? When originally introduced, **Napster** was a file-exchange site created to correct some of the small annoyances found by users of MP3.com and similar sites. One such annoyance was the limited availability of popular music in MP3 format. With the MP3 sites, if you found a song you wanted to download, often the links to the links to the sites the file was found on no longer worked. Napster differed from MP3.com because songs or locations of songs were not stored in a central public server but instead were "borrowed" directly from other users' computers. This process of users transferring files between

computers is referred to as **peer-to-peer (P2P) sharing**. Napster also provided a search engine dedicated to finding MP3 files. This direct search and sharing eliminated the inconvenience of searching links only to find them unavailable.

Why did Napster disappear for a while? The problem with Napster was that it was so good at what it did. Napster's convenient and reliable mechanism to find and download popular songs in MP3 format became a huge success. The rapid acceptance and use of Napster—at one point, it had nearly 60 million users—led the music industry to claim it was losing money. Recording companies and artists sued for copyright infringement, and Napster was closed in June 2002. Napster has since reopened as a music site that sells music downloads and is sanctioned by the recording industry.

If the original Napster site was illegal, why are there still Napster

TRENDS IN IT

EMERGING TECHNOLOGIES:
Wearing Your Applications on Your Sleeve

By now, most of us expect to have Internet access in our wristwatches and radio transmitters in our coat buttons in the not-so-distant future. But how about having computers woven into your clothes?

The idea may not be so far-fetched. Flexible synthetic "yarns" that can transmit electrical signals may soon be common components of cotton and polyester fabrics. Called *electrotextiles*, these textiles are already being woven into soldiers' vests to serve as radio antennas. Researchers see almost no limits to their possibilities and are working to make electrotextiles not only wearable but also washable, customizable, and even programmable. Experts predict that nearly every type of clothing will have some sort of electronic function in 10 years, ranging from Global Positioning Systems (GPSs) to medical sensors to fabrics that change colors and patterns at your command.

The new fibers are woven into fabric or sewn on in ribbon-like strips around the neck or sleeves of a

FIGURE 8.11

Someday you may be wearing your computer on your sleeve.

garment. They are then connected to chips and batteries so that, for instance, blankets and clothing can adapt to body temperature and car seat fabric can tell a car's air bags to adjust their force to match the passenger's weight. Researchers at the Georgia Institute of Technology are already working on a T-shirt for firefighters that tracks the heart rate, body temperature, and other vital signs of the person wearing it and transmits this data to a wearable pager. And scientists at Germany's Infineon Technologies have made a prototype of a hooded jacket (in stylish charcoal gray) that includes the electronic elements of an MP3 player in the pockets. The hood's drawstrings are used as the MP3 player's headphones, and controls are found on the sleeve (see Figure 8.11).

And just think: Once solar cells can be woven into fabric, you might be able to wear all your applications *and* your power source—in next year's hottest colors.

clones? While Napster was going through its legal turmoil, other P2P Web sites were quick to take advantage of a huge opportunity. Napster was "easy" to shut down because it used a central index server that queried other Napster computers for requested songs. Current P2P Web sites (such as Gnutella and Kazaa) differ from Napster in that they do not limit themselves to sharing only MP3 files. More important, these sites don't have a central index server. Instead, they operate in a true P2P sharing environment in which computers connect directly to other computers.

The argument these P2P networks make to defend their legality is that they do not run a central server like the original Napster but only facilitate connections between users. Therefore, they have no control over what the users trade, and not all P2P file sharing is illegal. Those against the file-sharing sites contend that the sites know their users are distributing illegal files. This argument has not yet been definitively settled.

Personal Digital Assistants (PDAs)

A **personal digital assistant (PDA)** is a small device that allows you to carry digital information. Often called *palm computers* or *handhelds*, PDAs are about the size of your hand and usually weigh less than 5 ounces. Although small, PDAs are quite powerful and can carry all sorts of information, from calendars to contact lists to specially designed personal productivity software programs (such as Excel and Word), to songs, photos, and games. And you can easily "synchronize" your PDA and your home computer so that the changes you make to your schedules and files on your PDA are made on your home or office computer files as well.

PDA HARDWARE

What hardware is inside a PDA? Like any computer, a PDA includes a processor (CPU), operating system software, storage capabilities, input and output devices, and ports. Because of their small size, PDAs (like cell phones) must use specially designed processors and operating system software. They store their operating system software in

ROM and their data and application programs (which are specially designed to run on the PDA) in random access memory (RAM).

What kinds of input devices do PDAs use? All PDAs feature touch-sensitive screens that allow you to enter data directly with a penlike device called a **stylus**. To make selections, you simply tap or write on the screen with the stylus. Other PDAs include integrated keyboards or support small, portable, folding keyboards. Figure 8.12 shows all of these input options.

With a touch screen and stylus, you can use either handwritten text or special notation systems to enter data into your PDA. One of the more popular notation systems is the **Graffiti** text system. As shown in

FIGURE 8.12

To enter text, PDAs offer different options: (a) a text entry window that you use together with a stylus, (b) an integrated keyboard (shown here on a Sharp Zaurus SL-5500), and (c) a folding keyboard accessory.

FIGURE 8.13

The Graffiti system uses special strokes to represent all the letters of the English alphabet.

Figure 8.13, with Graffiti, you must learn special strokes that represent each letter, such as an upside-down V for the letter A. Another popular system, **Microsoft Transcriber**, doesn't require special strokes and can recognize both printed and cursive writing with fairly decent accuracy. PDAs also support an on-screen keyboard so that you can use your stylus and "type" (tap out) messages.

Can I take photos with my PDA? Some newer PDAs (such as the Sony Clie shown in Figure 8.14) include digital cameras that can take photos and record videos. High-end models include digital cameras with flash, auto-focus, and red-eye-reduction features. They can record videos in the MPEG4 (Moving Picture Experts Group) format, a high quality standard for creating compressed video files, and play them back right on the PDA display or on a television through an audio/video output port.

What kinds of displays do PDAs have? PDAs come with LCD screens in a variety of resolutions. The more inexpensive models use 16 levels of gray (grayscale). For appointment schedules and to-do lists, this is fine. However, if you plan on using your PDA to display photos and play video clips, you should consider buying a PDA with a color display. High-end color displays can have resolutions as high as 320 x 480 and support for 65,000 colors.

How do I compare processors for PDAs? Popular PDA processors (CPUs) on the market today include the Motorola DragonBall, the Texas Instruments OMAP, and the Intel XScale processor. When comparing PDA processors, one consideration to keep in mind is **processor speed**. Processor speed, which is measured in hertz (Hz), is the number of operations (or cycles) the processor completes each second. For example, the Dell Axim X5 PDA uses an Intel XScale processor running at 400 megahertz (MHz), or 400 million cycles per second. The Palm Zire uses a Motorola DragonBall EZ processor running at 16 MHz. Just as with computers, you should get the fastest processor your budget will allow.

If you're interested in running demanding software on your PDA, such as games and image-editing applications, getting a fast processor is important. For basic PDA functions such as a to-do list and a calendar, a slower processor works fine, but if you will be doing large sets of calculations in Excel workbooks, the speed difference between a fast processor and a slower one is very noticeable. The type of application software you plan on running should help you determine whether the additional processing power is worth the cost.

However, processor speed is not the only aspect of the processor that affects performance. The internal design of the processor, both in the software commands it speaks and its internal hardware, are other factors. To measure performance, PDA reviewers often run the same task on competing PDAs and then compare the time it takes to complete the task. This process is called **benchmarking** and gives a good indication of the unit's overall system performance. When comparing PDAs, look for benchmarks in magazines (such as *PC Magazine*) in addition to online reviews (such as those found at **www.wired.com**).

As well as having different speeds, each processor uses different amounts of power, affecting how long the PDA can run on a single battery. When comparing PDAs, look for the expected operating time on one battery charge.

PDA OPERATING SYSTEMS

How do I compare PDA operating systems? The two main operating system competitors on the PDA market today are the **Palm OS** from Palm and the **Pocket PC**

FIGURE 8.14

New super PDAs combine many features into one device. The Sony Clie PEG-UX50 shown here runs the Palm OS and includes a digital camera, integrated Bluetooth and Wi-Fi, a QWERTY keyboard for easy entry, and can play back MP3 files. In addition, the swiveling screen folds down so that it can be used as a conventional PDA.

system from Microsoft (formerly called Windows CE). Which operating system is better depends on your personal needs. Palm OS is found on PDAs made by Palm and Sony. Pocket PC is used by Compaq, Hewlett-Packard, and Toshiba on their PDA models. As you can see in Figure 8.15, both operating systems offer you graphical user interfaces.

Palm OS is in some ways a better match to the PDA environment. It requires less memory, is easy to use, and focuses on supporting only the features most commonly used by PDA owners, such as a calendar, to-do list, and contact information. PDAs using the Palm OS can recognize and support Microsoft Word, Excel, and PowerPoint files, although this requires that you buy a software application named Documents To Go. Similarly, you can use the Palm OS to view movies or listen to MP3 files, but only with the purchase of separate application software.

Pocket PC is more of a scaled-down version of Windows. It supports versions of the Microsoft applications Word and Excel that can run on the Pocket PC. These applications are designed for the smaller PDA screen and have fewer features. Pocket PC PDAs can play MP3 files and video clips without installing any additional software. However, all of this comes at the cost of added memory requirements and added complexity. So, a Pocket PC PDA often ships with more base memory and is more expensive.

The PDA operating system affects you in another way. You may want to buy extra software for your PDA—a program to track your workouts at the gym or to provide driving directions, for example. Third-party companies, rather than the companies that built the PDAs, often develop software applications for PDAs. Because the Palm OS was the first PDA operating system on the market, much of the PDA software was originally designed for the Palm OS. Today, there are more than 13,000 software applications available for the Palm OS, and it still holds a dominant market share, outselling Pocket PC about 2 to 1. Although more software applications are now created for both operating systems, you should investigate exactly which applications you are interested in buying and make sure they're available for the operating system you're considering. Figure 8.16 lists the advantages and disadvantages of these operating systems.

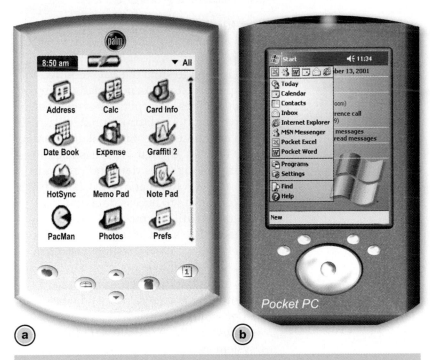

(a)   (b)

FIGURE 8.15

The two most popular operating systems for PDAs are (a) Palm OS and (b) Pocket PC.

FIGURE 8.16	**Comparing PDA Operating Systems**	
PDA OS	**ADVANTAGES**	**DISADVANTAGES**
PALM OS	• Requires less memory • Is easy to use • Is less expensive • Supports more third-party software applications	• Requires installation of separate Documents To Go software in order to support MS Word, Excel, and PowerPoint files • Requires installation of separate software to view video clips or listen to MP3 files
POCKET PC	• Supports specialized MS Office applications Word and Excel without installing additional software • Can play MP3 files and video clips without installing additional software	• Requires more memory • Is more expensive • Supports fewer third-party software applications

PDA MEMORY AND STORAGE

What kinds of memory does a PDA use? As you learned in earlier chapters, in desktop computers, nonvolatile memory (ROM) is used to store the data required to wake up the system. As nonvolatile memory, ROM saves these instructions even when the power is off. Desktop computers also contain a second form of nonvolatile storage: the hard drive. The hard drive is used to store large amounts of data and programs. Compared with ROM and RAM, hard drives take a long time to access data and load programs. Volatile memory (RAM), on the other hand, loses its contents when power is turned off, but it is incredibly fast. On a desktop computer, when a program is about to be executed, it is copied from the hard drive into RAM so it will run at the fastest speed possible.

In PDAs, ROM is used to hold the operating system as well as the most basic programs the PDA runs, such as the calendar, to-do list, and contact list. PDAs do not contain internal hard drives because it is too expensive to make a hard drive small enough and light enough to fit inside a PDA. Therefore, RAM holds additional applications and any data you load into the PDA. However, because RAM is volatile storage, and you do not want your data to disappear when you shut off your PDA, a small amount of power is taken from the battery to keep the data "alive" even while the PDA is off.

The main advantage of using RAM in this way is speed—RAM is incredibly fast compared with hard drives, so programs on a PDA load and run very quickly. The disadvantage is cost—RAM is expensive, so most PDAs have only 16 MB to 64 MB of RAM. In fact, applications for PDAs do not have all the functions that desktop versions include precisely because of their limited amount of RAM.

What if I need more memory on my PDA? Most PDAs cannot expand the amount of *internal* memory they contain. For memory needs beyond built-in RAM and ROM, PDAs use removable flash memory similar to that used in MP3 players. For example, if you want your PDA to hold a large MP3 collection, you might not have enough built-in RAM. But you could add the MP3s to your PDA by copying them onto flash memory and sliding the flash card into a special slot on the PDA, as shown in Figure 8.17.

FIGURE 8.17

Different PDAs use different types of flash memory. However, all flash memory cards slide into a specialized slot on the side of the PDA.

What types of flash memory are used in PDAs? PDAs feature all of the different types of flash memory. One manufacturer may support CompactFlash cards, whereas another may support SmartMedia cards. As is the case with MP3 players, Sony PDAs support their own brand of flash, the Memory Stick. The newest version, Memory Stick PRO, can hold between 256 MB and 1 GB of data. With a 1-GB Memory Stick PRO, your PDA can hold 16 CDs, 10 rolls of film, or 30 minutes of video. Not bad for a memory card smaller than your pinkie. Before buying a flash card, consult your PDA manual or manufacturer's Web site to make sure it's compatible with your PDA.

What battery sources are available for PDAs? Most PDAs use lithium ion batteries, which can be recharged. Newer model PDAs use a **smart battery**, a rechargeable lithium ion battery that can report the number of minutes of battery life remaining. You can also use AC adapters to plug your PDA into a wall outlet if you're near one.

PDA FILE TRANSFER AND SYNCHRONIZATION

How do I transfer data from my PDA to my desktop? If you're transferring data from your PDA to another computer and it accepts the type of flash card you are using, you can simply pull the flash card out of your PDA and slip it into the flash card reader on your computer. If your desktop does not include a built-in card reader, you can connect an external memory card reader to your computer using a USB port.

You can also transfer your data from your PDA to a desktop computer by using a special device called a **cradle**. Most PDAs come with a cradle, which connects the PDA to the desktop using either a USB port or a serial port, as shown in Figure 8.19. You can also use the PDA cradle to synchronize your PDA with your computer.

How do I synchronize a PDA with a desktop computer? To be truly valuable as mobile computing devices, PDAs provide a means by which you can coordinate the changes you make to your to-do lists, schedules, and other files with the files on your home computer. This process of updating your data so the files on your PDA and computer are the same is called **synchronizing**. To synchronize your desktop and PDA, you simply place the PDA in its cradle (which is connected to the desktop computer using a USB or serial port) and touch a "hot sync" button. This begins the process of data transfer (or synchronization) that updates both sets of files to the most current version.

Can I transfer files wirelessly from a PDA? Many PDAs include an infrared (IrDA) port that transmits data signals using infrared light waves. To transfer data between two PDAs, you can use the infrared port and "beam" data directly across. For example, if you missed a class, a fellow student could send you the assignment file by simply pointing her PDA at yours. The Sony PEG-NZ90 PDA expands on this infrared capability by incorporating a high-powered infrared control that you can use as a universal remote control to control the electronics in your home, such as your TV, VCR, and stereo.

Another type of wireless connection available for PDAs is **Bluetooth**. This technology uses radio waves to transmit data signals over short distances (up to about 30 feet). Many PDAs on the market today are Bluetooth-enabled, meaning they include a small Bluetooth chip that allows them to transfer data wirelessly to any other Bluetooth-enabled device. One benefit Bluetooth has over infrared is that direct line of sight does not have to be present between the two devices for them to communicate. You can also use Bluetooth to synchronize

BITS AND BYTES

Compact Memory More Powerful Than Flash

Although flash memory is powerful, the highest-density memory option available is actually not flash memory but a 1-inch portable hard drive. The Hitachi Microdrive, shown in Figure 8.18, allows you to store 4 GB of data in a CompactFlash-size cartridge. Devices that support the Microdrive allow it to slide right into a CompactFlash slot. With so much storage, you can keep videos, photographs, and hours of music, all on your mobile devices.

FIGURE 8.18

The 1-inch-square Hitachi Microdrive can hold 4 GB of data for a PDA, digital camera, or other portable device.

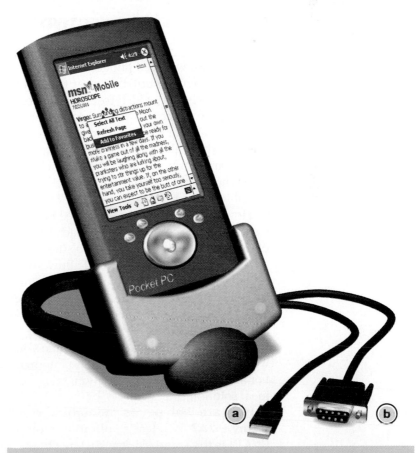

FIGURE 8.19

A cradle connects your PDA to your computer using either (a) a USB port or (b) a serial port.

your PDA with your home computer. No cradle to connect, no buttons to push: the Bluetooth-enabled PDA and desktop recognize each other and automatically begin the synchronization process.

What if my home computer or laptop computer doesn't have Bluetooth capabilities? Devices are now available that enable you to add Bluetooth capabilities to almost any computer. One is the Actiontec USB Bluetooth Adapter shown in Figure 8.20. When plugged into a computer's USB port, it adds wireless capability to your computer. The adapter comes with software that supports a wide range of Bluetooth services, including PDA synchronization, headset support, dial-up networking, network access, and file transfer.

FIGURE 8.20

Just plug the Actiontec USB Bluetooth Adapter into any USB port on your computer and install the Bluetooth manager software and you are ready to synchronize your PDA with your computer wirelessly.

PDA INTERNET CONNECTIVITY

How do PDAs connect to the Internet? As is the case with cell phones, connecting your PDA to the Internet requires that you have a wireless ISP, which costs an additional monthly fee. Once you're on the Internet, you can use your PDA to send and receive e-mail and use all the features you're familiar with from your desktop computer, including attachments, blind and carbon copies, and distribution lists.

However, you do not always need to be connected to the Internet to take advantage of its information resources. Web sites such as AvantGo (**www.avantgo.com**) allow you to download the content of many different Web sites from your home computer to your PDA. Popular channels include CNN.com and RollingStone.com. You can then read this downloaded information any time you want without having to access the Internet. For static Web-based information, this is an ideal solution.

How are Web pages "communicated" to my PDA? Wireless Application Protocol (WAP) is the standard that dictates how handheld devices will access information on the Internet. WAP supports all the major PDA operating systems, including Palm OS and Pocket PC. As mentioned earlier,

SOUND BYTE

PDA ON THE ROAD AND AT HOME

In this Sound Byte, you'll learn how to use your PDA as a powerful tool, how to use flash memory, and how to synchronize your PDA with your home computer.

mobile devices such as cell phones and PDAs run software applications called *microbrowsers* that allow them to access the Internet.

As noted previously, Web sites are beginning to provide specialized sites for mobile device users. In addition, a new technology called **Web clipping** allows you to extract the information you are interested in from a Web site and format it so it is more useful on smaller PDA displays. This conserves both the resources of your PDA for displaying information and the demand you are making for bandwidth in communicating between your PDA and the Web server. Because most wireless plans for PDAs charge an extra fee based on the amount of data you transfer, Web clipping can save you money. A list of sites that support Web clipping can be found at **www.palmone.com**.

PDA SOFTWARE AND ACCESSORIES

What PDA software is available? Most PDAs come with a standard collection of software such as a to-do list, contacts manager, and calendar. Software applications such as Word and Excel are also available for PDAs. Although these programs are not as full featured as their desktop counterparts, they can read and create files that can be transmitted to full-version applications on your home computer. In addition, a variety of games, tools, and reference applications are available for PDAs from numerous software companies. A good source to locate software applications for your PDA is **www.mobileplanet.com**. In addition, **www.download.com** includes a list of shareware and freeware applications for PDA platforms.

One new application of interest is Colligo Networks' **BlueBoard**. This application allows you to use your PDA display as a drawing board and instantly connect it with up to four other PDAs. You can each be working on your own screen, updating and adding comments, and the changes you make are instantly seen by the other BlueBoard users on their screens (see Figure 8.21). The information is shared wirelessly using Bluetooth technology.

What accessories can I add to my PDA? As PDAs become increasingly popular, more add-on accessories are becoming available. For example, Global Positioning System (GPS) attachments allow you to use your PDA as a navigation device when you're traveling. You can also attach a business card reader to your PDA that scans business cards directly into your PDA and stores them in your Outlook contacts database. You'll find other specialty PDA attachments such as pH-measurement devices and bar code readers that can be used in various industries.

PDA OR CELL PHONE?

Do I need both a PDA and a cell phone? A number of devices are being released that attempt to combine a cell phone and a PDA into one unit. For example, the Handspring Treo and the Sony Ericsson P800 are both cell phones that have added PDA features (see Figure 8.22). Both are steps toward the ideal device, but each is making some compromises: there are features available on the best cell phones that are missing on these two devices, and there are more powerful PDAs available than either of these items. However, they do strike a nice balance for people who need features from both phones and PDAs. Still, if your main need is voice communications, get a cell phone. If your needs are more along the lines of keeping track of facts and figures or using computer-like programs, then you probably should opt for a PDA.

Tablet PCs

A **tablet PC** is a portable computer that includes two special technologies: advanced handwriting recognition and speech recognition. Tablet PCs are available from a variety of manufacturers, come in a variety of designs, and are about the same size as a clipboard. They weigh just 3 pounds with

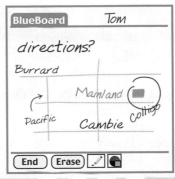

FIGURE 8.21

The BlueBoard application allows up to four people to use their PDAs as a mutual brainstorming drawing board.

FIGURE 8.22

The Handspring Treo (a) and the Sony Ericsson P800 (b) are part of a new generation of devices that merge the features of a cell phone and a PDA into one handheld.

DIG DEEPER

THE POWER OF GPS

Where in the world is Carmen San Diego? Or, more important, where in the world is the nearest gas station? Many people aren't whizzes at geography, but knowing your current location and the location of your destination can often come in handy. Luckily for those who are "directionally impaired," **Global Positioning System (GPS)** technology enables you to carry a powerful navigational aid in your pocket.

You've probably heard of GPS, but what is it exactly and how does it work? The Global Positioning System is a system of 21 satellites (plus three working spares), built and operated by the U.S. military, which constantly orbit the earth. GPS devices use an antenna to pick up the signals from these satellites and special software to transform those signals into latitude and longitude. Using the information obtained from the satellites, GPS devices can tell you what your geographical location is anywhere on the planet to within 10 feet (see Figure 8.23). Because they provide such detailed positioning information, GPS units are now used as navigational aids for aircraft, recreational boats, and automobiles, and they even come in handheld models for hikers.

Although this precise positioning information clearly redefines the fields of surveying and search and rescue operations, it has also changed other fields. Wildlife researchers now tag select animals and watch their migration patterns and how the population is distributed. Meanwhile, GPS was important to the two teams that created the Chunnel, the tunnel under the English Channel that connects England to France. One team worked from France toward England and the

FIGURE 8.23

GPS computes your location anywhere on earth from a system of orbiting satellites.

other from England toward France. They used GPS information along the way to make sure they were on target, and in 1990, the two sections joined to become

---

the removable keyboard attached, and just 2 pounds without it, making them much thinner and lighter than full-size laptops.

Why are they called tablet PCs? Tablet PCs are named such because the monitor can be used either in a traditional laptop mode or in "tablet mode," much like an electronic clipboard, as shown in Figure 8.24. Tablet PCs also can be connected to a full-size keyboard and monitor.

When would a tablet PC be the best mobile solution? A tablet PC can be the ideal solution when you require a lightweight, portable computer with full desktop processing power. Manufacturing sites, classrooms, and conference rooms are ideal settings for tablet PCs. They are very light

and, with their handwriting-recognition capabilities, allow you to take notes silently with no distracting keystrokes.

TABLET PC HARDWARE

What hardware is inside a tablet PC? Like any computer, a tablet PC includes a processor (CPU), operating system software, storage capabilities, input and output devices, and ports. What makes the tablet PC unique, however, is the way in which you input data into it.

How do I input data to a tablet PC? The most innovative input technology on the tablet is its use of **digital ink**. Digital ink is an extension of the text-entry systems

the first physical link between England and the continent of Europe since the Ice Age.

GPS has made its way into several commercial products as well. Hertz rental cars offer in-car GPS assistance with the NeverLost system. The unit is mounted on the front dashboard and displays your location on a map that is updated in real time as you drive. Enter your destination and a voice warns you of lane changes and approaching turns. If you miss a turn, it automatically reroutes you and gives you directions to get back on course. Flip to another screen and it shows you how far you have to drive to the next gas station, restaurant, or amusement park. Several car manufacturers such as Honda and Lexus are offering similar GPS navigation systems in their cars. And GPS navigation can be added to any vehicle using a PDA and a separate GPS accessory. You can purchase software maps for specific areas and get turn-by-turn driving directions from the PDA's speaker while your current location is displayed on the PDA screen.

The popularity of GPS units has even spawned a new hobby, called "geocaching." This hobby is a type of treasure hunt in which people with GPS-enabled devices try to reach specially hidden spots, or "geosites," at which a treasure, or "cache," is hidden. Participants visit geocaching Web sites such as **www.geocaching.com** to find the latitude and longitude coordinates for geosites around the world. They then take their GPS devices and they're off on their quest.

Although it sounds easy enough to find a geosite with a GPS device, reaching these sites can be another matter—some lie underwater, on the side of a cliff, or inside the basement of a city building. Once participants arrive at the geosite, they find the cache, which usually consists of a logbook in which other geocachers have left notes. Sometimes caches also contain trinkets, which geocachers can take as long as they leave one behind. When they get back home, geocachers e-mail the person who created the cache, reporting on the cache. The game can be expanded into multicaches—a treasure hunt leading players from one site to another—or a virtual cache, where the cache is a landmark and players have to answer a question from that spot to prove to the "cache owner" they were there.

However, having the ability to locate and track an object anywhere on earth does bring with it societal implications. The Federal Communications Commission (FCC) has mandated that by the end of 2005, every cell phone must include a GPS chip. This will enable the complete rollout of the Enhanced 911 (E911) program. E911 automatically provides dispatchers precision location information for any 911 call. It also means your cell phone records will include precise tracking information indicating where you are when you make a call.

In what ways could the tracking information provided by GPS devices be used unethically? Should the criteria for allowing government agencies to subpoena phone records be changed? Should users be allowed to turn off location information from their phones? Already, location records like these were used in determining that *New York Times* reporter Jayson Blair had been fabricating stories, resulting in his resignation. As we near the December 2005 FCC deadline, expect to see such privacy debates in the media.

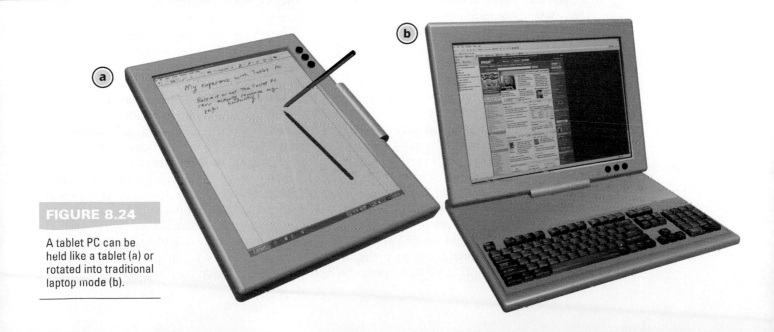

FIGURE 8.24

A tablet PC can be held like a tablet (a) or rotated into traditional laptop mode (b).

FIGURE 8.25

You input data into a tablet PC by writing on the touch-sensitive screen with a digital pen. The tablet then uses handwriting recognition to convert your writing to typewritten text.

used on PDA devices. Supporting digital ink, the tablet PC's entire screen is pressure-sensitive and reacts to a **digital pen**, allowing you to easily draw images and enter text, as shown in Figure 8.25. Once you enter text with the pen (using your own handwriting), you can convert it into typewritten text by tapping on the screen. You can also select blocks of text and move them around to a different location on the page, or erase text using a scribble motion.

Using the tablet PC's digital pen and ink, you can also annotate (or mark up) existing documents, such as a Word document, by importing them into special tablet PC ink-enabled programs, such as Windows Journal or Word 2003. The original document is unchanged, but your digital ink annotations on the document are also saved. Using this feature, you can mark up an article and send it to a coworker, add notes to a meeting agenda, or draw a route on a map.

How seamless is the use of digital ink and pens? There are delays between your pen movement and the text appearing and there are occasional mistakes in the handwriting recognition, so the experience

is not exactly like using pen on paper. Still, being able to have your notes translated into text is an appealing feature for many users. And if you prefer to use a keyboard, a software keyboard can appear on the screen and you can tap in text. Tablets also accept the Graffiti notation used in PDAs.

How do tablet PCs incorporate speech-recognition capabilities? As mentioned earlier, tablet PCs also come with integrated speech-recognition capabilities and software. The tablet can take dictation, recording your voice into a digital format. Your speech can then be converted into text for a word processor or can be interpreted as commands to the computer.

What are the storage and transfer options on tablets? Tablets are designed to be lightweight and to minimize the use of battery power, so they do not include a built-in DVD or CD drive. However, you can purchase external DVD/CD-RW (CD rewritable) drives so that you can transfer your files onto discs. Many tablets also include FireWire and USB 2.0 ports that enable you to attach high-speed peripherals such as external hard disk drives to your tablet PC. Some tablets offer flash memory slots as another option for storing and moving data, and some include built-in infrared ports that allow you to transfer data wirelessly at speeds up to 4.4 Mbps.

How can I quickly connect my tablet to my peripherals? A **docking station** is available for most tablet PC models. This piece of hardware allows you to connect printers, scanners, full-size monitors, mice, and other peripherals directly to the docking station (and therefore your tablet) very quickly. As shown in Figure 8.26, you simply slide your tablet into a docking station to connect it to all peripheral devices, rather than connecting all their cables individually.

What processors are used in tablet PCs? An important criterion for any portable tool like a tablet PC is low power consumption. Popular processors for tablet PCs include the Transmeta Crusoe 5800, which is used on the Compaq TC1000 tablet. The Crusoe processor uses very little power so the chip does not get as hot as ordinary CPU chips when it runs, thereby extending its life. The Gateway tablet uses the Intel Pentium M low-voltage processor specialized for mobile computing.

FIGURE 8.26

A docking station makes it easy to connect your tablet to your desktop monitor and any other peripherals. Just slide the tablet in place and you're ready to go.

Consuming less power also means the battery can last much longer. Battery life is extended to almost a full workday on one charge, and batteries can be "bridged." This means the tablet can be put into standby mode, not shut down, while you install a new battery.

How much memory can fit in a tablet? The amount of RAM designed for a specific model will vary by manufacturer. Several models on the market now begin with 256 MB of RAM but can be expanded up to 1 GB. Hard drives are offered in a range of capacities up to 60 GB or more.

TABLET SOFTWARE

Do tablet PCs have a special operating system? Tablet PCs run the Windows XP Tablet PC operating system. This operating system is based on the Windows XP Professional operating system but is expanded to include features unique to tablets, such as handwriting and speech recognition.

Can tablet PCs use the same software as desktop computers? Tablets can run any applications designed for Windows XP. All tablets include the Windows Journal application, which presents a legal pad-like interface you can use for note taking. The notes you take can be sent as e-mail or converted into appointments or tasks in Outlook. With Office you can add handwritten notes to any of the Office suite programs, including Word, Excel, Outlook, or PowerPoint.

TABLET OR PDA?

What benefits do tablet PCs have over PDAs and vice versa? Whereas tablet PCs have faster processors, a hard drive, and more RAM than PDAs, PDAs are smaller, lighter, and much cheaper. Thus, whether a tablet PC or a PDA is best for you depends on the needs you have for processing power and portability as well as your budget. Figure 8.27 compares these two devices.

FIGURE 8.27 Comparing PDAs and Tablets						
	SCREEN SIZE	CPU SPEED	RAM	HARD DISK	APPROXIMATE WEIGHT	COST
PDA	3" to 4"	400 MHz	64 MB	None	5 oz.	$100+
TABLET PC	12"	1,000 MHz	1 GB	60 GB	3 lbs.	$1,700+

BITS AND BYTES

Smart Displays

Want to be able to use your desktop computer in many different rooms of your house? "Smart displays," shown in Figure 8.28, are portable flat-screen monitors that allow you to access your regular desktop wirelessly from any room in your house, just like you can when you're sitting at your computer. These 3-pound, touch-sensitive monitors can run for up to four hours on a single battery charge, and some come with wireless keyboards and desktop docking stations. They are already cheaper than tablet PCs, and as prices continue to drop, you'll see them appearing in more homes and offices.

FIGURE 8.28

Smart displays are flat-panel monitors that connect wirelessly to your desktop computer, allowing you to access your desktop from any room in your house.

TRENDS IN IT

UBIQUITOUS NETWORKING: Wherever You Go, There You Are

Instead of having to move the files and programs you need onto mobile devices, how about having a network that "watches" your movements and moves the data so that it follows you? Researchers at the AT&T laboratories at Cambridge University are attempting to make this possible by creating a detection system that can track your location within a building, moving your files wherever you go. To take advantage of the network, users will carry a small device called a "bat," shown in Figure 8.29. This device will have a unique ID number and contain a radio transceiver and transmitter. A detection system (or central controller) installed in the building will keep track of the physical location of the bats and hence the people who carry them.

How does this system work? Suppose you go into a conference room that contains a computer and a phone. The controller is tracking the bat you have in your pocket, so it knows you entered the conference room and therefore routes all your phone calls to the phone in the conference room. It also sends your files and desktop settings to the computer in the conference room.

FIGURE 8.29

Bats are about the size of a pager device and therefore small enough to be carried comfortably. They allow the detection system to locate the bat owners wherever they roam in the facility.

What if two people are in the conference room at the same time? The controller assigns available devices to the first person who enters the room. However, using interactive buttons on your bat, you can indicate to the controller that you wish to take temporary possession of a device assigned to another person.

Ubiquitous networks such as this will force us to rethink our territorial approach to work and living spaces, as well as some of our ideas about privacy. In the future, because connectivity will follow us around, access to information may always be right where we are.

Laptops

The most powerful mobile computing solution is a **laptop computer**, sometimes called a **notebook computer**. Laptops offer large displays and all of the computing power of a full desktop system (see Figure 8.30). Although weighing just 6 pounds, laptops are still much heavier than the 2- or 3-pound tablet PCs.

This difference is important if you're carrying the unit all day, but not if you're going to be working on a desk where the laptop can rest.

LAPTOP HARDWARE

What hardware comes in a laptop?

Laptops can be equipped with DVD/CD-RW drives, large hard drives, and up to 1 GB of

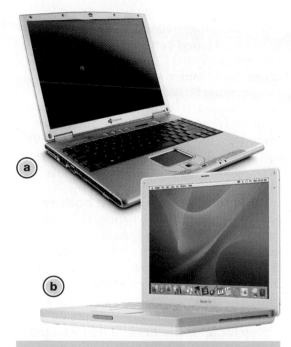

Laptop computers offer larger displays and more powerful processors than desktops could offer just a few years ago. Here you see (a) a PC laptop and (b) an Apple laptop.

slower than the latest available CPU offered for desktop units. Whereas existing desktops can currently run a 3.4-GHz processor, most laptop CPUs run at speeds less than 2.4 GHz. You won't notice the difference if you're using word processing programs, but if you run many applications at the same time or use programs that make heavy demands on the CPU (such as video-editing software), the laptop's performance may seem sluggish compared with a desktop computer.

Many laptop systems use low-power processors such as the Intel Pentium M series, designed to consume less power and extend battery life. The Pentium M can be combined with two additional components, the Intel 855 chipset and the Intel PRO/Wireless network connection, in a package called the Intel Centrino. The Centrino is optimized to work in a highly mobile setting because it uses less power, is more stable, and provides integrated wireless capability.

LAPTOP OPERATING SYSTEMS AND PORTS

RAM. Although the size of a laptop might prohibit it from having all of the drives you're interested in, newer models feature **hot-swappable bays**. This means that while the laptop is running, you can remove a DVD drive and exchange it with a Zip disk drive, for example, allowing the laptop to be much more versatile. As we discussed in Chapter 2, input devices on laptops include keyboards with built-in mouse functionality. In terms of output devices, many laptops include large display screens measuring up to 17 inches diagonally.

What are popular CPUs for laptops? CPUs available for laptops are usually a bit

Are there special operating systems for laptops? Laptops use the same operating systems that run on desktop systems. However, laptop operating systems do have some special settings, such as power management profiles. A power management profile contains recommended power-saving settings, such as turning off your hard drive after 15 minutes of no use, shutting down the display after 20 minutes of no movement, and switching the machine to standby or hibernation mode after a certain length of time.

Can laptops connect to other devices easily? As you can see in Figure 8.31, laptops include a full set of ports,

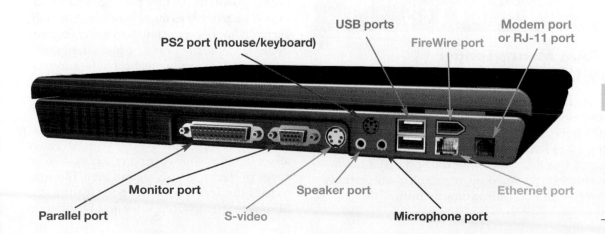

USB ports

PS2 port (mouse/keyboard)

FireWire port

Modem port or RJ-11 port

Monitor port

Speaker port

Parallel port

S-video

Microphone port

Ethernet port

Laptops include FireWire, USB 1.0 and 2.0, Ethernet, serial, parallel, and IrDA ports, as well as RJ-11 jacks for a modem connection.

including FireWire, USB 1.0 and 2.0, serial, parallel, infrared (IrDA); RJ-11 jacks for a modem connection; and Ethernet ports for wired networking connections. A newer version of FireWire, FireWire 800, is beginning to appear on laptop units as well. This port allows transfer speeds of twice the original FireWire connection, up to 800 Mbps.

Often, the size limitations of laptops mean that they don't offer as many of each type of port as in a desktop system. Therefore, if you buy a laptop you should consider how you will use your machine and whether you will need an expansion hub. An expansion hub is a device that connects to a USB port, creating three or four USB ports from one. If you will be connecting a USB mouse, printer, and scanner to your laptop, you may be short one USB port, in which case a hub would come in handy.

How do laptops connect to wireless networks? Most laptops have integrated support for wireless connectivity. As we discussed in Chapter 7, the 802.11b Wi-Fi wireless standard is the standard used in most wireless networks, whereas the faster 802.11g Wi-Fi standard is also becoming available on laptops. The 802.11g standard allows wireless connections to operate at up to 54 Mbps instead of the 11 Mbps offered in the 802.11b standard. Several laptops also offer built-in Bluetooth chips that allow you to connect to other Bluetooth-enabled devices.

LAPTOP BATTERIES AND ACCESSORIES

What types of batteries are there for laptops? Rechargeable batteries are lithium based (Li-ion batteries) or nickel-based (Ni-Cad). Lithium-based batteries are lighter than nickel-based batteries and do not show the "memory effect" that nickel-based batteries do. **Memory effect** means that the battery must be completely used up before it is recharged. If not, the battery won't hold as much charge as it originally did. Unless budget is a serious consideration, you should opt for the more expensive lithium batteries because low weight and lack of memory effect are significant advantages.

How long does a laptop battery last? The capacity of a battery is measured in ampere-hours (A-hrs). Ampere is a measure of current flow, so a battery rated at 5 A-hrs can provide 5 amps of current for an hour. Battery power depends on the device you're using and the work you're doing. A high-performance battery can operate a laptop for up to five hours if fully charged. However, using the laptop's DVD drive can consume a high-performance battery in as little as 90 minutes. Some laptop systems allow you to install two batteries at the same time, doubling the battery life but forcing you to purchase a second battery and have both fully charged.

Do I need to use my battery everywhere I go? Some environments support easy access to power for laptops. For example, you can use an AC/DC or DC/DC converter to enable a laptop to run in a car without using battery power. In addition, many airplanes offer laptop power connections at each seat, although to use such a connection you have to buy a power converter and adapter.

What if I need laptop computing power but in a smaller, lighter configuration? Just coming on the market are devices known as **subnotebook computers** such as the Sony Vaio U101 shown in Figure 8.32. Subnotebooks pack major computing power into a tiny package and try to extend battery life as far as possible. Although currently more expensive than many conventional laptops, they may be just what you need if size is your biggest consideration.

What special purchases might a laptop require? Because a laptop is so easily stolen, purchasing a security lock is a wise investment. And as is the case with regular desktops, power surges can adversely affect laptops, so investing in a portable surge protector is also a good idea. (Be sure to read the Technology in Focus feature "Protecting Your Computer and Backing

BITS AND BYTES

More RAM Means Longer Battery Life for Your Laptop

Your laptop stores data both in RAM and on the hard disk drive. Increasing your RAM capacity makes your laptop perform more quickly because data can be read from RAM much faster than from a hard drive. Adding more RAM to your laptop will also make your battery last longer. This is because if the data needed is not in RAM, the hard drive must be powered up, requiring about 30 times as much battery power as simply reading directly from RAM.

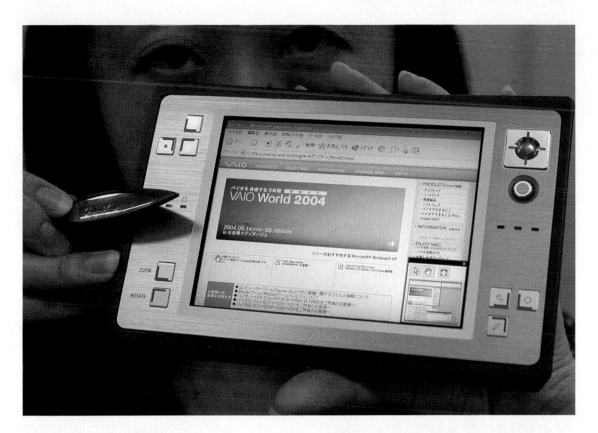

FIGURE 8.32

The Sony Vaio U is a subnotebook computer with a 600-MHz processor, 256 MB of RAM, 30 GB of storage, integrated Wi-Fi, and a 7.1-inch screen.

Up Your Data" for more information about protecting your laptop.)

If you frequently make presentations to large groups, adding a lightweight projector to your laptop might prove useful. Printers have also become travel-sized. Figure 8.33 shows some of these special laptop accessories.

SOUND BYTE

TABLET AND LAPTOP TOUR

In this Sound Byte, you'll take a tour of a tablet PC and a laptop computer, learning about the unique features and ports available on each.

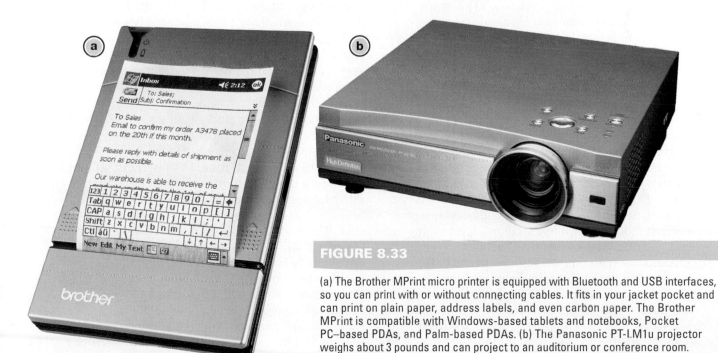

FIGURE 8.33

(a) The Brother MPrint micro printer is equipped with Bluetooth and USB interfaces, so you can print with or without connecting cables. It fits in your jacket pocket and can print on plain paper, address labels, and even carbon paper. The Brother MPrint is compatible with Windows-based tablets and notebooks, Pocket PC–based PDAs, and Palm-based PDAs. (b) The Panasonic PT-LM1u projector weighs about 3 pounds and can project to an auditorium or conference room.

LAPTOP OR DESKTOP?

How does a laptop compare to a desktop? Desktop systems are invariably a better value than laptops. Because of the laptop's small **footprint** (the amount of space on the desk it takes up), you pay more for each component. Each piece has had extra engineering time invested to make sure it fits in the smallest space. In addition, a desktop system offers you more expandability options. It's easier to add new ports and devices because of the amount of room available in the desktop computer's design.

Desktop systems are also more reliable. Because of the amount of vibration that a laptop experiences, as well as the added exposure to dust, water, and temperature fluctuations, laptops do not last as long as desktop computers. Manufacturers offer extended warranty plans that cover accidental damage and unexpected drops, although at a price.

How long should I be able to keep my laptop? The answer to that question depends on how easy it is to upgrade your system. Take note of the maximum amount of memory you can install in your laptop. Internal hard disks are not easy to upgrade in a laptop, but if you have a FireWire or USB 2.0 port, you can add an external hard drive for more storage space. Most laptops are equipped with PC Card slots, which are slots on the side of the laptop that accept special credit card–sized devices called **PC Cards**, shown in Figure 8.34. PC Cards can add fax modems, network connections, wireless adapters, USB 2.0 and FireWire ports, and other capabilities to your laptop.

You can also add a device that allows you to read flash memory cards, such as

TRENDS IN IT

EMERGING TECHNOLOGIES:
Nanotubes: The Next Big Thing Is Pretty Darn Small!

In the classic 1967 film *The Graduate*, Dustin Hoffman is a young man uncertain about which career he should embark upon. At a cocktail party, an older gentleman provides him with some career advice, telling him, "I've got just one word for you . . . plastics!" This made sense at the time because plastics were coming on strong as a replacement for metal. If *The Graduate* were remade today, the advice would be, "I've got just one word for you . . . nanotubes!"

As you learned in Chapter 1, *nanoscience* involves the study of molecules and structures (called *nanostructures*) whose size ranges from 1 to 100 nanometers (or one-billionth of a meter). Using nanotechnology, scientists are hoping to one day build resources from the molecular level by manipulating individual atoms instead of using raw materials already found in nature (such as wood or iron ore). This would allow us to create microscopic computers, the ultimate in portable devices. Imagine nano-sized robotic computers swimming through your arteries clearing them of plaque. Consider carrying a supercomputer with you the size of a pencil eraser, or even better, having the power of your desktop computer implanted in your body as a nano-sized chip.

The possibilities of miniaturization are endless, but from what would the computer circuits for these devices be constructed? Carbon nanotubes are poised to be the building blocks of the future. You're familiar with carbon from pencils. The graphite core in a pencil is composed of sheets of carbon atoms laid out in a honeycomb pattern. Individual sheets of graphite are very strong, but don't bond well to other sheets. This makes them ideal for use in a pencil because, as you write, the graphite flakes off and leaves marks on the paper. Unfortunately, graphite doesn't conduct electricity very well. This, coupled with the lack of strong bonding principles, makes graphite unsuitable as a material to manufacture circuits.

In 1991, carbon nanotubes were discovered. Nanotubes are essentially a sheet of carbon atoms (much like graphite) laid out in a honeycomb pattern but rolled into a spherical tube, as shown in Figure 8.35. Arranging the carbon in a tube increases its strength astronomically. It is estimated that carbon nanotubes are 10 to 100 times stronger per unit of weight than steel. This should make them ideal for constructing many types of devices and building materials. Some day we may have earthquake-proof buildings constructed from nanotubes or virtually indestructible clothing woven from nanotube fibers.

But how does this help us build a computer? Aside from strength, the most interesting property of nanotubes is that they are good conductors of electricity.

Compact Flash, Memory Sticks, and Secure Digital cards. As new types of ports and devices are introduced, many will be manufactured in PC Card formats so that you can make sure your laptop is not obsolete before its time.

FIGURE 8.34

PC Cards add functionality to your laptop.

Nanotubes are actually classified as semimetal, meaning they can have properties that are a cross between semiconductors (such as silicon, which is used to create computer chips) and metals. In fact, depending on how a nanotube is constructed, it can change from a semiconductor to a metal along the length of the tube. These properties make it vastly superior to silicon for the construction of transistor pathways in computer chips, because it provides engineers with more versatility.

In addition, although the smallest silicon transistors that are likely to be produced in the future will be millions of atoms wide, scientists believe that transistors constructed of nanotubes would be only 100 to 1,000 atoms wide. This represents a quantum leap in miniaturization even surpassing the original invention of the transistor. Just imagine what can be done when nanotube transistors replace silicon transistors!

So, when can you buy that pencil eraser–sized computer? Not for quite a while. At this point, researchers can manufacture nanotubes only in extremely small quantities at a large cost. But the U.S. government and many multinational corporations are expected to pour billions of dollars into nanoscience research over the next five years. The ongoing research will hopefully lead to breakthroughs in manufacturing technology that will result in nano-scale computers within your lifetime.

FIGURE 8.35

Here is a highly magnified close-up of a carbon nanotube. Rolling the sheets of carbon atoms into a tube shape gives them incredible strength.

Summary

1. What are the advantages and limitations of mobile computing?

Mobile computing allows you to communicate with others, remain productive, and have access to your personal information and schedules, Internet-based information, and important software no matter where you are. However, because mobile devices have been miniaturized, they are more expensive and less rugged than desktop equipment. In addition, battery life limits the usefulness of mobile devices, the screen area is small on most devices, the speed of Internet connection is currently very low, and wireless Internet coverage is limited.

2. What are the various mobile computing devices?

There is a range of mobile computing devices on the market today, including paging devices (pagers), cellular phones, MP3 players, personal digital assistants (PDAs), tablet PCs, and laptop (notebook) computers.

3. What can pagers do and who uses them?

A pager is a small wireless device that allows you to receive numeric (and sometimes text) messages on a small display screen. Two-way pagers support both receiving and sending messages. Pagers have long battery lives, are very compact, and are the most inexpensive mobile computing device. People who need to be reachable but want an inexpensive and lightweight device are the primary market for pagers.

4. How do cell phone components resemble a traditional computer and how do cell phones work?

Just like a computer system, cell phones include a processor (CPU), memory, input and output devices, software, and an operating system. When you speak into a cell phone, the sound enters as a sound wave. Analog sound waves need to be digitized, so an analog-to-digital converter chip converts these sound waves into digital signals. The digital information is then compressed (by a digital signal processor) so that it transmits more quickly to another phone. Finally, the digital information is transmitted as a radio wave through the cellular network to the destination phone.

5. What can I carry in an MP3 player and how does it store data?

An MP3 player is a device that enables you to carry MP3 files around with you. MP3 players store mainly digital music files, but some players also allow you to carry contact databases, images, and video and image files. The most inexpensive players use only memory chips to store data, whereas more expensive models use a built-in hard drive, which provides more storage. Some MP3 players allow you to add removable memory called flash memory.

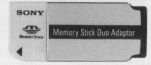

6. What can I use a PDA for and what internal components and features does it have?

PDAs are powerful devices that can carry calendars, contact lists, personal productivity software programs, songs, photos, games, and more. Like any computer, a PDA includes a processor, operating system software, input and output devices, and ports. All PDAs feature touch-sensitive screens that allow you to enter data with a stylus. You can use either handwritten text or special notation systems to enter data into a PDA. In terms of output devices, PDAs come with LCD screens in a variety of resolutions. The two main PDA operating systems are the Palm OS and the Pocket PC system. PDAs do not come with built-in hard drives, but for memory needs beyond their built-in RAM and ROM, PDAs use removable flash memory.

7. How can I synchronize my PDA with my desktop computer?

The process of updating your data so the files on your mobile device and desktop computer are the same is called synchronizing. To synchronize your desktop and PDA, you place the PDA in a cradle and touch a "hot sync" button. This begins the process of information transfer (or synchronization) that updates both sets of files to the most current version. Other options for synchronizing or transferring files include using IrDA ports and the newer Bluetooth wireless connectivity option.

8. What is a tablet PC and why would I want to use one?

A tablet PC is a portable computer that includes advanced handwriting and speech recognition. Tablet PCs are named such because the display monitor can be used either in a traditional laptop mode or in tablet mode. The most innovative input technology on the tablet PC is digital ink. Supporting digital ink, the tablet's screen is pressure-sensitive and reacts to a digital pen. A tablet PC can be the ideal solution when you require a lightweight, portable computer with full desktop processing power.

9. How powerful are laptops and how do they compare to desktop computers?

The most powerful mobile computing solution is a laptop (or notebook) computer. Laptops offer large displays and can be equipped with DVD/CD-RW drives, hard drives, and up to 1 GB of RAM. Many models feature hot-swappable bays and a full set of ports. Still, desktop systems are more reliable and cost-effective than laptops. In addition, it is easier to upgrade and add new ports and devices to a desktop than to a laptop. And although powerful, CPUs for laptops are usually a bit slower than the latest CPU offered for desktop units. Still, many users feel the mobility laptops offer is worth the added expense.

Key Terms

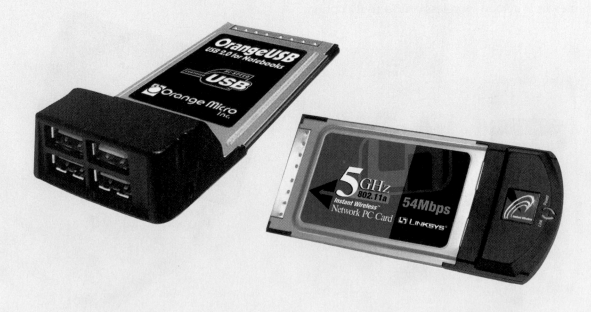

Buzz Words

Word Bank

- mobile switching center
- WML
- processor speed
- microbrowser
- tablet PC
- PDA
- memory effect
- flash memory card

- SMS
- synchronize
- stylus
- MP3 player
- laptop
- GPS
- mobile device(s)
- analog-to-digital
  converter chip

- Pocket PC
- MMS
- cradle
- Bluetooth
- cell phone
- Graffiti
- pager
- Palm OS
- digital ink

Instructions: Fill in the blanks using the words from the Word Bank.

Kathleen's new job as a sales rep is going to mean a lot of travel. She'll need to start thinking about using (1)_____ to stay productive when she's out of the office. Because she needs voice communication and not just text exchange, she'll be selecting a (2)_____ rather than a (3)_____. With her cell phone, she will be able to exchange quick text messages with her coworkers using (4)_____. When she accesses the Internet from her cell phone, she will use (5)_____ software to check the latest stock prices.

Because she travels a lot and loves music, she has been considering investing in a digital (6)_____. However, she has instead decided to purchase a more expensive, more powerful (7)_____ that includes MP3 capabilities. That way, she can also use the device as more than just an MP3 player. Seeing that she needs more storage room, she also invests in a removable (8)_____ on which she'll store her MP3 files. Because she's a hiker, she wants to use her PDA as a navigation device, so she has purchased a (9)_____ accessory to go with it.

To make sure she is getting the best device with the most powerful processor, Kathleen has been comparing benchmarks that measure (10)_____. She knows this is an important part of getting the most powerful device. In addition, she wants to make sure she can (11)_____ her PDA with her desktop computer, so the files on both always match. Thus, she bought a PDA that includes the wireless (12)_____ technology, as well as an external (13)_____ that connects her PDA to her computer through a USB port.

Because she still needs to run powerful software packages when she's out of the office, she bought a (14)_____ as well. It was a better choice than a full-sized (15)_____ because she carries it with her all day, taking notes while standing on the production floor.

Organizing Key Terms

Instructions: This chapter introduces many new terms and concepts. In the following illustration, fill in each of the blanks with key terms or concepts from the chapter in order to show how categories of ideas fit together.

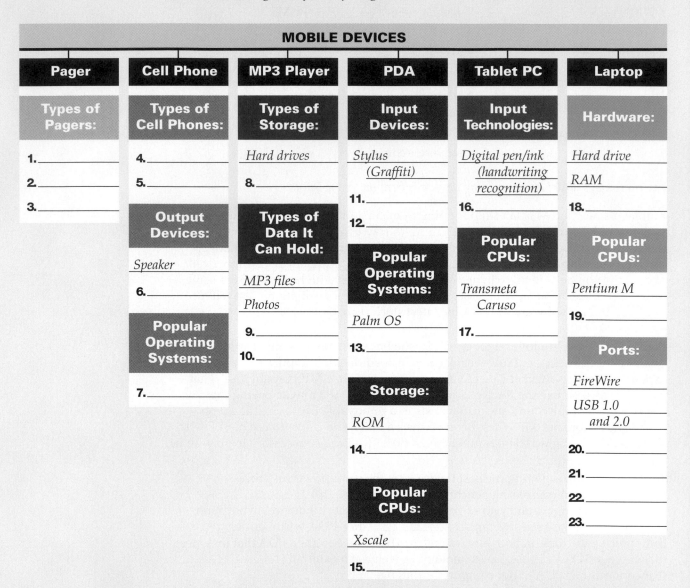

MOBILE DEVICES

Pager	Cell Phone	MP3 Player	PDA	Tablet PC	Laptop
Types of Pagers:	**Types of Cell Phones:**	**Types of Storage:**	**Input Devices:**	**Input Technologies:**	**Hardware:**
1._____	4._____	*Hard drives*	*Stylus (Graffiti)*	*Digital pen/ink (handwriting recognition)*	*Hard drive*
2._____	5._____	8._____	11._____	16._____	*RAM*
3._____			12._____		18._____
	Output Devices:	**Types of Data It Can Hold:**	**Popular Operating Systems:**	**Popular CPUs:**	**Popular CPUs:**
	Speaker	*MP3 files*	*Palm OS*	*Transmeta Caruso*	*Pentium M*
	6._____	*Photos*	13._____	17._____	19._____
	Popular Operating Systems:	9._____	**Storage:**		**Ports:**
		10._____	*ROM*		*FireWire*
	7._____		14._____		*USB 1.0 and 2.0*
			Popular CPUs:		20._____
			Xscale		21._____
			15._____		22._____
					23._____

Becoming Computer Fluent

You have a job as a sales representative at a large publishing company. Your boss is considering investing in some kind of mobile device with Internet access to help you perform your duties. However, first she requires a justification. What mobile device(s) would be best suited for your position? Why would you need (or not need) Internet access for your mobile device? Does it depend on which type of device you are using? Does it depend on your job responsibilities? What advantages would there be to the company? What hardware would be required?

Instructions: Using the preceding scenario, write a report using as many of the key words from the chapter as you can. Be sure the sentences are grammatically and technically correct.

Making the Transition to . . . Next Semester

1. Choosing Devices to Fit Your Needs

As a student, which devices discussed in this chapter would have the most immediate impact on the work you do each day? Which would provide the best value (that is, the most increase in productivity and organization per dollar spent)?

2. Choosing the Best Laptop

Compare the Apple PowerBook series of laptop computers with the Dell Inspiron 8500 series. Consider price, performance, expandability, and portability. Explain which would be the better investment for your needs next semester.

3. Choosing the Best Cell Phone Plan

Major national cellular providers include AT&T, Verizon, T-Mobile, and Sprint. Visit their Web sites and compare the prices and features of their popular cellular plans for both minimal users and power users. Based on your research, which cell phone plan would be best for your needs?

4. Choosing the Best PDA

Visit the Electronics store at Amazon.com and locate the PDA section. Compare three different PDA models and list their price, input and output devices, operating systems, built-in memory, processor speed, and other special features.

a. Which of the three models you compared is the best value for your needs?

b. What special features does that PDA have? What accessories would you buy for your PDA to make it more useful?

c. Would you consider buying a used PDA? Why or why not?

d. Next, investigate PDA software on sites such as **www.download.com**. What software would you buy for a PDA and which operating system does that software require?

5. How Many MP3 Files Can You Fit?

Fill out the following table to determine how many minutes of MP3 files you could store depending on the sampling rate of the MP3 files. Use the following to help you fill in the table:

- Say you sample music at 192 kilobits per second. There are 8 bits in one byte, so 192 kilobits per second = 192/8 = 24 KB per second.

- There are 60 seconds in one minute, so the number of kilobytes per minute is equal to 24 KB per second times 60 seconds = 1,440 KB per minute.

- With 256 MB of space, which is 256,000 KB, there would be room for 256,000 KB divided by 1,440 KB per minute = approximately 177 minutes of songs that can be stored.

SAMPLING RATE, KILOBITS PER SECOND	NUMBER OF KILOBYTES PER SECOND (KB/SEC)	NUMBER OF KILOBYTES (KB) PER MINUTE	FLASH CARD MEMORY	MINUTES OF SONGS THAT CAN BE STORED
192 Kbps	192/8 = 24 KBps	24 KBps * 60 seconds = 1,440 KB per minute	256 MB	256,000 KB / 1,440 KB per minute = 177 minutes
128 Kbps			256 MB	
96 Kbps			256 MB	
64 Kbps			256 MB	

Making the Transition to . . . The Workplace

1. Corporate Mobile Computing Needs

Imagine your company is boosting its sales force and looking to the future of mobile technology. Your boss has asked you to research the following issues surrounding mobile computing for the company:

a. Do mobile computing devices present increased security risks? What would happen if you left a flash memory card at a meeting and a competitor picked it up? Are there ways to protect your data on mobile devices?

b. Can viruses attack mobile devices? Is there any special software on the market to protect mobile devices from viruses?

c. Is there a role for mobile computing devices even if employees don't leave the building? Which devices would be important for a company to consider for use within corporate offices?

2. 3G Communications

The next generation of telecommunications (nicknamed "3G" for "third generation") allows the speed of cellular network transmissions to rise from 144 Kbps to 2 Mbps. How does that compare to dial-up and cable modem access for wired networks? What implications does it have on information access and e-commerce?

3. Mobile Speed Limits

Research the Internet and determine what speed limitations are expected to exist in the future with regards to mobile devices.

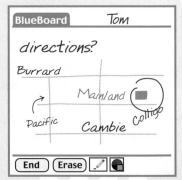

Critical Thinking Questions

Instructions: Albert Einstein used "Gedanken experiments," or critical thinking questions, to develop his theory of relativity. Some ideas are best understood by experimenting with them in our own minds. The following critical thinking questions are designed to demand your full attention but require only a comfortable chair—no technology.

1. Mobile Devices and Society

Do you think we will ever become a completely wireless society? Will there always be a need for some land lines (physical wired connections)? What social changes do you predict from increased mobile access to information? Will there be more social interaction? Less? Will mobile computing promote increased understanding between people? More isolation?

2. The Ultimate Mobile Devices

As devices become lighter and smaller we are seeing a combining of multiple functions into one device.

a. What would the ultimate convergent mobile device be for you? Is there a limit in weight, size, or complexity?

b. America Online Instant Messenger (AIM) service is now available on some cellular phone systems (for example, T-Mobile provides this service). Would the ability to be alerted to IM buddies on your cell phone be useful to you? What would you be willing to pay for this feature?

3. Protecting Intellectual Property

The recording industry, recording artists, and consumers find themselves in a complex discussion when the topic of peer-to-peer sharing systems is brought up.

a. What kind of solution would you propose to safeguard the business interests of the industry, the intellectual property rights of the musicians, and the freedoms of the consumers?

b. Have you ever downloaded music off the Web? If so, did you download the music from a legal site? Do you think illegal download sites should be allowed to exist?

4. Privacy Concerns: Bats

Consider the implications of the bat tracking device we discussed in the Trends in IT feature. Would you agree to be "tracked" at work if it meant a more convenient way to use communication tools? What sorts of privacy risks do such devices pose?

5. Privacy Concerns: GPS

Consider the following questions related to GPS security risks:

a. Your employer asks you to carry a GPS-enabled cell phone. The GPS chip inside allows a private service (**www.ulocate.com**) to gather information on your last location, the path you took to get there, and your average speed from point to point. What are the privacy issues this presents? Would you agree to take the phone?

b. Would you agree to insert a GPS-enabled tracking device into your pet? Your child? What legislation would be required if tracking data were available on you? Would you be willing to sell that information to marketing agencies? Should that data be available to the government if you were suspected of a crime?

Team Time   Assessing Mobile Computing Needs

Problem:

You have formed a consulting team that advises clients on how to move their businesses into the new mobile computing age.

Task:

Each team will be defined as an expert resource in one of the mobile devices presented in this chapter: cell phones, PDAs, tablet PCs, or laptops. For each of the scenarios described by a client, the team should assess how strong a fit their device is to that client's needs.

Process:

Divide the class into three or four teams and assign each team a different mobile device (cell phone, PDA, tablet PC, or laptop).

1. Research the current features and prices for the mobile device your team has been assigned.
2. Consider the following three clients:
   - An elementary classroom that wants to have students carry mobile devices to the nearby creek to do a science project on water quality
   - A manufacturing plant that wants managers using a mobile device to be able to report back hourly on the production line's performance and problems
   - A pharmaceutical company that wants to outfit its sales reps with the devices they need to be prepared to promote their products when they visit physicians

   Discuss the advantages and disadvantages of your device for each of these clients. Consider value, reliability, computing needs, and communication needs as well as expandability for the future.
3. Prepare a final report for the team that considers the costs, availability, and unique features of the device that led you to recommend or not recommend it for each client.
4. Bring the research materials from the individual team meetings to class. Looking at the clients' needs, make final decisions as to which mobile device is best suited for each client.

Conclusion:

There are a number of mobile computing devices on the market today. Finding the best mobile device to use in any given situation depends on factors such as value, reliability, expandability, and the computing and communication needs of the client.

Materials on the Web

In addition to the review materials presented here, you'll find extra materials on the book's companion Web site (**www.prenhall.com/techinaction**) that will help reinforce your understanding of the chapter content. These materials include the following:

Sound Byte Lab Guides

For each Sound Byte mentioned in the chapter, there is a corresponding lab guide located on the book's companion Web site. These guides review the material presented in the Sound Byte and direct you to various Web resources that examine the material. The Sound Byte Lab Guides for this chapter include these:

- PDAs on the Road and at Home
- Tablet and Laptop Tour

True/False and Multiple-Choice Quizzes

The book's Web site includes a true/false and a multiple-choice quiz for this chapter. You can take these quizzes, automatically check the results, and e-mail the results to your instructor.

Web Research Projects

The book's Web site also includes a number of Web research projects for this chapter. These projects ask you to search the Web for information on computer-related careers, milestones in computer history, important people and companies, emerging technologies, and the applications and implications of different technologies.

Technology in Action also features unique interactive Help Desk training, in which you'll assume the role of Help Desk operator taking calls about concepts learned in each chapter. The Help Desk calls for this chapter include:

- Using MP3 Players
- Using PDAs

CHAPTER 9

OBJECTIVES

After reading this chapter, you should be able to answer the following questions:

- **What is a switch and how does it work in a computer? (pp. 356–357)**

- **What is the binary number system and what role does it play in a computer system? (pp. 357–361)**

- **What is inside the CPU and how do these components operate? (pp. 361–362)**

- **How does a CPU process data and instructions? (pp. 363–366)**

- **What is cache memory? (p. 364)**

- **What types of RAM are there? (pp. 366–369)**

- **What is a bus and how does it function in a computer system? (pp. 371–373)**

- **How do manufacturers make CPUs so that they run faster? (pp. 373–375)**

SOUND BYTES

Behind the Scenes:

Inside the System Unit

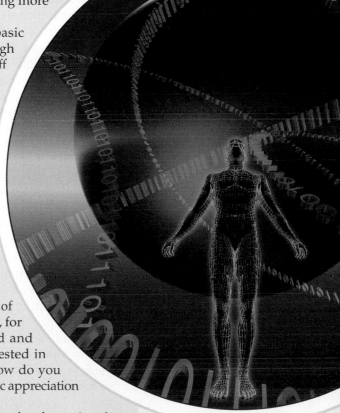

Although twins, Jim and Joe are completely different in certain ways. Joe checks the oil in his car regularly, knows the air pressure in his tires, and can tell when the fan belt should be replaced. Jim, on the other hand, asks, "Oil level? What oil?" and drives from place to place relying on service departments to keep his car running. Although Jim's lack of maintenance hasn't resulted in any catastrophic problems, Joe warns his brother that by not learning a few things about cars, he'll end up paying more to keep up his car, if it even lasts that long.

Similarly, after taking a class in college, Joe has a strong but basic understanding of his computer and keeps his PC running well through periodic maintenance and upgrades. Not surprisingly, Jim is hands-off when it comes to his computer. He's happy to just turn it on and open the files he needs. He can't be bothered with all the acronyms: CPU, RAM, and all the rest. When there's a problem, Jim just calls his brother. He hates waiting and paying for technical service and is afraid he'll mess up his system if he tries to fix things himself. But after making another 2:00 A.M. call to Joe after his computer crashed, Joe told him, "Take a class or pay a technician!"

When it comes to your computer, are you most like Jim or Joe? Joe found out how easy it is to understand his computer and isn't dependent on anyone else to keep it running. But if you use a computer without understanding the hardware inside, you'll have to pay a technician to fix or upgrade it. Meanwhile, it won't be as efficient as if you were fine-tuning it yourself, and you may find yourself buying a new computer earlier than necessary.

There are other advantages to having a deeper understanding of computer hardware. If you're preparing for a career in programming, for example, understanding computer hardware will affect the speed and efficiency of the programs you design. In addition, if you're interested in computers, you're no doubt excited by advances you hear about. How do you evaluate the impact of a new type of memory or a new processor? A basic appreciation of how a computer system is built and designed is a good start.

In this chapter, we'll build on what you've learned about computer hardware in other chapters and go behind the scenes, looking at your system unit's components in more detail. First we examine how computers translate the commands you input into the digits they can understand: 1s and 0s. Next, we analyze the internal workings of the central processing unit (CPU) and memory. We then look at buses, the highways that transport data between the CPU, memory, and other devices connected to the computer. But first, let's look at the building blocks of computers: switches.

Digital Data: Switches and Bits

In earlier chapters, you learned that the **system unit** is the box that contains the central electronic components of the computer, including the central processing unit (CPU), memory, motherboard, and many other circuit boards that help the computer to function. But how exactly does the computer perform all of its tasks? How does it process the data you input? In this section, we discuss how the CPU performs its functions—adding, subtracting, moving data around the system, and so on—using nothing but a large number of on/off switches. In fact, as you'll learn, a computer system can be viewed as just an enormous collection of on/off switches.

ELECTRONIC SWITCHES

What are switches and what do they do? You learned earlier that unlike humans, computers work exclusively with numbers (not words). To process data into information, computers need to work in a language they understand. This language, called **binary language**, consists of just two numbers: 0 and 1. Everything a computer does (such as process data or print a report) is broken down into a series of 0s and 1s.

Why do computers use 0s and 1s to process data? Because modern computers are electronic, digital machines, they understand only two states of existence: on and off. Computers represent these two possibilities, or states, using the numbers (or digits) 1 and 0. **Electronic switches** are devices inside the computer that can be flipped between these two states: 1 or 0, on or off.

Although the notion of switches may seem complex, you use various forms of switches every day. For example, a button is a mechanical switch: pushed in, it could represent the value 1, whereas popped out, it could represent the value 0. Another switch you use each day is a water faucet. As shown in Figure 9.1, shutting it off so no water flows could represent the value 0, whereas turning it on could represent the value 1.

Because computers are built from a huge collection of switches, using buttons or water faucets obviously would limit the amount of data computers could store. It would also make computers very large and

On

Off

FIGURE 9.1

Water faucets can be used to represent binary switches. Turning the faucet on could represent the value 1, whereas shutting the faucet off so no water flows could represent the value 0.

cause them to run at very slow speeds. Thus, the history of computers is really a story about creating smaller and faster sets of electronic switches so that more data can be stored and manipulated quickly.

What were the first switches used in computers? The earliest generation of electronic computers used devices called **vacuum tubes** as switches, as shown in Figure 9.2a. Vacuum tubes act as computer switches by allowing or blocking the flow of electrical current. The problem with vacuum tubes is that they take up a lot of space. The first high-speed digital computer, the Electronic Numerical Integrator and Computer (referred to as the ENIAC), was deployed in 1945 and used nearly 18,000 vacuum tubes as switches, which filled approximately 1,800 square feet of floor space. In addition to being very large, vacuum tubes produce a lot of heat. Thus, although they are still used as switches in some high-end audio equipment, they make for impractical switching devices in personal computers.

What do personal computers use as switching devices? Since the vacuum tubes of the ENIAC, two major revolutions have occurred in the design of switches, and consequently computers, to make them smaller and faster: the invention of the *transistor* and the fabrication of *integrated circuits*.

What are transistors? Transistors are electrical switches that are built out of layers of a special type of material called a **semiconductor**. A semiconductor is any material that can be controlled to either conduct electricity or act as an insulator (not allow electricity to pass through). Silicon, which is found in common sand, is the semiconductor material used to make transistors.

By itself, silicon does not conduct electricity particularly well, but if specific chemicals are added in a controlled way to the silicon, it begins to behave like a switch. It allows electrical current to flow easily when a certain voltage is applied, and it prevents electrical current from flowing otherwise, thus behaving as an on/off switch. This kind of behavior is exactly what is needed to store digital information, the 1s and 0s in binary language.

Early transistors were built in separate units as small metal cans, each can acting as a single on/off switch, as shown in Figure 9.2b. These first transistors were much smaller than vacuum tubes, produced very little heat, and could be switched from on to off (allowing or blocking electrical current) very quickly. They were also less expensive than vacuum tubes.

However, it wasn't long before transistors reached their limits. Continuing advances in technology began to require more transistors than circuit boards at the time could reasonably handle. Something was needed to pack more transistor capacity into a smaller space. Thus, integrated circuits, the next technical revolution in switches, developed.

What are integrated circuits? **Integrated circuits** (or chips) are very small regions of semiconductor material, such as silicon, that support a huge number of transistors, as shown in Figure 9.2c. Along with all the many transistors, other components critical to a circuit board (such as resistors, capacitors, and diodes) are also located on the integrated circuit. Most integrated circuits are no more than a quarter inch in size.

Why are integrated circuits important? Because so many transistors can fit into such a small area, integrated circuits have enabled computer designers to create small yet powerful **microprocessors**, which are chips that contain a CPU. In 1971, the Intel 4004 was the first complete microprocessor to be located on a single integrated circuit chip, marking the beginning of true miniaturization of computers. The Intel 4004 contained slightly more than 2,300 transistors. Today more than 220 *million* transistors can be manufactured in a space as tiny as the nail of your pinky finger!

This incredible feat has fueled an industry like none other. In 1951, the Univac I computer was 10 feet high by 10 feet wide by 10 feet long (or 1,000 cubic feet) and cost $1 million. Thanks to advances in integrated circuits, the IBM PC released just 30 years later took up just 1 cubic foot of space, cost $3,000, and performed 155,000 times more quickly. (For more information about computer history, see the Technology in Focus feature "The History of the PC.")

But how can computers store information in a set of on/off switches? You understand that computers use on/off switches to perform their functions. But how can these simple switches be organized so that they enable us to use a computer to pay our bills online or write an essay? How could a set of switches describe a number or a word or give a computer the command to perform addition? Recall that to manipulate the on/off switches, the computer works in binary language, which uses only two digits,

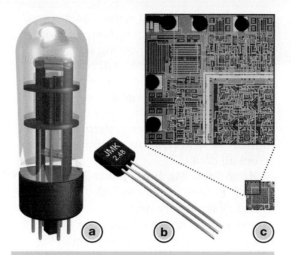

FIGURE 9.2

Electronic switches have become smaller and faster over time, from (a) vacuum tubes to (b) discrete single transistors to (c) integrated circuits that can hold more than 220 million transistors.

0 and 1. Therefore, to understand how a computer works, we must first look at how the computer uses a special numbering system called the *binary number system* to represent all of its programs and data.

THE BINARY NUMBER SYSTEM

What is a number system? A **number system** is an organized plan for representing a number. Although you may not realize it, you are already familiar with one number system. The **base 10 number system**, also known as **decimal notation**, is the system you use to represent all of the numeric values you use each day. It's called "base 10" because it uses 10 digits, 0 through 9, to represent any value.

To represent a number in base 10, you break the number down into groups of ones, tens, hundreds, thousands, and so on. Each digit has a place value depending on where it shows up in the number. For example, using base 10, in the whole number 6,954, there are 6 sets of thousands, 9 sets of hundreds, 5 sets of tens, and 4 sets of ones. Working from right to left, each place in a number represents an increasing power of 10, as shown here:

$$6,954 = 6 * (1,000) + 9 * (100) + 5 * (10) + 4 * (1)$$
$$= 6 * 10^3 + 9 * 10^2 + 5 * 10^1 + 4 * 10^0$$

Anthropologists theorize that humans developed a base 10 number system because we have 10 fingers. But computer systems, with their huge collections of on/off switches, are not well suited to thinking about numbers in groups of 10. Instead, computers describe a number as powers of 2 because each switch can be in one of two positions: on or off. This numbering system is referred to as the **binary number system**. It is the number system used by computers to represent all data.

How does the binary number system work? Because it only includes two digits (0 and 1), the binary number system is also referred to as the **base 2 number system**. However, even with just two digits, the binary number system can still represent all the same values that a base 10 number system can. Instead of breaking the number down into sets of ones, tens, hundreds, and thousands, as is done in base 10 notation, the binary number system describes a number as the sum of powers of 2. Binary numbers are used to represent every piece of data stored in a computer: all of the numbers, all of the letters, and all of the instructions that the computer uses to execute work.

Representing Numbers in the Binary Number System

How does the binary number system represent a whole number? As noted earlier, in the base 10 number system, a whole number is represented as the sum of ones, tens, hundreds, thousands, or the sums of powers of 10. The binary system works in the same way but describes a value as the sum of powers of 2: 1, 2, 4, 8, 16, 32, 64, and so on. Let's look at the number 67. In base 10, the number 67 would be 6 sets of tens and 7 sets of ones, as follows:

$$\text{Base 10: } 67 = 6 * 10^1 + 7 * 10^0$$

In base 2, we work from the largest possible power of 2 that could be in the number 67. Therefore,

67 has	1	group of	64	(leaving 3) and
3 has	0	groups of	32	
		0	groups of	16	
		0	groups of	8	
		0	groups of	4	
		1	group of	2	(leaving 1) and
1 has	1	group of	1	(leaving 0)

Therefore, the binary number for 67 is 1000011 as follows:

$$\text{Base 2: } 67 = 64 + 0 + 0 + 0 + 0 + 2 + 1$$
$$= (1 * 2^6) + (0 * 2^5) + (0 * 2^4) + (0 * 2^3) + (0 * 2^2) + (1 * 2^1) + (1 * 2^0)$$
$$= (1000011) \text{ base 2}$$

SOUND BYTE

BINARY NUMBERS INTERACTIVE

This Sound Byte helps remove the mystery surrounding binary numbers. You'll learn about base conversion between decimal, binary, and hexadecimal interactively using colors, sounds, and images.

SOUND BYTE

WHERE DOES BINARY SHOW UP?

In this Sound Byte, you'll learn how to use tools that come with the Windows operating system to work with binary, decimal, and hexadecimal numbers. You'll also learn where you might see binary and hexadecimal values showing up as you use a computer.

Is there an easier way to convert a base 10 number to a base 2 number? You can convert base 10 numbers to binary manually by repeatedly dividing the number by 2 and examining the remainder at each stage. An example will make this clearer. Let's convert the base 10 number 67 into binary:

67 ÷ 2 = 33	remainder 1
33 ÷ 2 = 16	remainder 1
16 ÷ 2 = 8	remainder 0
8 ÷ 2 = 4	remainder 0
4 ÷ 2 = 2	remainder 0
2 ÷ 2 = 1	remainder 0
1 ÷ 2 = 0	remainder 1
1 0 0 0 0 1 1		

The binary number is then read from left to right. Therefore, 100011 is the binary (base 2) equivalent of the base 10 number 67.

Is there a faster way to convert between base 10 and binary? Programmers and engineers who work with binary codes daily learn to convert between decimal and binary mentally. However, if you use binary notation less often, it is easier to use a calculator. Some calculators identify this operation with a button labeled DEC (for decimal) and one labeled BIN (for binary). In Windows, you can access a scientific calculator that supports base conversion between decimal (base 10) and binary (base 2) by choosing Start, Programs, Accessories, then choosing Calculator, then clicking the View menu to select the Scientific Calculator.

DIG DEEPER

Advanced Binary and Hexadecimal Notations

You understand how the binary number system represents a positive number, but how can it represent a negative number? In the decimal (base 10) system, a negative value is represented with a special symbol, the minus sign (–). In the binary (base 2) system, one way to represent a negative value is to place an extra bit (or digit) in front of the binary number. This extra bit is referred to as a sign bit. The sign bit is set to 1 if the binary number has a negative value and is set to 0 if the binary number has a positive value. Therefore, using a sign bit, the base 10 number +13 is written as 01101 in binary, whereas the number –13 is written as 11101 in binary. This is referred to as signed integer notation and is one way to represent negative numbers in binary.

But how does the computer know that what it is looking at is a negative number and not just a longer binary number? The binary pattern 11101 can represent more than one number. If we know it is a binary number using a sign bit, we read the first bit (the sign bit) as 1 and therefore know that the number is a negative number. Following the sign bit are the digits that represent the value of the number itself. Because 1101 in binary (base 2) has the value 13 in base 10, the final interpretation of the bits 11101 would be –13.

But what if we were told in advance that 11101 is definitely a positive number? We would then read this number differently and compute 1 * 16 + 1 * 8 + 1 * 4 + 0 * 2 + 1 * 1 and get the base 10 value of 29. The bits themselves are exactly the same. The only thing that has changed is our agreement on what the same five digits mean: the first time they represented a negative number, and the second time they represented a positive number.

The binary number system can also represent a decimal number. How can a string of 1s and 0s capture the information in a value like 99.368? Because every computer must store such numbers in the same way, the Institute of Electrical and Electronics Engineers (IEEE) has established a standard called the floating-point standard that describes how numbers with

fractional parts should be represented in the binary number system. Using a 32-bit system, an incredibly wide range of numbers can be represented. The method dictated by the standard works the same for any number with a decimal point, such as the number –0.75. The first digit, or bit (the sign bit), is used to indicate whether the number is positive or negative. The next eight bits store the *magnitude* of the number, indicating whether the number is in the hundreds or millions, for example. The standard says to use the next 23 bits to store the *value* of the number.

As you can imagine, some numbers in binary result in quite a long string of 0s and 1s. For example, the number 123,456 is a 17-digit sequence of 1s and 0s in binary code, 11110001001000000. When working with these long strings of 0s and 1s it is easy for a human to make a mistake. Thus, many computer scientists use **hexadecimal notation**, another commonly used number system, as a form of shorthand.

Hexadecimal notation is a base 16 number system, meaning it uses 16 digits to represent numbers instead of the 10 digits used in base 10 or the 2 digits used in base 2. The 16 digits it uses are the 10 numeric digits, 0 to 9, plus six extra symbols: A, B, C, D, E, F, with each of the letters, A through F, corresponding to a numeric value. So, A equals 10, B equals 11, and so on. Looking back at the number we started with: 123,456 is represented as 1E240 in hexadecimal notation. This is much easier for computer scientists to use than the long string of binary code. The scientific calculator in Windows XP (mentioned earlier) can also perform conversions to hexadecimal notation.

When will you ever use hexadecimal notation? Unless you write your own Web pages (where hexadecimal notation is used to represent colors), your only likely encounter with hexadecimal notation will be when you see an error code on your computer. Generally, the location of the error will be represented in hexadecimal notation.

Representing Letters and Symbols: ASCII and Unicode

How can the binary number system represent letters and punctuation symbols? We have just been converting numbers from base 10, which we understand, to base 2, or binary state that the computer understands. Similarly, we need a system that converts letters and other symbols that we understand to a binary

state that the computer understands. To provide a consistent means for representing letters and other characters, there are codes that dictate how to represent characters in binary format. Older mainframe computers use Extended Binary-Coded Decimal Interchange Code (EBCDIC, pronounced "Eb sih dik"). However, most of today's personal computers use the American National Standards Institute (ANSI) standard code,

BITS AND BYTES

Do I Ever See Binary Numbers on My Computer?

Internally, the computer "thinks" in binary numbers and stores all of your data and all the commands it is given in binary code. However, because computers interface with human users, who don't think in terms of binary code, messages and user interfaces are always presented in a style that is more comfortable to us. The only time most computer users ever encounter binary or hexadecimal code is when certain error messages appear, describing what the internal machine settings look like when an error occurred. Although confusing to most users, these strings of code can be useful to service technicians working to understand and correct computer problems. If you ever encounter such an error code, write down the complete error message so that you can better work with technicians to solve your problem.

called the **American Standard Code for Information Interchange (ASCII code)**, to represent each letter or character as an 8-bit (or 1-byte) binary code.

As you know by now, binary digits correspond to the on and off states of your computer's switches. Each of these digits is called a **binary digit**, or **bit** for short. Eight binary digits (or bits) combine to create one **byte**. In the previous discussions, we have been converting base 10 numbers to a binary format. In such cases, the binary format has no standard length. For example, the binary format for the number 2 is two digits (10), whereas the binary format for the number 10 is four digits (1010). Although binary

numbers can have more or less than 8 bits, each single alphabetic or special character is 1 byte (or 8 bits) of data and consists of a unique combination of a total of eight 0s and 1s. Eight bits is the standard length upon which computers are built.

The ASCII code represents the 26 uppercase letters and 26 lowercase letters used in the English language, along with a number of punctuation symbols and other special characters, using 8 bits. Figure 9.3 shows a number of examples of ASCII code representation of letters and characters.

Can ASCII represent the alphabets of different languages? Because it represents letters and characters using only 8 bits, the ASCII code can assign only 256 (or 2^8) different codes for unique characters and letters. Although this is enough to represent English and many other characters found in the world's languages, ASCII code cannot represent *all* languages and symbols. Thus, a new encoding scheme, called **Unicode**, was created. By using 16 bits instead of the 8 bits used in ASCII, Unicode can represent more than 65,000 unique character symbols, enabling it to represent the alphabets of all modern languages and all historic languages and notational systems, including such languages as Tibetan, Tagalog, Japanese, and Canadian-Aboriginal syllabics. As we continue to become a more global society, it is anticipated that Unicode will replace ASCII as the standard character formatting code.

So *all* data inside the computer is stored as bits? Yes! As noted in the Dig Deeper feature, positive and negative numbers can be stored using signed integer notation, with the first bit (the sign bit) indicating the sign and the rest of the bits indicating the value of the number. Decimal numbers are stored according to the IEEE floating-point standard, whereas letters and symbols are stored according to the ASCII code or Unicode. All of these different number systems and codes exist so that computers can store different types of information in their on/off switches. No matter what kind of data you input in a computer—a color, a musical note, or a street address—that information will be stored as a string of 1s and 0s. The important lesson is that the *interpretation* of 1s and 0s is what matters. The same binary pattern could represent a positive number, a negative number, a fraction, or a letter.

FIGURE 9.3   ASCII Standard Code for a Sample of Letters and Characters

ASCII CODE	REPRESENTS THIS SYMBOL	ASCII CODE	REPRESENTS THIS SYMBOL
01000001	A	01100001	a
01000010	B	01100010	b
01000011	C	01100011	c
01011010	Z	00100011	#
00100001	!	00100100	$
00100010	"	00100101	%

How does the computer know which interpretation to use for the 1s and 0s? When your brain processes language, it takes sounds you hear and uses the rules of English along with other clues to build an interpretation of the sound as a word. If you are in New York City and hear someone shout, "Hey, Lori!" you expect someone is saying hello to a friend. If you are in London and hear the same sound—"Hey! Lorry!"—you jump out of the way because a truck is coming at you! You knew which interpretation to apply to the same sound because you had some other information—that you were in England.

Likewise, the CPU is designed to understand a specific language, a set of instructions. But certain instructions tell the CPU to expect a negative number next or to interpret the following bit pattern as a character. Because of this extra information, the CPU always knows which interpretation to use for a series of bits. This all happens without any extra work on the part of the user or the programmer because of the work the CPU design team has done.

The CPU: Processing Digital Information

The **central processing unit (CPU or processor)**, the "brains" of the computer, executes every instruction given to your computer. As you learned earlier, the entire CPU fits on a tiny chip, called the microprocessor, which contains all of the hardware responsible for processing information, including millions of transistors (the switches we discussed earlier).

The CPU is located in the system unit on the computer's **motherboard**, the main circuit board that connects all of the electronic components of the system: the CPU, memory, the expansion slots where you can insert expansion (or adapter) cards, and all of the electrical paths that connect these components together. Figure 9.4 shows a typical motherboard and the location of each of these components.

Looking at a CPU chip gives you very little information about how exactly it accomplishes its work. However, understanding more about how the CPU is designed and

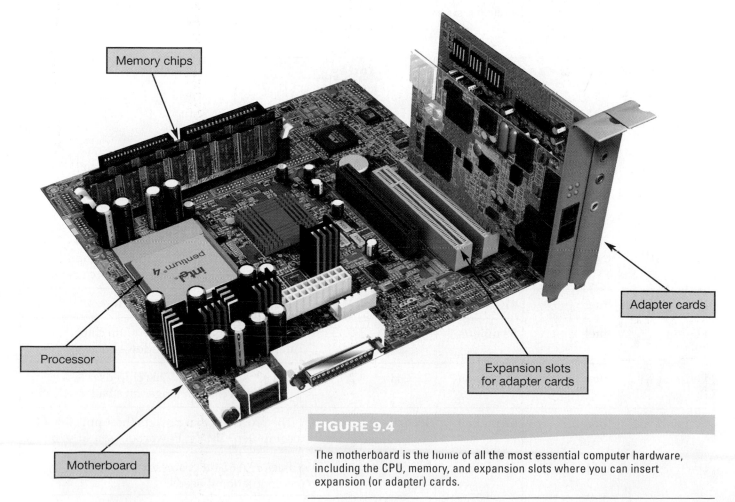

Memory chips · Processor · Motherboard · Adapter cards · Expansion slots for adapter cards

FIGURE 9.4

The motherboard is the home of all the most essential computer hardware, including the CPU, memory, and expansion slots where you can insert expansion (or adapter) cards.

how it operates will give you greater insight into how computers work, what their limitations are, and what technological advances may be possible in the future.

What CPUs are used in desktop computers? Only a few major companies manufacture CPUs for desktop computers. Intel manufactures the Xeon, Celeron, and Pentium processors (including the Pentium II, III, and 4), shown in Figure 9.5a.

Advanced Micro Devices (AMD) produces the AMD-K6, the Athlon XP, and the Athlon 64 FX processors. Both Intel and AMD chips are used in the majority of Windows-based PCs.

Apple computer systems (such as the iMac and PowerBook series of computers) use a very different CPU design. Until recently, the Motorola PowerPC G4 chip was the only CPU chip for Apple computers. However, IBM now manufactures the PowerPC G5 chip installed in the newest Apple desktop computers, shown in Figure 9.5b. As you learned in earlier chapters, the processor used on a computer also determines the operating system used. The combination of operating system and processor is referred to as a computer's *platform*.

What makes CPUs different? The primary distinction between CPUs is processing power, which is determined by the number of transistors on each CPU. In addition, as you'll learn in the next section, other factors differentiate CPUs, but the greatest differentiators are how quickly the processor can work (called its *clock speed*) and the amount of immediate access memory the CPU has (called its *cache memory*). Figure 9.6 shows the basic specifications of several of the major processors on the market today.

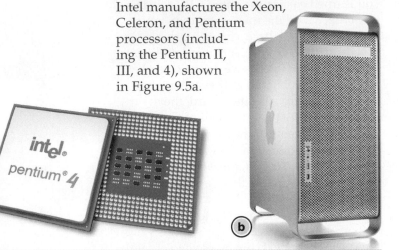

FIGURE 9.5

Externally a CPU chip reveals nothing about its internal architecture. (a) The Pentium 4 chip is used in many Windows-based PCs. (b) The Motorola PowerPC G5 chip is used in the most powerful Apple desktop systems.

FIGURE 9.6	Processors on the Market Today				
PROCESSOR	MANUFACTURER	NUMBER OF TRANSISTORS	CLOCK SPEED	LEVELS OF CACHE STORAGE	NOTES
Athlon XP	AMD	54.3 million	2.2 GHz	2	AMD processor that competes against the Intel Pentium 4.
Athlon 64 FX	AMD	106 million	2.4 GHz	2	64-bit processor for heavy computation and demanding video gaming needs.
Centrino	Intel	77 million	1.7 GHz	2	Designed specifically for mobile computers; has built-in wireless local network capabilities.
Itanium 2	Intel	410 million	1.5 GHz	3	Seen in high-end server computers.
Pentium 4	Intel	55 million	3.2 GHz	2	The latest version of the Pentium chip. It has the largest market in Windows home user PCs.
Pentium 4 Processor-M	Intel	55 million	2.6 GHz	2	The M is for mobile. This chip uses less power so it can run longer on a battery charge.
PowerPC G4	Motorola	57 million	1.0 GHz	3	The processor that powers the Apple line of computers (iMacs, PowerBooks, and so on).
PowerPC G5	IBM	58 million	2.0 GHz	2	Powerful 64-bit processor for heavy computational needs.

THE CPU MACHINE CYCLE

What exactly does the CPU do? Any program you run on your computer is actually a long series of binary code, 1s and 0s, describing a specific set of commands the CPU must perform. Each CPU is a bit different in the exact steps it follows to perform its tasks, but all CPUs must perform a series of similar general steps. These steps, referred to as a CPU **machine cycle (or processing cycle)**, are shown in Figure 9.7 and are described here:

- **Fetch:** When any program begins to run, the 1s and 0s that make up the program's binary code must be "fetched" from their temporary storage location in random access memory (RAM) and moved to the CPU before they can be executed.

- **Decode:** Once the program's binary code is in the CPU, it is decoded into the commands the CPU understands.

- **Execute:** Next, the CPU actually performs the work described in the command. Specialized hardware on the CPU performs addition, subtraction, multiplication, division, and other mathematical and logical operations at incredible speeds.

- **Store:** The result is stored in **registers**, special memory storage areas built into the CPU, which are the most expensive, fastest memory in your computer. The CPU is then ready to fetch the next set of bits encoding the next instruction.

No matter what program you are running, be it an Internet browser or a word processing program, and no matter how many programs you are using at one time, the CPU performs these four steps over and over at incredibly high speeds. Shortly, we'll look at each stage in more detail so you can understand the complexity of the CPU's design, how to compare different CPUs on the market, and what enhancements to expect in CPU designs of the future. But first, let's examine a few other components of the CPU that help it perform its tasks.

The System Clock
How does the CPU know when to begin the next stage in the machine cycle? To move from one stage of the machine cycle to the next, the motherboard

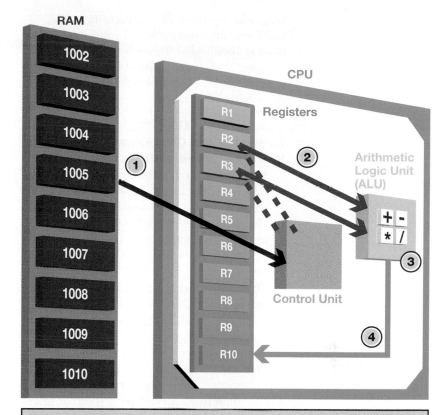

Step 1: FETCH: When a program begins to run, the program's binary code must be "fetched" from RAM and moved to the CPU's control unit before it can be executed.

Step 2: DECODE: Once the program's binary code is in the CPU, it is "decoded" into the commands the CPU understands. The control unit then tells the registers which data to feed to the arithmetic logic unit (ALU), the part of the CPU designed to perform mathematical operations.

Step 3: EXECUTE: The ALU performs the work described in the command.

Step 4: STORE: The result is stored in the registers. The CPU is then ready to fetch the next set of bits encoding the next instruction.

FIGURE 9.7

The CPU Machine Cycle

contains a built-in **system clock**. This internal clock is actually a special crystal that shouts out "Next! . . . Next! . . . Next! . . ." over and over, thereby controlling when the CPU moves to the next stage of processing.

These "ticks" of the system clock, known as the **clock cycle**, set the pace by which the computer moves from process to process. The pace, known as **clock speed**, is measured in hertz (Hz), a unit of measure that describes how many times something happens per second. Today's system clocks are measured in megahertz (MHz), or one million clock ticks per second, and gigahertz (GHz), or one billion clock ticks per second. Therefore, in a 3-GHz system, there are three billion clock ticks each second. Computers with older processors would sometimes need one or more cycles to process one instruction. Today, however, CPUs are designed to handle more instructions more efficiently, therefore executing more than one instruction per cycle.

The Control Unit
How does the CPU know which stage in the machine cycle is next? The CPU, like any part of the computer system, is designed from a collection of switches. How can simple on/off switches "remember" the fetch-decode-execute-store sequence of the CPU machine cycle? How can they perform the work required in each of these stages?

The **control unit** of the CPU manages the switches inside the CPU. It is programmed by CPU designers to remember the sequence of processing stages for that CPU and how each switch in the CPU should be set, on or off, for each stage. As soon as the system clock shouts "Next!" the control unit moves each switch to its correct setting (on or off) and then performs the work of that stage.

Let's now look at each of the stages in the machine cycle in a bit more depth.

STAGE 1: THE FETCH STAGE

Where does the CPU find the necessary information? The data and program instructions the CPU needs are stored in different areas in the computer system. Data and program instructions move between these areas as needed or not needed by the CPU for processing. Programs (such as Microsoft Word) are permanently stored on the hard disk because the hard disk offers nonvolatile storage, meaning the programs remain stored there even when you turn the power off. However, when you launch a program (that is, when you double-click an icon to execute the program), the program, or sometimes only the essential parts of a program, is transferred from the hard disk into RAM.

The program moves to RAM because the CPU can access the data and program instructions stored in RAM more than one million times faster than if they are left on the hard drive. This is because RAM is much closer to the CPU than is the hard drive. As specific instructions from the program are needed, they are moved from RAM into *registers* (the special storage areas located on the CPU itself), where they wait to be executed.

Why doesn't the CPU chip just contain enough memory to store an entire program? The CPU's storage area is not big enough to hold everything it needs to process at the same time. If enough memory were located on the CPU chip itself, an entire program could be copied to the CPU from RAM before it was executed. This certainly would add to the computer's speed and efficiency because there would not be any delay to stop and fetch instructions from RAM to the CPU. However, including so much memory on a CPU chip would make these chips very expensive. CPU design is so complex that there is only a limited amount of storage space available on the CPU itself.

Cache Memory
So, the CPU needs to fetch every instruction from RAM each time it goes through a cycle? Actually, there is another layer of storage that has even faster access than RAM, called **cache memory**. The word *cache* (pronounced "cash") is derived from the French word *cacher*, meaning "to hide." Cache memory consists of small blocks of memory located directly on and next to the CPU chip. These memory blocks are holding places for recently or frequently used instructions or data that the CPU needs the most. When these instructions or data are stored in cache memory, the CPU can more quickly retrieve them than if it had to access the instructions or data in RAM.

Taking data you think you'll be using soon and storing it nearby is a simple idea but a powerful one. This is a strategy that shows up other places in your computer system. For example, when you are browsing Web pages, images take a long time to download. Your browser software automatically stores images on your hard drive so you don't have to wait to download them again if you want to go back and view a page you've already visited. Although this cache of files is not related to the cache storage space designed into the CPU chip, the idea is the same.

How does cache memory work? Modern CPU designs include a number of types of cache memory. If the next instruction to be fetched is not already located in a CPU register, instead of looking directly to RAM to find it, the CPU first searches Level 1 cache. *Level 1 cache* is a block of memory that is built onto the CPU chip for the storage of data or commands that have just been used.

If the command is not located in Level 1 cache, the CPU searches Level 2 cache. Depending on the design of the CPU, *Level 2 cache* is located on the CPU chip but is slightly farther away from the registers, or it's on a separate chip next to the CPU and therefore takes somewhat longer to access. Level 2 cache contains more storage area than does Level 1 cache. For the Intel Pentium 4, for example, the Level 1 cache is 8 kilobytes (KB) and the Level 2 cache is 512 KB.

Only if the CPU doesn't find the next instruction to be fetched in either Level 1 or Level 2 cache will it make the long journey to RAM to access it, as shown in Figure 9.8.

Are there any other types of cache memory? The current direction of design in processors is toward larger and larger multilevel CPU cache structures. Therefore, some newer CPUs have an additional third level of cache memory storage, called *Level 3 cache*. On computers with Level 3 cache, the CPU checks this area for instructions and data after it looks in Level 1 and Level 2 cache, but before it makes the longer trip to RAM. The Level 3 cache holds between 2 megabytes (MB) and 4 MB of data. With 4 MB of Level 3 cache, there is almost enough storage for an entire program to be transferred to the CPU for its execution.

How do I use cache memory? As an end user of computer programs, you do nothing special to use cache memory. In fact, you will not even be able to notice that caching is being used—nothing special lights up on your system unit or keyboard. However, the advantage of having more cache memory is that you'll experience better performance because the CPU won't have to make the longer trip to RAM to get data and instructions as often. Unfortunately, because it is built into the CPU chip or motherboard, you can't upgrade cache: it is part of the original design of the computer system. Therefore, like RAM, it's important when buying a computer to consider buying the one, if everything else is equal, with the most cache memory.

STAGE 2: THE DECODE STAGE

What happens during the decode stage? The main goal of the decode stage is for the CPU's control unit to translate (or decode) the program's instructions into commands the CPU can understand. A CPU can understand only a very small set of

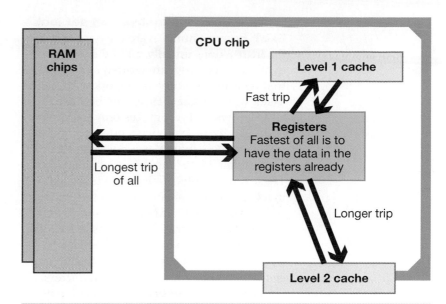

FIGURE 9.8

Modern CPUs have two or more levels of cache memory, which leads to faster CPU processing.

commands. The collection of commands a specific CPU can execute is called the **instruction set** for that system. Each CPU has its own unique instruction set. For example, the G4 processor used in an Apple PowerBook has a different instruction set than does the Intel Pentium 4 used in a Dell Inspiron laptop. The control unit interprets the code's bits according to the instruction set the CPU designers laid out for that particular CPU. Based on this process of translation, the control unit then knows how to set up all the switches on the CPU so that the proper operation will occur.

BITS AND BYTES

Why Does Caching Work?

Did you know that 80 percent of the time your CPU spends processing, it is working on the same 20 percent of code? Software monitoring programs have been built to test this conjecture for specific systems and it generally holds up well. This is the concept that cache memory exploits. It would be much too expensive to design a system with enough memory on the CPU to store an entire program. But if careful management of a cache of fast memory can make sure that the 20 percent of the program used the most often is already sitting in the cache (and is therefore closer to the CPU), the improvement in overall performance is great.

What does the instruction set look like? Because humans are the ones to write the instructions initially, all of the commands in an instruction set are written in a language that is easier for humans to work with, called **assembly language**. However, because the CPU knows and recognizes only patterns of 0s and 1s, it cannot understand assembly language, so these human-readable instructions are translated into long strings of binary code. These long strings of binary code, called **machine language**, are used by the control unit to set up the hardware in the CPU for the rest of the operations it needs to perform. Machine language is a binary code for computer *instructions* much like the ASCII code is a binary code for letters and characters. Similar to each letter or character having its own unique combination of 0s and 1s assigned to it, a CPU has a table of codes consisting of combinations of 0s and 1s for each of its commands. If the CPU sees that pattern of bits arrive, it knows the work it must do. Figure 9.9 shows a few commands in both assembly language and machine language.

Many CPUs have similar commands in their instruction sets, including ADD (add), SUB (subtract), MUL (multiply), DIV (divide), MOVE (move data to RAM), STORE (move data to a CPU register), and EQU (check if equal). CPUs differ in the choice of additional assembly language commands selected for the instruction set. Each CPU design team works to develop an instruction set that is both powerful and speedy.

STAGE 3: THE EXECUTE STAGE

Where are the calculations performed in the CPU? The arithmetic logic unit (ALU) is the part of the CPU designed to perform mathematical operations such as addition, subtraction, multiplication, and division and to test comparing values as greater than, less than, or equal to. For example, in performing its calculations, the ALU would decide whether the grade point average of 3.9 was greater than, less than, or equal to the grade point average of 3.5. The ALU also performs logical OR, AND, and NOT operations. For example, in determining whether a student can graduate, the computer would need to ascertain whether the student has taken all required courses AND obtained a passing grade in each of them. The ALU is specially designed to execute such calculations flawlessly and with incredible speed.

The ALU is fed data from the CPU's registers. The amount of data a CPU can process at a time is based in part on the amount of data each register can hold. The number of bits a computer can work with at a time is referred to as its **word size**. Therefore, a 64-bit processor can process more information faster than a 32-bit processor.

STAGE 4: THE STORE STAGE

What happens in the last stage of CPU processing? In the final stage, the result produced by the ALU is stored back in the registers. The instruction itself will explain which register should be used to store the answer. Now the entire instruction has completed. The next instruction will be fetched and the sequence fetch-decode-execute-store will begin again.

RAM: The Next Level of Temporary Storage

By now you are aware of **random access memory (RAM)** and the role it plays in your computer system. As you'll recall, RAM is volatile, meaning that when you turn off your computer, the data stored in RAM is erased. RAM is located as a set of chips on the system unit's motherboard and its capacity is measured in megabytes, with most modern systems containing around 256 MB to 512 MB of RAM. The type of memory chips your computer uses is tied to the type and speed of your CPU.

Figure 9.10 shows a hierarchy of the different types of memory found in your

FIGURE 9.9   Representations of Sample CPU Commands

HUMAN LANGUAGE FOR COMMAND	CPU COMMAND IN ASSEMBLY LANGUAGE (LANGUAGE USED BY PROGRAMMERS)	CPU COMMAND IN THE MACHINE LANGUAGE (LANGUAGE USED IN CPU'S INSTRUCTION SET)
Add	ADD	1110 1010
Subtract	SUB	0001 0101
Multiply	MUL	1111 0000
Divide	DIV	0000 1111

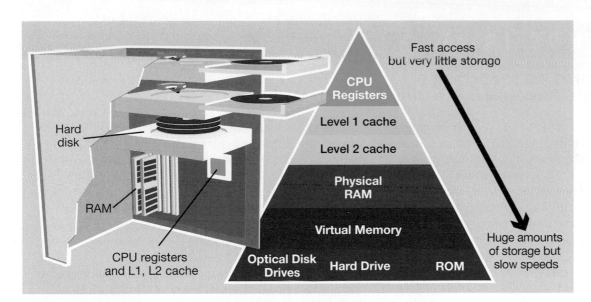

FIGURE 9.10

There are many different levels of memory in a computer system, ranging from the very small amounts in the CPU to the much slower but more plentiful storage of a hard disk drive.

computer system in addition to the more permanent storage devices. You've already read about the top two tiers: CPU registers and cache memory. The following section is about the various types of physical RAM in your system.

The time it takes the CPU to access RAM is very fast, which is why your computer uses RAM as a temporary storage location for data and instructions. The time it takes a device to locate data and instructions and make those data and instructions available to the CPU for processing is known as its **access time**. Recall that getting data and instructions from the hard disk drive to the CPU takes about 10 milliseconds (ms), or ten-thousandths of a second. The time it takes to get instructions from RAM to the CPU is expressed in nanoseconds (ns), or billionths of seconds. RAM is fast! However, although RAM always has faster access times than the hard drive, not all RAM is the same.

TYPES OF RAM

Why are there different types of RAM?
Like all other components of your computer, over time, improvements have been made to the design of RAM. Today, there are several kinds of RAM. Each type of RAM has a very different internal design, allowing some types to work at much faster speeds and to transfer data much more quickly than others.

Therefore, not all systems need the same type of RAM. Low-end computer systems may have one type of RAM, whereas more expensive computer systems that are

designed for heavy multimedia use may have another type. If you compare ads for computer systems, you'll see a number of different acronyms describing the various types of memory, including DRAM, SRAM, SDRAM, DDR SDRAM, and Rambus DRAM (RDRAM). Despite their differences in design, all of these forms of random access memory have the same purpose in a computer system: to store data and allow it to be quickly accessed by the CPU. Understanding the different types of RAM will make you a more knowledgeable consumer and will prepare you to evaluate future memory technologies.

What is the most basic type of RAM? The cheapest and most basic type of RAM is **dynamic RAM (DRAM)**. It is used in older systems or in systems in which cost is an important factor. DRAM offers access times on the order of 60 ns. This means that when the CPU requests a piece of information, it experiences a delay of 60 billionths of a second while the data is retrieved from DRAM.

How does DRAM work? In storing 1 bit of data inside DRAM, a transistor and a capacitor are used. As you learned earlier,

SOUND BYTE

MEMORY HIERARCHY INTERACTIVE

There are so many different types of memory in a computer—cache, registers, RAM, the hard drive. This Sound Byte focuses on the differences in each of these types of memory and how they can be upgraded to improve performance.

TRENDS IN IT

EMERGING TECHNOLOGIES
Printable Processors: The Ultimate in Flexibility

You know that the CPU is the "brains" of the computer. Without this important little chip, the computer couldn't process information. The innovations of the transistor and then the integrated circuit have shrunk the processor to a size so small that even a penlike instrument can house computer processing capabilities. Miniaturization has made technology very much a part of our lives.

Manufacturing tiny bits of electronic circuitry on silicon is a time-consuming and costly process. But imagine if making microprocessors were as easy as printing them out on your ink-jet printer. Or for larger projects, imagine printing out computer components on rolls similar to those that are fed through newspaper presses. Sound crazy? Not to Michael Sauvante and Jim Sheats, founders of Rolltronics Corporation. Their visions of what will one day be possible with computer technology make even the *Jetsons* seem old-fashioned.

According to Rolltronics, if computer processors could be printed out on common materials, such as flexible plastic or even paper, rather than manufactured on silicon, computers could be cheaper, smaller, and more completely incorporated into objects we use every day. In fact, the computer would be nearly invisible. You might, for example, download a processor from the Internet, then print this processor directly onto a plastic-type substance using your desktop printer. You could then incorporate these plastic-based processors into everything—even wallpaper that could change images or provide lighting for a room.

Printable processors might even have uses you would expect to see in a James Bond movie, such as wearable computers. Your jacket might have a processor with a built-in thermostat that "reads" your body temperature, and your sunglasses could include processors in the lenses that display visual information.

Sauvante and Sheats anticipate their technology will lead to other innovations, such as lightweight medical devices such as programmable heart and blood pressure

monitors, food cans that could tell you when they are out of date, high-capacity memory devices, ultrathin batteries that are safe and inexpensive, and flexible information devices (like today's personal digital assistants) that could roll up and fit inside your purse or pocket. They also anticipate that printable processors will become extremely cheap, lowering the price as well as the size of most computing devices and helping to close the so-called digital divide.

Realistically, flexible processors are several years out from actual production. The use of flexible electronic technology, however, is already being seen in other applications. For example, in 2004, a consortium of government, academic, and technological innovators agreed to combine their efforts to produce ultrathin, flexible displays. The intention is to integrate this technology in a wide variety of applications, military being at the top of the list. The new technology would enable the production of rollable maps and display-embedded uniforms. Anticipated commerce uses include improving upon current automotive displays as well as other mobile displays for phones, tablet PCs, personal digital assistants (PDAs), and so on. Similar strides are being made in developing memory chips on plastic that are then printed using roll-to-roll technology.

Possibilities like these represent only the tip of the iceberg in terms of printable electronics. Another company, Plastic Logic, is also working on printing electronic circuitry onto plastic. In addition to the new and creative applications that plastic microprocessors would produce, Plastic Logic touts an added environmental benefit of printable processors. The technology to make them doesn't use toxic or environmentally damaging materials that are currently used in manufacturing silicon chips. So, in a few years, when the coat you're wearing senses that you're still cold and turns on a built-in heater, you may be able to thank the innovative processes of printable processors!

---

a transistor is a switch that can be turned on (allowing electrical current to flow) or off (blocking current). A capacitor is an electronic device that is easily fabricated from silicon and that acts like a huge bathtub, or storage space, for the charged electrons coming from the transistors. To store a 1 (or an "on" bit), the transistor is turned to the "on" position and it fills the capacitor with charge. When a capacitor is full of charge, it will be read as a 1,

whereas when the capacitor is empty, or without charge, it will be read as a 0.

Why is DRAM referred to as "dynamic" RAM? Like a leaky bathtub, capacitors leak charge all the time. If the capacitor is just filled with charge once, it eventually loses all its charge. The data being stored in memory is read by looking at a specific capacitor for each bit. If the capacitor at that location is filled with enough

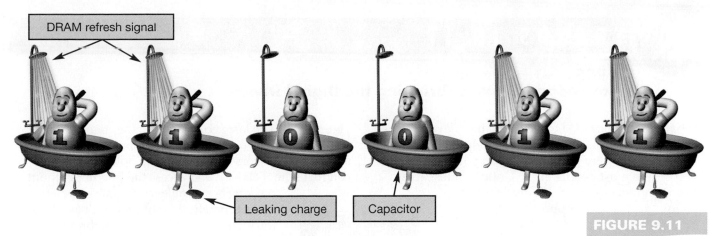

charge to be called "on" (that is, if the "bath-tub" has been filled with "water"), that bit is read as a 1. If that capacitor *should* be holding a 1 value, but has been sitting there for a while, it may have lost all its charge (that is, the charge may have leaked away over time). The bit would now be read as a 0 and the data stored there would be corrupted.

To make sure each capacitor holding a 1 value is filled with enough charge to be read as a 1 at any time, a refresh signal is applied. The refresh will flood current through the open transistors to refill the capacitors so they continue to store a valid 1. This is the dynamic factor in DRAM: the fact that capacitors leak charge and therefore must be recharged as they are used so the data they hold keeps its true value. This process is illustrated in Figure 9.11.

Are there different kinds of DRAM? Not all DRAM is of the same design. A variety of types of DRAM is currently on the market, each with different performance levels and prices. Synchronous DRAM (SDRAM), which is much faster than DRAM, is the current standard and provides the level of perfor-mance most home users require. Double data rate synchronous DRAM (DDR SDRAM) is faster than SDRAM but not as fast as Rambus DRAM (RDRAM), which is the fastest and the most recent entry on the market. RDRAM is found on multimedia machines because its speed is necessary to transfer large multi-media files efficiently. Each of these types of DRAM increases the speed with which the CPU can access data, but also increases the cost of the memory modules.

Is there a faster RAM than DRAM? All of the refresh signals required to keep the data "fresh" in DRAM take time. A faster type of RAM is **static RAM (SRAM)**. In SRAM, more transistors are used to store a

single bit, but no capacitor is needed. This eliminates the need for a refresh signal (thereby avoiding recharging), thus making SRAM much faster than DRAM. However, because it is more expensive than DRAM, it is used only in locations such as the CPU's cache, where the system demands the fastest possible storage.

What kind of memory should I buy for my system? You really do not have a choice in the type of RAM that comes with your system. As described earlier, the sys-tem manufacturer installs the specific type of RAM and it will vary depending on the system's performance requirements. As noted in Chapter 6, if you decide to pur-chase additional memory for your system you'll need to be sure to match the kind of RAM already installed. A system with SDRAM will not be compatible with the new RDRAM technology, for example.

Does ROM help the CPU work? As you've learned, **read-only memory (ROM)** is a set of memory chips located on the motherboard that stores data and instruc-tions that cannot be changed or erased. ROM chips can be found on most digital devices and usually contain the start-up instructions the computer needs to boot up. ROM chips do not provide any other form of data storage.

SOUND BYTE
COMPUTER ARCHITECTURE

In this Sound Byte, you'll take animated tours that illustrate many of the hardware concepts introduced in this chapter. Along the way you'll learn about the machine cycle of the CPU, the movement of data between RAM and the CPU, and the hierarchy of the different types of memory in computer systems.

FIGURE 9.11

The binary data 110011 is stored in DRAM using capacitors. However, like a bathtub with a leaky drain, these capacitors leak charge, so the DRAM must be refreshed (the bathtub refilled) with charge every clock cycle.

TRENDS IN IT

ETHICS
Knowledge Is Power: Bridging the Digital Divide

What would your life be like if you had never touched a computer because you simply couldn't afford one? What if there were no computers in your town? If you're like most people in the United States, access to computers is a given. But for many people, access to the opportunities and knowledge computers and the Internet offer is an impossibility.

The discrepancy between the "haves" and "have-nots" with regards to computer technology is commonly referred to as the *digital divide*. This discrepancy is a growing problem. People with access to computers and the Internet (that is, those who can afford it) are poised to take advantage of the many new developments technology offers, whereas poorer individuals, communities, and school systems that can't afford computer systems and Internet access are being left behind.

Bridging the digital divide is a thorny problem. It is difficult for families to spend money on computer equipment and Internet access when they're struggling to put food on the table. But without such access, schoolchildren and their parents are at a serious disadvantage compared with their affluent peers. For example, in the United States, more teachers are using the Internet to communicate with parents than ever before. E-mail updates on student progress, Web sites with homework postings that allow parents to keep tabs on assignments, and even online parent/teacher conferences are becoming popular. Unwired parents and students are left out of the loop. In the United States, children who do not have access to the Internet and computers won't be prepared for future employment, contributing to the continuing cycle of poverty.

But the digital divide isn't always caused by low income. Terrain can be a factor that inhibits connectivity. In Nepal's mountainous terrain, even though a village might be only a few miles away "as the crow flies," it might take two days to hike there because of the lack of roads. With these kinds of conditions, there aren't any phone lines in the villages either. Volunteers, funded by a generous donor, have installed 12 outdoor access points complete with directional antennas to connect a series of villages to the Internet using a wireless network (see

FIGURE 9.12

High-gain antennas and wireless access points are connecting remote villagers in Nepal to the information superhighway.

Figure 9.12). The last access point in the connectivity chain connects to an Internet service provider 22 miles away. The villagers are now able to hold meetings, conduct school classes, and access the Internet without trekking across miles of mountainous terrain. Unfortunately, this solution isn't available throughout Nepal . . . or even throughout some areas of the United States.

So, the United States must be the most wired country in the world with the smallest gap in the digital divide, right? Guess again. Although 15 percent of American households have broadband connections (either cable or DSL), a whopping two-thirds of South Korean households have high-speed connections. This widespread connectivity is changing the face of Korean society. Government agencies, once known for long lines and mind-numbing paperwork, have installed efficient Web sites to streamline processes. And approximately 23 million of the country's 30 million cell phones are Web enabled. In fact, during the last South Korean presidential campaign staffers were routinely sending text messages to 800,000 people with a few keystrokes. And while we're still in the test-marketing phase of video-on-demand in a few markets in the United States, South Koreans routinely download movies and watch them whenever they want.

So, what is being done to bridge the digital divide in rural and poor areas of the world? Some organizations are attempting to increase local and global Internet and computer access, while more and more community organizations such as libraries and recreation centers are providing free Internet access to the general public. Meanwhile, others are sponsoring referendums and funding that increase Internet capacity in schools. These organizations are e-mailing their local and state representatives, urging them to back legislation to provide funding for computer equipment in struggling neighborhoods and school systems. Others suggest computer users donate their old computers to a charity that refurbishes and distributes them to needy families. To help bridge the digital divide, you can start by supporting such programs and institutions (such as your local library) in your area that are attempting to increase Internet and computer access.

Buses: The CPU's Data Highway

A **bus** is an electrical wire in the computer's circuitry—the highway that data (or bits) travels on between the computer's various components. Computers have two different kinds of buses. **Local buses** are on the motherboard and run between the CPU and the main system memory. Most systems also have another type of bus, called an **expansion bus**, which expands the capabilities of your computer by allowing a range of different expansion cards (such as video cards and sound cards) to communicate with the motherboard.

Do buses affect a computer's performance? Some buses move data along more quickly than others, whereas some can move more data at one time. The rate of speed that data moves from one location to another, known as *bus clock speed*, affects the overall performance of the computer. Bus clock speed is measured in units of megahertz (MHz), or millions of clock cycles per second. The width of the bus (or the **bus width**) determines how many bits of data can be sent along a given bus at any one time. The wider the bus, the more data that can be sent at one time.

Bus width is measured in terms of bits, so a 32-bit bus can carry more data at one time than a 16-bit bus. Together, bus clock speed and bus width determine how quickly any given amount of data can be transferred on a bus (see Figure 9.13). This data transfer rate (measured in units of megabytes per second) is calculated by multiplying the speed of the bus by the bus width.

The bus width also affects the processor's word size, or the number of bits a processor can manipulate at one time. Even if a processor can manipulate 64 bits at a time, if the bus width allows only 32 bits of data to be sent at one time, the processor's performance will be affected.

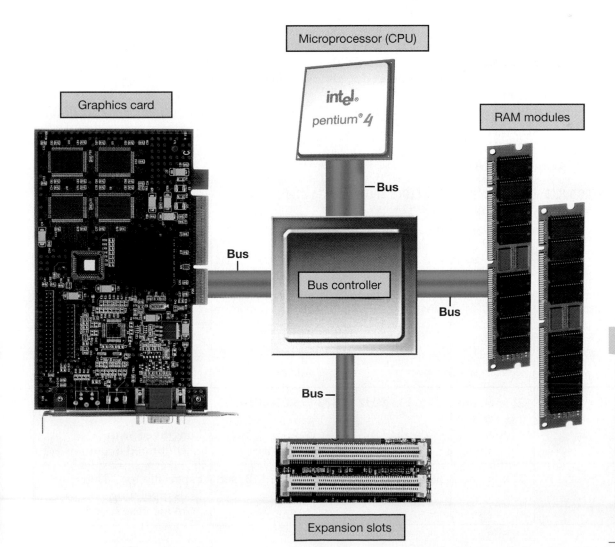

FIGURE 9.13

Buses connect components in your computer so that data can move between them. The width of the bus (bus width) determines how many bits of data can be sent along a given bus at any one time. The wider the bus, the more data that can be sent at one time.

What kinds of expansion buses do I need to know about? As noted earlier, the motherboard contains expansion slots in which you insert expansion cards. These expansion cards enable you to connect peripheral devices (such as a monitor) to your computer. For the peripherals to be able to communicate (send and receive data) with your CPU, the motherboard includes expansion buses. The expansion buses provide the pathways that enable the CPU to communicate with the peripheral devices attached through the cards.

Expansion buses have evolved to provide faster transfer speeds and wider bit widths to deliver higher data transfer rates to the many peripheral devices you may connect to your computer. There are several types of expansion buses. Older computers include buses such as the **Industry Standard Architecture (ISA) bus** and the **Extended Industry Standard Architecture (EISA) bus** to connect devices such as the mouse, modem, and sound cards. These are being replaced by faster, more efficient connections.

In a modern computer system, you'll find **Peripheral Component Interconnect (PCI) buses**. PCI expansion buses connect directly to the CPU and support such devices as network cards and sound cards. They have been the standard bus for much of the past decade and continue to be redesigned to increase their performance.

On modern systems, you'll also find **Accelerated Graphics Port (AGP) buses**. The AGP bus design was specialized to help move three-dimensional graphics data quickly. It establishes a direct pathway between the graphics card and main memory so that data does not have to ride on the PCI bus, clogging up other system data being moved about.

Figure 9.14 lists the many bus architectures and their respective features.

What will the next type of bus be? Newer versions of PCI and proposed new releases of AGP will keep these buses popular and allow them to accommodate the increasing user demands for information such as streaming video. Intel's proposal for a newer, revised version of AGP, named AGP 3.0, allows the AGP bus to support data transfer at more than 2,100 MB per second (or 2.1 GB per second). The PCI bus has been extended with the introduction of PCI-X, which can deliver data at 4.3 GB per second. This ultrafast bus design is currently seen only in server computers.

The next generation of bus designs will include HyperTransport, an open specification

FIGURE 9.14   Bus Design Evolution

BUS ARCHITECTURE	INTRODUCED	BUS WIDTH	BUS CLOCK SPEED	DATA TRANSFER RATE	NOTES
ISA (Industry Standard Architecture)	1982	8 or 16 bits	8 MHz	16 MB/sec	Increased performance from the original PC bus design
EISA (Extended Industry Standard Architecture)	Late 1980s	32 bits	8 MHz	32 MB/sec	Next evolution of ISA standard
PCI (Peripheral Component Interconnect)	Early 1990s	32 or 64 bits	33 to 133 MHz	133 to 1,024 MB/sec	Made popular with Windows 95 Long-lived with continued evolution
AGP (Accelerated Graphics Port)	1997	32 bits	66 to 533 MHz	266 to 2,133 MB/sec	Especially for 3-D graphics Uses pipelining to increase speed

that supports high-speed chip-to-chip communication, and Intel's proposed 3GIO (Third Generation I/O) standard. The first version of 3GIO that will be released will support data transfer rates at 0.5 GB per second but will later be scaled up to 8 GB per second. The HyperTransport bus will support data transfer rates up to 12.8 GB per second. These buses will provide a very different computer experience for users of high-performance graphics systems and peripherals, because data will be able to move at speeds more than 12 times faster than what current desktop systems allow.

Making Computers Even Faster: Advanced CPU Designs

Knowing how to build a CPU that can run faster than the competition can make a company rich. However, building a faster CPU is not easy. When a company decides to design a faster processor, it must take into consideration the time it will take to design, manufacture, and test that processor. When the processor finally hits the market, it must be faster than the competition to even hope to make a profit. To create a CPU that will be released 36 months from now, it must be built to perform at least twice as fast as anything currently available.

In fact, as you learned in Chapter 6, Gordon Moore, the cofounder of processor manufacturer Intel, predicted more than 25 years ago that the number of transistors on a processor would double every 18 months. Known as Moore's Law, this prediction has been remarkably accurate—but not without much engineering ingenuity. The first 8086 chip had only 29,000 transistors and ran at 5 MHz. Advances in the number of transistors on processors through the 1970s, 1980s, and 1990s continued to align with Moore's prediction.

However, there was a time near the turn of the twenty-first century when skeptics questioned how much longer Moore's Law would hold true. These skeptics were proved wrong with the continued growth in power of the microprocessor. Today's Pentium 4 chip has 55 million transistors and runs at 3.06 GHz—nearly 300 times faster than its

original counterpart. How much longer can Moore's prediction hold true? Only time will tell. One thing is for certain, though: CPU design is an area where companies can make great profits, but they risk great fortunes at the same time.

How can processors be designed so they are faster? There are many different ways processor manufacturers can increase CPU performance. One approach is to use a technique called *pipelining* to boost performance. Another approach is to design the CPU's instruction set so that it contains specialized, faster instructions for handling multimedia and graphics. In addition, some systems are being designed so that they use more than one CPU at the same time. Other problems can be attacked with more than one machine working on them at the same time.

PIPELINING

Earlier in the chapter you learned that as an instruction is processed, the CPU runs through the four stages of processing in a sequential order: fetch, decode, execute, store. **Pipelining** is a technique that allows the CPU to work on more than one instruction (or stage of processing) at a time, thereby boosting CPU performance.

For example, without pipelining, it may take four clock cycles to complete one instruction (one clock cycle for each of the four processing stages). However, with a four-stage pipeline, the computer can process four instructions *at the same time*. Like a car assembly line, instead of waiting for one car to go completely through each process of assembly, painting, and so on, you can have four cars going through the assembly line at the same time. When every component of the assembly line is done with its process, the cars all move on to the next stage.

Pipelined architectures allow several instructions to be processed at the same time. The computer allows several instructions to be processed at the same time. The ticks of the system clock (the clock cycle) indicate when all instructions move to the next process. The secret of pipelining is that the CPU is allowed to be fetching one instruction while it is simultaneously decoding another, executing a third, storing a fourth, and so on. Using pipelining, a four-stage processor can therefore potentially run up to four times faster because some instruction is finishing every clock cycle rather than waiting four cycles for each instruction to finish, as shown in Figure 9.15.

How many stages can a pipeline be? This depends entirely on design decisions. In this chapter we discussed a CPU that went through four stages in the execution of an instruction. The Intel Pentium 4 features a 20-stage pipeline and the Apple G4 processor uses a 13-stage pipeline. Thus, similar to an assembly line, in a 20-stage pipeline, there can be up to 20 different instructions being processed at any given time, making the processing of information much faster. However, because so many aspects of the CPU design interact, you cannot predict performance based solely on the number of stages in a pipeline.

Are there drawbacks to pipelining? There is a cost to pipelining a CPU. The CPU must be designed so that each stage (fetch, decode, execute, store) is independent. This means that each stage must be able to run at the same time as the other three stages are running. This requires more transistors and a more complicated hardware design. Despite this added cost, all processors on the market today feature some form of pipelined design.

SPECIALIZED MULTIMEDIA INSTRUCTIONS

How are some processors designed to process multimedia more quickly than others? Each design team developing a new CPU tries to imagine what the greatest needs of users will be in four or five years. Currently, several processors on the market reflect this in the incorporation of specialized multimedia instructions into the basic instruction set. The hardware engineers have redesigned the chip so that there are new commands in the instruction set that are specially designed to speed up the

FIGURE 9.15

The Effects of Pipelining

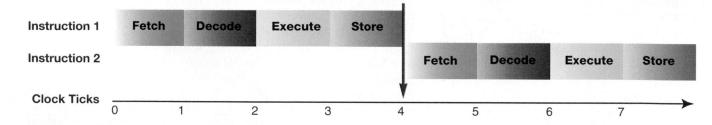

(a) Instruction Cycle, Non-Pipelined: At the end of four clock cycles, Instruction 1 has completed a cycle and Instruction 2 is about to be fetched from RAM.

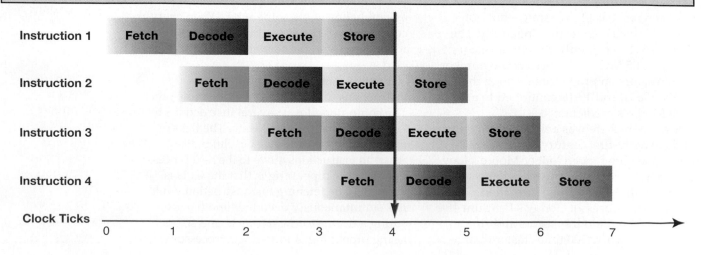

(b) Instruction Cycle, Pipelined: At the end of four clock cycles, Instruction 1 has completed a cycle, Instruction 2 has just finished executing, Instruction 3 has finished decoding, and Instruction 4 has been fetched from RAM.

work needed for video and audio processing. For example, Intel has integrated the Streaming Single Instruction Multiple Data (SIMD) Extensions 2 set of commands into its Pentium 4 processor design, adding a special group of 144 commands to the base instruction set. These multimedia-specific instructions work to accelerate video, speech, and image processing in the CPU.

MULTIPLE PROCESSING EFFORTS

Can I have more than one CPU in my desktop computer? Although the vast majority of home and work desktop systems today use only one processor, it is becoming increasingly common to use dual processors. A **dual-processor** design has two separate CPU chips installed on the same system. Operating systems such as Windows XP Professional or Apple's Mac OS X are able to work with dual processors and automatically decide how to share the workload between them.

Dual-processor systems are also becoming less expensive. Computers such as the Apple Power Mac G5 with dual processors are now available for as little as $2,500. Many high-end server systems also employ dual processors. Often, these server systems can later be scaled so that they can accommodate four, six, or even eight processors. Some of the most powerful mainframes support up to 32 processors!

When are dual processors used? Dual- or multiple-processor systems are often used when intensive computational problems need to be solved in such areas as computer simulations, video production, and graphics processing. Having two processors allows the work to be done *almost* twice as quickly, but not quite. It is not quite twice as fast because the system must do some extra work to decide which processor will work on which part of the problem and to recombine the results each CPU produces.

Could I have more than one machine working on a single task? Certain types of problems are well suited to a parallel-processing environment. In parallel processing, there is a large network of computers, with each computer working on a portion of the same problem simultaneously. To be a good candidate for **parallel processing**, a problem must be one that can be divided into a set of tasks that can be run simultaneously. If the next step of an algorithm can be started only after the results of the previous step have been computed, parallel processing will present no advantages.

A simple analogy of parallel processing is a laundromat. Instead of taking all day to do five loads of laundry with one machine, you can bring all your laundry to a laundromat, load it in five separate machines, and finish it all in approximately the same time it would have taken you to do just one load on a single machine. In real life, parallel processing is used for complex weather forecasting to run calculations over many different regions around the globe; in the airline industry to analyze customer information in an effort to forecast demand; and by the government in census data compilation.

For Information about scientists working on a supercomputer made of Sony PlayStation 2 consoles, see "PS2 Supercomputer," a TechTV clip found at www.prenhall.com/techinaction

BITS AND BYTES

Today's Supercomputers: The Fastest of the Fast

Supercomputers are the biggest and most powerful type of computer. Scientists and engineers use these computers to solve complex problems or to perform massive computations. Some supercomputers are single computers with multiple processors, whereas others consist of multiple computers that work together. The fastest supercomputer today is the Japanese-developed NEC Earth Simulator, which is used for climate modeling. It operates at nearly 40 teraflops (or 40 trillion operations per second).

That's almost 40,000 times faster than the average personal computer! The supercomputer ASCI Q operates at 30 teraflops and is the fourth supercomputer in the U.S. Department of Energy's five-stage Advanced Simulation and Computing Initiative (ASCI). The final objective for the DOE is development of a supercomputer that will achieve a 1 petaflop (1,000 teraflop) speed. These ASCI supercomputers are designed to maintain the safety and reliability of the U.S. nuclear supply and to avoid underground testing.

TRENDS IN IT

EMERGING TECHNOLOGIES
Computer Technology Changing the Face of Medicine

As you know by now, computers aren't just for gaming and spreadsheets any longer. Microprocessors, nanotechnology and other technologies developed during the personal computing explosion of the last two decades are rapidly being adapted to the medical field. Aside from the surgical robotic techniques and patient simulators discussed in Chapter 1, you can look forward to the following medical advancements appearing within the next decade:

1. **Printer mechanisms delivering drugs.**
   Although drugs such as insulin are self-administered by patients, the current injection delivery method can be uncomfortable or difficult to handle, especially for young and elderly patients. Inhalation of insulin is viewed by many physicians as the answer (because most people do not find this unpleasant) but the difficulty is in developing an efficient aerosol delivery method. Aradigm, a California manufacturer, is developing an inhaler called AerX that uses the same technology as ink-jet printer nozzles to process liquid medication into an aerosol (required for appropriate absorption of the medication through the membranes in the lungs). For many, this may mean saying good-bye to syringes.

2. **An implantable chip that lets you forget to take your pills.**
   Many drugs must be delivered in precise doses on a regular basis to be effective in treating disease. Although you may be able to remember to take a pill three times a day, not everyone in America's aging population is capable of adhering to this schedule. Therefore, researchers are developing new technologies to deliver medication automatically without any patient intervention. One such promising technology is a dime-sized silicon wafer implant being developed by MicroCHIPS, a Massachusetts-based company. The implants, which are produced using the same methods used to produce silicon microchips for CPUs, contain hundreds of storage areas (called microwells) that store individual doses of medication. The chips are implanted beneath the skin in your abdominal area. Preprogrammed microprocessors on the chip tell the wafer when to administer the doses of medication. No human interaction needed!

3. **Less-invasive medical procedures.**
   If you need to have an endoscopy (an examination of your gastrointestinal tract), doctors today normally insert a rather large hose into your body that holds a camera. Recently, the Food and Drug Administration approved a camera that uses small-scale (not yet nano-scale) computer technologies to shrink the camera down to the size of a small pill. In the very near future, you will merely swallow the camera, which will beam images to your doctor through wireless technology. Now that's an easier pill to swallow.

4. **DNA computers monitoring your body functions.**
   Israeli scientists have devised a computer that runs on DNA molecules and enzymes as opposed to silicon chips. The computer, although having no practical applications just yet, is extremely fast—in fact, it can perform 330 trillion operations per second, approximately 100,000 times as fast as any personal computer on the market today. Also, where silicon chips are reaching their limit of miniaturization, DNA computers can be constructed using only a few molecules . . . you don't get much smaller than that! As shown in Figure 9.16, DNA computers look just like an ordinary drop of water. But within the drop, chemical reactions are taking place in billions of DNA computers that generate data and perform rudimentary calculations.

   DNA computers use chemical reactions caused by mixing enzymes and DNA molecules. The reactions are designed to provide data and the energy for any calculations needed. Because chemical reactions can be measured precisely and their outcomes predicted reliably, there is no need for conventional hardware and software. All information can be passed at the molecular level. Although DNA computing is in its infancy today, in the future, doctors envision devices constructed from DNA computers that will patrol our bodies and make repairs (such as clearing plaque from arteries) as soon as a problem is detected.

So, as you can see, computing technology can be used not only to improve the quality of your life, but will some day improve the quality of your health as well.

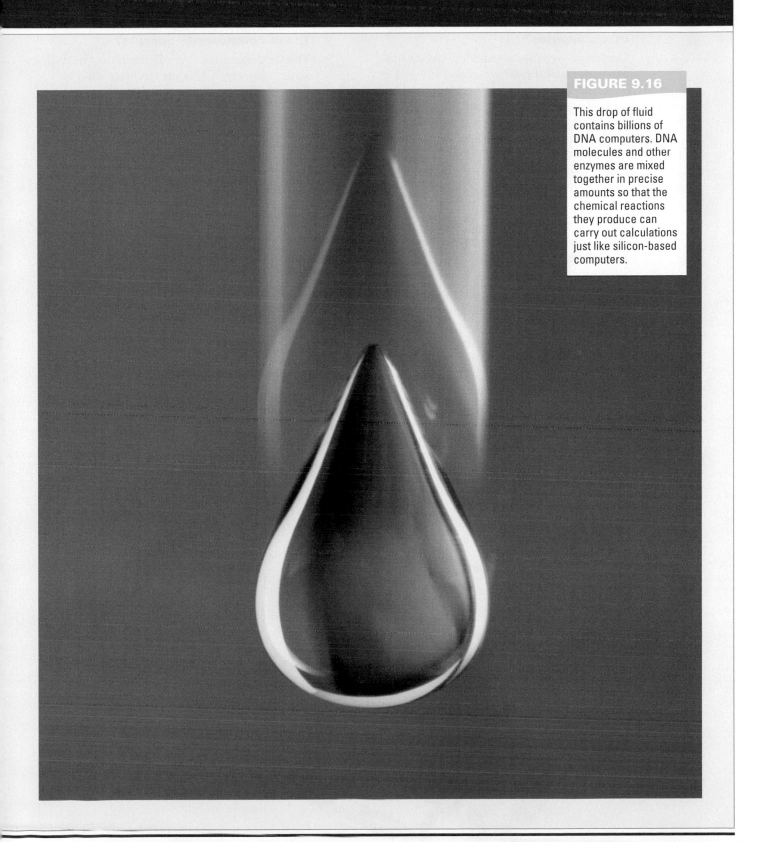

FIGURE 9.16

This drop of fluid contains billions of DNA computers. DNA molecules and other enzymes are mixed together in precise amounts so that the chemical reactions they produce can carry out calculations just like silicon-based computers.

Summary

1. What is a switch and how does it work in a computer?

Electronic switches are devices inside the computer that flip between two states: 1 or 0, on or off. Transistors are switches built out of layers of semiconductor. Integrated circuits (or chips) are very small regions of semiconductor material that support a huge number of transistors. Integrated circuits enable computer designers to fit millions of transistors into a very small area.

2. What is the binary number system and what role does it play in a computer system?

The binary number system uses only two digits, 0 and 1. It is used instead of the base 10 number system to manipulate the on/off switches that control the computer's actions. Even with just two digits, the binary number system can still represent all the same values that a base 10 number system can. To provide a consistent means for representing letters and other characters, codes dictate how to represent characters in binary format. The ASCII code uses 8 bits (0s and 1s) to represent 255 characters. Unicode uses 16 bits of data for each character and can represent more than 65,000 character symbols.

3. What is inside the CPU and how do these components operate?

The CPU executes every instruction given to your computer. CPUs are differentiated by their processing power (how many transistors are on the microprocessor chip), how quickly the processor can work (called clock speed), and the amount of immediate access memory the CPU has (called cache memory). The CPU consists of two primary units: the control unit controls the switches inside the CPU, and the arithmetic logic unit (ALU) performs logical and arithmetic calculations.

4. How does a CPU process data and instructions?

All CPUs must perform a series of similar general steps. These steps, referred to as a CPU machine cycle, include: fetch (loading program and data binary code into the CPU), decode (translating the binary code into commands the CPU can understand), execute (carrying out the commands), and store (placing the results in special memory storage areas, called registers, before the process starts again).

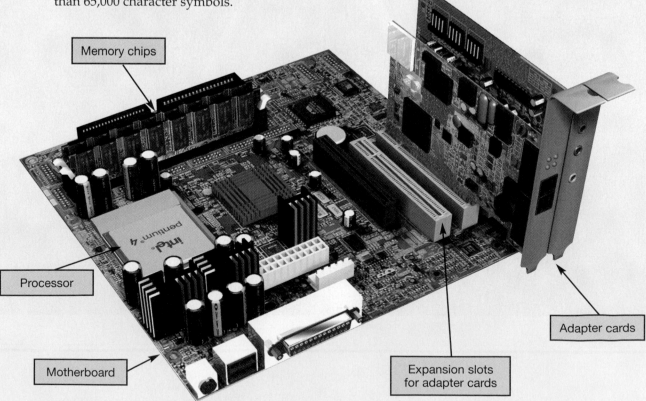

Memory chips

Processor

Motherboard

Expansion slots for adapter cards

Adapter cards

5. What is cache memory?

Cache memory consists of small blocks of memory located directly on and next to the CPU chip that hold recently or frequently used instructions or data that the CPU needs the most. The CPU can more quickly retrieve data and instructions from cache than from RAM.

6. What types of RAM are there?

RAM is volatile storage, meaning that when you turn off your computer, the data stored there is erased. The cheapest and most basic type of RAM is DRAM (dynamic RAM). Other types of RAM include SDRAM, DDR RAM, and Rambus DRAM (RDRAM). All of these forms of RAM store data that the CPU can access quickly.

7. What is a bus and how does it function in a computer system?

A bus is an electrical wire in the computer's circuitry through which data (or bits) travels between the computer's various components. Local buses are on the motherboard and run between the CPU and the main system memory. Expansion buses expand the capabilities of your computer by allowing a range of different expansion cards to connect to the motherboard. The width of the bus (or the bus width) determines how many bits of data can be sent along a given bus at any one time.

8. How do manufacturers make CPUs so that they run faster?

Pipelining is a technique that allows the CPU to work on more than one instruction (or stage of processing) at a time, thereby boosting CPU performance. A dual-processor design has two separate CPU chips installed on the same system. Dual- or multiple-processor systems are often used when intensive computational problems need to be solved. In parallel processing, computers in a large network each work on a portion of the same problem at the same time.

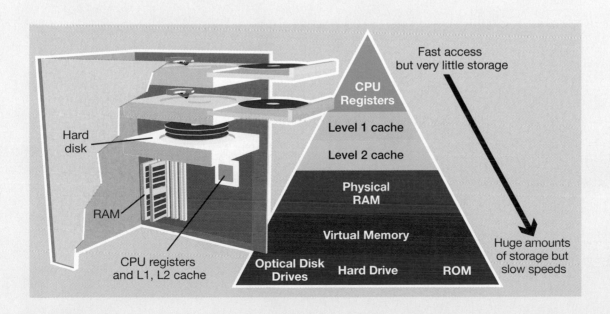

Key Terms

Buzz Words

Word Bank

- binary
- ALU
- AGP
- PCI
- registers
- bytes
- instruction set
- DDR SDRAM
- expansion bus

- ASCII
- control unit
- decoded
- DRAM
- data transfer rates
- buses
- hexadecimal
- fetch
- Level 1 cache

- dual processors
- supercomputer
- number system
- cache
- RDRAM
- pipelining
- Level 2 cache
- Centrino
- PowerPC G5

Instructions: Fill in the blanks using the words from the Word Bank.

Computers are based on a system of switches, which can be either on or off. The (1)_____ number system, which has only two digits, models this well. A (2)_____ is a set of rules for the representation of numbers. Bits are organized into groups of eight, or (3)_____, so they are easier to work with. The (4)_____ code organizes bytes in unique combinations of 0s and 1s to represent characters, letters, and numerals.

The CPU organizes switches to execute the basic commands of the system. No matter what command is being executed, the CPU steps through the same four processing stages. First it needs to (5)_____ the instruction from RAM. Next the instruction is (6)_____, and the (7)_____ sets up all of the CPU hardware to perform that particular command. The actual execution takes place in the (8)_____. The result is then saved by storing it in the (9)_____ on the CPU. Another form of memory the CPU uses is (10)_____ _____ memory. (11)_____ is the form of this type of memory located closest to the CPU. (12)_____ is located a bit farther from the CPU.

RAM comes in several different types. (13)_____ must be refreshed each cycle to keep the data it stores valid. The pathways connecting the CPU to memory are known as (14)_____. The speeds at which they can move data, or the data transfer rates, vary. (15)_____ is a bus designed primarily to move three-dimensional graphics data quickly.

Organizing Key Terms

Instructions: This chapter introduces many new terms and concepts. In the following illustration, fill in each of the blanks with key terms or concepts from the chapter in order to show how categories of ideas fit together.

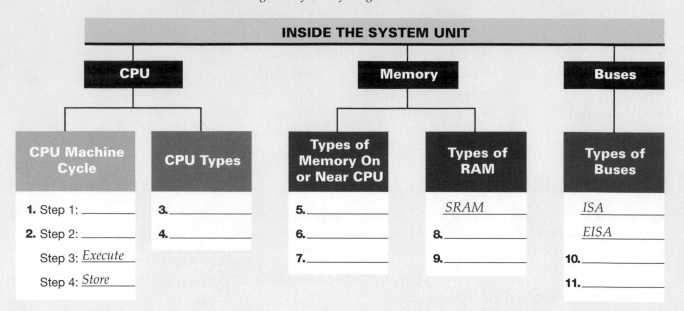

INSIDE THE SYSTEM UNIT

CPU | **Memory** | **Buses**

CPU Machine Cycle
1. Step 1: _____
2. Step 2: _____
   Step 3: *Execute*
   Step 4: *Store*

CPU Types
3. _____
4. _____

Types of Memory On or Near CPU
5. _____
6. _____
7. _____

Types of RAM
SRAM
8. _____
9. _____

Types of Buses
ISA
EISA
10. _____
11. _____

Becoming Computer Fluent

Some Apple Macintosh users develop a "religious" attachment to their machines. Apple has a reputation for elegant design but has made other business decisions that have limited its penetration into the business and home marketplace. Several of the revolutionary features of operating system and hardware design that have begun at Apple are now available from many PC clone vendors. Your new boss is unsure what the differences between high-end systems are and would like you to compile a report on two high-end systems, a G5 Macintosh and a Windows-based PC. She has asked you to compare the price/performance ratio, the hardware features including CPU design, and memory capacities.

Instructions: Using the preceding scenario, write a report using as many of the key words from the chapter as you can. Be sure the sentences are grammatically correct and technically meaningful.

Making the Transition to . . . Next Semester

1. Upgrading RAM

As your collegiate career continues, are you finding your computer needs to do more and more? Upgrading the RAM in your machine can greatly improve performance. What kind of RAM is installed in the computer you use for schoolwork (your own or the lab system you use)? How much would an upgrade to 512 MB of RAM cost for that type of RAM? An upgrade to 1 GB of RAM? Use the supplier Crucial Technology (**www.crucial.com**) to get information about the type of RAM in your system.

2. Lab Processors

It is always challenging for administrators to keep computer laboratories up-to-date. Investigate the type of processor installed in the computer systems you use in your lab. Visit the manufacturer's Web site to get detailed specifications about the design of that processor—how many levels of cache it has, how much total cache memory it has, its speed, and the number of pipeline stages in the CPU. How does that processor compare with the latest model available from the manufacturer?

3. Comparison Shopping for Systems

Do some comparison shopping. Pick three relatively comparable, moderately priced computer systems. Create a spreadsheet that outlines all the specific features of each machine. What kind of processor does each machine include? How fast is it? How many levels of cache and how much storage capacity does each cache level have? Look at the RAM: what kind and how much RAM does each machine have? What is the bus architecture of each machine?

Making the Transition to . . . The Workplace

1. Finding Your Network Adapter Address

Almost every business today uses networks to connect the computer systems they own. Each machine is assigned its own identifying number, called a network adapter address. This value is a long binary number that uniquely labels each adapter card in the business. On the networked machine, click Start, click Run, then type "command" in the Open text box of the Run dialog box. Then type "ipconfig" in the console window to find your own network adapter address. Is it presented in binary? hexadecimal? decimal? Why?

2. CPUs: The Next Generation

In an effort to stay technologically current, you have been asked to research the most recently released CPUs to determine whether it's worth buying new machines with the new CPUs or waiting for perhaps the next generation. Investigate the newest CPUs released by Intel, Motorola, and IBM. Compare these new CPUs with the current "best" CPUs. What technological advancements are present in the latest CPUs? From a cost perspective, does it make sense to replace the old systems with these new CPUs? What is the buzz on the next-generation CPUs? Would it be better to wait for these future CPUs to come out?

3. Using Pipelining

You work in a car assembly plant, so production lines are a familiar concept to your boss. However, he still doesn't understand the concept of pipelining and how it expedites a computer's processing cycle. Create a presentation for your boss that describes pipelining in enough detail so your boss will understand it. In doing so, compare it with the automobile assembly process.

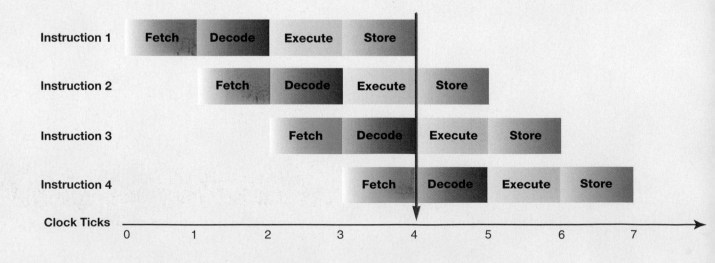

Critical Thinking Questions

Instructions: Albert Einstein used "Gedanken experiments," or critical thinking questions, to develop his theory of relativity. Some ideas are best understood by experimenting with them in our own minds. The following critical thinking questions are designed to demand your full attention but require only a comfortable chair—no technology.

1. Processors of the Future

Consider the current limitations of the design of memory, how it is organized, and how a CPU operates. Think radically—what extreme ideas can you propose for the future of processor design? What do you think the limit of clock speed for a processor will be? How could a CPU communicate more quickly with memory? What could future cache designs look like?

2. Increasing Processor Speed

SIMD and 3DNow! (used by AMD in its processors) are two approaches to modifying the instruction set to speed up graphics operations. What do you think will be the next important type of processing users will expect from computers? How could you customize the commands the CPU understands so that processing occurs faster on the CPU you are designing?

3. The Impact of Registers

How would computer systems be different if we could place 1 GB of registers on a single CPU? How would that impact the design of video cards? Would it change the way RAM is used in the system?

4. The CPU Processing Cycle

The four stages of the CPU processing cycle are fetch, decode, execute, and store. Think of some real-world tasks you perform that could be described the same way. For each example, describe how it would be changed if it were pipelined. What additional resources would the pipelined task require?

5. Binary Style

Binary events, things that can be in one of only two positions, happen around you all the time. A common example is a light switch that is toggled on or off. How about a coin? It must always be either heads up or heads down. What other events or objects behave in a binary style?

Team Time   Balancing Systems

Problem:

For a system to be effective, it must be balanced—that is, the performance of each subsystem must be well matched so that there are no bottlenecks in the overall performance. In this exercise, teams will develop balanced hardware designs for specific systems within several different price ranges.

Task:

Each group will select one part of a computer—either the CPU, the memory, or the bus architecture. The group will be responsible for researching the available options and collecting information on both price and performance specifications. The group will write a report that recommends a specific product for each of three price ranges—entry level, mid-range, and high performance. Finally, the three groups will combine their reports so that the team has developed a specification for the entire system.

Process:

1. Divide into three groups: processor, memory, and bus design.
2. Consider the following three price ranges:

   - $500 to $1,000
   - $1,001 to $2,500
   - Unlimited

   For each price range, try to specify at least two components that would keep the system cost in range and would provide the best performance. Keep track of all performance information so you can later meet with the other groups and make sure each subsystem is well matched.

3. Bring the research materials from the group meetings to one final team meeting. Looking at the system level, make final decisions on the system design for each of the three price ranges. Each range is the sum of total cost that can be expended for hardware for the system unit (monitor and other peripherals not included). The system case, power supply, motherboard, RAM, video card, and storage must be included. Research vendors that supply parts to home developers, such as TigerDirect.com.

4. Produce a report that documents the decisions and trade-offs evaluated en route to your final selections.

Conclusion:

A performance increase in one subsystem contributes to the overall performance, but only in proportion to how often it is used. This affects system design and how limited financial resources can be spent to provide the most balanced, best-performing system.

Materials on the Web

In addition to the review materials presented here, you'll find extra materials on the book's companion Web site (**www.prenhall.com/techinaction**) that will help reinforce your understanding of the chapter content. These materials include the following:

Sound Byte Lab Guides

For each Sound Byte mentioned in the chapter, there is a corresponding lab guide located on the book's companion Web site. These guides review the material presented in the Sound Byte and direct you to various Web resources that examine the material. The Sound Byte Lab Guides for this chapter include these:

- Binary
- Where Does Binary Show Up?
- Memory Hierarchy
- Computer Architecture

True/False and Multiple-Choice Quizzes

The book's Web site includes a true/false and a multiple-choice quiz for this chapter. You can take these quizzes, automatically check the results, and e-mail the results to your instructor.

Web Research Projects

The book's Web site also includes a number of Web research projects for this chapter. These projects ask you to search the Web for information on computer-related careers, milestones in computer history, important people and companies, emerging technologies, and the applications and implications of different technologies.

Technology in Action also features unique interactive Help Desk training, in which you'll assume the role of Help Desk operator taking calls about concepts learned in each chapter. The Help Desk calls for this chapter include:

- Understanding the CPU
- Understanding Types of RAM

GLOSSARY

3-D sound card Enables a computer to produce a sound that is omnidirectional, or three-dimensional.

802.11 standard A wireless standard established in 1997 by the Institute of Electrical and Electronics Engineers; also known as Wi-Fi (short for Wireless Fidelity), it enables wireless network devices to work seamlessly with other networks and devices.

A

academic fair use A provision that gives teachers and students special consideration regarding copyright violations. As long as the material is being used for educational purposes, limited copying and distribution are allowed.

Accelerated Graphics Port (AGP) bus The AGP bus design was specialized to help move three-dimensional graphics data quickly. It establishes a direct pathway between the graphics card and main memory so that data does not have to travel on the Peripheral Component Interconnect (PCI) bus, which already handles transferring a great deal of system data being moved through the computer.

access method Established to control which computer is allowed to use the transmission media at a certain time.

access time The time it takes a storage device to locate its stored data.

accounting software An application program that helps small business owners manage their finances more efficiently by providing tools for tracking accounting transactions such as sales, accounts receivable, inventory purchases, and accounts payable.

active-matrix displays With a monitor using active-matrix technology, each pixel is charged individually, as needed. The result is that an active-matrix display produces a clearer, brighter image than a passive-matrix display.

Active Server Pages (ASP) A scripting environment in which users combine Hypertext Markup Language (HTML), scripts, and reusable Microsoft ActiveX server components to create dynamic Web pages.

active topology A network topology in which each node on the network is responsible for retransmitting the token, or the data, to other nodes.

Advanced Research Products Agency Network (ARPANET) A U.S. government-funded project for the military in the 1960s, ARPANET was the first attempt to enable computers to communicate over vast distances in a reliable manner.

algorithm A set of specific, sequential steps that describe in natural language exactly what the computer program must do to complete its task.

alphabetic check Confirms that only textual characters are entered in a database field.

alphanumeric pagers Devices that display numbers and text messages on their screens. Like numeric pagers, alphanumeric pagers do not allow the user to send messages.

Alt key One of the function keys used with other keys for shortcuts and special tasks.

American Standard Code for Information Interchange (ASCII) A format for representing each letter or character as an 8-bit (or 1-byte) binary code.

analog-to-digital converter chip Converts analog signals into digital signals.

antivirus software Software that is specifically designed to detect viruses and protect a computer and files from harm.

APIs *See application programming interfaces (APIs)*

applet A small program designed to be run from within another application. Java applets are often run on your computer by your browser through the Java Virtual Machine (an application built into current browsers).

application programming interfaces (APIs) Blocks of code in the operating system that software applications need to interact with it.

application server A server that acts as a repository for application software.

application software The set of programs on a computer that helps a user carry out tasks such as word processing, sending e-mail, balancing a budget, creating presentations, editing photos, taking an online course, and playing games.

arithmetic logic unit (ALU) Part of the central processing unit (CPU) that is designed to perform mathematical operations such as addition, subtraction, multiplication, and division and to perform comparison operations such as greater than, less than, and equal to.

artificial intelligence (AI) The science that attempts to produce computers that display the same type of reasoning and intelligence that humans do.

ASCII *See American Standard Code for Information Interchange (ASCII)*

ASP *See Active Server Pages (ASP)*

assembly languages Languages that enable programmers to write their programs using a set of short, English-like commands that speak directly to the central processing unit (CPU) and give the programmer very direct control of hardware resources.

Asymmetrical Digital Subscriber Line (ADSL) A typical Digital Subscriber Line (DSL) transmission that downloads (or receives) data from the Internet faster than it uploads (or sends) data.

authentication The process that takes place after a user types in his or her login name and password and the computer system determines whether the computer is an authorized user and what level of access is to be granted on the network.

authentication servers Servers that keep track of who is logging on to the network and which services on the network are available to each user.

B

Back button A button on a Web browser used to return to a Web page viewed previously.

backdoor program A program that enables a hacker to take complete control of a computer without the legitimate user's knowledge or permission.

backup utility A utility that creates a duplicate copy of selected data on the hard disk and copies it to another storage device.

bandwidth (or throughput or data transfer rate) The amount of data that can be transmitted across a transmission medium in a certain amount of time.

base class The original object class.

base 2 number system (or binary system) A number system that uses two digits, 0 and 1, to represent any value. Also called the binary number system.

base 10 number system (or decimal notation) A number system that uses 10 digits, 0 through 9, to represent any value.

base transceiver station A large communications tower with antennas, amplifiers, and receivers/transmitters.

basic input/output system (BIOS) A program that manages the data between the operating system and all the input and output devices attached to the system. BIOS is also responsible for loading the operating system (OS) from its permanent location on the hard drive to random access memory (RAM).

bastion host A heavily secured server located on a special perimeter network between the company's secure internal network and the firewall.

batch processing Accumulating transaction data until a certain point is reached, then processing those transactions all at once.

benchmarking A process used to measure performance in which two devices or systems run the same task and the times are compared.

beta versions Early versions of software programs that are still under development. Beta versions are usually provided free of charge in return for user feedback.

binary decisions Decision points that can be answered in one of only two ways: yes (true) or no (false).

binary digit (or bit) A digit that corresponds to the on and off states of a computer's switches. A bit contains either a value of 0 or 1.

binary language The language computers use to process information, consisting of only the values 0 and 1.

binary number system The number system used by computers to represent all data. Because it includes only two digits (0 and 1), the binary number system is also referred to as the base 2 number system.

biometric access devices Devices that use some unique characteristic of human biology to identify authorized users.

BIOS *See basic input/output system (BIOS)*

bistable display A display that has the ability to retain its image even when the power is turned off.

bit depth The number of bits the video card uses to store data about each pixel on the monitor.

black-hat hackers Hackers who use their knowledge to destroy information or for illegal gain.

blog *See Weblog (blog)*

BlueBoard An application developed by Colligo Networks that enables a personal digital assistant (PDA) display to be used as a drawing board and be instantly connected with up to four other PDAs.

Bluetooth Technology that uses radio waves to transmit data over short distances.

Bookmark A feature in the Netscape browser that places a marker of a Web site's Uniform Resource Locator (URL) in an easily retrievable list in the browser's toolbar (called Favorites in Microsoft Internet Explorer).

Boolean operators Words used to refine Internet searches. These words—AND, NOT, and OR—describe the relationships between keywords in a search.

boot process (or start-up process) Process for loading the operating system into random access memory (RAM) when the computer is turned on.

boot-sector viruses Viruses that replicate themselves into the Master Boot Record of a floppy or hard drive.

breadcrumb list A list that shows the hierarchy of Web pages above the Web page that you are currently visiting. Shown at the top of some Web pages, it provides an aid to Web site navigation.

bridges Network devices that are used to send data between two different local area networks (LANs) or two segments of the same LAN.

broadband connections High-speed Internet connections, including cable, satellite, and Digital Subscriber Line (DSL).

browsing (1) Viewing database records. (2) "Surfing" the Web.

brute force attacks Attacks delivered by specialized hacking software that tries many combinations of letters, numbers, and pieces of a user ID in an attempt to discover a user password.

bus A group of electrical pathways inside a computer that provide high-speed communications between various parts of a computer and the central processing unit (CPU) and main memory.

bus (or linear bus) topology Networking topology in which all devices are connected to a central cable called the bus (or backbone).

bus width How many bits of data can be transferred along the data pathway at one time.

business-to-business (B2B) E-commerce transactions between businesses.

business-to-consumer (B2C) E-commerce transactions between businesses and consumers.

byte Eight binary digits (or bits).

C

C The predecessor language of C++, developed originally for system programmers by Brian Kernighan and Dennis Ritchie of AT&T Bell Laboratories in 1978. It provides higher-level programming language features (such as if statements and for loops) but still allows programmers to manipulate the system memory and central processing unit (CPU) registers directly.

C++ The successor language to C, developed by Bjarne Stroustrup. It uses all of the same symbols and keywords as C but extends the language with additional keywords, better security, and more support for the reuse of existing code through object-oriented design.

cable modem A device that modulates and demodulates the cable signal into digital data and back again. The cable TV signal and Internet data can share the same line.

cache memory Small blocks of memory located directly on and next to the central processing unit (CPU) chip that act as holding places for recently or frequently used instructions or data that the CPU accesses the most. When these instructions or data are stored in cache memory, the CPU can more quickly retrieve them than if it had to access the instructions or data from random access memory (RAM).

CAD *See computer-aided design (CAD)*

Carrier Sense Multiple Access with Collision Detection (CSMA/CD) A protocol that nodes on a network can use. With CSMA/CD, a node connected to the network listens (that is, has carrier sense) to determine that no other nodes are currently transmitting data signals. If the node doesn't hear any other signals, it assumes it is safe to transmit data. All devices on the network have the same right (that is, they have multiple access) to transmit data when they deem it safe. It is therefore possible for two devices to begin transmitting data signals at the same time. If this happens, the two signals collide. When signals collide, a node on the network alerts the other nodes.

cathode-ray tube (CRT) A picture tube device in a computer monitor; very similar to the picture tube in a conventional television set. A CRT screen is a grid made up of millions of pixels, or tiny dots. The pixels are illuminated by an electron beam that passes back and forth across the back of the screen very quickly so that the pixels appear to glow continuously.

CD-R (Compact Disc-Recordable) disc A portable, optical storage device that can be written to once and can be used with either a CD-R drive or a CD-RW drive.

CD-R drive A drive for reading and writing CD-R discs.

CD-ROM A portable, read-only optical storage device.

CD-ROM drive A drive for reading compact discs (CDs).

CD-RW (Compact Disc-Read/Writable) disc A portable, optical storage device that can be written and rewritten to many times.

CD-RW drive A drive that can both read and write data to CDs.

cell phones Telephones that operate over a wireless network. Cell phones can also offer Internet access, text messaging, personal information management (PIM) features, and more.

cells Individual boxes formed by the columns and rows in a spreadsheet. Each cell can be uniquely identified according to its column and row position.

central processing unit (CPU) The part of the system unit of a computer that is responsible for data processing (or the "brains" of the computer); it is the largest and most important chip in the computer. It controls all the functions performed by the computer's other components and processes all the commands issued to it by software instructions.

centralized A type of network design in which users are neither responsible for creating their own data backups nor for providing security for their computers; instead, those tasks are handled by a centralized server, software, and a system administrator.

chat room An area on the Web where people come together to communicate online. The conversations are in real time and are visible to everyone in the chat room.

cgi-bin A directory where Common Gateway Interface (CGI) scripts are normally placed.

CGI scripts Computer programs that conform to the Common Gateway Interface (CGI) specification, which provides a method for sending data between end users (using browsers) and Web servers.

circuit switching A method of communication in which a dedicated connection is formed between two points (such as two people on telephones) and the connection remains active for the duration of the transmission.

classes Categories of objects that define the common properties of all objects belonging to the class.

click-and-brick businesses Traditional stores that have an online presence.

clickstream data Information captured about each click that users make as they navigate a Web site.

client A computer that requests information (such as your computer when you are connected to the Internet).

client-based e-mail E-mail that is dependent on an e-mail account provided by an Internet service provider (ISP) and a client software program, such as Microsoft Outlook or Eudora.

client/server network A network that consists of client and server computers, in which the clients make requests of the server and the server "serves up" the response.

client-side application A computer program that runs on the client and requires no interaction with a Web server.

clip art A gallery of images that is often included with software packages.

clock cycle The "ticks" of the system clock. One cycle equals one "tick."

clock speed The steady and constant pace at which a computer goes through machine cycles, measured in hertz (Hz).

coaxial cable A single copper wire surrounded by layers of plastic insulation and sheathing.

code editing The step in which programmers actually type the code into the computer.

coding Translating an algorithm into a programming language.

cold boot A complete power down and restart of a computer.

command-driven interface An interface in which the user enters commands to communicate with the computer system.

comments (or remarks) Plain English notations inserted into program code for documentation. The comments are not ever seen by the compiler.

commerce servers Computers that host software that enables consumers to purchase goods and services over the Web. These servers generally use special security protocols to protect sensitive information (such as credit card numbers) from being intercepted.

Common Gateway Interface (CGI) Provides a methodology by which a browser can request that a program file be executed (or run) instead of just being delivered to the browser.

communications server A server that handles all communications between the network and other networks, including managing Internet connectivity.

Compact Flash Memory cards about the size of a matchbook that can hold between 64 megabytes (MB) and 1 gigabyte (GB) of data.

compilation The process by which code is converted into machine language, the language the central processing unit (CPU) can understand.

compiler The program that understands both the syntax of the programming language and the exact structure of the central processing unit (CPU) and its machine language. It can "read" the source code and translate the source code directly into machine language.

completeness check Ensures that all fields defined as "required" have data entered into them.

computed field (or computational field) A numeric field in a database that is filled as the result of a computation.

computer A data processing device that gathers, processes, outputs, and stores data and information.

computer-aided design (CAD) 3-D modeling programs used to create automated designs, technical drawings, and model visualizations.

computer fluent Describes a person who understands the capabilities and limitations of computers and knows how to use them to accomplish tasks.

computer forensics The application of computer systems and techniques to gather potential legal evidence; a law-enforcement specialty used to fight high-tech crime.

computer network Two or more computers that are connected by software and communications media so they can communicate.

computer protocol A set of rules for accomplishing electronic information exchange. If the Internet is the information superhighway, protocols are the driving rules.

computer virus A computer program that attaches itself to another computer program (known as the host program) or pretends to be an innocuous program and attempts to spread itself to other computers when files are exchanged.

connectionless protocol A protocol that a host computer can use to send data over the network without establishing a direct connection with any specific recipient computer.

connection-oriented protocol A protocol that requires two computers to exchange control packets, which set up the parameters of the data exchange session, prior to sending packets that contain data.

connectivity port A port that enables the computer (or other device) to be connected to other devices or systems such as networks, modems, and the Internet.

consistency check Comparing the value of data in a field against established parameters to determine whether the value is reasonable.

consumer-to-consumer (C2C) E-commerce transactions between consumers through online sites such as eBay.com.

Control (Ctrl) key One of the function keys that is used in combination with other keys to perform shortcuts and special tasks.

control unit A component that controls the switches inside the central processing unit (CPU).

cookies Small text files that some Web sites automatically store on a client computer's hard drive when a user visits the site.

copyright violation When one person uses another person's material for their own personal economic benefit, or when someone diminishes the economic benefits of the originator.

course management software Programs that provide traditional classroom tools such as calendars and grade books over the Internet, as well as areas for students to exchange ideas and information in chat rooms, discussion forums, and using e-mail.

CPU *See central processing unit (CPU)*

CPU usage The percentage of time a central processing unit (CPU) is working.

cradle Connects a personal digital assistant (PDA) to a computer using either a universal serial bus (USB) port or a serial port.

CRT *See cathode-ray tube (CRT)*

cursor The flashing | symbol that indicates where the next character will be inserted.

cursor control keys The set of special keys on a keyboard, generally marked by arrows, that move the cursor one space at a time, either up, down, left, or right within a document. Other cursor control keys move the cursor up or down one full page or to the beginning or end of a line.

custom installation Installing only those features of a software program that a user wants on the hard drive, thereby saving space on the hard drive.

customer relationship management (CRM) software A business program used for storing sales and client contact information in one central database.

cybercrime Any criminal action perpetrated primarily through the use of a computer.

cybercriminals Individuals who use computers, networks, and the Internet to perpetrate crime.

cyberterrorists Terrorists who use computers to accomplish their goals.

D

data Numbers, words, pictures, or sounds that represent facts or ideas.

data collisions When two computers send data at the same time and the sets of data collide somewhere in the media.

data dictionary (or database schema) Defines the name, data type, and length of each field in the database.

data inconsistency Differences in data in lists caused when data exists in multiple lists and not all lists are updated when a piece of data changes.

data integrity When data contained in a database is accurate and reliable.

data marts Small slices of a data warehouse.

data mining The process by which great amounts of data are analyzed and investigated to spot significant patterns or trends within the data that would otherwise not be obvious.

data redundancy When the same data exists in more than one place in a database.

data staging A three-step process: extracting data from source databases, transforming (reformatting) the data, and storing the data in a data warehouse.

data transfer rate (or throughput) The speed at which a storage device transfers data to other computer components, expressed in kilobits per second (Kbps) or megabits per second (Mbps).

data type (or field type) Indicates what type of data can be stored in the database field or memory location.

data warehouse A large-scale electronic repository of data that contains and organizes in one place all the data related to an organization.

database Electronic collections of related data that are organized and searchable.

database administrator (or database designer) An individual trained in the design, construction, and maintenance of databases.

database management system (DBMS) Specially designed application software (such as Oracle or Microsoft Access) that interacts with the user, other applications, and the database to capture and analyze data.

database query An inquiry the user poses to the database so that it provides the data the user wishes to view.

database server A server that provides client computers with access to information stored in a database.

database software An electronic filing system best used for larger and more complicated groups of data that require more than one table, and where it's necessary to group, sort, and retrieve data, and to generate reports.

date fields Fields in a database that hold date data such as birthdays, due dates, and so on.

debugger A tool that helps programmers step through a program as it runs to locate errors.

debugging The process of running the program over and over to find errors and to make sure the program behaves in the way it should.

decentralized A type of network in which users are responsible for creating their own data backups and for providing security for their computers.

decision points Points at which a computer program must choose from an array of different actions based on the value of its current inputs.

decision support system (DSS) A system designed to help managers develop solutions for specific problems.

dedicated servers Servers used to fulfill one specific function (such as handling e-mail).

Deep Space Network Comprises three antenna installations located in California, Spain, and Australia. These installations provide for almost continuous transmission of data to outer space, regardless of the orbital position of the earth.

default values The values a database will use for fields unless the user enters another value.

denial of service (DoS) attack An attack that occurs when legitimate users are denied access to a computer system because a hacker is repeatedly making requests of that computer system to tie up its resources and deny legitimate users access.

derived class A class created based on a previously existing class (i.e., base class). Derived classes inherit all of the member variables and methods of the base class from which they are derived.

desktop As its name implies, your computer's desktop puts at your fingertips all of the elements necessary for a productive work session that are typically found on or near the top of a traditional desk, such as files and folders.

desktop box The most common style of system unit for desktop computers, which sit horizontally on top of a desk.

desktop publishing (DTP) software Programs for incorporating and arranging graphics and text to produce creative documents.

detail report A report generated with data from a database that shows the individual transactions that occurred during a certain time period.

device driver Software that facilitates the communication between a device and the operating system.

dial-up connection A connection to the Internet using a standard telephone line.

digital ink An extension of the text-entry systems used on personal digital assistant (PDA) devices.

digital pen A device for drawing images and entering text in a tablet PC.

digital signal processor A specialized chip that processes digital information and transmits signals very quickly.

Digital Subscriber Line (DSL) A technology that uses telephone lines to connect to the Internet and provide higher throughput. DSL enables phone and data transmission to share the same telephone line.

Digital Subscriber Line (DSL) modem A modem that uses modulation techniques to separate the types of signals into voice and data signals so they can travel in the right "lane" on the twisted pair wiring. Voice data is sent at the lower speed, whereas digital data is sent at frequencies ranging from 128 kilobits per second (Kbps) to 1.5 megabits per second (Mbps).

digital video-editing software Programs for editing digital video.

directories Hierarchical structures that include files, folders, and drives, used to create a more organized and efficient computer.

Disk Cleanup A Windows utility that cleans unnecessary files from your hard drive.

disk defragmenter utilities Utilities that regroup related pieces of files together on the hard disk, enabling faster retrieval of the data.

distributed denial of service (DDoS) attacks Automated attacks that are launched from more than one zombie computer at the same time.

docking station Hardware for connecting a portable computing device to printers, scanners, full-size monitors, mice, and other peripherals.

documentation A description of the development and technical details of a computer program, including how the code works and how the user interacts with the program.

domain name Part of a Uniform Resource Locator (URL). Domain names consist of two parts: The first part indicates who the site's host is; the second part is a three-letter suffix that indicates the type of organization. (Example: www.popsci.com)

Domain Name System (DNS) server A server that contains location information for domains on the Internet and functions like a phone book for the Internet.

DoS attack *See denial of service (DoS) attack*

dot-matrix printer The first type of computer printer, which has tiny hammer-like keys that strike the paper through an inked ribbon.

dot pitch The diagonal distance, measured in millimeters, between pixels of the same color on the screen. A smaller dot pitch means that there is less blank space between pixels, and thus a sharper, clearer image.

dotted decimal numbers The numbers in an Internet Protocol (IP) address.

double data rate synchronous DRAM (DDR SDRAM) Memory chips that are faster than SDRAM but not as fast as RDRAM.

drawing software (or illustration software) Programs for creating or editing two-dimensional line-based drawings.

drive bays Special shelves inside computers designed to hold storage devices.

DSL *See Digital Subscriber Line (DSL)*

DSL/cable routers Routers that are specifically designed to connect to Digital Subscriber Line (DSL) or cable modems.

DSL modem *See Digital Subscriber Line (DSL) modem*

dual processor A design that has two separate central processing unit (CPU) chips installed on the same system.

DVD drive A drive that enables the computer to read digital video discs (DVDs). A DVD±R/RW drive can write DVDs as well as read them.

DVD-RW drive A drive that enables the computer to read and write to DVDs.

Dvorak keyboard A leading alternative keyboard that puts the most commonly used letters in the English language on "home keys," the keys in the middle row of the keyboard. It is designed to reduce the distance your fingers travel for most keystrokes, increasing typing speed.

dynamic addressing The process of assigning Internet Protocol (IP) addresses when users log on using their Internet service provider (ISP). The computer is assigned an address from an available pool of IP addresses, which is common today.

Dynamic Host Configuration Protocol (DHCP) Handles dynamic addressing. Part of the Transmission Control Protocol/Internet Protocol (TCP/IP) protocol suite, DHCP takes a pool of IP addresses and shares them with hosts on the network on an as-needed basis.

dynamic RAM (DRAM) The most basic type of random access memory (RAM); used in older systems or in systems for which cost is an important factor. DRAM offers access times on the order of 60 nanoseconds.

E

editor A tool that helps programmers as they enter the code, highlighting keywords and alerting the programmers to typos.

educational software Applications that offer some form of instruction or training.

edutainment Software that both educates and entertains the user.

electronic commerce (e-commerce) Conducting business online for purposes ranging from fund-raising to advertising to selling products.

electronic switches Devices inside the computer that can be flipped between two states: 1 or 0, on or off.

elements In Hypertext Markup Language (HTML), elements are the tags and the text between them.

e-mail (electronic mail) Internet-based communication in which senders and recipients correspond.

e-mail server A server that processes and delivers incoming and outgoing e-mail.

e-mail virus A virus transmitted by e-mail that often uses the address book in the victim's e-mail system to distribute itself.

encryption The process of encoding data (ciphering) so that only the person with a corresponding decryption key (the intended recipient) can decode (or decipher) and read the message.

entertainment software Programs designed to provide users with entertainment; computer games make up the vast majority of entertainment software.

ergonomics Refers to how a user sets up his or her computer and other equipment to minimize risk of injury or discomfort.

error handling In programming, the instructions that the program runs if the input data is incorrect or another error is encountered.

Ethernet networks Networks that use the Ethernet protocol as the means (or standard) by which the nodes on the network communicate.

Ethernet port A port that is slightly larger than a standard phone jack and transfers data at speeds of up to 1,000 megabits per second (Mbps). It is used to connect a computer to a cable modem or a network.

event Every keystroke, every mouse click, and each signal to the printer creates an action, or event, in the respective device (keyboard, mouse, or printer) to which the operating system responds.

exception reports Reports that show conditions that are unusual or that need attention by users of a system.

executable program The binary sequence (code) that instructs the central processing unit (CPU) to perform certain calculations.

expansion bus An electrical pathway that expands the capabilities of a computer by enabling a range of different expansion cards (such as video cards and sound cards) to communicate with the motherboard.

expansion cards (or adapter cards) Circuit boards with specific functions that augment the computer's basic functions as well as provide connections to other devices.

expansion hub A device that connects to one port, such as a universal serial bus (USB) port, to provide additional new ports, similar to a multi-plug extension cord for electrical appliances.

expert system Designed to replicate the decision-making processes of human experts to solve specific problems.

export Putting data into an electronic file in a format that another application can understand.

Extended Industry Standard Architecture (EISA) bus An older expansion bus for connecting devices such as the mouse, modem, and sound cards.

Extensible Hypertext Markup Language (XHTML) A new standard recently released by the World Wide Web Consortium (WC3) that combines elements from both Extensible Markup Language (XML) and Hypertext Markup Language (HTML). XHTML has much more stringent rules than HTML does regarding tagging (for instance, all elements require an end tag in XHTML).

Extensible Markup Language (XML) A language that enables designers to define their own tags, making it much easier to transfer data between Web sites and Web servers.

extension (or file type) In a filename, the three letters that follow the user-supplied filename after the dot (.) ; the extension identifies what kind of family of files the file belongs to or which application should be used to read the file.

extranets Pieces of intranets that only certain corporations or individuals can access. The owner of the extranet decides who will be permitted to access it.

F

Favorites A feature in Microsoft Internet Explorer that places a marker of a Web site's Uniform Resource Locator (URL) in an easily retrievable list in the browser's toolbar. (Called Bookmarks in Netscape.)

fiber-optic line (or cable) Lines that transmit data at close to the speed of light along glass or plastic fibers.

field Where a category of information in a database is stored. Fields are displayed in columns.

field constraints Properties that must be satisfied for an entry to be accepted into the field.

field name An identifying name assigned to each field in a database.

field size The maximum number of characters (or numbers) that a field in a database can contain.

fifth-generation languages (5GLs) Considered the most "natural" of languages. With 5GLs, instructions closely resemble human speech or are visual in nature so that little programming knowledge is necessary.

file A collection of related pieces of information stored together for easy reference.

file allocation table (FAT) An index of all sector numbers that the hard drive stores in a table to keep track of which sectors hold which files.

file compression utility A program that takes out redundancies in a file to reduce the file size.

file management Providing organizational structure to the computer's contents.

file path Identifies the exact location of a file, starting with the drive in which the file is located, and including all folders, subfolders (if any), the filename, and extension. (Example: C:\My Documents\Spring 2005\ English Comp\Term Paper\Illustrations\ EBronte.jpg)

file servers Computers deployed to provide remote storage space or to act as a repository for files that users can access.

File Transfer Protocol (FTP) A protocol used to upload and download files from one computer to another over the Internet.

filename The first part of the label applied to a file, similar to our first names; it is generally the name a user assigns to the file when saving it.

financial and business-related software Software used by businesses or individuals that helps them perform specific or general business tasks.

financial planning software Programs for managing finances, such as Intuit's Quicken and Microsoft Money, which include electronic checkbook registers and automatic bill payment tools.

firewalls Software programs or hardware devices designed to prevent unauthorized access to computers or networks.

FireWire 800 One of the fastest ports available, moving data at 800 megabits per second (Mbps).

FireWire port (previously called the IEEE 1394 port) A port based on a standard developed by the Institute of Electrical and Electronics Engineers (IEEE), with a transfer rate of 400 megabits per second (Mbps). Today, it is most commonly used to connect digital video devices such as digital cameras to the computer.

first-generation languages (1GLs) The actual machine languages of a central processing unit (CPU), the sequence of bits—1s and 0s— that the CPU understands.

flash drive Drives that plug into a universal serial bus (USB) port on a computer and store data digitally. Also called USB drives.

flash memory Portable, nonvolatile memory.

flash memory card A form of portable storage. This removable memory card is often used in digital cameras, MP3 players, and personal digital assistants (PDAs).

floppy disk A portable 3.5-inch storage format, with a storage capacity of 1.44 megabytes (MB).

floppy disk drive A drive bay for a floppy disk.

flowcharts Visual representations of the patterns an algorithm comprises.

folder A collections of files stored on a computer.

footprint The amount of physical space on the desk a computer takes up.

For and Next Keywords in Visual Basic to implement a loop.

foreign key The primary key of another database table that is included for purposes of establishing relationships with that other table.

format To design or change the appearance of a document by changing fonts, font styles, and/or sizes; adding colors to text; adjusting the margins; adding borders to portions of text or whole pages; inserting bulleted and numbered lists; organizing text into columns, and so forth.

formula An equation a spreadsheet user builds using addition, subtraction, multiplication, and division, as well as values and cell references.

Forward button A button on a Web browser toolbar that enables you to return to a Web page after going back using the Back button.

fourth-generation languages (4GLs) Computer languages that are nonprocedural: They specify what is to be accomplished without determining how. Many database query languages and report generators are 4GLs.

frames Containers designed to hold multiple data packets.

freeware Any copyrighted software that can be used for free.

frequently asked questions (FAQs) A list of answers to the most common questions.

FTP *See File Transfer Protocol (FTP)*

full installation Installing all the files and programs from the distribution CD to the computer's hard drive.

function keys Act as shortcut keys to perform special tasks; they are sometimes referred to as the "F" keys because they start with the letter *F* followed by a number.

fuzzy logic Allows the interjection of experiential learning into the equation by considering probabilities.

G

gigabyte (GB) About a billion bytes.

gigahertz (GHz) One billion hertz.

Global Positioning System (GPS) A system of 21 satellites (plus three working spares), built and operated by the U.S. military, that constantly orbit the earth. They provide information to GPS-capable devices to pinpoint locations on the earth.

Graffiti One of the more popular notation systems for entering data into a personal digital assistant (PDA).

graphical user interface (or GUI, pronounced "gooey") Unlike the command- and menu-driven interfaces used earlier, GUIs display graphics and use the point-and-click technology of the mouse and cursor, making them much more user-friendly.

graphics and multimedia software Programs to design and create attractive documents, images, illustrations, and Web pages, as well as three-dimensional models and drawings.

grid computing A form of networking that enables linked computers to use idle processors of other networked computers.

groupware Software that helps people who are in different locations work together using e-mail and online scheduling tools.

H

hacker (or cracker) Anyone who breaks into a computer system (whether an individual computer or a network) unlawfully.

handshaking The process of two computers exchanging control packets that set up the parameters of a data exchange.

hard disk drive (or hard drive) Holds all permanently stored programs and data; is located inside the system unit.

hardware Any part of the computer you can physically touch.

head crash A stoppage of the hard disk drive that often results in data loss.

hexadecimal notation A number system that uses 16 digits to represent numbers; also called a base 16 number system.

hibernation When a computer is in a state of deeper sleep. Pushing the power button awakens the computer from hibernation, at which time the computer reloads everything to the desktop exactly as it was before it went into hibernation.

high-level languages Third-, fourth-, and fifth-generation computer languages.

historical data Data that shows trends over time.

History list A feature on a browser's toolbar that shows all the Web sites and pages visited over a certain period of time.

hits A list of sites (or results) that match an Internet search.

home page The main or opening page of a Web site.

home phoneline network adapter (also HPNA adapter) A device that attaches to computers and peripherals on a phoneline network to enable them to communicate using phone lines.

host Organization that maintains the Web server on which a particular Web site is stored.

hot-swappable bays Bays that provide the ability to remove one drive and exchange it with another drive while the laptop computer is running.

HTML *See Hypertext Markup Language (HTML)*

HTML embedded scripting language A language used to embed programming language code directly within the Hypertext Markup Language (HTML) code of a Web page.

HTTP *See Hypertext Transfer Protocol (HTTP)*

hubs Simple amplification devices that receive data packets and retransmit them to all nodes on the same network (not between different networks).

hyperlink fields Fields in a database that store hyperlinks to Web pages.

hyperlinks Specially coded text that, when clicked, enables a user to jump from one location, or Web page, to another within the Web site or to another Web site altogether.

hypertext Text that is linked to other documents or media (such as video clips, pictures, and so on).

Hypertext Markup Language (HTML) A set of rules for marking up blocks of text so that a Web browser knows how to display them. It uses a series of tags that define the display of text on a Web page.

Hypertext Transfer Protocol (HTTP) The protocol a browser uses to send requests to a Web server; created especially for the transfer of hypertext documents over the Internet.

I

icons Pictures on the desktop that represent an object such as a software application or a file or folder.

identity theft Occurs when someone uses personal information about someone else (such as the victim's name, address, and social security number) to assume the victim's identity for the purpose of defrauding others.

if else Keywords in the programming language C++; used for binary decisions.

image-editing software (sometimes called photo-editing software) Programs for editing photographs and other images.

impact printers Printers that have tiny hammer-like keys that strike the paper through an inked ribbon, thus making a mark on the paper. The most common impact printer is the dot-matrix printer.

import To bring data into an application from another source.

indexer A program in a search engine that organizes into a large database the information a spider collects on the Internet.

Industry Standard Architecture (ISA) bus An older expansion bus used for connecting devices such as the mouse, modem, and sound cards.

information Data that has been organized or presented in a meaningful fashion.

information system A system that includes data, people, procedures, hardware, and software and is used to gather and analyze information.

inheritance The ability of a new class of object to automatically pick up all of the data and methods of an existing class, and then extend and customize those to fit its own specific needs.

initial value A beginning point in a loop.

ink-jet printer A nonimpact printer that sprays tiny drops of ink onto paper.

input device Hardware device used to enter, or input, data (text, images, and sounds) and instructions (user responses and commands) into a computer; input devices include keyboards, mice, scanners, microphones, and digital cameras.

input form Provides a view of the data fields to be filled in a database, with appropriate labels to assist database users in populating the database.

instant messaging (IM) services Programs that enable users to communicate in real time with others who are also online.

instruction set The collection of commands a specific central processing unit (CPU) can run.

instructions The steps and tasks the computer needs to process data into usable information.

integrated circuits (or chips) Very small regions of semiconductor material, such as silicon, that support a huge number of transistors.

integrated development environment (IDE) A developmental tool that helps programmers write, compile, and test their programs.

integrated software application A single software program that incorporates the most commonly used tools of many productivity software programs into one integrated stand-alone program.

Internet A network of networks and the largest network in the world, connecting millions of computers from more than 65 countries.

Internet2 An ongoing project sponsored by more than 200 universities (supported by government and industry partners) to develop new Internet technologies and disseminate them as rapidly as possible to the rest of the Internet community. The Internet2 backbone supports extremely high-speed communications (up to 9.6 gigabits per second [Gbps]).

Internet backbone The main pathway of high-speed communications lines over which all Internet traffic flows.

Internet Explorer (IE) A popular graphical browser from Microsoft Corporation for displaying different Web sites, or locations, on the Web; it can display pictures (graphics) in addition to text, as well as other forms of multimedia, such as sound and video.

Internet hoaxes E-mail messages that contain information that is untrue.

Internet Protocol (IP) A protocol for sending data between computers on the Internet.

Internet Protocol address (IP address) The means by which all computers connected to the Internet identify each other. It consists of a unique set of four numbers separated by dots, such as 123.45.678.91.

Internet Protocol version 4 (IPv4) The original IP addressing scheme.

Internet Protocol version 6 (IPv6) A proposed IP addressing scheme that makes IP addresses longer, thereby providing more available IP addresses. It uses eight groups of 16-bit numbers.

Internet service providers (ISPs) National, regional, or local companies that connect individuals, groups, and other companies to the Internet.

Internet telephony Hardware and software that enables people to use the Internet to transmit telephone calls.

interpreter Translates source code into an intermediate form, line by line. Each line is then executed as it is translated.

interrupt A signal that tells the operating system that it is in need of immediate attention.

interrupt handler A special numerical code that prioritizes requests to the operating system.

interrupt table A place in the computer's primary memory (or random access memory, RAM) where interrupt requests are placed.

intranet A private corporate network that is used exclusively by company employees to facilitate information sharing, database access, group scheduling, videoconferencing, or other employee collaboration.

IP *See Internet Protocol (IP)*

IP address *See Internet Protocol address (IP address)*

IrDA port A port based on a standard developed by the Infrared Data Association for transmitting data. IrDA ports enable you to transmit data between two devices using infrared light waves, similar to a TV remote control. IrDA ports have a maximum throughput of 4 megabits per second (Mbps) and require that a line of sight be maintained between the two ports.

J

jam signal A special signal sent to all network nodes, alerting them that a collision has occurred.

Java A platform-independent programming language that Sun Microsystems introduced in the early 1990s. It quickly became popular because its object-oriented model enables Java programmers to benefit from its set of existing classes.

Java applets Small Java-based programs.

Java Server Pages (JSP) An extension of the Java servlet technology with dynamic scripting capability.

JavaScript A programming language often used to add interactivity to Web pages. JavaScript is not as full-featured as Java, but its syntax, keywords, data types, and operators are a subset of Java's.

join query A query that links (or joins) two tables using a common field in both tables and extracts the relevant data from each.

K

kernel (or supervisor program) The essential component of the operating system, responsible for managing the processor and all other components of the computer system. Because it stays in random access memory (RAM) the entire time your computer is powered on, the kernel is called memory resident.

kernel memory The memory that the computer's operating system uses.

key pair A public and a private key used for coding and decoding messages.

keyboard Used to enter typed data and commands into a computer.

keywords (1) Specific words a user wishes to query (or look for) in an Internet search. (2) The set of specific words that have predefined meanings for a particular programming language.

kilobyte (KB) Approximately 1,000 bytes.

knowledge-based system A support system that provides additional intelligence that supplements the user's own intellect and makes the decision support system (DSS) more effective.

L

label Descriptive text that identifies the components of a spreadsheet.

LANs *See local area networks (LANs)*

laptop computer (or notebook computer) A portable computer that offers a large display and all of the computing power of a full desktop system.

Large Scale Networking (LSN) A program created by the U.S. government, the objective of which is to fund the research and development of cutting-edge networking technologies. Major goals of the program are the development of enhanced wireless technologies and increased network throughput.

laser printer A nonimpact printer known for quick and quiet production and high-quality printouts; it uses laser beams to make marks on paper.

latency (or rotational delay) Occurs after the read/write head locates the correct track, then waits for the correct sector to spin to the read/write head.

Level 1 cache A block of memory that is built onto the central processing unit (CPU) chip for the storage of data or commands that have just been used.

Level 2 cache A block of memory that is located on the central processing unit (CPU) chip but slightly farther away from the CPU (or on a separate chip next to the CPU). It therefore takes somewhat longer to access than the CPU registers. Level 2 cache contains more storage area than Level 1 cache.

Level 3 cache On computers with Level 3 cache, the central processing unit (CPU) checks this area for instructions and data after it looks in Level 1 and Level 2 cache, but before it makes the longer trip to random access memory (RAM). The Level 3 cache holds between 2 megabytes (MB) and 4 MB of data.

Linux An open-source operating system based on UNIX. Because of the stable nature of this operating system, it is often used on Web servers.

liquid crystal display (LCD) Technology used in flat-panel computer monitors.

local area networks (LANs) Networks in which the nodes are located within a small geographic area.

local buses Located on the motherboard, these buses run between the central processing unit (CPU) and the main system memory.

logic bombs Computer viruses that run when a certain set of conditions is met, such as specific dates keyed off of the computer's internal clock.

logical port A virtual communications gateway or path that enables a computer to organize requests for information (such as Web page downloads, e-mail routing, and so on) from other networks or computers.

logical port blocking When a firewall is configured to ignore all incoming packets that request access to port 25 (the port designated for File Transfer Protocol [FTP] traffic), so no FTP requests will get through to the computer.

loop An algorithm that, when asked a question and the answer is yes, performs a set of actions. Once the set of actions has been performed, the question is asked again (creating a loop). As long as the answer to the question is yes, the algorithm will continue to loop around and repeat the set of actions. When the answer to the question is no, the algorithm breaks free of the looping and moves on to the next step.

M

Mac OS Apple Computer's operating system. In 1984, Mac OS became the first operating system to incorporate the user-friendly point-and-click technology in a commercially affordable computer. The most recent version of the Mac operating system, Mac OS X, is based on the UNIX operating system. Previous Mac operating systems had been based on Apple's own proprietary program.

machine cycle (or processing cycle) The steps a central processing unit (CPU) follows to perform its tasks.

machine language Long strings of binary code used by the control unit to set up the hardware in the central processing unit (CPU) for the rest of the operations it needs to perform.

macro viruses Viruses that are distributed by hiding them inside a macro.

Macromedia Flash A software product from Macromedia for developing Web-based multimedia.

macros Small programs that group a series of commands to run as a single command.

magnetic card readers Devices that read information from a magnetic strip on the back of a credit card–like access card (such as a student ID card). The card reader, which can control the lock on a door, is programmed to admit only authorized personnel to the area.

magnetic media Portable storage devices, such as floppy disks and Zip disks, that use a magnetized film to store data.

mainframes Large, expensive computers that support hundreds or thousands of users simultaneously.

management information system (MIS) A system that provides timely and accurate information that enables managers to make critical business decisions.

mapping programs Software that provides street maps and written directions to locations.

Master Boot Record A program that runs whenever a computer boots up.

Media Access Control (MAC) address A physical address similar to a serial number on an appliance that is assigned to each network adapter; it is made up of six 2-digit numbers such as 01:40:87:44:79:A5.

megabyte (MB) About a million bytes.

megahertz (MHz) One million hertz; hertz is the unit of measure for processor speed, or machine cycles per second.

memo fields Text fields in a database that are used to hold long pieces of text.

memory A component inside the system unit that helps process data into information; memory chips hold (or store) the instructions or data that the central processing unit (CPU) processes.

memory bound A system that is limited in how fast it can send data to the central processing unit (CPU) because there's not enough random access memory (RAM) installed.

memory card reader An external device for reading flash memory cards.

memory effect The result of a battery needing to be completely used up before it is recharged or it won't hold as much charge as it originally did.

memory modules (or memory cards) Small circuit boards that hold a series of random access memory (RAM) chips.

Memory Stick Sony's brand of flash memory; the cards measure just 2 inches by 1 inch and weigh a fraction of an ounce.

menu-driven interface A user interface in which the user chooses a command from menus displayed on the screen.

menus Lists of commands that appear on the screen.

meta search engine A search engine that searches other search engines rather than individual Web sites.

metadata Data that describes other data.

methods (or behaviors) Actions associated with a class of objects.

metropolitan area networks (MANs) Wide area networks (WANs) that link users in a specific geographic area (such as within a city or county).

microbrowser Software that makes it possible to access the Internet from a cell phone or personal digital assistant (PDA).

microphone A device for capturing sound waves (such as voice) and transferring them to digital format on a computer.

microprocessors Chips that contain a central processing unit (CPU).

Microsoft Disk Operating System (MS-DOS) A single-user, single-task operating system created by Microsoft. MS-DOS was the first widely installed operating system in personal computers.

Microsoft Visual Basic (VB) A powerful programming language used to build a wide range of Windows applications. VB's strengths include a simple, quick interface that is easy for a programmer to learn and use. It has grown from its roots in the language BASIC to become a sophisticated and full-featured object-oriented language.

Microsoft Windows The most popular operating system for desktop computers.

MIME See Multipurpose Internet Mail Extensions (MIME)

mobile computing devices Portable electronic tools such as cell phones, personal digital assistants (PDAs), and laptops.

mobile switching center A central location that receives cell phone requests for service from a base station.

model management system Software that assists in building management models in decision support systems (DSSs).

modem A device that converts (modulates) the digital signals the computer understands to the analog signals that can travel over phone lines.

modem card A device that provides the computer with a connection to the Internet.

modem port A port that uses a traditional telephone signal to connect two computers.

monitor (or display screen) A common output device that displays text, graphics, and video as "soft copies" (copies that can be seen only on-screen).

Moore's Law A mathematical rule, named after Gordon Moore, the cofounder of the central processing unit (CPU) chip manufacturer Intel, that predicts that the number of transistors inside a CPU will increase so fast that CPU capacity will double every 18 months.

motherboard A special circuit board in the system unit that contains the central processing unit (CPU), the memory (RAM) chips, and the slots available for expansion cards. It is the largest printed circuit board; all of the other boards (video cards, sound cards, and so on) connect to it to receive power and to communicate.

mouse A device used to enter user responses and commands into a computer.

MP3 player A small portable device for storing MP3 files (digital music).

MS Transcriber A notation system for personal digital assistants (PDAs) that doesn't require special strokes and can recognize both printed and cursive writing with fairly decent accuracy.

multifunction printer A device that combines the functions of a printer, scanner, fax machine, and copier into one machine.

multimedia Anything that involves one or more forms of media plus text.

multimedia cards (MMCs) Thin, small, rugged cards used as portable memory that can hold up to 128 megabytes (MB) of data.

Multimedia Message Service (MMS) An extension of Short Message Service (SMS) that enables messages that include text, sound, images, and video clips to be sent from a cell phone or PDA to other phones or e-mail addresses.

multipartite viruses Literally meaning "multipart" viruses, this type of computer virus attempts to infect both the boot sector and executable files at the same time.

Multipurpose Internet Mail Extensions (MIME) A specification that was introduced in 1991 to simplify attachments to e-mail messages. All e-mail client software now uses this protocol for attaching files.

multitasking When the operating system allows a user to perform more than one task at a time.

multiuser operating system (or network operating system) Enables more than one user to access the computer system at one time by efficiently juggling all the requests from multiple users.

Musical Instrument Digital Interface (MIDI) port A port for connecting electronic musical instruments (such as synthesizers) to a computer.

N

nanoscience The study of molecules and nanostructures whose size ranges from 1 to 100 nanometers.

nanotechnology The science revolving around the use of nanostructures to build devices on an extremely small scale.

Napster The most well-known file-exchange site for digital music. Peer-to-peer sharing technology previously allowed users to exchange files, rather than downloading from a public server. Napster was purchased, shut down, and then reopened for downloading music that a user purchases, in compliance with copyright provisions.

natural language processing (NLP) system A system that enables users to communicate with computer systems using a natural spoken or written language as opposed to using computer programming languages.

negative acknowledgment (nack) What computer Y sends to computer X if a packet is unreadable, indicating the packet was not received in understandable form.

netiquette General rules of etiquette for Internet chat rooms and other online forums.

Netscape Navigator A popular graphical browser from Netscape Communications for displaying different Web sites, or locations, on the Web; it can display pictures (graphics) in addition to text, as well as other forms of multimedia, such as sound and video.

network A group of two or more computers (or nodes) that are configured to share information and resources such as printers, files, and databases.

network access points (NAPs) The points of connection between Internet service providers (ISPs).

network adapters Adapters that enable the computer (or peripheral) to communicate with the network using a common data communication language, or protocol.

Network Address Translation (NAT) A process firewalls use to assign internal Internet Protocol (IP) addresses on a network.

network administrator Someone who has training in computer and peripheral maintenance and repair, network design, and the installation of network software.

network architecture The design of a network.

network interface card (NIC) An expansion (or adapter) card that enables a computer to connect with a network.

network navigation devices Devices on a network such as routers, hubs, and switches that move data signals around the network.

network operating system (NOS) Software that handles requests for information, Internet access, and the use of peripherals for the rest of the network nodes.

network topology The layout and structure of the network.

New Technology File System (NTFS) A file system in Windows XP that differs from File Allocation Table (FAT). NTFS was developed with the Windows NT version and has been used in Windows 2000 and Windows XP.

newsgroup (or discussion group) An online discussion forum in which people "post" messages and read and reply to messages from other members of the newsgroup.

NIC *See network interface card (NIC)*

nodes Devices connected to a network, such as a computer, a peripheral (such as a printer), or a communications device (such as a modem).

nonimpact printers Printers that spray ink or use laser beams to make marks on the paper. The most common nonimpact printers are ink-jet and laser printers.

nonvolatile storage Permanent storage, as in read-only memory (ROM).

normalization The process of recording data only once to reduce data redundancy.

number system An organized plan for representing a number.

numeric check Confirms that only numbers are entered in a database field.

numeric fields Fields in a database that store numbers.

numeric keypad Section of a keyboard that enables a user to enter numbers quickly.

numeric pagers Paging devices that display only numbers on their screens, telling the user that he or she has received a page and providing the number to call. Numeric pagers do not allow the user to send a response.

object A class. Each object in a specific class shares similar data and methods with the other objects in the class.

object fields Fields in a database that hold objects such as pictures, video clips, or entire documents.

object-oriented analysis The process when programmers first identify all of the categories of inputs that are part of the problem the program is trying to solve.

object-oriented database A database that stores data in objects, not in tables.

object-relational database A hybrid between a relational and an object-oriented database. It is based primarily on the relational database model, but it is better able to store and manipulate unstructured data such as audio and video clips.

octet The four numbers in the dotted decimal notation of an Internet Protocol (IP) address.

office support system (OSS) A system (such as Microsoft Office) designed to assist employees in accomplishing their day-to-day tasks and to improve communications.

online service providers (OSPs) Internet access providers such as America Online (AOL) that have their own proprietary online content and often offer special services and areas that only their subscribers can access.

online transaction processing (OLTP) The immediate processing of user requests or transactions.

open-source program A program that is available for developers to use or modify as they wish; it is typically free of charge.

open systems Systems whose designs are public, enabling access by any interested party.

operating system (OS) System software that controls the way in which a computer system functions, including the management of hardware, peripherals, and software.

operators The coding symbols that represent the fundamental actions of a computer language.

optical media Portable storage devices that use a laser to read and write data, such as CDs and DVDs.

optical mouse A mouse that uses an internal sensor or laser to control the mouse's movement. The sensor sends signals to the computer, telling it where to move the pointer on the screen.

organic light-emitting displays (OLEDs) These displays, currently used in some Kodak cameras, use organic compounds that produce light when exposed to an electrical current.

output device A device that sends processed data and information out of a computer in the form of text, pictures (graphics), sounds (audio), and/or video.

P

packet A small segment of data that is bundled to be sent over transmission media. Each packet contains the address of the computer or peripheral device to which it is being sent.

packet filtering A process firewalls perform to filter out packets sent to specific logical ports.

packet screening Involves examining incoming data packets to ensure they originated from or are authorized by valid users on the internal network.

packet sniffer A program that looks at (or sniffs) each data packet as it travels on the Internet.

packet switching A communications methodology in which data is broken into small chunks (called packets) and sent over various routes at the same time. When the packets reach their destination, they are reassembled by the receiving computer.

page file The file the operating system builds on the hard drive when it is using virtual memory to enable processing to continue.

paging If the data and/or instructions that have been placed in the swap file are needed later, the operating system swaps them back into active random access memory (RAM) and replaces them in the hard drive's swap file with less active data or instructions.

paging device (or pager) A small wireless device that enables a user to receive and sometimes send numeric (and sometimes text) messages on a small display screen.

painting software Programs for modifying photographs.

Palm OS One of the two main operating systems for personal digital assistants (PDAs), made by 3Com.

parallel port A port that sends data between devices in groups of bits at speeds of 92 kilobits per second (Kbps). Parallel ports are often used to connect printers to computers.

parallel processing A network computer environment in which each computer works on a portion of the same problem simultaneously.

Parcel Transfer Protocol (PTP) A new transmission protocol under development by a team of scientists and computer professionals. The protocol must be designed to keep running even if packets are lost in transmission and to block out noise that can be picked up while data is traversing millions of miles. PTP stores data at the receiver until all data is received and accounted for, then transmits it to the proper destination.

Pascal The only modern computer language that was specifically designed as a teaching language; it is seldom taught at the college level any longer.

passive-matrix displays Computer monitor technology in which electrical current passes through the liquid crystal solution and charges groups of pixels, either in a row or a column. This causes the screen to brighten with each pass of electrical current and subsequently to fade.

passive topology When data merely travels the entire length of the communications medium and is received by all network devices.

path (or subdirectory) The information following the slash in a Uniform Resource Locator (URL).

path separators The backslash marks (\) used by Microsoft Windows and DOS in file names. Mac files use a colon (:), and UNIX and Linux use the forward slash (/) as the path separator.

patient simulator A computer-controlled mannequin that simulates human body functions and reactions. Patient simulators are used in training doctors, nurses, and emergency services personnel to simulate dangerous situations that would normally put live patients at risk.

PC cards (or PCMCIA, which stands for Personal Computer Memory Card International Association) Credit card-sized cards that enable users to add fax modems, network connections, wireless adapters, USB 2.0 and FireWire ports, and other capabilities primarily to laptops.

PDA *See personal digital assistant (PDA)*

peer-to-peer (P2P) network A network in which each node connected to the network can communicate directly with every other node on the network.

peer-to-peer (P2P) sharing The process of users transferring files between computers.

Peripheral Component Interconnect (PCI) buses Expansion buses that connect directly to the central processing unit (CPU) and support such devices as network cards and sound cards. They have been the standard bus for much of the past decade and continue to be redesigned to increase their performance.

peripheral devices Devices such as monitors, printers, and keyboards that connect to the system unit through ports.

personal area networks (PANs) Networks used to connect wireless devices (such as Bluetooth-enabled devices) in close proximity to each other.

personal digital assistant (PDA) A small device that enables a user to carry digital information. Often called palm computers or handhelds, PDAs are about the size of a hand and usually weigh less than 5 ounces.

personal firewalls Firewalls specifically designed for home networks.

personal information manager (PIM) software Programs such as Microsoft Outlook or Lotus Organizer that strive to replace the various management tools found on a traditional desk, such as a calendar, address book, notepad, and to-do lists.

phoneline networks Networks that use conventional phone lines to connect the nodes in a network.

physical memory The amount of random access memory (RAM) that is actually available on memory modules in a computer.

pipelining A technique that enables the central processing unit (CPU) to work on more than one instruction (or stage of processing) at a time, thereby boosting CPU performance.

pixels Illuminated, tiny dots that create the images you seen on a computer monitor. Pixels are illuminated by an electron beam that passes back and forth across the back of the screen very quickly—60 to 75 times a second—so that the pixels appear to glow continuously.

plagiarism When someone uses someone else's ideas or words and represents them as his or her own.

platform The combination of a computer's operating system and processor. The two most common platform types are the PC and the Apple Macintosh.

platter Thin, round metallic plates stacked onto the hard disk drive spindle.

plotters Large printers that use a computer-controlled pen to produce oversize pictures that require precise continuous lines to be drawn, such as in maps or architectural plans.

Plug and Play Technology that enables the operating system, once the system is booted up, to recognize automatically any new peripherals and configure them to work with the system.

plug-in (or player) A small software program that "plugs in" to a Web browser to enable a specific function; for example, to view and hear some multimedia files on the Web.

Pocket PC (formerly Windows CE) One of the two main operating systems for personal digital assistants (PDAs), made by Microsoft.

point of presence (POP) A bank of modems through which many users can connect to an Internet service provider (ISP) simultaneously.

pointer The I-beam or arrow that appears on the computer screen.

polymorphic viruses A virus that changes its virus signature (the binary pattern that makes the virus identifiable) every time it infects a new file. This makes it more difficult for antivirus programs to detect the virus.

port An interface through which external devices are connected to the computer.

portability The capability to move a completed solution easily from one type of computer to another.

portal A subject directory on the Internet that is part of a larger Web site that focuses on offering its visitors a variety of information, such as the weather, news, sports, and shopping guides.

positive acknowledgment (ack) What computer Y sends when it receives a data packet that it can read from computer X.

powerline network Network that uses the electrical wiring in a home to connect the nodes in the network.

powerline network adapter An adapter that is attached to each computer or peripheral that is part of a powerline network.

power-on self-test (POST) The first job the basic input/output system (BIOS) performs, ensuring that essential peripheral devices are attached and operational. This process consists of a test on the video card and video memory, a BIOS identification process (during which the BIOS version, manufacturer, and data are displayed on the monitor), and a memory test to ensure memory chips are working properly.

power supply Used to regulate the wall voltage to the voltages required by computer chips; it is housed inside the system unit.

presentation software An application program for creating dynamic slide shows, such as Microsoft PowerPoint or Corel Presentations.

Pretty Good Privacy (PGP) A public-key package.

primary key (or key field) The unique field that each database record must have.

print server A server that manages all client-requested printing jobs for all printers on the network.

printer A common output device that creates tangible or hard copies of text and graphics.

private key One-half of a pair of binary files that is needed to decrypt an encrypted message. The private key is kept only by the individual who created the key pair and is never distributed to anyone else. The private key is used to decrypt messages created with the corresponding public key.

private-key encryption A procedure in which only the two parties involved in sending a message have the code. This could be a simple shift code where letters of the alphabet are shifted to a new position.

problem statement A very clear description of which tasks the computer program must accomplish and how the program will execute these tasks and respond to unusual situations. It is the starting point of programming work.

processor speed The number of operations (or cycles) the processor completes each second, measured in hertz (Hz).

productivity software Programs that enable a user to perform various tasks generally required in home, school, and business. This category includes word processing, spreadsheet, presentation, personal information management (PIM), and database programs.

program Instruction set that provides a means for users to interact with and use the computer, all without specialized computer programming skills.

program development life cycle (PDLC) A number of stages, from conception to final deployment, a programming project follows.

programming The process of translating a task into a series of commands a computer will use to perform that task.

programming language A kind of "code" for the set of instructions the central processing unit (CPU) knows how to perform.

project management software An application program such as Microsoft Project that helps project managers easily create and modify project management scheduling charts.

proprietary software A program that is owned and controlled by the company it is created by or for.

proprietary (or private) systems Systems whose design is not made available for public access.

protocol (1) A set of rules for exchanging data and communication. (2) The first part of the Uniform Resource Locator (URL) indicating the set of rules used to retrieve the specified document. The protocol is generally followed by a colon, two forward slashes, www (indicating World Wide Web), and then the domain name.

prototype A small model of a computer program, often built at the beginning of a large project.

proxy server Acts as a go-between for computers on the internal network and the external network (the Internet).

pseudocode A text-based approach to documenting an algorithm.

public key One-half of a pair of binary files that is needed to decrypt an encrypted message. After creating the keys, the user distributes the public key to anyone he wishes to send him encrypted messages. A message encrypted with a public key can be unencrypted only using the corresponding private key.

public-key encryption A procedure in which the key for coding is generally distributed as a public key that may be placed on a Web site. Anyone wishing to send a message codes it using the public key. The recipient decodes the message with a private key.

Q

query The processing of requesting information from a database.

query language Language used to retrieve and display records. A query language consists of its own vocabulary and sentence structure, used to frame the requests.

QWERTY keyboard A keyboard that gets its name from the first six letters on the top-left row of alphabetic keys on the keyboard.

R

Rambus DRAM (RDRAM) The fastest and the most recent type of RAM on the market. RDRAM is found on multimedia machines because its speed is necessary to transfer large multimedia files efficiently.

random access memory (RAM) The computer's temporary storage space or short-term memory. It is located as a set of chips on the system unit's motherboard, and its capacity is measured in megabytes, with most modern systems containing around 256 megabyte (MB) to 512 MB of RAM.

range checks A type of data validation used in databases to ensure that a value entered falls within a specified range (such as requiring a person's age to fall in a range of between 1 and 120).

rapid application development (RAD) A method of system development in which developers create a prototype first and generate system documents as they use and remodel the product.

read-only memory (ROM) A set of memory chips located on the motherboard that stores data and instructions that cannot be changed or erased; it holds all the instructions the computer needs to start up.

read/write heads The read/write heads move from the outer edge of the spinning platters to the center, up to 50 times per second, to retrieve (read) and record (write) the magnetic data to and from the hard disk.

real-time operating system (RTOS) A program with a specific purpose that must guarantee certain response times for particular computing tasks, or the machine's application is useless. Real-time operating systems are found in many types of robotic equipment.

real-time processing The process of querying a database and updating it while the transaction is taking place.

record In database software, a collection of related fields.

recycle bin A folder on a PC's desktop where deleted files from the hard drive reside until permanently purged from the system.

reference software A software application that acts as a source for reference materials, such as standard atlases, dictionaries, and thesauri.

referential integrity For each value in the foreign key of one table, there is a corresponding value in the primary key of the related table.

refresh rate (or vertical refresh rate) The number of times per second an electron beam scans the monitor and recharges the illumination of each pixel.

registers Special memory storage areas built into the central processing unit (CPU).

registry Contains all the different configurations (settings) used by the operating system (OS) as well as by other applications.

relational algebra The use of English-like expressions that have variables and operations, much like algebraic equations.

relational database Organizes data in table format by logically grouping similar data into relations (or tables that contain related data).

relations Tables that contain related data.

relationships In relational databases, the links between tables that define how the data are related.

repeaters Devices that are installed on long cable runs to amplify a signal.

resolution The clearness or sharpness of an image, which is controlled by the number of pixels displayed on the screen.

restore point The snapshot of the entire system's settings that Windows XP creates every time the computer is started, or when a new application or driver is installed.

reusability The ability to reuse existing classes of objects from other projects, enabling programmers to produce new code quickly.

ring (or loop) topology Networked computers and peripherals that are laid out in a circle. Data flows around the circle from device to device in one direction only.

ROM *See read-only memory (ROM)*

root directory The C drive, which is the top of the filing structure of the computer system.

root domain name servers Servers that know the location of all the name servers that contain the master listings for an entire top-level domain.

routers Devices that route packets of data between two or more networks.

runtime (or logic) errors The kinds of errors in the problem logic that are only caught when the program executes.

S

Safe mode A special diagnostic mode designed for troubleshooting errors that occur during the boot process.

sampling rate The number of times per second a signal is measured and converted to a digital value. Sampling rates are measured in kilobits per second.

satellite Internet A way to connect to the Internet using a small satellite dish, which is placed outside the home and connects to a computer with coaxial cable. The satellite company then sends the data to a satellite orbiting the earth. The satellite, in turn, sends the data back to the satellite dish and to the computer.

scalable network A type of network that enables the easy addition of users without affecting the performance of the other network nodes (computers or peripherals).

ScanDisk A Windows utility that checks for lost files and fragments as well as physical errors on the hard drive.

screen savers Animated images that appear on a computer monitor when no user activity has been sensed for a certain time.

script kiddies Amateur hackers without sophisticated computer skills; typically teenagers, who don't create programs used to hack into computer systems but instead use tools created by skilled hackers that enable unskilled novices to wreak the same havoc as professional hackers.

scripts Lists of commands (miniprograms) that are executed on a computer without the user's knowledge.

scrollbars On the desktop, bars that appear at the side or bottom of the screen that control which part of the information is displayed on the screen.

search engine A set of programs that searches the Web for specific words (or keywords) you wish to query (or look for) and then returns a list of the Web sites on which those keywords are found.

second-generation languages (2GLs) Also known as assembly languages. 2GLs deal directly with system hardware but provide acronyms which are easier for human programmers to work with.

second-level domains Domains that fall within top-level domains of the Internet. Each second-level domain needs to be unique within that particular domain, but not necessarily unique to all top-level domains.

sectors A section of a hard disk drive platter, wedge-shaped from the center of the platter to the edge.

Secure Digital A newer type of memory card that is faster and offers encryption capabilities so data is secure even if the user loses the card. The stamp-sized Secure Digital cards can hold up to 256 megabytes (MB) of data.

Secure Sockets Layer (SSL) A protocol that provides for the encryption of data transmitted using Transmission Control Protocol/Internet Protocol (TCP/IP) protocols such as Hypertext Transfer Protocol (HTTP). All major Web browsers support SSL.

seek time The time it takes for the read/write heads to move over the surface of the disk, between tracks, to the correct track.

select query A query that displays a subset of data from a table based on the criteria the user specifies.

semiconductor Any material that can be controlled to either conduct electricity or act as an insulator (not allowing electricity to pass through).

serial port A port that enables the transfer of data, one bit at a time, over a single wire at speeds of up to 56 kilobits per second (Kbps); it is often used to connect modems to the computer.

server A computer that provides resources to other computers on a network.

server-side application A program that runs on the Web server as opposed to running inside a browser on a client machine.

shareware Software that enables users to "test" software by running it for a limited time free of charge.

shielded twisted pair (STP) cable Twisted pair cable that contains a layer of foil shielding to reduce interference.

Short Message Service (SMS) (or text messaging) Technology that enables short text messages (up to 160 characters) to be sent over mobile networks.

Simple Mail Transfer Protocol (SMTP) A protocol for sending e-mail along the Internet to its destination.

single-user, multitask operating system An operating system that allows only one person to work on a computer at a time, but the system can perform a variety of tasks simultaneously.

single-user, single-task operating system An operating system that allows only one user to work on a computer at a time to perform just one task at a time.

smart battery A rechargeable lithium ion battery used in a personal digital assistant (PDA) that can report the number of minutes of battery life remaining.

SmartMedia A type of flash memory card that is especially thin and light. SmartMedia cards can hold up to 128 megabytes (MB) of data.

SMTP *See Simple Mail Transfer Protocol (SMTP)*

software The set of computer programs or instructions that tells the computer what to do and enables it to perform different tasks.

software licenses Agreements between the user and the software developer that must be accepted prior to installing the software on a computer.

software piracy Violating a software license agreement by copying an application onto more computers than the license agreement permits.

software suite A collection of software programs that have been bundled together as a package.

software updates (or service packs) Small downloadable software modules that repair errors identified in commercial program code.

sort (or index) The process of organizing a database into a particular order.

sound card An expansion card that attaches to the motherboard inside the system unit that enables the computer to produce sounds.

source code The instructions programmers write in a higher-level language.

spam Unwanted or junk e-mail.

speech-recognition software (or voice-recognition software) Software that translates spoken words into typed text.

speech-recognition system A computer that can be operated through a microphone, with a user telling the computer to perform specific commands (such as to open a file) or to translate spoken words into data input.

spider (or crawler or bot) A program that constantly collects information on the Web, following links in Web sites and reading Web pages. Spiders got their name because they crawl over the Web using multiple "legs" to visit many sites simultaneously.

spreadsheet software An application program such as Microsoft Excel or Lotus 1-2-3 that enables a user to do calculations and numerical analyses easily.

SSL *See Secure Sockets Layer (SSL)*

standby mode When a computer's more power-hungry components, such as the monitor and hard drive, are put in idle.

star topology The most widely deployed client/server network layout in businesses.

In a star topology, the nodes connect to a central communications device called a hub. The hub receives a signal from the sending node and retransmits it to all other nodes on the network. The network nodes examine data and pick up only the transmissions addressed to them. Because the hub retransmits data signals, a star topology is an active topology.

statements Sentences in programming code.

static addressing Assigning an Internet Protocol (IP) address for a computer that never changes and is most likely assigned manually by a network administrator.

static RAM (SRAM) A type of random access memory that is faster than DRAM. In SRAM, more transistors are used to store a single bit, but no capacitor is needed.

stealth viruses Viruses that temporarily erase their code from the files where they reside and hide in the active memory of the computer.

storage devices Devices such as hard disk drives, floppy disk drives, and CD drives for storing data and information.

streaming audio Technology that enables audio files to be fed to a browser continuously. This avoids users having to download the entire file before listening to it.

streaming video Technology that enables video files to be fed to a browser continuously. This avoids users having to download the entire file before viewing it.

structured (analytical) data Relational databases excel in the storage of structured (analytical) data (such as "Bill" or "345"). However, object-oriented databases are more adept at handling unstructured data. Unstructured data includes nontraditional data such as audio clips (including MP3 files), video clips, pictures, and extremely large documents. Data of this type is known as a binary large object (BLOB) because it is actually encoded in binary form.

Structured Query Language (SQL) The most popular database query language today.

stylus A device used to tap or write on touch-sensitive screens.

subject directory A structured outline of Web sites organized by topics and subtopics. Yahoo! is a popular subject directory.

subnotebook computers Portable computers that are smaller and weigh less than normal notebook computers. Usually, these feature smaller displays and keyboards.

subwoofer A special type of speaker designed to more faithfully reproduce low-frequency sounds.

summary data reports *See summary reports*

summary reports A report that summarizes data in some fashion (such as a total of the day's concession sales at an amusement park).

supercomputers Specially designed computers that can perform complex calculations extremely rapidly. They are used in situations where complex models requiring intensive mathematical calculations are needed (such as weather forecasting or atomic energy research).

swap file (or page file) A temporary storage area on the hard drive where the operating system "swaps out" or moves the data or instructions from random access memory (RAM) that have not recently been used; this process takes place when more RAM space is needed.

switch A smart hub. It makes decisions, based on the Media Access Control (MAC) address of the data, as to where the data is to be sent.

Symbian OS A popular operating system for full-featured cell phones.

Symmetrical Digital Subscriber Line (SDSL) A Digital Subscriber Line (DSL) transmission that uploads and downloads data at the same speed.

synchronizing The process of updating data so the files on different systems are the same.

synchronous DRAM (SDRAM) Much faster than DRAM, it is the current memory standard and provides the level of performance most home users require.

syntax An agreed-upon set of rules defining how a programming language must be structured.

syntax errors Violations of the strict, precise set of rules that define a programming language.

system clock A computer's internal clock.

system development life cycle (SDLC) An organized process (or set of steps) for developing an information processing system.

system evaluation The process of looking at a computer's subsystems, what they do, and how they perform to determine whether the computer system has the right hardware components to do what the user ultimately wants it to do.

system files The main files of the operating system.

system requirements Minimum storage, memory capacity, and processing standards recommended by the software manufacturer to ensure proper operation of a software application.

System Restore A utility in Windows XP that lets you restore your system settings to a specific previous date when everything was working properly.

system software The set of programs that enables a computer's hardware devices and application software to work together; it includes the operating system and utility programs.

system unit The metal or plastic case that holds all the physical parts of the computer together, including the computer's processor (its brains), its memory, and the many circuit boards that help the computer function.

T

T lines High-speed fiber-optic communications lines that are designed to provide much higher throughput than conventional voice (telephone) and data (DSL) lines.

T-1 lines High-speed fiber-optic communications lines that can support 24 simultaneous voice or data channels and achieve a maximum throughput of 1.544 megabits per second (Mbps).

T-2 lines High-speed fiber-optic communications lines composed of four T-1 lines that deliver a throughput of approximately 6.3 megabits per second (Mbps).

T-3 lines Fiber-optic communications lines often used by Tier 1 and Tier 2 Internet service providers (ISPs) and very large businesses; they consist of a bundle of 28 T-1 lines. T-3 lines deliver 44.736 megabits per second (Mbps) of bandwidth.

T-4 lines Fiber-optic communications lines that contain 168 T-1 lines and provide 274.176 megabits per second (Mbps) of throughput.

table In database software, a group of related records.

tablet PC A portable computer that includes two special technologies: advanced handwriting recognition and speech recognition.

tags In Hypertext Markup Language (HTML), a way to indicate how the text should look (such as <b> and </b> to indicate boldface text).

Task Manager A Windows utility that checks on a program if it has stopped working and exits the nonresponding program when you click End Task.

Task Scheduler A Windows utility that enables you to schedule tasks to run automatically at predetermined times, with no interaction necessary on your part.

tax-preparation software An application program such as Intuit's TurboTax and H&R Block's TaxCut for preparing state and federal taxes. Each program offers a complete set of tax forms and instructions as well as expert advice on how to complete each form.

TCP/IP *See Transmission Control Protocol/Internet Protocol (TCP/IP)*

telephony software Software that, combined with the Internet, speakers, and a microphone, turns a computer into a high-tech phone and answering service.

Telnet Both a protocol for connecting to a remote computer and a Transmission Control Protocol/Internet Protocol (TCP/IP) service that runs on a remote computer to make it accessible to other computers.

templates Forms included in many productivity applications that provide the basic structure for a particular kind of document, spreadsheet, or presentation.

terminator A device that absorbs a signal so it is not reflected back onto parts of the network that have already received it.

test condition A check to see whether a loop is completed.

testing plan In the problem statement, a plan that lists specific input numbers the program would typically expect the user to enter. It then lists the precise output values that a perfect program would return for those input values.

text fields Fields in a database that can hold any combination of alphanumeric data (letters or numbers) and are most often used to hold text.

thermal printer A printer that works by either melting wax-based ink onto ordinary paper (in a process called thermal wax transfer printing) or by burning dots onto specially coated paper (in a process called direct thermal printing).

third-generation languages (3GLs, or high-level languages) Computer languages that use symbols and commands to help programmers tell the computer what to do, making 3GL languages easier to read and remember. Programmers are relieved of the burden of having to understand everything about the hardware of the computer to give it directions. In addition, 3GLs enable programmers to name storage locations in memory with their own names so they are more meaningful to them.

thrashing A condition of excessive paging in which the operating system becomes sluggish.

three-way handshake A process Transmission Control Protocol (TCP) uses to establish a connection.

Tier 1 ISPs Internet service providers that route a large percentage of the traffic on the Internet and have extremely high-speed connections with other ISPs, sometimes in the 2.5 to 10 gigabits per second (Gbps) range.

Tier 2 ISPs Internet service providers that usually have a regional or national focus. Therefore, to enable their customers to reach any possible point on the global Internet, Tier 2 ISPs must route at least a portion of their traffic through the global Tier 1 ISPs.

Tier 3 ISPs Internet service providers that provide Internet access to homes or to small to medium-size businesses. These ISPs normally cover a local geographical area. All Tier 3 ISPs need to be connected to at least one Tier 2 ISP.

time-variant data Data that doesn't all pertain to one period in time, such as data in a data warehouse.

toggle key A keyboard key whose function changes each time it's pressed; it "toggles" between two function.

token A special data packet used to pass data in a token-ring network.

token method The access method that ring networks use to avoid data collisions.

token-ring topology A network layout in which data is passed using a special data packet called a token.

toolbars On the desktop, groups of icons collected together in a small box.

top-down design A systematic approach in which a programming problem is broken down into a series of high-level tasks.

top-level domain (TLD) The three-letter suffix in the domain name (such as .com or .edu) that indicates the kind of organization the host is.

touchpad A small, touch-sensitive screen at the base of the keyboard. To use the touchpad, you simply move your finger across the pad to direct the cursor.

tower configuration A style of system unit on a desktop computer that typically sits vertically on the floor below a desk.

trackball mouse A mouse with a rollerball on top instead of on the bottom. Because you move the trackball with your fingers, it doesn't require much wrist motion, so it's considered healthier for your wrists than a traditional mouse.

trackpoint A small, joystick-like nub that enables you to move the cursor with the tip of your finger.

tracks Concentric circles on a hard disk drive platter.

transaction processing system (TPS) A system used to keep track of everyday business activities.

transceiver In a wireless network, a device that translates the electronic data that needs to be sent along the network into radio waves and then broadcasts these radio waves to other network nodes.

transistors Electrical switches that are built out of layers of a special type of material called a semiconductor.

Transmission Control Protocol (TCP) A protocol for preparing data for transmission; it provides for error checking and resending lost data.

Transmission Control Protocol/Internet Protocol (TCP/IP) The main suite of protocols used on the Internet.

transmission media The cable or wireless lines that transport data on a network.

Trojan horse A computer program that appears to be something useful or desirable (such as a game or a screen saver), but at the same time does something malicious in the background without the user's knowledge.

twisted pair wiring (or twisted pair cable) Telephone lines made of copper wires that are twisted around each other and surrounded by a plastic jacket.

two-way pagers Devices that support both receiving and sending text messages.

U

Unicode An encoding scheme that uses 16 bits instead of the 8 bits used in ASCII. Unicode can represent more than 65,000 unique character symbols, enabling it to represent the alphabets of all modern languages and all historic languages and notational systems.

Uniform Resource Locator (URL) A Web site's unique address, such as www.microsoft.com.

universal serial bus (USB) port A port that can connect a wide variety of peripherals to the computer, including keyboards, printers, Zip drives, and digital cameras. USB 2.0 transfers data at 480 megabits per second (Mbps) and is approximately 40 times faster than the original USB port.

UNIX An operating system originally conceived in 1969 by Ken Thompson and Dennis Ritchie of AT&T's Bell Labs. In 1974, the UNIX code was rewritten in the standard programming language C. Today there are various commercial versions of UNIX.

unshielded twisted pair (UTP) cable The most popular transmission media option for Ethernet networks. UTP cable is composed of four pairs of wires that are twisted around each other to reduce electrical interference.

unstructured data Nontraditional database data such as audio clips (including MP3 files), video clips, pictures, and extremely large documents. Data of this type is known as a binary large objects (BLOBs) because it is actually encoded in binary form.

URL *See Uniform Resource Locator (URL)*

USB *See universal serial port (USB)*

USB 2.0 External bus that supports a data throughput of 480 megabits per second (Mbps). These buses are backward compatible with buses using the original universal serial bus (USB) standard.

User Datagram Protocol (UDP) A protocol that prepares data for transmission but has no re-sending capabilities.

user interface Part of the operating system that enables you to interact with your computer.

Utility Manager A utility in the Accessories folder of Windows XP that enables you to magnify the screen image; you can also have screen contents read out loud or display an on-screen keyboard.

utility programs Small programs that perform many of the general housekeeping tasks for the computer, such as system maintenance and file compression.

V

vacuum tubes Used in early computers, vacuum tubes act as computer switches by allowing or blocking the flow of electrical current.

validation The process of ensuring that data entered into a database is correct (or at least reasonable) and complete.

validation rules Rules that are set up in a database to alert the user to clearly wrong entries.

value Numeric data either entered in to a spreadsheet directly or as a result of a calculation.

variable declaration Tells the operating system that the program needs to allocate storage space in random access memory (RAM).

variables Input and output items that a computer program manipulates.

VBScript A subset of Visual Basic; also used to introduce interactivity to a Web page.

video card (or video adapter) An expansion card that is installed inside a system unit to translate binary data (the 1s and 0s your computer uses) into the images viewed on the monitor.

video RAM (VRAM) The random access memory included with a video.

videoconferencing Technology that enables a person sitting at a computer and equipped with a personal video camera and a microphone to transmit video and audio across the Internet (or other communications medium). All computers participating in a videoconference need to have a microphone and speakers installed so that participants can hear one another.

virtual memory The space on the hard drive that the operating system stores data to if you don't have enough random access memory (RAM) to hold all of the programs you're currently trying to run.

virtual private network (VPN) Utilizes the public Internet communications infrastructure to build a secure, private network between various locations.

virtual reality programs Software that turns an artificial environment into a realistic experience.

virus signatures Signatures in files that are portions of the virus code that are unique to a particular computer virus.

visual programming A technique for automatically writing code when the programmer says the layout is complete. It helps programmers produce a final application much more quickly.

Voice over IP (VoIP) The transmission of phone calls over the same data lines and networks that make up the Internet. Also called Internet telephony.

voice pager A device that offers all the features of a numeric pager but also enables the user to receive voice messages.

volatile storage Temporary storage, such as in random access memory (RAM); when the power is off, the data in volatile storage is cleared out.

VPN *See virtual private network (VPN)*

W

WAN *See wide area network (WAN)*

WAP *See Wireless Application Protocol (WAP)*

warm boot The process of restarting the system while it's powered on.

Web-based e-mail E-mail that uses the Internet as the client; therefore, a user can access a Web-based e-mail account from any computer that has access to the Web—no special client software is needed.

Web browser Software that enables a user to access the Web.

Web clipping Technology for extracting the information from a Web site and formatting it so it is more useful on smaller personal digital assistant (PDA) displays.

Web-enabled The capability of a device, such as a desktop computer, laptop, or mobile device, to access the Internet.

Web page authoring software Programs you can use to design interactive Web pages without knowing any Hypertext Markup Language (HTML) code.

Web server A computer running a specialized operating system that enables it to host Web pages (and other information) and provide requested Web pages to clients.

Web site A location on the Web.

Weblog (blog) Personal logs or journal entries posted on the Web.

"what-if" analysis Testing the effects that different variables have on a spreadsheet analysis, using the recalculation feature.

white-hat hackers Hackers who break into systems just for the challenge of it (and who don't wish to steal or wreak havoc on the systems). They tout themselves as experts who are performing a needed service for society by helping companies realize the vulnerabilities that exist in their systems.

wide area network (WAN) A network made up of local area networks (LANs) connected over long distances.

Wi-Fi (Wireless Fidelity) The 802.11 standard established by the Institute of Electrical and Electronics Engineers (IEEE).

wildcards Symbols used in an Internet search when the user is unsure of the keyword's spelling or when a word can be spelled in different ways or can contain different endings. The asterisk (*) is used to replace a series of letters and the percent sign (%) to replace a single letter in a word.

windows In a graphical user interface, rectangular boxes that contain programs displayed on the screen.

Windows Explorer The program in Microsoft Windows that helps a user manage files and folders by showing the location and contents of every drive, folder, and file on the computer.

Windows key A function key specific to the Windows operating system. Used alone, it brings up the Start menu; however, it's used most often in combination with other keys as shortcuts.

wireless access point A device similar to a hub in an Ethernet network. It takes the place of a wireless network adapter and helps to relay data between network nodes.

Wireless Application Protocol (WAP) The standard that dictates how handheld devices will access information on the Internet.

wireless DSL/cable router A device that enables wireless and wired nodes to be connected to the same network.

wireless Internet service provider Providers such as Verizon or T-Mobile that offer their subscribers wireless access to the Internet.

Wireless Markup Language (WML) A format for writing content viewed on a cellular phone or personal digital assistant (PDA) that is text-based and contains no graphics.

wireless media Communications media that do not use cables but instead rely on radio waves to communicate.

wireless network A network that uses radio waves instead of wires or cable as its transmission medium.

wireless network adapter Devices that are required for each node on a wireless network for the node to be able to communicate with other nodes on the network.

wireless network interface cards (wireless NICs) Cards installed in a system that connect with wireless access points on the network.

wizards Step-by-step guides that walk you through the necessary steps to complete a complicated task.

WML *See Wireless Markup Language (WML)*

word processing software Programs used to create and edit written documents such as papers, letters, and résumés.

word size The number of bits a computer can work with at a time.

worksheet The basic element in a spreadsheet program; it is a grid consisting of columns and rows.

World Wide Web (WWW or Web) The part of the Internet used the most. What distinguishes the Web from the rest of the Internet is (1) its use of common communication protocols (such as Transmission Control Protocol/Internet Protocol, or TCP/IP) and special languages (such as the Hypertext Markup Language, or HTML) that enable different computers to talk to each other and display information in compatible formats, and (2) its use of special links (called hyperlinks) that enable users to jump from one place to another in the Web.

worm A program that attempts to travel between systems through network connections to spread infections. Worms can run independently of host file execution and are active in spreading themselves.

WWW *See World Wide Web (WWW or Web)*

X

XML *See Extensible Markup Language (XML)*

Z

Zip disk A portable storage medium with storage capacities ranging from 100 megabytes (MB) to 750 MB.

Zip disk drive A drive bay for a Zip disk.

zombies Computers that are controlled by hackers who used a backdoor program to take control.

INDEX

edutainment, 143
EISA (Extended Industry Standard
    Architecture) bus, 372
electronic commerce. *See* e-commerce
electronic mail. *See* e-mail
Electronic Numerical Integrator and
    Computer (ENIAC), 80–81
electronic spreadsheet programs, 76.
    See also Excel (Microsoft)
electronic switches, 356–357
electrotextiles, 326
Encarta, 144
ENIAC (Electronic Numerical Integrator
    and Computer), 80–81
entertainment (Web entertainment), 109–110
entertainment software, 144–145
    edutainment, 143
    games, 144–145
    MP3, 145
    specialized hardware, 144
Entertainment Software Rating Board
    (ESRB), 144
ergonomics, 56–57
error handling in boot process, 193–195
ESRB (Entertainment Software Rating
    Board), 144
Ethernet networks, 268–271
    cabling/node connections, 269–270
    creating, 269
    hubs, 270–271
    routers, 270–271
Ethernet ports, 53, 243
    laptops, 339–340
ethics
    copying CDs/DVDs, 236
    hacking, 299
    MP3 players, 325–327
    software licensing, 152, 161
        used software, 149
evaluating computer systems, 221
    audio subsystems, 240
        sound cards, 241–242
        speakers, 240–241
    buying versus upgrading, 222–223
        assessing value, 248–249
    CPUs, 224–226
        upgrading, 226–227
    determining your ideal computer, 223–224
    memory, 227–230
        evaluating RAM, 227–229
        upgrading RAM, 230–231
        virtual memory, 229–230
    port connectivity, 242–245
        upgrading, 245–246
    storage media, 231–237
        CD/DVD drives, 235–237
        flash drives, 234
        floppy/Zip drives, 233–235
        hard drives, 231–233
    system reliability, 246–247
    video subsystems, 238–240
        monitors, 239–240
        video cards, 238–239
events, 188
Excel (Microsoft), 76, 126–128
    history, 76
execute stage (CPU machine cycle), 363, 366
expansion buses, 371–372

expansion cards, 54–55
    adding additional ports, 245
    sound cards, 241–242
expansion hubs, 245
exporting digital video, 176–177
Extended Industry Standard Architecture
    (EISA) bus, 372
extension, 200–201

F

fans (CPUs), 226
FAQs (frequently asked questions), 147
FAT (File Allocation Table), 206–207
Favorites (Web browsers), 95–96
fetch stage (CPU machine cycle), 363–365
fiber-optic cable, 264
File Allocation Table (FAT), 206–207
file compression utilities, 204–205
file management, 197–202
    deleting files, 202
    File Allocation Table (FAT), 206–207
    keyboard shortcuts, 41
    naming/renaming files, 200–202
    organizing files, 197–199
    viewing/sorting files/folders, 199–200
file paths, 201–202
file swapping, 325–327
File Transfer Protocol (FTP), 94
file types, 200–201
    digital video, 176
files, 197
    extensions, 200–201
    finding, 200
    managing. *See* file management
    transferring. *See* transferring files
financial/business software, 135–137
    database software, 129
    general business, 136–137
    personal finance, 135–136
    specialized business applications, 137
    spreadsheet software, 76, 126–128
Find in File (Search) tool, 41
finding
    files/folders, 200
    Web sites
        evaluating found sites, 100
        search engines, 96–99
        subject directories, 98–99
fingerprint authentication devices, 308
firewalls, 284–286, 308
    functioning, 284–285
    installing personal firewalls, 285
    types, 285–286
FireWire, 54
    laptops, 339–340
FireWire 800, 54
FireWire ports, 242. *See also* ports
    external hard drives, 237
First Internet Software House, 149
first-generation computers, 81
flash drives, 52, 234
flash memory, 52, 234, 237
    digital cameras, 168–169
    MP3 players, 325
    PDAs, 330–331
flat-panel monitors.
    See LCD (liquid crystal display) monitors

flexible OLEDs (FOLEDs), 58–59
flexible processors, 368
flexible screens, 58–59
floppy disk drives, 52, 233–235
    care for disks, 234
    history, 75, 77
folders, 197. *See also* file management
FOLEDs (flexible OLEDs), 58–59
footprints, 342
forensics, 11–12
formatting text, keyboard shortcuts, 41
formulas, spreadsheet software, 126–127
fourth-generation computers, 81
Frankston, Bob, 76
freeware, 149–150
frequently asked questions (FAQs), 147
Friendster Web site, 279
Friendzy Web site, 279
FTP (File Transfer Protocol), 94
full installations, 152
function keys, 39
functions, spreadsheet software, 126–127
future of Internet, 110–111
    power-line connectivity, 92

G

gaming
    careers, importance of computer
        fluency, 14–15
    joysticks/game controls, 42
    software, 144–145
    surgeons' use of three-dimensional
        gaming technology, 9
Gates, Bill, 75
gateways (wireless networks), 273
GBs (gigabytes), 20–21
geocaching, 335
GHSA (Governors Highway Safety
    Association) Web site, 321
GHz (gigahertz), 225
Gibson Research Web site, 286
gigabytes (GBs), 20–21
gigahertz (GHz), 225
gizmodo.com Web site, 104
Global Positioning System (GPS), 334–335
GNOME user interface (Linux), 187
Google, 97
gov Web sites, 94
Governors Highway Safety Association
    (GHSA) Web site, 321
GPS (Global Positioning System), 334–335
    privacy, 351
Graffiti text system (PDAs), 327–328
graphical user interfaces (GUIs), 186–188
    history, 76–77
graphics
    digital photography, 168–173
        advantages, 172
        downloading pictures to computers, 170
        editing images/adding special effects,
            170–171
        printing, 171–172
        resolution, 168
        scanners, 171
        storage/memory, 168–169
        taking pictures, 170

privacy. *See also* security
  cookies, 108
  donating old computers, 248
  GPS, 351
  Identity Theft, 280–281
pro Web sites, 94
processing cycle (CPUs), 363.
        See also machine cycle (CPUs)
processors. *See* CPUs
productivity software, 124–135
  database software, 129
  integrated software applications, 130–131
  personal information manager (PIM)
        software, 129
  presentation software, 128
  productivity tips and tricks, 130
  productivity tools, 129–130
  software suites, 131, 134–135
  spreadsheet applications, 126–128
  word processing, 124–126
program files, backups, 312
programming. *See* languages
programs, 124. *See also* software
Project (Microsoft), 137
project management software, 136–137
projectors (laptops), 341
Properties dialog box, hard drives, 233
proprietary software, 137
protecting computers
  backups, 311–313
  online use
    pop-ups, 310
    spam, 309
    spam filters, 309–310
    spyware/adware, 310–311
    viruses, 308. *See also* viruses
  physical protection
    surge protectors, 303–304
    uninterruptible power supplies
        (UPSs), 304
  theft protection, 305–306
  unauthorized access protection
    biometric authentication devices, 308
    firewalls, 308
    passwords, 306–307
protocols
  URLs, 94
  Voice over Internet Protocol (VoIP), 147
  Wireless Application Protocol (WAP), 332
publishing (desktop) software, 138–139

Q

QDOS (Quick and Dirty Operating System), 75
QuarkXPress, 138–139
Quick and Dirty Operating System (QDOS), 75
QuickBooks, 136
Quicken, 135–136
QuickLaunch toolbar, 153
QuickTime, 109, 176. *See also* video
QWERTY keyboards, 38

R

RAM (random access
        memory), 55, 227–229, 366–369
  access time, 367
  amount of RAM needed, 229

evaluating memory subsystems, 229–230
laptops, 340
operating system memory/storage
        management, 189
OS loading during boot process, 193
PDAs, 330
rate of capacity growth, 222
tablet PCs, 337
types of RAM, 367, 369
upgrading, 230–231, 383
video RAM (VRAM), 238
virtual memory, 189, 229–230
Rambus inline memory modules (RIMMs), 228
random access memory. *See* RAM
read-only memory (ROM), 55, 369
  PDAs, 330
real-time operating systems (RTOS), 181
RealOne, 109
Recycle Bin, 202
recycling computers, 257
Red Hat Linux, 185–186
reference/educational software, 142–144
refresh rate, 44, 240
registers, 363
registry, 193
repeaters, 270
resolution
  digital cameras, 168
  monitors, 44, 239–240
  printers, 47
restore points, 208
restore utilities, 208
restoring deleted files, 202
retail careers, importance of computer
        fluency, 6
RIMMs (Rambus inline memory modules), 228
ripping software, 145
RJ-45 connectors, Ethernet networks, 269
robots
  Artificial intelligence (AI), 17–18
  home maintenance, 15
  surgeons' use of computer-guided robots, 10
ROM (read-only memory), 55, 369
  PDAs, 330
root directories, 198
rottentomatoes.com, 104
routers, 265
  DSL/cable routers, 271
    wireless, 273–274
  Ethernet networks, 270–271
  phone line networks, 268
  power line networks, 266
  wireless networks, 273–274
RTOS (real-time operating systems), 181

S

Safe mode, 194–195
safety, cell phones, 321
sampling rate, 167, 323, 349
satellites
  Global Positioning System (GPS), 334–335
  satellite Internet, 89–90
saving documents/files, 201–202
  keyboard shortcut, 41
  Save versus Save As, 126
savvy computer users/consumers, 4–5
ScanDisk, 207

scanners, 171
science
  careers, importance of computer fluency, 14
  nanoscience, 16
Scientific Calculator, 358
screen resolution, 239–240
screen savers, 204
script kiddies, 279
script viruses, 288
scripts, 288
scrollbars, 196
SDSL (Symmetrical Digital Subscriber
        Line), 87, 90
Search for Extra Terrestrial Intelligence (SETI)
        Institute Web site, 297
searching files/folders, 200
  Find in File keyboard shortcut, 41
searching the Web
  evaluating found sites, 100
  search engines, 96–99
  subject directories, 98–99
second-generation computers, 81
Secure Digital cards, 325
security, 277–278. *See also* protecting computers
  authentication/passwords, 306–308
  computer security careers, 291
  cyberterrorism, 280
  donating old computers, 248
  e-commerce, 107–108
  firewalls, 284–286, 308
    functioning, 284–285
    installing personal firewalls, 285
    types, 285–286
  hackers, 278–283
    denial of service (DoS) attacks, 282–283
    ethics, 299
    methods of access, 283
    packet sniffing, 280
    trojan horses, 280, 282
    types, 278, 280
  Identity Theft, 280–281
  passwords, 193, 306–308
  social networking Web sites, 279
  testing security, 286
  theft protection, 305–306
  VeriChip personal ID chips, 17
  viruses, 287
    antivirus software, 289–290, 308
    boot-sector viruses, 288
    classifications, 289
    freeware/shareware, 150
    logic bombs, 288
    script/macro viruses, 288
    symptoms of infection, 288
    trojan horses, 280, 282, 289
    worms, 288
  wireless networks, 308
seek time (hard drives), 232
semiconductors, 356
Senx device (Sensory Enhanced Net
        Experience), 111
serial ports, 53, 242–243
servers, 23, 263
  client/server networks, 263–264
  Internet, 84–85
shareware, 149–150
sharing Internet connections via
        networks, 262

CREDITS

Chapter 1

Chapter Opener © Mendola/Doug Chezem/Corbis

Figure 1.1 © Chuck Savage/Corbis

Figure 1.3 Courtesy of Hewlett Packard/tablet PC

Figure 1.3 Courtesy of Nokia/telephone

Figure 1.4 © Michael Newman/Photo Edit

Figure 1.5a Getty Images (Royalty Free) label

Figure 1.5b This image is reproduced with permission of United Parcel Service of America, Inc. © United Parcel Service of America, Inc. All rights reserved.

Figure 1.5c Courtesy of Symbol Corporation

Figure 1.7 COPYRIGHT 2003 GEORGIA TECH, CREDIT: STANLEY LEARY

Figure 1.8 'Liquid Time Series Tokyo' (2001) interactive installation by Camille Utterback

Figure 1.9 Medical Education Technologies, Inc. © 2003

Figure 1.10 Courtesy of Intuitive Surgical da Vinci Surgical System

Figure 1.12 Courtesy of Rhino Parking Systems, Inc., Oakland, California

Figure 1.13 © Wyeknot, Inc.

Figure 1.14 National Museum of America History, Behring Center. © Smithsonian Institution.

Figure 1.15 © 2004 Antenna Audio

Figure 1.16 Reprinted by permission of NCSA University of Illinois

Figure 1.17 University of Ferrara, Dept. of Architecture-Cy-Ark Foundation Pompeii

Figure 1.18 © NewTek, Inc.

Figure 1.19a Courtesy of White Box Robotics

Figure 1.19b Friendly Robotics® and Robomower® are registered trademarks of F. Robotics Acquisitions Ltd.

Figure 1.19c © iRobot

Figure 1.20 Courtesy of C. Durkan, University of Cambridge

Figure 1.21 © Dr. Peter Harris/Photo Researchers

Figure 1.22 © MPI Bio Chemistry/Volker Steger/Photo Researchers, Inc.

Figure 1.23 Image of VeriChip courtesy of Applied Digital Solutions

Figure 1.24 © David Parker/Photo Researchers, Inc.

Figure 1.26 © Chuck Savage/Corbis

Figure 1.28 Courtesy of International Business Machines Corporation. Unauthorized use not permitted.

Figure 1.29 Adobe Illustrator box shot reprinted with permission of Adobe Systems, Inc.

Figure 1.29 CorelDraw Graphics box shot reprinted with permission of Corel Corporation.

Figure 1.29 Microsoft box shot reprinted with permission of Microsoft Corporation.

Figure 1.29 Adobe PageMaker box shot reprinted with permission of Adobe Systems, Inc.

Figure 1.29 Microsoft Works Suite box shot reprinted with permission of Microsoft Corporation.

Figure 1.29 Lotus Smart Suite box shot courtesy of International Business Machines Corporations. Unauthorized use not permitted.

Chapter 2

Chapter Opener	© Randy Farris/Corbis
Figure 2.1	Courtesy of International Business Machines Corporation. Unauthorized use not permitted. (inside system unit)
Figure 2.1	Courtesy of Hewlett Packard (printer)
Figure 2.4a	Reprinted by permission of Gateway
Figure 2.4b	Courtesy of Datadesk Technologies, Inc.
Figure 2.8	Courtesy of Maples Communications/Targus
Figure 2.17	Photo courtesy of Apple Computer, Inc.
Figure 2.19	Screen shots reprinted by permission from Microsoft Corporation.
Figure 2.22	Courtesy of International Business Machines Corporation. Unauthorized use not permitted.
Figure 2.23	Courtesy of International Business Machines Corporation. Unauthorized use not permitted.
Figure 2.26	Courtesy of Datadesk Technologies, Inc.
Figure 2.28	Courtesy of Universal Display Corporation
Figure 2.29	Courtesy of MicroOpitcal Corporation

Chapter 3

Chapter Opener	© Larry Williams/Corbis
Figure 3.2a	MuVo is a registered trademark of Creative Technology Ltd. in the United States and/or others countries. NOMAD is registered trademark of Aonix and is used by Creative Technology Ltd. and/or its affiliates under license.
Figure 3.3	© IEI03
Figure 3.8a	Screen shot reprinted by permission from Microsoft Corporation. © 2004 Netscape Communications Corporation. Used with permission. Netscape Communications has not authorized, sponsored, endorsed, or approved this publication and is not responsible for its content.
Figure 3.8b	Screen shot reprinted by permission from Microsoft Corporation.
Figure 3.11	© 2004 by Yahoo! Inc. YAHOO! and the YAHOO! logo are trademarks of Yahoo! Inc.
Figure 3.12	Screen shot reprinted by permission from Microsoft Corporation.
Figure 3.18	© 2004, Librarians' Index to the Internet, **lii.org**. All rights reserved.
Figure 3.19	Screen shot reprinted by permission from Microsoft Corporation.
Figure 3.22	AOL screenshots © 2004 America Online, Inc. Used with permission.
Figure 3.23	© 2004 Harleysville Savings Bank. All rights reserved.
Figure 3.24	Screen shot reprinted by permission from Microsoft Corporation.

Chapter 4

Chapter Opener	© Sanford/Agliolo/Corbis
Figure 4.2	Screen shot reprinted by permission from Microsoft Corporation.
Figure 4.3	Screen shot reprinted by permission from Microsoft Corporation.
Figure 4.4	Screen shot reprinted by permission from Microsoft Corporation.
Figure 4.5	Screen shot reprinted by permission from Microsoft Corporation.
Figure 4.6a	Screen shot reprinted by permission from Microsoft Corporation.
Figure 4.6b	Screen shot reprinted by permission from Microsoft Corporation.
Figure 4.6c	Screen shot reprinted by permission from Microsoft Corporation.
Figure 4.7	Screen shot reprinted by permission from Microsoft Corporation.
Figure 4.8a	Screen shot reprinted by permission from Microsoft Corporation.
Figure 4.8b	Screen shot reprinted by permission from Microsoft Corporation.
Figure 4.9	Microsoft Office box shot reprinted with permission of Microsoft Corporation.
Figure 4.9	Louts Smart Suite box shot courtesy of International Business Machines Corporation. Unauthorized use not permitted.
Figure 4.9	WordPerfect box shot reprinted with permission of Corel Corporation.
Figure 4.9	StarOffice box shot © Sun Microsystems 2003.
Figure 4.10b	Screen shot reprinted by permission from Microsoft Corporation.
Figure 4.13	Screen shot reprinted by permission from Microsoft Corporation.
Figure 4.14	Screen shot reprinted by permission from Microsoft Corporation.
Figure 4.16	© 2004 Quark, Inc. and Quark Media House Sàrl, Switzerland. All rights reserved.
Figure 4.17	Screen shot reprinted by permission from Microsoft Corporation.
Figure 4.18	Screen shot reprinted by permission from Microsoft Corporation.
Figure 4.19	Screen shot reprinted by permission from Microsoft Corporation.
Figure 4.22	Screen shot reprinted by permission from Microsoft Corporation.
Figure 4.23a	Reprinted with permission Logitech (joystick)
Figure 4.23b	i-0Display Systems, LLC (goggles)
Figure 4.26	Getty Images
Figure 4.27	Screen shot reprinted by permission from Microsoft Corporation.
Figure 4.28	© 2004 by Yahoo! Inc. YAHOO! and the YAHOO! logo are trademarks of Yahoo! Inc.
Figure 4.29a	Screen shot reprinted by permission from Microsoft Corporation.
Figure 4.29b	Screen shot reprinted by permission from Microsoft Corporation.
Figure 4.29c	Screen shot reprinted by permission from Microsoft Corporation.
Figure 4.30a	Screen shot reprinted by permission from Microsoft Corporation.
Figure 4.30b	Screen shot reprinted by permission from Microsoft Corporation.

Chapter 5

Chapter 6

Chapter Opener	© Colin Anderson/Brand X Pictures/PictureQuest
Figure 6.5	Screen shot reprinted by permission from Microsoft Corporation.
Figure 6.6	Screen shot reprinted by permission from Microsoft Corporation.
Figure 6.9	Screen shot reprinted by permission from Microsoft Corporation.
Figure 6.11	Screen shot reprinted by permission from Microsoft Corporation.
Figure 6.12	© Terra Nova Designs
Figure 6.13	Courtesy of International Business Machines Corporation. Unauthorized use not permitted.
Figure 6.15	Screen shot reprinted by permission from Microsoft Corporation.
Figure 6.18	Courtesy of Victorinox
Figure 6.20	Courtesy of Archos
Figure 6.21	Courtesy of SanDisk
Figure 6.24	Screen shot reprinted by permission from Microsoft Corporation.
Figure 6.25	Screen shot reprinted by permission from Microsoft Corporation.
Figure 6.26	Klipsch Audio Technologies
Figure 6.28	© Creative Technology Ltd. Copyright 2003
Figure 6.29a	Courtesy of Hack In The Box, **www.hackinthebox.org**
Figure 6.29b	Courtesy of Hack In The Box, **www.hackinthebox.org**
Figure 6.29c	Courtesy of Hack In The Box, **www.hackinthebox.org**
Figure 6.29d	© Terra Nova Designs
Figure 6.29e	Courtesy of Hack In The Box, **www.hackinthebox.org**
Figure 6.29f	Courtesy of Hack In The Box, **www.hackinthebox.org**
Figure 6.29g	Courtesy of Hack In The Box, **www.hackinthebox.org**
Figure 6.29h	Courtesy of Hack In The Box, **www.hackinthebox.org**
Figure 6.29i	Courtesy of Hack In The Box, **www.hackinthebox.org**
Figure 6.29j	Courtesy of Hack In The Box, **www.hackinthebox.org**
Figure 6.29k	Courtesy of Hack In The Box, **www.hackinthebox.org**
Figure 6.29l	Courtesy of Hack In The Box, **www.hackinthebox.org**
Figure 6.35	Courtesy of Koutech

Chapter 7

Chapter Opener	© H. Prinz/Corbis
Figure 7.2a	Screen shot reprinted by permission from Microsoft Corporation.
Figure 7.2b	Screen shot reprinted by permission from Microsoft Corporation.
Figure 7.21	Screen shot reprinted by permission from Microsoft Corporation.
Figure 7.27	© 2003 Gibson Research Corporation, Laguna Hills, CA, USA.
Figure 7.31	Screen shot reprinted by permission from Microsoft Corporation.

Chapter 8

Chapter Opener	© Peter Griffith/Masterfile
Figure 8.1	© 2004 T-Mobile. All rights reserved
Figure 8.4	Reproduced with permission of Motorola, Inc. © 2003 Motorola, Inc.
Figure 8.6a	Kyocera 7135 Smartphone courtesy of Kyocera Wireless Corp.
Figure 8.6b	Nokia, Inc.
Figure 8.6c	Reproduced with permission of Motorola, Inc. © 2003 Motorola, Inc.
Figure 8.8	Courtesy of SoftSource LLC
Figure 8.9a	MuVo is a registered trademark of Creative Technology Ltd. in the United States and other countries. Nomad is a registered trademark of Aonix and is used by Creative Technology Ltd. and/or its affiliates under license.
Figure 8.9b	Courtesy of Soul Player
Figure 8.9c	Courtesy of Apple © Apple
Figure 8.9d	Getty Images
Figure 8.9e	Copyright 2003 Archos, Inc.
Figure 8.10a	Courtesy of SanDisk
Figure 8.10b	Courtesy of SanDisk
Figure 8.10c	Courtesy of Sony Corporation
Figure 8.10d	Courtesy of Porter Novelli/Calli
Figure 8.11	Courtesy of Infineon Technologies
Figure 8.12b	AP/Wide World Photos
Figure 8.14	Courtesy of Sony Corporation
Figure 8.17	Image used with permission of Palm, Inc. Palm is a trademark of Palm, Inc.
Figure 8.18	Courtesy of Hitachi Global Storage Technologies.
Figure 8.20	S&S Public Relations/Actiontec Electronics
Figure 8.22a	Photo courtesy of Handspring, Inc.
Figure 8.22b	Courtesy of Sony Corporation
Figure 8.25	© Reuters NewMedia/Corbis
Figure 8.28	© Microsoft Corporation
Figure 8.29	Laboratory for Communications Engineering, Cambridge.
Figure 8.32	Courtesy of Icube
Figure 8.33a	Brother UK Ltd.
Figure 8.33b	Courtesy of Panasonic
Figure 8.35	© Photo Researchers

Chapter 9

Chapter Opener	© Denis Scott/Corbis
Figure 9.2c	© Ferranti Electronics/A. Sternberg/Photo Researchers
Figure 9.5a	Courtesy of Intel Corporation
Figure 9.5b	Courtesy of Apple © Apple
Figure 9.12	© Kim Kulish/Corbis
Figure 9.16	© Fukuhara/Corbis

Technology in Focus: The History of the PC

Figure 1	Courtesy of Apple2history.org	**Figure 11**	Courtesy of Dan Bricklin and Bob Frankston.
Figure 2a	Getty Images	**Figure 13**	© The Computer History Museum
Figure 2b	© Roger Ressmeyer/Corbis	**Figure 14**	Photo courtesy of Apple Computer, Inc.
Figure 3	Photo courtesy of Apple Computer, Inc.	**Figure 15**	Photo courtesy of Apple Computer, Inc.
Figure 4	Photo courtesy of Apple Computer, Inc.	**Figure 16**	© The Computer History Museum.
Figure 6	© Jerry Mason/Photo Researchers, Inc.	**Figure 17**	© The Computer History Museum
Figure 7	© The Computer History Museum	**Figure 18**	Courtesy of Ames Laboratory
Figure 8	© The Computer History Museum	**Figure 19**	Naval Historical Center
Figure 9	Time Magazine, Copyright Time, Inc.	**Figure 20**	© The Computer History Museum
Figure 10	© David Wilson/Corbis	**Figure 21**	Intel Corportation

Technology in Focus: Digital Technology

Figure 2a	Screen shot reprinted by permission from Microsoft Corporation.	**Figure 11a**	"CANON", the Canon logo, Powershot and Elura are trademarks of Canon Inc. all rights reserved. Used by permission.
Figure 2b	Screen shot reprinted by permission from Microsoft Corporation.	**Figure 11b**	Olympus America, Inc.
Figure 5	Photo of Nikon SQ courtesy of MWW Group	**Figure 13a**	RCA camcorder photo courtesy of Thomson.
Figure 5	Photo © Konica Minolta Photo Imaging U. S. A., Inc.	**Figure 13b**	"CANON", the Canon logo, Canon EOS Rebel are trademarks of Canon Inc. All rights reserved. Used by permission.
Figure 5	"CANON", the Canon logo, Canon EOS Rebel are trademarks of Canon Inc. All rights reserved. Used by permission.	**Figure 14a**	Courtesy of Pinnacle
		Figure 14b	©Iomega
Figure 5	Image courtesy of © Kodak.	**Figure 15a**	Screen shot reprinted by permission from Microsoft Corporation.
Figure 8	Courtesy of Sandisk	**Figure 15b**	Screen shot reprinted by permission from Microsoft Corporation.
Figure 9	Courtesy of Hewlett Packard	**Figure 16**	Adobe product screen shot reprinted with permission from Adobe Systems Incorporated.
Figure 10	Copyright © 1995–2003, Jasc Software, Inc.		

Technology in Focus: Protecting Your Computer and Backing Up Your Data

Figure 3	Image courtesy of American Power Conversion Corporation	**Figure 14**	© 2002–2004 PestPatrol, Inc. All rights reserved.
Figure 8	Screen shot reprinted by permission from Microsoft Corporation.	**Figure 15**	Screen shot reprinted by permission from Microsoft Corporation.
Figure 12	© 2004 by Yahoo! Inc. YAHOO! and the YAHOO! logo are trademarks of Yahoo! Inc.		

Front matter